Washington, DC

timeout.com/washingtondc

Published by Time Out Guides Ltd, a wholly owned subsidiary of Time Out Group Ltd.
Time Out and the Time Out logo are trademarks of Time Out Group Ltd.

© Time Out Group Ltd 2004
Previous editions 1999, 2001

10 9 8 7 6 5 4 3 2 1

This edition first published in Great Britain in 2004 by Ebury
Ebury is a division of The Random House Group Ltd,
20 Vauxhall Bridge Road, London SW1V 2SA

Random House Australia Pty Limited, 20 Alfred Street, Milsons Point, Sydney, New South Wales 2061, Australia
Random House New Zealand Limited, 18 Poland Road, Glenfield, Auckland 10, New Zealand
Random House South Africa (Pty) Limited, Endulini, 5A Jubilee Road, Parktown 2193, South Africa

Random House UK Limited Reg. No. 954009

Distributed in USA by Publishers Group West
1700 Fourth Street, Berkeley, California 94710

Distributed in Canada by Penguin Canada Ltd
10 Alcorn Avenue, Toronto, Ontario, Canada M4V 3B2

For further distribution details, see www.timeout.com

ISBN 1-904978-20-7

A CIP catalogue record for this book is available from the British Library

Colour reprographics by Icon, Crowne House, 56-58 Southwark Street, London SE1 1UN

Printed and bound by Cayfosa-Quebecor, Ctra. De Caldes, KM 3 08 130 Sta, Perpètua de Mogoda, Barcelona, Spain

Time Out Guides Limited
Universal House
251 Tottenham Court Road
London W1T 7AB
Tel + 44 (0)20 7813 3000
Fax + 44 (0)20 7813 6001
Email guides@timeout.com
www.timeout.com

Editorial

Editor Ros Sales
Consultant Editors Mark Jenkins, Bradford McKee
Deputy Editor Lesley McCave
Listings Editors Patrick Foster, Denise Kersten
Proofreader John Watson
Indexer Anna Raikes

Editorial/Managing Director Peter Fiennes
Series Editor Ruth Jarvis
Deputy Series Editor Lesley McCave
Business Manager Gareth Garner
Guides Co-ordinator Anna Norman
Accountants Sarah Bostock, Abdus Sadique

Design

Art Director Mandy Martin
Deputy Art Director Scott Moore
Senior Designer Tracey Ridgewell
Designer Oliver Knight
Junior Designer Chrissy Mouncey
Digital Imaging Dan Conway, Tessa Kar
Ad Make-up Charlotte Blythe

Picture Desk

Picture Editor Jael Marschner
Deputy Picture Editor Tracey Kerrigan
Picture Researcher Ivy Lahon
Picture Desk Assistant/Librarian Kate Knighton

Advertising

Sales Director Mark Phillips
International Sales Manager Ross Canadé
International Sales Executive James Tuson
Advertising Sales (Washington) Suzonne Davids
Advertising Assistant Lucy Butler

Marketing

Marketing Manager Mandy Martinez
US Publicity & Marketing Associate Rosella Albanese

Production

Production Director Mark Lamond
Production Controller Samantha Furniss

Time Out Group

Chairman Tony Elliott
Managing Director Mike Hardwick
Group Financial Director Richard Waterlow
Group Commercial Director Lesley Gill
Group Marketing Director Christine Cort
Group General Manager Nichola Coulthard
Group Art Director John Oakey
Online Managing Director David Pepper
Group Production Director Steve Proctor
Group IT Director Simon Chappell

Contributors

Introduction Bradford McKee. **History** Mark Jenkins (*Marching on Washington* Steve Ackerman). **Washington Today** Mark Jenkins. **Government Town** Mark Jenkins. **Architecture** Mark Jenkins. **Where to Stay** Denise Kersten. **Sightseeing** Steve Ackerman. **Museums** Jessica Dawson. **Restaurants & Cafés** Kate Gibbs, Kim O'Donnel (*Get your claws out, Nothing beats Latin eats, Hood hangouts* Kate Gibbs). **Bars** Ivan Sciupac. **Shops & Services** Bradford McKee. **Festivals & Events** Trey Graham. **Children** Patrick Foster. **Film** Mark Jenkins. **Galleries** Jessica Dawson. **Gay & Lesbian** Steve Gdula. **Music** Glenn Dixon. **Nightlife** Kate Gibbs. **Sport & Fitness** Brooke Foster. **Theatre & Dance** Trey Graham. **Trips Out of Town** Don Graff. **Directory** Patrick Foster (*Diplomatic impunity, SPAN-ing the country* Steve Ellman).

Maps JS Graphics (john@jsgraphics.co.uk).

Photography by Alys Tomlinson, except: pages 10, 15, 16, 26, 74 Corbis; page 20 Rex Features; pages 28, 29 Getty Images; page 67 Don Ripper (Latoff Inc.)/American Battle Monuments Commission; page 86 Cultural Heritage Tourism Collection; page 90 Washington DC Convention & Tourism Corporation; page 222 Daniel Cima. The following image was provided by the featured establishment/artist: page 228.

The Editor would like to thank Ismay Atkins, Janet Zmroczek, Rob Norman, the Radisson Barceló Hotel.

Contents

Introduction

Washington, DC, loves its visitors – all 20 million of them who pile into town every year to see the seat of the US government, visit the hallowed monuments, browse the world-class museums, and immerse themselves in the city's beguiling landscape. This is a place that likes to spoil its tourists, now more than ever. Washingtonians perhaps took for granted the volume of human traffic filling their streets until the terror attacks of September 2001. After those disasters struck so close to home, locals looked at the empty museums, restaurants and hotels, and wondered, wistfully, when tourists would start coming back.

To everyone's delight, they are back – in droves. And they have come at an excellent time, because DC has never been so vibrant. The financial and political problems that dogged the city for decades are being resolved. And while plenty of ills remain in the local school system and public services, there's every reason to feel confident about the future.

In many ways, the Washington of today is a completely different city from the Washington of only five years ago. A breathtaking amount of new construction – not all of it welcomed by residents, but a positive step on the whole – has transformed downtown and the neighbourhoods beyond it. Where huge swathes of land had stood empty for years, new apartments, offices, shops, restaurants and cultural outlets now animate entire blocks. The monumental core has also undergone vast renovations with the arrival of the new World War II Memorial, construction of a new US Capitol visitors' centre, and the completion of the National Museum of the American Indian.

Any dutiful Washingtonian, however, would urge you to see all the national treasures you can squeeze in but to also save time to get out into the city's lively neighbourhoods, such as Dupont Circle, Adams Morgan, Logan Circle and Shaw, to name a few. These areas are full of cool, shady streets lined by stately houses and small, intimate parks. And don't miss the mother of all green spaces, Rock Creek Park, which winds its way up through the centre of the District. Here, hundreds of acres of woods and walking trails provide respite just a short walk from some of the city's most populated corridors.

If it's drama you want, you've come to the right place. DC is a bona fide theatre town, but reserves its best performances for the street. During your stay, you may happen upon a march of people demanding political action of one sort or another; you may hear a storm of sirens clearing the streets ahead of a VIP's motorcade; or you may simply catch a brass band performance outside a Metro station – be sure to throw a dollar into the bucket.

But above all, Washington is a real city. The still photos and sound bites that usually represent it scarcely do it justice. Indeed, if it were as rational and conservative as it appeared, no one would ever visit. Both the lifers and those who pass by briefly will tell you one thing: to really get to know the place you have to jump in, feet first and eyes open.

ABOUT TIME OUT CITY GUIDES

Time Out Washington, DC is one of an expanding series of travel guides produced by the people behind London and New York's successful listings magazines. Our guides are all written and updated by resident experts who have striven to provide you with all the most up-to-date information you'll need to explore the city, whether you're a local or first-time visitor.

THE LOWDOWN ON THE LISTINGS

Above all, we've tried to make this book as useful as possible. Websites, telephone numbers, transport information, opening times, admission prices and credit card details are all included in our listings. And, as far as possible, we've given details of facilities, services and events, all checked and correct at the time we went to press. However, owners and managers can change their arrangements at any time. Before you go out of your way, we'd strongly advise you to call and check opening times, dates of exhibitions and other particulars. While every effort has been made to ensure the accuracy of the information contained in this guide, the publishers cannot accept responsibility for any errors it may contain.

PRICES AND PAYMENT

We have noted whether venues such as shops, hotels and restaurants accept credit cards or not but have only listed the major cards – American Express (AmEx), Diners Club (DC), Discovery (Disc), MasterCard (MC) and Visa (V). Many businesses will also accept other cards, including Switch/Maestro or Delta, JCB, Discover and Carte Blanche. Virtually all shops, restaurants and attractions will accept dollar travellers' cheques issued by a major financial institution (such as American Express).

The prices we've supplied should be treated as guidelines, not gospel. Fluctuating exchange rates and inflation can cause prices, in shops and restaurants particularly, to change rapidly. If prices vary wildly from those we've quoted, ask whether there's a good reason. If not, go elsewhere. Then please write and let us know. We aim to give the best and most up-to-date advice, so we always want to know if you've been badly treated or overcharged.

THE LIE OF THE LAND

We have broken down the city into its best-known sections, and many of our chapters are divided according to these areas. We've included cross streets in all our addresses, so you can find your way about more easily; we've also included zip codes for any venue you might want to write to.

TELEPHONE NUMBERS

The area code for Washington, DC is 202. Maryland and Virginia use a variety of different area codes. We've included these codes in all telephone numbers printed in this guide. Numbers preceded by 1-800 can be called free of charge from within the US, and some of them can be dialled (though not all free of charge) from the UK.

To dial numbers as given in this book from abroad, use your country's exit code (00 in the UK), followed by the country code for the United States. For more details of phone codes and charges, *see p262*.

ESSENTIAL INFORMATION

For all the practical information you might need for visiting the city – including visa and customs information, disabled access, emergency telephone numbers, a list of useful websites and the lowdown on the local transport network – turn to the Directory chapter at the back of this guide. It starts on p230.

Advertisers

MAPS

We've included a series of fully indexed colour street maps to the city at the back of this guide – they start on p280. Where possible, we've printed a grid reference with each address that map of the city, a map of appears on the maps. There is also an overview the surrounding countryside and a Metro transport map at the back of the guide on p288.

LET US KNOW WHAT YOU THINK

We hope you enjoy *Time Out Washington, DC* and we'd like to know what you think of it. We welcome tips for places that you consider we should include in future editions and take notice of your criticism of our choices. You can email us on guides@timeout.com.

There is an online version of this book, along with guides to over 45 other international cities, at **www.timeout.com**.

In Context

Union troops in the Civil War.

History

Politics and people converge.

Symbolically, Washington is the heart of American democracy. More than 200 years after its founding, however, democracy for its own residents is only partial: DC's citizens can participate in presidential elections, but have no voting representation in the US Congress. This awkward circumstance is rooted in the city's founding, which was a political compromise between Northern and Southern states.

The Revolutionary War left the North with substantial debts that it pressed the new federal government to assume. In exchange, the Northerners abandoned their hopes of locating the government in a large Northern city such as New York or Philadelphia, each of which had served as the capital for a time. Instead, they agreed to construct a new city on the border between North and South. The actual choice was left to President George Washington.

THE NEW CAPITAL

The first president was not the earliest person to recognise that the confluence of the Potomac and Anacostia rivers was a natural crossroads. The area was an Indian meeting and trading

place a millennium before the Federal City was conceived. Still, the Algonquin Indians who lived in the area when Europeans first arrived in the early 17th century left little besides the names of the two rivers.

Within the new city were two port towns that had been founded around 1750: Georgetown on the Maryland side and Alexandria in Virginia. Both were incorporated into the new District of Columbia, a diamond-shaped 100-square-mile (259-square-kilometre) precinct that took 70 square miles from Maryland and 30 from Virginia. But the new capital, which came to be known as Washington, would be built from scratch on land that was mostly farmland or forest – contrary to the popular belief that the city is built on a swamp, hence the summer humidity. Washington hired a former member of his army staff, Pierre-Charles L'Enfant, to design the new city (see p36 **The man with the plan**).

Construction of the White House and Capitol began in 1792-93, but neither was finished when John Adams, the country's second president, took office in 1800. Adams and other members of the new government were the first to notice the gap between the grandeur of L'Enfant's baroque street plan and the reality: a muddy frontier town of a mere 14,000 inhabitants, most of them living in Georgetown and Alexandria.

After 1801, residents of the District of Columbia lost their right to vote in Maryland or Virginia. The Constitution specified that Congress alone would control 'the federal district', although it's unclear that the document's drafters actually intended to disenfranchise the District's residents. The city of Washington was incorporated, with an elected city council and mayor appointed by the president. In 1820, the city's residents were allowed to elect the mayor as well. This was the first of many tinkerings with the local form of government.

'By 1800, around a quarter of the city's population was African American.'

What progress had been made in creating the new capital was largely undone during the War of 1812. In 1814, after defeating local resistance at the Battle of Bladensburg, British troops marched unopposed into the city and burned most of the significant buildings. President Madison fled the White House for the Octagon, the nearby home of Colonel John Tayloe. It was there that he ratified the Treaty of Ghent, which ended the war. Among the things destroyed by the British was the original collection of the Library of Congress, which didn't yet have its own building; former president Thomas Jefferson sold the nation his library as the basis for a new collection.

After the War of 1812 re-confirmed American sovereignty, European guests began to arrive to inspect the new capital. They were unimpressed. Visiting in 1842, Charles Dickens provided the most withering sobriquet for pre-Civil War Washington: 'the city of magnificent intentions'. It was another Englishman, however, who made the greatest impact on the city in this period. In 1829 James Smithson, a professor of chemistry at Oxford who never visited the United States, left his estate to the new nation for the founding of an educational institution. Congress was so bewildered by this bequest that it didn't act on it for more than a decade, but the Smithsonian Institution was finally founded in 1846. Its original building opened in 1855.

While the Smithsonian laid one of the earliest foundations for Washington's contemporary position as an information hub, the city showed few signs of becoming a centre of commerce. In an attempt to increase trade, the Chesapeake & Ohio Canal was built, paralleling the Potomac

River for 185 miles (296 kilometres) to Cumberland, Maryland. Ground was broken in 1828, and the canal's Georgetown terminus opened in 1840. The canal continued to operate into the early 20th century, but its importance was soon diminished by the Baltimore & Ohio Railroad, the country's first railway, which began operation in 1830 and arrived in Washington in 1835.

The other event of this period that had long-term significance for Washington was the 1846 retrocession to Virginia of the southern third of the District; the area now encompasses Arlington County and part of the city of Alexandria. Among residents' grievances was Congress's refusal to loan money to construct a Virginia-side canal connecting Alexandria to the west. The Virginia state government was more inclined to support the project than Congress, which has always been reluctant to spend money on people without any voting representatives in the Capitol. (The canal project was ultimately reduced to an aqueduct connecting Alexandria to the C&O Canal.) An underlying issue, however, was some Virginians' anticipation that Congress would soon restrict the slave trade in the District.

From its founding, Washington had a large African American population. By 1800 around a quarter of the city's population was African American, and most of those were slaves. By 1840 the ratio of white to black was similar, but there were almost twice as many free blacks as slaves. Free blacks and runaway slaves arrived in Washington to escape the horrors of life on Southern plantations, and quickly set up institutions to help their compatriots. Washington became a more attractive destination in 1850, when Congress did ban slave-trading (but not slavery itself). A year before Abraham Lincoln's 1863 Emancipation Proclamation, Congress abolished slavery in the District.

Despite the presence of some relatively prosperous free blacks, Washington was hardly a safe haven for former slaves. African Americans were sometimes kidnapped off the city's streets and sold into slavery, the papers certifying their free status having been destroyed by their captors. Those who escaped this fate still had to live under the onerous 'black codes' adopted by Congress from the laws of Virginia and Maryland. These restricted African Americans' property ownership, employment and trades, public meetings, and even use of profane language. Being arrested for an infraction of these laws could result in a permanent loss of liberty, since jail wardens were authorised to sell their black prisoners to pay the cost of their incarceration.

CIVIL WAR CONSEQUENCES

The Civil War transformed Washington from a sleepy part-time capital into the command centre of an energised country – the first (but not the last) time that a national crisis actually benefited the city. New residents flooded into the city, and such DC inhabitants as photographer Matthew Brady became nationally known for their war work. Among the new Washingtonians was poet Walt Whitman, who initially came to care for his wounded brother and then became a volunteer at the makeshift hospitals in the converted Patent Office and Washington Armory. (Whitman remained in the city for 12 years, working as a clerk at various federal agencies; he was fired from the Bureau of Indian Affairs when the new Secretary of the Interior deemed *Leaves of Grass* to violate 'the rules of decorum & propriety prescribed by a Christian Civilisation'.)

Several Civil War battles were fought near Washington, notably the two engagements at Manassas, now a local commuter-rail stop. A string of forts was built to protect the District, but only one saw action: Fort Stevens, site of the 1864 skirmish. The city's most significant war-related incident, the 1865 assassination of President Lincoln at Ford's Theatre, actually occurred five days after the South surrendered.

After the war, a Congress dominated by 'radical Republicans' made some efforts to atone for slavery. The Freedman's Bureau was established to help former slaves make the transition to freedom, and in 1867 Howard University was chartered for African American students. All adult male DC residents were granted local suffrage in 1866, and 9,800 white and 8,200 'colored' men registered to vote.

Congress, however, did not address Washingtonians' lack of Congressional representation. In 1871 it reclassified the city as a territory, but quieted the latest round of rumours that it intended to move the capital west by authorising the construction of the massive State, War & Navy Departments Building (now the Old Executive Office Building). A prominent local real-estate developer, Alexander Shepherd, was appointed to the territory's Board of Public Works, which he soon dominated. 'Boss' Shepherd began an ambitious programme of street grading and paving, sewer-building and tree-planting, transforming the city but also quickly bankrupting it.

Only three years after establishing the territorial government, Congress abandoned it, putting the city under the control of three presidentially appointed commissioners. Local voting rights were eliminated, a move that one local newspaper welcomed as ending the 'curse' of African American suffrage. President Grant,

still a Shepherd supporter, nominated the 'Boss' to be one of the three new commissioners, but the Senate wouldn't confirm him. In 1876 Shepherd moved to Mexico, leaving behind a city that was beginning to look like modern Washington.

The next major round of civic improvements was inspired by severe flooding in 1881. A land-reclamation and flood-control project led to the building of Hains Point and West Potomac Park, literally creating the ground that would become the home of such Washington landmarks as the Lincoln and Jefferson memorials. That same year, President Garfield was shot at the Baltimore & Potomac Railroad station (now the site of the National Gallery of Art) by a disgruntled job-seeker. Garfield died two months later in New Jersey, where he had been taken for the supposedly rehabilitative effect of sea air.

Following Shepherd's modernisation of the city, many improvement projects were undertaken. The Washington Monument was finally finished in 1885, and electric streetcars began operation in 1888, opening the areas beyond Boundary Street (now Florida Avenue) to development as suburbs. In 1889, the National Zoological Park was founded in Rock Creek Park, which was officially established the following year.

NEW CENTURY AND NEW DEAL

Washington's 1900 centennial brought major plans to remake the city. Under the influence of the 'City Beautiful' movement, the Congressionally chartered McMillan Commission proposed restoring the primacy of the oft-ignored L'Enfant Plan and developing the neglected Mall and nearby areas along the river. Some of the city's poorest and most dangerous neighbourhoods were to be bulldozed to create a grand greensward, and such unseemly intrusions as the Baltimore & Potomac Railroad station were to be banished from the Mall. The result of the latter dictum was Union Station, which upon its 1908 opening consolidated the city's several downtown rail 'road stations on a site north of the Capitol. In 1910 the Fine Arts Commission was established to ensure the aesthetic worthiness of new federal structures, and an act was passed to limit the height of buildings.

A practical challenge to the McMillan Plan came with World War I, which prompted another Washington building boom. Dozens of 'temporary' structures were erected, including some on the western part of the Mall. Many of these buildings were used not only during World War I but World War II as well. The last of them was torn down in 1971, and part of the space they occupied became Constitution Gardens, which opened in 1976.

The large numbers of unemployed sailors and soldiers demobilised in Washington after World War I are often cited as one of the causes of the race riots that convulsed the city in the summer of 1919. Nine people were killed in the worst disturbance, which began after false rumours spread that a black man had raped a white woman. Much of the violence spread from the Navy Yard into the predominantly African American neighbourhoods nearby in Southwest.

Race relations were strained by the riots, but they were precarious even before them. Most of

I spy

Washington may not seem as exotic as Istanbul and Shanghai, or as ominous as Cold War-era Moscow and Berlin. Yet a former chief of the FBI's Washington Field Office, Ray Mislock, recently claimed that 'there are more foreign spies in Washington, DC than in any other city in the world.'

Although espionage didn't become a full-time vocation in Washington until World War I, the city is actually named after a spy master. During the American Revolutionary War, the Culper Ring operated in New York City and Long Island, passing intelligence on British activities to George Washington.

During the American Civil War, DC hostess Rose O'Neal Greenhow spied for the rebels, providing information that Confederate President Jefferson Davis credited with helping to win the battle of Manassas.

In 1917 Herbert O Yardley became a cryptologic officer with the American Expeditionary Forces in France. After the war, he was hired to create the first US peacetime code-breaking office, MI-8, also known as the Black Chamber. Its operations were very successful, but MI-8 was eliminated in 1929 by Secretary of State Henry Stimson, who supposedly announced, 'Gentlemen do not read each other's mail'. The impoverished Yardley wrote a controversial 1931 exposé, *The American Black Chamber*, and a lot of countries quickly changed their codes.

During the next World War, avoiding a potential spy scandal may have furthered John F Kennedy's presidential ambitions. As a young Naval Intelligence officer, JFK fervently romanced the glamorous Inga Arvad, a suspected Nazi operative. While FBI chief (and Kennedy nemesis) J Edgar Hoover kept the couple under surveillance, the future president's alarmed father, Joseph Kennedy Sr, pulled some strings to have his son transferred to active duty in the Pacific. There, his PT boat was sunk by the Japanese, an event that gave Kennedy war-hero status.

His affair with Arvad wasn't the only time the famously libidinous Kennedy entangled eros and intrigue. In 1964 one of the recently assassinated president's former lovers, Mary Pinchot Meyer, was mysteriously murdered on the C&O Canal towpath in Georgetown. While the slaying was never solved, two top CIA officials quickly arrived at Meyer's house to seize her diary. They were Cord Meyer, the victim's ex-husband, and James Angleton, CIA counterintelligence chief who had allowed free access to the agency for his close friend Kim Philby, first secretary of the British Embassy in Washington from 1949 to 1951 – and a Soviet agent who had been exposed in 1963.

Georgetown figures in more than a few Washington spy stories, even though the USA's own spies all operate from suburbs: the CIA is based in nearby McLean, Virginia; the Defense Intelligence Agency is headquartered at the Pentagon; and the National Security Agency snoops from Fort Meade, Maryland, which is near Baltimore-Washington International Airport. But Georgetown has been a frequent meeting place for spies and handlers, from Soviet courier Elizabeth Bentley in the '30s to US Navy analyst Jonathan Pollard, who a half-century later met his Israeli contact at Dumbarton Oaks. In 1985, CIA agent Aldrich Ames divulged the names of 20 agency informants in the Soviet bloc to a KGB man at Chadwick's, a K Street restaurant. The same year, the highest-ranking KGB agent ever to defect to the US, Vitaly Yurchenko, took leave of his CIA escort, slipped out through the kitchen and hailed a cab to the Soviet Embassy, where he de-defected.

The largest setback to American intelligence in recent years was the work of Robert Philip Hanssen, an FBI agent arrested in 2001 for supplying copious secret documents to the KGB. Hanssen spent much of his illegal income sending his children to expensive private schools affiliated with Opus Dei, a conservative Catholic organisation, and on stripper Priscilla Sue Galey, a supposedly platonic friend, who worked at Joanna's 1819 Club, near Dupont Circle. It's still there, a reminder of the diverse activities that can occur behind closed doors in Washington.

WOW!

Great value holiday car hire to North America.

Get these great rates today at www.hertz.co.u

The '**Bonus Army**' of jobless World War I veterans march for back pay.

the advances for African Americans in the post-Civil War era had been turned back by the early 20th century, and President Woodrow Wilson, hailed as a visionary in foreign policy, was a reactionary on matters of race. Federal government agencies were rigidly segregated, as were most of the capital's public facilities – although its libraries, trolleys and buses, and baseball stadium (but not the teams that played there) were integrated.

In 1922, when the Lincoln Memorial opened, the man who freed the slaves was commemorated by a racially segregated crowd; Tuskegee Institute President Robert Moten, an official invitee, was brusquely ushered to the 'negro' section. Three years later, 25,000 hooded Ku Klux Klansmen marched down Pennsylvania Avenue, although the founding of a local Klan chapter drew little support. In 1926, the local superior court upheld the legality of voluntary covenants designed to prevent blacks from buying property in predominantly white neighbourhoods.

Women won the vote in 1920, although not if they were DC residents. Meanwhile, separate and unequal African American Washington boomed, with the Harlem Renaissance mirrored on U Street, known as the 'Great Black Way'. The Howard and other theatres frequently presented such performers as Ella Fitzgerald, Eubie Blake and Washington native Duke Ellington. The city's African American neighbourhoods were swelled by

dispossessed Cotton Belt agricultural workers, and the Depression was soon to send more Southern blacks to town.

In central Washington, the work begun by the McMillan Commission continued. Beginning in 1926, the construction of the Federal Triangle displaced the city's Chinatown and one of its roughest neighbourhoods, 'Murder Bay', while creating an area of monumental federal office buildings unified by their Beaux Arts style. Other events boosted the capital's national prestige: in 1924 and 1925, the Washington Senators baseball team (now defunct) made their first two of three trips to the World Series. (They won only in 1924.) In 1927, the first Cherry Blossom Festival was held, calling attention to the city's new ornamental riverfront.

The Depression soon ended the major civic improvement projects and made Washington the focus for a different sort of national attention. In 1931, a group called the Hunger Marchers arrived in the city; it was followed by some 20,000 jobless World War I veterans who became known as the 'Bonus Army'. They camped at various places around the city, sometimes with their families, waiting for Congress to pass legislation awarding them back pay. Eventually troops under the command of General Douglas MacArthur dispersed the camps with bayonets and tear gas. Four people were killed, two of them young children.

In 1932, Franklin D Roosevelt was elected president and his New Deal created new programmes and jobs. Again, Washington benefited from national adversity. Local construction crews began to work again, erecting the National Archives and the Supreme Court, both finished in 1935. Meanwhile, some of the president's cabinet members and top advisers discovered Georgetown, which fitted the 1930s vogue for the colonial style; the old port town, which then had a large African American population, became the first Washington neighbourhood to be gentrified.

The New Dealers took a more liberal stand on racial issues. Although the Roosevelts were reluctant to antagonise segregationists with major changes, they did sometimes invite black leaders to receptions – and black musicians to perform – at the White House. In 1939, when the Daughters of the American Revolution refused to let famed African American contralto Marian Anderson perform at the group's Constitution

Hall, Secretary of the Interior Harold Ickes immediately approved a concert at the Lincoln Memorial. Anderson performed there for an integrated crowd of 75,000.

World War II added to the city's bustle, as thousands of workers and volunteers arrived to further the war effort. National Airport opened in 1941, and the Pentagon (still the nation's largest federal office building) was rapidly constructed for the military command. (The Pentagon was built with separate bathrooms for white and black employees, but after FDR protested, signs distinguishing the facilities were never added to the doors.) Also opening in this period were two less martial structures: the Jefferson Memorial and the National Gallery of Art. The arts kept a low profile for the remainder of the war, however, as such institutions as Dumbarton Oaks were requisitioned by wartime agencies.

Marching on Washington

The main stage, usually, is the national Mall; the main event, the march on Washington. That phrase instantly conjures images of the 1963 March for Jobs and Freedom, and Dr Martin Luther King's 'I have a dream' speech. Although indelibly the most memorable, the 1963 march was neither the first, nor the largest, nor the most immediately effective march on Washington.

For a century, Americans had petitioned their government from a distance. Citizens either sent small delegations to present a resolution to Washington or 'mailed it in'. In an economic depression in 1894

Despite fears of a post-war depression, the city continued to boom in the late 1940s. As the Korean War began, the 1950 census put the District's population at 800,000, its highest point. Washington's new position as an imperial capital in a polarised world was emphasised by a series of controversial hearings on alleged Communist infiltration of the federal government.

In the 1950s, suburbanisation began to transform the land around Washington, most of it farms or woodland. Aided by new highways and federally guaranteed home mortgages, residential developments grew rapidly in the (now) inner suburbs, followed by commercial development. Congress authorised the Interstate Highway System and supported plans for an extensive system of urban freeways for Washington that would destroy neighbourhoods and overwhelm the proportions of L'Enfant's plan.

Automobile, petroleum and rubber interests that worked quietly to destroy transit systems in other American cities had no need for subtlety in DC, which still had no elected local government. Corporate envoys influenced lawmakers to eliminate trolleys in favour of 'modern' cars and buses. Under Congressional pressure, streetcar lines were abandoned throughout the decade, with the final routes cut in 1962.

While the suburbs grew, Congress turned again to removing embarrassing examples of poverty in the vicinity of the Capitol. Thousands of working-class inhabitants were displaced from Southwest Washington as a result of 'urban renewal'. (Critics called it 'urban removal'.) Southwest also became a focus for federal development, with massive new headquarters buildings erected near the new L'Enfant Plaza.

everything changed, when a ragtag 'Army of the Unemployed' led by Ohio merchant Jacob Coxey converged on the city to present what was called a 'a petition in boots', urging the government to create employment through a national road-building campaign. Congress wasn't amused. Coxey was arrested under a hastily enacted law banning treading on the grass of the Capitol grounds.

The next notable marchers arrived in 1913, when elaborately costumed and staged demonstrations demanding women's suffrage greeted the crowds gathered for the inauguration of President Woodrow Wilson. The spectacle of white-clad females behaving aggressively shook the social conventions of the time, but women were voting by the election of 1920.

The Ku Klux Klan flexed its muscle in a brazen march down Pennsylvania Avenue in 1925, and the Depression brought protests from the jobless with a hunger march on the city in 1931. This was followed by the arrival of the Bonus Army of 1932. World War I veterans jobless in the Great Depression came to demand early payment of a cash bonus promised them in 1946. Fearing a communist plot, President Hoover drove them from town with tanks and cavalry, to his cost at the next election.

The most immediately effective march on Washington never happened. Black labour

leader A Philip Randolph threatened a demonstration in 1941 protesting at racial discrimination in America's war industries. To avoid embarrassment in an awkward international situation, President Roosevelt issued a corrective order. Randolph took the lesson, and went on to engineer the famous 1963 march.

A Poor People's March in 1968 failed to revive the spirit of 1963, but a sequence of marches protesting the war in Vietnam soon grabbed the headlines. The impressive Vietnam Veterans Against the War demonstrations of 1971 started the political rise of John Kerry, culminating in his presidential candidacy three decades later.

By the late 20th century, marching on Washington had become so ritualised that many such exercises became ends in themselves: the male morality rallies of the Promise Keepers or the Million Man March had no specific demands to present to the government. But cliché or not, the marchers keep coming. An abortion rights march in 2004 certainly drew half a million people, and possibly almost twice that number. If you want to publicise an issue, stage a celebration, assert your identity or make a show of strength, the nation agrees that the Mall is the place to do it. Over 3,000 groups apply for special event permits yearly.

Ethnic Washington

In 1975, just a few years after the US Census Bureau declared Washington more than 70 per cent African American, the funk band Parliament recorded an album named after the then-popular tag for DC: 'Chocolate City'. Aside from a few diplomats and foreign students, black and white seemed to be the only colours in town.

That ethnic shift had come quickly, spurred by the end of World War II and the 1954 racial integration of DC's public schools. In the 19th century, Washington had developed the sort of ethnic neighbourhoods typical of other East Coast cities, including German, Italian, Irish and Jewish enclaves. During the post-war building boom, however, long-standing ethnic bonds were shattered by affluence, assimilation and suburbanisation. Only Chinatown survived, and that is now rapidly being consumed by non-Chinese businesses and residents. And, as the Maryland and Virginia suburbs grew at a fantastic rate, most inner-city wards were transformed.

In the last 25 years, much of the inner city has been transformed again. DC is now a little less than 60 per cent African American, which makes the city's principal ethnic minority a dwindling majority. Blacks have been departing Washington for two decades, while the white population has increased slightly and new-immigrant groups have burgeoned. Many African Americans moved to adjacent Prince George's County, Maryland, which in the 1990s became the country's first predominantly black suburban county.

An influx of foreign-born residents has considerably altered such neighbourhoods as Adams Morgan, Mount Pleasant, Columbia Heights, Shaw and Petworth. The largest contingent comes from Latin America, especially El Salvador. (Ironically, many of them moved to Washington to flee the death squads that were instruments of US policy in Central America.) Although they share a language and some customs with the new arrivals from Peru, Nicaragua and other Latin countries, some Salvadorans have essentially reproduced their home villages in DC, working and socialising with their neighbours from the old country. Other nations that have sent many newcomers to Washington include Vietnam, Jamaica, Afghanistan, Ethiopia and Eritrea.

The metropolitan area is also home to substantial numbers of immigrants from India, China, Iran and Korea, but those groups live mostly in the suburbs. In large part, this is a matter of economics. Immigrants from these countries tend to be professionals and proprietors who see the suburbs as the natural habitat of the American middle and upper classes. Central Washington has principally drawn poorer immigrants, although working-class newcomers also live in such suburban neighbourhoods as Maryland's Langley Park/Hyattsville, Silver Spring and Wheaton, and Virginia's Arlandria, South Arlington and Seven Corners/Bailey's Crossroads. The latter is home to Eden Center, the area's biggest Asian retail district.

There are other suburban shopping areas that cater to foreign-born Washingtonians, but U, 18th and Mount Pleasant Streets, NW, and Columbia Road, NW, are the principal arteries of immigrant DC. Salvadoran groceries, Ethiopian restaurants and African record stores line these thoroughfares, providing the city with a wealth of flavours beyond chocolate and vanilla. You'll have to go to Baltimore for a Little Italy or a Greektown, but Washington's ethnic mix is both lively and singular.

RIGHTS AND RIOTS

The city's white population began to decline precipitously in 1954, after the Supreme Court outlawed racial segregation. While many jurisdictions resisted the ruling, Washington quickly came into compliance. It was soon a majority black city, with a poverty rate that mortified federal officials.

Under Presidents John F Kennedy and Lyndon Johnson, the capital became both the symbolic focus and a conspicuous test case of the civil rights movement and the 'war on poverty'.

In 1963, Martin Luther King Jr led a 200,000-person March for Jobs and Freedom to Washington, and delivered his 'I have a dream' speech at the Lincoln Memorial. Neither race relations nor inner-city economies improved significantly in the mid 1960s, and some feared the capital would soon experience the same sort of riots that had already scarred other major cities. The spark was the 1968 assassination of Martin Luther King Jr: Washington and other cities erupted in flames. Twelve people were killed as rioters burned many small businesses in predominantly black sections of the city.

Congress had already made tentative steps toward enfranchising Washington residents. In 1961, a Constitutional amendment had given Washington residents the right to vote in presidential elections, and in 1967 Congress restored the mayor-and-council system of government, but with all officials appointed by the president. Despite post-1968 fears that Washington would explode again, progress in establishing an elected local government was slow. Finally, in 1975, Walter Washington become the city's first elected mayor of the 20th century and its first African American one.

The 'Free DC' battle for local voting rights was rooted in, and interconnected with, the larger civil rights movement. Many of the city's first elected officials – notably Marion Barry, who began the first of four terms as mayor in 1979 – were civil rights veterans. Almost as important, however, was the anti-freeway campaign. An ad hoc citizens' group managed to stop most of the proposed highways through the city. Protests halted a planned freeway bridge across the Potomac River, and the slogan 'white men's roads through black men's homes' prevented an eight-lane thoroughfare through Upper Northeast.

Local activists preferred a mostly underground rapid-rail system, which had already been discussed for half a century. Congress funded the system that would become the Metro, but influential congressmen held up financing until city residents also accepted the freeway system. They never did, and the Metro finally opened its long-delayed first section in 1976.

In the 1970s, Washington served as a backdrop for several national struggles, notably the one over the Vietnam War. President Richard Nixon, who recognised his local unpopularity, stressed 'law and order' – considered code words for racial fears – and painted the majority-black city as the nation's 'crime capital'. Then five burglars working indirectly for Nixon were arrested during a break-in at the Democratic National Committee campaign headquarters in the Watergate office building, and 'Watergate' gradually became synonymous with Washington.

The city's reputation was supposed to have been bolstered by the 1976 celebration of the nation's bicentennial, but most people skipped the party, perhaps frightened by reports of crowds that never materialised. Still, the year saw the opening of the National Air & Space Museum, which soon became the country's most popular museum.

> **'Reagan was ideologically opposed to big government and temperamentally averse to Washington.'**

The following year, members of a small black Islamic group, the Hanafi Movement, seized the District Building, the B'Nai Brith Building and the Washington Islamic Center in a protest against an obscure film depicting the prophet Mohamed. In the attack on the District Building, then the headquarters of the mayor and the city council, a journalist was killed and councilman Marion Barry was wounded.

Faced with pressure from the DC statehood movement, in 1978 Congress passed a constitutional amendment that would have given the District voting representation in both the House and the Senate. The amendment was ratified by only 16 of the necessary 35 states, however, and expired in 1985.

In 1981, Ronald Reagan became president and, that same year, survived an assassination attempt outside the Washington Hilton Hotel. Reagan was ideologically opposed to big government and temperamentally averse to Washington. Nonetheless, after surviving the major recession of Reagan's first term, the region enjoyed a building boom, as new office buildings rose in the city and the suburbs, especially in Virginia. Tenants of the latter were known as 'Beltway Bandits', after their proximity to the circumferential highway completed in 1964; many of them were government contractors benefiting from the Reagan administration's large military build-up.

Damage to the **Pentagon** after the hijacked plane crash of 11 September 2001.

Although the city benefited from the tax revenues flowing from the new developments, Barry spent much of the money on assuring his political invulnerability. Years of rumours about the mayor's nocturnal activities were validated in 1990, when Barry was arrested after being videotaped smoking crack. Many Barry supporters were angered by the FBI sting, however, charging entrapment. When brought to trial, Barry was convicted of only a misdemeanour, making him eligible for office at the end of his jail term.

DC IN THE 1990S

The city's white population has grown slightly in recent years, but middle-class blacks departed in large numbers during the 1980s and '90s. The 2000 census put DC's population at 572,000, a figure that surely undercounts the illegal immigrants, many of whom fled Central America in the 1980s. Among Washington's foreign-born recent arrivals, Latinos are the fastest-growing group. The tension between these new residents and the city's predominantly black police force erupted in 1991, with two days of anti-police rioting in the largely Latino Mount Pleasant, Adams Morgan and Columbia Heights neighbourhoods.

Barry did indeed run again in 1994, winning re-election in a vote polarised along racial and class lines. He showed little interest in the job, however, and Congress had no patience for the notorious mayor. With revenues diminished by the early 1990s real-estate slump, the city was at great fiscal risk. Congress took advantage of the crisis to seize control of the city, putting a financial control board in charge of most municipal business.

When Barry was replaced by the sober, low-key Anthony Williams in 1999, Congressional leaders backed off. The cost-cutting, pro-business Williams has antagonised many residents – notably by shutting the public hospital that treated the city's poor – but his administration met the requirement to produce three years of balanced budgets, thus causing the financial control board to disappear in 2001.

BEYOND 2001

George W Bush won the 2000 presidential election, despite having been outpolled by rival Al Gore to the tune of half a million votes. In what many judged as a politically motivated decision, the Supreme Court voted to stop a recount of votes in Florida, effectively sealing victory for Bush in the Electoral College. He was inaugurated in January 2001.

On September 11 of that year, a hijacked airliner smashed into the Pentagon in nearby Virginia, killing 184. Although overshadowed by the much greater death toll in New York, the Pentagon attack – and the possibility that a fourth plane was supposed to hit the Capitol or the White House – put the federal government on high alert, where it essentially remains. Security was tightened, barriers went up around federal buildings, and permanent new crowd-control methods were hastily planned. Tourism fell dramatically, but as of spring 2004 has rebounded to former levels. While the monumental core has never looked less welcoming, some inner-city neighbourhoods are rapidly gentrifying. More than 200 years after the Federal District absorbed local towns, official Washington and hometown DC remain on separate tracks.

Key events

circa 700 Indians use the confluence of the Potomac and Anacostia rivers as a meeting place.
1608 Captain John Smith is the first known European to explore the Potomac, although he was apparently preceded by fur traders.
1749 Alexandria founded by Scottish settlers.
1790 The US Congress votes to establish a Federal City and to move the capital there from Philadelphia.
1791-92 Pierre-Charles L'Enfant plans the new city, but is soon fired.
1800 President John Adams moves to the District of Columbia, the new capital.
1802 The City of Washington is incorporated, with local government by an elected council and a mayor appointed by the president.
1814 British troops invade Washington.
1820 Congress allows Washington's 30,000 residents to elect the city's mayor.
1829 Englishman James Smithson leaves his estate to the new nation for the founding of an educational institution.
1846 The portion of the District south of the Potomac is ceded back to Virginia.
1850 Congress abolishes slave trade in Washington, but not slave ownership.
1861-65 The Civil War greatly expands Washington's influence and size.
1862 Congress bans slavery in the District.
1865 President Lincoln is assassinated at Ford's Theatre.
1871 Congress converts Washington to a territorial government.
1874 Congress abandons territorial government, eliminates local voting rights and gives control of the city to three presidentially appointed commissioners.
1881 President Garfield assassinated.
1888 Electric streetcars begin operation.
1902 The McMillan Commission begins to restore the L'Enfant Plan.
1908 Union Station opens.
1912 The first of 2,000 cherry trees, a gift from Japan, are planted near the Tidal Basin.
1917 America's entry into World War I spurs another population and building boom.
1919 Inflamed by false rumours of a black man's rape of a white woman, white rioters attack black neighbourhoods. Nine are killed.
1922 In the city's worst natural disaster, 97 people are killed when the roof of the Knickerbocker Theater collapses during a 26in (66cm) snowfall.

1926 The Federal Triangle building programme begins.
1928 The first licensed TV station in the US opens in Washington on an experimental basis.
1932 The federal government grows dramatically under Franklin D Roosevelt's New Deal. Jobless World War I veterans camp in Washington and are eventually dispersed by troops, killing four.
1943 The Pentagon is completed.
1950 During the Korean War, the population of the District grows to 800,000, its highest point.
1954 DC schools and recreation facilities desegregated.
1961 A constitutional amendment gives Washington residents the right to vote in presidential elections.
1962 The last lines of the local trolley system, shut down by Congressional edict, close.
1963 Martin Luther King Jr delivers his 'I have a dream' speech at the Lincoln Memorial.
1964 The Capital Beltway is completed.
1967 Congress re-establishes the mayor and council system of government for the city, but with all officials appointed by the president.
1968 Riots follow Martin Luther King Jr's assassination. Twelve people are killed.
1970 Several anti-Vietnam War protests.
1971 The Kennedy Center opens.
1972 Burglars working indirectly for President Richard Nixon are arrested during a break-in at the Watergate office building.
1975 Walter Washington becomes the city's first elected mayor of the 20th century and its first African American one.
1976 The first segment of the Metro rapid-rail system opens.
1981 President Reagan is wounded by a would-be assassin outside the Washington Hilton Hotel.
1990 Mayor Marion Barry is arrested in an FBI sting after being videotaped smoking crack.
1994 After serving prison time for a misdemeanour, Marion Barry is re-elected as mayor.
1995 Congress appoints a control board to run most of the city government.
1999 Anthony Williams becomes mayor.
2001 The final segment of the planned 103-mile Metro system opens; the control board closes. A hijacked plane hits the Pentagon, killing 184.
2002 Despite not qualifying for the primary ballot, Anthony Williams is re-elected.

Washington Today

Complex and multi-layered, Washington has its problems. But it's not done fighting yet.

Everyone seems to agree that there are two Washingtons, but which two? There are the black and white Washingtons, but though this divide remains crucial for some, its sharp contrast is fading as the city becomes home to a multi-hued citizenry with origins in Latin America, Asia and the Caribbean.

There are urban and suburban Washingtons, a split that's reflected nationwide but is particularly significant in the capital region, where suburbanites enjoy not only greater economic power but also the full political enfranchisement that DC residents lack.

Then there are federal and local Washingtons, a distinction that defines life along the Potomac, but is often misunderstood. While Washington is officially the 'federal city', a large portion of the national bureaucracy – and the bulk of its local employees – reside in Virginia and Maryland.

GETTING DEFENSIVE

September 11 created another two Washingtons: fortified and unfortified. Security procedures were in place before the attacks, of course, and it's been more than a century since private citizens could simply arrive unannounced at the White House. But the post-9/11 frenzy of shutting, barricading and scrutinising has transformed the White House, the Capitol, the Mall and adjacent areas.

Entrance to many buildings has been curtailed or entirely eliminated. Concrete bollards and barriers posing as planters now surround dozens of buildings. Streets have been closed around the Capitol and the White House, and the section of Pennsylvania Avenue in front of the latter is being converted to a public plaza/security perimeter. A scheme to build a moat around the Washington Monument, with access to the structure through a trench, was only narrowly averted – and may be introduced

again. Throughout the city, poorly trained (and often poorly paid) rent-a-cops reign officiously over the doorways to public spaces.

THRIVING AND REVIVING

In the same period that official Washington has been putting up the barricades, however, the unfortified city has been thriving. While visiting the monumental core has become more of a hassle, away from the national landmarks and major museums there are new shops, restaurants and nightclubs, as well as an upsurge in the construction and rehabilitation of inner-city housing.

Strikingly, DC's current boom began during a nationwide recession and a Republican administration. Since Richard Nixon's racially charged characterisation of DC as America's 'crime capital' more than 30 years ago, Republican candidates have demonised the overwhelmingly Democratic and majority African American District. A Republican in the White House is usually bad news for DC, but since George W Bush's inauguration, the city's economy has been robust. The most recent monthly statistics showed the Washington region with a 2.8 per cent unemployment rate, the lowest of any major US metropolitan area, and the largest number of new jobs. In 2003 local home values were up 13.3 per cent, the fourth-highest rate in the nation.

Yet the benefits of such growth are distributed unequally. That reflects fundamental inequities in the American economy, of course, but also dilemmas specific to Washington. After all, DC is by definition a most un-American place.

In fact, Washington is a unique city in many ways, and several of those ways are not to its benefit. Ultimate control of DC's laws and finances rests with the US Congress, which can overturn any local legislation and must approve the city's annual budget. Washingtonians' ability to influence Congressional oversight is exceptionally limited, since residents of DC are the only Americans who don't have voting representation in either the Senate or the House of Representatives. (A bill that would grant the city a single member in the House, in exchange for adding another Republican member from conservative Utah, was introduced in June 2004, but Congress is not expected to consider the measure before 2005.)

DC is also a relatively small city, in the midst of a sprawling, populous region. The Washington area contains nearly five million people, while DC's population is estimated at less than 600,000. According to the US Census Bureau in 2003 the number of DC inhabitants slipped to 563,864, making it the 25th-largest US city. City government officials argue that this figure is too low, and they're probably right. After all, the 2000 census found 50,000 more inhabitants than the federal counters had estimated the year before.

While the Washington area encompasses much of Maryland and Virginia and bits of West Virginia, Pennsylvania and Delaware, DC itself is only 68 square miles (176 square kilometres) – tiny compared with most US cities. It's the only major American metropolis to have actually lost area since it was founded (in 1846, the southern third of the District was retroceded to Virginia).

Visitors who are familiar with dense cities of Asia, Europe or Latin America may consider Washington a wide open space. Buildings over 15 storeys are not permitted, and a high percentage of the housing consists of detached homes. By American standards, however, DC is unusually urban. Its public transport system has the second highest ridership of any US city, after New York's. A recent study indicated that DC's motorists drive fewer miles annually than residents of any US state except Alaska and Hawaii, neither of which have many roads.

Washington's urban qualities are drawing new residents, at least in the western half of the city. New houses and apartment buildings are rising on the few plots of available land in the mostly built-up areas west of 16th Street, but the major construction boom is in the areas near the U Street/African-American Civil War

Memorial/Cardozo, Mount Vernon Square/
7th Street-Convention Center and Columbia
Heights Metro stations.

Restaurants, coffeeshops, supermarkets
and home-furnishing stores are opening to
serve this new population, changing the face
of streets that once featured thrift shops, auto-
parts stores and empty lots. With employment
growth higher in the suburbs than in DC, such
rapidly changing neighbourhoods as Logan
Circle are a new sort of bedroom community,
with some of their residents commuting
against the tide to suburban jobs.

HOME OF HIGH-TECH

Washington's biggest business remains
government, but the federal purse's significance
has dramatically decreased over the past 30
years (although military spending grew under
Reagan and is escalating again under George W
Bush). Federal employment declined throughout
the '90s, while the local service and information
industries boomed. Today more than 80 per
cent of the area's jobs are in the private sector.
Most of these are well-paid professional or
technical positions. The Washington area
contains the fourth-largest supply of office space
in the world, after Tokyo, New York and Paris.

Many of the high-tech businesses that took
root in the DC area did so because of the
proximity of federal agencies: biotechnology
companies developed near the National
Institutes of Health, while satellite and
telecommunications enterprises orbit around the
Federal Communications Commission and the
recently privatised Intelsat. Yet such industries
have grown to the point where they have their
own critical mass. The area has slightly more
computer programmers than lawyers – and
approximately twice as many of each per capita
than the country at large. Energy, hospitality,
defence and media companies are still among the
DC area's largest, but in recent years the region
has been best known as 'the home of the internet'.

Two of the area's largest information-
technology companies, AOL and MCI, suffered
major setbacks after the tech-stock bubble burst
in 2001. The shakeout was most agonising in
the area around Dulles Airport, home to many
internet companies, but it was felt in the city
as well. Yet the area wasn't hit as hard as,
say, Silicon Valley. Many stock options
evaporated, but most jobs didn't. The rise
of net, telecom and other high-tech businesses
has permanently altered the local economy.

CITY VS SUBURBS

Despite DC's improved financial condition,
the divide between the city and its contiguous
suburbs in Maryland and Virginia remains one

of the region's central dilemmas. As a practical
matter, there is little difference between living
in Dupont Circle or Takoma Park, Capitol
Hill or Arlington, but the political gap is
vast. As long as DC continues to have no voting
representation in Congress, the residents of 'the
capital of the free world' will always be under
the thumb of their suburban neighbours.

When they're not politically overpowering
the District, the city's suburbs just make it
look bad by comparison. Although DC does
have crime, destitution and dangerous areas,
its long-standing reputation as an urban pit
of despair has been overstated. The city's per
capita income and education rates are actually
above average for major American cities,
while its poverty rate is below average. Yet
DC just can't compete demographically with its
suburbs, which contain some of the country's
most affluent, best-educated inhabitants.

The contrast is most striking when
the city's generally upscale suburbs are
compared to its most impoverished areas.
As the neighbourhoods immediately north
of Downtown gain new homes and boutiques,
DC's neglected precincts – mostly far off the
tourist map in Southeast and Northeast – have
seen few improvements. Mayor Tony Williams,
the mild-mannered but high-handed successor
to the flamboyant, self-indulgent Marion Barry,
managed to balance the city's books, thus
retrieving control of DC's finances from
a Congressionally imposed control board.
But he has had little effect on the city's lousy
public schools, mismanaged police department
and ineffective redevelopment efforts.

All Washington mayors face the challenges
of Congressional meddling and a severely limited
tax base. More than half of the city's land is
exempt from property taxes because it belongs to
the federal government or universities, religious
institutions, and other non-profit organisations.
In addition, the federal law that gave DC limited
autonomy forbids its government to tax the
income of non-residents, who earn 60 per cent
of the wages paid in the city.

Suburbanites pay income tax only to
the jurisdictions in which they live, not to
the one in which they work. (Most large
American cities, including New York, tax
non-resident workers.) Lower income tax
rates in the suburbs, especially Virginia,
undercut DC revenues, encouraging people
to live in the suburbs and even lead some
people who maintain homes in the city to
claim legal residence outside it.

DC and its suburbs are entwined in
numerous ways, yet their respective
governments co-operate very little. The Metro
rail and bus system is the only significant local

public entity run by a regional group, and it was recently forced to raise fares by Maryland's new anti-transit Republican governor.

The other significant area authority, the Council of Governments, plays an essentially advisory role. Real regional government won't happen any time soon, because the sovereign states of Virginia and Maryland resist ceding any of their power to the politically disenfranchised city-state at the region's centre.

LOVE THY NEIGHBOUR

In the past two decades Washington has become the new home for Central Americans, Ethiopians, Vietnamese and others. The newcomers who have recently pushed up the prices of rowhouses in Shaw and Mount Pleasant, however, are mostly white. This in-migration conjures the spectre of 'The Plan', a secret scheme that some black Washingtonians believe is designed to displace the African American population of all the city's more appealing and convenient neighbourhoods.

> ### 'Most of the strife in the city's more diverse areas seems to be within groups rather than between them.'

Passions sometimes become overheated on this topic, but if there is a Plan, there's no organised resistance to it. Indeed, the city's three-decade demographic shift from over 70 to less than 60 per cent black is mostly the result of middle-class African American flight to the suburbs, principally Prince George's County, Maryland. Since 1998 majority-black DC has been overseen by a majority-white city council. This may be just a fluke, but it's not exactly a sign that the forces of reaction are reclaiming Washington. Two of the council's members are openly gay, and several white council members are – on some issues, at least – notably more liberal than their black colleagues. Still, an era has clearly passed: the DC government is no longer rooted in, and vaguely yearning to be a continuation of, the civil rights movement.

Relations between long-time African American residents and the new immigrants are sometimes strained, but most of the strife in the city's more diverse areas seems to be within groups rather than between them. Perhaps because so many of the different groups of new immigrants have located in the same areas, rather than form their own one-ethnicity precincts as in other cities, the newcomers don't have exclusive turf to defend. The gaps of language and culture can be wide, but neighbourhoods like Columbia Heights have little choice but to serve as a melting pot.

Washington has long attracted a different sort of immigrant, of course: ambitious young people hoping to make a career in politics or a related field. The preponderance of these transients is exaggerated, however.

Contrary to legend, there are native-born Washingtonians, from the old-money aristocrat whose grandmother used to have tea regularly at the White House to the blue-collar worker whose grandfather used to take the trolley to Griffith Stadium to see Negro League baseball.

CRIME CAPITAL?

Since the late 1980s the second biggest story in the District has been crime (the federal government is always the first). Around 15 years ago DC briefly had the highest homicide rate in the country, and though the current rate is acceptable only by comparison to the early '90s, the fact is that it has declined dramatically. Since its 1991 peak of 489 per year, the homicide rate dropped to 248 in 2003. Violent crime, much of it drug-related, tends to be ghettoised in poor areas, and preventing it seems an intractable problem. The high gun-crime rate in part stems from the city's proximity to Virginia, whose lax laws make it the prime East Coast source of guns used to commit crimes.

Although the crime situation is serious, it is in part a demographic anomaly. Washington serves as the region's centre for vice – drugs, prostitution, alcohol and associated offences – but the per capita crime rate is factored against the city's official population. Excluded from the stats are the hundreds of thousands of people who enter the city every day to work, and to play.

The perception of danger in Washington also reflects the city's international prominence. In late 2002, when a rifleman began to shoot people at random in Maryland and Virginia, he was widely dubbed the 'Washington sniper'. In fact, there were two snipers, and they killed or seriously wounded at least 15 people in five states; only one of these victims was shot in DC. And when the hijacked jetliner hit the Pentagon on 9/11, the US military headquarters were usually identified as being in Washington, although it's actually in Virginia.

The crash at the Pentagon was indeed intended as an attack on one of the many Washingtons – the metaphorical hub of American power. That Washington has responded forcefully, blockading itself behind barriers, metal detectors and newly locked doors. There are, however, other Washingtons to explore, ones that are more lively and welcoming, if potentially more harmful to preconceptions.

Government Town

The eyes of the world are permanently fixed on US politics... with Washington centre stage.

The way the US government works can seem unfathomable at times, even to the country's own citizens. But a grasp of the subject is essential to understanding the way America (and Washington DC in particular) is run. Here we explain the evolution of a system of government that began with a single simple document.

THE CONSTITUTION

Suspicious of central control, the original 13 states initially agreed on a weak affiliation called the Articles of Confederation in the late 1770s. That arrangement proved inadequate to govern foreign affairs and interstate relations, so in 1787 the whole system was revamped during a general convention in Philadelphia.

The new plan of government was inaugurated by the **Constitution of the United States**. This document established a federal system, with rights and responsibilities split between the state governments and a national government in 'the federal city'. The

Constitution is defined as the 'supreme law of the land' but the proper balance of state and federal power has been debated ever since.

The Founding Fathers (as the conventioneers are called) created a system that rests on two fundamental, related principles: separation of powers, and checks and balances. Federal power is split between three branches: legislative (Congress) to write the laws; judicial (the Supreme Court) to interpret them; and executive (the Presidency) to administer them. The divided functions are meant to block any one branch from predominating.

The Constitution has been appended with 27 Amendments – the first ten are known as the Bill of Rights – but its underlying structure is essentially unchanged.

CONGRESS

The legislative branch is the bicameral Congress, with equal representation of every state in the upper chamber, the Senate, and proportional representation in the lower chamber, the House of Representatives. This system, known as the Great Compromise, was devised to reconcile the claims of the more populous states with the fears of the smaller ones.

The House of Representatives (known as the House) has 435 members, each representing an electoral district of roughly 650,000 voters. Each state is guaranteed at least one representative. House members stand for office every two years. They have always been chosen by popular election. All terms run concurrently, so the whole House stands for office simultaneously.

The Senate has 100 members, two from each state (regardless of its population). Senatorial terms are six years long, with one-third of the Senators standing for re-election every two years. Senators were originally chosen by their state's legislatures, but in 1913 the Constitution was amended to specify direct, popular election.

Both Houses are organised in a system of committees and sub-committees responsible for discussing specific areas of legislation. Committee assignments are determined in the separate caucuses of the two major political parties, which also draft competing legislative programmes. Committee chairmanships are extremely powerful positions, usually assigned to the senior member of the majority party on each committee.

'Almost 25,000 lobbyists work the suites of DC, spending more than $1.5 billion annually.'

The presiding officer of the House of Representatives is the Speaker of the House, the leader of that body's majority party. There have been many powerful Speakers of the House, from Henry Clay in the early 19th century to, most recently, Newt Gingrich. At the time of writing, however, Speaker Dennis Hastert is widely considered less influential than majority leader Tom DeLay.

The vice-president serves as the presiding officer in the Senate. His function is usually more symbolic than real, but he casts the deciding vote when the Senate is tied.

Congress is authorised to tax and borrow, to coin money, establish a postal system, regulate patents and raise armed forces. Because the Constitution includes the accordion-like directive that Congress shall 'make all laws necessary and proper for carrying into execution' the enumerated powers, its legislative reach has grown enormously since 1787.

The Senate has exclusive power over the ratification of treaties, so it has more influence than the House in foreign affairs. Two-thirds of the Senate must concur for a treaty to become law. The Senate also has right of approval over presidential nominees to the Cabinet, to ambassadorships and to the federal judiciary. The House has more control of the federal purse, since all revenue bills originate there.

Legislative proposals are introduced under the signature of individual legislators, though they're often drafted by the executive branch or by individuals and organisations completely outside government. Bills are numbered, distributed to members and assigned to whatever committee has appropriate jurisdiction. Committee hearings are a period for public comment and expert testimony on the necessity and possible impact of the legislation. This is also the period where lobbyists exert most of their influence (for more on lobbying, *see p31*). If passed by committee, a bill goes to the powerful Rules Committee, which assigns the time and rules of its debate on the chamber floor. At this point it may be debated, further amended and voted up or down. Votes often follow party lines, although some split along other divides (urban versus rural, for example).

Bills passed by one house go through a nearly identical series of steps in the other. If the second house passes the legislation with amendments, it is returned to the first for re-approval. If the two houses cannot agree on a bill, a conference committee is formed to attempt some reconciliation. If that doesn't work, the bill is dead, although usually some sort of accommodation is reached.

No legislation passes into law unless signed by the president, with two exceptions: if his signature is withheld while Congress is in session, it becomes law by default after ten days; if, on the other hand, he vetoes a bill, it can be overridden by a two-thirds vote of both houses. If the president's signature is withheld and Congress adjourns before ten days expire, the bill dies by 'pocket veto'.

Investigation has become almost as significant to Congressional activity as legislation, and decidedly more high-profile, particularly with the televising of hearings. Supposedly undertaken to help in the writing of legislation, investigations have become one of Congress's chief tools for enforcing executive branch accountability – such as during the Iran-Contra hearings of the Reagan era. The investigative function also yielded, however, Joe McCarthy's anti-Communist witch-hunts and the vehement Republican crusade desperate to prove President Bill Clinton guilty of something – anything.

THE HOUSE AND THE SENATE
Because members of the House stand for office so often, it is the more populist of the two bodies. House members are by definition more parochial, since they represent smaller constituencies. To compensate for the House's unruly size, procedures are very formal and tightly directed.

The Senate is the more aristocratic body, so overwhelmingly white and wealthy that it is sometimes called the Millionaires' Club

(although lately it's a bit less male, with a record 14 women members). Because of the length of their terms and because members' elections are staggered, the Senate tends to be more collegial than the House and more resistant to executive branch or party direction. Senators can bypass the committee system and bring legislation directly to the floor. They work with minimal limitation on debate and can amend bills freely.

Two nations, under God

George W Bush has been the most hated president of the United States since, well, Bill Clinton. This is not mere happenstance. Although the two men's policies and personalities have certainly contributed to their unpopularity, the widespread hostility also reflects the growing spitefulness of the country's political culture.

As the ever more powerful leader of the world's most powerful nation, the American president embodies both the country's dominant political creed and its self-image. Although Bush represents the platform of the Republican Party, just as Clinton symbolised the Democratic agenda, political parties are not as important in the US system as in a parliamentary government. If a major initiative misfires, it's the president, not his party, who is regarded a failure. Many Americans now see themselves as independent, meaning they often choose candidates based on their dispositions as much as their positions.

Thus Clinton was both embraced and assailed as a 'liberal', even though he was overwhelmingly a centrist. (He retreated quickly from the two most controversial proposals of his first term: national health insurance and allowing gays to serve openly in the military.) To Clinton's enemies, his warmth, intelligence, unabashed avoidance of service in Vietnam and regard for minority groups were as infuriating as his slippery way with inconvenient facts. Almost as soon as Clinton took office, the adversaries that First Lady Hillary Clinton was to characterise as a 'vast right-wing conspiracy' began accusing him of graft, adultery – well, they were right about that one – and even murder.

Bush presents a very different image: laconic, resolute and ideologically – perhaps intellectually – simple-minded. Just as they did with Reagan before him, American conservatives took Bush's aversion to subtlety as a sign of strength. ('I don't do

THE PRESIDENCY

The president is elected for a four-year term and can serve only two terms in total. Since the whole House and one-third of the Senate stands for election every two years, every presidential election coincides with the election of the new House and one Senate class.

As the nation's chief administrative officer, the president commands millions of civilian employees in 100 or so separate departments, agencies and bureaus. The most important are the Cabinet departments, whose chiefs are appointed by the president, with Senatorial advice and consent. There are now 15 departments, gradually expanded from the original four. The newest is Homeland Security, hastily assembled from mostly existing agencies after 9/11. Cabinet secretaries and other major executive-branch officers may be elected officials (in which case they would resign their previous

nuance', the president is on record as saying.) Yet Bush's unwillingness to admit error, or even acknowledge contrasting viewpoints, has outraged his detractors. He is widely seen as a cowboy, loyal to a manly code more appropriate to the gruff hero of a John Ford movie than to a contemporary world leader.

Of course, many Americans like cowboys. By spring 2004, Bush's numerous miscalculations – notably those concerning the US invasion and occupation of Iraq – had dramatically decreased his job-approval ratings. Yet his position within his own party did not seem to be in any danger.

In fact, in the run-up to the November 2004 election, Bush still had a strong base of support. Conservatives have developed a media support system of talk-radio shows, gossipy websites and even a cable-TV network – Rupert Murdoch's Fox News – that bolsters the president's policies and status.

Although the country's mainstream newspapers and news programmes barely questioned Bush's claims in the run-up to the Iraq War, many on the American right now dismiss the merest hint of criticism from these so-called 'liberal media' as being tainted by anti-Americanism and, indeed, a hatred of the president.

The current cultural and political polarisation is reflected in the changing nature of the two major parties. Although there are still moderate Republicans (found mostly in New England) and conservative Democrats (largely in the South), the parties – and the country – are now splitting along parallel geographical and ideological lines: the conservative South, Plains and Mountain states are increasingly Republican, while the liberal East and West coasts and Great Lakes states tend to go Democratic. The flashpoint, however, remains the president. After all, he's the man Americans love to hate.

offices) but can be chosen from any field. They are subject to approval by the Senate, but rarely rejected. Lesser officials and employees of the executive branch – some 85 per cent of the total – are career civil servants exempt from dismissal through a change of regime.

The Constitution's description of presidential powers is surprisingly limited. The president submits an annual budget to Congress and can submit, approve or veto legislation. In addition, he is commander-in-chief of the armed forces, receives foreign ministers and grants federal pardons. The president also negotiates foreign treaties – but their approval requires a two-thirds vote in the Senate. The president appoints federal judges – but that also requires the Senate's 'advice and consent'. Presidents have nominal leadership of their political party – but may face a Congress that is under the control of the opposition party, as has frequently been the case in the post-war era.

The US president is simultaneously prime minister and head of state, and the pomp surrounding him skews the perception of his merely managerial functions. The man in the White House has enormous power to influence, but he can also become the scapegoat for circumstances outside his control. Presidential power has evolved over time in step with the immense growth of the federal government.

The framers of the Constitution envisioned the chief executive as a check upon legislative excess. But with America's emergence as a world power, the 'Imperial Presidency' has become the most overreaching of the three branches. For example, Congress has the exclusive power to declare war, but the president is commander-in-chief and he alone deals directly with foreign nations. As US military involvements grew, the effective understanding was that Congressional dissent ended when American forces went into combat. Throughout the 20th century US troops have gone into action at the president's directive and without Congress declaring war. This balance shifted somewhat when domestic political discontent over Vietnam finally emboldened Congress to reassert its prerogatives and limit presidential war-making authority with the War Powers Act of 1973. Still, the executive retains enough leeway that Ronald Reagan was free to invade Grenada, Bill Clinton to police the former Yugoslavia and George W Bush to attack Afghanistan and Iraq – all without formal declarations of war.

THE COURTS

The judicial branch of American federal government consists of three levels of tribunals. Numerous district courts are seated throughout the states, an intermediate level of appellate

courts sits in 'circuits' above them, and the Supreme Court – consisting of a chief justice and eight associate justices – sits in Washington, DC. Over the centuries the number of justices has varied from six to ten but has been steady at nine for nearly 100 years.

Federal judges are chosen through nomination by the president and confirmation by the Senate. Since appointments are for life (with the proviso of 'good behaviour', an exception rarely invoked), it is during the confirmation process that controversies around the courts are most heated. Both Clinton and Bush Jr have battled to get judicial appointments approved, sometimes turning to 'recess appointments' when Congress was out of session.

The federal appeals courts do not rule directly on law, but on cases arising under the law. Any dispute that hinges on matters in which federal law is at issue or where an aggrieved party claims an infringement of constitutionally specified rights can be heard in these courts. As cases make their way up this legal ladder, the constitutional validity of particular acts of Congress or the executive may be determined.

The Supreme Court aspires to an Olympian detachment, but as its decisions frequently touch on fiercely contested matters – abortion, racial issues – it is an inescapably political institution. In the 1960s and '70s it was social conservatives who decried the Court's 'judicial activism' – school desegregation orders, for example – while in the 1930s FDR damned the conservatism of the 'nine old men' and tried to pack the court with new appointees more to his liking.

Many observers felt that the political biases of the Supreme Court were evident in its decision on the Florida ballot recount case of the 2000 election. In its ruling, a conservative, five-justice majority (the product of years of Republican presidential nominations) overturned a Florida supreme court decision that favoured the Gore camp's claims.

DEMOCRATS AND REPUBLICANS

US politics is based on a two-party system, with neither party possessing a clear-cut ideology. Broadly speaking, the Democratic Party is located (a bit) to the left of the spectrum, traditionally perceived as the friend of the common man and the advocate of activist government; the Republican Party is to the right, the representative of social conservatism, big business and small government.

The need for compromise among the parties' various internal factions is one reason both groups end up more similar than not. It was George Wallace, Alabama's segregationist governor, who remarked, 'there ain't a dime's worth of difference between the two'.

Parties are national but their real strength rests in the individual state party organisations. Candidates work their way up the ladder of office from local to state to national, though people with sufficient fame have leapfrogged the process. The party system arose completely outside governmental regulation, though laws regarding their structure and function were gradually adopted.

Big-city political bosses and state party organisations once had firm control of the spoils of victory – jobs on the public payroll and influence over judicial and regulatory decisions. Reform movements gradually put an end to this source of party discipline, however, and party loyalty has shown a steady decline. A growing number of Americans now forgo party affiliation entirely and identify themselves as political independents, although in practice the overwhelming majority vote for either Democrat or Republican candidates.

INTEREST GROUPS

The demonisation of 'special interests' is a recurring feature of US political rhetoric. As the development of modern telecommunications has democratised the possibility of mass organisation, interest groups with conflicting public policy solutions have sprung up around every significant issue in American life.

These advocacy organisations function both as individual caucuses within the parties and as pressure groups outside them. Ethnic minorities, women's and gay rights groups, environmentalists and organised labour provide support for the Democratic Party. The Republicans are based around an uneasy alliance of social conservatives and economic libertarians. Right-wing Christian groups, chiefly fundamentalist Protestants, are especially strong in the Republican Party.

Interest groups attempt to influence government using various methods. These include petitions, letters and emails from the general membership, advertising and public relations campaigns and, in the judicial arena, lawsuits. Many organisations also maintain offices in DC whose job it is to appeal directly to individual legislators and their staffs, testify at committee hearings and cultivate the press.

Interest groups cover the broadest swathe of policy through the quasi-academic institutions known as think tanks, which generally reflect an overall ideological orientation. Some tend to the left, such as the Brookings Institution, which G Gordon Liddy offered to firebomb on behalf of the Nixon administration, but most are on the right, including the Heritage Foundation, from which the Reagan government lifted its policy programme.

The lights are on... but is anybody home?

LOBBYISTS

The effort to tilt policy and influence legislation has spawned another peculiarly Washington figure: the lobbyist. These freelance political operatives work on behalf of industry trade groups, individual corporations and foreign nations, in addition to traditional political organisations. As of 2002 almost 25,000 lobbyists worked the suites of DC, spending more than $1.5 billion annually – that's 47 lobbyists and $3.5 million per Congressperson.

Because so much of a lobbyist's work depends on access to government officials, the most powerful firms are replete with erstwhile officials who have passed through the 'revolving door'. It's not unusual for former political opponents to become partners in lobbying concerns or law firms whose speciality is influencing the political process.

Lobbyists' ability to open doors often stems from their involvement in the fundraising process. Many firms have political action committees (*see p32*) of their own, which enable them to make large contributions to campaigns.

Effective lobbying requires political acumen as well as pure access, and fundraising prowess. Carefully crafted position statements from full-time propagandists are an easy out for over-burdened officials, for whom lobbyists also serve as freelance political strategists and researchers. While groups with mass memberships can stimulate genuine 'grassroots' action, lobbyists have perfected a kind of pseudo-grassroots technique: they use databases and phone banks to identify supporters on particular issues and patch them through to Congressional offices, charging their clients a fee per call.

CAMPAIGN FINANCES

Finance is a major issue in American politics. The enormous cost of campaigning, chiefly due to the expense of TV advertising, means that a typical run for the Senate today requires tens of millions of dollars, House races remaining a bargain in the mere millions.

There is extensive federal regulation of contributions, and a ceaseless search for loopholes in such laws. When post-Watergate restrictions placed a $1,000 limit on individual and corporate donations to congressional campaigns, the result was the creation of political action committees, or PACs, which enable contributions to go through a third party. Corporate, union and other interest groups currently sponsor thousands of such committees.

A 1976 Supreme Court decision created another substantial campaign finance loophole by affirming the argument that political money was the equivalent of free speech and abolishing any restrictions on issues-related advertising. This allowed groups organised around set topics – such as abortion rights or gun control – to spend unlimited sums on 'issue ads' in support of like-minded candidates, as long as the groups remain formally unaffiliated with the candidates' parties or campaign organisations.

The latest development, whose implications are still being explored, is the 2002 McCain-Feingold Act (named for its two Senate sponsors). The law bans political parties from raising 'soft money', cash that was solicited for general party purposes but often used to support individual candidates.

Under the new law, groups known as '527s' (named for a section of the tax code) have been fundraising to support certain causes. So far, the majority of 527s are working on issues associated with the Democrats. But the Republicans remain the hard-money champions, thanks to their big-business connections.

MEDIA INVOLVEMENT

As much as big money, the mass media has altered the political equation. It has enabled individuals with deep pockets and political

Politics in progress

For almost 200 years, the US Capitol was remarkably accessible to visitors. That changed on September 11, 2001, when all people without official business were abruptly barred. The Capitol is now open again, but on a much more limited basis. For information on public access for guided tours and visits to the galleries overlooking the House and Senate floors, see p72.

Congress is in session 11 months of the year, with a midsummer break in August and recesses at Easter, Christmas, Thanksgiving and election time (November, but sometimes starting earlier in the autumn). The largest proportion of floor activity occurs towards the end of legislative sessions and at the approach of holidays, when there's a rush to finish old business.

Each day's session begins at 9am or 10am, with a ringing of bells in the Capitol. Lights and bells throughout the building announce votes and quorum calls. Both houses open with prayers from their respective chaplains, followed by short speeches from the majority and minority leaders in the Senate, and 'One Minute Speeches' by designated Representatives in the House. Members sit grouped by party affiliation on the floor of the House and by individually assigned seats in the Senate.

If the chambers appear surprisingly empty while measures are debated, it's because most of the work of legislation is accomplished in committee meetings. For more controversial hearings, the meeting rooms often can't hold all the interested observers, and lines form early for admittance. The Senate committees meet in the Senate office buildings north of the Capitol; House committees meet in the House office buildings across Independence Avenue to the south. These buildings remain open to members of the public who have ID. It is no longer possible for visitors to travel between the Capitol and the Senate office buildings via the connecting tunnel.

For schedule information for both houses and all committees, see the *Washington Post*'s 'Today in Congress' panel. There are also listings on the House of Representatives website (www.house.gov) and the Senate website (www.senate.gov), and more information on the websites of the Library of Congress (http://thomas.loc.gov) and the Architect of the Capitol (www.aoc.gov).

In Context

ambitions to buy their way into the public arena, with or without party support. In 1992 Ross Perot's war chest linked electronic communications to a vein of populist discontent and created a new party. (It didn't last, however.)

Long before cable TV and the internet, American politicians began using the electronic media. The process began with Franklin D Roosevelt's weekly radio addresses, dubbed the 'fireside chats'. In the post-war years, Dwight Eisenhower initiated regular, televised news conferences, in which he submitted to questioning from the press. John F Kennedy perfected the practice with his wit and sophistication but subsequent presidents fared less well. Among the most un-telegenic were the maudlin Lyndon Johnson, and Richard Nixon, whose dark sense of aggrievement fairly radiated contempt for the fourth estate. This, combined with five o'clock shadow, is said to have contributed to his narrow loss of the 1960 election to the undeniably more attractive JFK.

'Since its 1960 peak of 63 per cent, turnout has fallen at every election except 1992.'

Later administrations, consequently, turned from the uncertainties of spontaneous cross-examination to the never-never land of the media event, an approximation of reality in which the setting is carefully chosen and the audience thoroughly screened. Examples include Clinton's well-publicised walk on the Normandy beaches on the 50th anniversary of D-Day and – a successful photo-op that backfired in retrospect – Bush's landing on an aircraft carrier in May 2003 to announce the end of 'major hostilities' in Iraq.

An alternative method of dealing with the press is the 'Rose Garden' strategy, in which an incumbent presidential candidate simply stays home. Reagan's successful 1984 re-election effort, for instance, forswore public appearances in favour of the 'Morning In America' TV ad campaign, which consisted of little more than reassuring tableaux of amber waves of grain and no substantive discussion of issues whatsoever.

The present juncture holds a world of 24-hour TV news channels, round-the-dial (chiefly right-wing) talk radio and factoid rumour-mongering on the internet. The speed and pervasiveness of electronic news has forced the hand of more traditional sources such as the *New York Times* and the *Washington Post*. The inescapable prominence of even an unconfirmed rumour in tabloids such as the *National Enquirer* or Matt

Drudge's online gossip mill becomes news in itself. This hall of mirrors reached dizzying proportions during the Lewinsky scandal, when the very intensity of the story became the story.

THE POWER OF SPIN
At that political pole where the media sun never sets, the campaign goes on forever. The consequence is that every politician of ambition, and the president most of all, counts among his closest consultants professional spin doctors, who practise Machiavellian media manipulation or 'spin control'.

It is the duty of spin doctors to 'frame the issue' and 'set the terms of debate'. Is abortion about 'the right to life' or 'a woman's right to choose'? Is trade with China 'constructive engagement' or 'kowtowing to dictators'? The spin doctor's ultimate prescription is the soundbite, the pithy phrase that encapsulates an argument, although not always accurately. The 'war on terror' is a favourite of recent years, used by the Bush administration to characterise nearly all its actions.

Spin utilises the tools first perfected in the market research divisions of Madison Avenue. Scientific polling methods assess the mood of the target audience. 'Focus groups' of average Americans are formed to determine their reaction to various presentations of public issues. Journalists are courted with promises of access and threats of its denial. The most visible administrators of spin are the press spokesmen of the various cabinet agencies and, pre-eminently, the president's press secretary. Other figures enter the spotlight occasionally, usually as hatchetmen – a job often designated for vice-presidents, including the Bush administration VP, Dick Cheney.

The pre-eminent public forum for DC spin is the Sunday morning TV talk shows, where Congressional leaders and presidential emissaries make their case to the public and submit to questioning from the press. The shows' panels of journalists, collectively known as the 'punditocracy', suffer from a surfeit of conventional thought but Washington provides no other occasion where one can see public officials regularly cross-examined by the press.

Widespread revulsion with the DC media circus is symptomatic of a cynicism in the body politic that threatens the whole system. The most revealing fact about US politics today is the steady decline of citizen participation in the political process. A smaller percentage of America's citizens exercise their right to vote than that of almost any other industrial nation. Since its 1960 peak of 63 per cent, turnout has fallen at every election except 1992, a clear sign that democracy here stands in need of renewal.

The **White House**. *See p35.*

Architecture

Neo-classical solemnity and just a touch of modernism.

Washington's two best-known buildings are the Capitol and the White House, which symbolise American government and, specifically, Congress and the President. That's not all they represent, however. They also exemplify the city's dedication to a formal, traditional (and low-rise) style that's at odds with the look of most American cities. Despite some forays into modernism, the practice of architecture in Washington is an ongoing debate about neo-classicism.

Although Washington was the first major Western capital designed from scratch, it never occurred to its founders to build a city free of classical precedents. Such founding fathers as Thomas Jefferson (an avid, if self-educated, architect) insisted on architectural styles that recalled democratic Athens and republican Rome. George Washington hired Pierre-Charles L'Enfant to design a baroque street plan (*see p36* **The man with the plan**). He also mandated that the new capital's structures be built of brick, marble and stone, thus conveying a sense of permanence in a city – and a country – that in its early days seemed a bit wobbly.

FIRST BUILDINGS

Washington's oldest buildings actually precede the founding of the city. The river ports of Georgetown and Alexandria existed prior to their incorporation into the District of Columbia, and they contain most of the area's examples of 18th-century architecture. The city's only surviving pre-Revolutionary War structure is Georgetown's **Old Stone House**, a modest 1765 cottage with a pleasant garden.

Although Georgetown has the feel of a colonial-era village, most of its structures date from the 19th and early 20th centuries. Many are Victorian, but some are in the Federal style, a common early 19th-century American mode that adds such classical elements as columns, pediments and porticoes to vernacular structures usually made of brick or wood.

Over the river in Old Town Alexandria, which was once part of DC, there are some larger pre-Revolutionary War structures, such as **Carlyle House** and **Christ Church**, a Georgian-style edifice where George Washington was a vestryman. Like Georgetown, however, most of Old Town is of 19th- and 20th-century vintage.

Further south is George Washington's plantation, **Mount Vernon** (*see p244* **Through the keyhole**), now a museum about Washington and the life of colonial-era gentry. This Georgian estate is one of the finest extant examples of an 18th-century American plantation. Back closer to town, next to Arlington National Cemetery, is **Arlington House** (also known as the Lee-Custis House), a neo-classical mansion that was once the home of Confederate general Robert E Lee.

Washington's two most metonymic structures, the White House and the Capitol, were both first occupied in 1800 and have been substantially remodelled and expanded since. James Hoban was the original architect of the **White House**, but Thomas Jefferson, who lost the competition to design what was at first simply called the President's House, tinkered with the plans while in residence from 1801 to 1809. The most significant additions during this time were new monumental north and south porticoes, designed in 1807 by Benjamin Latrobe but not built until the 1820s. Many additions followed, with some of the more recent ones (for offices and security equipment) out of sight. The structure apparently got its current name after it was whitewashed to cover damage from being burned in 1814 by British troops, although the sandstone façade was first whitewashed in 1797, while still under construction.

'The Capitol's Corinthian columns make the case that the building is a temple to democracy.'

The **United States Capitol**, at the centre of the city's grid, has grown dramatically from William Thornton's modest original design. Since the cornerstone was laid in 1793, virtually every visible part of the structure has been replaced, from the dome to the east and west façades. The last major renovation of the exterior was carried out in 1987, and a new underground visitors' centre is now under construction. Despite its grander scale, the Capitol remains true to the original neo-classical concept, with Corinthian columns making the case that the building is a temple to democracy.

Other local buildings that survive from the Federal period are less august. Built in 1800, the **Octagon** gives a distinctive shape to the Federal style. Actually a hexagon with a semicircular portico, the house was designed by Capitol architect Thornton. Both the **Sewall-Belmont House** and **Dumbarton Oaks** are fine examples of the Federal style, although

they have been altered considerably since they were built, respectively, in 1790 and 1801 (though parts of Sewall-Belmont House date to 1750). All three structures are now museums.

Washington's first business district developed around the intersection of Pennsylvania Avenue and Seventh Street, NW, and there are still some examples of pre-Civil War vernacular architecture in this area. The buildings near the intersections of Seventh Street with Indiana Avenue, E Street and H Street in nearby Chinatown all offer examples of the period.

Also noteworthy is the 500 block of Tenth Street, NW, whose most imposing structure is the 1863 **Ford's Theatre**, site of Abraham Lincoln's assassination.

The government buildings erected in the first half of the 19th century generally adhered to the Greek Revival style, which modelled itself on such Athenian edifices as the Parthenon, rediscovered by European architects in the mid 18th century. Two of these structures, the **Patent Office** and the **Tariff Commission Building**, face each other at Seventh and F Streets, NW. Both are early examples of the city's official style – also known in the US and especially in DC as neo-Grec – and both were designed at least in part by Robert Mills, who is best known for the Washington Monument. In 2002 the long-neglected Tariff Commission Building became the Hotel Monaco. The Patent Office, the once and future home of the National Portrait Gallery and the Smithsonian American Art Museum, is under renovation; it will reopen in 2006 with a new canopy, devised by Norman Foster, over its central courtyard.

Mills also designed the **US Treasury Building**, with its 466-foot (142-metre) Ionic colonnade along 15th Street. In the first major divergence from the L'Enfant Plan, this edifice was sited directly east of the White House, thus blocking the symbolic vista between the building and the Capitol. Construction began in 1836 and wasn't completed until 1871, but that's almost speedy compared to the progress of Mills' **Washington Monument**. Started in 1845, it was finished (after a 20-year break due to lack of funds) in 1884. The highest structure in the world at its completion, the 600-foot (183-metre) monument is unusually stark by the standards of 19th-century local architecture. That's because the colonnaded base of Mills' plan was never built, leaving only a tower modelled on an Egyptian obelisk.

> ▶ Unless an address is given in brackets, buildings in **bold** are covered in more detail in the Sightseeing chapters (*pp62-119*).

Other examples of the pre-Civil War era are **St John's Church**, designed in 1816 by Benjamin Latrobe; **Old City Hall** (now occupied by Superior District Court offices); and the modest but elegant Georgetown **Custom House & Post Office**, derived from Italian Renaissance palazzos and typical of small US government buildings of the period.

AFTER THE CIVIL WAR

The more exuberant styles that flourished after the Civil War are presaged by the first **Smithsonian Institution** building, which was designed by James Renwick in 1846. Its red sandstone suits the turreted neo-medieval style, which has earned it the nickname 'the Castle'.

Fifteen years later, Renwick designed the original building of the Corcoran Museum, now the **Renwick Gallery**. Modelled loosely on the Louvre, it is considered the first major French-inspired building in the US. The Renwick is a compatible neighbour to a more extravagant Second Empire structure, the **Old Executive Office Building**. The lavish interior of the structure, originally the State, War and Navy Building, is open for tours by appointment on Saturdays; call 1-202 395 5895 for details.

The Civil War led directly to the construction of the Pension Building, which was designed by Montgomery Meigs in 1882 to house the agency that paid stipends to veterans and their families. Now the **National Building Museum**, this structure was based on Rome's Palazzo Farnese, but is twice the size. Outside is a frieze that depicts advancing Union Army troops; inside is an impressive courtyard, featuring the world's largest Corinthian columns. The atrium was once essential to one of the building's marvels, its highly efficient passive ventilation system, now supplanted by air-conditioning.

The man with the plan

The fountainhead of Washington's design is the street layout conceived by Pierre-Charles L'Enfant, a young Frenchman who had been a member of George Washington's army staff. The resulting L'Enfant Plan is the city's single most influential architectural document, even though no one alive has ever seen a copy of it.

Washington hired L'Enfant in 1791 but was forced to fire him a year later after he overspent his budget and dealt imperiously with some of the city's largest landowners. L'Enfant (who began signing his first name 'Peter' after moving to America) took his plan with him; the version that exists today was probably drafted by one his assistants, Benjamin Ellicott.

Most historians of the document think that the adopted plan differs only slightly from L'Enfant's intentions, although a few disagree. The baroque scheme attributed to L'Enfant is a rectangular street grid with broad diagonal avenues radiating from ceremonial circles and squares, the two essential structures, the White House and the Capitol. The plan is often likened to Baron Haussmann's design for Paris, although L'Enfant conceived his 100-foot (30-metre)-wide avenues a half-century before Haussmann began redefining the French capital by driving grand boulevards though neighbourhoods of narrow medieval streets.

The original plan dictated the layout of only the City of Washington, which is defined by the Potomac and Anacostia rivers, Rock Creek and Florida Avenue (originally Boundary Street). As the city expanded beyond these borders, attempts were made to follow L'Enfant's method, but difficult topography and sheer lack of interest sometimes overcame deference to the plan.

L'Enfant's avenues were named for the 15 states of the union as of 1790; streets have subsequently been chosen to bear the names of the other 35, although admittedly some are quite modest.

At the city's first centennial, in 1902, Washington rededicated itself to the L'Enfant Plan with the McMillan Commission Plan, which banished such intrusions as a railroad line and station on the Mall. Today the National Capital Planning Commission watches over the L'Enfant Plan, while the 1910 Height Limitation Act continues to prevent buildings from towering so high that they overwhelm the plan's horizontal emphasis. (The maximum height is 150 feet (about 46 metres), although such non-functional embellishments as spires are allowed to go higher.)

L'Enfant didn't live to see how influential his blueprint would become. Washington was still a very humble place when the designer died in 1825, penniless after refusing the offer of $2,500 for his services. In 1909 his remains were transferred to Arlington National Cemetery (see p102), the final resting place of many of the country's heroes.

Daniel Burnham's **Union Station** – still stunning after its 1988 revamp. *See p38.*

The Old Executive Office Building and the Pension Building were disparaged by both classicists and modernists, who often proposed razing them. Equally unpopular was the **Old Post Office**, which now houses various shops, restaurants and offices. The 1899 building is an example of the Romanesque Revival, which adapted the rounded arches, dramatic massing and grand vaults of 11th- and 12th-century northern European cathedrals. The structure contrasts with its Federal Triangle neighbours, which were all built in a more sedate style in the 1920s, and was threatened with demolition in that decade and again in the '60s.

Second Empire, Romanesque Revival and other ornate styles are still well represented in the Logan Circle, Dupont Circle, Sheridan Circle and Kalorama Triangle areas. Many palatial homes were built in these areas in the late 19th and early 20th centuries, and some survive as embassies, museums and private clubs. Those open to the public include the **Heurich Mansion** (1307 New Hampshire Avenue, NW, 1-202 429 1894); the **Phillips Collection**; and **Anderson House** (2118 Massachusetts Avenue, NW, 1-202 785 2040), which is home to the Society of the Cincinnati, a group founded by Revolutionary War veterans.

One of the city's most remarkable architectural fantasies is the **Scottish Rite Temple** (1733 16th Street, NW, 1-202 232 3579), finished in 1915 and modelled on the mausoleum at Halicarnassus. It was designed by John Russell Pope, later the architect of some of the city's most prominent buildings. His work includes the **National Archives**, the neo-classical temple that holds the country's most important documents.

The Archives is the tallest structure erected during Washington's first large urban renewal project, which during the 1920s converted one of the city's most notorious precincts into the government office district known as the Federal Triangle. The Triangle's massive structures provided the headquarters for most of the executive branch departments, and reiterated the federal government's preference for classicism. The project, which stretches from Sixth to 15th Streets, between Pennsylvania and Constitution Avenues, NW, was interrupted by the Depression, and its completion was then debated for 50 years. Eventually the government committed to a design for the final structure, the **Ronald Reagan Building**, a hulking mediocrity that opened in 1998. It, too, is in classical drag, albeit with some tricky angles to show that it's the work of the prominent architectural firm of Pei Cobb Freed.

Pope went on to design several more neo-classical temples, including the 1941 original (now called West) building of the **National Gallery of Art** and the 1943 **Jefferson Memorial**. The latter is partially derived from Rome's Pantheon, while its 1922 predecessor, the **Lincoln Memorial**, is modelled on the Parthenon in Athens.

World Bank Headquarters. See p39.

The bustling cousin of these contemplative edifices is **Union Station**, the 1908 structure whose Daniel Burnham design borrows from two Roman landmarks: the Arch of Constantine and the Baths of Diocletian. Dramatically remodelled before reopening in 1988, the building's interior still features many of its original architectural details – including statues of centurions, whose nudity is hidden only by shields – but now incorporates shops, eateries and a cinema. Most of the train-related functions have been moved to an undistinguished new hall to the rear of the building.

> **'L'Enfant Plaza was one of several questionable designs by IM Pei.'**

Other notable neo-classical structures of the period are the 1928 **Freer Gallery of Art** and the 1932 **Folger Shakespeare Library**, an example of Paul Cret's art deco-influenced 'stripped classicism'.

THE ARRIVAL OF MODERNISM

Modernism reached Washington after World War II, but couldn't get comfortable. One dilemma was – and still is – the city's Height Limitation Act, which bans skyscrapers. A variety of subterfuges have been employed in an effort to get an extra storey here or there, but no 'inhabitable' space is allowed above the 150-foot (46-metre) limit.

In the 1950s modernist notions of design and planning were applied to another urban-renewal project, the New Southwest, with awkward results. A lively (if hardly upscale) mixed-use area was obliterated in favour of sterile apartment buildings and a shopping mall. Modernism also guided the nearby **L'Enfant Plaza**, a huge office, hotel and retail complex (bordered by Independence Avenue, Ninth Street and various freeway approaches); its plan was the first of several questionable Washington designs by IM Pei, later one of the founders of Pei Cobb Freed. This ironically named assault on the L'Enfant Plan was followed by many stark, bleak buildings in Southwest, most of which were rented to the federal government.

In the 1960s and '70s modernist architects designed some of the city's least popular structures, including the **J Edgar Hoover FBI Building**, a brutalist concrete fortress finished in 1972, the year of Hoover's death. Perhaps more damaging to the style's reputation, however, was the profusion of mediocre office buildings in the 'New Downtown' along K Street and Connecticut Avenue, NW. Built with little consideration for Washington's distinctive street plan and without strategies for adapting the Bauhaus-derived American skyscraper style to the city's height limitation, these blank-walled knock-offs look like New York or Chicago office blocks inexplicably stunted at the 12th floor.

Most of these buildings were designed by local architects, but nationally renowned modernists and postmodernists are also

These 'background buildings' set a precedent for design in the city's older districts; several local firms came to specialise in contextual postmodern structures that often incorporated façades of existing buildings. Examples include Shalom Baranes's remake of the **Army-Navy Club** (901 17th Street, NW) and Hartman-Cox's **1001 Pennsylvania Avenue**, NW, which were both finished in 1987. Such 'façadomies' were widely criticised, especially when the new construction dwarfed the historic component; one conspicuous example of this is **Red Lion Row** (2000 Pennsylvania Avenue, NW).

Today the city's historicist architects are still influential, but no single style currently dominates. An updated, less dogmatic modernism is showcased in such structures as Kohn Pederson Fox's asymmetrical, vaguely industrial 1997 **World Bank Headquarters** (1818 H Street, NW, 1-202 473 1806; tours by appointment). Two other striking, recent buildings are embassies: Mikko Heikkinen and Markku Komonen's 1994 **Embassy of Finland** (3301 Massachusetts Avenue, NW, 1-202 298 5824; tours by appointment) features a trellis façade, dramatic atrium and glass-wall overlook on to Rock Creek Park. Sartogo Architetti Associati's 2000 **Embassy of Italy** (3000 Whitehaven Street, NW) uses a glass atrium to link two postmodern *palazzi*. The Corcoran Museum is still raising money to build an addition designed by one of the world's most flamboyant contemporary architects, Frank Gehry. The celebrity designer who has been busiest in the District, however, is postmodernist Michael Graves. In addition to his 1997 **International Finance Corporation Building** (2121 Pennsylvania Avenue, NW), he recently designed the **E Barrett Prettyman Courthouse Annex** (Third Street and Pennsylvania Avenue, NW), an oversized series of silos that ends in a neo-classical rotunda, and is working on a Department of Transportation headquarters near the Washington Navy Yard.

The huge new **Washington Convention Center** opened in 2003, but the shops that are supposed to enliven the three-block-long north–south walls have yet to arrive. More distinctive is the 2004 **Museum of the American Indian**, adapted from a design by Douglas Cardinal; clad in multi-hued limestone, the rough, undulating façade suggests Southwestern mesas. On the other side of the Mall – and the architectural spectrum – is Friedrich St Florian's 2004 **World War II Memorial**. With its circular array of pillars and arches tucked into the vista between the Washington Monument and the Lincoln Memorial, this imperial-style shrine is the latest evidence of official Washington's taste for the crypto-classical.

responsible for lacklustre work in Washington, including Mies van der Rohe's 1972 black-box **Martin Luther King Jr Memorial Library** and Marcel Breuer's 1976 precast concrete **Hubert H Humphrey Building** (Second Street and Independence Avenue, SW).

One of modernism's local successes is actually far from the District: **Washington-Dulles International Airport**, designed by Eero Saarinen in 1962 and now being expanded in accordance with his famous gull-wing design. Others include IM Pei's 1978 **National Gallery of Art East Building** and Harry Weese's **Metro system**. The latter two designs succeed in part because they are sensitive to their Washington context: the East Building's overlapping triangles play off the trapezoidal plot created by the L'Enfant street plan, while the Metro stations' coffered vaults are simply an extreme example of stripped classicism.

For a complete contrast to modernism, look to Georgetown, which became a fashionable neighbourhood when it began to be gentrified in the 1930s, or to Lafayette Square, which is surrounded by Federal-period houses. In the '60s, when demand for office surged, a proposal was drawn up to replace the Lafayette Square houses with new office buildings. The eventual compromise was to erect two large structures just off the square, John Carl Warneke's 1969 **New Executive Office Building** and the **Court of Claims Building**, which would defer to their older neighbours in form and material, if not in size.

Where to Stay

Where to Stay

New luxury resorts and boutique properties – along with make-overs for tired old places – mean the DC hotel scene is finally worth talking about.

Washington has always been rich in grand, elegant – and sometimes stuffy – hotels. At the Hay-Adams, the Mayflower and the Willard InterContinental – a few of the best – you might see congressmen puffing cigars in a mahogany-panelled corner, or socialites nibbling sandwiches and sipping tea. In recent years, though, DC has come into its own as a cosmopolitan city. Sure, it's still got its fair share of chain hotels (the best of which are reviewed in this chapter), but the once-sleepy political capital continues to attract new and more daring places to stay.

The **Mandarin Oriental** opened its doors in spring of 2004. The 400-room deluxe resort features an Asian twist and a more modern feel than traditional Washington luxury hotels. And the Ritz-Carlton opened a second property in the District, a splashy Georgetown hotel complete with martini lounge. Another newcomer is the Kimpton Group. Its six unique hotels – including the gorgeous, brightly coloured **Hotel Monaco** – cater to guests' every whim. Other hotels have had a facelift, such as the **River Inn**, which went from low-budget blah to sleek and fabulous when DC's hottest design firm gave it a make-over.

RATES AND SERVICES

Because many visitors swoop into town on business and leave by Friday, rooms cost more during the week. At weekends, rates can drop by as much as half. Although prices are displayed in the rooms, in practice there is no such thing as a fixed hotel rate in DC – almost no one pays the figure posted. All in all, rates vary according to the time of year, the day of the week and what discounts you can finagle. The price categories below are for the cheapest room. Most hotels offer special weekend packages that can include breakfast, dinner, champagne or even spa treatments (unless otherwise stated, rates below do not include breakfast). Rates decrease during summer – when locals flee the humidity – and late autumn, and are rock-bottom around Christmas. They are at their highest in spring, when DC sees a flux of school groups and cherry blossom gazers. Bear in mind that sales tax is added to prices quoted.

When booking your room, ask about a corporate rate even if your company has no formal arrangement with the hotel. If relevant, enquire about senior rates too: some hotels offer up to 50 per cent off to guests over 65. Also mention any and all associations or frequent-flyer schemes you belong to, or – especially at quiet times – just ask straight out if there are any discounts available.

Some chains have reductions for bookings completed online, and internet wholesalers such as www.priceline.com and www.wdcahotels.com offer hotel rooms at short notice or to the highest bidder. You can also reserve during office hours through Capitol Reservations (1-202 452 1270; 8.30am-6pm weekdays) or Washington, DC Accommodations (1-202 289 2220; 9am-5.30pm weekdays), which can sometimes track down discounts and find a room even when the city's full to bursting with conferences.

In a place where the term 'presidential suite' might mean just that, there are few really low-budget options. DC has no campsites or RV/caravan sites, although there are a few well within an hour's drive, in Maryland and Virginia. And there is only one official youth hostel in town (Hostelling International Washington, DC; *see p55*), but thankfully it's a very good one.

Prices drop slightly as you go further away from the centre. If you don't mind staying outside of the city itself, you could do worse

Hotels

For political junkies
Willard InterContinental, *see p43.*

For spotting celebrities
Ritz-Carlton, Washington, DC, *see p44.*

For never leaving the hotel
Mandarin Oriental, *see p43.*

For roof-top cocktails
Hotel Washington, *see p45.*

For a tryst
Hotel Rouge, *see p48.*

Mandarin Oriental: for all-out luxury.

than opt for one of the suburbs. The Rosslyn, Clarendon and Courthouse neighbourhoods of Arlington, Virginia, have shops, dining and nightlife of their own and are well served by the Metro. The same goes for the Maryland suburb of Bethesda. Hotels are mushrooming here; they're slightly cheaper than in the city centre, but the downside is the concrete, strip-mall environment.

Recently, many hotels have taken guest relations a step further, welcoming pets or banning cigarettes. If you have a strong preference for anything, be sure to ask when making your reservation. All hotels except for the smallest B&Bs have access for the disabled, but only those marked 'disabled: adapted rooms' in this chapter are specially designed for wheelchair-users (and, even so, we strongly recommend that travellers with disabilities check first with their chosen hotel). Most rooms have a clock radio and a safe or safety deposit boxes at the front desk. And if you're coming to DC for work purposes, it's worth finding what business amenities establishments offer – they can range from a communal fax machine to full conference facilities. A last word of warning – hotels change hands – and names – often in Washington, so double-check the name and address when you book.

Very expensive (over $250)

The Federal Triangle

Willard InterContinental
1401 Pennsylvania Avenue, NW, at 14th Street, DC 20004 (reservations 1-800 327 0200/front desk 1-202 628 9100/fax 1-202 637 7326/ www.washington.interconti.com). Metro Center Metro. **Rates** $450-$620 single/double; $850-$4,200 suite. **Credit** AmEx, DC, Disc, MC, V. **Map** p284 H6. As one of the very best hotels in DC, the Willard has hosted scores of figures of historical note, from Lincoln to Martin Luther King; since 1853 practically every US president has stayed here. The 341 oversized rooms and suites, all renovated at the end of 2000, are stocked with modern amenities like high-speed internet and CD players, while antique mirrors and four-poster beds maintain an old-fashioned dignity. Some have partial views of the White House or Capitol.
Hotel services *Bars (2). Business services. Disabled: adapted rooms. Gym. Parking ($23 per night). Restaurants (2).* **Room services** *High-speed internet. Minibar. Telephone. TV: cable, pay movies. VCR.*

South of the Mall

Mandarin Oriental
1330 Maryland Avenue, SW, at 12th Street, DC 20004 (front desk 1-202 554 8588/fax 1-202 554 8999/www.mandarinoriental.com). Smithsonian

Metro. **Rates** $350-$695 single/double; $900-$8,000 suite. **Credit** AmEx, DC, Disc, MC, V. **Map** p284 H7.

More than a few Washingtonians raised an eyebrow when the Mandarin chose a spot surrounded by government office buildings and a seafood market for its new 400-room hotel. But the international chain saw potential in the site – which, in fairness, is only a few blocks from the Mall and a Metro station – and went about proving that location isn't everything. This vast resort is sumptuous in every detail, from the gorgeous spa, indoor pool and top-notch restaurant to the bed linens and bathroom toiletries. It gives the Willard InterContinental, long the undisputed 'best' hotel in DC, a run for its money in terms of service and luxury. Some rooms have views of monuments and the Tidal Basin.

Hotel services *Bars (2). Business services. Disabled: adapted rooms. Gym. Parking ($30 per night). Restaurants (2). Spa. Wireless internet.* **Room services** *DVD. High-speed internet. Minibar. Telephone. TV: cable, pay movies.*

Foggy Bottom

Ritz-Carlton, Washington, DC

1150 22nd Street, NW, at M Street, DC 20037 (reservations 1-800 241 3333/front desk 1-202 835 0500/fax 1-202 835 1588/www.ritz-carlton.com). Foggy Bottom-GWU Metro. **Rates** $329-$499 single/double; $579-$4,500 suite. **Credit** AmEx, DC, Disc, MC, V. **Map** p284 G5.

Something is always happening at the Ritz-Carlton. Various local celebs have joined the state-of-the-art fitness centre, the Sports Club LA, to which guests

have access. You'll see Secret Service men and beautiful people mingling in the lobby and in the intimate, luxurious lounges. Even the lowliest of rooms are labelled deluxe (they, like all other rooms, boast marble baths and high-speed net access). If your company's paying (and thinks highly of you), go for the Club experience, which offers a private lounge and 24-hour butler service. The immediate neighbourhood is slightly dull, but the Ritz is its own chic island, so who cares?

Hotel services *Babysitting. Bar. Beauty salon. Business services. Disabled: adapted rooms. Parking ($28 per night). Restaurant.* **Room services** *High-speed internet. Minibar. Telephone. TV: cable, pay movies. VCR.*

Downtown

Hay-Adams Hotel

800 Lafayette Square, NW, at 16th & H Streets, DC 20006 (front desk 1-202 638 6600/fax 1-202 638 2716/www.hayadams.com). Farragut North or McPherson Square Metro. **Rates** $425-$875 single/double; $895-$5,500 suite. **Credit** AmEx, DC, Disc, MC, V. **Map** p284 H5.

A recent $19 million renovation only enhanced the grandeur of one of Washington's most elegant hotels. Its location on Lafayette Square provides great people-watching opportunities, as various anti-presidential protests take place in the park. The hotel played a central role in the infamous Iran-Contra scandal in the 1980s, when millions of dollars of 'fundraising' changed hands in its leathery lounges. The roof deck has a great view of the White House, and the basement bar oozes with class.

Ritz-Carlton, Washington, DC.

Hotel services *Bar. Business services. Gym. Parking ($29 per night). Restaurant. Wireless internet.* **Room services** *DVD (some rooms). High-speed internet. Telephone. TV: cable, pay movies, web TV.*

The Madison

15th & M Streets, NW, DC 20005 (reservations 1-800 424 8577/front desk 1-202 862 1600/ fax 1-202 785 1255/www.themadisondc.com). McPherson Square Metro. **Rates** $289-$379 single/double; $429-$3,800 suite. **Credit** AmEx, DC, Disc, MC, V. **Map** p282 H5.

The Madison reopened in 2004 following a major renovation. This downtown hotel has a luxurious and very traditional feel – just as founding father James Madison would have wanted it – which helps make it popular with foreign dignitaries. The hotel sponsors a polo team and offers guests polo lessons and trail rides out in the country. One of its two restaurants, Palette, is sleek and modern – a departure from the hotel's otherwise classical feel.
Hotel services *Bars (2). Business services. Gym. Parking ($26 per night). Restaurants (2). Spa.* **Room services** *High-speed internet. Telephone. TV: cable, pay movies.*

Georgetown

Four Seasons

2800 Pennsylvania Avenue, NW, between 28th & 29th Streets, DC 20007 (reservations 1-800 332 3442/front desk 1-202 342 0444/fax 1-202 944 2076/www.fourseasons.com). Foggy Bottom-GWU Metro then 30, 32, 34, 35, 36, Georgetown Metro Connection bus. **Rates** $345-$650 single/ double; $750-$5,500 suite. **Credit** AmEx, DC, Disc, MC, V. **Map** p281 F5.

This discreetly off-street Four Seasons is one of DC's most comfortable hotels. It has long attracted VIP guests and pampers them with every luxury or facility they may desire. A massive renovation scheduled for completion in December 2004 will expand the size of guest rooms. The health spa is both serious and sybaritic, and high-class art is displayed throughout. Even if you're not lucky enough to be staying here, at least treat yourself to a glass of wine during live jazz performances on Wednesday evenings or afternoon tea in the Garden Terrace.
Hotel services *Business services. Disabled: adapted rooms. Gym. Parking ($26 per night). Swimming pool (indoor). Wireless internet.* **Room services** *High-speed internet. Minibar. Telephone. TV: cable, pay movies, web TV. VCR.*

Ritz-Carlton, Georgetown

3100 South Street, NW, at 31st Street, DC 20007 (1-202 912 4100/fax 1-202 912 4199/www.ritz carlton.com/hotels/georgetown). Foggy Bottom-GWU Metro then 30, 32, 34, Georgetown Metro Connection bus. **Rates** $475-$500 single/double; $895-$5,000 suite. **Credit** AmEx, DC, Disc, MC, V. **Map** p281 E5.

With just 86 guest rooms – about a third of which are executive suites – the Ritz's new Georgetown property is more intimate than its Foggy Bottom

sister. Located near the Potomac River waterfront, the hotel is housed in a renovated red-brick building with a 130ft (40m) smokestack. The industrial architecture makes an appropriate, slightly unusual backdrop for the chic modern furnishings. Some rooms have views of downtown and the river. The building also houses a cinema, spa and coffee shop, plus a restaurant (Fahrenheit) and martini lounge (Degrees). The posh neighbourhood is not convenient to the Metro, but there's plenty right here to keep you entertained.
Hotel services *Babysitting. Bar. Business services. Disabled: adapted rooms. Parking ($28 per night). Restaurant.* **Room services** *Dataport. DVD. Minibar. Telephone. TV: cable, pay movies, web TV.*

Upper Northwest

Marriott Wardman Park

2660 Woodley Road, NW, at Connecticut Avenue, DC 20008 (reservations 1-800 228 9290/front desk 1-202 328 2000/fax 1-202 387 5397/ www.marriott.com). Woodley Park-Zoo/Adams Morgan Metro. **Rates** $289-$329 single/double; $475-$750 suite. **Credit** AmEx, DC, Disc, MC, V. **Map** p281 F2.

A huge (more than 1,300 rooms) and labyrinthine hotel perched on a hill near the Woodley Park-Zoo/Adams Morgan Metro stops. If you get lost (as you inevitably will), ask the friendly staff, who seem to be everywhere. Although the 1918 building is gorgeous and surrounded by luscious greenery, the larger wing of the complex is monolithic and lacks character. On the plus side, the rooms have been upgraded with new bathrooms and beds and the hotel has a large new fitness centre. Expect to see weddings or conferences here; the hotel has extensive facilities for the latter.
Hotel services *Bars (2). Business services. Disabled: adapted rooms. Gym. Parking ($22 per night). Restaurants (3). Swimming pool (outdoor).* **Room services** *High-speed internet. Minibar. Telephone. TV: cable, pay movies.*

Expensive ($159-$250)

The White House & around

Hotel Washington

515 15th Street, NW, at Pennsylvania Avenue, DC 20004 (reservations 1-800 424 9540/ front desk 1-202 638 5900/fax 1-202 638 1595/ www.hotelwashington.com). Metro Center Metro. **Rates** $195-$275 single/double; $495-$700 suite. **Credit** AmEx, DC, Disc, MC, V. **Map** p284 H5.

Famous for its lovely rooftop bar, the Terrace Café, the historic Hotel Washington (completed in 1918) has 350 large rooms and friendly, down-to-earth staff. Though not as upscale as the nearby Willard (*see p43*), the hotel does boast marble baths and mahogany furnishings.

Hotel services *Bars (2). Beauty salon. Business services. Gym. Parking ($25 per night). Restaurant.* Room services *Dataport. Telephone. TV: cable, pay movies, web TV.*

Union Station & around

Phoenix Park Hotel

520 North Capitol Street, NW, at Massachusetts Avenue, DC 20001 (reservations 1-800 527 8483/ front desk 1-202 638 6900/fax 1-202 393 3236). Union Station Metro. Rates *$159-$319 single; $189-$349 double.* Credit *AmEx, DC, Disc, MC, V.* Map *p285 K6.*
A couple of blocks from the Capitol and across from Union Station, this hotel has one major plus point: the massive Dubliner pub below it. The local Hill workers seem to like it, though the Irish theme can be a tad overwhelming at times.
Hotel services *Business services. Gym. Parking ($25 per night).* Room services *Dataport. Minibar. Telephone. TV: cable, pay movies.*

South of the Mall

Loews L'Enfant Plaza

480 L'Enfant Plaza, SW, DC 20024 (reservations 1-800 635 5065/front desk 1-202 484 1000/fax 1-202 466 4456/www.loewshotels.com). L'Enfant Plaza Metro. Rates *$159-$329 single/double; $375-$795 suite.* Credit *AmEx, DC, Disc, MC, V.* Map *p285 J7.*
A large opulent hotel located near the Mall and the Capitol. The balconies offer great views but the business-heavy area largely shuts down at night. That said, the hotel goes out of its way to make all members of the family welcome: kids under 18 stay in parent's room for free, grandparents travelling with grandchildren are offered special rates for adjoining rooms, and cats and dogs get their own room service menu. Business travellers are very well catered to, while the rooftop swimming pool is perfect for downtime. The hotel also has its own entrance to the Metro.
Hotel services *Bars (2). Business services. Disabled: adapted rooms. Gym. Parking ($14 per night). Restaurants (2). Swimming pool (indoor/outdoor).* Room services *Minibar. Telephone. TV: cable, pay movies. VCR.*
Other locations: Jefferson Hotel 1200 16th Street, NW, at M Street, Downtown DC 20036, (reservations 1-800 555 8000/front desk 1-202 347 2200/fax 1-202 331 7982).

Foggy Bottom

The Fairmont

2401 M Street, NW, at 24th Street, DC 20037 (reservations 1-877 222 2266/1-202 429 2400/ fax 1-202 457 5010/www.fairmont.com/washington). Foggy Bottom-GWU Metro. Rates *(incl breakfast) $199-$429 single/double; $299-$529 Fairmont Gold single/double; $1,099-$3,099 suite.* Credit *AmEx, DC, Disc, MC, V.* Map *p284 F5.*

The Fairmont's sunny, marble-floored lobby, so full of plants it looks like a greenhouse, instantly lifts the spirits. The pool, garden patio and vast, bright rooms do the rest. The exceptional fitness centre offers a lap pool, squash and racquetball courts, aerobics classes, massages and a juice bar. Everyone, staff and guests alike, seem happy in this 415-room hotel located on a quiet street. The Fairmont Gold, a 'hotel within a hotel', is a club floor with separate check-in, and free continental breakfast, afternoon tea and evening cocktails in the private lounge.
Hotel services *Business services. Disabled: adapted rooms. Gym. Parking ($23 per night). Restaurant. Swimming pool (indoor). Wireless internet.* Room services *Dataport. Minibar. Telephone. TV: cable, pay movies.*

Hotel Lombardy

2019 Pennsylvania Avenue, NW, at I Street, DC 20006 (reservations 1-800 424 5486/ front desk 1-202 828 2600/fax 1-202 872 0503/ www.hotellombardy.com). Farragut West Metro. Rates *$179-$249 single/double.* Credit *AmEx, DC, Disc, MC, V.* Map *p284 G5.*
Formerly a grand apartment building, this 127-unit boutique hotel retains some charm, with old-fashioned touches such as brass fixtures and crystal doorknobs, and a Middle Eastern-style bar. The Lombardy shares the neighbourhood with the World Bank and has an international feel. The views over Pennsylvania Avenue are good, but try not to get stuck in a room at the back of the building. There's also an attendant-operated lift – when was the last time you saw that in a hotel? Access to the pool at nearby the Washington Plaza Hotel is included.
Hotel services *Parking ($25 night).* Room services *Dataport. Kitchen (suites). Telephone. TV: cable.*

One Washington Circle Hotel

1 Washington Circle, NW, between 23rd Street & New Hampshire Avenue, DC 20037 (reservations 1-800 424 9671/front desk 1-202 872 1680/fax 1-202 887 4989/www.onewashcirclehotel.com). Foggy Bottom-GWU Metro. Rates *$159-$309 suite.* Credit *AmEx, DC, Disc, MC, V.* Map *p284 F5.*
Nixon used to stay in this underrated suite hotel. The hotel has upgraded its restaurant: the new Circle Bistro has already drawn a raft of praise. Many of the 151 suites are large and some have their own balconies, though one drawback is that you can hear ambulances passing by en route to GW University Hospital from some of them (ask for a suite on the L Street side if you think noise will be a problem).
Hotel services *Business services. Parking ($18 per night). Swimming pool (outdoor).* Room services *Dataport. Kitchen. Telephone. TV: pay movies.*

Park Hyatt

1201 24th Street, NW, at M Street, DC 20037 (reservations 1-800 233 1234/front desk 1-202 789 1234/fax 1-202 457 8823/www.hyatt.com). Foggy Bottom-GWU Metro. Rates *$199-$330 single/double; $224-$370 suite; $595 park suite.* Credit *AmEx, DC, Disc, MC, V.* Map *p284 F5.*

Boutique chic

While Washington has always been home to numerous chain hotels, there's now a new type of property springing up across town. Yep, the boutique hotel has finally made it to the District, thanks largely to the Kimpton Group, which owns all of the properties below except the River Inn. Small, hip and design-conscious, they have been an instant hit within fashionable circles. Many are found in neighbourhoods with great dining and nightlife, but also themselves boast bars that attract locals as well as out-of-towners. Whether your tastes tend toward classic glam, minimalist modern or playful retro, there'll be a property to match. Other Kimpton properties listed in this chapter are **Hotel Monaco** (see below) and **Hotel Madera** (see p50).

Hotel George

15 E Street, NW, at North Capitol Street, Judiciary Square area, DC 20001 (reservations 1-800 576 8331/front desk 1-202 347 4200/fax 1-202 347 4213/www.hotelgeorge.com). Union Station Metro. **Rates** $179-$375 single; $25 each additional person; $750-$900 suite. **Credit** AmEx, DC, Disc, MC, V. **Map** p285 K6.
The first Kimpton Group property in DC, the George set the bar high. From the sleek, white lobby with grand piano to the hip, buzzy bar and restaurant-bistro Bis (see p126), it generally hits the spot. Rooms vary, but are quite generously sized and decorated with refreshing restraint and style – not a floral in sight, and the only flourish is a Warhol-like wall print of a dollar bill.
Hotel services *Bar. Business services. Disabled: adapted rooms. Parking ($26 per night). Restaurant.* **Room services** *High-speed internet. Minibar. Telephone. TV: pay movies.*

Hotel Helix

1430 Rhode Island Avenue, NW, between 14th & 15th Streets: Logan Circle, DC 20005 (reservations 1-800 706 1202/front desk 1-202 462 9001/fax 1-202 332 3519/www.hotelhelix.com). McPherson Square Metro. **Rates** from $159 weekdays; from $129 weekends. **Credit** AmEx, DC, Disc, MC, V. **Map** p282 H5.
Pop culture is the theme at this fun and funky hotel – which pays homage to Andy Warhol – in the newly hip Logan Circle neighbourhood. Expect bright colours, mod furniture, oversized photos, lots of plastic and great design. Catering to a twenty- and thirtysomething clientele, the hotel has wisely placed flat-screen TVs and Nintendo video game systems in all the rooms. At the nightly 'Hour of Bubbles', staff serve complimentary champagne and wine. The Metro is a bit of a hike, but the neighbourhood itself is quite vibrant.
Hotel services *Bar. Business services. Gym. Parking ($22 per night).* **Room services** *High-speed internet. Minibar. Telephone. TV: pay movies.*

Hotel Rouge

1315 16th Street, NW, at Massachusetts Avenue & Scott Circle, Dupont Circle, DC 20036 (reservations 1-800 738 1202/front desk 1-202 232 8000/fax 1-202 667 9827/www.rougehotel.com). **Rates** $139-$329 single/double. **Credit** AmEx, DC, Disc, MC, V. **Map** p282 G4.
There's nothing refined about Rouge, which prides itself on being brash and playful, but chances are you won't mind. The decor verges on camp – with ten white Venus statues outside and white leather chairs inside – in a retro chic sort of way. The hotel offers a complimentary wine hour on weekdays and

If you crave wide open spaces, stay at the Park Hyatt, where everything – rooms, lobby, pool – seems oversized. The hotel has the kind of lobby that makes you want to whisper, and a clientele straight out of the horsey 'dahling' set – think Scarlett O'Hara, with a European education. The restaurant has an outdoor café, where you can gaze across the street at… two other hotels. Some suites have jacuzzi tubs.
Hotel services *Bar. Beauty salon. Business services. Disabled: adapted rooms. Gym. Parking ($25 per night). Restaurant. Swimming pool (indoor).* **Room services** *Dataport. Minibar. Telephone. TV: pay movies. VCR.*

Downtown

Hotel Monaco

700 F Street, NW, at 7th Street, DC 20004 (1-202 628 7177/reservations 1-877 202 5411/fax 1-202 628 7277/www.monaco-dc.com). Gallery Place-Chinatown Metro. **Rates** from $169 single/double; $525 suite. **Credit** AmEx, DC, Disc, MC, V. **Map** p285 J6.
The transformation of Washington's landmark General Post Office building into a high-end hotel (with an equally top-notch restaurant, Poste) was a

Hotel Helix. *See p48.*

Blood Marys on weekend mornings, and Bar Rouge is one of the best hotel bars in town. The immediate surroundings are lacklustre, but Dupont Circle is nearby.
Hotel services *Bar. Business services. Gym. Parking ($22 per night).* **Room services** *High-speed internet. Minibar. Telephone. TV: pay movies.*

River Inn

924 25th Street, NW, between I & K Streets, Foggy Bottom, DC 20037 (reservations 1-800 424 2741/front desk 1-202 337 7600/fax 1-202 337 6520/www.theriverinn.com). Foggy Bottom-GWU Metro. **Rates** $169-$225 suite. **Credit** AmEx, DC, MC, V. **Map** p284 F5.
Once a family-friendly lodging that drew primarily government and university types, this boutique hotel was reinvented by Washington's hottest design firm, Adamstein/Demetriou. The new look exudes modern elegance, with dark wood and clean lines. The hotel pampers guests with plush robes, a video/CD library and in-room coffee makers; and its restaurant, Dish, serves up nostalgic American fare. Some of the upper-floor rooms have amazing views of Georgetown, and the location is convenient.

Hotel services *Bar. Business services. Parking ($20 per night). Restaurant.* **Room services** *DVD. Disabled: adapted rooms. High-speed internet. Kitchen. TV: cable, pay movies, web TV.*

Topaz Hotel

1733 N Street, NW, on Embassy Row, Dupont Circle, DC 20036 (reservations 1-800 424 2950/front desk 1-202 393 3000/fax 1-202 785 9581/www.topazhotel.com). Dupont Circle Metro. **Rates** $149-$359 double. **Credit** AmEx, DC, Disc, MC, V. **Map** p282 G4.
Topaz bills itself as DC's 'most enlightened boutique hotel', a theme that plays out with daily horoscope readings, morning energy drinks and speciality yoga rooms (on request), which come furnished with mats and blocks, dimmer switches and instructional videos. It's not just for health nuts, though: in the evening, the small Topaz Bar comes to life with cocktails, Asian-influenced fare and dance music.
Hotel services *Bar. Business services. Parking ($24 per night).* **Room services** *High-speed internet. Minibar. Telephone. TV: pay movies.*

colossal undertaking for the Kimpton Group. The result, however, is stunning – vivid colours and modern furniture in a monumental-scale classical building. The surrounding neighbourhood is vivid too, with the MCI Center, International Spy Museum and Mall all close by. Rooms come equipped with high-speed internet (and suites have CD players), but the hotel's signature touch is the goldfish it lends to guests who could use the company.
Hotel services *Bar. Business services. Gym. Parking ($27 per night). Restaurant.* **Room services** *High-speed internet. Minibar. Telephone. TV: pay movies.*

Renaissance Mayflower Hotel

1127 Connecticut Avenue, NW, between L & M Streets, DC 20036 (reservations 1-800 228 9290/front desk 1-202 347 3000/fax 1-202 776 9182/www.renaissancehotels.com). Farragut North Metro. **Rates** $199-$399 single/double; $299-$499 suite. **Credit** AmEx, DC, Disc, MC, V. **Map** p284 G5.
With its grand floral displays, excellent food and professional, warm staff, the Mayflower epitomises Southern hospitality. Both Kennedy and Eisenhower lived here before they moved to the White House, and FDR, Winston Churchill, Charles de Gaulle, Queen Elizabeth and Jimmy Stewart have all enjoyed the

Hotel Rouge: for red-hued decadence. *See p48.*

hotel's shimmering hospitality over the years. The property recently underwent a $9 million renovation, which means updated rooms and the addition of a VIP club floor. High tea, served every day at 3pm, is a Mayflower tradition.
Hotel services *Bar. Business services. Gym. Parking ($26 per night). Restaurant.* **Room services** *High-speed internet. Minibar. Telephone. TV: cable, pay movies.*

The St Regis
923 16th Street, NW, at K Street, DC 20006 (reservations 1-800 562 5661/front desk 1-202 638 2626/fax 1-202 638 4231/www.luxurycollection. com). **Rates** $189-$550 single/double; $500-$3,500 suite. **Credit** AmEx, DC, Disc, MC, V. **Map** p284 H5.
Sink into one of the exquisite couches in the lobby, stare at the ornate gilded ceiling and stay a while. Modelled after an Italian palazzo, this 193-room hotel is located two blocks from the White House. The baroque theme continues in the sumptuously furnished rooms. The hotel's restaurant, Timothy Dean, is admired by locals and visiting celebs.
Hotel services *Bar. Business services. Disabled: adapted rooms. Parking ($28 per night). Restaurant.* **Room services** *High-speed internet. Minibar. Telephone. TV: cable, pay movies. VCR.*

Dupont Circle

Governor's House Hotel
1615 Rhode Island Avenue, NW, at 17th Street, DC 20036 (reservations 1-800 821 4367/front desk 1-202 296 2100/www.governorshousewdc.com). Dupont Circle or Farragut North Metro. **Rates** $189-$259 single/double; $229-$259 suite. **Credit** AmEx, DC, Disc, MC, V. **Map** p282 G/H4.

Governor's offers 149 generously sized rooms and a refined Federalist-style lobby (plenty of leaves and dark wood). The staff are as warm as the decor. Elbow up to the popular outdoor bar with *National Geographic* photographers – they room here and then stop in for happy hour. It's convenient for Connecticut Avenue shopping and a short stroll to the White House. Passes to the YMCA on request.
Hotel services *Bar. Business services. Disabled: adapted rooms. Parking ($15/$21 per night).* **Room services** *High-speed internet. Kitchen (some rooms). Telephone. TV: cable, pay movies, web TV.*

HH Leonards Mansion
2020 O Street, NW, between 20th & 21st Streets, DC 20036 (front desk 1-202 496 2000/fax 1-202 659 0547). Dupont Circle Metro. **Rates** (incl breakfast) $250-$2,000 suite. **Credit** AmEx, Disc, MC, V. **Map** p282 G4.
This beautiful 18-room B&B is hidden on a residential side street, with no sign to announce its presence. Each room in the three interconnected townhouses has a different theme: the Log Cabin suite, for example, has huge log beams, cowhide rugs and a Frederic Remington sculpture. The owner is also an antiques dealer, so just about everything you see, from the furniture to the wall hangings, is for sale.
Hotel services *Parking ($15-$20 per night). Swimming pool (outdoor).* **Room services** *High-speed internet. Telephone. TV: cable.*

Hotel Madera
1310 New Hampshire Avenue, NW, between N & 20th Streets, DC 20036 (reservations 1-800 368 5691/front desk 1-202 296 7600/fax 1-202 293 2476/www.hotelmadera.com). Dupont Circle Metro. **Rates** from $189 weekdays; $149 weekends. **Credit** AmEx, DC, Disc, MC, V. **Map** p282 G4.

More muted than the other Kimpton properties, Madera plays with natural hues and materials for a soothing, sophisticated ambiance. Unlike the others, though, the guest rooms here are prone to look rather, well, ordinary. Still, the Dupont Circle location is hard to beat, the restaurant/bar Firefly is highly rated, and the speciality rooms include extras such as exercise equipment and kitchenette. The hotel also offers a free wine hour.
Hotel services *Bar. Business services. Parking ($24 per night). Restaurant.* **Room services** *High-speed internet. Minibar. Telephone. TV: pay movies.*

Adams Morgan

Washington Hilton

1919 Connecticut Avenue, NW, at T Street, DC 20009 (reservations 1-800 445 8667/front desk 1-202 483 3000/fax 1-202 232 0438/ www.washington.hilton.com). Dupont Circle Metro then 42 bus. **Rates** *$204-$339 single/double; $475-$970 suite; $750-$1,220 2-bedroom suite.* **Credit** AmEx, DC, Disc, MC, V. **Map** p282 G3.
With more than a thousand rooms, this vast hotel complex caters to conventions, so there are always three or four events under way. Nicknamed the 'Hinckley Hilton' after President Reagan's would-be assassin, who shot him outside in 1981, the hotel is normally filled with delegates – be prepared to see plenty of people wandering the sleek lobby wearing name tags. The two restaurants and two bars should keep you busy, and the upper-level rooms have great city views. The hotel also has a heated pool, and is one of the few in town to boast tennis courts.
Hotel services *Bars (2). Business services. Disabled: adapted rooms. Gym. Parking ($21 per night). Restaurants (2). Swimming pool (outdoor).* **Room services** *High-speed internet. Minibar. Telephone. TV: cable, pay movies.*

Georgetown

Hotel Monticello

1075 Thomas Jefferson Street, NW, between M & K Streets, DC 20007 (reservations 1-800 388 2410/ front desk 1-202 337 0900/fax 1-202 333 6526). Foggy Bottom-GWU Metro then 30, 32, 34, 35, 36 bus. **Rates** (incl breakfast) $169-$350 single/double. **Credit** AmEx, DC, MC, V. **Map** p281 F5.
Formerly the Georgetown Dutch Inn, the charming Hotel Monticello, named after Thomas Jefferson's country estate (the man himself once lived on this street), offers quiet rooms amid the hubbub of Georgetown. All 47 gorgeous suites have roomy living areas, complete with microwave and mini-fridge, and big, modern bathrooms with upmarket toiletries and fluffy robes. Get a room with a view of M Street and indulge in a spot of people-watching from your window.
Hotel services *Disabled: adapted rooms. Gym. Parking ($20 per night). Swimming pool (indoor).* **Room services** *Kitchen. Minibar. Telephone. TV: cable.*

Arlington, VA

Key Bridge Marriott

1401 Lee Highway, at Wilson Street, VA 22209 (reservations 1-800 228 9290/front desk 1-703 524 6400/fax 1-703 524 8964/www.marriott.com). Rosslyn Metro. **Rates** $219-$259 single/double; $375-$400 suite. **Credit** AmEx, DC, Disc, MC, V.
You won't find a better view of the Washington skyline at night than from the restaurant at the top of the Key Bridge Marriott. A large and luxurious hotel built for conventions (it has 17 meeting rooms), it's about a mile from Arlington National Cemetery and a quick walk across the bridge to Georgetown. The Metro, too, is nearby. A recent $13 million renovation included an expanded 24-hour fitness centre and an improved business centre. Be sure to request a room with a city view.
Hotel services *Bar. Business services. Parking ($10 per night). Restaurants (2). Swimming pool (indoor/outdoor).* **Room services** *High-speed internet. Telephone. TV: cable, pay movies.*

Bethesda, MD

Residence Inn Bethesda-Downtown

7335 Wisconsin Avenue, between Waverly Street & Montgomery Lane, Bethseda, MD 20814 (reservations 1-800 331 3131/front desk 1-301 718 0200/fax 1-301 718 0679). Bethesda Metro. **Rates** (incl breakfast) $249-$309 suite. **Credit** AmEx, DC, Disc, MC, V.

Hotel Monaco. See p48.

They don't call this the Residence Inn for nothing: all of the 187 suites in this hotel are spacious and so well equipped you could live here. Indeed, it's a home away from home for many business types. Rates decrease for longer stays (phone for details).
Hotel services *Business services. Gym. Parking ($15 per night). Swimming pool (outdoor).*
Room services *High-speed internet. Kitchen. Telephone. TV: cable, pay movies.*

Moderate ($100-$158)

The Capitol & around

Capitol Hill Suites
200 C Street, SE, at Second Street, DC 20003 (reservations 1-800 424 9165/front desk 1-202 543 6000/fax 1-202 547 2608/www.capitolhillsuites.com). Capitol South Metro. **Rates** (incl breakfast) $139-$219 single suite; $179-$239 double suite. **Credit** AmEx, DC, Disc, MC, V. **Map** p285 K7.
An all-suite hotel comprising two conjoined apartment buildings on a quiet street in a decent neighbourhood, within walking distance of the Metro and the Mall. Passes to a nearby gym are available for $10. Accommodation varies widely – the best suites have full kitchens and separate living spaces.
Hotel services *Parking ($28 per night).* **Room services** *Kitchen. Telephone. TV: pay movies.*

Foggy Bottom

St Gregory Luxury Hotel & Suites
2033 M Street, NW, at 21st Street, DC 20036 (reservations 1-800 829 5034/front desk 1-202 223 0200/fax 1-202 223 0580/www.stgregoryhotelwdc. com). Dupont Circle or Foggy Bottom-GWU Metro. **Rates** $139-$289 suite. **Credit** AmEx, DC, Disc, MC, V. **Map** p284 G5.
There aren't many hotels in Washington like this whimsically stylish, elegant boutique hotel whose lobby features a life-sized statue of Marilyn, skirt up. The experienced staff treat everyone like a VIP. Each of the 154 rooms and suites looks as if it was decorated by a pro; the proprietors, who also own the Governor's House Hotel (*see p50*), spared no expense with the high-quality furniture and original floral displays. Many rooms have full kitchens; some have balconies. All bathrooms are spacious and have a TV, in case bathing turns to boredom.
Hotel services *Bar. Business services. High-speed internet. Disabled: adapted rooms. Gym. Kitchen. Parking ($15-$22 per night).* **Room services** *Telephone. TV: cable, pay movies. VCR.*

Downtown

Comfort Inn Downtown/ Convention Center
1201 13th Street, NW, at M Street, DC 20005 (1-202 682 5300/fax 1-202 371 9624/ www.choicehotels.com). McPherson Square Metro. **Rates** (incl breakfast) $149-$199 single/double. **Credit** AmEx, DC, Disc, MC, V. **Map** p284 H5.
This well-appointed Comfort Inn is a surprisingly decent 100-room hotel in an up-and-coming neighbourhood three blocks from the convention centre. The cheerful staff serve a free continental breakfast every morning.
Hotel services *Business services. Gym. Parking ($22 per night).* **Room services** *High-speed internet. Telephone. TV: cable.*

Hamilton Crowne Plaza
1001 14th Street, at K Street, NW, DC 20005 (front desk 1-202 682 0111/reservations 1-800 637 3788/fax 1-202 682 9525/www.basshotels.com/ crowneplaza). McPherson Square Metro. **Rates** $130-$260 single/double; $290-$350 suite. **Credit** AmEx, DC, Disc, MC, V. **Map** p284 H5.
This Beaux Arts building on Franklin Square dates from the 1920s, and its gorgeous architecture matches the 381 small but elegantly appointed rooms and suites inside. Some of the rooms boast skyline views, but it's the Crowne Plaza's location that really makes it a winner. 'Club level' guests get a private elevator, plus free breakfast and use of the club lounge.
Hotel services *Bar. Business services. Disabled: adapted rooms. Gym. Parking ($26 per night). Restaurant.* **Room services** *High-speed internet (some rooms). Telephone. TV: pay movies, web TV.*

Morrison-Clark Inn
1015 L Street, NW, between 11th Street & Massachusetts Avenue, DC 20001 (reservations 1-800 332 7898/front desk 1-202 898 1200/fax 1-202 289 8576). Metro Center Metro. **Rates** (incl breakfast) $155-$325 single/double. **Credit** AmEx, DC, Disc, MC, V. **Map** p284 J5.
This Victorian manse has 54 uniquely designed and individually decorated rooms and suites. The antique furnishings add to the traditional feel – the inn is on the National Register of Historic Places. The hotel restaurant is a favourite spot for locals. Afternoon tea is included.
Hotel services *Bar. Gym. Internet. Parking ($22 per night).* **Room services** *Telephone. TV: cable.*

Sofitel Lafayette Square
806 15th Street, NW, at H Street, DC 20005 (1-202 730 8800/fax 1-202 730 8500/ www.sofitel.com). McPherson Square Metro. **Rates** $119-$320 single/double; $450-$600 suite. **Credit** AmEx, MC, V. **Map** p282 H5.
This new hotel close to the White House holds itself to standards as high as some of Washington's more expensive accommodation. The contemporary design in its 220 rooms and 17 suites is worthy of a posh boutique hotel, and the French cuisine at Café 15 draws diners who aren't staying here.
Hotel services *Bar. Business services. Gym. Parking ($26 per night). Restaurant.* **Room services** *Disabled: adapted rooms. High-speed internet. Minibar. Telephone. TV: cable.*

Judiciary Square area

Holiday Inn on the Hill

415 New Jersey Avenue, NW, between D & E Streets, DC 20001 (reservations 1-800 638 1116/ front desk 1-202 638 1616/fax 1-202 638 0707/ www.basshotels.com/holiday-inn). Union Station Metro. **Rates** $109-$225 single/double. **Credit** AmEx, DC, Disc, MC, V. **Map** p285 K6.

Possibly Washington, DC's most family-friendly hotel. Under-19s stay free in a parent's room and under-12s don't pay to eat in the restaurant. The hotel also provides 10,000sq ft (930sq m) of meeting space as well as plenty of amenities for the business traveller. Rooms and bathrooms are not huge, but you won't bump into the walls. It's also near the Mall and all major attractions, as well as the Metro. Overall, you'll be hard pressed to find more for your money.

Hotel services *Bar. Business services. Disabled: adapted rooms. Gym. Parking ($22 per night). Restaurant. Swimming pool (outdoor).* **Room services** *High speed internet. Telephone. TV: cable, pay movies.*

Dupont Circle

Dupont at the Circle

1604 19th Street, NW, between Q & Corcoran Streets, DC 20009 (reservations 1-888 412 0100/front desk 1-202 332 5251/fax 1-202 332 3244/www.dupontatthecircle.com). Dupont Circle Metro. **Rates** (incl breakfast) $140-$260 single/double. **Credit** AmEx, Disc, MC, V. **Map** p282 G4.

Just off bustling Dupont Circle, this elegant B&B is housed in two connected townhouses dating from 1883. Thickly blanketed beds, a luxurious parlour and a charming family-style dining room make the place feel ritzy but homely. The owner is friendly and helpful, and the location is great.

Hotel services *Business services. Gym. Parking ($15 per night).* **Room services** *High-speed internet. Telephone.*

Jurys Washington Hotel

1500 New Hampshire Avenue, NW, at Dupont Circle, DC 20036 (reservations 1-800 423 6953/ front desk 1-202 483 6000/fax 1-202 328 3265/ www.jurys.com). Dupont Circle Metro. **Rates** $125-$275 single/double; $300-$1,200 suite. **Credit** AmEx, DC, Disc, MC, V. **Map** p282 G4.

You'll not find a better view of Dupont Circle than from this hip hotel perched right in the middle of the action. It's owned by the Irish hotel chain, but this is no shamrock-and-claddagh affair; instead, funky furnishings adorn the lobby, and the 314 sunny rooms are modern and fully equipped. Dupont Grille, the hotel's stunning new restaurant, complete with floor-to-ceiling windows, serves an eclectic mix of cuisines. Biddy Mulligans, an Irish bar popular with locals, serves what has to be the best pint of Guinness in town.

Key Bridge Marriott. *See p51.*

Hotel services *Bar. Business services. Gym. Parking ($15 per night). Restaurants (2).* **Room services** *High-speed internet. Telephone. TV: cable, pay movies.*

Swann House

1808 New Hampshire Avenue, NW, at 18th Street, DC 20009 (1-202 265 4414/fax 1-202 265 6755/ www.swannhouse.com). Dupont Circle Metro. **Rates** (incl breakfast) $140-$295. **Credit** AmEx, DC, Disc, MC, V. **Map** p282 G4.

Unlike some of Washington's other townhouse B&Bs, the Swann House, built in 1883, is a free-standing mansion, which means the hallways aren't cramped and the lighting is good throughout. The pleasant rooms, which vary in their colour schemes, are romantic without being twee and some have working fireplaces and jacuzzis. A small swimming pool nestles in a brick courtyard at the back. Although it's a four-block walk to the nearest Metro station, you are rewarded with a beautiful tree-lined neighbourhood within an easy stroll of the trendy bars on U Street and the hip strip of 17th Street. Swann House is no-smoking throughout, but there are plenty of decks and porches. Room prices include breakfast, afternoon nibbles and an evening sherry. Note: children are tolerated but not really encouraged.

Hotel services *Business services. Parking ($12 per night). Swimming pool (outdoor).* **Room services** *Dataport. Kitchen (suites). Telephone. TV: cable. VCR.*

Where to Stay

Georgetown

Georgetown Suites

1111 30th Street, NW, at M Street, DC 20007 (reservations 1-800 348 7203/front desk 1-202 298 7800/fax 1-202 333 5792/www.georgetownsuites. com). Foggy Bottom-GWU Metro then Georgetown Metro Connection bus. **Rates** (incl breakfast) $150-$300 suite. **Credit** AmEx, DC, Disc, MC, V. **Map** p281 F5.

This 217-suite hotel, divided into two buildings, is set on a quiet street off the main drag of M Street. Formerly condominiums, each suite is well equipped with full kitchens and some units have patios too. It's also well situated for forays into Georgetown and along the C&O Canal. The rooms are bright and spacious – some of them are absolutely huge – and the bathrooms have been newly renovated (though the '80s-looking pastel decor is downright dismaying).
Hotel services *Business services. Gym. Parking ($18 per night).* **Room services** *Dataport. Telephone. TV: cable, pay movies. VCR.*

Budget ($99 or under)

The Capitol & around

Bull Moose Bed & Breakfast on Capitol Hill

101 Fifth Street, NE, at A Street, DC 20002 (reservations 1-800 261 2768/1-202 547 1050/ fax 1-202 548 9741/www.bullmoose-b-and-b.com). Union Station Metro. **Rates** (incl breakfast) $89-$209 single/double; from $350 per wk. **Credit** AmEx, Disc, MC, V. **Map** p285 L6.

Located just five blocks from the Capitol on a lovely tree-lined street, this 1890 townhouse inn pays homage to Teddy Roosevelt (and his Bull Moose Reform Party). Its ten cleverly decorated rooms, with names like 'The Sequoia' and 'John Stevens and the Big Ditch', will teach you a thing or two about TR's presidency, as will the Teddy memorabilia on the walls. Unlike most B&Bs, this one has a bright parlour filled with hip, funky furnishings by local artisans. You may be offered sherry, but there are no dusty velvet curtains here.
Hotel services *Parking (free with 48hrs' notice). Pay phone.*

Foggy Bottom

Allen Lee Hotel

2224 F Street, NW, at 23rd Street, DC 20037 (reservations 1-800 462 0186/front desk 1-202 331 1224/fax 1-202 296 3518/www.allenleehotel.com). Foggy Bottom-GWU Metro. **Rates** $45-$58 single; $62-$74 double; $71-$85 triple; $85-$98 quad. **Credit** AmEx, DC, MC, V, Disc. **Map** p284 F6.
Full of backpackers and students, the Allen Lee has small, spartan rooms with rather shabby furniture. It's basically a step up from a hostel – most rooms

have shared bathrooms but also TVs and phones. Service is on the brusque side, but at these prices you can't expect white gloves.
Hotel services *Payphone.*

Downtown

Hostelling International Washington, DC

1009 11th Street, NW, at K Street, DC 20001 (reservations 1-800 909 4776, ext 927/ front desk 1-202 737 2333/fax 1-202 737 1508/ www.hiwashingtondc.org). Metro Center Metro. **Rates** (incl breakfast) $20-$29 per person. **Credit** MC, V. **Map** p284 J5.
A top-notch, dirt-cheap hostel close to the Metro, Hostelling International offers 270 beds divided between single-sex rooms and four-bed 'family' rooms. Kitchens, lockers and a laundry (self-service) are at your disposal during your stay, and the staff arrange group walking tours and theatre outings. Most importantly, there is no lock-out time. You'll have to book well in advance to get a place, because this is the only official hostel in town. Rates include linen.
Hotel services *Disabled: adapted rooms. High-speed internet. Kitchen. Payphone. TV.*

Where to Stay

Discreet **HH Leonards Mansion.** *See p50.*

Hotel Harrington

436 11th Street, NW, at E Street, DC 20004 (1-202 628 8140/reservations 1-800 424 8532/fax 1-202 347 3924/www.hotel-harrington.com). Metro Center Metro. **Rates** $95 single/double; $105-$155 family room. **Credit** AmEx, DC, Disc, MC, V. **Map** p284 J6.
Harrington is a budget hotel, plain and simple. The lobby and rooms are clean but outdated and the staff are welcoming and helpful. People choose to stay here for two reasons: price and location. The hotel is conveniently downtown, surrounded by a neighbourhood where you'll never get bored. The Smithsonian museums and the Mall are also within easy reach. Family rooms sleep up to eight people. **Hotel services** *Bar. Parking ($10 per night). Restaurants (2).* **Room services** *Telephone. TV: cable.*

Dupont Circle

Brickskeller Inn

1523 22nd Street, NW, between P & Q Streets, DC 20037 (front desk 1-202 293 1885/fax 1-202 293 0996). Dupont Circle Metro. **Rates** $54-$73 single/double (shared bath); $73-$92 single/double (private bath). **Credit** AmEx, DC, Disc, MC, V. **Map** p282 G4.
Don't be put off by the buzzed entry here: the bar (serving 800 beers) and restaurant below the hotel make it a necessity. Cheap and, well, moderately cheerful, the 400-room hotel is near Rock Creek Park and tons of restaurants on P Street. Most rooms have shared baths, but not all have TVs.
Room services *Telephone.*

Radisson Barcelô Hotel

2121 P Street, NW, at 21st Street, DC 20037 (reservations 1-800 333 3333/front desk 1-202 293 3100/fax 1-202 857 0134/www.radisson.com). Dupont Circle Metro. **Rates** $99-$299 single/double; $259-$1,000 suite. **Credit** AmEx, DC, Disc, MC, V. **Map** p282 G4.

Located plum in the middle of P Street's cruising corridor, the Barcelô is a calm oasis steps from Rock Creek Park and the restaurants and cafés of Dupont Circle. Its major selling point: gigantic rooms. With 301 large rooms, 77 suites, and conference facilities measuring 7,000sq ft (651 sq m), it's big – but not impersonal. There's a rooftop sundeck and a popular Spanish/Latin American restaurant, Gabriel.
Hotel services *Babysitting. Bar. Business services. Disabled: adapted room. Gym. Parking ($22 per night). Restaurant. Swimming pool (outdoor).* **Room services** *Dataport. Telephone. TV: cable, pay movies. VCR (on request).*

Tabard Inn

1739 N Street, NW, at Connecticut Avenue, DC 20036 (front desk 1-202 785 1277/fax 1-202 785 6173/www.tabardinn.com). Dupont Circle Metro. **Rates** (incl breakfast) $86-$120 single/double (shared bath); $125-$190 single/double (private bath). **Credit** AmEx, MC, V. **Map** p282 G4.
The Tabard Inn employs a full-time interior designer – and it shows. Each of the 42 rooms is decorated in brilliant colours with a hotchpotch of slightly chipped antiques. Unique and classy, the Tabard draws locals with its excellent restaurant (*see p130*) and offers a garden courtyard in summer and a roaring fire in winter. It's made up of three 19th-century townhouses and is the oldest continuously operated hotel in the District; the floors and doors squeak and there's no lift or TVs (the latter are available on request). Guests get use of the nearby YMCA. All in all, a great deal.
Hotel services *Bar. Parking ($22 per night). Restaurant.* **Room services** *Dataport. Telephone.*

Adams Morgan

Adam's Inn

1744 Lanier Place, NW, at 18th Street, DC 20009 (1-202 745 3600/reservations 1-800 578 6807/fax 1-202 319 7958/www.adamsinn.com). Woodley Park-

Tabard Inn.

single (private bath); $60-$75 double (shared bath); $80-$100 double (private bath); $95-$135 suite. **Credit** AmEx, DC, Disc, MC, V. **Map** p282 G3.
This B&B is successful because it's such a good deal. The 29-unit property is situated in prime real estate, close enough to Columbia Road for nightlife but far enough for quiet. There's a garden patio out back.
Hotel services *Parking ($7 per night). Payphone.*
Other locations: 2700 Cathedral Avenue, NW, at 27th Street, Woodley Park, DC 20008 (1-202 328 0860/fax 1-202 328 8730).

Arlington, VA

Days Inn

2201 Arlington Boulevard, at Route 50 & Fort Myer Drive, Arlington, VA 22201 (1-703 525 0300/fax 1-703 525 5671/www.daysinn.com). Rosslyn Metro then hotel shuttle. **Rates** $68-$96 single/double. **Credit** AmEx, DC, Disc, MC, V.
No frills here – just a good bargain. The hotel is located next to a highway and looks a bit run-down. But there's free parking and a shuttle to the Rosslyn Metro station. Under-17s stay free in a parent's room, staff are friendly and the hotel has an outdoor pool.
Hotel services *Bar. Business services. Parking (free). Restaurant. Swimming pool (outdoor).*
Room services *Dataport. Telephone. TV: cable.*

Bethesda, MD

Four Points Sheraton

8400 Wisconsin Avenue, at Woodmont Avenue, Bethesda, MD 20814 (1-301 654 1000/reservations 1-800 325 3535/fax 1-301 654 0751/www.four points.com). Medical Center Metro. **Rates** $79-$264 single/double. **Credit** AmEx, DC, Disc, MC, V.
A few blocks from the Metro station and what passes for 'bustle' along Wisconsin Avenue, this large and rather anonymous chain hotel has 164 rooms and suites. It's geared more for business than pleasure, but is a real bargain. The Olympic-sized outdoor pool is a plus, Chatters sports bar less so.
Hotel services *Business services. Disabled: adapted rooms. Gym. Parking ($7 per night). Swimming pool (outdoor).* **Room services** *High-speed internet. Telephone. TV: cable, pay movies.*

Hyatt Regency Bethesda

One Bethesda Metro Center, Wisconsin Avenue at Old Georgetown Road, MD 20814 (reservations 1-800 223 1234/front desk 1-301 657 1234/fax 1-301 657 6453/www.hyatt.com). Rates $89-$300 single/double. **Credit** AmEx, DC, Disc, MC, V.
Kids will adore this luxurious hotel for its rooftop pool, thrilling 11-storey atrium lobby and three speedy glass elevators. Each of the 389 rooms has huge desks and black-and-white photographs of the city's monuments – the best hotel art in the DC area.
Hotel services *Bar. Business services. Disabled: adapted rooms. Gym. Parking ($8-$10 per night). Restaurant. Swimming pool (indoor).* **Room services** *Dataport. Telephone. TV: cable, pay movies.*

Kalorama Guest House – cheap and good.

Zoo/Adams Morgan Metro then 90, 92, 93, bus. **Rates** (incl breakfast) $75-$85 single; $10 per extra person. **Credit** AmEx, DC, Disc, MC, V. **Map** p282 G2.
Simple and clean rooms fill this three-storey B&B in a quiet part of Adams Morgan. The flea-market furnishings and fireplaces make it cosy, and though rooms don't have phones or TVs, there is a common lounge and kitchen if you crave company.
Hotel services *Kitchen. Parking ($10 per night). Payphone.*

Jurys Normandy

2118 Wyoming Avenue, NW, at Connecticut Avenue, DC 20008 (front desk 1-202 483 1350/fax 1-202 387 8241). Dupont Circle Metro then L1 bus. **Rates** $79-$180 single/double. **Credit** AmEx, DC, Disc, MC, V. **Map** p282 G3.
Jurys Normandy is a small hotel with gracious touches: the garden patio and glass conservatory are just a couple of the unexpected pleasures. Though none of the 75 rooms have views to speak of, they're nicely decorated in rich tones and feature mahogany furniture.
Hotel services *Parking ($15 per night). Swimming pool (outdoor).* **Room services** *High-speed internet. Telephone. TV: cable.*

Kalorama Guest House

1854 Mintwood Place, NW, at Columbia Road, DC 20009 (front desk 1-202 667 6369/fax 1-202 319 1262). Woodley Park-Zoo/Adams Morgan Metro or Dupont Circle Metro then 42 bus. **Rates** (incl breakfast) $55-$70 single (shared bath); $75-$95

 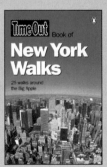 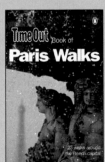

Sightseeing

Features

Introduction

You can still frolic freely in the nation's capital – it just takes adaptability and a sense of humour.

It's hard now to picture the days in the 19th century when visitors could stroll freely into the White House – and maybe even meet the president. Security was stepped up in stages, but in today's locked-down, post-9/11 DC, it's tighter than ever.

Unpredictable security crackdowns, keyed to a colour-coded security index (*see p262* **On the alert**), aren't the only variables faced by today's tourist. Demonstrations, marathons and all kinds of festival can shut down important buildings and major thoroughfares. Wise is the visitor who consults www.washington.org, the morning paper or the TV news for the latest information.

It's worth the effort. Major government buildings and museums are free, although of late some privately funded attractions have started to charge admission fees. And, more recently, visitors have begun to look beyond the traditional attractions of the National Mall into the life of the city itself, where security measures are far less intrusive.

On the Mall, security measures are quirky and inconsistent: some museums have airport-style metal detectors, others don't. It's a good idea to keep your keys, change and other heavy metal in a small bag to breeze through the monitors. More than ever, visitors must make reservations, often weeks in advance, for public tours or over-subscribed events and exhibitions. For some bookings (including tours of the White House and Capitol), Americans find aid in their congressional representatives; foreigners

may find their embassies can help (foreign passport holders can only see the White House by arranging a tour through their embassy). For a list of local embassies, *see p255*, or go to www.embassy.org. Ask the Convention & Tourism Corporation (*see p263*) for a copy of its calendar, which details forthcoming events.

ORIENTATION AND NEIGHBOURHOODS

DC's logical street-naming system makes finding your destination easy – if you master a couple of basic rules (which are explained on p251).

The National Mall and its institutions are on a walkable scale (if you enjoy walking, that is – pack some comfy shoes), and forays further afield are not a problem given the efficient Metro subway system and relatively low cab fares. The must-see monuments and museums on and around the Mall are covered in our **Monumental Centre** chapter, starting on p62.

DC Neighbourhoods, on pp76-95, covers the rest of the District, including the corporate downtown zone and Dupont Circle, a residential area with a buzzing street scene. Further north are Adams Morgan (lively and ethnically diverse) and the U Street/14th Street Corridor in Shaw – the hip, historic hub of DC's African American culture. West of Rock Creek is Georgetown, long on elegance but short on Metro stations.

The parts of Virginia and Maryland bordering Washington are included in **DC Suburbs**, starting on p96.

Our street maps begin on p280.

Lincoln Memorial. *See p62.*

Guided tours

DC has more than its fair share of tour companies, which between them offer a huge variety of guided (and self-guided tours). A great place to start is the **Cultural Tourism DC** website (www.culturaltourismdc.org), which has a full list of tours (including links to some of those listed below).

The following tours are also recommended. Where the company provides only one tour we have listed the cost; for others you should call or check the website for details of prices. Booking is advised for all.

For bicycle tours, see p216; for kayak tours, see p214; for African American heritage tours, see p86 **Parallel lives**.

Anecdotal History Walks

1-301 294 9514/www.dcsightseeing.com.
Cost $15.
Anthony Pitch, British journalist turned DC historian, gives personally narrated walking tours most Sundays from 11am to 1pm.

Bike the Sites

1-202 842 2452/www.bikethesites.com.
Guided tours by various types of bike (or even electric scooters, aka 'personal convenience vehicles' – great for the mobility-impaired). Tours leave from the Old Post Office Pavilion (12th Street & Pennsylvania Avenue, NW).

C&O Canal Barge Rides

1057 Thomas Jefferson Street, NW, at M Street, Georgetown (1-202 653 5190).
Cost $8; $5-$6 concessions.
Leisurely, mule-drawn canal boat rides on the C&O Canal between Georgetown and Great Falls, Maryland. Runs daily April to October.

Duck Tours

1-202 832 9800/www.trolleytours.com.
Cost $28; $14 concessions; free under-4s.
A narrated tour of the monuments in a World War II amphibious vehicle, which navigates the streets, then floats on the Potomac. The 90-minute tour leaves from the front of Union Station every hour on the hour from 10am to 3pm daily.

Nina's Dandy Cruises

Zero Prince Street, between King & Duke Streets, Alexandria, VA (1-703 683 6076/ http://www.dandydinnerboat.com).
Dinner, lunch or brunch cruises past the major monuments, sailing out of Old Town Alexandria year-round.

Old Town Trolley Tours

1-202 832 9800/www.trolleytours.com.
Cost $24; $12 concessions; free under-4s.
Trolleys – actually buses in twee disguise – run every half hour. Stops aren't marked, but you can hop on at will (though you can only make the full circle once).

Potomac Riverboat Company

1-703 548 9000/www.potomacriverboat co.com.
One-way or round-trip narrated boat tours of Alexandria, Mount Vernon or DC. Trips run most days, from mid March to October, and most leave from Alexandria Docks.

Scandal Tour

1-202 783 7212/www.gnpcomedy.com.
Cost $35.
This 90-minute tour features costumed performers acting out different scandals that took place in DC, such as the Watergate break-in. It kicks off at 1pm on Saturdays at the Old Post Office Pavilion (12th Street & Pennsylvania Avenue, NW).

Spies of Washington Tour

1-703 273 2381/www.spytour.com.
Cost $45.
Periodic explorations of the haunts of espionage under the auspices of Francis Gary Powers Jr, son of the U-2 spy-plane pilot shot down over the USSR in 1959.

Tour DC

1-301 588 8999/www.tourdc.com.
A range of tours (Georgetown, Embassy Row, Dupont Circle) run by happily downshifted attorney Mary Kay Ricks.

Tourmobile

1-202 544 5100/www.tourmobile.com.
Guided bus tours around the major sights (including Arlington National Cemetery), with options to get off and reboard at any point on the circuit. Twilight tours are also available.

Washington Photo Safari

1-877 512 5969/1-202 537 0937/ www.washingtonphotosafari.com.
Sick of blurry holiday photos? Combine sightseeing with snapping by booking one of the many half-day or day-long tours offered by experienced photographer E David Luria. Elaborate equipment isn't necessary: even a disposable camera will do.

Sightseeing

The Monumental Centre

The symbolic – and actual – hub of American power is both a working centre of government and a series of stunning monuments.

Lincoln Memorial. *See p64.*

The Mall & Tidal Basin

Map p284 & p285

Famous the world over, the Mall is the nexus of iconic picture-postcard Washington, a central tree-lined greenway flanked by imposing museums and crowned by the US Capitol. Some visitors see it less grandly. 'If this is the Mall, where are all the stores?' always makes the National Park Service's list of top ten dumb questions asked by tourists. But the only stores are garish vendor carts now banished to the periphery and the promising gift shops (*see p157* **Cultural commodities**) to be found inside many of the Mall's museums, repositories of the American experience.

The bigger picture is more inspiring. One of the four radii branching from the Capitol – the formal if not geographical centre of the city – the Mall thrusts due west for a mile, originally ending at the Potomac shore, which was then just beyond the Washington Monument at 17th Street. In 1921 the Lincoln Memorial rose on reclaimed marshland, and the vista was extended to the new river bank. Arlington Memorial Bridge, a symbolic link between a North and South still estranged by the Civil War, continues the Mall line to Arlington House.

The National Mall was integral to the city's original blueprint, the L'Enfant Plan of 1791 (*see p36* **The man with the plan**), commissioned by President Washington to give the capital an appropriately stately layout. In 1902 the McMillan Plan reimposed – and reinterpreted – L'Enfant's largely neglected vision, and now the National Capital Planning Commission referees the continual development debates over this quasi-sacred space (*see p66* **Turf wars**).

The Mall from west to east

At the western end of the mall, the first defining monument is the **Lincoln Memorial**, in front of the long Reflecting Pool. Beyond rises the needle of the Washington Monument and, finally, at the eastern end of the Mall, the Capitol, two miles (3.2 kilometres) away. The previously uncluttered vista between the two ends was interrupted in 2004 by the new **National World War II Memorial** (*see p64*) – the siting of the monument, needless to say, was heavily criticised.

Starting south-east of the Lincoln Memorial, on the far side of the Tidal Basin, is the circular **Jefferson Memorial** (*see p64*), commemorating the brainy third US president and author of the Declaration of Independence. Tucked just south is a new monument to Jefferson's friend, local Revolutionary-era thinker **George Mason**, relaxing on a bench with his ever-present books.

The **Franklin Delano Roosevelt Memorial** (*see below*) enlivens West Potomac Park, across the cherry tree-rimmed Tidal Basin (paddleboats for rent). Nearby is the site designated for a memorial to civil rights leader **Martin Luther King**, slated to involve a relief bust and excerpts from his speeches.

It was at the revered **Lincoln Memorial**, a neo-classical monument to the assassinated president, that King delivered his 'I have a dream' speech more than four decades ago.

Two war monuments flank Lincoln's. To the north-east is the celebrated V-shaped black wedge of the **Vietnam Veterans Memorial** (*see p65*); to the south-east is the evocative **Korean War Veterans Memorial** (*see p64*). Walking east past Constitution Gardens on the Mall's northern border, you first encounter the new, controversially sited **National World War II Memorial** (*see p64*). Next is the starkly impressive **Washington Monument** (*see p65*), honouring the 'father of his country', who selected this site for his capital.

To the north spreads the **Ellipse**, formally the President's Park South. It contains the **Boy Scout Memorial**, which recalls the Socialist Realist style of the former USSR, and the **First Division Memorial**, an 80-foot (23-metre) monument to the soldiers of the First Division of the US Army. Atop is a gilded bronze Victory. On the north of the Ellipse is the **Zero Milestone**, from which highway distances from the capital are measured.

The Washington Monument looks down into museumland. The turreted red fortress, guarded by a carousel, is the **Smithsonian Castle** (*see p113*), which houses an information centre with maps of the Smithsonian Institution's 16 museums (two are in New York), as well as the crypt for Smithsonian benefactor James Smithson.

Clustered about the Castle are the palazzo-like **Freer Gallery** (Asian art, *see p107*), its younger sibling, the subterranean **Arthur M Sackler Gallery** (*see p106*), the Sackler's twin, the **National Museum of African Art** (*see p110*), and the old **Arts & Industries Building** (now an exhibition space, currently closed for renovation). Behind the Castle blooms the **Enid Haupt Garden**, in an area that was used as a buffalo pen before the opening of the National Zoo. Further along are the doughnut-shaped **Hirshhorn Museum & Sculpture Garden** (*see p109*), the modernist marble of the **National Air & Space Museum** (*see p118*), the world's most visited museum, stacked with all manner of returned space hardware, and the new **National Museum of the American Indian** (*see p115*).

On the Mall's north side are the **National Museum of American History** (*see p115*), dubbed the 'Pink Palace' for the colour of its stone after rain, and the **National Museum of Natural History** (*see p118*). A sculpture garden, whose central pool doubles as an ice rink in winter, punctuates the line-up. Next comes the neo-classical **National Gallery of Art** (*see p109*), connecting to the angular geometry of its East Building, which displays the contemporary collection and special exhibitions.

On the far side of the Capitol Reflecting Pool, at the foot of Capitol Hill, stands a sprawling sculptural group that features an equestrian statue of Ulysses S Grant, the Union general who won the war for Mr Lincoln, modelled after the Victor Emmanuel memorial in Rome. Crowning the hill is the **United States Capitol** (*see p72*), whose dome Lincoln insisted be finished during the Civil War as a symbol of the Union's durability.

Franklin Delano Roosevelt Memorial

Off West Basin Drive, SW, at the Tidal Basin (1-202 426 6841/www.nps.gov/fdrm). Smithsonian Metro. **Map** p284 G7.

FDR, who led the country through the Great Depression and World War II and is the only president to be elected four times, is honoured in this monument, opened in 1997. Despite Roosevelt's own preference, for a simple desk-sized memorial slab (which was made, and placed outside the National Archives), designer Lawrence Halprin has created a grander and more striking monument here. The four 'galleries' combine waterfalls, giant stones engraved with memorable quotations and sculptures (including a statue of Eleanor Roosevelt, the first First Lady

Sightseeing

Don't miss Sights

Lincoln Memorial
A monumental Lincoln presides over all he surveys. See p64.

Jefferson Memorial
Modelled on the Roman Pantheon. See p64.

National World War II Memorial
Love it or hate it, you can't miss it. See p64.

United States Capitol
House (and Senate) on the hill. See p72.

Vietnam Veterans Memorial
Moving but not martial. See p65.

to be so honoured in a national memorial). The site is particularly alluring when it's lit up at night.

A monument open to the sky and dotted with trees, its peacefulness belies the controversy behind it. Disabled advocates objected that the somewhat dyspeptic statue of the polio-stricken president all but concealed his flowing cloak two tiny wheels, hinting that he used a wheelchair. Many historians countered that he concealed his disability so carefully that only two photographs survive revealing his wheelchair. (Other historians maintain that his disability was actually well known). In response to the controversy, a second, jauntier FDR, with wheels in full view, joined the display in 2000.

Jefferson Memorial

Southern end of 15th Street, SW, at the Tidal Basin & East Basin Drive (1-202 426 6841/www.nps.gov/thje). Smithsonian Metro. **Map** p284 H8.

FDR promoted this 1942 shrine to the founder of the Democratic Party in part to balance that to the Republicans' icon, Lincoln. It's a favourite of Washingtonians, and Roosevelt himself liked it so much he had trees cleared so he could see it from the Oval Office. Like Roosevelt, Jefferson asked for only a small memorial. Instead, John Russell Pope designed an adaptation (sneered at by the monument's few detractors as 'Jefferson's muffin') of the Roman Pantheon that the architect Jefferson so adored. It also recalls the president's own design for his home, Monticello (*see p244*), and for the rotunda at what he considered his finest achievement, the University of Virginia in Charlottesville.

The white, Georgia marble walls surrounding Jefferson's 19ft (5.5m) likeness are inscribed with his enduring words. For the record, the 92-word quote from the Declaration of Independence contains 11 spelling mistakes and other inaccuracies. Why? Space limitations, no doubt; a problem Jefferson knew all too well, since his original version was heavily edited and cut by some 500 words. A modest museum beneath the monument is a primer on Jefferson's legacy.

Korean War Veterans Memorial

The Mall, SW, just south of Reflecting Pool, at Daniel French Drive & Independence Avenue (1-202 426 6841/www.nps.gov/kwvm). Smithsonian Metro. **Map** p284 G7.

This monument, which honours the 12 million Americans who fought in the inconclusive, bloody 'police action' to prevent communist takeover of South Korea, is quite moving. It features 19 battle-clad, seven-foot (two-metre) soldiers slogging across a V-shaped field towards a distant US flag. Fatigue and pain show in the soldiers' finely detailed faces (which are particularly eerie at night), and the outlines of full battle packs are visible beneath their ponchos. Reflected in the polished granite wall beside them, the 19 become 38 – in reference to the 38th parallel separating North and South Korea. Unlike the wall at the Vietnam Veterans Memorial, the one here is a subtle mural sandblasted into rock.

Based on real photos, it's a montage of the support troops – drivers and medics, nurses and chaplains – and the equipment they used. Opposite the mural are the names of all the countries that served under the UN command. The field slopes up to a circular 'pool of remembrance'.

Lincoln Memorial

The Mall, 23rd Street, NW, between Henry Bacon Drive & Daniel French Drive (1-202 426 6841/www.nps.gov/linc). Smithsonian of Foggy Bottom-GWU Metro. **Map** p284 F7.

Despite its appearance on the penny and the $5 bill, the Lincoln Memorial is perhaps best known as the site of historic protests and demonstrations. In 1939, when the Daughters of the American Revolution barred the African American contralto Marian Anderson from singing in their Constitution Hall, she performed for more than 75,000 people from these steps. It was here that Martin Luther King Jr delivered his 'I have a dream' speech in 1963. Just a few months later, President Lyndon Johnson led candle-carrying crowds in ceremonies concluding national mourning for John F Kennedy. Half a century of debate followed Lincoln's assassination in 1865 before Henry Bacon's classical design was chosen in 1911 (over proposals ranging from a triumphal arch to a memorial highway from Washington to Gettysburg).

Stastistics don't prepare visitors for the drama of the monument – yet another that is most striking at night. The 'cage' surrounding Lincoln has one Doric column representing each of the 36 states in the Union at the time of his death; their names are inscribed above. The 19ft- (5.5m)-high marble statue of Lincoln himself, by Daniel Chester French, peers out over the Reflecting Pool, his facial expression seeming to change at different times of day. Cut into the wall to the left of the entrance is Lincoln's Gettysburg Address; to the right is his second inaugural address.

National World War II Memorial

The Mall, 17th Street, from Independence to Constitution Avenues (1-202 426 6841/www.wwiimemorial.com). Farragut West of Smithsonian Metro. **Map** p284 G6/7.

Dedicated on 29 May 2004, the monument honouring America's 'Greatest Generation', a rather grandiose affair on a 7.4-acre plot, features a granite space dominated by the central Rainbow Pool between two 43ft (13m) triumphal arches, representing the Atlantic and Pacific theatres of war. Fifty-six wreath-crowned pillars represent the US states and territories (which then included the Philippines), while a bronze Freedom Wall displays 4,000 gold stars, each signifying 100 war dead. The ceremonial entrance, descending from 17th Street, passes 24 bronze bas-reliefs depicting events of the global conflict. A more subdued (superfluous?) Circle of Remembrance garden off to the north-west is designed for quiet reflection. A visitor kiosk and restrooms clutter the periphery.

Strictly neo-classical: the **Jefferson Memorial** is inspired by the Roman Pantheon. *See p65.*

The memorial attracted controversy right from the outset. First, the location means that it interrupts the green sweep of the Mall. Second, it is so vulnerable to sinking into the reclaimed land that pumps have to work overtime. And last but not least, the design itself, a heavily neo-classical creation by Austrian-born Friedrich St Florian, has drawn flack for its style of totalitarian assertiveness. *See also p66* **Turf wars**.

The memorial's apologia for its controversial location is engraved in granite at the 17th Street entrance – an explanation of why it belongs between heroes Washington from the 18th century and Lincoln from the 19th. In an effort to preserve the open vista, the memorial was placed below street level. But from within the submerged plaza, there's little sense of the Mall's sweep; and from street level, its marble monumentalism pokes from its trench as an impressive interruption of the Mall's continuity.

Vietnam Veterans Memorial

West Potomac Park, just north of the Reflecting Pool at Henry Bacon Drive & Constitution Avenue, NW (1-202 462 6841/www.nps.gov/vive). Smithsonian Metro. Map p284 G6.

In the two decades since it opened, the sombre black granite walls of the privately funded Vietnam Veterans Memorial have become a shrine, with pilgrims coming to touch the more than 58,000 names, make pencil rubbings and leave flowers, letters and flags. Few would have predicted such public veneration when Maya Ying Lin won the nationwide design contest in 1981. Lin was a 21-year-old Yale University senior whose abstract design – two walls, each just over 246ft (75m) long – was angled to enfold the Washington Monument and the Lincoln Memorial in a symbolic embrace. Political pressures forced later additions to the striking design: first, a

flagpole plus a sculpture by Frederick Hart of three Vietnam GIs. In 1993 came the Vietnam Women's Memorial sculpture of two uniformed women tending a wounded male soldier, while a third woman kneels in the distance: a group inspired by Michelangelo's *Pietà*. Happily, these additional elements were tactfully spaced so as not to clash with one another or the central wall. Proponents of a shrine to the dogs of the Vietnam conflict so far have failed to secure another addition, but a subterranean 'education center' has been approved.

The names on the wall appear in the chronological order that they became casualties, but there's a directory to locate individuals. A diamond symbol means the death has been confirmed; a cross means the person has been designated missing. To descend gradually past the thousands of names to the nadir, then slowly emerge, is to follow symbolically America's journey into an increasingly ferocious war, only to try to 'wind it down' over years. It can be a genuinely touching experience.

Washington Monument

The Mall, between 15th & 17th Streets, & Constitution & Independence Avenues (1-202 426 6841/www.nps.gov/wamo). Smithsonian Metro. **Open** 9am-5pm daily. Map p284 H7.

The Washington Monument was completed in 1884, 101 years after Congress authorised it. It rises in a straight line between the Capitol and the Lincoln Memorial, but is off-centre between the White House and the Jefferson Memorial because the original site was too marshy to build on. Private funding ran out in the 1850s, when only the stump of the obelisk had been erected. In 1876 the Army resumed building, which is why you can see a slight change in the colour of the marble about a third of the way up. In 1884, the 555ft (170m) monument – the tallest free-standing masonry structure in the world – was capped with solid aluminium, which was then a rare material. There's an information centre about George Washington at the 490ft (149m) level, just below the 500ft (152m) observation deck. You'll need a ticket to go up in the elevator. They're free, and available from 7.30am in summer and 8.30am from autumn through to spring. Tickets are timed, and if you're not fussy about when in the day you go, you shouldn't have a problem; if you need a specific time during high season, you'll need to get in line early. Alternatively, you can pre-book by phoning the National Park Reservation Service on 1-800 967 2283 for an admin fee of $1.50 per ticket plus 50¢ per order.

Recent national security measures are all too evident here. Barriers surround the formerly open grounds and spy cameras have been crammed into the already skimpy windows at the top. The German-American friendship garden, just north on Constitution Avenue, has been significantly overwhelmed in the Iraq II security frenzy, with cameras and fences virtually obliterating the space.

South of the monument, a cast-iron plate near the light box covers a hole containing a 162in (4.11m) miniature of the monument. It's used to measure the rate at which the big version is sinking into the ground: around a quarter-inch every 30 years.

The White House & around

Set above the Ellipse to the north of the Mall, and flanked by august federal buildings, the **White House** (*see p68*) opens up the rectangular dynamic of the Mall with north–south sightlines to the Washington Monument and Jefferson Memorial. Directly north of it is Lafayette Park, named after the Marquis de Lafayette, who aided in the American Revolution. Workers and tourists fill its benches at lunchtime; a round-the-clock anti-nuclear protest has camped here continuously since 1981. Despite President Bush's 2000 platform promise to reopen it, the stretch of Pennsylvania Avenue separating the park from the White House seems to be closed to traffic for good, converted to a pedestrian walk.

Turf wars

Washingtonians didn't always revere the National Mall. Aside from some fussy Romantic landscaping hedging around the Smithsonian in the 1850s, 'the Reservation' was then a soggy tract appropriated by ad hoc stockyards, a railroad station and 'the most active and importunate squatters'. The 1902 McMillan Commission revisited L'Enfant's vision of a grand *allée* from the Capitol to the Washington Monument, then extended it on an extra mile of land reclaimed from the Potomac to the 'damned swamp' where the Lincoln Memorial now stands.

Over the decades, the Mall imperceptibly morphed from swamp to sacred space, the theatre for great national events. Here, at the Lincoln Memorial, Martin Luther King delivered his 'I have a dream' oration in 1963 (on the same site of Marian Anderson's dramatic Easter recital of 1939). In 1979 Pope John Paul II celebrated Mass here. And in 1981 the site of the presidential inauguration was moved from the East Front of the Capitol to the West, adding extra gravitas to these grounds.

And, of course, the Mall is famous as the site of demonstrations, among them the anti-Vietnam War protests in the 1960s, the 'tractorcades' of discontented farmers in the '70s, the nuclear freeze advocates of the '80s, the Million Man and Million Mom marchers of the '90s, and the anti-globalisation activists of the 2000s.

From the 1960s onwards the annual Smithsonian Folklife Festival has made the Mall a cultural playground as well, but this levity was judged to have gone a step too far in 2002, when the National Football League staged a corporate-logoed festival for private ticketholders, enlivened by the gyrations of Britney Spears. Policies were subsequently introduced to restrict further commercial banalisation.

Its growing status as America's altar has put extra pressure on the Mall, as groups bent on canonising pet concepts or secular saints vie for their share of the turf. Obscure Revolutionary War thinker George Mason snarfed a spot by the Jefferson Memorial, while a nearby swatch by the Tidal Basin awaits a Dr King monument. A memorial to the two presidents Adams and an African American Museum have also been approved, though to date without specified sites. Conservative zealots have pressed for a Reagan memorial square in the centre of the Mall, while partisans of other worthies covet surrounding ground. To avert impending clutter, a report has identified more than 100 sites suitable for statuary around town, but everybody still wants to plant their standard on the monumental main drag.

Though the park is named after Lafayette, its most prominent statue – the hero on the horse in the middle – is Andrew Jackson at the Battle of New Orleans in 1814. This was the first equestrian statue cast in the US at the time of its unveiling in 1853. His four companions are European heroes of the American Revolution: Lafayette (south-east corner), Comte de Rochambeau (south-west corner), General Thaddeus Kosciusko (north-east) and Baron von Steuben (north-west).

The mellow yellow **St John's Church**, on H Street north of the square, dates from 1816, and every president since James Madison has attended at least one service there. A brass plate at pew 54 marks the place reserved for them.

TV news-watchers might recognise the green awning across Jackson Place to the west of the square: this is **Blair House** (1660 Pennsylvania Avenue, NW), where visiting heads of state bunk. Next door, is the **Renwick Gallery** (*see p111*), at Pennsylvania and 17th Street – an 1859 building in the French Second

Empire mode, named after its architect, James Renwick. Part of the Smithsonian, it houses a collection of 20th-century crafts. It originally housed William Wilson Corcoran's art collection, but at the end of the 19th century this moved three blocks south into the purpose-built **Corcoran Museum of Art** (*see p106*), the Beaux Arts building on the south-west corner of 17th and E Streets. Just west of here, crossing into Foggy Bottom, is the **Octagon** (*see p77*).

The four-storey townhouse known as **Decatur House** (*see p68*) at 748 Jackson Place was home to naval hero Stephen Decatur, as well as French, British and Russian diplomats, 19th-century statesmen Henry Clay and Martin Van Buren. On the other side of the square, at H Street and Madison Place, is the **Dolley Madison House** (closed to the public), home of the widowed first lady until her death.

The two office buildings that bookend Lafayette Square on the west and east are the **New Executive Office Building** (whose recently replaced faux-mansard

The biggest blow-up of all involved the National World War II Memorial (*see p64*); the fight over this one lasted longer than the war itself. Many criticised the design, with the German press observing that the grandiose construct of arches and columns, reminiscent of Albert Speer, makes it look as if Hitler had won. Locals deplored the sharp interruption of the Mall's grand openness (and controversial security barriers at the Washington Monument and the Lincoln Memorial further slice up the

green and pleasant strand). Planning boards, official commissions, acts of Congress, protests and lawsuits fought to a stalemate.

But while the opening of the monument in May 2004 seemed to mark the end of this particular debate, the recent go-ahead for a subterranean education centre at the Vietnam memorial seems likely to prompt demands for a Korean War mate, with further requests bound to follow. Never was the phrase 'watch this space' more literally spoken.

roof hides anti-aircraft missile batteries) and the **United States Court of Claims**.

West of the White House is the Dwight D Eisenhower Executive Office Building, aka the **Old Executive Office Building** (OEOB). With its 900 Doric columns and French Empire bombast, this was the largest office building in the world in 1888, housing the entire State, War and Navy departments. Unfortunately, the public aren't allowed to tour it any more. President Bush maintained a hideaway here, with National Security Advisor Condoleeza Rice and Vice-President Cheney. Here too schemed the 'Strategery Group', political operatives named for their boss's rhetorical lapses.

East of it is the **United States Treasury**, the third-oldest federal office building in Washington. It interrupts Pennsylvania Avenue because the ornery President Jackson, exasperated at endless debate, declared, 'Put it there!' Sadly, post-9/11 paranoia means that the building is now closed to the public, with no plans to reopen.

Surrounding the Treasury is a cluster of banks and former banks – mostly neo-classical buildings – vestiges of the city's old financial district, once known as 'Washington's Wall Street'. The area is now part of the 15th Street Financial Historic District.

Decatur House

748 Jackson Place, NW, at H Street (1-202 842 0920/www.decaturhouse.org). Farragut West Metro. **Open** 10am-5pm Tue-Sat; noon-4pm Sun. **Guided tours** depart every hr, 15mins past the hr. **Admission** free; suggested donation. **Credit** AmEx, MC, V. **Map** p284 H5.

Admiral Nelson declared Stephen Decatur 'the greatest hero of the age' for his raids that crippled the 'Barbary' pirates in 1804. It was Decatur who uttered the famous toast concluding 'my country, right or wrong'; he burnished his laurels in the War of 1812, only to die in a needless duel in 1820. (Ghost-hunters take note: Decatur's mournful face has reportedly been seen gazing from one of the bricked-up windows above H Street). Portions of his home are still open during restoration work, which is scheduled to last a few years. Out front, a tablet commemorates the work of Jacqueline Kennedy to preserve the historic homes facing Lafayette Square.

The White House

1600 Pennsylvania Avenue, NW, between 15th & 17th Streets (1-202 456 7041/www.whitehouse.gov). McPherson Square Metro. **Open** *Tours* 7.30-11.30am Tue-Sat. Booking essential; see review below. *Visitors' centre* 7.30am-4pm daily. **Admission** free. **Map** p284 H6.

Part showplace, part workplace, the White House is sometimes called 'the people's house'. Until the 19th century the public could walk freely into the building; the grounds were open until World War II.

Today the Executive Mansion is open only to pre-arranged groups of ten or more, who only get to peek at a scant eight rooms out of the house's 132, and with little time to linger. The public tour is self-guided (though highly regimented) and there's not much in the way of interpretation, but the nation proudly clings to keeping its leader's residence open to the public. (That said, the tours and other White House events were suspended post 9/11. It was only when the traditional Easter Monday Egg Roll for children was revived in 2004 that it became clear the building had partially recovered from the terrorist jitters). To arrange a tour, US citizens should contact their Senator or Representative; some may help by putting individuals together to make a group. Visitors with foreign passports should contact their nation's embassy. Tours will be scheduled around a month before the appointed date.

Inspired by the Duke of Leinster's house in architect James Hoban's native Dublin, the White House was finished in 1800 and has been home to every US president except George Washington (he died the year before). Early presidents lived and worked above the shop, with visitors casually wandering into their offices and apartments. In 1902 Teddy Roosevelt added the East Gallery and the West Wing, which grew to include today's renowned (or, perhaps, infamous) Oval Office.

Each new first lady can furnish the White House as she pleases: Jacqueline Kennedy, for example, replaced the B Altman department store furniture and frilly florals of her predecessors, the Trumans and Eisenhowers, with plain blues and whites. Her overall refurbishment of the White House restored many historic furnishings and artworks to the rooms. Her tour on national television was a triumph. Each president, meanwhile, imposes his character on the Oval Office, bringing in favourite furniture and personal selections from the White House art collection.

There are also offices for around 200 executive branch staffers, and recreational facilities, including a cinema, tennis courts, putting green, bowling alley and, courtesy of the elder George Bush, a horseshoe pitch. All told, there are 32 bathrooms, 413 doors, three elevators, seven staircases and a staff of more than 100, including florists, carpenters and cooks.

On the tour, you may get a look in the China Room, the pantry for presidential crockery. Don't miss Nancy Reagan's $952-per-setting red-rimmed china, which sparked a controversy about conspicuous consumption – as had Mrs Lincoln's previously.

Up the marble stairs, visitors enter the cavernous East Room, which holds the sole item from the original White House: the 1797 portrait of George Washington that Dolley Madison rescued just before the British burned the place on 24 August 1814. The East Room is the ceremonial room where seven presidents have lain in state – and where Abigail Adams, wife of the second president, John, hung her laundry. At 3,200sq ft (960sq m), the space could hold the average American home.

Next is the Green Room, once Jefferson's dining room, and where James Madison did his politicking after Dolley had liquored up important guests in the Red Room, the tour's next stop, decorated as an American Empire parlour of 1810-30. It was here that Mary Todd Lincoln held a seance to contact her dead sons and where President Grant and his former generals refought the Civil War on the carpet using salt shakers and nut dishes as troops.

The colour naming scheme continues in the Blue Room – although it actually has yellow walls. The furnishings here, the traditional home of the White House Christmas tree, were ordered in 1817 by President Monroe. Last stop: the cream and gold State Dining Rooms, which can seat up to 140. Then you're out the door.

You can't penetrate the family quarters unless you're a mega-bucks political contributor, but Hollywood, of course, managed to. To film the sappy-sweet Michael Douglas/Annette Bening movie *An American President*, filmmakers were allowed unprecedented access to the White House to create a replica that's now referred to as Hollywood's 'White House West' as it has been used in many productions, among them *The West Wing*. Nowadays tourists repair to the White House Visitors Center, in the dignified former search room of the Patent Office, at 15th and E Streets, NW, which has historical displays and even living history re-enactments. In some ways, the new arrangements tell visitors more than the old walk-throughs ever did.

Alternatively, you can stop at the White House Historical Association offices (740 Jackson Place NW, on the west side of Lafayette Park, 1-202 737 8292; open 9am-4pm Mon-Fri) to pick up an extensive guide to the mansion, a CD-ROM, or the definitive books by official historian William Seale.

The Capitol & around

An angry senator once scolded President Lincoln that his administration was on the road to hell – or, more precisely, just a mile from it. Lincoln shot back that that was almost exactly the distance from the White House to the Capitol. The Legislative Branch on the east end of Pennsylvania Avenue balances the Executive on the west.

Standing at the east end of the Mall is the commanding presence of the **United States Capitol** (*see p72*). Achieving both dignity and grace from every angle – though the walk along the Mall via the Capitol Reflecting Pool and its ducks shouldn't be missed – the Capitol rises elegantly to the occasion.

The **United States Botanic Garden** (*see p71*) at the foot of the Capitol has been splendidly revamped with high-tech climate controls to pamper fussy flora from around the globe. Its highlight is the central rainforest room, now equipped with a catwalk affording

United States Capitol. *See p72.*

tree-top views. This glass palace coddles tropical and subtropical plants, cacti, ferns, palm trees, shrubs and flowers, including its hallmark 500 varieties of orchid.

North of the Capitol, the grounds extend towards Union Station (*see p72*). Downhill is a carillon dedicated to 'Mr Republican', Ohio Senator Robert A Taft. Son of a president, he came closest to recapturing that office in 1952, when he lost the Republican nomination to Dwight Eisenhower.

Around the Capitol throbs a civic city of Congressional office buildings (the Senate's to the north on Constitution Avenue, the House's to the south along Independence). In its eastern lee are the restrained, rectangular **Supreme Court** (*see p71*) and the lavish **Library of Congress** (*see p70*), its refurbished copper dome now moving towards a green patina. Beside the art deco Adams Building annex is the incomparable **Folger Shakespeare Library** (*see p70*). Books here are available only to scholars, but the Elizabethan Garden (*see p90* **Wild at Heart**) and the museum are open to the public. So far, the librarians have refrained from turning the outdoor statue of Puck, exclaiming 'What fools these mortals be!' around so as to face Congress.

Adjoining the Senate offices is the **Sewall-Belmont House** (144 Constitution Avenue, NE; *see also p35*), a three-storey Federal Period townhouse, with a museum detailing women's struggle to get the vote and pass the Equal Rights Amendment.

Library of Congress, a gloriously gaudy temple to the written word.

Folger Shakespeare Library

201 East Capitol Street, SE, between Second & Third Streets (1-202 544 4600/www.folger.edu). Capitol South or Union Station Metro. **Open** *Great Hall 10am-4pm Mon-Sat. Library 11am-4pm Mon-Sat.* **Guided tours** 11am Mon-Fri; 11am, 1pm Sat. **Admission** free. **Map** p285 L7.

The marble façade of this classic art deco building sports bas-reliefs of scenes from Shakespeare's plays. To the east of the building is the understated Elizabethan Garden. Inside is the world's largest collection of the playwright's works, including the 79-volume First Folio collection. Everything was given by Standard Oil chairman Henry Clay Folger, who fell in love with Shakespeare after hearing Ralph Waldo Emerson lecture on him. Items include musical instruments, costumes and films, as well as 27,000 paintings, drawings and prints. The Tudor-style rooms that house them include the oak-panelled Great Hall, with its hand-carved walls, tile floors and recurring motifs. The reading room, open during the library's annual celebration of Shakespeare's birthday in April, has a copy of a bust of the Bard from Stratford's Trinity Church and a stained-glass window that portrays the Seven Ages of Man as described in *As You Like It*. The intimate theatre (*see p223*) is a wooden, three-tiered replica of one from the yard of an Elizabethan inn.

Library of Congress

Visitors Center, Jefferson Building, First Street & Independence Avenue, SE (1-202 707 8000/ www.loc.gov). Capitol South Metro. **Open** 10am-5.30pm Mon-Sat. **Guided tours** 10.30am, 11.30am, 1.30pm, 2.30pm, 3.30pm Mon-Fri; 10.30am, 11.30am, 1.30pm, 2.30pm Sat. **Admission** free. **Map** p284 L7.

The national library of the US, the Library of Congress is the world's largest. Its three buildings bulge with some 100 million items – including the papers of 23 US presidents – along 535 miles (861km) of bookshelves. Alas, the popular notion that the Library of Congress has a copy of every book ever printed is untrue, although its heaving shelves are still impressive.

To get to grips with the place, it's best to start with the 20-minute film in the ground-floor visitors' centre, excerpted from a TV documentary, which provides a clear picture of the place's scope and size. An even better option is to join a guided tour (note that they are limited to 50 people). To use any of the specialised research rooms or enter the grand main reading room, you have to register as a reader.

Begun in 1800 with a $5,000 grant from Congress, the original Library was crammed into the Capitol. Ransacked by the British in 1814, it revived when president-scholar Thomas Jefferson offered his collection of 6,487 books. The Thomas Jefferson Building – the main one – was finished in 1897 and splendidly restored upon its centennial. Based on the Paris Opera House, the Library has granite walls supporting an octagonal dome, which rises to 160ft (49m) above the spectacular marble and wood reading room. Gloriously gaudy mosaics, frescos and statues overwhelm the visitor with a gush of 19th-century high culture. A permanent rotating exhibition, 'American Treasures of the Library of Congress', displays significant items from America's past – from the contents of Lincoln's pockets the night he died to film of a youngster frolicking in the Library's Neptune Fountain in 1906. The Bob Hope and American Variety gallery traces the life of the popular entertainer. A visitors' gallery overlooks the stunning Great Hall – white marble with red and gold roof panels – adorned with brass zodiac symbols, neo-Greek mosaics, mermen, nymphs and Muses. This can only be viewed on a guided tour. The main reading room has classic marble archways and great plaster figures of disciplines (Philosophy, Religion, Art, History – all women) flanked by bronze images of their mortal instruments (Plato, Moses, Homer, Shakespeare – all men).

Directly across Independence Avenue is the James Madison Building, opened in 1980, which encloses an area greater than 35 football fields. It displaced Ptomaine Row, a block of dubious luncheonettes catering to Congressional staffers before the House opened its own employee cafeterias. It houses the copyright office, manuscript room, film and TV viewing rooms and the incredible photography collections. Staff run frequent lunchtime 'language tables' where regulars, students and strangers drop in to converse in tongues ranging from Ukrainian to Swahili. Diagonally opposite is the 1939 John Adams Building, which contains the Science and Business reading rooms. On a mural near the ceiling, Chaucer's Canterbury pilgrims trudge perpetually.

Anyone with photo ID can register for a library card – the process takes about 15 minutes. You can't wander all the shelves yourself: a librarian will dig out your selected text for you. The Library catalogue is also available online at www.lcweb.loc.gov, though many of the old card-catalogue entries have been overlooked.

The Library also stages free concerts, poetry readings, films, lectures and presentations by celebrated authors; *see p188 and p206.*

Supreme Court

First Street & Maryland Avenue, NW (1-202 479 3211/www.supremecourtus.gov). Capitol South or Union Station Metro. **Open** 9am-4.30pm Mon-Fri. **Map** p285 L6.

The ultimate judicial and constitutional authority, the United States Supreme Court pays homage in its architecture to the rule of law. Justices are appointed for life, and their temple reflects their eminence. Designed by Cass Gilbert in the early 1930s, its classical façade incorporates Corinthian columns supporting a pediment decorated with bas-reliefs representing Liberty, Law, Order and a crew of historical figures. In the white marble courtroom, overhead friezes depict the faces of renowned lawmakers from the pre-Christian and Christian eras. The sober style conceals whimsy in the shape of sculpted turtles lurking to express the 'deliberate pace' of judicial deliberations. There are also ferocious lions – enough said.

You can tour the building any time, entering from the Maryland Avenue entrance. The ground level has a cafeteria, an introductory video show, and a gift shop. The regular tour lacks heavy Law and Order theatrics, but the venue is awesome. The cathedral-like entrance hall daunts one into hushed tones. The sober courtroom, with its heavy burgundy velvet draperies and marble pillars, is where the nine judges hear around 120 of the more than 6,500 cases submitted to the court each year. The black-robed figures appear as the Court Marshal announces 'Oyez! Oyez! Oyez!' and sit in seats of varying height, handcrafted to their personal preferences. Goose-quill pens still grace the lawyers' tables, for tradition's sake.

When the court is in session, from October to April, visitors can see cases being argued on Mondays, Tuesdays and Wednesdays from 10am to 3pm. Two lines form in the plaza in front of the building: one for those who want to hear the whole argument (better be there by 8am), and the 'three-minute line', for those who just want a peek at the court in session. In May and June, 'opinions' are handed down on Tuesdays, Wednesdays and sometimes on other days. Check the newspapers' Supreme Court calendars to see what cases are scheduled. Controversial cases – like the Florida recount case deciding the disputed 2000 presidential election – draw massive queues to get in. When the court is out of session, there are regular lectures in the courtroom about court procedure and the building's architecture. The private levels above the courtroom contain a gym and offices, and are closed to the public.

United States Botanic Garden

245 First Street, at Maryland Avenue (1-202 225 8333/www.usbg.gov). Federal Center SW Metro. **Open** 10am-5pm daily. **Admission** free. **Map** p285 K7.

In 1842 the Navy's Wilkes Expedition returned from exploring Fiji and South America, and showered Congress with a cornucopia of exotic flora. The collection endured until the present conservatory was erected in 1930. Its recent renovation introduced state-of-the-art climate controls and a catwalk giving a bird's-eye view of the delightful central rainforest.

The renewed conservatory displays 4,000 plants: tropical and subtropical, with a feature on endangered species. It also honours its origins with specimens from the Wilkes expedition. Themed displays feature the desert and the oasis, plant adaptations and the primeval garden. The orchid collection is a particular delight. Across Independence Avenue, Bartholdi Park displays plants more suited to Washington's climate, ranged around a central fountain that was created by Frederic Bartholdi, sculptor of the Statue of Liberty, for the US Centennial in 1876. The proposed National Garden emerging immediately to the west aims to be a showcase for 'unusual, useful, and ornamental plants that grow well in the mid-Atlantic region'.

Sightseeing

United States Capitol

Capitol Hill, between Constitution & Independence Avenues (recorded tour information 1-202 225 6827/www.aoc.gov). Capitol South or Union Station Metro. **Open** *Guided tours* 9am-4.30pm Mon-Sat (last ticket 3.30pm). **Admission** free. **Map** p285 K7.

French architect Major Pierre L'Enfant, hired by President Washington to plan the federal city, selected Capitol Hill – a plateau, actually – as 'a pedestal waiting for a monument'. Indeed it was. In 1793 George Washington and an entourage of local masons laid the building's long-lost cornerstone, then celebrated by barbecuing a 500-pound ox. Thirty-one years later, despite a fire, a shortage of funds and the War of 1812, the structure was complete. But as the Union grew, so did the number of legislators. By 1850 architects projected the Capitol would have to double its size. In 1857 they added wings for the Senate (north) and the House of Representatives (south). An iron dome (a 600-gallon paint job each year makes it look like marble) replaced the wooden one in 1865. Abe Lincoln insisted it be finished during the Civil War as a symbol of the durability of the Union.

Today the Capitol – which has 540 rooms, 658 windows (108 in the dome alone) and 850 doorways – is a small city. As well as the 535 elected lawmakers, an estimated 20,000 workers toil daily among the six buildings (not including the Capitol itself) – all connected by tunnels – that make up the complex. Within this massive workforce is a 1,200-member police department, doctors, nurses, electricians, carpenters, day-care personnel and more. There are power plants, libraries, shops, restaurants, gyms and maintenance workshops. A US flag flies over the Senate and House wings when either is in session; at night a lantern glows in the Capitol dome.

There are now only two ways for visitors to enter the Capitol: with an official tour, or with a pass to the visitors' galleries that overlook the House and Senate floors. Both are free and available daily on a first-come, first-served basis. Tickets for the one-hour, 40-person tours are distributed between 9am and 3.30pm from a kiosk on the southwest corner of the Capitol grounds, near the Botanic Garden. For US citizens, gallery passes are available from the office of the visitor's Senator or Representative. Those with foreign passports may get passes from the South Screening Facility, a kiosk on the southeast side of the building. You will be asked to check in bags and follow guidelines to avoid disrupting proceedings (no pagers, mobile phones or cameras allowed). For more details on attending Congressional sessions, *see p32* **Politics in progress**.

Before 9/11, a massive underground visitors' centre was planned. This controversial structure, which is currently under construction (and well over budget) on the Capitol's east side, was subsequently redefined and redesigned as a integral part of the building's security system. Visitors will enter through the centre upon its completion, currently set for spring 2006.

Union Station & around

Uniting the scattered depots of rival railroads, and matching some of the city's more striking monuments in its beauty, is Daniel Burnham's Beaux Arts-style **Union Station** (*see below*). The **Thurgood Marshall Judiciary Building** east of Union Station complements the former City Post Office – now the **National Postal Museum** (*see p117*) – also built by Burnham, to present an elegant urban vista. In front of the trio, the flags of all the US states and territories are ranged around the central Columbus Memorial Fountain, which dates from 1912. The landscaped Union Station Plaza in front of the station stretches all the way to the Capitol.

The neighbourhood around Union Station was once a shantytown of Irish railroad labourers, who christened their marshy abode 'Swampoodle' after its swamps and puddles. The **Phoenix Park Hotel** (*see p47*) and bars such as the **Dubliner** and **Kelly's Irish Times** (*see pp145-52*) keep up the Hibernian connection, while across North Capitol Street, on the corner of Massachusetts Avenue, is the new **National Guard Memorial Museum** (*see p113*), preserving the heritage of America's local militias from colonial days to present.

Union Station

50 Massachusetts Avenue, NE (1-202 371 9441/ www.unionstationdc.com). Metro Union Station. **Open** *Station* 24hrs daily. *Shops* 10am-9pm Mon-Sat; noon-6pm Sun. **Map** p285 K/L 5/6.

Built in 1908, Union Station grandiosely reflects its inspiration – the Baths of Diocletian in Rome. Envisioning the most splendid terminal in the country, architect Daniel 'Make no small plans' Burnham lavished the building with amenities, including a nursery, a swimming pool and even a mortuary for defunct out-of-towners. The Main Hall is a huge rectangular space, with a 96ft (29m)-high barrel-vaulted ceiling and a balcony with 36 sculptures of Roman legionnaires.

The station languished when rail travel declined. The President's Room, reserved for chief executives welcoming incoming dignitaries such as King George VI and Haile Selassie, is now a restaurant. In 1953 a decidedly non-stop express train bound for Eisenhower's inauguration smashed into the crowded concourse; incredibly, nobody was killed. Two decades later, a deliberate but also disastrous hole was sunk in the Great Hall to make way for the multi-screen video set-up of an ill-conceived (and short-lived) visitors' centre. At this stage, despite its lingering grandeur, the station seemed doomed to the wrecking ball.

But in 1988 a painstaking $165-million restoration programme was begun, during which time entertainment came into play. There are now shops, amusements and eateries of all sorts, and even a multi-screen cinema. Rents are high and some of the shops have failed, but successors always seem to come along and more sales per square foot move through the shops here than any other DC mall. It's easy to forget that the marble and gilt palace's main function is still as a railway station – with lines to New York, Chicago, Miami and New Orleans, as well as the suburbs – though the crowds at rush hour will bring you back to your senses.

The Federal Triangle

The nine-block-long triangle of monolithic federal buildings wedged between Pennsylvania Avenue, NW, and the Mall is known as the Federal Triangle. The federal government bulldozed the whole district in the 1920s, claiming 'eminent domain' (the right of compulsory purchase), and today the Federal Triangle is the ballpark for the heavy hitters of the government machine, housing within its 70 acres 28,000 office workers – and counting. The triangle is both a labyrinth and a fortress. Security is tight, and visitors usually end up asking about six different people before finally making it to their destination. Wags call it the Bermuda Triangle.

All but three of the buildings in the Triangle were built between 1927 and 1938 as massive Beaux Arts limestone structures, complete with high-minded inscriptions, to house various federal agencies, such as the **Departments of Commerce** and **Justice**, and the **National Archives** (*see below*). The **Internal Revenue Service** headquarters are inscribed with the not-so-comforting words of former chief justice Oliver Wendell Holmes: 'Taxes are what we pay for a civilised society.'

The three exceptions are the **John Wilson (District) Building** (the city hall, on the corner of 14th and E Streets), the **Ronald Reagan Building**, and the **Old Post Office** (*see p75*). Once sneered at as the 'old tooth' and slated for demolition, the latter now sports a tourist mall and a brilliant view from the top of its 315ft (96m) tower.

Built in the 1990s, the **Ronald Reagan Building & International Trade Center** (on 14th Street, opposite the Department of Commerce) is the most expensive building ever constructed in the US for federal use, at a cost of over $700 million. It was supposed to symbolise Reagan's passion for free enterprise and global trade, but it's really an embodiment of big government, with one-and-a-half times the floorspace of the Empire State Building. The **DC Chamber of Commerce Visitor Information Centre** is located here, along with a fast-food court. In the basement of the

Commerce Department, an unexpected novelty is the **National Aquarium of Washington, DC**, an old-fashioned exhibit that affords a closer look at sea creatures than many more modern aquaria (*see p183*).

National Archives

Constitution Avenue, NW, between Seventh & Ninth Streets (1-866 272 6272/www.archives.gov). Archives-Navy Memorial Metro. **Open** *Apr-late May* 10am-7pm daily. *Late May-early Sept* 10am-9pm daily. *Early Sept-Mar* 10am-5.30pm daily. **Admission** free. **Map** p285 J6.

The vast collection of the National Archive & Record Administration (NARA) represents the physical record of the birth and growth of a nation in original documents, maps, photos, recordings, films and a miscellany of objects. The catalogue resonates with national iconography and historic gravitas (and pathos): it includes the Louisiana Purchase, maps of Lewis and Clark's explorations, the Japanese World War II surrender document, the gun that shot JFK, the Watergate tapes and documents of national identity, among them the Declaration of Independence, Constitution and Bill of Rights (collectively known as the Charters of Freedom).

The building that houses them, opened in 1935 and designed to harmonise with existing DC landmarks (in other words neo-classical), was the work of John Russell Pope. In a city of monumental architecture, where the NARA's 72 columns barely raise an eyebrow, the most distinctive features are the bronze doors at the Constitution Avenue entrance. Each weighs six and a half tons and is 38ft (12m) high and 11in (28cm) thick. Though security is their main function, they also remind the visitor of the importance of the contents. Unless you're a history junkie, skip the rote tour, which basically consists of a guide displaying copies of the various documents held in the stacks, and cut straight to the main attraction. That's the Rotunda, where the original Charters of Freedom are mounted, triptych-like, in a glass case at the centre of a roped-off horseshoe containing other key documents. A renovation completed in 2003 now protects them with high-tech preservation and security measures. A semi-circular gallery running behind the Rotunda stages temporary exhibitions, but only an infinitesimal fraction of the Archives' holdings are on display. As for the rest, research access (photo ID required) is via the door on Pennsylvania Avenue.

Note that many documents – including all post-World War II records – were transferred a few years back to Archives II, a facility at College Park, Maryland (*see p104*); several free shuttle buses run every day from NARA to the less-accessible site.

Old Post Office

1100 Pennsylvania Avenue, NW, between 11th & 12th Streets (1-202 606 8691/www.nps.gov/opot). Federal Triangle Metro. **Open** *Sept-Mar* 9am-4.45pm Mon-Fri; 10am-5.45pm Sat, Sun. *Apr-Aug* 9am-7.45pm Mon-Fri; 10am-5.45pm Sat, Sun. **Admission** free. **Map** p284 J6.

First residents

The opening of the **National Museum of the American Indian** (*see p115*) brings together artefacts and art work by and about the first Americans in a new building on the Mall – the latest addition to its historic museums.

The Mall site symbolises America's eventual recognition of the place of its colonised indigenous people in its history, but many generations before the Mall existed, Indians had made their mark on the land here.

Washington has been inhabited for at least 12,000 years, though its Native American heritage is obscure. What is known is that Eastern Woodland Indians of this region dwelt in communal longhouses sturdily made from reed wattle over wooden frameworks. They fished, farmed and traded extensively. When Captain John Smith led Jamestown explorers as far as Georgetown in 1608, he encountered thriving trade between Powhatan's confederacy in Virginia and the Conoy people in Maryland.

Archeologists have also found ancient villages or campsites on Theodore Roosevelt (or Analostan) Island, at the Pentagon Lagoon, and lining the east bank of the Anacostia River. The Algonquian language group dominates the map with names like Potomac, Chesapeake, Piscataway, and Anacostia. And when President Ford had a swimming pool built at the White House in 1976, the bulldozers unearthed Indian artefacts.

A few other vestiges of Native culture can be found around the District. **Soapstone Trail**, starting on Albemarle Street, NW, just east of Connecticut Avenue, follows a woodland stream that ancient people mined for rock implements. A seasonal fishing camp 2,000-4,000 years ago, **Gulf Branch Nature Center** (3608 North Military Road, Arlington, Virginia, 1-703 228-3203; open 10am-5pm Tue-Sat, noon-5pm Sun) exhibits artefacts on the site where they were found. Further afield, the **Mattaponi** and **Pamunkey** reservations (www.baylink.org/Mattaponi and www.baylink.org/Pamunkey), established in King William County, Virginia, as long ago as the mid 1600s, preserve ancient heritage through

museums and educational programmes. At Pamunkey, the craft of pottery is preserved and developed by today's craftspeople; pieces are for sale.

More authentic artwork is available at the Indian Craft Shop in the **Department of the Interior Museum** (*see p112*), which also maintains its Indian displays. Note, though, that the shop carries work from western reservations rather than local artists.

For more experience of the lifestyle of Washington area Indians, **St Mary's City** in Maryland (www.stmaryscity.org) has a painstakingly reconstructed Yaocomaco hamlet, while the **Piscataway Indian Museum** at Waldorf, Maryland (16816 Country Lane, Waldorf, 1-301 782 7622; by appointment) occupies a former Nike missile base; its highlight is an indoor replica of a longhouse. The former launcher base now serves as the dance circle during powwows.

Washington's Native American community gathers for numerous local powwows, many open to the public, with Indian food, crafts and dancing. The American Indian Society of Washington, DC (www.aisdc.org) has information on forthcoming events.

Washington's best views may be from the Washington Monument, but from here you get to see the Monument itself as well. It's a 47-second ride to the ninth floor; you then change to another elevator bound for the 12th, and top, floor. The Post Office Pavilion below is a mix of shops, eateries and a performing arts stage.

The Northwest Rectangle

The Northwest Rectangle is not an official appellation, but it's sometimes used to describe the rectangle of federal buildings west of the Ellipse and south of E Street that roughly mirrors the Federal Triangle to the east. It's really just part of Foggy Bottom (see p76), an industrial immigrant area in the 19th century, but any original character the area has retained emerges only further north.

In this southern part, it's grandiose federal anonymity all the way. From west to east, the buildings of interest are the **State Department**, whose opulent reception rooms can be toured by arrangement (see below); then, dropping down to Constitution Avenue, the **American Pharmaceutical Association**, the **National Academy of Sciences**, with its invitingly climbable statue of Einstein, the **Federal Reserve Board** and the **Organization of American States (OAS)**.

Behind the OAS annex is the **Department of the Interior** (see p112), housing in its museum examples of Native American arts, with authentic goods for sale in its craft shop. Attempting to improve its PR, the **IMF Center** (see below) — scene of an annual siege by anti-globalisation protesters – offers displays explaining international financial policy.

IMF Center

720 19th Street, NW, between G & H Streets (1-202 623 6869/www.imf.org/center). Farragut West Metro. **Open** 9am-4.30pm Mon-Fri. **Admission** free. **Map** p284 G5.

A permanent display traces the development of world monetary policies, while special exhibits follow the history of various countries, reflected in their currencies. The coin collection includes an impressive array on long-term loan from the Smithsonian.

State Department Diplomatic Reception Rooms

C & 22nd Streets, NW (1-202 647 3241/www.state. gov/www/about_state/diprooms/index.html). Foggy Bottom-GWU Metro. **Guided tours** 9.30am, 10.30am, 2.45pm Mon-Fri. **Admission** free. **Map** p284 G6.

When the State Department was finished in 1951, the wife of the Secretary of State reportedly wept when she looked at the chrome, glass and concrete walls and tasteless furniture. Not any more. The three diplomatic reception rooms, which are used to receive foreign visitors, are described by some as

Washington's best-kept secret – a nirvana for serious fine arts and antiques lovers. They contain one of the finest collections of national treasures from 1740 to 1830, valued at some $90 million. Among the collection are Chippendale pieces; the English Sheraton desk on which the Treaty of Paris was signed in 1783, ending the Revolutionary War; and a table-desk used by Thomas Jefferson. There are also some none-too-exciting exhibits in the lobby on the history of the State Department, which is the oldest of the cabinet departments. Note that you can only visit by guided tour, for which reservations are required (call four weeks in advance).

South of the Mall

The area south of the Mall is filled with unremarkable federal buildings (Federal Aviation Administration, Transportation Department and so on). The principal exceptions are the **United States Holocaust Memorial Museum** (see p117) and the **Bureau of Engraving & Printing** (see below), where the greenback is printed. Both are to the west near the Tidal Basin.

To the east, **L'Enfant Plaza** is ironically named, considering that it's supposed to honour the man whose city plan made Washington so stately (see p36 **The man with the plan**) – this modern, grey expanse is primarily notable for its unremarkable underground shopping mall. From the Plaza, L'Enfant Promenade leads across US395 to Benjamin Banneker Memorial Circle, overlooking the river.

Bureau of Engraving & Printing

14th Street, SW, at C Street, (1-202 874 2330/ www.moneyfactory.com). Smithsonian Metro. **Tours** 10am-2pm every 15mins Mon-Fri. **Admission** free. **Map** p284 H6.

As the sign says, 'The Buck Starts Here!' The printing in the title refers to hard currency: this is where the dollar bill is born. The Bureau produces stamps and other stuff too, and there's a pretty interesting visitors' centre, but make no mistake, it's the prospect of seeing the creation of cash that draws the crowds. The 40-minute guided tour provides a glimpse into the printing, cutting and stacking of the 37 million banknotes produced daily. It's all done behind the thickest plate glass you've ever seen, with enough guards and security cameras to make the White House look positively easy-access.

In the off-season (September to April) you should be able to go in with a minimal wait; in summer, you'll need a ticket for a timed tour. These are given out from 8am to 1.40pm (and also from 3.30-6.40pm from June to August) from the ticket booth just outside in Raoul Wallenberg Place (in summer you'll probably have to queue). Go at 7.45am to be sure of getting on a tour, or, if you are a US citizen, ask your Congressional representative to get you on one of the 'VIP' tours in advance.

DC Neighbourhoods

Behind the façade of monuments and museums lies the real city.

Japanese-American Memorial. *See p82.*

Even before post-9/11 security made the Mall a bit of a hassle, visitors were looking beyond the monuments to explore a genuine, rather quirky city, populated by people rather than politicians, made more of brick than marble. However artificial its origins, 'old DC' very much has its own character, and the preoccupations of its residents are often oblivious to geopolitics. The city is divided into quadrants, taking the Capitol – which is slightly east of centre – as its nexus.

Northwest

By far the largest quadrant, Northwest is also the most affluent, with the majority of the city's residential hinterlands, streetlife and nightlife within it. It is roughly bisected, from south to north, by Rock Creek and the widening wedge of parkland sheltering it. The Northwest section of this chapter starts with the city's neighbourhoods nearest the Monumental Centre, then heads north and then across to Rock Creek Park to Georgetown and further suburbs.

Foggy Bottom

Map p284

West and south-west of the White House down to the Potomac River, Foggy Bottom takes its name either from its original marshy riverside location or for the emissions from the factories that used to stand here (or, possibly, both). Its fame, however, it owes to the Department of State, which moved into the recently renamed Truman Building just south of here (2201 C Street, NW) in 1950. The immigrant settlers who once worked in the factories here wouldn't recognise its current hauteur. A historic district on the National Registry since 1987 because of the design of its rowhouses, these days Foggy Bottom is home to highly transient foreign service workers, federal appointees, college students and performing artists – along with older long-term residents. And sprawling over more than 20 blocks of the neighbourhood is **George Washington University** (GWU), once dubbed 'The Thing That Ate Foggy Bottom' because of its relentless expansion, and ever an irritant to locals.

Near the dock where the US government first arrived in its muddy new capital in 1800, the white marble box of the John F Kennedy Center for the Performing Arts (known as the **Kennedy Center**, *see below*) rises above the river. North of the Kennedy Center lie the swirling contours of the **Watergate** complex (at 26th Street and Virginia Avenue, NW), site of the eponymous 1972 burglary that unravelled Richard Nixon's presidency. Scandal seems to have followed the Watergate since: it was the home of Monica Lewinsky. Shops and delis line its courtyard. The humble Howard Johnson motel across the street, from where Tricky Dick's 'plumbers' monitored the break-in, is now a GWU dorm.

At Virginia and New Hampshire Avenues, a statue of valiant Mexican President Benito Juarez points symbolically towards the distant monument to George Washington, the man who inspired him.

Above stately Virginia Avenue, Foggy Bottom seeps from monumental into urban Washington. Although many of the neighbourhood's characteristic tiny townhouses were bulldozed to make way for George Washington University, some neat pockets – such as the area between New Hampshire Avenue and K Street – survive.

The **Octagon** was President James Madison's refuge for seven months after the British invaders torched the executive mansion in 1814. The **Arts Club of Washington** (2017 I Street, NW, 1-202 331 7282) was home to his successor, James Monroe, until the charred mansion was rebuilt.

Around Pennsylvania Avenue, Foggy Bottom frequently succumbs to 'façadism', token retention of the fronts of historic buildings to satisfy preservation rules, with massive modern structures ballooning behind. The blatant **Mexican Chancery** (1911 Pennsylvania Avenue, NW) and slightly subtler **Red Lion Row** (2000 Pennsylvania Avenue, NW) are prime examples. The **Spanish Chancery** on Washington Circle is subtler still, and more stylish.

North of Pennsylvania Avenue, the 'New Downtown' to the west of Farragut Square is the haunt of the 'K Street lawyer' lobbyists. Although recent spending limits on entertaining members of Congress have pinched a bit, their expense-account hangouts still aren't cheap. A stroll down the block-long promenade of the **Renaissance Mayflower Hotel** (1127 Connecticut Avenue, NW; *see p49*), renovated to its pristine 1925 chic, may also yield a glimpse of celebrity clientele.

To keep K Street fit for Guccis to tread, the self-taxing 38-block Golden Triangle Business Improvement District, centred on Farragut Square, tidies streetscapes here. A corps of cheery uniformed functionaries give directions and keep an eye on pesky panhandlers.

Kennedy Center

2700 F Street, NW, at New Hampshire Avenue & Rock Creek Parkway (1-800 444 1324/1-202 467 4600/www.kennedy-center.org). Foggy Bottom-GWU Metro. **Open** 10am-11pm daily. **Map** p284 F6.
Festooned with decorative gifts from many nations, 'Ken Cen' is as much a spectacle as the shows it presents, with its six theatres and concert halls, three rooftop restaurants and great views from the open-air terrace. Free concerts (6pm daily) liven up the Millennium Stage, and free 45-minute guided tours (10am-4.45pm Mon-Fri; 10am-12.45pm Sat, Sun) leave from Parking Lobby A, opposite the gift shop. Parking is inadequate when several shows are playing at once – better to walk or take the free shuttle bus from the Foggy Bottom-GWU Metro stop. A major reconfiguration of the site along the freeway to the east promises other complications but eventual relief. *See also p207 and p222.*

The Octagon

1799 New York Avenue, NW, at 18th Street (1-202 638 3221/recorded information 1-202 638 3105/www.theoctagon.org). Farragut North or Farragut West Metro. **Open** 10am-4pm Tue-Sun. **Admission** $5; $3 concessions; free under-6s. **No credit cards. Map** p284 G6.
Designed to fit its odd-shaped lot by Dr William Thornton, first architect of the Capitol, this elegant brick mansion is the city's oldest, completed in 1800. The aristocratic Tayloes offered it to a fellow Virginian, President Madison, when he was made homeless by the 1814 White House fire. More like a pregnant hexagon than an octagon, the house – reputedly haunted – is a gem of light and proportion. The related American Institute of Architects headquarters are next door; hence the Octagon hosts topical architectural exhibitions as well as Madison-era furnishings – including the desk where Madison signed the Treaty of Ghent in 1815, ending the war between the US and Britain. *See also p35 and p117.*

Downtown

Map p284 & p285

DC's 'Old Downtown' east of the White House is now distinguished from 'New Downtown' north of Foggy Bottom. Once synonymous with F Street's theatres, restaurants and department stores, the area was bustling until the 1980s, when redevelopment drove out most of the retail businesses. In 1985 the Hecht Company opened at 12th and G Streets, the first freestanding department store built in an American downtown in four decades. No others have followed its lead.

Recently, though, Old Downtown has rebounded emphatically. An influx of law firms

Sightseeing

spawned such power-lunch hangouts as **DC Coast** at K and 14th Streets and **Oceanaire Seafood Room** at F and 12th. Cultural Tourism DC (www.culturaltourismdc.org), an organisation concerned with promoting the city's heritage, kicked off a campaign of posting historical background and illustrations on kerbside signs here, linked to its published walking tours. At Franklin Square (14th and I Streets, NW), strip clubs long ago gave way to posh offices, which chip in to maintain the park. Even its statue facing 14th Street of Irishman John Barry, Father of the US Navy, got a polish.

The **National Theatre** (1321 Pennsylvania Avenue, NW; *see p222*) flourishes afresh after years as a Ken Cen colony, while the **Warner Theatre** (at 13th and E Streets, NW; *see p209*) reflects a thorough restoration. At 511 Tenth Street, NW, is **Ford's Theatre** (*see p80*). Still a functioning theatre, its main claim to fame is as the site of Lincoln's assassination.

The **National Press Club** (14th and F Streets, NW), opened in 1924, still draws reporters, and sponsors speeches by newsmakers, foreign and domestic. Recently it opened its so-so restaurant to anyone who wishes to hobnob with the scribes. The **Washington Post**, at 1150 15th Street, NW (1-202 334 6000), can be toured by arrangement.

The oddly shaped **Octagon**. *See p77.*

One block west is the home of the venerable **National Geographic Society** (*see p80*).

Half a block south of the National Geographic is the **Russian Embassy** (1125 16th Street, NW, between L and M Streets). A wedding gift for the daughter of sleeping-car tycoon George Pullman, the gushy palazzo became the Tsarist Russian embassy in 1917. With US recognition in 1934, the USSR moved in, planting hammer-and-sickle motifs amid the gilt cherubs adorning the walls. The red flag finally came down in 1991. This Russian Embassy is now only the ceremonial appendage of the working compound on Wisconsin Avenue at Calvert Street. That US spies had burrowed a surveillance tunnel under the latter building came to light, embarrassingly, in 2001. Sixteenth Street is also notable for its procession of handsome houses of worship, which line it all the way to Maryland.

The former Greyhound bus terminal at 12th Street and New York Avenue used to be a wino magnet. Now its streamlined façade, treasured by Washington's legion of art deco devotees, fronts an office building complementing its lines. Street-level tenants include many restaurants and bars. **The National Museum of Women in the Arts** (*see p111*) arrived in 1987 to redeem a dignified 80-year-old Renaissance Revival Masonic lodge that had become a cinema.

The gigantic new **Convention Center** north of Mount Vernon Square replaced a drab, punier predecessor at Ninth Street and New York Avenue. On the square itself, the old wedding-cake Carnegie Library now houses the **City Museum of Washington, DC** (*see p118*). Skip the corny video, with its extra charge; instead, go for the delightful displays about life in old 'Mudville'. The successor as central public library, the **Martin Luther King Jr Memorial Library** (*see p80*), sparks passionate controversy. The last design of Bauhaus guru Mies van der Rohe, the 1972 black box inspires both defenders, who insist it's an architectural masterpiece, and detractors, who dismiss it as a dysfunctional disaster demanding rapid replacement.

The **National Museum of American Art** and the **National Portrait Gallery**, which split the historic **Patent Office** building at Seventh and F Streets, are reopening in 2006 after extensive renovations. Opposite, across Seventh Street, looms the **MCI Center** (*see p80*). The arena has triggered an explosive revival along Seventh Street, with escalating rents blowing some old Chinese businesses out of Chinatown. Although their names may be written in Chinese characters, chains like Legal Sea Foods and even Hooters don't quite pass the

Back to the city

In the 1960s Black Power activists fulminated against the Plan, an apocryphal plot by developers and politicians to drive minorities and the poor out of the city centre and into invisibility north and east of Massachusetts Avenue. Their fears gave the alleged plotters too much credit for efficiency.

Yet economic forces have now outdone the Plan. Space is at a premium, and tracts of previously despised territory are being reclaimed by young guns for whom the suburbs would be anathema. A prime example of this is NoMa (*see p80*), until recently a nameless wasteland north of Massachusetts Avenue, east of Mount Vernon Square – and now the place to be. All over the District and the older, close-in suburbs, rampant gentrification is morphing city blocks in borderline neighbourhoods and transforming large empty structures – such as old public schoolhouses and deconsecrated churches – into luxury loft condominiums.

The success of the MCI Center in stirring the former backwater of Chinatown into a nightlife hub, the emergence of offices north of Union Station, and the revival of Shaw as a residential magnet all rendered the redevelopment of the neighbouring NoMa inevitable. In the near suburbs, the same process is transforming pockets of land, especially those near Metro stations, such as Ballston and Silver Spring.

Mayor Anthony Williams' proposals to reverse the District's long population decline by attracting 100,000 new residents inspired sceptical derision, yet an influx of young affluent singles is changing the face of the city. Reaction against suburbia, with its long commutes, as well as decreased urban crime and renewed enthusiasm for city living, are among the draws.

Not even security concerns have slowed the frantic pace. Although it's presumably terrorist target number one, the average price of a single-family house on Capitol Hill soared from $154,000 to $418,000 between 1996 and 2003, without even a pause at 9/11. Other less-prominent neighbourhoods are also experiencing huge property price hikes. Unable to absorb soaring rents, neighbourhood shops give way to Starbucks or video rental chains, and the poor find themselves pushed further and further north and east.

The developers chafe under a District law giving tenants the first right to buy their buildings. Landlords in hot markets like Columbia Heights can 'flip' low-rent tenements by giving less-affluent residents lump-sum buyouts – the developer pays the tenant to surrender his rights and is then able to resell overnight at a huge profit. In, say, Columbia Heights, these tenants might well be vulnerable Latinos who speak little English. The sudden offer of $5,000 or $10,000 to move out seems like a fortune, though of course they'd be far better off in the long run if they stayed put.

Already developed areas aren't safe from the bulldozer either. In neighbourhoods whose homes are unprotected by Historic District building restrictions, builders find it sufficiently lucrative to tear down a good house on a nice street and cram as large and gaudy a replacement as possible on to the lot, dwarfing its neighbours. Thus the McMansion is born.

chopstick test. Gaudy chinoiserie still obscures some quite old house façades; Wok-n'-Roll restaurant (604 H Street, NW, 1-202 347 4656) occupies Mary Surratt's boarding house, where in 1865 John Wilkes Booth met co-conspirators to plot Abe Lincoln's doom. Texan barbecue restaurants and Irish eateries now thrive within sight of the world's largest Chinese arch (over H Street, at Seventh Street), given by the People's Republic of China. A large chunk of the arch broke away a few years ago; happily, nobody was injured, but the Taiwanese revelled in a symbolic interpretation of the event. DC's Chinese population has largely dispersed through the suburbs, but Chinatown remains the community's spiritual centre and site of dragon dancing at Chinese New Year.

Nearby places of worship are reminders of Washington's immigrant past, particularly **St Mary's Mother of God** (727 Fifth Street, NW), a downsized copy of Germany's Ulm Cathedral, ministering to German-speaking Catholic immigrants. **St Patrick's Catholic Church** (619 Tenth Street, NW) was established in 1794 to serve the Irish immigrants who came to build the White House; the present building rose a century later. **Holy Rosary Church** (595 Third Street, NW) has masses in Italian, plus cultural events at its Casa Italiana next door. In 2004 a cluster of Jewish congregations bought back the historic **synagogue** at Sixth and I Streets from the black Baptist congregation that had long occupied – then outgrown – it.

Dating from 1876, Washington's first synagogue now houses the **Jewish Historical Society** and its museum (*see p112*). The District's long-frustrated goal of a 'living downtown' popped into reality at the turn of the 21st century in this vicinity, as recent urban deserts bloomed with condos. The hottest coming property is north-east of Mount Vernon Square, in NoMa (named with envious eyes like Manhattan's Soho, for NOrth of MAssachusetts Avenue).

Ford's Theatre & Lincoln Museum

511 Tenth Street, NW, between E & F Streets (box office 1-202 347 4833/Park Service 1-202 426 6924/www.fordstheatre.org or www.nps.gov/foth). *Gallery Place-Chinatown or Metro Center Metro.* **Open** 9am-5pm daily. **Admission** free. **Map** p284 J6.
On Good Friday, 1865, President Abraham Lincoln sat in a rocking chair in Ford's Theatre watching the comedy *Our American Cousin*, when actor and Southern sympathiser John Wilkes Booth entered the presidential box and shot him. Booth jumped on to the stage, breaking his leg on landing. He escaped painfully on horseback, only to be killed by US troops 12 days later. Today's theatre is decorated as it was that day, although less-punishing chairs offer

a concession to tender modern derrières. Exhibits in the Lincoln Museum downstairs include Booth's Derringer pistol, Lincoln's bloodstained clothes and the tools used to seal his coffin. Cross the street to Petersen House (516 Tenth Street, NW; 1-202 426 6924), where Lincoln was taken after the shooting. He expired there at 7.22am the next morning. *See also p223.*

Martin Luther King Jr Memorial Library

901 G Street, NW, between Ninth & Tenth Streets (general information 1-202 727 1111/reference 1-202 727 1126/www.dclibrary.org/mlk). Gallery Place-Chinatown Metro. **Open** 9.30am-9pm Mon-Thur; 9.30am-5.30pm Fri, Sat; 1-5pm Sun. **Map** p285 J6.
The centre of DC's public library system contains the third-floor Washingtoniana Room, where extraordinary reference librarians help sort through books, historical directories, maps and more than 13 million newspaper clippings concerning the District of Columbia and vicinity. You may have to walk up, since the library's elevators are rarely all in working order at the same time.

MCI Center

601 F Street, NW, at Seventh Street (1-202 628 3200). Gallery Place-Chinatown Metro. **Open** events only. **Map** p285 J6.
This huge, $200-million arena hosts some 200 public events a year, including concerts, family entertainment, horse shows and local college athletics, as well as pro games by the Washington Capitals NHL hockey team and the Washington Wizards NBA basketball team. It involves all the economic excesses now de rigueur in American professional sport: startling admission prices, 110 exorbitant skyboxes for corporate entertaining, restaurants restricting admission to top-end ticketholders and other money- and class-based novelties. Still, it's well designed and conveniently atop a Metro station. Seating is comfortable and angled to afford even stratospheric spectators a good view. *See also p220.*

National Geographic Society

Gilbert H Grosvenor Auditorium *1600 M Street, NW, at 16th Street (1-202 857 7700/ www.nationalgeographic.com/explorer).* **Explorers Hall** *1145 17th Street, NW, at M Street (1-202 857 7588/www.nationalgeographic.com/explorer).* **Both** *Farragut North Metro.* **Open** 9am-5pm Mon-Sat; 10am-5pm Sun. **Admission** free. **Map** p284 H5.
Founded in 1890 by local patricians, the Geographic has funded nearly 6,000 exploration and research projects to destinations from China to Peru and pole to pole. It also publishes the *National Geographic Magazine*, the rather stodgy but nevertheless iconic vehicle that brought the outside world to generations of Americans. The Grosvenor Auditorium hosts traditional lecture series by slide-showing adventurers, but now also presents international concerts and videos, even beer tastings.

Highlights of America's naval history at the **US Navy Memorial**. *See p82.*

The adjacent Explorers Hall is a free museum with changing exhibitions on subjects as diverse as 17th-century pirate life, dinosaurs of the Sahara, and Lucy, the oldest humanoid.

Penn Quarter

Map p284 & p285

North of Federal Triangle, this developer-dubbed area is known simply as 'downtown' to residents, who recall it as the main shopping district. In recent years, the area has blossomed with new restaurants, developments, displays and theatres.

Nineteenth-century District residents shopped along Pennsylvania Avenue and Seventh Street. But then the success of the fixed-price Woodward & Lothrop department store after 1882 made F Street the principal shopping street, while business on the Avenue declined. Distressed by the tawdriness of Pennsylvania Avenue as he rode in his 1961 inaugural procession, President Kennedy set up a commission charged with revamping 'America's Main Street'. In time, the Pennsylvania Avenue Development Corporation rose to the task.

The elegant water crane perched on the quirky Temperance Fountain at Seventh Street and Pennsylvania Avenue punctuates the Seventh Street arts corridor of galleries and studios blooming behind Victorian cast-iron storefronts. The former Lansburgh's department store now houses posh apartments above the **Shakespeare Theatre** (450 Seventh Street, NW; *see p223*). The **US Navy Memorial** (*see p82*) plaza nicely frames the Eighth Street axis between the National Portrait Gallery and the **National Archives** (*see p73*). The **International Spy Museum** (*see p119*) at Ninth and F has been a smash hit, despite its decidedly un-Washington admission fees. Near the White House, grand old hotels like the **Washington** (515 15th Street, NW; *see p45*) with its famous rooftop bar, and the lavish **Willard Inter-Continental** (1401 Pennsylvania Avenue, NW; *see p43*) have recovered their lost lustre. JFK would have been pleased.

The **J Edgar Hoover FBI Building** (935 Pennsylvania Avenue, NW, between Ninth and Tenth Streets, 1-202 324 3447, www.fbi.gov) presents a sterile streetscape because Hoover himself vetoed the planned street-level shops and restaurants as potential security threats. Resumption of the tours of the building, first cancelled over 9/11 security concerns, was under consideration at the time of writing.

A locally popular pastime across E Street is attending the day-long Wednesday auctions that have been conducted at **Weschler's** (909 E Street, NW, 1-202 628 1281) for over a century. Treasures, trash and grab bags keep the bidders lively.

US Navy Memorial & Heritage Center

701 Pennsylvania Avenue, NW, between Seventh & Ninth Streets (1-202 737 2300/www.lonesailor.org). Archives-Navy Memorial Metro. **Open** 9.30am-5pm Mon-Sat. **Admission** free. **Map** p285 J6.

Dedicated on the Navy's 212th birthday in 1987, this memorial features the world's biggest map of itself – a flat granite circular map 100ft (30m) across, with this very spot at its centre. The surrounding sculptured wall has 22 bas-reliefs depicting naval highlights like the Great White Fleet sent around the world by Theodore Roosevelt in 1907, Commodore Perry's 1854 expedition to Japan and the 'Silent Service' of submarines. Off-centre stands a statue of the Lone Sailor, stolid in his pea jacket. The subterranean visitor centre contains a cinema with a 52ft (15.6m) screen, showing an all-too-authentically noisy depiction of life at sea. The amphitheatre hosts free summer concerts by military bands.

Judiciary Square area

Map p285

Judiciary Square is the hub of the city's courts. The **National Building Museum** (*see p112*) occupies the 1883 Pension Building, built in the style of a Renaissance palace, with an extraordinary frieze of Civil War troops perpetually patrolling the premises. Its atrium is spectacular and its gift shop imaginative. Across F Street, bronze lions flank the **National Law Enforcement Officers Memorial** to the nearly 15,000 cops killed in the line of duty since 1794. To help make sense of the memorial, which assigns no chronological or alphabetical order to the names, grab a brochure from the visitors' centre (605 E Street, NW, 1-202 737 3213). It explains the system, pointing out policemen slain by notorious criminals such as Bonnie and Clyde.

Flanking the area is the dwindling domain of bail bondsmen and 'Fifth Street lawyers' (not to be confused with the sleek K Street set): cut-rate but street-savvy attorneys hustling over to the criminal courts to prevent clients' incarceration. The **Court of Appeals** building (Fifth & D Streets) was once Washington's city hall, a chaste 1820 Greek Revival design by British architect George Hadfield. Lincoln's statue at the front is significant as the first public memorial to the murdered president, sculpted by his acquaintance, Lot Flannery, and dedicated on the third anniversary of his death in 1868. Flannery knew how Lincoln looked, and he worked fast, so the oratorical posture is likely to be accurate.

Down the stairs that constitute Fourth Street, beside the statue of Chief Justice John Marshall that once graced the Capitol grounds, the

Canadian Embassy (501 Pennsylvania Avenue, NW) – awarded its prominent site in honour of close bi-national relations – houses a gallery spotlighting Canadian artists. The new **Newseum**, a grander incarnation of the previous museum, rises adjacent to it at Sixth Street and Pennsylvania Avenue. It's due to open in 2006.

Protected by statues of General Meade, the victorious commander at Gettysburg, and master legal commentator Sir William Blackstone, the **US Court House** opposite the embassy is gradually losing its 'Watergate Courthouse' identity as subsequent scandals unfold before interminable grand juries, while a new wing to the east alters its appearance. The **Frances Perkins Department of Labor Building** (*see below*) to the east houses a noteworthy but small Labor Hall of Fame.

The triangle at D Street and Louisiana Avenues contains the **Japanese-American Memorial**, dedicated to the Americans of Japanese descent who were interned during World War II, and the Japanese-American Nisei regiments of their sons, who fought for the US. An eloquent sculpture captures two traditional Japanese cranes struggling against barbed-wire entanglements.

Frances Perkins Department of Labor Building

200 Constitution Avenue, NW, at Third Street (1-202 693 4650). Judiciary Square Metro. **Open** 8.30am-4.45pm Mon-Fri. **Admission** free (photo ID required). **Map** p285 K6.

Named for FDR's confidant and the first female US cabinet officer (1933-45), this building displays personal artefacts of leaders ranging from radical activist Mother Jones to unorthodox industrialist Henry J Kaiser.

Dupont Circle

Map p282

Dupont Circle is perhaps the most cosmopolitan of all DC's neighbourhoods. Long a centre of the city's affluent gay community, its bars and bistros cater to a diverse public. The circle itself is a lively green space, with a collection of chess tables in constant use.

In the middle of it all, a white marble fountain sprays into the air in honour of Civil War admiral Samuel Francis Dupont. In the 19th century, Dupont Circle was a backwater on the outskirts of downtown. By the turn of the 20th, mansions began sprouting along the dirt roads. The area experienced a bout of radicalism in the 1960s, when anti-Vietnam War protesters and black power activists claimed the circle for demonstrations; anti-globalists seek the old energy there today.

Malcolm X Park. *See p85.*

Dupont Circle. *See p82.*

By and large, though, the neighbourhood remains calm, well-mannered and well-heeled.

Chain stores have infiltrated Connecticut Avenue, but enough idiosyncratic bookstores and bistros survive to reward a wander. The debut of one chain, a Krispy Kreme doughnut bakery, inspired general joy.

Large hotels and apartment buildings start to dominate the landscape about four blocks north, heading towards Adams Morgan (*see p85*). The pavement outside the Washington Hilton on the corner of Connecticut Avenue and T Street was the site of John Hinckley's attempted assassination of President Ronald Reagan in 1981.

Off Connecticut Avenue, the blocks north of the circle consist largely of well-kept Victorian rowhouses, art galleries and gorgeous mansions now occupied by embassies or the non-profit associations represented in the nation's capital. If the weather is nice, amble northwards through the blocks west of Connecticut Avenue – known as **Kalorama** – to check out the impressive architecture and exhibitions. The galleries display contemporary, experimental and traditional art, from painting to sculpture to photography. At the heart of them all is the **Phillips Collection** (*see p111*), opened in 1921 as the first permanent museum of modern art in America. For more information on other galleries, *see pp189-96*.

Massachusetts Avenue, from Scott Circle, East of Dupont Circle, through to Upper Northwest (*see p88*) is known as 'Embassy Row'. For a cheap tour, catch any westbound 'N' Metrobus at Dupont Circle and cruise past the mosque established for diplomats in the 1950s (No.2551, at Belmont Road, Kalorama), the embassies of Turkey, the Netherlands, Brazil, the Vatican, and others. Further on, into Upper Northwest, the British Embassy (No.3100) sports a statue of Churchill, with one foot on British soil (all embassies are deemed their nations' territory) and the other on American, reflecting his ancestry. The US confiscated the former Iranian Embassy across the way following the seizure of the American Embassy in Tehran and the holding of its staff hostage in 1979. It is now rented out for extremely expensive parties and wedding receptions.

Although for security the US has encouraged embassies to move to new quarters in the International Drive enclave further north, many cling to the now cramped but elegant millionaires' mansions of yesteryear. Lots of these embassies open their doors for concerts, art displays, and charity events (see www.embassyseries.org). Foreign heroes patrol this strand: there's a statue of Gandhi at 21st Street, opposite the Indian embassy;

Czechoslovakian leader Marsyk adorns 22nd Street; and, further north, political martyr Robert Emmet gazes toward the Irish Embassy from the 2200 block.

Adams Morgan

Map p282

To the east of Dupont Circle, 18th Street becomes the main strip of lively Adams Morgan some nine walkable blocks north. The area is known for its ethnic restaurants and militant diversity. Soaring rents haven't yet scotched its bohemianism, and it continues to attract young, mainly white, transplants too sophisticated or too poor for the homogeneity of Georgetown or the suburbs. Few button-down shirts grace its streets and restaurants; with so few offices nearby, the weekday lunch hour stretches into several. The streetlife is leisurely Latino, notably Central American. Everything changes at night, though, when 18th Street (up to and including the spots along Columbia Road, which intersects 18th Street at the top of the hill) morphs into a big bar and dining scene. Nowhere else in the city can you hop from one joint to the next with better results. The bars range from flat-out frat-boy hangouts to salsa and reggae clubs, and on warm summer evenings outdoor cafés pack in the customers.

In the 1920s and '30s what is now Adams Morgan was an elite neighbourhood of rowhouses stacked on a hill. The elevation made for precious breezes in the sweltering summers and, for some houses, a charming view of the city. The neighbourhood got its name in the 1950s, when progressive-minded residents opted to integrate the white Adams school with the black Morgan school. The area is still home to a wide range of nationalities and races. DC is home to the largest community of Ethiopians outside Ethiopia, and many have opened bars and restaurants in Adams Morgan, joining the numerous Thai, Vietnamese, Indian and Cajun restaurants in the area.

One place in Adams Morgan that is always lively during the day is **Malcolm X Park** – officially Meridian Hill Park (bordered by 16th, Euclid, 15th and W Streets, NW), a space that's often throbbing to the competing sounds of ad hoc African, Brazilian and Puerto Rican percussion groups.

Shaw

Map p282 & p283

Bounded by North Capitol Street and 16th Street on the east and west, and by Irving Street and M Street to the north and south, Shaw embraces historic neighbourhoods, including

Howard University, the U Street Corridor and Logan Circle. All were bastions of African American DC, fostering black businesses, churches and scholarship during the dismal decades of racial segregation. Today Shaw has bounced back after decades of slow decline, which culminated in the disastrous 1968 riots (*see p19*). And if U Street hasn't quite returned to its days as America's 'Black Broadway', it's getting there pretty fast.

Logan Circle

This neighbourhood – bordered by S Street to the north, M Street to the south, Ninth Street to the east and 16th Street to the west – was once a fashionable vicinity for the wealthy, who built lavish Victorian homes here in the 1870s and 1880s. Many have now been expensively restored. White 'urban pioneers' have joined with longtime black residents to reclaim this turf from prostitutes working the area after dark.

U Street/14th Street Corridor

U Street has been reborn as a centre of trendy commerce and nightlife, surrounded by rowhouses that have become interracial magnets for the city's hipsters. The neighbourhood is bisected by 14th Street – which has experienced its own revival, albeit in less dramatic style.

Anchored by nearby Howard University, the neighbourhood became the hub of African American culture. Poet Langston Hughes and jazz great Duke Ellington both grew up here. Along with Ella Fitzgerald, Nat King Cole and Redd Foxx, they made U Street bars world-famous with their performances. During the 1930s, trendy You Street was a cultural hub of black America, echoing on a small scale New York's Harlem renaissance. Recently, historical signs and photo displays in store windows have evoked those glory days.

Ben's Chili Bowl, on U Street between 12th and 13th Streets (*see p134*), is an old-school diner frequented by celebs such as Bill Cosby and ex-mayor Marion Barry. It's a greasy dive famous for its chilli dogs and atmosphere, which only gets busier as the night goes on. The **Lincoln Theatre** (*see p209*), next door, was once a grand stage for black performances in the age of segregation. At the U Street-Cardozo Metro station is an African American Civil War Memorial. On U and 13th Streets is the **Republic Gardens** bar/restaurant (*see p213*), which always draws a huge crowd of African Americans. Nearby, on 14th Street, aside from a couple of swanky new lounges, the main attraction is the **Black Cat** (*see p204*),

Sightseeing

Parallel lives

Black history was born in Washington in 1926, when the acerbic Dr Carter G Woodson launched Negro History Week to counter the assumption that his race didn't have any. Soon afterwards, Howard University professor Alaine Locke sparked the New Negro cultural revival. In the 1930s the New Negro Alliance broke significant political and legal ground, with action by pickets forcing Washington businesses to desegregate. Meanwhile, native son Duke Ellington was playing his progressive jazz to audiences nationwide. The Harlem Renaissance in New York may be better known, but Washington arguably played a broader and deeper role in stirring African American consciousness between the wars.

Sheer population numbers had helped establish Washington as a hub of black America. During the Civil War, DC's blacks were joined by thousands of freedmen who flooded into the city from the South. Evidence of the influx remains in the dwellings known as alley houses – cheap, tiny houses hastily thrown up by developers in the spacious alleys providing rear access to Washington homes. (Remaining alley houses include Rumsey Court, at the 100 block of First Street, SE; Terrace Court, behind the Supreme Court, at the 200 block of A Street, NE; and Archibald Walk, at the 600 block of E Street, SE).

Congress ruled that the city's expanding black population should be educated – though not, needless to say, alongside whites. The result was free public school education, producing what were arguably the only genuinely 'separate but equal' schools in the nation. With its federal funding, **Howard University** (*see p87*) offered the best black higher education anywhere. From this core grew an affluent, sophisticated African American elite of merchants and

professionals, a virtually separate city within a larger, racially segregated Washington. And U Street (*see p85*) – was at its heart.

After World War II, Howard alumni and faculty were prominent in the legal war against race discrimination. As legal director of the NAACP, former HU law professor Thurgood Marshall argued the case against segregation in the Supreme Court in Brown vs Board of Education, the landmark case that led to desegregation of public schools; in 1967 he became the first black US Supreme Court justice. Others excelled in arts, culture and commerce.

The 1968 riots were a massive setback, driving middle-class African Americans out of the city and marking the end of an era for black Washington. But today, Washington's eminence as a centre of African American life and culture is getting a fresh look. Virtually every local jurisdiction distributes free black history maps or booklets. Perhaps the handiest is the African American Heritage Trail booklet, supplemented by a database at www.culturaltourismdc.org. Rather than a contiguous route, the trail is a series of 14 neighbourhood guides. For themed guided tours on topics like U Street culture, the Civil Rights movement or the Underground Railroad, try Site Seeing Tours (http://siteseeingtoursinc.com, 1-301 445 2098) or Capitol Entertainment Services (www.washington-dc-tours.com, 1-202 636 9203).

which continues to be a centre for the city's punk bands. A block north on V Street at Ninth Street is the **9:30 Club** (*see p203*), DC's premier venue for big-name bands.

U Street wasn't always a mecca for black artists and club-hopping kids. It has seen some very dark days, going into a steep decline after the riots triggered by Martin Luther King Jr's assassination in 1968. Middle-class blacks all but vanished. Much of the 14th Street corridor burned to the ground. In its current gentrifying guise, those days seem to be well and truly over.

Howard University & around

Many famous students, professors and alumni have lived a short walk south of the university in LeDroit Park. This small neighbourhood extends from Florida Avenue in the south, Elm Street in the north, Second Street in the east and Bohrer Street in the west. A long list of black activists, including the Reverend Jesse Jackson, owned houses here beside the homes of other upper-class black ministers, lawyers, businessmen and Howard professors.

Howard University

2400 Sixth Street, NW, at Howard Place (1-202 806 6100/www.howard.edu). Shaw-Howard University Metro then 70, 71 bus. **Map** p283 J2.

With a hall of fame that includes former mayors and Supreme Court justices, Howard University has a legacy to brag about. The school was chartered in 1867 with government funds as a theological seminary to train black ministers, who could in turn help guide the newly emancipated slaves after the Civil War. By 1940 half of African Americans in college were Howard students. Much of the leadership that planned the legal assault on Jim Crow segregation came from Howard. Ironically, their success in opening educational opportunities eventually forced them to compete for top African American students, now lured by other prestigious universities.

Howard holds some of the best collections on African history and art in the country at the Howard University Museum on the first floor of the Founders Library, and the Howard University Gallery in the College of Fine Arts.

Mount Pleasant & north

Map p282

Mount Pleasant's streets are lined with trees and row after row of modest homes with front porches. The neighbourhood is bounded in the north by Rock Creek Park, in the south by Harvard Street, in the west by Adams Mill Road and in the east by 16th Street. It is a largely residential area, and a preferred location for DC's punks and hipsters. The

neighbourhood also has strong Salvadorean and Vietnamese populations, living in houses and apartments surrounding the main drag, Mount Pleasant Street.

North of Mount Pleasant, unremarkable residential blocks stretch out towards the Maryland line. Some of the streets are more dangerous than others (pockets east of 16th Street are among DC's high-crime areas), but most are just row after row of homes. One historic neighbourhood is the **Gold Coast**, a stretch of 16th Street north of Shepherd Street. The mansions and upscale homes of the Gold Coast have long been status symbols for the city's black upper-middle class. The only tourist draws are the preserved bastion of **Fort Stevens** at 13th and Quackenbos Streets, active in repelling a Confederate attack in 1864, and the **National Museum of Health & Medicine** in the grounds of Walter Reed Army Medical Center at Georgia and Elder (*see p106*).

In the nearby section of Rock Creek Park is the **Carter Barron Amphitheatre** (*see p89*).

Georgetown

Map p280 & p281

George, Maryland, was laid out in 1751 around the large block between the current 30th and 31st, M and N Streets. Although reluctantly included in Washington in 1871, today's Georgetown is unlike the rest of the city, with its tranquil mansion-lined streets and haughty boutiques. Its physical division from the rest of the District by Rock Creek enhances its sense of insularity.

At the upriver limit of navigation for ocean vessels, the town started life as a colonial tobacco port. Oxen pulled huge cylinders of 'sot weed' down its 'rolling road', which is now Wisconsin Avenue.

From the mid 1800s until the turn of the century, black Georgetown thrived south of P Street between Rock Creek and 31st Street. Some 1,000 African American families slept there at night, working by day as cooks, domestics and stable boys. Although it's hard to fathom now, Georgetown was dwindling into slumishness by the 1930s. Then, a 'colonial revival' made Federal-style homes fashionable again. Many of FDR's New Dealers moved in amid the multi-generation 'cliff dwellers', turning Georgetown into a chic address.

A fine way to sample the flavour of the place is to follow the self-guided walking tour available free from www.georgetowndc.com, called The Kennedys' Georgetown. Starting in 1951, young congressman John F Kennedy lived in half a dozen houses in the area, on some of the most distinctive blocks.

The prestigious **Georgetown University** (*see below*) is an academically rigorous and media savvy institution; its students still find time to enjoy the local nightlife, though.

Yet for some, all the power and wealth makes Georgetown rather stuffy, by day or night. The two main strips are M Street and Wisconsin Avenue, which intersect one another. The sidewalks are crowded at weekends with people throwing money around at the chic clothing stores. Built by cabinet-maker Christopher Layman in 1765, the **Old Stone House** (3051 M Street, NW, 1-202 426 6851) is the oldest home in DC, its tiny garden offering repose to the weary consumer. Stately **Tudor Place** (1644 31st Street, NW) rests serenely isolated on extensive grounds. **Dumbarton Oaks** (*see p107*) is home to a first-class collection of Byzantine and pre-Columbian art. Landscape architect Beatrix Farrand designed its celebrated formal gardens. Separating it from Montrose Park, a long, steep path called Lovers' Lane descends towards Rock Creek.

The **C&O Canal towpath**, roughly parallel to M Street, also makes for a lovely, shaded walk. The canal, which was begun in 1828, parallels the Potomac for over 184 miles (276 kilometres) to Cumberland, Maryland – as far as it had gone when its newfangled competitor, the railroad, beat it to the Ohio River. The canal finally ceased commercial use in 1924. In 1954 Supreme Court Justice William O Douglas led a hike to demonstrate the canal's natural beauty and abundant wildlife, countering proposals to pave it for a parkway. Today the C&O Canal is a long and very thin National Historical Park, with summertime mule-drawn barge trips a popular attraction in the watered section above Georgetown.

At night Georgetown jumps with dozens of bars and restaurants filled with suburban twentysomethings and international jetsetters. In the summer, garish **Washington Harbour**, at the southern end of Wisconsin Avenue on the Potomac River, is overrun with people looking to eat, drink and flirt. The restaurants are forgettable and the drinks overpriced, but the warm breezes off the Potomac make the boardwalk a nice stroll. **House of Sweden**, a combination embassy and cultural centre, has taken the last available riverside space to the east. Just west of here, **Jack's Boathouse** (*see p215*) still rents canoes for aquatic sightseeing. A splendid view of the Potomac may be had from the **Francis Scott Key Memorial Park** (34th and M Streets), celebrating the writer of the US national anthem, who lived on a house on this site.

Georgetown University

37th & O Streets, NW (1-202 687 0100). Dupont Circle Metro then G2 bus. **Map** p281 D4.
A Jesuit institution founded in 1789 by John Carroll, first Catholic bishop in the United States. Alumni fought on both sides in the Civil War, inspiring the school colours, blue and grey. Equally polarised alumni of more recent vintage include Bill Clinton and conservative pundit Pat Buchanan. Georgetown Law School across town is highly ranked; the School of Foreign Service draws top geopolitical junkies.

Upper Northwest

Map p280 & p281

The large swathe of land west of Connecticut Avenue and north of Georgetown and Dupont Circle is often referred to as 'West of the Park', the park being the extensive, leafy landscape of **Rock Creek Park** (*see below*). It is home to some of the city's wealthiest residents. Massive homes and posh boutiques stack up, one after another, streets such as Foxhall Road and upper Wisconsin Avenue.

Washington National Cathedral (*see p89*) is the sixth-largest church in the world and the second-largest in the US. On the cathedral grounds are two selective prep schools favoured by the children of the ruling elite: St Alban's and National Cathedral School. Beyond lies another, Sidwell Friends (once Chelsea Clinton's choice).

Nearby are the **Khalil Gibran Peace Garden** (*see p90* **Wild at heart**) and the **US Naval Observatory** (3450 Massachusetts Avenue, NW, 1-202 762 1467), housing the official residence of the vice-president. Its first occupant, multimillionaire Nelson Rockefeller, reportedly found the mansion too small. At Massachusetts and Nebraska Avenues is the campus of the **American University**. It's not a national icon as the name suggests, but it is a respectable school, attracting hundreds of budding politicos because of its established internship programmes within the halls of government.

Still further north, just before the Maryland border, **Friendship Heights** is another well-heeled residential area with a strip of glitzy shops that attempts to be DC's version of Rodeo Drive. If you're desperate to spend wads of cash, this is the place to go.

Rock Creek Park

Upper Northwest (1-202 895 6070/www.nps. gov/rocr). **Open** *Park* dawn-dusk daily. *Nature Center & Planetarium* 9am-5pm Wed-Sun. Closed some holidays. **Map** p281 F3.
Nestled between sprawling condo corridors and busy commercial strips lies 1,750 acres of urban forest called Rock Creek Park, following that stream all

the way to the city line to join an extension into Maryland. One of the largest such preserves in the nation, its 29 miles (47km) of hiking trails and ten miles (16.5km) of horse trails intersect a net of bicycle trails. At weekends, several park roads close to motor vehicles. Its central thoroughfare, Beach Drive, a major commuter cut on weekday rush hour, is a quiet route to picnic groves (some with barbecue facilities) and playing fields at other times.

The park is a magnet for wildlife, with fox and deer as well as smaller creatures. The Nature Center just off Military Road details its history and ecology, offering daily nature walks and similar events. The planetarium offers free star-gazing sessions from April to November (*see also p183*). The staff can also provide directions to some of the other attractions concealed in the park's foliage: tennis courts, a golf course, walking and biking trails, even the remains of Civil War fortifications. Bird-watchers can obtain directions to Picnic Groves 17 and 18 just south, prime perches from which to observe the warblers migrating during the spring and autumn. The District's only public riding stable (*see p218*), sharing the Nature Center parking lot, offers guided trail rides through the hilly terrain.

Continue north in the park to Carter Barron Amphitheatre, which stages low-cost summertime shows, from free Shakespeare in the Park productions to R&B and gospel concerts. Nearby, a state-of-the-art tennis centre hosts major competitions. For more on the Rock Creek's sporting facilities, *see pp214-20*.

Washington National Cathedral

Massachusetts & Wisconsin Avenues, NW (1-202 537 6200/www.cathedral.org/cathedral). Bus 30, 32, 34, 35, 36. **Open** *Sept-May* 10am-5.30pm Mon-Fri; 10am-4.30pm Sat; 8am-6.30pm Sun. *June-Aug* 10am-8pm Mon-Fri; 10am-4.30pm Sat; 8am-6.30pm Sun. **Admission** free; suggested donation $3. **Credit** AmEx, Disc, MC, V. **Map** p281 E2.

Washington National Cathedral was built in 14th-century Gothic style, stone upon stone, without structural steel, an exercise that took most of the 20th century and was only finished in 1990. It's a bit overbearing, but the design makes a nice contrast to the Federal neo-classicism rampant downtown. Its medievalism has been somewhat updated: there's a gargoyle in the shape of Darth Vader in the north-west corner, while the much-admired stained-glass Space Window contains a piece of lunar rock. The top of the tower is the highest point in DC; there are great views from the observation gallery. Afternoon tea can be taken here on Tuesdays and Wednesdays at 1.30pm (reservations required).

The cathedral has introduced self-paced CD-based audio tours ($5); alternatively, join one of various guided tours, held at regular intervals. Special events can often mean that certain parts of the cathedral are closed at short notice, so it's best to phone first to check (the same applies if you have a specific tour in mind).

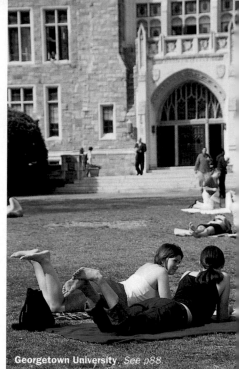

Georgetown University. *See p88.*

Wild at heart

The White House Rose Garden may be Washington's most famous garden, but it's hardly its most stunning. The capital is filled with an extraordinary array of horticultural gems, often hidden away, but nevertheless far more accessible than the president's patch of turf.

In many of these shady refuges it's easy to forget you're in the city. The Washington climate allows all but tropical plants to grow here, and the city's location on the Eastern Flyway means that many migratory birds join the year-round residents to enliven garden environments.

The city's several house museums tend to sit on landscapes suited to their periods. For instance, **Hillwood** (*see p107*) nestles between a formal French *parterre* in front and a flowing Japanese garden to the rear. **Dumbarton Oaks** (*see p107*) rests amid a series of garden rooms by master gardener Beatrix Farrand, harmonising with the open terrain of Montrose Park next door.

Washington National Cathedral (*see p89*) includes the popular Bishop's Garden (with shop) on the grounds laid out by landscaping legend Frederick Law Olmsted, while the gorgeous gardens of the **Franciscan Monastery** (*see p92*) contain replicas of religious sites from the Holy Land such as the Garden of Gethsemane and the Holy Sepulchre, and the grotto at Lourdes, too, for good measure.

Opposite the British Embassy (*see p84*), the **Khalil Gibran Peace Garden** is adorned with the poet's words. It has a structural layout that's based on walls and paths rather than plants, and is as peaceful as its name suggests (its distance from the city centre and lack of nearby parking facilities means it attracts fewer visitors). Not so the sculpture gardens at the **Hirshhorn Museum** (*see p113*), part of the Smithsonian Institute, on south fringe of the National Mall, which are usually bustling.

The **United States Botanic Garden** (*see p69*), with its great glass dome, preserves a glimpse of greenery even in winter and offers lectures and demonstrations year-round. Less well known is the South American garden and atrium of the **Organisation of American States** (OAS) at 17th and Constitution, NW,

facing the Ellipse. The **Folger Shakespeare Library** (*see p70*) has a small Elizabethan garden, which also contains sculptures evocative of the Bard's characters.

The **National Arboretum** occupies 37 hilly acres in Northeast (*see p92*), with a variety of environments and collections of scarce miniature plants, azaleas and bonsai. The original columns of the US Capitol preside, somewhat bizarrely, over the scene, while the administration building seems to float on a severe pond filled with enormous koi.

Across the Anacostia River is **Kenilworth Aquatic Gardens** (*see p92*). A network of dozens of ponds teem with aquatic flora, including hardy and tropical lilies and lotuses, some revived from oriental seeds 5,000 years old. No exotic fish are stocked, but frogs and ornate insects populate the murky waters, and the bird life is impressive. As with other gardens around town, June is probably the time of year to see the optimum number of blooms.

The Episcopalian cathedral holds some 1,200 services a year, yet has no membership of its own. It is meant to be a church for all. Every president since Theodore Roosevelt has visited, as have Martin Luther King Jr and the Dalai Lama. Funeral services of distinguished national figures (including, in June 2004, Ronald Reagan) have also been held here. Medieval gardens appropriately adorn the spacious grounds, supporting a popular herb shop.

Woodley Park

East towards Connecticut Avenue before Rock Creek Park, Woodley Park is a small but bustling neighbourhood featuring upscale homes, varied restaurants and the **National Zoo**. Conventioneers fill the restaurants along the short strip by the Metro station on Connecticut Avenue, and the handful of outdoor cafés make the area a popular spot on summer nights. In truth, though, there's not much else to do apart from visit the zoo.

National Zoo

3001 block of Connecticut Avenue, NW, at Rock Creek Park (1-202 357 2700/information 1-202 673 4800/www.natzoo.si.edu). Woodley Park-Zoo/Adams Morgan Metro. **Open** *Grounds* Nov-Mar 6am-6pm daily. Apr-Oct 6am-8pm daily. *Buildings* Nov-Mar 10am-4.30pm daily. Apr-Oct 10am-6pm daily. **Admission** free. **Map** p281 F2.

The great thing about the National Zoo is that it's free. It makes a diverting escape, even for just half an hour. Particularly during the off-season, when the paths are not cluttered by pushchairs, the zoo is a perfect place to stroll, away from the bustle of Connecticut Avenue. Tree-shaded paths wind through the margins past the various animals. Two of the most well-known residents are a pair of pandas, here since 2001, who imitate their predecessors by failing to mate every spring, despite a series of redesigns to make their lair more alluring. Still, they're wildly popular, even inspiring a 2004 competition with artists decorating giant panda statues placed all over town. Recent new habitats include the Amazonia rain forest and the American Prairie area. A distressing series of animal deaths in 2003 made for much official embarrassment.

Cleveland Park

Further north is Cleveland Park, home to even wealthier residents than Woodley Park, but similarly organised around a central strip of stores and restaurants along Connecticut Avenue. The main reason to visit the area is for mellow night-time entertainment. There are a couple of excellent restaurants here , as well as various coffeehouses and some good, cheap pizza and sandwich places. The **Cineplex Odeon Uptown** (*see p187*), also on this strip, is possibly the best cinema in the

city of Washington DC, with an obscenely large screen, two tiers and comfy seats.

North of Cleveland Park is the beautifully restored **Hillwood Museum & Gardens** (*see p107*), with late socialite Marjorie Merriweather Post's stunning collection of Russian objets d'art and serene Japanese landscaping.

Northeast

Map p283

The most industrial sector of a non-industrial city, Northeast Washington is bisected by railroad tracks and railyards serving warehouses and distribution centres. Some of these buildings have now been converted to offices and 'server farms' for new high-tech businesses. Beyond the tracks, however, Northeast is principally a residential area.

A couple of blocks east of the Supreme Court is the **Frederick Douglass Museum** (316 A Street, NE, 1-202 547 4273), the first Washington residence of the famous abolitionist. The original site of the Museum of African Art, the building now houses the Caring Foundation, which recognises worthy philanthropists. One room is maintained as it was in Douglass's time. Constantino Brumidi, the artist who painted the frescos in the Capitol, lived nearby, at 326 A Street. A crumbling curiosity abutting the Amtrak line just north of Union Station is the former Washington Coliseum (Second and K Streets, NE), lately reduced to a trash transfer station, but in February 1964 it was the site of the Beatles' American concert debut.

The main commercial street on the Hill's north side is Massachusetts Avenue, which has many restaurants and bars. The avenue is interrupted by Stanton Park, the neighbourhood's principal green area, located between Fourth and Sixth Streets. Further north is H Street, a working-class African American commercial strip that's making a comeback. Further east is **Gallaudet University** (800 Florida Avenue, NE), established in 1857 and one of the world's few liberal arts college for hearing-impaired students. The school's grounds were designed by landscape-architecture pioneer Frederick Law Olmsted.

The largest Northeast campus belongs to the **Catholic University of America** (620 Michigan Avenue, NE), a pontifical institution known for some graduate programmes and its famous drama school, which stages notable productions in its **Hartke Theatre**. The large tracts of land the church purchased for the university in the 1870s now hold a number of religious institutions, notably the **National Shrine of the Immaculate Conception**, the eighth-largest church in the world (400 Michigan Avenue, NE, 1-202 526 8300). Begun in 1914 in a Byzantine style rarely seen in US Catholic churches, the basilica was only completed in 1959.

Across Harewood Road at No.4250 gleam the traditional golden domes of the **Ukrainian Catholic National Shrine of the Holy Family** (1-202 526 3737). Downhill is the ambitious **Pope John Paul II Cultural Center** (3900 Harewood Road, NE, 1-202 635 5400), displaying not only mementos of the beloved pontiff, but also interactive exhibits aiming to bring religious doctrines to life.

Across North Capitol Street is the Armed Forces Retirement Home, founded as Soldiers' Home with booty from the Mexican War. Its pastoral grounds are normally closed to the public, but Cultural Tourism DC's special tours (www.culturaltourismdc.org) occasionally inspect preservation work on the cottage that President Lincoln used as his summer retreat.

Just south of the university is the converted warehouse that is home to **Dance Place** (*see p228*), the city's leading presenter of avant-garde and African dance.

Brookland is a diverse, moderate-income section, with many of its sprawling bungalows converted into convents of Catholic religious orders. Its highlight is the **Franciscan Monastery** (1400 Quincy Street, NE, 1-202 526 6800). It has a glorious mixture of influences: the church is modelled on Hagia Sophia in Istanbul, while beneath is a replica of the catacombs of Rome; the garden's hilly paths connect replicas of religious sites. *See also p90* **Wild at heart**.

Along the west bank of the Anacostia, DC's previously neglected river now enjoying ecological restoration, is the **United States National Arboretum** (*see below*), a 440-acre enclave containing both local and exotic foliage. Near the arboretum is **Mount Olivet Cemetery** (1300 Bladensburg Road, NE, between Montana Avenue and Mount Olivet Road, 1-202 399 3000), final resting place of White House architect James Hoban and of Mary Suratt, who was hanged for her alleged role in Lincoln's assassination. On the New York Avenue side of the arboretum, one brick kiln stands as a reminder of the brickyards that constituted Northeast's first major industry. Anacostia Park follows the river's east bank and contains **Kenilworth Aquatic Gardens** (*see below and p90* **Wild at heart**). Although located near a highway that shares its name, the gardens are a quiet retreat full of aquatic plants, including lilies and lotuses. Now that

Eastern Market. *See p94.*

the Anacostia is getting cleaner, this area attracts all sorts of reptiles, amphibians and water-loving mammals.

Kenilworth Aquatic Gardens

Anacostia Avenue & Douglas Street, NE, at Quarles Street (1-202 426 6905/www.nps.gov/nace/keaq). Deanwood Metro. **Open** 7am-4pm daily. **Admission** free.

Kenilworth Aquatic Gardens is a 12-acre garden with a network of ponds displaying a variety of aquatic plants. A one-armed Civil War veteran started water gardening here as a hobby in 1880; then, in the 1920s, the public – and President Coolidge – began to visit for a stroll. On the northern boundary, a path leads to the Anacostia River. On the southern boundary, a boardwalk leads to vistas of the reviving wetlands. During the week you may have the place to yourself. It's off the beaten track, and shunned by some who assume the low-income neighbourhood at the approach is dangerous.

United States National Arboretum

3501 New York Avenue, NE, entrance at Bladensburg Road & R Street (1-202 245 2726/www.usna. usda.gov). Stadium-Armory Metro then B2 bus. **Open** *Grounds* 8am-5pm daily. *National Bonsai Collection* 10am-3.30pm daily. **Admission** free.

Technically a research division of the Agriculture Department, this haven always has many more trees than people, even on its busiest days during the spring azalea season. Highlights include a boxwood collection, dwarf conifers, an Asian collection, a herb garden and 'herbarium' of dried plants, as well as the National Bonsai Collection, which contains more than 200 trees donated by Japan and is said to be

worth something in the order of $5 million. Also on display, somewhat incongruously, are 22 columns removed from the Capitol's East Front during its 1958 expansion. See the website for details of tours, talks and other events such as the (very popular) full-moon hikes.

Southeast

There's Southeast and then there's 'Southeast'. The latter usually refers not to the whole quadrant but to some of the city's rougher neighbourhoods, across the Anacostia River and far from the centre of town. The Congress Heights and Southern Avenue Green Line stations that opened in early 2001 serve areas of little interest to visitors, who seldom travel beyond Capitol Hill.

Capitol Hill

Map p285

Bounded to the west by the Capitol building and South and North Capitol Streets, to the south by the Southeast Freeway, to the north by H Street, NE, and to the east by 11th Street, this genteel neighbourhood overlays two quadrants – Southeast and Northeast. Since more of it falls into the former, most of it is dealt with here; the northern extremities are covered in Union Station & around (see p72) and Northeast (see p91) and the federal institutions behind the Capitol in The Capitol & around (see p69).

Primarily a residential area of late 19th-century stone and brick townhouses, Capitol Hill is a pleasant area for walking, quieter and more domestic than areas to the west. The businesses along Pennsylvania Avenue, the main drag on this side of the Hill, include many bars and restaurants that attract a youthful, politics-obsessed crowd. There are still a few vintage hangouts such as the **Tune Inn** (331 Pennsylvania Avenue, SE, 1-202 543 2725), which show little evidence of change since VJ Day. The neighbourhood's non-Federal centrepiece is **Eastern Market** (see p94), now complemented by the revived Barracks Row on Eighth Street between Pennsylvania Avenue and M Street. The vicinity's growing restaurant roster offers a dozen cuisines – including Belgian, Salvadorean and Turkish – available without the congestion of Adams Morgan or Dupont Circle.

The Hill is home to many senators and representatives, but they don't tend to be conspicuous. Red-baiting senator Joe McCarthy lived at 20 Third Street, and presidential candidate Gary Hart was resident at 517 Sixth Street when he dared the press to prove him an adulterer. (It promptly did.) Several of the early presidents attended **Christ Church** (620 G Street, SE), built in 1806 and probably the oldest surviving church in the city. **St Mark's Episcopal Church** (corner of Third and A Streets, SE), where President Lyndon Johnson was a frequent worshipper, was built in 1888. St Mark's is renowned for its stained-glass windows, especially the one designed by Louis Comfort Tiffany. The **Ebenezer United Methodist Church** on Fourth and D Streets was built in 1838 and served as the first schoolhouse for blacks in Washington.

Aside from Pennsylvania Avenue itself, the Hill's principal shopping streets are Seventh Street near Eastern Market and Eighth Street just below, featuring speciality food stores, galleries and craft shops. At the end of that commercial strip is the **US Marine Barracks** (Eighth and I Streets, SE), which has been on this site since 1801, although none of its extant buildings is that old. On Friday nights from May to September, an impressive Marine parade drill is held (reservations required; call 1-202 433 6060).

Capitol Hill's largest open space is **Lincoln Park**, which interrupts East Capitol Street (the road that divides Southeast and Northeast) between 11th and 13th Streets. This haven for kids and dog-walkers has a relaxed feel, but its statues commemorate the major trauma of US history. The **Emancipation Monument**, sculpted in 1876, depicting Abraham Lincoln and a newly freed slave, was paid for by contributions from the grateful freedmen. Nearby is a sculpture of African American educator Mary McLeod Bethune, flanked by delighted children. At Seward Square, Fifth and D Streets, a modern church displays a soaring stained-glass J Edgar Hoover memorial window, on the site of the top G-Man's birthplace.

Stately East Capitol Street is mostly residential, but it does contain the **Folger Shakespeare Library** (*see p70*), which has the world's largest collection of the bard's plays and poetry. A bank-turned-residence at No.822 is wrapped in a 'New American landscape'-style garden, with an emphasis on asymmetrical layouts, garden art, and the use of rocks and grasses in preference to grass. At the other end of this axis is the **DC Armory** (2001 East Capitol Street, SE, 1-202 547 9077), headquarters of the DC National Guard but better known as a site for concerts, circuses and the occasional rave. Adjacent is **RFK Stadium** (*see p220*), which straddles Southeast and Northeast; it was built in 1961 for baseball and football, neither of which is now regularly played there. Today it's home to the DC United soccer team and occasional rock shows.

A few blocks south-west of the Stadium-Armory complex is **Congressional Cemetery** (1801 E Street, SE), the resting place of such eminent Washingtonians as photographer Matthew Brady, FBI chief J Edgar Hoover, Choctaw chief Pushmataha

and march composer John Philip Sousa. Look for free guide pamphlets at the gatehouse.

South of the Hill – and separated from it by the Southwest Freeway – is an area that's been largely industrial ever since the **Washington Navy Yard** (*see below*) set up here in 1799. Now the Navy Yard's factories are being brilliantly converted for military office use, principally by the 4,000 employees of the Naval Sea Systems Command, relocated from Arlington. Defence contractors following them are thrusting up their own offices across M Street. The recycled warehouses near the Navy Yard Metro station, lately home to edgy dance clubs such as **Nation** (*see p213*), seem doomed by rapid development, as do some adjacent, trouble-plagued public-housing tracts. Ships are no longer built at the Navy Yard, but guns and weaponry were being manufactured there as recently as the 1991 Gulf War. Navy and Marine museums record the Yard's heritage.

Eastern Market

225 Seventh Street, SE, between C Street & North Carolina Avenue (1-202 544 0083). Eastern Market Metro. **Open** dawn-late afternoon Sat, Sun. *Permanent inside stalls* 10am-6pm Tue-Fri; 8am-6pm Sat; 8am-4pm Sun. **Map** p285 L7.
Of the three remaining structures from the city's 19th-century market system, this is the only one still being used for its original purpose. Constructed in 1873 on the site of a previous market established in 1801, the building holds produce, meat and fish stalls, as well as the popular Market Lunch lunch counter. Artists and craftsmen also sell their work here. The spot is liveliest on Sunday, when a flea market operates outside. *See also p138 and p172.*

Washington Navy Yard

Eleventh & O Street, SE. Navy Yard Metro. **Map** p285 L8.
The US Navy's oldest shore facility was torched by British forces in 1814. Rebuilt, it produced the big guns for American ships in World War II. Post-9/11 restrictions were lifted – partly – in 2004, but visiting involves running a security gauntlet. Located on the base are the Navy Museum (Building 76, 901 M Street, SE, 1-202 433 4882), which has a permanent exhibition on US naval history spanning the period from the Revolutionary War to the present, and the Marine Corps Historical Center (Building 58, 1-202 433 3840), where the top attraction is the flag raised on Mount Suribachi during the battle for the island of Iwo Jima in World War II. For security purposes visits must be arranged in advance: for the Navy Museum, call 1-202 433 6897; for the Historical Center, phone 1-202 433 0731. You can also tour the USS *Barry*, a decommissioned 1960s-vintage destroyer. The Yard is also the site of Quarters 'A', the official residence of the Chief of Naval Operations, the top uniformed post in the US Navy, but that's off-limits.

Anacostia

Across the Anacostia River is a section of Southeast popularly known as Anacostia, although its historic name is 'Uniontown' (and, just to confuse things, some people consider Anacostia to mean the whole area of DC south of the river). It is bordered by the Anacostia River to the west, Suitland Parkway to the south, Good Hope Road to the north and Fort Stanton Park to the east. Anacostia's signatures are the 20-foot (six-metre) 'world's largest chair', erected by a now-defunct furniture outlet at Martin Luther King Avenue and V Street, and St Elizabeth's Hospital (2700 Martin Luther King Avenue, SE). Former psychiatric patients include Ezra Pound; John Hinckley, Reagan's would-be assassin, is a current resident.

The areas south and east of Anacostia contain many of Washington's meanest streets, but also middle-class neighbourhoods of detached homes, mature trees and rolling hills. On top of one of these is **Cedar Hill** (*see below*), home of abolitionist, journalist and diplomat Frederick Douglass. Nearby is the **Anacostia Museum** (*see p112*), which sits on a hill in Fort Stanton Park, one of the numerous open spaces east of the river. The two largest parks are **Anacostia Park**, on the east bank, and **Fort Dupont Park**, which in summer is the site of outdoor jazz and R&B concerts.

Frederick Douglass National Historic Site (Cedar Hill)

1411 W Street, SE, at 14th Street (1-202 426 5961/ www.nps.gov/frdo/freddoug.html). Anacostia Metro then B2 bus. **Open** *mid Oct-mid Apr* 9am-4pm daily. *Mid Apr-mid Oct* 9am-5pm daily. **Admission** $2. **Credit** MC, V.

Built in 1854, this Victorian country house was the home of abolitionist and author Frederick Douglass, who lived here from 1877 until his death in 1895. Born a slave in Maryland, Douglass taught himself to read, founded an abolitionist newspaper and became an adviser to Abraham Lincoln and other presidents. A small visitor centre at the bottom of the hill provides an introduction to Douglass's life and work. The house itself, open for guided tours on the hour, is preserved largely as Douglass left it, and includes his 1,200-volume library as well as gifts from Mary Todd Lincoln, Harriet Beecher Stowe and others. Cedar Hill also provides an excellent view of central Washington.

Southwest

Map p285

Hugely truncated when Virginia took its chunk of DC back, and degraded by a large-scale 1950s 'urban renewal project' that

bulldozed residential areas in favour of office space, the Southwest quadrant is now known mostly for containing the western elbow of the National Mall, cradling the Potomac in its curve. Its primary draws are the museums and federal buildings to the south of the Mall, and the Tidal Basin, which are covered – down to the Eisenhower Freeway – in the Monumental Centre chapter (*see pp62-75*). The debut of the five-star **Mandarin Oriental** hotel in 2004 (*see p43*), plus projects to reconfigure the waterfront, promise to make the Island (as it was once called) less insular. Banneker Circle, capping the L'Enfant Plaza promenade along Tenth Street, affords a sweeping vista of the quarter.

The **East Potomac Park** peninsula sports tennis facilities and a modest golf course. Army engineers dredged Hains Point from malarial mud-flats in the 1880s, creating Washington Channel. Below 14th Street Bridge rests the Cuban-American Friendship Urn presented in 1926.In 1982 an Air Florida jet clipped the bridge after taking off from National Airport during a blizzard. The southbound span is dedicated to Arlan Williams, who drowned rescuing another passenger.

Fishing boats have hawked their catch near the Tidal Basin inlet continuously since 1790, before there was a city. You can still get seafood at the **Fish & Seafood Market** (1-202 686 1068), just south of the Francis Case Memorial Bridge; some vendors will even cook it up for you. The ponderous **Waterfront** development, largely comprising oversized tour-bus restaurants, conceals a lively houseboat colony. Past the tour-boat piers, the promenade climaxes at the willowy memorial to the gentlemen who gave ladies their seats on the *Titanic*'s lifeboats.

Inland, **Wheat Row** (1315-21 Fourth Street, SW) is a curiosity of the 1950s urban renewal programme. Built in 1794, these distinguished residences were incorporated into a modern apartment complex. This theoretical juxtaposition of rich and poor populations did not uniformly foster the envisioned social harmony. **Law House** (1252 Sixth Street), dubbed 'Honeymoon House' in 1796 when its prominent owners moved in, kept the tag, despite their messy celebrity divorce a while later. Nearby, the pioneering theatre company **Arena Stage** (1101 Sixth Street, SW; *see p222*) continues its vital dramatic presence and in-the-round productions; after flirting with relocation elsewhere, the theatre has decided instead to construct a larger premises on its current site. South of the Waterfront is **Fort McNair** (1791), the army's oldest post, no longer open to visitors.

Sightseeing

DC Suburbs

Beyond the District, out to the Beltway.

George Washington Masonic National Memorial. *See p99.*

Virginia

More politically conservative and more socially Southern than Maryland, its neighbour across the Potomac, Virginia was England's first permanent colony in the present USA. A bastion of reaction after Civil War defeat, northern Virginia emerged from the doldrums as DC's suburbs mushroomed after World War II.

Arlington and Alexandria filled out the original District of Columbia diamond from 1800 to 1846, when they retroceded to the Old Dominion, claiming federal neglect, but covertly fearing that Congress might ban slavery in the capital. **Arlington** still seems like part of DC in its character and transport links – as the view of the Pentagon from the Yellow Line Metro bridge over the Potomac, with Arlington Cemetery rising up behind it, reminds you.

A visit to self-consciously quaint **Alexandria**, a restored riverport with a

history that predates the capital (except Georgetown) by half a century, can make a welcome break from all that federal seriousness.

Arlington

Arlington has its martial version of DC's ceremonial core, along the Potomac, centring on Memorial Bridge (1932), decorously connecting Lincoln's monument to the home of Confederate icon Robert E Lee, in symbolic reconciliation of North and South. As the bridge makes landfall among the trees of Columbia Island, home of Lady Bird Johnson Park and Lyndon B Johnson's discreet Memorial Grove, the **Pentagon** (*see p97*) looms to the south and **Arlington National Cemetery** (*see p102*) lies ahead, with **Fort Myer** army base (*see p97*) in its lee.

The cemetery is serene today, and until relatively recently its surroundings were countrified: the Arlington neighbourhood was a semi-rural pocket transformed into solid suburbia only after World War II. As more distant neighbourhoods became fashionable, immigrants replaced many older inhabitants in the ageing housing here: first Latinos, then Vietnamese. Now young professionals rush into costly new condos: the so-called 'smart growth' development along the Metro lines.

The benefit to visitors of this mini melting pot has been a potpourri of inexpensive ethnic eateries along Wilson Boulevard. Lately, many have given way to upscale bars and bistros. A stroll downhill from Clarendon station (on the Orange Line) passes the (bargain) foreign, the funky, and the fashionable eateries in Arlington's thriving nightlife strip.

Rosslyn used to be just a trolley terminal squatting amid seedy bars and pawnshops exiled here by DC's usury regulations. Today it's an over-developed concrete mass, with high buildings alarmingly close to the flight path of National Airport.

Dropping to the south of the cemetery, following the Blue Line round, is the **Pentagon City** development, which contains the ritzy **Fashion Centre at Pentagon City** mall (*see p154*) and, behind it, **Pentagon Row**, home of Arlington's handy new visitors' centre (1301 S Joyce Street, 1-800 677 6267). A two-block walk away (or catch the hotel shuttle bus) is the **Doubletree Hotel**, where the glassed-in circular Skydome lounge bar rotates 360° every hour and provides a lovely view of the Pentagon, Arlington National Cemetery and the city. The **Drug Enforcement Administration Museum** (*see p118*) draws cop-groupies who feel deprived since the FBI cancelled its tours.

One Metro stop later is **Crystal City**, an unremarkable office/apartment development connected by bizarre tunnels, filled with fast-food outlets and shops.

Across Jefferson Davis Highway, **23rd Street** sports an eclectic alternative strip of a dozen moderately priced restaurants, serving almost as many cuisines. On the other side of Crystal City is **Ronald Reagan Washington National Airport** (*see p248*). Its old art moderne main terminal from the 1930s oddly complements an airy north wing capped with 'Jeffersonian' domes. Locals still call the airport National, despite the partisan renaming for the Gipper. Good for views of the city (and its runways), the airport houses the ruins of an 18th-century plantation house, a curiously contemplative place amid the airport's bustle.

In planning a trip to Arlington, note that even though some of its attractions are close together, uncrossable highways and often absent sidewalks make walking between them often impractical. The area is well served by Metro, but you often have to change, so allow lots of time, especially at weekends.

Fort Myer: The Old Guard Museum

Building 249, Sheridan Avenue, at Macomb Street, Fort Myer (1-703 696 6670). Rosslyn Metro then 4A bus. **Open** 9am-4pm Mon-Sat; 1-4pm Sun. **Admission** free.

The army's oldest active infantry regiment, the Old Guard (Third US Infantry) is a spit-and-polish troop dignifying state occasions and funerals at Arlington. They're not just tin soldiers, though, having started in 1784 patrolling the nation's bloody Western frontiers and later fighting in Vietnam. Exhibits at the museum include a video explaining the significance of flags and military ceremony, along with displays on the history of both the unit and the fort. A Civil War bastion, the parade ground nearby was the scene of the world's first fatal aeroplane crash. On 3 September 1908, a demonstration flight killed Lieutenant Thomas Selfridge and seriously injured inventor Orville Wright. The army bought some 'Wright Flyers' nonetheless.

Pentagon

I-395. Pentagon Metro.

The Pentagon is open now only to select groups, but it's an extraordinary sight, even from the outside. Thrown up in an incredible 15 months to meet the demands of World War II, the 34-acre, five-sided, five-storey-high pile may seem the work of a mad numerologist, but it has served well for five decades.

It's still the world's largest government building, and indeed office building, housing up to 25,000 employees along 172 miles (277km) of confusing corridors. Now each thread of the giant screw is being modernised in turn, with plumbing suitable for today's electronic warmaking.

The hijacked plane of 11 September 2001 blasted into a section of the building that was being modernised, which perhaps reduced casualties. The 184 who perished here are to be commemorated in as many metallic benches set in a contemplative copse facing the side of the impact.

Alexandria

Established in 1749 by Scots traders, Alexandria celebrated its 250th anniversary in 1999. This was also the year it marked the bicentennial of the death of its prime homie, George Washington, who surveyed its street layout. Snoozing into slumishness after World War II, its Old Town awoke to its colonial charm first in the 1930s, slept again, then reawoke in the '60s, when neglected warehouses were meticulously restored and vacant warehouses along King Street began to sprout bars, boutiques and antique shops. Commerce now extends 19 blocks from the river to King Street Metro station, and the overall feel is lively yet leisurely.

Revival has had its comic aspects. Cobblestone streets that had survived more from lethargy than historical sensibility have been re-cobbled at vast expense. Then there is the ever-ongoing dispute between householders keen on parking and zoning limitations and merchants anxious to attract and accommodate customers and visitors. Indeed, the town's official tag is 'the fun side of the Potomac'; for more information go to www.funside.com.

'Flounder houses', dwellings with half-gable roofs descending asymmetrically, are characteristic of Alexandria. At least 40 of these anomalies from the 18th and early 19th centuries mingle with standard Georgian neighbours. Newer housing includes at least several dozen neo-flounders as a local signature.

The Civil War indelibly marked this swiftly conquered community; reminders include the Confederate Statue (1888), glowering in the middle of the intersection of South Washington and Prince Streets, its back defiantly turned on the Nation's Capital. The Virginia legislature declared its location 'perpetual and lasting' in 1890. A free map of local war sites is available at the nearby **Lyceum, Alexandria's History Museum** (*see p100*).

Old Town rewards random wanderings, and there are abundant opportunities to eat, drink and shop. Make your first stop the visitors' centre in historic **Ramsay House** (221 King

Street, 1-703 838 4200), which offers guided tours and pamphlets detailing self-guided tours.

Just north, at 121 N Fairfax Street, is the 18th-century **Carlyle House** (*see below*), important in colonial history. Next door, the old Bank of Virginia has been restored for use – as a bank. Across the street is **Gadsby's Tavern Museum** (*see p99*).

George Washington prayed as well as played in Alexandria, attending **Christ Church** (*see below*). He was also a patron of the company of **Friendship Fire House** (*see p99*), west on King Street. From 1792 until the Depression overwhelmed them, Quaker druggist Edward Stabler's family made nostrums for patrons including Washington and Lee. Today the **Stabler-Leadbeater**

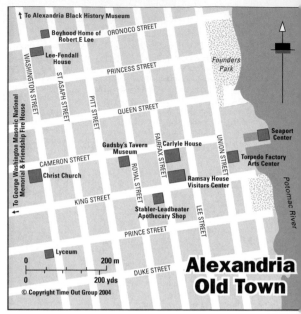

Apothecary Shop on Fairfax Street (*see p100*) appears just as it was when it ceased business in 1933. Further north are **Lee-Fendall House** (*see p99*) and **Alexandria Black History Museum** (formerly the Black History Resource Center; *see below*).

Bordering the Potomac to the east are the **Seaport Center** (*see p100*), preserving Alexandria's seafaring heritage, and, nearby, the **Torpedo Factory Art Center** (*see p100*), where local artists have worked for 30 years. A new glory of the 'Fun Side' is the **Museum of Otolaryngology**, for ear, nose and throat groupies to view antique medical apparatus (1-703 836 4444, www.entnet.org/museum).

Back towards King Street Metro station, Dulany Street is the new home of the **United States Patent & Trademark Museum**; (*see p100*), which moved here from Crystal City, Arlington, as this guide went to press.

Just west of town, a federal camp occupied Shuter's Hill, now crowned by the **George Washington Masonic National Memorial** (*see p99*). Around three miles (five kilometres) further north-west, is **Fort Ward** (*see below*), part of the interconnected 162-fort ring thrown up around the capital in 1861.

Alexandria Black History Museum

638 N Alfred Street, at Wythe Street (1-703 838 4356/http://oha.ci.alexandria.va.us/bhrc). Braddock Road Metro. **Open** 10am-4pm Tue-Sat. **Admission** free.
This museum of Virginia's African American heritage occupies the former Robinson Library, a Jim

Crow institution built to escape racially integrating the Alexandria Public Library (717 Queen Street, 1-703 838 4555), now the city's historical repository.

Carlyle House

121 N Fairfax Street, between King & Cameron Streets (1-703 549 2997). King Street Metro then 29K bus or Dash bus AT2, AT3, AT5, AT7. **Open** 10am-4.30pm Tue-Sat; noon-4.30pm Sun. *Guided tours every half hr.* **Admission** $4; $2 concessions; free under-11s. **No credit cards.**
John Carlyle, a Scottish merchant, built his Scottish-Palladian stone palace here in 1751. General Edward Braddock convened a council of British colonial governors at the house to plot a campaign against French forces squeezing the Crown's claims to the Ohio River Valley. Braddock Road follows the path of his march west, towards Pennsylvania – and disaster.

Christ Church

Cameron & N Washington Streets (1-703 549 1450/ www.historicchristchurch.org). King Street Metro then 29K bus or Dash bus AT2, AT3, AT5, AT7. **Open** 9am-4pm Mon-Sat; 2-4pm Sun. **Admission** free, $5 donation suggested for adults.
Dubbed 'The Church in the Woods' in 1773 , this Anglican house of worship has been in continuous service since. The pew assigned to George Washington, No.15, is preserved in its original high-backed eminence. In January 2004 Archbishop Desmond Tutu ordained his daughter as a priest here.

Fort Ward

4301 West Braddock Road (1-703 838 4848/ http://oha.ci.alexandria.va.us/fortward). King Street Metro then Dash bus AT5. **Open** 9am-5pm Tue-Sat; noon-5pm Sun. **Admission** free; donations accepted.

One of the major posts in Lincoln's belligerent belt-way, Fort Ward retains around 90% of its earthwork walls, and the north-west bastion has been restored to its original state. The site also contains a reconstructed officers' hut with period furnishings and a museum with Civil War exhibits.

Friendship Fire House

107 S Alfred Street, between King & Prince Streets (1-703 838 3891/http://oha.ci.alexandria.va.us/ friendship). King Street Metro then 29K bus or Dash bus AT2, AT3, AT5, AT7. **Open** 10am-4pm Fri, Sat; 1-4pm Sun. **Admission** free.
Formed in 1774, the volunteer fire brigade built this snug station in 1855. Very early hand-drawn engines feature in the displays.

Gadsby's Tavern Museum

134 N Royal Street, between King & Cameron Streets (1-703 838 4242/http://oha.ci.alexandria. va.us/gadsby). King Street Metro then 29K bus or Dash bus AT2, AT3, AT5, AT7. **Open** *Nov-Mar* 11am-4pm Wed-Sat; 1-4pm Sun. *Apr-Oct* 10am-5pm Tue-Sat; 1-5pm Mon, Sun. *Guided tours* every 30mins. **Admission** $4; $2 concessions; free under-11s. **Credit** MC, V.
These two buildings comprise a tavern dating from 1785 and a hotel built in 1792. Towards the end of the 18th century they were joined together and run by Englishman John Gadsby. They soon became a local hot spot, and in 1798 George Washington graced a ball here, the first public celebration of his birthday. The older building preserves the life of a first-rate hostelry of the 18th century. The 'ordinary' next door serves colonial-style food and drink, to the tune of period entertainment. A rare specimen of primitive refrigeration, the ice cellar permitted mint juleps that made steamy summers endurable.

George Washington Masonic National Memorial

101 Callahan Drive, between King & Duke Streets (1-703 683 2007/www.gwmemorial.org). King Street Metro. **Open** 9am-5pm daily. **Guided tours** 9.30am, 11am, 1pm, 2.30pm, 4pm daily. **Admission** free.
Sitting on a hill dominating low-lying Alexandria, the George Washington Masonic National Memorial (which was dedicated in 1932) is unlike the iconic monument on the National Mall in DC. That one is starkly imposing; this one is more laboured, though nonetheless striking. Displaying memorabilia of Washington's activity as a Freemason, including a reconstruction of the lodge hall he frequented, the museum also commemorates later presidents involved with the Brotherhood. Don't miss the huge bronze statue of Washington in the Memorial Hall. The view from the top of the monument (only accessible as part of a guided tour) is impressive.

Lee-Fendall House

614 Oronoco Street, at Washington Street (1-703 548-1789/www.leefendallhouse.org). Braddock Road Metro then 10A, 10B bus or Dash Bus AT2, AT3,

AT4, AT5. **Open** 10am-4pm Tue-Sat; 1-4pm Sun. **Admission** $4; $2 concessions; free under-11s. **No credit cards**.
The aristocratic Lees were quintessential First Families of Virginia – or FFVs. Francis Lightfoot Lee and Richard Henry Lee were the only brothers to sign the Declaration of Independence, while kinsman 'Lighthorse' Harry Lee was a cavalry hero. His son, General Robert E Lee, was a Confederate military genius.
Harry Lee sold the lot on which No.614 is built to the second husband of his mother-in-law; she built the house in 1785, and it was later remodelled to its Federal-period look. In the 20th century fiery United Mine Workers leader John L Lewis bunked here. Lee-Fendall House is open to the public, furnished as it would have been in the mid 1800s.
The Revolution wrecked Harry financially and he was twice jailed for debt. Losing his magnificent plantation, Stratford Hall, he found his family a more modest house at 607 Oronoco Street, then fled to Barbados, ostensibly for his health. He left behind a classic toast to Washington ('first in war, first in peace, first in the hearts of his countrymen'). Long an under-funded museum, the home was controversially sold as a private residence in 2000.
Nearby 609 Washington Street (privately owned) was the home of yet another Lee, Harry's brother Edmund Jennings, Alexandria's mayor in 1814. This 'Lee's Corners' intersection evokes the cosy world of Virginia's old aristocracy.

Christ Church. *See p98.*

Torpedo Factory Art Center.

The Lyceum, Alexandria's History Museum

201 S Washington Street, at Prince Street (1-703 838 4994/http://oha.ci.alexandria.va.us/lyceum). King Street Metro then 29K bus or Dash bus AT2, AT3, AT5, AT7. **Open** 10am-5pm Mon-Sat; 1-5pm Sun. **Admission** free.

In 1839 local culture-vultures built this Greek Revival library-auditorium for debates, concerts and literary soirées. Today it celebrates Alexandria's heritage with changing displays such as local silverware and furniture. An alternative perspective is given at the Alexandria Black History Museum (*see p98*).

Seaport Center

Thompsons Alley, at the Potomac River, north of Torpedo Factory (1-703 549 7078). King Street Metro then 29K bus or Dash bus AT2, AT3, AT5, AT7. **Open** 9am-5pm daily. **Admission** free.

In colonial days Alexandria was briefly the third-largest port in British North America. In recent decades it has embraced its maritime origins, opening access to the Potomac. The Alexandria Seaport Foundation was formed in 1983, and the Swedish schooner *Lindo* was converted into the city's flagship. Rechristened the *Alexandria*, she sank off Cape Hatteras in December 1996. In 1999 the foundation rallied with its floating Seaport Center, with demonstrations of boat-building and other exhibits.

Stabler-Leadbeater Apothecary Shop

105-107 Fairfax Street, at King Street (1-703 836 3713/www.apothecarymuseum.org). King Street Metro then 29K bus or Dash bus AT2, AT3, AT5, AT7. **Open** 10am-4pm Mon-Sat; 1-5pm Sun. **Admission** phone for details. **Credit** AmEx, Disc, MC, V.

Stabler-Leadbeater Apothecary Shop is a time capsule of old-time medications, with modern pharmaceuticals alongside Native American herbals in their original jars. The revival of 'alternative therapies' puts the dated remedies into intriguing perspective. The gift shop sells odd, old collectibles. The museum was closed for renovation as this guide went to press, so check it has reopened before you visit.

Torpedo Factory Art Center

105 N Union Street, at King Street (1-703 838 4565/www.torpedofactory.org). King Street Metro then 29K bus or Dash bus AT2, AT3, AT5, AT7. **Open** 10am-5pm daily. *Guided tours* phone for details. **Admission** free. **Tours** $2; free concessions. **Credit** MC, V.

A World War I munitions plant, the Torpedo Factory now spawns arts, not arms, with three storeys of studios and galleries. Exhibits of the old war work line the lobby, including a signature torpedo. Alexandria Archeology operates a small 'hands-on' museum upstairs, where volunteers and guests help clean and preserve cultural detritus excavated from colonial privies. There are excursion boats and snack vendors on the riverside promenade.

United States Patent & Trademark Museum

400 Dulany Street (1-703 305 8341/www.uspto. gov/web/offices/ac/ahrpa/opa/museum/welcome.html). King Street Metro. **Open** 9am-4pm Mon-Fri; also by appointment. **Admission** free.

This paean to Yankee ingenuity, which moved here from its former home in Crystal City as this guide went to press, is small, witty and surprisingly fun. It celebrates the history of patents granted in the US since Samuel Hopkins received the first one, for a method of making potash, in 1790. Here are charming early samples of everything from folding beds to dental plates. But the champ of gizmos has to be Thomas Edison, who patented a vote-counting device in 1879, followed by 1,092 other handy widgets, including the phonograph and the lightbulb.

Out to the Beltway

Travelled by over 175,000 cars each day, the Capital Beltway (I-495) makes a wide loop around Washington, DC, encompassing the large chunks of Virginia and Maryland that are considered part of the Washington metropolitan area. 'The Beltway' was the catchier term for 'The Circumferential Highway' that planners mapped in the 1950s, then built piecemeal. When the Woodrow Wilson Bridge across the Potomac River finally closed the circle in 1961, the omens were bad. En route to the span's dedication, President Wilson's widow, Edith, suffered a fatal stroke.

Her de facto memorial also developed circulatory problems, such as by the notorious 'Mixing Bowl' at Springfield to the south, a snarl-prone tangle of highways and exit ramps at the intersection of I-395 and the Beltway that's still undergoing massive reconstruction.

I-95 – which joins the Beltway as it swings east around DC – is the major north–south transport corridor of the eastern US, and its double duty as a commuter route makes it especially congested in the Virginia suburbs. The larger eight-lane replacement for the bridge, meanwhile, is rising south of the old span.

Arlington and Old Town Alexandria aside, most of Virginia inside the Beltway is white-bread suburbia. The closer-in 'burbs abound with 'Broyhill Boxes', named for their developer: basic houses with two bedrooms and a den upstairs designed to qualify for federal veterans' housing loans after World War II. The growth of larger development beyond was so neverending that the term 'Fairfaxization', named after Fairfax County (Virginia), is now used to describe generic, featureless suburban sprawl.

In the northern sector (and an easy detour if you're driving to Dulles) is the chic enclave of **McLean**, with its wooded estates (including Bobby and Ethel Kennedy's Hickory Hill) lining Chain Bridge Road.

On the other side of the Georgetown Pike (Route 193) is **Langley**, home of the CIA, which doesn't exactly welcome visitors (you can take the 15K and 15L bus through the compound but you're not allowed to get off in the grounds). The sign designating the renamed George Bush Center for Intelligence – honouring Bush Senior – draws chuckles from cynics.

Further south is the modest early suburb of **Falls Church**, home to sizeable Vietnamese and later Muslim communities. The eponymous church was constructed in 1767 at what even then was a major crossroads and served in the Revolutionary War as a recruitment agency and in the Civil War as a stables.

Maryland

Maryland inside the Beltway contains historic towns dating from British colonial times alongside modern suburban spaces. **Montgomery County** borders the Potomac River across from Virginia on the north-west and moves eastwards around the DC border to **Prince George's County**, which wraps around DC, reuniting with the Potomac to the south-east.

Maryland donated the bulk of the land when the diamond-shaped federal District was formed in 1791. Although its part of the metropolitan area is serviced by the Metro and various bus systems, the easiest way to explore is by car.

The District's original boundaries are marked with boundary stones; one of the original stones was rediscovered in May 1999 by volunteers cleaning up an area overgrown with weeds and

Sightseeing

strewn with garbage, on the exact eastern corner of DC, at Eastern and Southern Avenues, where the District runs into Prince George's County.

Near the bottom of Montgomery County, right next to the Potomac River, **Glen Echo** is a unique combination of history and entertainment. An amusement park from 1899 until 1968, **Glen Echo Park** (7300 MacArthur Boulevard, 1-301 492 6229, www.nps.gov/glec) used to have a swimming pool that could hold 3,000 people. The pool and amusement park are now closed, but the site is administered by the National Park Service. A 1921 carousel with 52 hand-carved animals is open in summer. The art deco Spanish Ballroom has been refurbished and is again one of the premier dance venues in the area, hosting popular swing dances on Saturdays. Frequent folk festivals liven things up and a puppet company and children's theatre operate year-round (*see p184*).

Arlington National Cemetery

The Valhalla of America's heroes, Arlington National Cemetery started out in a gesture of vengeance. Union forces seized the estate of Confederate General Robert E Lee in 1861, appreciating its position commanding the capital. In 1864 the Feds started burying soldiers so close to the Arlington House residence as to render it unsuitable as a home should the Lees ever return, even filling Mrs Lee's rose garden with unknown soldiers. Intending further insult, they opened Freedman's Village here to resettle liberated slaves, also burying them nearby. Only time transformed Arlington into a place of honour. Now it is the right of anyone killed in action in any branch of military service, or who served for 20 years, to be buried here, along with their spouse (the criteria used to be more generous but, with 1,000 World War II veterans dying daily, Arlington faces daunting space problems).

Built in 1802-1816 by Martha Washington's grandson, George Washington Parke Custis, Arlington House seeks gravity in the massive pillars of its portico. Lee married Custis's adopted daughter, Mary Custis (who was Martha's great-granddaughter by her first marriage) in the family parlour in 1831 and lived here thereafter. Now a museum (open 9.30am-4.30pm daily), the house has been restored to its appearance in the Lees' times, featuring several of Custis's pedestrian paintings.

Entranced by the view of the city across the river, President Kennedy murmured: 'I could stay here forever.' Upon his assassination shortly after, his remark was honoured in his

gravesite, just below the house. The simple flame and inscription is still a place of pilgrimage for Americans. Kennedy is buried with his wife, Jacqueline Kennedy Onassis, their son Patrick, and an unnamed stillborn daughter (John Junior was buried at sea); nearby is the simple grave of his brother, Robert, who also died at the hands of an assassin (in 1968).

The other beacon for visitors, in the imposing marble Amphitheater, is the Tomb

Adjoining is the **Clara Barton National Historic Site** (*see p104*), home of the founder of the American Red Cross.

North-east from Glen Echo lies **Bethesda**, whose downtown has a lively array of intriguing restaurants. Despite warnings of naysayers, Montgomery County's draconian ban on smoking hasn't yet killed off the area's after-hours vitality. **Bethesda Metro Center Plaza**, at the central intersection of Old

Georgetown Road and Wisconsin Avenue, hosts dance concerts on Fridays in summer. In winter an ice skating rink is open every day. Bethesda also has promising bookshops, clothing stores and thrift shops (*see p158* **Rich pickings**).

The campus of the **National Institutes of Health**, a medical research dynamo, borders downtown Bethesda on the north. The **National Library of Medicine** offers interactive displays and free tours (1-301 496

Sightseeing

of the Unknowns, erected following World War I, then expanded to include unidentified casualties of other conflicts. In 1998, DNA identification caused removal of the Vietnam representative. Today the Pentagon keeps DNA samples of all troops, making future unknowns unlikely. The changing of the guard on the hour (which takes place every half an hour from April to September, and every hour between October and March) remains moving in its reverent precision, as are occasional wreath-layings by dignitaries at the Tomb and the processions of ordinary funerals elsewhere, with flag-draped caskets borne on horse-drawn caissons to the haunting bugle strains of 'Taps'.

Tombs range from plain white headstones, such as actor Lee Marvin's, to sculpted personal memorials, like that of heavyweight boxing champion Joe Louis (both World War II army veterans), next to it. The Tourmobile route (*see below*) naturally features celebrity sites, but discovery of more obscure heroes rewards the contemplative stroller. There's ex-slave James Parks, born and buried at Arlington; John Clem – the youngest US soldier ever, who entered service as a nine-year-old drummer and retired in 1916 a major-general; Vinnie Ream, a 17-year-old sculptress who managed to have President Lincoln sit for her; detective novelist Dashiell Hammett of *Maltese Falcon* fame; and countless other worthies. Memorials include the mast of the battleship *Maine* (whose explosion in Havana harbour sparked the Spanish-American War), the monument to the Navaho Code Talkers (whose language baffled Japanese codebreakers during World War II), and commemorations of the Iran Rescue Mission and the Space Shuttle Columbia casualties.

At the north end is the Netherlands Carillon, a Dutch gift thanking the US for liberation from the Nazis. Beyond is the US Marines'

Iwo Jima Memorial, a giant recreation of the famous photo of leathernecks raising the flag on Mount Suribachi in the furious 1942 battle.

Opened in 1997, the Women in Military Service to America Memorial (1-800 222 2294) was brilliantly inset behind the decorous (but deteriorating) Main Gate retaining wall to create a light-flooded arch with 16 display niches. At present there are three permanent displays, two dedicated to World War II and one to the Korean War. Notables currently represented on the memorial include Mary Walker, trouser-clad Civil War surgeon, so far the only female recipient of the Congressional Medal of Honor; Sarah Osborne, Revolutionary army cook who survived to be photographed at the age of 104; and Lieutenant Sharon Lane, the only female trooper killed by enemy fire in Vietnam. At the heart is a growing registry of over 200,000 women who served.

Arlington Cemetery's visitors' centre is just past the entrance on Memorial Avenue. Here you can enquire about the location of particular graves or pick up maps here if you prefer to wander the cemetery on foot (pleasant, practicable and somehow appropriate, but note that some of the significant graves are a mile or more uphill). Alternatively, you can buy tickets for the Tourmobile coach circuit ($5.25; $2.50 concessions; *see also p61*). The coach makes brief stops at each major point of interest, but to avoid that cattle-drive feeling, take your time and reboard the subsequent service (tickets are valid).

Arlington National Cemetery

(1-703 695 3250/Tourmobile info 1-703 979 0690/www.arlingtoncemetery.com). Arlington Cemetery Metro. **Open** *Apr-Sept* 8am-7pm daily. *Oct-Mar* 8am-5pm daily. **Admission** free.

7771, www.nlm.nih.gov). Across Wisconsin Avenue rises the tower of Bethesda Naval Medical Center, designed by an amateur architect, a certain Franklin D Roosevelt.

Chevy Chase is bordered by Bethesda in the west, Kensington in the north-west, Silver Spring in the east and the DC/Maryland border in the south. Upscale neighbourhoods surround posh country clubs and Chevy Chase's own mini 'Fifth Avenue' along the stretch of Wisconsin Avenue extending south across the DC border, with stores such as Tiffany and Versace. North of the Beltway, along Connecticut Avenue, **Kensington** harbours lovely Victorian homes and an antiques row centred on Howard Avenue.

Maryland's **Rock Creek Park** follows the meanderings of Rock Creek and joins the national park at the District line, where the greensward continues all the way to the Potomac River. The three-mile (four-and-a-half-kilometre) Maryland section of the park from the Beltway to Boundary Bridge on the DC border has a deep-in-the-woods feeling, far from the city noise and pollution. A paved path attracts hikers, bikers and rollerbladers (*see p215*).

The striking white towers of the **Temple of the Church of Jesus Christ of Latter-Day Saints** are visible through the trees just outside the Beltway. The $15-million temple is sheathed in 173,000 square feet (16,089 square metres) of white marble. The highest of the six gold-plated steel spires supports a gold-leaf statue of Moroni, the Mormon angel and prophet. The temple is closed to non-Mormons, but a visitors' centre (9900 Stoneybrook Drive, off Capitol View Lane, 1-301 587 0144) is open daily.

Neighbouring **Silver Spring** is bouncing back from a declining inner suburb to a trendy enclave with the opening of the headquarters of cable-TV giant Discovery Communications, right by the Metro station with its beloved 'Penguin Rush Hour' mural, an avian depiction of the daily commute. The American Film Institute has restored the Silver Theatre to screen classic cinema (*see p188*).

To the south-east, the East–West Highway (Route 410) turns into Philadelphia Avenue in **Takoma Park**, aka 'The People's Republic', a beguilingly quirky town of regal Victorian houses, modest bungalows, ageing hippies and a self-declared Nuclear Free Zone. Soaring real-estate prices are now threatening its bohemian character. Adventurous counter-culturalists are starting to drift east to Mount Rainier, where US Route 1 crosses the DC line and affordable bungalows cry out for restoration.

Sligo Creek Park runs through Takoma Park, from Silver Spring into Prince George's County. It features miles of scenic hiking and biking on a paved streamside trail.

University Boulevard runs east, from where Takoma Park borders run-down Langley Park, to **College Park**, home of the lately prestigious University of Maryland, one of the nation's first land-grant universities. It is also the location of the world's oldest continuously operating airport, established in 1909 when Wilbur Wright taught military officers to fly the government's first airplane. Post-9/11 restrictions have radically stifled the private plane traffic here. The **College Park Aviation Museum** (1985 Corporal Frank Scott Drive, between US 1 and Kenilworth Avenue, 1-301 864 6029) is open daily. **Archives II** (8601 Adelphi Road, 1-866 272 6272), part of the National Archives, where you can listen to the legendary Watergate tapes, is also in College Park. *See p75*.

West of College Park is **Greenbelt**, an experimental 'new town' for working people planned around green paths and curving drives as part of FDR's New Deal. Ebenezer Howard's 'garden city' concept, embodied in Letchworth and Welwyn in England, was a major inspiration. The original art deco style thrives at the shopping centre and surrounding homes, one of which is preserved as a museum with 1930s furnishings (15 Crescent Road, 1-301 507 6582, www.greenbeltmuseum.org). Just 12 miles (19 kilometres) from downtown DC, **Greenbelt Regional Park** (6565 Greenbelt Road, 1-301 344 3948) is a quiet forest haven with walking trails and camping and picnic facilities.

South of Greenbelt on the Baltimore-Washington Parkway (State Route 295) is the historic port of **Bladensburg**, site of the first hot-air balloon launch in the US, in 1784. The town was near 'dark and bloody duelling grounds', where affairs of honour were pursued until the mid 19th century. An exhibition at the marina recalls the colonial seaport and the British invasion of 1814, along with Anacostia river ecology.

In Landover, **FedEx Field** – formerly Jack Kent Cooke Stadium – was erected in 1997 and is home to the Washington Redskins, DC's NFL football team. Built by the late 'billionaire bully' Redskins owner, the ill-planned, grandiose arena dropped his name when new owners came in after his death. *See p219*.

Clara Barton National Historic Site

5801 Oxford Road, off MacArthur Boulevard (1-301 492 6245/www.nps.gov/clba). Friendship Heights Metro then Ride On bus 29. **Open** 10am-5pm daily. **Admission** free.

Barton, who founded the American Red Cross in 1881, lived here until her death in 1912. The 1891 Victorian house served as a warehouse for Red Cross supplies and as the American Red Cross HQ. The house is furnished as it was during Barton's last years.

Museums

World-class collections and quirky compilations.

Visitors to Washington today will find the mood in the museum community positively buoyant – thanks to a trove of brand-new houses of culture that have set up shop around the city. The hotly anticipated **National Museum of the American Indian**, on the National Mall's east end, completes DC's already impressive museum core by filling one of the last available spots on the famous greensward. The museum's neighbour to the west, the National Air & Space Museum, added its own shiny annex: the impressive **Steven F Udvar-Hazy Center**, in the distant suburb of Chantilly, Virginia, where massive flying craft sprawl inside cavernous exhibition halls. Elsewhere in Washington's downtown, new attractions have sprung up, including the **International Spy Museum** with its fun, undercover kitsch, and the small but glossy **Marian Koshland Science Museum**.

Washington's museums experienced a big dip in attendance after the 9/11 attacks, which devastated the city's tourism. Nowadays, visitor numbers have climbed but museum-goers continue to notice the tragedy's ramifications: security screenings at museum entrances are compulsory, as are the now-ubiquitous stands of concrete barriers guarding Mall museum entrances. Though some security obstacles have been beautified, they remain unwelcome signs of the times.

One thing that has not changed, thankfully, is the city's high-calibre – if safe – exhibitions programme. DC boasts some of the country's best art galleries and museums, housed in buildings designed by renowned architects. Here, museum research departments, libraries and collections of acknowledged genius thrive. That they remain adequately funded to maintain these standards is largely attributable to the city's penchant for pleasing the notoriously conservative government, which controls the purse strings of many institutions (most museums receive a mix of federal and private funding; the Smithsonian is actually owned by the government).

The city's traditionalist bent means you'll find unparalleled selections of well-known masterpieces. Institutional holdings are strong, and important touring exhibitions usually stop at one of the larger art museums in town. The privately funded **National Gallery of Art**

presents a superlative survey of painting and sculpture from the 1300s to the present. Although its 20th-century collections and one-off exhibitions rarely stride the cutting edge, the one-offs prove consistent blockbusters with wide appeal. Meanwhile, the intimately scaled **Phillips Collection** serves up its own mini-blockbusters of Impressionist painting.

But the city's main draw is undoubtedly the **Smithsonian** (*see p113*). You simply cannot visit Washington without bumping into this venerable and unique organisation in some way. The country's largest museum complex, the Institution comprises 15 museums and the National Zoo in DC, plus two museums in New York (the Smithsonian's museums are designated in the listings below by 'S' in parentheses after their name); together, they drew a grand total of 24 million visitors in 2003 – that's down significantly from pre-9/11 levels, but still strong.

Although sometimes overshadowed by the Mall museums, the District's quirkier venues merit attention. The **National Building Museum** devotes itself to bricks and mortar,

The best Museums

For indulging your inner secret agent
International Spy Museum. See p119.

For sumptuous Ming-style furniture and sculptures of Hindu gods
Arthur M Sackler Gallery. See p106.

For unparalleled 20th-century art inside a groovy building
Hirshhorn Museum & Sculpture Garden. See p109.

For a close look at priceless Leonardos and Titians
National Gallery of Art (West Building). See p109.

For an unusual bite to eat
National Museum of the American Indian. See p115.

Sightseeing

Dumbarton Oaks. *See p107.*

the **Textile Museum** to the fibre arts. For those set on seeing the truly unusual, the **Squished Penny Museum** and the **National Museum of Health & Medicine** offer tastes of the silly and the bizarre, respectively.

PRACTICAL INFORMATION

For further museum listings, including temporary exhibitions, consult the *Washington Post* and the free *Washington City Paper*.

Note that on federal holidays, certain museums are closed (though the Smithsonian's buildings shut only on Christmas Day), so ring first to check. Museums may be fully or partially closed at short notice for press conferences and special events – it's always best to phone to check before you turn up. During busy periods you should also consider booking tickets in advance.

Disabled visitors or those with special needs are advised to phone individual museums about facilities. Also, though the US is generally extremely child-friendly, a few museums do not allow children under a certain age.

In terms of specific museums, the **American Art Museum** and the **National Portrait Gallery** – both Smithsonian museums, housed together in the same building – were closed for renovation as this guide went to press, and were scheduled to reopen in 2006 with a striking new

glass-covered courtyard designed by London architect Norman Foster. In the meantime, their collections are circulating in travelling exhibitions and some will rotate into available gallery space at the **Renwick Gallery**.

Fine art

Arthur M Sackler Gallery (S)

1050 Independence Avenue, SW, between 11th & 12th Streets, The Mall & Tidal Basin (1-202 633 4880/www.asia.si.edu). Smithsonian Metro. **Open** *mid June-July* 10am-5.30pm Mon-Wed, Fri-Sun; 10am-8pm Thur. *Aug-mid June* 10am-5.30pm daily. **Admission** free. **Map** p284 J7.

Opened in 1987, the Sackler is seen as the younger, hipper Asian art museum sibling to its neighbour, the Freer Gallery. That's because the Sackler's mandate, unlike the Freer's, allows an active roster of international loan exhibits of ancient through to contemporary Asian art. Connected to the Freer by an underground passageway and sharing its director and administration, the Sackler was built up around a 1,000-piece Asian art gift from Dr Arthur M Sackler, a New York City research physician and medical publisher.

Visitors enter through architects Shepley Bulfinch Richardson and Abbott's first-floor granite pavilion (a similar pavilion, by the same firm, is at the National Museum of African Art). You then head below ground into a maze of overlapping bridges and long passageways that give the feel of an ancient temple, albeit underground. Artefacts on permanent display include pieces from China – such as lacquered tropical hardwood Ming-style furniture (1368-1644) and a late 17th-century Qing dynasty rosewood armchair – and sculpture from South and South-east Asia, including 12th-century Hindu temple sculpture and fifth-century BC Jainist religious figures. The museum recently invigorated its contemporary art programme with an installation by whimsical Japanese artist Yayoi Kusama, who covered the museum's first-floor entrance walls with bright red dots.

Corcoran Museum of Art

500 17th Street, NW, between New York Avenue & E Street, The White House & around (1-202 639 1700/www.corcoran.org). Farragut West Metro. **Open** 10am-5pm Mon, Wed, Fri-Sun; 10am-9pm Thur. **Admission** $6.75; $12 family. Free Mon, after 5pm Thur. **Credit** AmEx, MC, V. **Map** p284 G6.

When District financier William Wilson Corcoran's collection outgrew its original space (now the Renwick Gallery), gallery trustees engaged architect Ernest Flagg to design its current Beaux Arts building, which opened in 1897. Despite a handful of significant bequests that added the minor Renoirs and Pissarros that now grace the wood-panelled Clark Landing, the Corcoran's strength remains its 19th-century American painting collection, featuring landscapes of the American West by Albert

Bierstadt, Frederick Church and Winslow Homer. Church's mammoth oil, *Niagara*, and Bierstadt's *Mount Corcoran* capture Americans' reverence for the natural world.

The museum's 6,000 pieces also include contemporary art, photography, prints, drawings and sculpture. Notable displays include the Evans-Tibbs collection of African American art and drawings by John Singer Sargent. The museum's contemporary collection was recently bolstered by the purchase of husband-and-wife sound artist team Janet Cardiff and George Bures Miller's 'The Paradise Institute', an enclosed multimedia installation recalling a 1940s-era movie theatre, where on-screen characters speak to the artwork's real-life audience: you. The museum is expected to close for 30 months beginning summer 2006, while work on a stunning Frank Gehry-designed addition is carried out.

Dumbarton Oaks Research Library & Collections

1703 32nd Street, NW, between R & S Streets, Georgetown (1-202 339 6401/www.doaks.org). Bus 30, 32, 34, 36. **Open** *Museum* 2-5pm Tue-Sun. *Garden* mid Mar-Oct 2-6pm Tue-Sun. Nov-mid Mar 2-5pm Tue-Sun. **Admission** *Museum* $1. *Garden* $6; $4 concessions. **No credit cards. Map** p281 E4.

Wealthy art connoisseurs Mildred and Robert Woods Bliss purchased the 19th-century Federal-style brick mansion Dumbarton Oaks in 1920. In 1940 they commissioned architects McKim, Mead and White to build an addition, which they filled with their modest-sized collection of Byzantine art. The array of portable, sumptuous Byzantine objects, including rare sixth-century ecclesiastical silver, is one of the world's finest. That same year the Blisses gave the property, collections and a newly endowed research library to Harvard University.

In 1963 the octagonal Philip Johnson-designed wing was completed; today it houses the pre-Columbian collection in galleries encircling a central fountain. Unmissable exhibits include a miraculously preserved Peruvian burial mantle from 400 BC and the grotesque 'Head of a Maize God', originally crafted in AD 775 for a Honduran temple. The 16 acres of flora-filled formal gardens skirting the mansion, the creation of Beatrix Farrand, are also open to the public and worth a wander.

Freer Gallery of Art (S)

Jefferson Drive, SW, at 12th Street, The Mall & Tidal Basin (1-202 633 4880/www.asia.si.edu). Smithsonian Metro. **Open** *mid June-July* 10am-5.30pm Mon-Wed, Fri-Sun; 10am-8pm Thur. *Aug-mid June* 10am-5.30pm daily. **Admission** free. **Map** p284 J7.

When Detroit business magnate Charles Lang Freer (1854-1919) began collecting the works of American painter James McNeill Whistler in the 1880s, the artist encouraged him to collect Asian art while on his travels to the Middle and Far East. Freer did so, amassing neolithic Chinese pottery, Japanese screens and Hindu temple sculpture, along with works by

19th-century American painters. In 1904 he offered his collection to the Smithsonian, which commissioned this dignified, grey granite, Renaissance palazzo-style building from architect Charles Adam Platt to house the collection; it opened in 1923. The collection's mandate precludes any lending of its 26,500-piece holdings, so selections are rotated every six months. Occasional special exhibitions are small but smart: one detailing Japanese tea ceremonies proved a hit. An underground passage connects the Freer to the neighbouring Sackler Gallery.

Hillwood Museum & Gardens

4155 Linnean Avenue, NW, between Tilden & Upton Streets, Upper Northwest (1-202 686 8500/ reservations 1-202 686 5807/www.hillwoodmuseum. org). Van Ness-UDC Metro. **Open** 9.30am-5pm Tue-Sat (reservations required). Admission (reservation deposit) $12; $7-$10 concessions; $5 under-18s. **Credit** AmEx, MC, V.

This stunning house and garden, purchased by cereal heiress Marjorie Merriweather Post in 1955 to house her extensive collection of French and Russian decorative art, reward those willing to trek uptown to this quiet residential neighbourhood. Seduced by Russian culture after living there for 18 months in the 1930s, Post amassed the largest collection of imperial Russian art objects outside that country. Portraits of tsars and tsarinas, palace furnishings and a porcelain service commissioned by Catherine the Great are displayed in Hillwood's

Hirshhorn Sculpture Garden. *See p109.*

gilt and wood-panelled rooms. The French collection includes Sèvres porcelain, 18th-century furniture and Beauvais tapestries.

Visitors can also roam the 12-acre manicured grounds, including a Japanese-style garden with plunging waterfall. Guided evening tours, when offered, are not to be missed: the waning light makes for romantic strolls in the gardens. Demonstrations, talks and other special events complete the programme. Note that you must book in advance for the museum, and that children under the age of six are only allowed in the gardens, not the museum. You can ask for the return of your deposit after your visit, or donate the sum to the museum.

Hirshhorn Museum & Sculpture Garden (S)

Independence Avenue, SW, at Seventh Street, The Mall & Tidal Basin (1-202 633 4674/http:// hirshhorn.si.edu). L'Enfant Plaza Metro. **Open** *July* 10am-5.30pm Mon-Wed, Fri-Sun; 10am-8pm Thur. *Aug-June* 10am-5.30pm daily. **Admission** free. **Map** p285 J7.

This spectacular, aggressively modern cylindrical building by Skidmore, Owings and Merrill enlivens the predominantly neo-classical architecture lining the Mall. The purpose of the structure, which was completed in 1974, was to house self-made Wall Street millionaire Joseph Hirshhorn's collection of 20th-century painting and sculpture. SOM's chief architect, Gordon Bunshaft, has created a three-storey hollow concrete drum supported on four curvilinear piers. In keeping with the modernist tradition, there is no ceremonial entrance, only a utilitarian revolving door (strictly speaking there are two, but usually only one is in use). And now, bowing to post-9/11 security concerns, you'll find a set of barriers incorporated, as stylishly as possible, into the small plaza out front.

The third-floor galleries (with some exhibits on the second floor) present a predominantly chronological survey of international modern art, beginning with American realists such as Edward Hopper through Sigmar Polke's capitalist realism. Particular strengths include a significant Giacometti collection, the largest public collection of works by Thomas Eakins outside the artist's native Philadelphia, and a pair of Willem de Kooning's rare 'door paintings' (the museum boasts the largest public collection of his work in the world).

The museum reserves its basement for rotating installations of contemporary art from its permanent collection, including *At the Hub of Things*, a stunning blue pigment-filled orb by Englishman Anish Kapoor. Second-floor galleries host major travelling exhibitions, many of which are solos of great living artists; recent examples include Scotsman Douglas Gordon and South African William Kentridge. The museum also offers the well-regarded Directions series, spotlighting unusual or cutting-edge artists; past shows have featured Ernesto Neto and Marina Abramovic, for example.

Kreeger Museum

2401 Foxhall Road, NW, between Dexter & W Streets, Upper Northwest (1-202 337 3050/ reservations 1-202 338 3552/www.kreegermuseum. com). D6 bus. **Open** 10am-4pm Sat. *Guided tours* 10am-1.30pm Tue-Fri (reservations required); frequently Sat. **Admission** suggested donation $8; $5 concessions. **Credit** AmEx, MC, V. **Map** p280 C3.

This intimate museum, housed in a spectacular 1967 Philip Johnson-designed travertine home nestled in woods, is best visited on one of its small, 90-minute guided tours. Alternatively, visitors may stop in during the day on Saturday. Either way, it's worth it: The late insurance magnate David Lloyd Kreeger and his wife Carmen amassed a small but striking collection of 180 works by 19th- and 20th-century heavyweights. The museum's scale allows visitors to savour the details of works by Kandinsky, Chagall, Stella and Braque; two rooms showcase Monet's cliffside landscapes. The Kreegers also collected African ceremonial art, and their outdoor sculpture terrace overlooking verdant woodland has bronzes by Henry Moore, Jean Arp and Aristide Maillol. An annual special exhibition augments permanent collection gems. Public transport doesn't take you very close to the museum; it's probably easier to take a cab. Note that children under 12 are only allowed to visit on Saturday afternoons. See the website for details of Open House events.

National Gallery of Art

West Building: Constitution Avenue, between Fourth & Seventh Streets, NW; East Building: Constitution Avenue & Fourth Street, NW, The Mall & Tidal Basin (1-202 737 4215/www.nga.gov). Archives-Navy Memorial, Judiciary Square or Smithsonian Metro. **Open** 10am-5pm Mon-Sat; 11am-6pm Sun. **Admission** free. **Map** p285 J6.

Pittsburgh investment banker and industrialist Andrew Mellon was born the son of a poor Irish immigrant but went on to serve as US Treasury Secretary from 1921-32. In 1941 he presented the National Gallery's West Building as a gift to the nation. Mellon's son, Paul, created the gallery's East Building in 1978. Mellon junior, who had donated over 900 artworks during his lifetime, bequeathed $75 million and 100 paintings – including works by Monet, Renoir and Cézanne – on his death in 1999.

In designing the Tennessee marble West Building, architect John Russell Pope borrowed motifs from the temple architecture of the Roman Pantheon. The white marble stairs at the Constitution Avenue entrance lead to the main-floor rotunda, with its impressive green Italian marble floors and columns around a bubbling fountain encircled by fragrant flora and greenery. On this level, galleries lead off the building's 782ft (238m) longitudinal spine. The ground level houses artificially lit galleries as well as a gift shop and garden court café. An underground concourse has a cafeteria, another shop and a moving walkway that connects the West Building to the skylit, IM Pei-designed East Building.

The West Building's skylit main floor reads like an art history text: masterworks from the 14th to the 19th century pepper practically every gallery. Late medieval Flemish highlights include Jan Van Eyck's *Annunciation* and Rogier van der Weyden's tiny *St George and the Dragon*. Pre- through high-Renaissance Italian works represent a large proportion of the collection. Giotto's seminal *Madonna and Child* hangs here, as does Leonardo da Vinci's almond-eyed portrait of Ginevra de' Benci and Botticelli's *Adoration of the Magi*. Giovanni Bellini and Titian's *Feast of the Gods* commands Gallery 17, to the north of the West Garden Court.

Snaking westwards, galleries mainly devoted to Titian hold his luscious *Venus with a Mirror* and the terrifying *St John the Evangelist on Patmos*. Rembrandt's 1659 self-portrait, with his intent gaze, hangs among 17th-century Dutch and Flemish works, which also include a solid selection of Van Dyck. Goya's portraits of Spanish notables, meanwhile, are showcased nearby. Downstairs, the West Wing sculpture galleries, which occupy the entire northwest quadrant of the building's ground floor, now register 24,000sq ft (2,232sq m) divided into 22 galleries, following a major expansion completed in 2002. More than 900 works are on view, including masterpieces from the Middle Ages to the early 20th century. Visitors entering from the museum's Sixth Street entrance encounter works by Auguste Rodin and Augustus Saint-Gaudens. From there, they move in reverse chronological order from the 19th century to the Middle Ages, with detours into a pair of galleries housing early modern sculpture. Highlights of the collection include Leone Battista Alberti's bronze *Self-Portrait* plaque (c1435); Honoré Daumier's entire bronze sculptural oeuvre, including all 36 of his caricatures of French government officials, and the world's largest collection of Edgar Degas original wax and mixed-media sculptures.

The East Building's triple-height, skylit atrium, usually dominated by Alexander Calder's 32ft by 81ft (9m by 23m) aluminum and steel mobile, will be without its striking attraction until the end of 2005, while the piece is refurbished. The gallery's small but strong collection of 20th-century art includes several must-sees on view in the concourse-level galleries. Don't miss Barnett Newman's minimalist Stations of the Cross, a 15-panel installation of monochromatic paintings that ring the walls of a dedicated room. You'll also want to visit *Angel of History*, Anselm Kiefer's massive, elegiac lead sculpture of a fighter jet – the piece weighs 2,000lb (906kg).

The Micro Gallery, just inside the West Building's main-floor Mall entrance, has 15 individual cubicles with touch-screen colour monitors where visitors can learn more about individual works, movements and artists. There are also thorough explanations of conservation techniques. In addition, you can assemble up to ten works in a 'personal tour', which can then be printed on to a gallery map showing each selection's exact location.

The gallery opened a sculpture garden in 1998 on a six-acre square across Seventh Street from the West Building. Designed by Philadelphia landscape architect Laurie Olin, the garden's circular fountain bubbles in summer, and is transformed into an ice-skating rink in winter. Nestled among the Lebanon cedars and linden trees are Louise Bourgeois' 10ft (3m) bronze cast *Spider*, whose spindly legs span 24ft (7m), Sol LeWitt's 15ft (4m)-high concrete *Four-Sided Pyramid*, and Tony Smith's stout *Moondog*.

National Museum of African Art (S)

950 Independence Avenue, SW, between Seventh & 12th Streets, The Mall & Tidal Basin (1-202 633 4600/www.nmafa.si.edu). Smithsonian Metro. **Open** 10am-5.30pm daily. **Admission** free.
Map p284 J7.

This museum's entrance pavilion, designed by Shepley Bulfinch Richardson and Abbott, lies across the amazing Enid Haupt Garden from its twin, the Sackler. The primary focus of the collection, which opened in 1987, is ancient and contemporary work from sub-Saharan Africa, although it also collects arts from other African areas, including a particularly strong array of royal Benin art. The Point of View gallery is devoted to thematic explorations of objects in the collection, while temporary shows present a wide variety of African visual arts, including sculpture, textiles, ceramics and photos. Recent

National Museum of African Art.

surveys of contemporary art have included some of the finest artists practising today, including South African photographer Zwelethu Mthethwa and Ethiopian-born painter Julie Mehretu.

National Museum of Women in the Arts

1250 New York Avenue, NW, at 13th Street, Downtown (1-202 783 5000/www.nmwa.org). Metro Center Metro. **Open** 10am-5pm Mon-Sat; noon-5pm Sun. **Admission** $8; $6 concessions; free members. **Credit** AmEx, MC, V. **Map** p284 H5.

Though it was founded in 1981 by Wallace and Wilhelmina Holladay to showcase important art by women, the museum didn't occupy its current 70,000sq ft (6,510sq m) Renaissance Revival building (by Waddy Butler Wood) until six years later. The museum provides a survey of art by women from the 1700s to the present. Highlights include Renaissance artist Lavinia Fontana's dynamic *Holy Family with St John* and Frida Kahlo's defiant 1937 self-portrait *Between the Curtains*. Artists Helen Frankenthaler, Camille Claudel and Elisabeth Vigee-LeBrun are also represented. Though it has sometimes been faulted for its touchy-feely programming, the museum of late has offered more sophisticated fare, including Nordic Cool: Hot Women Designers, a survey of Scandinavian women designers from the mid 20th century onwards.

Phillips Collection

1600 21st Street, NW, at Q Street, Dupont Circle (1-202 387 2151/www.phillipscollection.org). Dupont Circle Metro. **Open** 10am-5pm Tue, Wed, Fri, Sat; 10am-8.30pm Thur; noon-7pm (noon-5pm June-Sept) Sun. **Admission** *Sat, Sun & special exhibitions* $8; $6 concessions; free under-18s. *Mon-Fri (permanent collection only)* free; suggested donation equivalent to weekend prices. **Credit** AmEx, MC, V. **Map** p282 G4.

This mansion was opened as a gallery in the 1920s by Marjorie and Duncan Phillips as a memorial to his father. The building was remodelled in the 1960s and underwent further renovation in the '80s, when a modern addition extended its space by almost 20,000sq ft (1,860sq m). Now the museum is undergoing yet another renovation and expansion, adding galleries, an art and technology laboratory and digital holdings database, as well as an auditorium. Central to the expansion is the proposed Center for Studies in Modern Art, which promises to become a centre for art scholarship.The museum's signature painting, Renoir's *Luncheon of the Boating Party*, will return home in 2005 in time for the opening of the new facilities. The mansion remains open during renovation; here, significant Van Gogh oils rub shoulders with Steiglitz prints and there is a solid selection of lesser-known works by Picasso, Bacon, Vuillard and Rothko – that is, if a travelling show hasn't deposed them temporarily. The historical surveys and one-person shows held here tend to be conservative – Impressionists and 20th-century photography, say, or 20th-century standbys such as painter Milton Avery.

National Gallery of Art. *See p109.*

Renwick Gallery of the Smithsonian American Art Museum (S)

17th Street & Pennsylvania Avenue, NW, The White House & around (1-202 633 2850//http://americanart. si.edu/renwick/renwick_about.cfm). Farragut North or Farragut West Metro. **Open** 10am-5.30pm daily. **Admission** free. **Map** p284 G5.

This mansarded building, modelled on the Louvre, was built across from the White House in 1859 by architect James Renwick to house the art collection of financier and philanthropist William Wilson Corcoran. The space soon became too small for the displays, and it changed hands several times before opening in 1972 as the Smithsonian's craft museum. The exhibition of 20th-century American crafts – defined as objects created from materials associated with trades and industries, such as clay, glass, metal and fibre – often showcases striking work. In the mansion's refurbished Grand Salon picture gallery, paintings that exemplify the taste of wealthy late 19th-century collectors hang in gilt frames stacked two and three high; works on view rotate regularly. Temporary exhibitions, which are held downstairs, survey artistic movements or artists; 2004's High Fiber explored how materials such as metal, plastic and glass could be used in weaving and quilting. The Renwick is the only accessible part of the Smithsonian American Art Museum until the latter reopens in 2006.

National Museum of the American Indian. See p115.

History & culture

Anacostia Museum & Center for African American History & Culture (S)

1901 Fort Place, SE, at Martin Luther King Jr Avenue, Anacostia, Southeast (1-202 287 3306/ www.si.edu/anacostia). Anacostia Metro then W2 bus. **Open** 10am-5pm daily. **Admission** free.

Housed in an unprepossessing red-brick building at the top of a hill in the District's historically black Anacostia neighbourhood, this modest museum hosts changing thematic exhibitions spotlighting history, culture and creative expression from an African American perspective. Recent acquisitions include the 19th-century diary of one-time slave Adam Francis Plummer, who wrote of his foiled plan to escape on the Underground Railroad. The Center for African American History & Culture also presents exhibits in the Smithsonian's Arts & Industries Building on the Mall. Free events such as poetry slams help boost the museum's profile.

Black Fashion Museum

2007 Vermont Avenue, NW, between U & V Streets, U Street/14th Street Corridor (1-202 667 0744/ www.bfmdc.org). U Street/African-American Civil War Memorial/Cardozo Metro. **Open** by appointment only 10am-4pm Mon-Wed, Fri, Sat. **Admission** suggested donation $2; $1 concessions. **No credit cards. Map** p282 J3.

Black fashion designer Lois Alexander founded this museum in New York's Harlem neighbourhood in 1979; in 1996 ill health forced her to relocate the collection to this DC townhouse, where her daughter Joyce Bailey now presides. Rotating exhibits in the tiny space spotlight important black fashion designers, many of whose work is in the museum's 5,500-piece collection. The yellow-flowered dress that civil rights icon and seamstress Rosa Parks sewed the day she refused to cede her seat on an Alabama bus to a white man is on permanent display. One past exhibition featured garments made by abolitionist – and seamstress – Sojourner Truth.

Department of the Interior Museum

1849 C Street, NW, between 18th & 19th Streets, The Northwest Rectangle (1-202 208 4743). Farragut West Metro. **Open** 8.30am-4.30pm Mon-Fri. **Admission** free. **Map** p284 G6.

The Department of the Interior's exhibits are a hotchpotch of Indian arts and crafts: Pueblo drums; Apache basketwork; Cheyenne arrows that a soldier plucked from dying buffaloes at Fort Sill Indian Territory (Oklahoma) in 1868. You can also see early land bounties and exhibits about endangered species, complete with shoes made from crocodile skin. The gift shop, one of Washington's best-kept secrets, is over 60 years old and contains wares from 40 Indian tribes, from Navajo folk art to Alaskan ivory. Note that tours are by reservation only and that photo ID is required.

Jewish Historical Society of Greater Washington

701 Third Street, NW, at G Street, Judiciary Square area (1-202 789 0900/www.jhsgw.org). Judiciary Square Metro. **Open** by appointment only. **Admission** suggested donation $3. **Credit** MC, V. **Map** p285 K6.

Exhibits of local Jewish history organised by the Jewish Historical Society occupy the ground floor of this now-landmarked former synagogue – the oldest in Washington. Built in 1876 of red brick, the structure was adopted by the Society in 1960; its sanctuary was restored in the 1970s, preserving the original ark, pine benches, and slender columns that support the women's balcony.

National Building Museum

4401 F Street, NW, between Fourth & Fifth Streets, Judiciary Square area (1-202 272 2448/ www.nbm.org). Judiciary Square Metro. **Open** 10am-5pm Mon-Sat; 11am-5pm Sun. **Admission** suggested donation $5. **Credit** AmEx, MC, V. **Map** p285 J6.

This privately run museum produces smart, note-worthy exhibits focusing on architects and urban design concerns, both contemporary and historical. However, the main attraction is without doubt the building's Italian Renaissance-style Great Hall, with its central fountain and eight colossal 75ft (23m)-high Corinthian columns: visitors crane their necks for a vertiginous glance of the ceiling 15 storeys above. The red-brick building, designed as the US Pension Building, was completed in 1887. One of the permanent exhibitions relates the history of the building; another documents changing architectural styles. The museum shop offers the quirkiest museum buys in town, with all manner of gadgets and gizmos up for grabs.

National Guard Memorial Museum

1 Massachusetts Avenue, NW, at North Capitol Street, Judiciary Square area (1-888 226 4287/ www.ngef.org). Union Station Metro. **Open** 10am-4pm Mon-Fri. **Admission** free. **Map** p285 K6.
From the Jamestown settlement of 1607 to the Iraq War of 2003, local and state militias have won many of America's military laurels, chronicled here

The Smithsonian

Founded by wealthy British chemist and mineralogist James Smithson (1765-1829), who conferred his fortune of $515,169 to the United States government, the Smithsonian Institution was created by an act of Congress in 1846. Smithson requested that it would be an institution promoting research and the dispersal of academic knowledge, nonetheless, his motives for founding it remain unclear: he had never set foot on American soil (save one posthumous journey: he was disinterred from an Italian cemetery in 1904 and relocated to a crypt below the Smithsonian Castle, where he remains).

Architect James Renwick designed the first building, known as the Castle because its combination of late Romanesque and early Gothic styles included signature turrets, on a prime piece of national real estate on the verdant Mall. Completed in 1855, the Castle now serves as the Smithsonian Information Center and administrative hub – and should be the first port of call for any visitor. The Victorian red-brick Arts & Industries Building, designed as the Smithsonian's first hall devoted solely to exhibitions, was added in 1881 (though until recently a venue for rotating exhibitions, the building is closed indefinitely for major renovations). Over the years, collections shown here became large enough to warrant their own buildings. After the creation of the National Zoo in 1890, Congress began the steady erection of museums lining the Mall, beginning with the Museum of Natural History in 1910. From 1923 to 1993, 11 new museums entered the Smithsonian portfolio, most of them holding fine art.

Today the Smithsonian owns more than 140 million objects (plus a further 128 million in its libraries and archive collections), covering everything from ancient Chinese pottery to dinosaurs, Italian Renaissance painting to moon landings, so you're bound to find at least one collection that interests you. Scholars are also attracted to the Institution's extensive research facilities: the

remit of the National Museum of Natural History's 500 scientists and scholars encompasses everything from helping the federal government compile its endangered species lists to researching biodiversity. The Sackler and Freer galleries, meanwhile, house the largest Asian art research library in the US. The Institution's modern art arm, the Hirshhorn Museum & Sculpture Garden, boasts a strong 19th- and 20th-century collection.

INFORMATION

There is one central phone number – 1-202 357 2700 – where you can get information on all the Smithsonian's museums. The website – www.si.edu – is also useful and has links to the individual museums' homepages. All museums are free, open 10am-5.30pm daily (except the Anacostia, which shuts at 5pm) and close only on Christmas Day. Some have extended hours in summer. Many museums get very crowded; the best time to visit is usually just after opening time. Also, don't try to 'do' the Smithsonian in one go – you could easily spend a day at each museum.

Smithsonian Access, a brochure detailing the disabled facilities at the museums, is available at each museum – or call 1-202 786 2942. If you need to arrange special facilities – such as a sign-language interpreter – call the museum two weeks in advance.

From June to August, the Smithsonian's Hirshhorn Museum, Sackler Gallery, Freer Gallery and National Museum of African Art participate in Art Night on the Mall, hosting activities such as concerts, talks and films.

Smithsonian Information Center

Smithsonian Institution Building (The Castle), 1000 Jefferson Drive, SW, between Seventh & 12th Streets, The Mall & Tidal Basin (1-202 357 2700/24hr recorded information 1-202 357 2020/www.si.edu). Smithsonian Metro. **Open** 8.30am-5.30pm daily. **Map** p312 J7.
Opens an hour and a half before the museums to give you time to plan your visit.

Sightseeing

Smithsonian
Anacostia Museum and Center
for African American History and Culture

1901 Fort Place, SE. www.anacostia.si.edu. 202.287.3306
www.anacostia.si.edu. The museum is accessible by Metrorail.

Sculpture by Allen Uzikee Nelson entitled *Real Justice -The Spirit of Thurgood Marshall* is on loan to the museum through 2009. The fifteen-foot iron ancestral sculpture was created in honor of the late supreme court justice Thurgood Marshall. It was dedicated to mark the 50th year commemorating *Brown v. Board of Education* and the end of segregation in public schools.

Photographs by
Steven M. Cummings

through six rooms of displays and memorabilia. Nineteen US presidents served in the Guard or its previous incarnations, including such improbable warriors as Thomas Jefferson and James Madison. George W Bush also features.

National Museum of American History (S)

Constitution Avenue & 14th Street, The Mall & Tidal Basin (1-202 633 1000/www.american history.si.edu). Federal Triangle Metro. **Open** *June-Aug* 10am-6.30pm daily. *Sept-May* 10am-5.30pm daily. **Admission** free. **Map** p284 H6.

Camp dioramas and quirky displays make this a retro-chic haven – for now. The museum began a multi-stage renovation in January 2004 that will refurbish the Military History Hall, create a permanent display site for the restored Star Spangled Banner, and update continuing exhibitions. Phase one should be complete by late 2004; phases two and three between 2006 and 2007. The museum remains open during the project, although selected galleries may close intermittently.

Gems among the museum's permanent collection reflect aspects of American culture both venal and endearing: the lunch counter from Greensboro, North Carolina, where black students staged a sit-in in 1960 protesting segregation; Judy Garland's ruby slippers from *The Wizard of Oz* (which look better on screen, it has to be said). There's also an interesting programme of events, including music performances. Beware the legions of children that descend at weekends and on holidays.

National Museum of the American Indian

Independence Avenue & Fourth Street, SW, The Mall & Tidal Basin (1-202 633 1000/ www.nmai.si.edu). L'Enfant Plaza Metro. **Open** 10am-5.30pm daily. **Admission** free. **Map** p285 J7.

Dedicated to America's colonised, historically abused, indigenous people, the museum marks the final addition to the Mall's museum ring. Occupying a triangle of land across the Mall from the National Gallery and directly east of the Air & Space Museum, the structure was designed by a Native American team; the building is as much a part of the message as the exhibits. The details are stunning: dramatic, Kasota limestone-clad undulating walls resemble a wind-carved mesa; the main entrance plaza plots the star configurations on 28 November 1989, the date federal legislation was introduced to create the museum.

Visitors enter at the dramatic Potomac Hall rotunda, with its soaring 120ft (37m) dome. The museum's permanent collection, exhibited on the third and fourth floors, orbits around thousands of works assembled at the turn of the 20th century by wealthy New Yorker George Gustav Heye, including intricate wood and stone carvings, hides and 18th-century materials from the Great Lakes region. Collections also include a substantial array of items from the Caribbean, Central and South America; highlights include carved jades from the Olmec and Maya and elaborate Amazonian featherwork. Contemporary prints and paintings round out the holdings.

The permanent exhibitions, Our Universes, Our Peoples, and Our Lives, feature segments devoted to cosmology, history and present-day life. Rotating temporary exhibitions augment permanent programming. Interactive technology allows visitors to access in-depth information about each object; a resource centre is open seven days a week. Two theatres screen films and multimedia presentations. And, as an alternative to the standard fries and burgers, the café features Native foods.

For more about the Washington area's Indian heritage, *see p74* **First residents**.

National Museum of American Jewish Military History

1811 R Street, NW, at 18th Street, Dupont Circle (1-202 265 6280/www.nmajmh.org). Dupont Circle Metro. **Open** 9am-5pm Mon-Fri; Sun by appointment. Closed Jewish holidays. **Admission** free. **Map** p282 G4.

This small museum recognises the contributions of American Jews to war efforts. Ongoing exhibits focus on Jewish women's role in the military and the history of Jewish war veterans; a recent temporary show highlighted Jewish American recipients of the Medal of Honor.

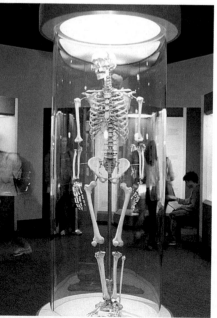

National Museum of Health & Medicine. See p117.

Nooks and crannies

Must-see rooms in DC's finest museums that offer an experience unto themselves.

Dining Room at Hillwood Museum & Gardens

This sumptuous room, covered in 18th-century French oak panels, has hosted some of Washington's most lavish dinner parties. Presided over by cereal heiress Marjorie Merriweather Post, meals here honoured presidents, politicians and visiting dignitaries. Though today the dining table is regularly set with spectacular displays of porcelain, silver and glassware, once a year the fineries are lifted and the gorgeous table uncovered. Spanning 28 feet (8.5 metres) long at its fullest length, the piece features around 70 types of mineral and marble set into its surface in glorious stylised floral motifs. For Hillwood Museum & Gardens, *see p107.*

Music Room at the Phillips Collection

Duncan Phillips's luxuriant 1897 mansion, a welcome escape from the Mall mêlée, holds a special treat: a refined, enveloping Music Room with spectacular oak wainscoting and ceiling coffers. Commissioned by Duncan's parents as an addition to the mansion, the room originally functioned as Duncan and his brother James's recreation room – and a very sophisticated rec room indeed. In 1941 it became a recital space, playing host to Sunday afternoon concerts. Emerging musical talents were often featured here; the room showcased early performances by the likes of Glenn Gould and Jessye Norman. Today the room continues to host Sunday concerts from September to May (*see p207*). For the Phillips Collection, *see p111.*

Peacock Room at the Freer Gallery of Art

An immersive experience transported from the Gilded Age, Whistler's stunning deep green and gilt Peacock Room (*pictured*) was purchased by Detroit business magnate Charles Lang Freer in 1904. The museum's only permanent installation, this 1876-77 dining room was transported wholesale from the London house of British shipowner Frederick R Leyland. Whistler covered the ceiling with gold leaf, overlaid with a peacock feather pattern, gilded the shelving, and finished the wooden shutters with immense

plumed peacocks. His Japonais-style canvas, *The Princess from the Land of Porcelain*, presides over the room. For the Freer Gallery of Art, *see p106.*

Salon Doré at the Corcoran Museum of Art

The 18th-century neo-classical Salon Doré – transported from the Hôtel de Clermont in Paris, complete with gilded and mirrored panelling decorated with garlands, Corinthian pilasters and trophy panels – is a feast for the eyes. Given to the museum by industrialist and US Senator William A Clark, the room was removed from its original location in aristocratic Faubourg St-Germain and brought to New York, where it was installed in Clark's Fifth Avenue mansion. Upon his death in 1925, the Corcoran built a wing to accommodate his sizeable bequest, which opened three years later. Though the room served as a bedroom for its original occupant, the widow of the Marquis de Saissac, it wasn't outfitted to its current gaudy glory until its purchase by Pierre-Gaspard-Marie Grimod, the count of Orsay, in 1768. A man inclined to flashiness, Grimod transformed the ground-floor bedroom into this opulent gem, which he enjoyed until his exile to Germany in the late 1780s. For the Corcoran Museum of Art, *see p106.*

National Museum of Health & Medicine

6900 Georgia Avenue, NW, at Elder Street, Upper Northwest (1-202 782 2200/http://nmhm. washingtondc.museum). Silver Spring Metro then 70, 71 bus/Takoma Park Metro then 52, 53, 54 or K2 bus. **Open** 10am-5.30pm daily. **Admission** free.

Highlights (if you can call them that) at this anatomical museum, which was founded as the Army Medical Museum in 1862, include an assortment of preserved organs, a coal miner's blackened lungs and live leeches bobbing about in a petri dish. The memorable exhibit on medicine during the Civil War includes the bullet that killed Abraham Lincoln, as well as a detailed account of Major General Daniel Sickles' annual visits to his formaldehyde-preserved amputated leg (lost during the Battle of Gettysburg). Among the more recent acquisitions are the latest clotting agents QuikClot and HemCon, both used by the US military during manoeuvres in Iraq and Afghanistan. Although a visit will prove more informative than stomach-churning, it's probably best not to head for dinner immediately afterwards.

National Postal Museum (S)

2 Massachusetts Avenue, NE, at First Street, Union Station & around (1-202 633 5555/www.si.edu/ postal). Union Station Metro. **Open** 10am-5.30pm daily. **Admission** free. **Map** p285 L6.

Audiovisual and interactive presentations in this family-friendly museum detail the invention and history of stamps, the postal service and stamp collecting. The frequent special exhibitions aren't likely to bowl over serious philatelists: one recent show, In the Line of Duty: Dangers, Disasters and Good Deeds, was dedicated to American postal workers. For a bit of fun you can send your own postcard electronically from the museum. Serious scholars, on the other hand, should head to the museum's huge library and research centre.

The Octagon

1799 New York Avenue, NW, at 18th Street, Foggy Bottom (1-202 638 3221/recorded information 1-202 638 3105/www.archfoundation.org/octagon/ index.htm). Farragut North or Farragut West Metro. **Open** 10am-4pm Tue-Sun. **Admission** $5; $3 concessions; free under-6s. **No credit cards.** **Map** p284 G6.

This museum of the American Architectural Foundation hosts occasional exhibitions of art-historical and architectural interest in its Federal-style house. The adjacent American Institute of Architects headquarters also has exhibitions, sometimes linked to the Octagon's. *See also p77.*

Textile Museum

2320 S Street, NW, between 23rd & 24th Streets, Dupont Circle (1-202 667 0441/www.textile museum.org). Dupont Circle Metro. **Open** 10am-5pm Mon-Sat; 1-5pm Sun. **Admission** suggested donation $5. **Credit** AmEx, MC, V. **Map** p282 F4.

This modest museum nestled amid regal town-houses has two permanent exhibitions: the Textile Learning Center describes the history and procedures of textile production, while the Collections Gallery rotates selections of historic rugs and textiles. Recent changing shows have been high-tech, with one about textiles made with digital technology. Every Saturday the museum hosts textile and rug appreciation programmes.

United States Holocaust Memorial Museum

100 Raoul Wallenberg Place, SW, at 14th Street, South of the Mall (1-202 488 0400/www.ushmm. org). Smithsonian Metro. **Open** Apr-mid June 10am-5.30pm Mon, Wed, Fri-Sun; 10am-8pm Tue, Thur. *Mid June-Mar* 10am-5.30pm daily. Closed Yom Kippur. **Admission** free. **Map** p284 H7.

Since its opening in 1993, the Holocaust Museum has attracted legions of visitors to its permanent exhibition, for which timed passes are required (call ahead to reserve; most same-day passes are distributed by 10am). The three-floor exhibition presents a chronological history of the Holocaust from the rise of Hitler and Nazism in the mid 1930s, the forced incarceration of Jews in ghettos and death camps in the early 1940s, through to the Allied liberation and subsequent war-crime trials. Visitors, assigned a Holocaust victim's identity card and biography referred to during their visit, are herded into a dimly lit, steel-clad freight elevator that deposits them into an environment of unparalleled sobriety. Photo- and text-intensive accounts of atrocities unfold dispassionately, but objects and symbols make powerful impressions: thousands of camp victims' shoes piled in a heap personalise the losses.

The building (designed by Pei Cobb Freed) incorporates red brick and slate-grey steel girders and catwalks, echoing death camp architecture; within the permanent exhibition, skylit zones alternate with claustrophobic darkness. Notable artworks include a Richard Serra sculpture and graceful Ellsworth Kelly and Sol LeWitt canvases.

Science & nature

Marian Koshland Science Museum of the National Academy of Sciences

Sixth Street & E Street, NW, Judiciary Square area (1-202 334 1201/www.koshland-science-museum.org). Gallery Place-Chinatown Metro. **Open** 10am-6pm Mon, Wed-Sun. **Admission** $5; $3 concessions. **Credit** MC, V. **Map** p285 J6.

Though modestly sized and featuring only three exhibitions (one permanent and two rotating), this museum, named after immunologist and molecular biologist Marian Koshland (1921-1997), proves something of an eye-opener. State-of-the-art, interactive displays teach visitors by doing, not just showing. You can, for instance, learn how to catch a criminal using DNA, or meet Bessy, a fibre-glass cow who shows how cow… er… emissions contribute to the phenomenon of global warming.

Sightseeing

National Air & Space Museum (S)

*Sixth Street & Independence Avenue, SW, The Mall
& Tidal Basin (1-202 357 2700/www.nasm.si.edu).
L'Enfant Plaza Metro.* **Open** *Sept-May* 10am-5.30pm
daily. **Admission** *Museum* free. *Planetarium* $8.
Credit AmEx, MC, V. **Map** p285 J7.

Opened in 1976, Air & Space tops visitors' to-do list,
year-in, year-out. Even the museum slump after 9/11
barely touched this crowd-pleaser, which still regis-
ters more than nine million visitors a year. The
imposing Tennessee marble modernist block, by
Hellmuth, Obata and Kassabaum, incorporates three
skylit, double-height galleries, which house missiles,
aircraft and space stations. In the central Milestones
of Flight hall, towering US Pershing-II and Soviet
SS-20 nuclear missiles stand next to the popular
moon rock station, where visitors can stroke a lunar
sample acquired on the 1972 Apollo 17 mission. The
1903 Wright Flyer – the first piloted craft to maintain controlled, sustained flight (if only for a few
seconds) – and Charles Lindbergh's *Spirit of St
Louis* are both suspended here.

Permanent exhibitions in the museum detail the
history of jet aviation and satellite communications.
Updates acknowledge contemporary information
technology, but most of the collection's low-tech presentation maintains the quaint optimism of the early
space age. A bevy of hands-on exhibits appeal to
children, who line up to pilot a full-size Cessna aircraft in the How Things Fly exhibit or to walk
through the research lab in the Skylab Space Station.
The Albert Einstein Planetarium offers half-hour
multimedia presentations about stars and outer
space; the Langley Theater shows IMAX films
on air and space flight. After an exhausting mission,
pick up some freeze-dried space food in the gift shop.

The museum's annex, the Steven F Udvar-Hazy
Center, named after its major donor, opened in
Chantilly, Virginia, in December 2003. Its hangar-
like halls hold the restored Enola Gay, the shimmering B-29 that dropped the first atomic bomb, and
the space shuttle Enterprise, among other large-scale
treasures. A shuttle bus service makes a round trip
between the two outposts several times a day (tickets cost $7, and you're strongly advised to book in
advance by calling 1-202 633 4629).

National Museum of Natural History (S)

*Tenth Street & Constitution Avenue, NW, The Mall
& Tidal Basin (1-202 357 2700/www.mnh.si.edu).
Smithsonian Metro.* **Open** *June-Aug* 10am-7.30pm
daily. *Sept-May* 10am-5.30pm daily. **Admission**
free. **Map** p284 J6.

This museum's gem is a state-of-the-art IMAX
cinema and an 80,000sq ft (7,440sq m) brushed-steel
and granite Discovery Center housing a cafeteria
and exhibition space. The rotunda, too, is impressive and is dominated by an eight-ton African elephant. A renovation in the late 1990s added chrome-
and halogen-filled galleries; more recently, in late
2003, the museum's restored west wing opened

its glistening, 25,000sq ft (2,325sq m) Kenneth E
Behring Hall featuring interactive displays alongside 274 taxidermied critters striking dramatic
poses. The gem and mineral collection attracts
gawking spectators, who ring two-deep the (well-
guarded) 45.52-carat cut blue Hope Diamond. The
museum is a real kid-magnet: Dinosaur Hall has an
assortment of fierce-looking dinosaur skeletons and
a 3.4-billion-year-old stromatolite; tarantulas and
other live arthropods ripe for petting inhabit the
Insect Zoo (*see p182* **Creature discomforts**).

Weird & wonderful

Bead Museum & Study Center

*Ground floor, 400 Seventh Street, NW, at D Street,
Penn Quarter (1-202 624 4500/www.beadmuseum
dc.org). Archives-Navy Memorial Metro.* **Open** 11am-
4pm Wed-Sat; 1-4pm Sun; also by appointment.
Admission free; $3 suggested donation. **Credit**
AmEx, MC, V. **Map** p285 J6.

Not just for bauble zealots, this one-room museum
and library dedicated to ornaments and beads hosts
themed shows of international jewellery. The bead
library and learning centre, however, will probably
only really appeal to aficionados.

City Museum of Washington, DC

*801 K Street, NW, between Seventh & Ninth Streets,
Downtown (1-202 383 1800/www.citymuseumdc.org).
Mt Vernon Square/7th St-Convention Center or
Gallery Place-Chinatown Metro.* **Open** 10am-5pm
Tue-Sun. **Admission** $5; $1 concessions. **Credit**
MC, V. **Map** p285 J5.

Housed in the restored Beaux Arts Carnegie Library,
which served as the city's central public library from
1903 to 1970, the Washington Historical Society's
City Museum offers an alternative to the pomp of
Government Town. Its 60,000sq ft (5,580sq m) exhibition space emphasises the local experience in this
historically black city. Visitors hear stories official
tours won't tell you, including residents' outrage at
their lack of voting rights in Congress and their
pride in the jazz and go-go music scenes. Screened
in a spacious theatre, the museum's multimedia presentation is a bit hokey but good fun. Second-floor
galleries host changing exhibits; past ones have
included sports and historic maps of the metropolitan area. A research library is open to scholars and
students, and the Griot Cinema hosts film series.

Drug Enforcement Administration Museum

*700 Army Navy Drive, Pentagon City, Arlington, VA
(1-202 307 3463/www.usdoj.gov/dea/deamuseum).
Pentagon City Metro.* **Open** 10am-4pm Tue-Fri.
Admission free.

This compact exhibition traces the history of drugs
and the law in America, primarily through relics of
20th-century drug culture collected by agents: drug
paraphernalia, narc (cop) disguises, and even a surf-
board with a hollow hull used in an ingenious albeit
unsuccessful 1977 smuggling attempt. Except for

International Spy Museum.

be asked questions later) – you've come to the right spot. Testing your sleuthing abilities, along with gawking at an array of funky spy gadgets, including KGB-issued poison pellet-shooting umbrellas and Germany's Steineck ABC wristwatch camera, adds up to fun for some folks – many of them under 20. Be aware that this is an 'event' museum: expect to be herded in groups and subjected to overhead public addresses at the beginning of your tour. Despite the racket, James Bond junkies will be in heaven – the groovy silver Aston Martin from 1964's *Goldfinger* assumes a central spot on the circuit. Special exhibitions have already included such gripping stuff as Terror in America: 1776 to Today, which displayed fragments of the planes that attacked the World Trade Center on September 11 2001. Not surprisingly, the museum has proved a huge hit since it opened in 2002; consider booking tickets in advance.

Society of the Cincinnati at Anderson House

2118 Massachusetts Avenue, NW, at 21st Street, Dupont Circle (1-202 785 2040). Dupont Circle Metro. **Open** 1-4pm Tue-Sat. **Admission** free. **Map** p282 G4.

Practically unknown to most Washingtonians, this museum, the former residence of American diplomat Larz Anderson III and his wife Isabel, contains works acquired on the couple's many trips to Asia and Europe. Anderson, a direct descendant of a founding member of the Society of the Cincinnati, bequeathed his house to that organisation, which was formed just after the American Revolution with the aim of sharing wealth among bereft army men who had fought for independence (the group included Founding Father George Washington). In 1902 the Andersons hired Boston firm Arthur Little and Herbert Browne to construct the limestone Beaux Arts mansion, and imported Italian artisans to carve and inlay wood and gilt floors and ceilings. Downstairs, a room devoted to rotating historical exhibitions about the American Revolution, and others hung with Japanese screens and wall frescoes, are open to the public. The upstairs rooms, which are only accessible on hourly guided tours, contain numerous bejewelled Chinese semi-precious stone and jade trees and Flemish Renaissance tapestries dating from the late 16th and early 17th centuries.

a kiosk offering messages from DEA officials, the display isn't particularly preachy. A gift shop (open 10am-3.30pm Tue, Thur) sells DEA-branded gear.

Freedom Park

1101 Wilson Boulevard, between Lynn & Nash Streets, Arlington, VA (1-703 284 3544/ www.newseum.org). Rosslyn Metro. **Open** dawn-dusk daily. **Admission** free.

Though the Newseum, the museum devoted to newspapers, is closed while a new building is being constructed in downtown Washington (it's slated to open in early 2007), the outdoor Freedom Park, a plaza dotted with glazed memorials to slain journalists and free-speech advocates, remains open. The dramatic Berlin Wall exhibit features eight pieces from the Cold War relic – the largest display of Wall pieces outside Germany.

International Spy Museum

800 F Street, NW, between 8th & 9th Streets, Penn Quarter (1-202 393 7798/www.spymuseum.org). Gallery Place-Chinatown Metro. **Open** *Mid Apr-mid Aug* 9am-8pm daily. *Mid Aug-Mid Oct* 10am-8pm daily. *Mid Nov-Mid Mar* 10am-6pm daily. Last admission 2hrs before closing. **Admission** $13; $10-$12 concessions; free under-4s, members. **Credit** AmEx, Disc, MC, V. **Map** p285 J6.

If your idea of a fun museum experience includes adopting a cover and memorising your alias's vitals – age, provenance, travel plans and itinerary (you'll

Squished Penny Museum

416 T Street, NW, at Fourth Street, Shaw (1-202 986 5644/www.squished.com). Shaw-Howard Metro. **Open** by appointment only. **Admission** free. **Map** p283 J3.

For the uninitiated, squished pennies are souvenirs made from machines that flatten and imprint pennies with tourist scenes or state mottoes. This museum's wacky proprietors, Pete and Christine, will guide you around their living room, which they've given over to the display of squished pennies. You'll have to call first to make an appointment, but they'll be thrilled to see you.

Sightseeing

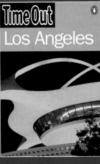

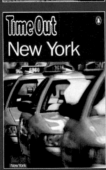

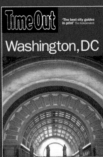

Eat, Drink, Shop

Restaurants & Cafés

Award-winning eateries are the city's bread and butter.

There was a time when dining establishments in Washington, DC traded in steaks for politicians and snooty French cuisine for their Georgetown ladies. That hasn't been true for a while now. In the last decade, the city has grown additional professional interests, new communities and legions of good restaurants. Residents and visitors can still eat their way around the globe. But the new Washington delights in four-star menus and low-key dining spots. In 2004 four of the five chefs short-listed in the Best Mid-Atlantic Chef category of the prestigious James Beard Awards were from DC, including the winner Ann Cashion (of **Cashion's Eat Place**). Furthermore, the Beard Foundation won the respect of late-night hot dog eaters everywhere when they designated **Ben's Chili Bowl** an 'American Classic'.

Good news, too, for suburbanites: DC's appetite has expanded into neighbouring Maryland and Virginia. Here an increasing number of destinations welcome both adventurous and casual diners.

Foggy Bottom

Asian

Kaz Sushi Bistro
1915 I Street, NW, between 19th & 20th Streets (1-202 530 5500/www.kazsushi.com). Farragut West Metro. **Open** 11.30am-2pm, 6-10pm Mon-Fri; 6-10pm Sat. **Main courses** $10-$16 lunch; $12-$20 dinner. **Credit** AmEx, MC, V. **Map** p284 G5.
Sushi king Kazuhiro Okochi made his mark at Sushi-Ko (*see p139*), successfully melding Asian and Western ingredients, before bringing his winning formula here. The sushi is top-notch – the fish is gorgeous and glistening, the rice has a touch of sweetness unlike anywhere else. There's also a bounty of wonderful cooked items, including Asian-style short ribs, ginger-cured duck confit and barbecued eel.

Cafés & coffeehouses

The Bread Line
1751 Pennsylvania Avenue, NW, between 17th & 18th Streets (1-202 822 8900). Farragut West Metro. **Open** 7.30am-3.30pm Mon-Fri. **Credit** AmEx, MC, V. **Map** p284 G5.

From empanadas and focaccia to Chinese pork buns and West African wraps, the Bread Line is the United Nations of sandwiches. Expect local, organic and upscale ingredients: the ham and cheese sandwich, for example, is actually prosciutto and mascarpone with fig jam. True to its name, there is some waiting, but it's worth it, as testified by the loyal crowd – which is as international as the menu.

Contemporary American

Equinox
818 Connecticut Avenue, NW, between H & I Streets (1-202 331 8118/www.equinoxrestaurant.com). Farragut West Metro. **Open** 11.30am-2pm, 5.30-10pm Mon-Fri; 5.30-10.30pm Sat; 5-9pm Sun. **Main courses** $30-$35. **Credit** AmEx, MC, V. **Map** p284 G5.
Once an upstart restaurant with moderate prices and a rising star chef, Equinox is now fully established as a power broker destination run by a

The best Restaurants

For classic Americana
Dogs, burgers, subs, chilli: it's **Ben's Chili Bowl**, *see p134*.

For contemporary cooking
Ann Cashion of **Cashion's Eat Place**, *see p133*, fuses some mighty fine flavours.

For easy living
Sink into an armchair with coffee and a sandwich at **Tryst**, *see p132*.

For Latin cooking
'Neuvo Latino' flavours at **Café Atlantico**, *see p126*.

For shameless romance
By the fire in winter, in the garden in summer, at the **Tabard Inn**, *see p130*.

For Southern comfort
Shrimp, grits and Shenandoah trout at **Vidalia**, *see p124*.

For a vegetarian feast
Find **Nirvana**, *see p123*: the owners sweep the subcontinent for the very best of India.

Eat, Drink, Shop

The spectacular **DC Coast**: seafood with regional influences. *See p124.*

big-time chef, Todd Gray. Prices reflect his rise to fame: entrées are $30 and up, which makes Equinox more of a special-occasion restaurant than an everyday eaterie. A thoughtfully designed tasting menu is always available – it's an interesting way to experience the scope of Gray's cooking, which reflects both his time spent in Italy and his roots in Virginia.

Kinkead's

2000 Pennsylvania Avenue, NW, between 20th & 21st Streets (1-202 296 7700/www.kinkead.com). Foggy Bottom-GWU Metro. **Open** 11.30am-2.30pm, 5.30-10pm Mon-Thur, Sun; 11.30am-2.30pm, 5.30-10.30pm Fri; 5.30-10.30pm Sat. **Main courses** $15-$21 lunch; $24-$32 dinner. **Credit** AmEx, DC, Disc, MC, V. **Map** p284 G5.

Recently renovated, Kinkead's remains popular among the World Bank set and upscale professionals. The bar area is lively, with nightly jazz piano/bass, and roomy enough to accommodate barside nibbling. Although seafood is the menu's focus, the meaty items carry their weight. Oyster lovers, take note: the raw bar gets top marks.

French

Marcel's

2401 Pennsylvania Avenue, NW, between 24th & 25th Streets (1-202 296 1166/www.marcelsdc.com). Foggy Bottom-GWU Metro. **Open** 5.30-10pm Mon-Thur; 5.30-11pm Fri, Sat; 5.30-9.30pm Sun. **Main courses** $13-$28. **Credit** AmEx, DC, MC, V. **Map** p284 F5.

Chef Robert Weidmaier (who named his restaurant after his son) calls his food 'French with a Belgian flair'. Subtle influences are evident in the extensive menu: the entrecôte, for example, is paired with a shallot tarte rather than traditional frites. The dining room is open and spacious, and there's even a limo service to whisk diners to the Kennedy Center by curtain time and back again for dessert and coffee afterwards.

Indian

Bombay Club

815 Connecticut Avenue, NW, between H & I Streets (1-202 659 3727/www.bombayclubdc.com). Farragut West or Farragut North Metro. **Open** 11.30am-2.30pm, 6-10.30pm Mon-Thur; 11.30am-2.30pm, 6-11pm Fri; 6-11pm Sat; 11.30am-2.30pm, 5.30-9pm Sun. **Main courses** $13-$19. **Set brunch** $18.50. **Credit** AmEx, DC, MC, V. **Map** p284 H5.

By far the swankiest Indian restaurant in town, Bombay Club is as famous for its elite setting as it is for its food. Located a block from the White House, it attracts Washington's money- and decision-makers. There's no sense of home-grown ethnic dining here: the aesthetic is British colonial – you can have a Pimm's at the bar or Sunday champagne brunch.

Nirvana

1810 K Street, NW, between 18th & 19th Streets (1-202 223 5043). Farragut West Metro. **Open** 11am-9pm Mon-Thur; 11am-10pm Fri; noon-10pm Sat, Sun. **Main courses** $8-$12. **Credit** AmEx, Disc, MC, V. **Map** p284 G5.

The silk-lined interior belies the budget vegetarian feast at Nirvana. Jain owners Jawahar and Doler Shah opened this oasis for adventurous diners in 2004. The menu spans everything from mild coconut-laced curries to fried peppers stuffed with nuts and cheese that sing with heat. Indeed, the menu is so expansive the Shahs change the optional buffet's theme daily: for example, Tuesdays nod to Gujarat, Fridays to Rajasthan. Great for singles or groups, or if you just fancy popping in for a lassi.

Italian

Galileo

1110 21st Street, NW, between L & M Streets (1-202 293 7191). Farragut North or Farragut West Metro. **Open** 11.30am-2pm, 5.30-10pm Mon-Fri; 5.30-10.30pm Sat; 5.30-10pm Sun. **Main courses** $15-$30. **Set meals** $60/$80. **Credit** AmEx, DC, Disc, MC, V. **Map** p284 G5.

Flagship of chef Roberto Donna, Galileo is famous for pastas and entrées inspired by the chef's native Piedmont, with fine wines – many by the glass – to match. Pasta alone can run as high as $30; the four- or six-course fixed-price menus are, by comparison, a deal. Several nights a week Donna experiments in Laboratorio, his kitchen-within-a-kitchen. The view of the action is peerless, the prices higher too. Shoestringers in the know lunch 'al Bar' on weekdays. Our choice: 'polpetti' (meatballs in ragu) – one pork, one tripe, one bread and one eggplant. A new, lower-priced osteria has recently opened on the premises.

Southern

Vidalia

1990 M Street, NW, between 19th & 20th Streets (1-202 659 1990/www.vidaliadc.com). Dupont Circle Metro. **Open** 11.30am-2.30pm, 5.30-10pm Mon-Thur; 11.30am-2.30pm, 5.30-10.30pm Fri; 5.30-10.30pm Sat; 5.30-10pm Sun. Closed Sun July, Aug. **Main courses** $12-$18 lunch; $18-$29 dinner. **Credit** AmEx, DC, Disc, MC, V. **Map** p284 G5.

Jeffrey Buben's Southern-infused menu has attracted power-lunching Washingtonians to his subterranean dining room for more than ten years. Here, Buben, who also runs French bistro Bis (*see p126*) in Hotel George, reworks staples like shrimp and grits into other-worldly dishes. Look out too for the local specialities such as Chesapeake crab and Shenandoah trout. A word of advice: when offered the lemon chess pie, don't say no. By the way, the upscale spot takes its name from Vidalia onions from Georgia.

Downtown

American

DC Coast

The Tower Building, 1401 K Street, NW, at 14th Street (1-202 216 5988/www.dccoast.com). McPherson Square Metro. **Open** 11.30am-2.30pm, 5.30-10.30pm Mon-Thur; 11.30am-2.30pm, 5.30-11pm Fri; 5.30-11pm Sat. **Main courses** $14-$19 lunch; $16-$28 dinner. **Credit** AmEx, MC, V. **Map** p284 H5.

Latin food at sophisticated and sexy **Ceiba**. *See p125.*

DC Coast remains one of the city's most hotly pursued restaurants. The interior is spectacular (it used to be a bank), with high ceilings, a long, sexy bar off to the side and a grand statue of a mermaid watching over things. Washington veteran Jeff Tunks serves mostly seafood with coastal American influences (hence the restaurant's name). Signature dishes include Chinese-style smoked lobster and chilled Malpeque oysters with iced, vodka-flavoured pickled ginger. Be warned: the prices are high and the scene is very mobile phone-centric. The owners also oversee Latin eaterie Ceiba (*see p125*).

Fish

Oceanaire Seafood Room

1201 F Street, NW, at 12th Street (1-202 347 2277). Metro Center Metro. **Open** 11.30am-3pm, 5-10pm Mon-Thur; 11.30am-3pm, 5-11pm Fri; 5-11pm Sat; 5-9pm Sun. **Main courses** $13-$16. **Credit** AmEx, DC, Disc, MC, V. **Map** p284 H6.
Seafood is given steakhouse treatment in this art deco-styled dining room that feels like a gentlemen's club. The menu changes daily, reflecting availability and seasonality of the goods. Ever tried moonfish? Here's your chance. Or how about the seafood sampler, resplendent with lobster, shrimp, mussels and oysters on the half shell, and big enough for three? Whatever you do, load up on jewels of the sea rather than hold out for dessert, which is served gargantuan-style and feels generic. And be sure to try the fresh horseradish sauce.

Fusion

Butterfield 9

600 14th Street, NW, between F & G Streets (1-202 289 8810/www.butterfield9.com). Metro Center Metro. **Open** 11.30am-2.30pm, 5.30-10pm Mon-Thur; 11.30am-2.30pm, 5.30-11pm Fri; 5.30-11pm Sat; 5.30-10pm Sun. **Main courses** $15-$35. **Credit** AmEx, DC, Disc, MC, V. **Map** p284 H6.
Butterfield 9 is decidedly fusion. Soft banquettes and black-and-white photos set a luxurious stage where food is the star. Chef Arthur Rivaldo's dishes comb America's bounty. From the south comes turtle soup snapping with sherry; from the west, bison hanger steak; from the north, Hudson Valley foie gras and fiddleheads (a rare green). California and Oregon wines are shining partners for all. Tom Cruise has eaten here when in town – it's got that kind of cachet… and price tag.

Latin/Caribbean

Ceiba

701 14th Street, NW, at G Street (1-202 393 3983/ www.ceibarestaurant.com). Metro Center Metro. **Open** 11.30am-2.30pm, 5.30-11pm Mon-Fri; 5.30-11pm Sat. **Main courses** $16-$27. **Credit** AmEx, DC, Disc, MC, V. **Map** p284 H6.

Sexy Ceiba is the latest darling from chef Jeff Tunks (of DC Coast fame). This time, the notes are Latin, elegant and tropical. Cocktails are a must, above all the Pisco Sour and the Batida (made with passion fruit). The menu lends itself to sharing, and groups can easily create a meal from appetisers. The ceviche sampler is a delightful quartet: raw tuna, shrimp, striped bass and grouper 'cooked' in lime juice and chillis on an icy bed. Grilled octopus salad is a knockout, as are the guava-glazed short ribs. Ceiba's good humour is present to the very end, when the bill arrives tucked in a basket of caramel corn.

Mediterranean

Zaytinya

Pepco Building, 701 Ninth Street, NW, at G Street (1-202 638 0800/www.zaytinya.com). Gallery Place-Chinatown Metro. **Open** 11.30am-10pm Mon, Sun; 11.30am-11.30pm Tue-Thur; 11.30am-midnight Fri, Sat. **Main courses** $4-$12. **Credit** AmEx, DC, Disc, MC, V. **Map** p285 J6.
With a chic white interior, this Chinatown hot-spot finds inspiration in Greece, Turkey and Lebanon. Zaytinya is uncommonly good for groups prepared to wait. A 'no reservations' policy keeps things noisy, but once parties are seated, cones of piping hot bread arrive with pomegranate dip, and the fun begins. The menu of 60-plus meze is kind to both vegetarians and carnivores. Our tips? Carrot, apricot and pine-nut fritters or Santorini fava beans to start, followed by braised lamb shank with eggplant purée. Belly dancers shake up the party on Thursdays.

Southern

Capital Q

707 H Street, NW, at Seventh Street (1-202 347 8396). Gallery Place-Chinatown Metro. **Open** 11am-8pm Mon-Thur; 11am-9pm Fri; 11am-11pm Sat. **Main courses** $8-$10. **Credit** ($15 minimum) AmEx, MC, V. **Map** p285 J5.
Texas barbecue in Chinatown? Yessiree! This no-frills stop is honestly priced and friendly as can be. Pick up a tray and choose from dry-smoked brisket, pork ribs wet with sauce, portobello caps hot from the grill, or smoked sausage flown in from Elgin, a small Texas town famous for its butchers. Sides solidify the cook-out vibe: potato salad, mac and cheese, coleslaw, cornbread, and so on. Shiner Bock is the beer to choose. This is no place for wimps.

Georgia Brown's

950 15th Street, NW, between I & K Streets (1-202 393 4499/www.gbrowns.com). McPherson Square Metro. **Open** 11.30am-10.30pm Mon-Thur; 11.30am-11.30pm Fri; 5.30-11.30pm Sat; 10am-2.30pm, 5.30-9pm Sun. **Main courses** $15-$22. **Set brunch** $26.95. **Credit** AmEx, DC, Disc, MC, V. **Map** p284 H5.
Low-country cuisine with modern twists. The fried chicken comes as a traditional platter with greens, cornbread and mashed potatoes, but also in a salad

Eat, Drink, Shop

with pecans, blue cheese, lots of greens and a buttermilk dressing. There are biscuits, sweet tea and grits with shrimp, but gussied up in very downtown digs. Power lunchers, including local sports celebs and politicos, tend to dominate during the day. The bar often buzzes after work with drinkers knocking back a bourbon or two. The Sunday brunch, with all the Southern trimmings, works well for big eaters.

Penn Quarter

Cafés & coffeehouses

Footnotes, A Café
Olsson's Books & Records, 418 Seventh Street, NW, between D & E Streets (1-202 638 7610). Archives-Navy Memorial or Gallery Place-Chinatown Metro. **Open** 9am-8pm Mon-Fri; 10am-8pm Sat; noon-7.30pm Sun. **Credit** AmEx, MC, V. **Map** p285 J6.
One of the last independent bookstores in the area has caught up with its corporate competition and now houses a café in two of its branches. It's a small space with a living-room feel, and makes a great pit-stop while gallery-hopping in the area. The menu is made up of decent salads and sandwiches.
Other locations: Café Matisse 2111 Wilson Boulevard, between North Courthouse Road & North Velton Street, Arlington, VA (1-703 525 4227).

Café Atlantico
405 Eighth Street, NW, at D Street (1-202 393 0812). Archives-Navy Memorial or Gallery Place-Chinatown Metro. **Open** 11.30am-2.30pm, 5-10pm Mon-Thur, Sun; 11.30am-2.30pm, 5-11pm Fri, Sat. **Main courses** $19-$25. **Credit** AmEx, Disc, MC, V. **Map** p285 J6.
The inspiration of chef José Andrés (Jaleo, Zaytinya) is 'neuvo Latino', a collage of New World ingredients, Old World prep, and even Japanese presentation. Sunday's 'Latin dim sum' is a prix-fixe ($34) parade of four courses (each course supported by as many as five smaller courses). Gourmands would be wise to make a reservation at Mini Bar, Andres' six-seat 'laboratory' within the restaurant. Here, his ceaseless sparkle and training at Spain's legendary El Bulli shines nightly.

Mediterranean

Jaleo
480 Seventh Street, NW, at E Street (1-202 628 7949/www.jaleo.com). Gallery Place-Chinatown or Archives Navy-Memorial Metro. **Open** 11.30am-10pm Mon, Sun; 11.30am-11.30pm Tue-Thur; 11.30am-midnight Fri, Sat. **Tapas** $3-$8. **Main courses** $10-$15. **Credit** AmEx, DC, Disc, MC, V. **Map** p285 J6.
With José Andrés (Café Atlantico, Zaytinya) at the helm, Jaleo focuses on tapas: garlic shrimp, chorizo with garlic mash, Catalan spinach with raisins and pine nuts, a Spanish-style Caesar salad with manchego cheese, to name a few. The bar area is often filled with a pre-theatre and after-work crowd enjoying a jug of sangria or a little nibble. Both the downtown and newer Bethesda locations offer reliable food and upbeat energy. The Seventh Street spot features flamenco dancers on Wednesday evenings.
Other locations: 7271 Woodmont Avenue, between Elm Street & Hampden Lane, Bethesda, MD (1-301 913 0003).

Judiciary Square area

Asian

Full Kee
509 H Street, NW, between Fifth & Sixth Streets (1-202 371 2233). Gallery Place-Chinatown Metro. **Open** 11am-1am Mon-Thur, Sun; 11am-3am Fri, Sat. **Main courses** $5-$16. **No credit cards**. **Map** p285 J5.
Full Kee is a throwback to pre-MCI Center Chinatown, to the days before the landlords squeezed out the Chinese business owners to make way for sleek chains trying to capitalise on the sports-fan traffic. The restaurant is rather dank, but the food, especially the soups and stews, is good, cheap and unapologetically authentic. (Yes, dear, that man *is* eating intestine.) Full Kee has no alcohol licence, but you can bring your own beer or wine (no corkage fee). It stays open late, so it's also popular with local chefs who are just getting off work.

French

Bis
Hotel George, 15 E Street, NW, between North Capitol Street & New Jersey Avenue (1-202 661 2700/www.bistrobis.com). Union Station or Judiciary Square Metro. **Open** 7-10am, 11.30am-2.30pm, 5.30-10.30pm daily. **Main courses** $7-$18 brunch; $13-$15 lunch; $17-$22 dinner. **Credit** AmEx, DC, Disc, MC, V. **Map** p285 K6.
Sit at the zinc bar and drink up the atmosphere. Chef Jeffrey Buben (of Southern-style Vidalia, *see p124*) serves up classic bistro fare, including steak-frites, foie gras terrine and an outstanding rôtisserie chicken, which comes out crispy and redolent of garlic and thyme, served with more of those wonderful fries. Soups, which come in huge portions, are also a forte. A hop from Union Station and the Capitol building, Bis is ideal for a special-occasion dinner, a power lunch or for simply taking it all in – Martini in hand – at that gorgeous bar.

Dupont Circle

Asian

City Lights of China
1731 Connecticut Avenue, NW, between R & S Streets (1-202 265 6688/www.citylightsofchina.com). Dupont Circle Metro. **Open** 11.30am-10.30pm Mon-Fri; noon-11pm Sat; noon-10.30pm Sun. **Main courses** $9-$40. **Credit** AmEx, MC, V. **Map** p282 G4.

Eat, Drink, Shop

Get your claws out

Blue crabs are the jewels of the Chesapeake Bay. Sweet and meaty, these nippers define the best of DC's regional cuisine. Crabbers and environmentalists monitor the annual harvest (both groups are eager to sustain this local treasure). The size of summer's harvest determines the price per bushel, but they're never cheap. Each male crab is categorised as small, medium or large. Tip: it's well worth the extra money for the large.

'Picking' crabs is a local sport. Blue crabs are boiled with Old Bay (a spicy mix that also makes a great present for friends at home) and served streaming on to picnic tables covered with layers of plain brown paper. Each diner whacks open the shell and legs with a wooden mallet. The meat is then eaten with bare hands, and washed down with cheap cold beer. **Bethesda Crab House** (4958 Bethesda Avenue, near Woodmond Avenue, 1-301 652 3382, Bethesda Metro), **Dancing Crab** (4611 Wisconsin Avenue, NW, between Brandywine & Chesapeake Roads, 1-202 244 1882, Tenleytown-AU Metro) and **Crisfield Seafood House** (8012 Georgia Avenue, at 13th Street, 1-301 589 1306, Silver Spring Metro) are the liveliest joints to 'pick.'

More so than the beloved 'hard tops', crab cakes are the stars of local menus. These soft, hand-formed patties of crab and modest amounts of herbs, cracker crumbs and mayonnaise appear on casual and upscale menus. Among the best are those taken away from **Market Lunch** (see p138), and those served up at **Johnny's Half Shell** (see p130) and the venerable **Kinkead's** (see p123).

Southerners were once fools for she-crab soup. Now a rarity, this creamy delicacy finished with sherry is on the menu at **Georgia Brown's** (see p125) and **Vidalia** (see p124).

If you're visiting Washington in spring and summer, order soft-shell crabs – those caught moulting. Flash fried and eaten whole, they are as delicious for breakfast at the **Tabard Inn** (see p130) as they are for dinner at **Sushi-Ko** (see p139) or **Kinkead's** (see p123).

For years, this restaurant was a local hangout, known for its consistency and take-out menu, as well as its proximity to shopping and bars. In the spring of 2004, City Lights expanded, adding a brightly lit sushi bar. It's basically a decent place for a beer and a quick, westernised Chinese meal (all the usual faves – spare ribs, shrimp tempura, hot and sour soup).

Sushi Taro

1503 17th Street, NW, at P Street (1-202 462 8999/www.sushitaro.com). Dupont Circle Metro. **Open** 11.30am-2pm, 5.30-10pm Mon-Thur; 11.30am-2pm, 5.30-10.30pm Fri; 5.30-10.30pm Sat. **Main courses** $7-$45. **Credit** AmEx, DC, Disc, MC, V. **Map** p282 G4.

With its open sushi bar and kitchen located right near the entrance, Sushi Taro is always busy – and a favourite with visiting Japanese journalists. In fact, kimono-clad servers are sometimes so rushed off their feet with larger groups that they forget the single diner. Perks include a hot towel as you're seated and a dish of edamame (boiled, salted soybeans – not everyone's cup of tea) to snack on while you wait for dinner to arrive. The extensive menu includes specialities such as lobster sashimi and home-made ginger, green tea and sweet bean ice-cream.

Thaiphoon

2011 S Street, NW, between 20th Street & Connecticut Avenue (1-202 667 3505/www. thaiphoon.com). Dupont Circle Metro. **Open** 11.30am-10.30pm Mon-Thur, Sun; 11.30am-11pm Fri, Sat. **Main courses** $9-$12. **Credit** MC, V. **Map** p282 G4.

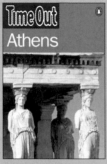

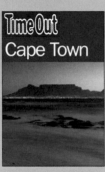

Shiny stainless steel and a striking front window invite you to be part of the buzz at this bright, bustling place, even during off hours. The menu is lengthy, covering many Thai classics, from papaya salad to fish steamed in banana leaves; the presentation is pretty and the flavours freshly assertive. Try the Thai iced coffee for dessert. Vegetarians are well fed here.
Other locations: Pentagon City, 1301 South Joyce Street, Arlington, VA (1-703 413 8200).

Cafés & coffeehouses

Cosi
1350 Connecticut Avenue, NW, between N Street & Dupont Circle (1-202 296 9341). Dupont Circle Metro. **Open** 6.30am-1am Mon-Thur, Sun; 6.30am-2am Fri, Sat. **Credit** AmEx, MC, V. **Map** p282 G4.
A step up from wham-bam-thank-you-ma'am Starbucks, this Connecticut-based company (formerly Xando) is spreading rapidly across the East Coast with its coffee bar/lounge concept. In the morning you can queue to get your java and a pastry (hit or miss) to go; if it's booze you're after, you'll have to wait till 4pm. There are lots of bright sofas and groovy outdoor seating. Big on coffee cocktails, the menu also features play food such as s'mores (complete with your own at-table hibachi for proper marshmallow toasting). It's loud, it's young and it's always jammed.
Other locations: throughout the city.

Teaism
2009 R Street, NW, at Connecticut Avenue (1-202 667 3827/www.teaism.com). Dupont Circle Metro. **Open** 8am-10pm Mon-Thur; 8am-11pm Fri; 9am-11pm Sat; 9am-10pm Sun. **Credit** AmEx, MC, V. **Map** p282 G4.
Freshly baked nan, oat cookies and Thai chicken curry are on offer at this café-style oasis from the bustle of urban living. After a cup of chai or a bento box, you'll feel ready to pound the pavement once again. The spacious Eighth Street branch lends more of a calming vibration, with its downstairs hideout. Check the website for details of open-mic poetry nights, and art and photo exhibitions.
Other locations: 800 Connecticut Avenue, NW, at H Street, Downtown (1-202 835 2233); 400 Eighth Street, NW, at D Street, Penn Quarter (1-202 638 6010).

Contemporary American

Komi
1509 17th Street, NW, between P & Q Streets (1-202 332 9200). Dupont Circle Metro. **Open** 11.30am-3pm, 5.30-10pm Mon-Thur; 11.30am-3pm, 5.30-11pm Fri, Sat. **Main courses** $10-$17. **Credit** AmEx, MC, V. **Map** p282 G4.
Komi is a twentysomething operation. From chef Johnny Monis to his partners and waitstaff, everyone looks fresh out of university or home from a trip backpacking around the world. The ever-present

Night bites
Top five

Ben's Chili Bowl
Fill up on chilli dogs and fixings at this famous diner until 2am Mon-Thur, and 4am Fri, Sat. *See p134.*

The Diner
Non-stop, round-the-clock staples (plus more adventurous fare) at this popular Adams Morgan spot. *See p131.*

Kramerbooks & Afterwords Café & Grill
This low-key DC stalwart doesn't shut up shop till 1am Mon-Thur, and stays open continuously from Friday morning till 1am Monday. *See p129.*

Leftbank
The laptop crowd come here for sushi, coffee and other modern goodies until 2am Mon-Thur, Sun, and 3am Fri, Sat. *See p131.*

Quick Pita
Does exactly what its name suggests, in a tiny space, until 3am Mon-Wed, Sun, and 4.30am Thur-Sat. *See p137.*

youth brings a vitality and a passion unique to Washington restaurants; the staff is so excited to tell you about an Australian cheese or a dessert wine they'll bring samples to taste. Little touches include an amuse-bouche, a basket of home-made breads and lollipops (yes, they make their own lollipops) given with the bill. The walls may be bare but they're a great balance for the top-notch, Italian-inspired food. The wine list is one of the more interesting in town.

Kramerbooks & Afterwords Café & Grill
1517 Connecticut Avenue, NW, at Q Street (1-202 387 1462/www.kramers.com). Dupont Circle Metro. **Open** 7.30am-1am Mon-Thur; 7.30am Fri-1am Mon continuously. **Main courses** $9-$15. **Credit** AmEx, Disc, MC, V. **Map** p282 G4.
The restaurant/bar part of the famed independent Kramerbooks (*see p159*), Afterwords remains a staple of Washington downtowners in search of a quick nosh, a couple of beers or an easy place to recharge after a long day. Chef Pete Barich is always looking to make his menu a conversation piece, with themes and quirky names of dishes. To wit: the 'sharezies', small dishes of which you pick three, then served on a three-tiered tower. Otherwise, go for pasta, salads, noodles, or kick off your Sunday with brunch fit for a king.

One of a kind: **Tabard Inn**.

Tabard Inn
1739 N Street, NW, between 17th & 18th Streets (1-202 833 2668/www.tabardinn.com). Dupont Circle Metro. **Open** 7-10am, 11.30am-2.30pm, 6-10pm Mon-Thur; 7-10am, 11.30am-2.30pm, 6-10.30pm Fri; 8-10am, 11am-2.30pm, 6-10.30pm Sat; 8-9.30am, 10.30am-2.30pm, 6-10pm Sun. **Main courses** $3-$8 breakfast; $5-$15 brunch; $9-$15 lunch; $18-$28 dinner. **Credit** AmEx, DC, MC, V. **Map** p282 G4.
Tucked at the back of a 19th-century brownstone, home for the last 25 years to a family-run hotel (*see p56*), the Tabard is an eclectic and shamelessly romantic destination. Dine in the lounge in front of the fireplace, in the garden under the shade of a silk parachute, or in the private dining room. The menu favours crisp and local ingredients: fried oysters top a salad of corn and baby spinach. Salmon and trout, both house-smoked, are an excellent standby. Sunday's crowds brunch on just-made doughnuts and eggs Benedict.

Fish

Johnny's Half Shell
2002 P Street, NW, at 20th Street (1-202 296 2021). Dupont Circle Metro. **Open** 11.30am-10.30pm Mon-Thur; 11.30am-11pm Fri, Sat. **Main courses** $9-$18. **Credit** AmEx, MC, V. **Map** p282 G4.
The second venture for Cashion's Eat Place partners Ann Cashion and John Fulchino, Johnny's is an East-Coast style seafood house that's looser around the collar than its more elegant sister in Adams Morgan. Traditional touches include the black-and-white tiled floor, the marble bar and the white-coated servers. But this is no stuffy place – fun, noisy and neighbourly, Johnny's offers up an unfussy sampler of raw and cooked seafood, from oysters on the half shell and garlicky roasted clams to shimmery bay scallops and pan-roasted cod. The po boy sarnies are legendary. Reservations not taken.

Greek

Mourayo
1732 Connecticut Avenue, NW, between R & S Streets (1-202 667 2100). Dupont Circle Metro. **Open** noon-3pm, 5.30-10.30pm Mon-Thur; noon-3pm, 5.30-11pm Fri; 5.30-11pm Sat; 5.30-10pm Sun. **Main courses** $13-$22. **Credit** AmEx, MC, V. **Map** p282 G4.
The message here is clear: eat from the sea. Long white walls are dotted with portholes, and servers wear sailors' uniforms. Happily, the gimmicks end. A whole grilled snapper wrapped with herbs and infused with lemon, and a bottle of young white wine, is a feast for two or three. Shrimp sautéed in a tomato and feta purée is popular; less so, but no less delicious, is the squid-ink soup. Roast lamb and feta triangles in home-made filo pastry is another moreish dish.

Italian

Obelisk
2029 P Street, NW, between 20th & 21st Streets (1-202 872 1180). Dupont Circle Metro. **Open** 6-10pm Tue-Sat. **Set dinner** $58. **Credit** DC, MC, V. **Map** p282 G4.
Chef Peter Pastan owns this prix-fixe-only trattoria as well as 2 Amys (*see p140*) but it's here that his purist sensibilities really shine. With just 12 tables (reservations are essential), the kitchen is able to focus on the night's four-course offering. Pastan, who makes his own butter, vinegar and bread sticks, highlights various regions of Italy. Pasta with nettles, skate in brown butter, and goat cheese quenelles will all blow your mind. Ladies, if possible, sneak a peek of the prints inside the men's room.

Pizzeria Paradiso
2029 P Street, NW, between 20th & 21st Streets (1-202 223 1245). Dupont Circle Metro. **Open** 11.30am-11pm Mon-Thur; 11.30am-midnight Fri; 11am-midnight Sat; noon-10pm Sun. **Main courses** $7-$14. **Credit** DC, MC, V. **Map** p282 G4.
Good quality, wood-oven pizza that keeps locals coming back for more. Expect to wait for a table, even at the larger Georgetown location. The salad of white beans and tuna, plus the antipasto plate of salami and Italian cheeses, are worth considering if pizza is not your thing. But do try the effervescent lemonade. All in all, a fun excursion. **Other locations:** 3282 M Street, NW, between Potomac & 33rd Streets, Georgetown (1-202 337 1245).

Latin/Caribbean

Lauriol Plaza
1835 18th Street, NW, at T Street (1-202 387 0035/ www.lauriolplaza.com). Dupont Circle Metro. **Open** 11.30am-11pm Mon-Thur, Sun; 11.30am-midnight Fri, Sat. **Main courses** $6.50-$15.95 brunch; $6-$17 dinner. **Credit** AmEx, DC, Disc, MC, V. **Map** p282 G3.
With a capacity for up to 350 diners in its two storeys (plus rooftop), the joint is jumping at Lauriol. Food is reasonably priced Spanish/Central American/Caribbean fare. From Margaritas and chips and salsa, to savoury tamales and frijoles negros, there's a little of everything for the Latin food fan. Sunday brunch is cheap, good and popular.

Adams Morgan

American

Asylum
2471 18th Street, NW, at Columbia Road (1-202 319 9353/www.asylumdc.com). Dupont Circle Metro then 42 bus or Woodley Park-Zoo/Adams Morgan Metro. **Open** 5pm-2am Mon-Thur; 5pm-3am Fri; 11am-3am Sat; noon-5pm Sun. **Main courses** $5-$9. **Credit** AmEx, MC, V. **Map** p282 G2.
Dark as a dungeon and staffed by friendly punks, Asylum is awash with absurdities. The roses on the table are dead, the sword on the wall is a rubber facsimile. But any place whose 'mission statement' is 'to have a fuckin' good time' gets our vote. The kitchen serves a damn fine burger and the city's best vegan brunch (noon-5pm Sun) at prices low enough to attract bikers and young journalists. Great for late-night feasts.

The Diner
2453 18th Street, NW, between Kalorama & Columbia Roads (1-202 232 8800). Dupont Circle Metro then 42 bus or Woodley Park-Zoo/Adams Morgan Metro. **Open** 24hrs daily. **Main courses** $5-$18. **Credit** MC, V. **Map** p282 G3.
The Diner is brought to you by the same folks who own coffee lounge Tryst *(see p132)* just two doors away. Open round the clock, this joint is constantly packed with neighbourhood hipsters and night owls. True to its name, there's home-style chow (and more), but we don't think it's the food that keeps people going back for more. It's those long counters, great for flirting, sipping coffee and playing with your food behind the Sunday paper.

Leftbank
2424 18th Street, NW, between Belmont & Columbia Roads (1-202 464 2100). Dupont Circle Metro then 42 bus or Woodley Park-Zoo/Adams Morgan Metro. **Open** 7am-2am Mon-Thur, Sun; 7am-3am Fri, Sat. **Main courses** $4-$18. **Credit** AmEx, Disc, MC, V. **Map** p282 G3.

Eat, Drink, Shop

A relaxed atmosphere, with traditional touches. Seafood at **Johnny's Half Shell**. *See p130.*

Nothing beats Latin eats

Latin Americans are the fastest-growing ethnic group in Washington. Their influence is indelible on the city's nightlife: locals flock to Spanish-language plays at Gala Hispanic Theatre (*see p227*) and movies at Visions (*see p187*); later, enlivened by Caipirinhas and Mojitos, they dance to salsa and bossa nova. Their presence has given rise to myriad Latin restaurants.

Street food runs from authentic to the Disney-fied. **Julia's Empanadas** (*see p133*) serves savoury pockets until the wee hours at four area locations. In our opinion, the Chilean-style (beef, raisins and green olives) and curried Jamaican versions are better than the doughier vegetarian options. **Chipotle Mexican Grill** (*see p140*), a national chain studding the metro area, rolls burritos the size of logs to order. The *carnitas* comprises pork perfumed with bay leaves; the *barbacoa* is beef with *adobo* and cloves; both are far superior to other fast food.

A seated feast can be had for a song at **MixTec** (1792 Columbia Road, NW, near 18th Street, 1-202 332 1011) in Adams Morgan. This is the real deal – chips and salsa do not come to the table. Rather, brave diners start with *menudo* (tripe soup), the rest of us tuck into tacos – *al carbón* (grilled beef) or *al pastor* (grilled pork) – with a side of charred spring onions. Add in a *lícuidos* (fruit juice), and dinner for two hovers around $20. **Austin Grill** (*see p141*) serves Tex-Mex standards with endless chips and salsa at equally modest prices.

The size of a car dealership, Dupont Circle's **Lauriol Plaza** (*see p131*) easily caters to 800 diners a night. On the Hill, the **Banana Café & Piano Bar** (*see p138*) serves a fraction of that number in punch-coloured rooms with live piano music. Regardless, neighbours pack both for frozen Margaritas (order a pink and white swirl) and Tex-Mex standards (though visitors would be better off listening to their server and ordering from the specials – dishes like Lauriol's cubes of pork roasted with bitter Seville oranges).

In 2003 two upscale Latin restaurants opened in DC's downtown core. A New York transplant, **Rosa Mexicano** (575 Seventh Street, NW, at F Street, Downtown, 1-202 783 5522), shimmers across the street from the MCI Center. The decor is a knock out: orange butterfies shimmer against azure tiles as a wall of water flows between the two. The food disappoints. The house cocktail, a pomegranate Margarita, is a sweet pink shiver. Salads wilt as if overwhelmed by the surrounding activity. Subtle and adult, **Ceiba** (*see p125*) has more charm and far superior food. The pan-Latin menu stretches from Cuba's black bean soup to a thin Argentine steak splashed with green chimichurri (a garlicky coriander sauce).

Café Atlantico (*see p126*) is the most deserving upscale Latin destination. As at Rosa Mexicano, Atlantico 'performs' guacamole tableside, an excellent start. All similarities end there, though. The inspiration of chef José Andrés – trained at Spain's legendary El Bullí – is 'neuvo Latino', an eclectic, contemporary mix of ingredients and preparation styles. The result, fantastic food.

From the outset, Leftbank was keen to wrestle the all-night crown from the Diner. The cavernous space arrived in the spring of 2003 fully loaded with every yuppie trick: Wi-Fi, mammoth espresso machines, a sushi counter. With a menu divided by 'garden', 'farm' and 'ocean', the likes of minute steaks, protein shakes, raspberry croissants and lobster-filled pasta are always available. Sink into an orange banquette or meet the locals (young, old, gay, straight) at a communal table.

Café & coffeehouses

So's Your Mom

1831 Columbia Road, NW, between Biltmore Street & Mintwood Place (1-202 462 3666). Dupont Circle Metro then 42 bus or Woodley Park-Zoo/Adams Morgan Metro then 90, 92, 93, L2 bus. **Open** *7am-8pm Mon-Fri; 8am-7pm Sat; 8am-3pm Sun.* **Main courses** *$4-$7.* **No credit cards. Map** *p282 G3.*
Meats and cheeses, cold drinks, gourmet potato chips and newspapers are the order of the sunny day at Mom's. The lox and white-fish are bagel-ready; tongue sandwiches lend an old-world charm. The sweet deals start early: 'Breakfast in a bag' (strong coffee, fresh OJ and a bagel) will start you up for the day. It may be a simple deli, but it's got spirit.

Tryst

2459 18th Street, NW, between Belmont & Columbia Roads (1-202 232 5500). Dupont Circle Metro then 42 bus, or Woodley Park-Zoo/Adams Morgan Metro then 90, 92, 93, L2 bus. **Open** *6.30am-2am Mon-Thur; 6.30am-3am Fri, Sat; 8am-2am Sun.* **Credit** *AmEx, Disc, MC, V.* **Map** *p282 G3.*

Not quite a club, a bar, or even a coffeehouse for that matter, Tryst is the ultimate community living room. Furnishings consist of overstuffed chairs, comfy sofas and country-style kitchen tables, creating a hip, relaxed vibe without feeling collegiate. If you want to drink alcohol, fine. If not, the coffee, served in enormous mugs, is very good. There are also a dozen sandwiches (half of which are vegetarian) on the menu and several small plates for nibbling. Chat to a stranger, work from your laptop or just people-watch.

Cajun/Creole

Bardia's New Orleans Café

2412 18th Street, NW, at Columbia Road (1-202 234 0420). Dupont Circle Metro then 42 bus or Woodley Park-Zoo/Adams Morgan Metro then 90, 92, 93, L2 bus. **Open** 11am-10pm Mon-Fri; 10am-10pm Sat, Sun. **Main courses** $5-$14. **Credit** AmEx, MC, V. **Map** p282 G3.

Weekend 'brunch' – when there is an open menu all day – is the best reason to hang out at this cosy nook. Order a plate of beignets, linger over coffee and try one of the Creole-style omelettes. The red beans and rice will make you yearn for Jazz Fest.

Contemporary

Cashion's Eat Place

1819 Columbia Road, NW, between Biltmore Street & Mintwood Place (1-202 797 1819). Dupont Circle Metro then 42 bus or Woodley Park-Zoo/Adams Morgan Metro then 90, 92, 93, L2 bus. **Open** 5.30-10pm Tue; 5.30-11pm Wed-Sat; 11.30am-2.30pm, 5.30-10pm Sun. **Main courses** $18-$28. **Credit** MC, V. **Map** p282 G3.

Chef/owner and award-winner Ann Cashion consistently puts on a good show, with classic food to match her classic dining room. The menu is seasonal and based on what her local purveyors have to hand. There are heavier meat choices (pork loin, lamb steak, buffalo) to balance the fish dishes. The influence is a little bit Euro, a little bit New Orleans, with a little bit of Asian thrown in for zest. There's room at the bar for eating, but if you want a table, be sure to book. In warm months, the outdoor seating area is one of the most festive in DC. For a fish-heavy menu, done Cashion style, try Johnny's Half Shell (*see p130*).

Ethiopian

Eighteenth Street in Adams Morgan is home to most of Washington's Ethiopian restaurants. In addition to **Fasika's** (*see below*), other good choices include **Addis Ababa** (No.2106, between Wyoming Avenue & California Street, 1-202 232 6092) or **Merkerem** (No.2434, between Columbia & Belmont Roads, 1-202 462 4100).

Fasika's

2447 18th Street, NW, between Columbia & Belmont Roads (1-202 797 7673). Dupont Cirle then 42 bus or Woodley Park-Zoo/Adams Morgan Metro then 90, 92, 93, L2 bus. **Open** 5-11.30pm Mon-Thur; 5pm-1am Fri; noon-1am Sat; noon-11.30pm Sun. **Main courses** $8-$22. **Map** 310 G3.

All the Ethiopian favourites are to be found in this lively restaurant: mostly meaty stews, scooped up with spongy, filling injera bread, plus salads. Food is served family-style on a big silver platter.

Fusion

Perry's

1811 Columbia Road, NW, at Biltmore Street (1-202 234 6218). Dupont Circle Metro then 42 bus or Woodley Park-Zoo/Adams Morgan Metro then 90, 92, 93, L2 bus. **Open** 5.30-10.30pm Mon-Thur; 5.30-11.30pm Fri, Sat; 10.30am-2.30pm, 5-10pm Sun. **Main courses** $6-$22.50. **Set brunch** $22.95. **Credit** AmEx, Disc, MC, V. **Map** p282 G3.

The biggest rooftop dining option in Adams Morgan, if not the city, is now one of the best, too. Once pretty ho-hum, Perry's received a boost in 2002 when the staff of Ruppert's (now defunct) took over here. Sushi chefs are still busy along the counter, but it's the entrées that stand out. Salad greens with duck prosciutto and roasted mushrooms on quinoa are a hit at a table, booth or bar. Sunday's brunch is a drag – queens take orders and the crowd lip-syncs into their waffles. Perry's does not accept reservations.

Italian

Pasta Mia

1790 Columbia Road, NW, at 18th Street (1-202 328 9114). Dupont Circle Metro then 42 bus or Woodley Park-Zoo/Adams Morgan Metro then 90, 92, 93 bus. **Open** 6.30-10.30pm Mon-Sat. **Main courses** $8-$12. **Credit** MC, V. **Map** p282 G2.

Red-checked tablecloths and Frank Sinatra or Tony Bennett playing on the speakers will set you up for an inexpensive, home-grown Italian dinner, complete with a carafe of house red and a basket of crusty bread. If you don't like pasta, you're out of luck – they do it 29 different ways here. And don't get smart and suggest a substitution. The menu is set – *capisce?*

Latin/Caribbean

See also p132 **MixTec**.

Julia's Empanadas

2452 18th Street, NW, at Columbia Road (1-202 328 6232). Dupont Circle Metro then L2 bus or Woodley Park-Zoo/Adams Morgan Metro then 90, 92, 93 bus. **Open** 10am-10.30pm Mon-Thur; 10am-4am Fri, Sat; 10.30am-8pm Sun. **Main courses** $3-$4. **No credit cards.** **Map** p282 G2.

As can be gathered from the name, empanadas are the main attraction here. With plenty of varieties, including one for vegetarians and one for dessert, these mostly baked, pie-like wonders are, as the sign says, 'made by hand... baked with love'. This branch is open very late on weekends for after-bar crowds; the other two cater more to the lunchtime office market and have more table seating.

Other locations: 1221 Connecticut Avenue, NW, between M & N Streets, Dupont Circle (1-202 861 8828), 1000 Vermont Avenue, NW, at K Street, Downtown (1-202 789 1878); 1410 U Street, NW, between 14th & 15th Streets, Shaw: U Street/14th Street Corridor (1-202 387 4100).

Shaw: Logan Circle

Asian

Rice

1608 14th Street, NW, between Q & Corcoran Streets (1-202 234 2400/www.ricerestaurant.com). Dupont Circle or U Stree/African-American Civil War Memorial/Cardozo Metro. **Open** 11.30am-2.30pm, 5-10.30pm Mon-Thur; 11am-11pm Fri, Sat; 11am-10.30pm Sun. **Main courses** $11-$14. **Credit** Disc, MC, V. **Map** p282 H4.

Rice is a welcome addition to this newly overhauled neighbourhood. The interior is dark and minimalist and evokes a sense of urban cool, but the staff keep things from getting pretentious. The menu offers Thai food three different ways: 'authentic', 'healthy green' and 'rice specialties'. Entrées come in bowls; the colourful, coconut milk-scented rice is shaped into beautifully garnished mounds on its own plate. In fact, this is possibly the only place you'll eat where you'll remember the rice (though the fruit salad with chillis is another contender). Vegetarians do very well here.

Shaw: U Street/ 14th Street Corridor

American

Ben's Chili Bowl

1213 U Street, NW, between 12th & 13th Streets (1-202 667 0909/www.benschilibowl.com). U Street/ African-American Civil War Memorial/Cardozo Metro. **Open** 6am-2am Mon-Thur; 7am-4am Fri, Sat; noon-8pm Sun. **Main courses** $3-$6. **No credit cards**. **Map** p282 H3.

Established in 1958, and a survivor of the MLK riots a decade later, this family business is a national institution. Dogs, burgers, subs, even regular or veggie chilli by the gallon, plus less-than-light sides of fries, slaw and more. Go and be part of the scenery: Bill Cosby does whenever he's in town (his favourite dish: the famous chilli half-smoke). With Motown playing on the jukebox and the counter stools swivelling, Ben's is a sure thing.

French

Café Saint-Ex

1847 14th Street, NW, at T Street (1-202 265 7839/ www.saint-ex.com). U Street/African-American Civil War Memorial/Cardozo Metro. **Open** 5pm-2am Mon-Fri; 11am-2am Sat, Sun. **Main courses** $4-$8 brunch; $7-$22 dinner. **Credit** AmEx, MC, V. **Map** p282 H3.

Named after *Little Prince* author and pilot Antoine de Saint-Exupéry, this casual brasserie took off in 2003. Owner Mike Benson may have gone wild with aviation memorabilia but once the yellow lights are dimmed and regulars order from the café classics (the likes of plates of olives and cheese, mussels with skinny frites), the atmosphere holds together. Diners relax at tables indoors and out; loungers help themselves to couches in 'Gate 54' in the basement. DJs and smokers are welcomed downstairs. Good for dinner before a Black Cat or 9.30 Club show.

Italian

Coppi's

1414 U Street, NW, between 14th & 15th Streets (1-202 319 7773). U Street/African-American Civil War Memorial/Cardozo Metro. **Open** 6-11pm Mon-Thur; 5pm-midnight Fri, Sat; 5-11pm Sun. **Main courses** $9-$18. **Credit** AmEx, Disc, MC, V. **Map** p282 H3.

Vegging out

The days of ghetto-ising vegetarian fare on menus are thankfully long gone. And while only one of the restaurants in this chapter is exclusively vegetarian (**Nirvana**; *see p123*), virtually all offer good choices for the meat-free crowd.

Indeed, Indian restaurants are famously welcoming to vegetarians. The **Bombay Club** (*see p123*) is a good upscale choice, while **Heritage India** (*see p139*) devotes a third of its menu to meat-free dishes – as does Logan Circle's Asian eaterie **Rice** (*see p134*).

Otherwise, pan-Asian style **Teaism** (*see p129*) and **Café Asia** (*see p141*); mezze at **Lebanese Taverna** (*see p140*), **Zaytinya** (*see p125*) and **Neyla** (*see p137*); sandwiches at low-key **Tryst** (*see p132*); Thai staples at **Thaiphoon** (*see p127*); noodles at **Pasta Mia** (*see p133*) and pizzas at **2 Amys** (*see p140*), **Coppi's** (*see p134*) and **Pizzeria Paradiso** (*see p130*) are good choices.

Even vegans get a look-in, at **Asylum**'s Sunday brunch (*see p131*).

Thai food is fun and the atmosphere unpretentious at **Rice**. *See p134.*

In 2002 the husband-and-wife team of Pierre Mattia and chef Elizabeth Bright decided to rework their ten-year-old pizza joint. No longer content to bake the finest pies in town, they closed their second restaurant and expanded the menu at their original U Street location, putting an emphasis on local organic produce. Lo and behold – a serious casual restaurant was born (but not too serious – staff are friendly and the customers happily chatting away). Bright has a knack with vegetables: new peas and fresh mint make for great salads in the spring; roasted chestnuts and mushrooms come into play in the autumn.

Kuna

1324 U Street, NW, between 13th & 14th Streets (1-202 797 7908). U Street/African-American Civil War Memorial/Cardozo Metro. **Open** 6-10pm Tue-Thur; 6-11pm Fri, Sat. **Main courses** $15-$20. **Credit** MC, V. **Map** p282 H3.

Arrive at this small neighbourhood dining room without a reservation and you'll be waved up to the bar to sample the house wines – which isn't such an onerous task. Owner and chef Mark Guiricich is a gregarious host who takes a great deal of trouble to keep his customers satisfied on a budget. A curve of house-cured bacon tops a plate of equally fat mushrooms; a splash of truffle oil lifts pasta with sausage, cabbage and cream to sublime levels. Silky panna cotta is flush with berries. Pass the grappa and enjoy!

Latin/Caribbean

Chi-Cha Lounge

1624 U Street, NW, between 16th & 17th Streets (1-202 234 8400). Dupont Circle or U-Street/African-American Civil War Memorial/Cardozo Metro. **Open** 5.30pm-1.30am Mon-Thur, Sun; 5.30pm-3am Fri, Sat. **Tapas** $4.75-$8.50. **Credit** AmEx, DC, Disc, MC, V. **Map** p282 H3.

Don't let the ambience fool you. Just as you're getting comfortable on one of the low-riding, 1970s-style couches, sipping on a cocktail and taking in the Latin/Cuban/Brazilian jazz mix, there's the menu to consider. Chi-Cha may be the only place in town to sample tapas from the Andes, so you can learn a little something too, as you nibble on ceviche, tamales or yapingacho (potato pancake stuffed with cheese and yucca), and watch under-35 Washington at play.

Georgetown

Asian

Basil Thai

1608 Wisconsin Avenue, NW, at Q Street (1-202 944 8660). Foggy Bottom-GWU Metro then 30, 32, 34, 35, 36 bus or Dupont Circle Metro then D1, D2, D3, D6, G2 bus. **Open** 11am-4pm, 5-10pm Mon-Sat; 4-10pm Sun. **Main courses** $9-$13. **Credit** AmEx, DC, MC, V. **Map** p281 E4.

Ben's Chili Bowl: an American classic. *See p134.*

Pale orange walls greet you in this charming, one-room storefront. To start, try a plate of fishcakes, fried and served with tangy cucumbers and peanut sauce. The chef's specials tend to be fun, such as a crispy duck in a spicy basil sauce jazzed up with lemongrass. Desserts include sweet sticky rice with mango and coconut-battered fritters with honey. Parking is a pain but it's worth persevering.

Cafés & coffeehouses

The café at **Dean & Deluca** (*see p169*) is also an excellent stop-off for hot drinks and cakes.

Pâtisserie Poupon

1645 Wisconsin Avenue, NW, between Q Street & Reservoir Road (1-202 342 3248). Foggy Bottom-GWU Metro then 30, 32, 34, 35, 36, Georgetown Metro Connection bus or Dupont Circle then D1, D2, D3, D6, G2 bus. **Open** 8am-6.30pm Tue-Sat; 8am-4pm Sun. **Credit** AmEx, MC, V. **Map** p281 E4.
Light and airy in an LA chic sort of way, PP gets points for presentation and attitude. The tarts and cakes are just like you'd find in Paris, and the menu is short but oh-so-French: salade niçoise, crudités, quiches and baguettes.

Contemporary American

Clyde's of Georgetown

3236 M Street, NW, between Wisconsin Avenue & Potomac Street (1-202 333 9180/www.clydes.com). Foggy Bottom-GWU Metro then 30, 32, 34, 35, 36, 38B, Georgetown Metro Connection bus or
Dupont Circle then D1, D2, D3, D6, G2 bus. **Open** 11.30am-10.30pm Mon-Thur; 11.30am-1am Fri; 9am-1am Sat; 9am-midnight Sun. **Main courses** $11-$16 lunch; $13-$18 dinner. **Credit** AmEx, DC, Disc, MC, V. **Map** p281 E5.
If ever there was a catch-all restaurant, this has to be it. It's dark and woody inside, with Americana hanging on the walls, and has a friendly and easy-going atmosphere. Between 4pm and 7pm on week-days you can have a snack at the bar and take advantage of incredible bargains, including a very tasty crabcake sandwich and one of the best burgers in the city. The first of many Clyde's branches to open in the area, this one prides itself on buying produce from local farms and does a nice job on local seafood.

1789 Restaurant

1226 36th Street, NW, at Prospect Street (1-202 965 1789/www.1789restaurant.com). Foggy Bottom-GWU Metro then 38B, Georgetown Metro Connection bus or Dupont Circle then D1, D2, D3, D6, G2 bus. **Open** 6-10pm Mon-Thur, Sun; 6-11pm Fri; 5.30-11pm Sat; 5.30-10pm Sun. **Main courses** $18-$32. **Credit** AmEx, DC, Disc, MC, V. **Map** p281 E5.
As many people come to this restaurant (part of the Clyde's group) for the setting – 18th-century Federal townhouse, working fireplaces, period furniture and china – as they do for the food, which is more contemporary than the furnishings. An alumnus of Kinkead's, chef Ris Lacoste is known for her way with fish, as well as true-blue American favourites, such as roast turkey with all the trimmings (1789 is a great Thanksgiving and Christmas Day destination).

French

Café La Ruche

1039 31st Street, NW, between K & M Streets (1-202 965 2684/www.cafelaruche.com). Foggy Bottom-GWU Metro then 30, 32, 34, 35, 36, 38B, Georgetown Metro Connection bus or Dupont Circle then D1, D2, D3, D6, G2 bus. **Open** 11.30am-11.30pm Mon-Thur; 11.30am-1am Fri, Sat; 10am-11.30pm Sun. **Main courses** $9-$14. **Set brunch** $10.95. **Credit** AmEx, MC, V. **Map** p281 E5.

Quaint from the outside, a little more hip on the inside, La Ruche is a comfort zone for Francophiles who don't want to drop a big wad of cash. The food comes café-style, with choices in the quiche/sandwich/salad range, plus a smattering of daily entrée specials such as mussels and duck à l'orange. Desserts, which include a range of traditional tarts, are made in house. Brunch (10am-3pm weekends) is popular, especially in the garden in warm weather.

Michel Richard Citronelle

Latham Hotel, 3000 M Street, NW, at 30th Street (1-202 625 2150/www.citronelledc.com). Foggy Bottom-GWU Metro then 30, 32, 34, 35, 36, 38B, Georgetown Metro Connection bus or Dupont Circle then D1, D2, D3, D6, G2 bus. **Open** 6.30-10.30am, 6.30-10pm Mon-Thur, Sun; 6.30-10.30am, 6.30-10.30pm Fri; 6.30-10.30am, 6-10.30pm Sat. **Main courses** $8-$17 breakfast; $12-$38 dinner. **Credit** AmEx, DC, Disc, MC, V. **Map** p281 F5.

This is the sort of place where diners come for an 'experience' rather than just a meal. Hailed as one of the country's best chefs, Michel Richard has built a reputation for innovative combinations. And while these might encompass the likes of foie gras and venison, dishes are light and imaginative, never heavy. The 8,000 or so bottles of wine, sitting comfortably in their state-of-the-art cellar, get equal billing. Be prepared to shell out in a big way.

Fusion

Mendocino Grill & Wine Bar

2917 M Street, NW, between 29th & 30th Streets (1-202 333 2912). Foggy Bottom-GWU Metro then 30, 32, 34, 35, 36, 38B, Georgetown Metro Connection bus. **Open** 11.30am-3pm, 5.30-10pm Mon-Thur; 11.30am-3pm, 5.30-11pm Fri, Sat; 5.30-10pm Sun. **Main courses** $7-$26. **Credit** AmEx, MC, V. **Map** p281 F5.

The name is a bit misleading. If you're thinking steaks and chops, think again. But if you're after a varied, intriguing wine list featuring small vintners, then you're in the right place. In some ways, the wines are more compelling than the menu, which is an ode to fusion cooking. Dishes like tandoori sushi-grade tuna and Caesar salad tower don't always translate at table, but the attempts are valiant and it's still worth exploring. Your best bet is to steer towards the simpler items, such as roast chicken and risotto. Service is highly competent and the date factor high – this space is just dark enough to be romantic.

Mediterranean

Moby Dick House of Kabob

1070 31st Street, NW, at M Street (1-202 333 4400). Foggy Bottom-GWU Metro then 30, 32, 34, 35, 36, 38B, Georgetown Metro Connection bus. **Open** 11am-10pm Mon-Thur, Sun; 11am-4am Fri, Sat. **Main courses** $4-$11. **No credit cards.** **Map** p281 E5.

There's not much to this eaterie – just the counter to place your order and two tables on the right. All the action is going on behind the scenes, from where the aromas of grilled meat and clay-oven-baked pita waft out. The food is earnest, tasty and authentic, and, not surprisingly, Middle East expats from all over the region are always queuing up for kubideh (ground beef), halal lamb or one of the daily specials. The servings are enormous – even the souvlaki sandwiches are big enough to share. Don't fret about the lack of seating: take your goodies home or stroll down to the C&O Canal.

Neyla

3206 N Street, NW, at Wisconsin Avenue (1-202 333 6353/www.neyla.com). Foggy Bottom-GWU Metro then 30, 32, 34, 35, 36, 38B, Georgetown Metro Connection bus or Dupont Circle Metro then D1, D2, D3, D6, G2 bus. **Open** 5-10.30pm Mon-Wed, Sun; 5-11.30pm Thur-Sat. **Main courses** $12-$27. **Credit** AmEx, MC, V. **Map** p281 E4.

This is the place to go on a hot date. Tapestries hang from the ceiling, pillows dress the romantic banquette corners and sultry music oozes through the speakers. A high-top, dressed-up communal table situated between the bar and the dining room adds to the nightclub feel of the space, which on a weekend night gets its share of glamourpusses. As for the menu, stick to the more traditional Middle Eastern plates, of which there are many designed for sharing, for parties of two to eight. The baba ganoush is memorable – gorgeously smoky, adorned with beads of pomegranates – and the Turkish coffee is proper. If you're feeling extra zesty, smoke a hookah out on the brick patio.

Quick Pita

1210 Potomac Street, NW, between M & Prospect Streets (1-202 338 7482/www.quickpita.com). Foggy Bottom-GWU Metro then 30, 32, 34, 35, 36, 38B, Georgetown Metro Connection bus. **Open** 11.30am-3am Mon-Wed, Sun; 11.30am-4.30am Thur-Sat. **Main courses** $3-$10. **Credit** AmEx, MC, V. **Map** p281 E5.

There are just seven seats in this tiny storefront restaurant, which offers authentic Lebanese staples including baba ganoush, falafel, tabbouleh and sandwiches such as shawarma, gyro and kebab combinations. The Quick Pita Special is an oddly delicious mixture of grilled cubes of chicken, garlic paste, tomatoes and french fries, rolled into a warm pita. Despite the limited seating, Quick Pita is good for a, well, quick pita while shopping, or a late-night snack. It's open late from Thursday to Saturday.

Eat, Drink, Shop

Capitol Hill

Latin/Caribbean

Banana Café & Piano Bar
500 Eighth Street, SE, at E Street (1-202 543 5906). Eastern Market Metro. **Open** 11.30am-2.30pm, 5-10.30pm Mon-Thur; 11.30am-2.30pm, 5-11pm Fri; 5-11pm Sat; 5-10.30pm Sun. **Main courses** $9-$12. **Credit** AmEx, DC, Disc, MC, V. **Map** p285 M7.

Home to the best Margaritas and Cuban food on the Hill, Banana Café packs a tropical punch. The menu is mostly Tex-Mex standards; insiders order the ropa vieja (shredded beef with cumin and chillis) along with equally spicy plaintain soup. Art by the owner and other local painters dots the lime-green walls and local musicians drop in to play the keyboards. This is an easy-going hangout in a hardworking 'hood.

French

Café Montmartre
327 Seventh Street, SE, between C Street & Pennsylvania Avenue (1-202 544 1244). Eastern Market Metro. **Open** 11.30am-2.30pm, 5.30-10pm Tue-Thur; 11.30am-2.30pm, 5.30-10.30pm Fri, Sat; 11.30am-2.30pm, 5.30-9pm Sun. **Main courses** $12-$22. **Credit** AmEx, Disc, MC, V. **Map** p285 L7.

In a restaurant-deprived neighbourhood, Montmartre is a welcome addition. The name is not the only thing that's French here: you are welcomed with a proper 'bonjour' and are seated with a menu that includes classic bistro items such as poulet rôti, quiche du jour, moules and tarte tatin. The light-filled dining room handles noise well and, when weather permits, you can enjoy people watching on the patio.

American

Market Lunch
Eastern Market, 225 Seventh Street, SE, between Pennsylvania & North Carolina Avenues (1-202 547 8444). Eastern Market Metro. **Open** 7.30am-3pm Tue-Sat; 11am-3pm Sun. **Main courses** $2-$5. **No credit cards. Map** p285 L7.

Eastern Market is a historic building housing a lively indoor farmers' market, with vendors selling cheese, poultry, seafood, produce and flowers. A must-do pit stop while shopping is Market Lunch, a lunch counter of very simple but satisfying proportions. Line up, place your order with the cashier, wait for your food, which comes on a paper plate, and join the rest of your fellow customers at the long communal-style table. Locals go for the crabcakes, fried fish and eggs, barbecued pork sandwich, and, of course, greasy burger. Go on the weekend, when vendors set up outside with local art, antiques and collectibles (*see p93*).

Pâtisserie Poupon. *See p136.*

Hood hangouts

You only have only to count the industrial cranes looming over the city to understand the magnitude of DC's real-estate boom. As area fortunes have risen, house prices have skyrocketed. Many younger and middle-income residents have taken refuge in once down-at-heel neighbourhoods (such as Logan Circle and Shaw: U Street/Cardozo), and brought their restaurants with them. These joints tend to be small and casual, and many turn into lounges after the kitchen closes. Join the locals – and get chatting to them while you're here – and try some of Washington's best budget cooking. Here we have suggested some foodie hotspots within easy reach of neighbourhood Metro stops.

Dupont Circle Metro

Dupont Circle likes to stay up late. At **Chi-Cha Lounge** (*see p135*) and **Cocoa** (*see p211*) diners are welcome to kick back and listen to live Latin jazz or electronica, respectively. Both kitchens serve small plates to a well-dressed crowd. At nearby **Komi** (*see p129*), chef Johny Monis is less interested in the look of his nightly crowd than the fashion on his plates. Both, however, impress. Visiting vegetarians are welcomed with myriad choices at **Rice** (*see p134*) in Logan Circle. This modern Thai restaurant is popular and elegant, the queue on the sidewalk friendly.

U Street/African-American Civil War Memorial/Cardozo Metro

A short walk up 14th Street yields **Café Saint-Ex** (*see p134*), a handsome yellow bistro serving burgers, mussels and perhaps the best brunch for the buck in the city. DJs pepper the basement with indie rock. At the neighbouring **Kuna** (*see p135*), the food, like the mood, is more mature. The menu is Italian farmhouse. Here, spicy southern wine helps bowls of lamb ragu to disappear (or is it vice versa?). Both spots are absurdly welcoming.

Eastern Market Metro

Bright, small and necessary, **Café Montmartre** (*see p138*) is Capitol Hill's best date destination. Steak-frites-salad and rabbit cassoulet draw bipartisan couples. After a morning poking through Eastern Market (antiques, crafts, fruit and veg), soup and omelettes make for a restorative Sunday brunch.

Rosslyn or Court House Metro

Before you head out for New York strip in Arlington, secure a reservation at **Ray's the Steaks** (*see p144*). Big cuts of prime beef served at honest (read: unbelievable) prices pack the modest space with a large, all-ages crowd. Ray's secret is out, city-wide.

Upper Northwest

Asian

Makoto
4822 MacArthur Boulevard, NW, at Reservoir Road (1-202 298 6866). Dupont Circle Metro then D3, D6 bus. **Open** noon-2pm, 6-10pm Tue-Sun. **Set meal** $42. **Credit** AmEx, MC, V. **Map** p280 B3.
When you make a reservation (which is highly recommended for this tiny space), you should be prepared for a very special experience. Entering Makoto is like stepping into a restaurant in Japan, where you must trade your shoes for slippers at the front door. Dinner is prix-fixe, a seemingly never-ending feast of delicate bites. The food is beautiful, clean and a great lesson in Japanese cuisine, from egg custards and seaweed to sashimi and aubergine. Note that the easiest way to get here is by taxi.

Sushi-Ko
2309 Wisconsin Avenue, NW, between Calvert Street & Observatory Lane, Glover Park (1-202 333 4187). Foggy Bottom-GWU Metro then 30, 32, 34, 35, 36

bus. **Open** 6-10.30pm Mon; noon-2.30pm, 6-10.30pm Tue-Thur; noon-2.30pm, 6-11pm Fri; 5.30-11pm Sat; 5.30-10pm Sun. **Main courses** $12-$21. **Credit** AmEx, MC, V. **Map** p281 D3.
Known to have one of the best-quality sushi bars in town, Sushi-Ko has been a mainstay in Washington for more than 20 years. Owner Daisuke Utagawa is committed to the fusion of Japanese and Western ingredients and techniques, as well as matching dishes with wines and premium sakes. The decor is stylish, with simple lines and pastels.

Indian

Heritage India
2400 Wisconsin Avenue, NW, at Calvert Street, Glover Park (1-202 333 3120). Farragut West Metro then 30, 32, 34, 35, 36 bus. **Open** 11.30am-2.30pm, 5.30-10.30pm Mon-Fri; 5.30-11pm Sat; 5.30-10.30pm Sun. **Main courses** $8-$22. **Credit** AmEx, Disc, MC, V. **Map** p281 D2.
Until Heritage opened in early 1999, the choices for local Indian restaurants were either very high-end or very low-end, local holes in the wall. Here you

can have the best of both worlds: top-quality, complex-flavoured Indian food (the chef is ex-Bombay Club) and an interesting wine list, but without the worry of having to get dressed up. Vegetarians will love Heritage India, where meatless dishes make up around a third of the menu, including the fabulous begumi khazana, a feast that's served on a silver platter.

Other locations: 1337 Connecticut Avenue, NW, between N Street & Dupont Circle, Dupont Circle (1-202 331 1414).

Italian/pizza

Palena

3529 Connecticut Avenue, NW, between Ordway & Porter Streets (1-202 537 9250/www. palenarestaurant.com). Cleveland Park Metro. **Open** 5.30-10pm Tue-Sat. **Set menus** $50, $57, $64. **Credit** AmEx, Disc, MC, V. **Map** p281 F1.
Chef Frank Ruta and pastry chef Ann Amernick met in the kitchen – the White House kitchen, that is, during Jimmy Carter's presidency. Together, these friends serve meals that are fit for presidents and queens at high but not unreasonable prices. Palena's prix-fixe menus are delivered with a whisper-light touch in the twinkling dining room. Humbler bank balances are not forgotten at Palena Café – house-made hot dog and sauerkraut, fine roast chicken and duck ragu with hand-rolled noodles ($9 an entrée) are served to patrons in the rosy glow of the bar area and front patio. Amernick's caramels are justly famous.

2 Amys

3715 Macomb Street, NW, at Wisconsin Avenue (1-202 885 5700). Farragut West Metro then 34, N2 bus. **Open** 11am-11pm Tue-Sun. **Main courses** $8-$14. **Credit** MC, V. **Map** p281 D1.
A slice of heaven for young families and gourmands, this white-tiled restaurant serves hand-tossed pizzas. The menu, which arrives printed on a single sheet of paper, is as spare as the decor. Owner Peter Pastan (Obelisk) offers few appetisers: olives, deviled eggs, salt cod fritters or a simple salad. It's the pizza that's serious business here. So serious, in fact, that Pastan's offerings – simply topped discs that arrive blistered from the oak-fire stove – have garnered the approval of the Associazione Verace Pizza Napoletana. Wines are moderately priced.

Latin/Caribbean

Chipotle Mexican Grill

2600 Connecticut Avenue, NW, at Calvert Street, Woodley Park (1-202 299 9111/www.chipotle.com). Woodley Park-Zoo/Adams Morgan Metro. **Open** 10am-11pm daily. **Main courses** $3-$7. **Credit** MC, V. **Map** p281 F2.
This Colorado-based chain (owned by McDonald's) has made its debut in Washington and surrounding suburbs with a bang, opening up all over the place

almost simultaneously. Filling a need for folks on the run, Chipotle ('chee-pot-lay', a smoked jalapeño chilli) offers upscale burritos and tacos (that's it, folks) in a slick, quick-paced setting. The quality of ingredients is several notches above fast food, but after a few minutes' waiting for someone to fill your order in assembly-line fashion, it's hard to avoid the burger joint feeling. That said, we urge you to try the barbacoa burrito, stuffed with pinto beans, shredded beef and a tomatillo sauce that will knock you for six. ¡Arriba!

Other locations: throughout the city.

Mediterranean

Lebanese Taverna

2641 Connecticut Avenue, NW, at Woodley Road, Woodley Park (1-202 265 8681/www. lebanesetaverna.com). Woodley Park-Zoo/Adams Morgan Metro. **Open** 11.30am-3pm, 5.30-10.30pm Mon-Thur; 11.30am-3pm, 5.30-11.30pm Fri; 11.30am-3.30pm, 5.30-11.30pm Sat; 5-10pm Sun. **Main courses** $9-$15. **Credit** AmEx, DC, Disc, MC, V. **Map** p281 F2.
This popular family-owned operation, part of a 25-year-old mini chain, starts filling up early for dinner. The friendly crowd is a mix of families, couples and more formal business groups. Make a meal of appetisers, which are quite substantial, fun to share and a bit more of a bargain. There's the familiar tabouleh and falafel as well as more interesting variations, such as moujawara bel shawarma, shankleesh (herbed and spiced feta with a tomato salad) and manakish b'sbanigh, a Lebanese-style pie topped with a spinach, pine nut and cheese mixture. Save room for baklava, and round things off with an Arabic coffee scented with cardamom.
Other locations: 5900 Washington Boulevard, between McKinley Road & Nicholas Street, Arlington, VA (1-703 241 8681); Pentagon Row, 1101 South Joyce Street, VA (1-703 415 8681).

Southern

Rocklands

2418 Wisconsin Avenue, NW, at Calvert Street, Glover Park (1-202 333 2558/www.rocklands.com). Foggy Bottom-GWU Metro then 30, 32, 34, 35, 36 bus. **Open** 11.30am-10pm Mon-Fri; 11am-10pm Sat; 11am-9pm Sun. **Main courses** $4-$10. **Credit** AmEx, MC, V. **Map** p281 D2.
A polished version of a barbecue shack, Rocklands offers a little bit of everything, from pulled pork and ribs to whole chickens. At the Glover Park branch, the seating is at a long communal table, where there are peanuts to shell and various hot sauces to share. Side dishes include baked beans, corn pudding, slaw, potato salad and all the stuff of a good picnic.
Other locations: 4000 North Fairfax Drive (inside carpool), at North Quincy Street, Arlington, VA (1-703 528 9663).

You can't beat the pita bread sandwiches at **Quick Pita**. *See p137.*

Tex-Mex

Austin Grill

2404 Wisconsin Avenue, NW, at Calvert Street, Glover Park (1-202 337 8080/www.austingrill.com). Foggy Bottom-GWU Metro then 30, 32, 34, 35, 36 bus. **Open** 11.30am-10.30pm Mon; 11.30am-11pm Tue-Thur; 11.30am-midnight Fri; 11am-midnight Sat; 11am-10.30pm Sun. **Main courses** $6-$14. **Credit** AmEx, DC, Disc, MC, V. **Map** p281 D2.

The Tex-Mex cousin of Jaleo (*see p126*), Austin Grill fills the gap between upscale dining and fast-food munching. It's popular with a variety of diners – families who don't want to deal with high-maintenance restaurants and singles who are looking for chow that doesn't interrupt meeting potential suitors. There are plenty of tequilas to sample and everything comes with chips and salsa.
Other locations: throughout the city.

Arlington, VA

Asian

Café Asia

1550 Wilson Boulevard, at Pierce Street, Rosslyn (1-703 741 0870/www.cafeasia.com). Rosslyn Metro. **Open** 11am-10pm Mon-Thur; 11am-11pm Fri, Sat; 5-10pm Sun. **Main courses** $6-$12. **Credit** AmEx, MC, V.

If you like your sushi loud, you'll like Café Asia. It's pretty hard to ignore the blaring music coming from the bar/lounge area, which always seems to be

hopping with singles. The pan-Asian menu is far from inspiring, but its coverage of the region is above average. The Rosslyn location has extensive sidewalk seating and one large bar area. The new downtown location has two floors, each with a bar, and offers communal tables for larger groups.
Other locations: 1721 I Street, NW, Downtown, between 17th & 18th Streets (1-202 659 2696).

Little Viet Garden

3012 Wilson Boulevard, between Highland & Garfield Streets (1-703 522 9686). Clarendon Metro. **Open** 11am-2.30pm, 5-10pm Mon-Fri; noon-10pm Sat, Sun. **Main courses** $5-$12. **Credit** AmEx, DC, Disc, MC, V.

There are plenty of Vietnamese restaurants in this area of Arlington, but Little Viet Garden gets points for ambience. It's an exotic hideaway, with white Christmas lights, tables pushed closely together to give a cosy café feel and, when the weather's warm, lovely garden seating. If it's busy (as it often is), consider eating at the bar, where service seems to be a tad more attentive than tableside. The menu runs the gamut, from noodles to shrimp toast; one dish always worth a look is the spicy fried tofu cooked in a clay pot, very flavourful and un-tofu-like in texture.

Minh's Vietnamese Restaurant

2500 Wilson Boulevard, at North Barton Street (1-703 525 2828). Court House Metro. **Open** 11am-10pm Mon-Thur, Sun; 11am-11pm Fri, Sat. **Main courses** $6-$12. **Credit** MC, V.

At first glance you don't expect much from this place because of its location on the ground of a nondescript office building. But forget the exterior:

The lunch bunch

Traipsing around the attractions on the National Mall can take a toll on your appetite. As little as three years ago, the selection of places to eat (and rest weary feet) was paltry. Not only have the choices inside the museums been smartened up, but several smaller restaurants have opened. Sadly, the immensely popular National Air & Space Museum only has a few tired fast-food options, including a McDonald's. Thankfully there's a bit more imagination elsewhere. Note, however, that departmental canteens inside federal buildings are no longer an open owing to increased security.

The **National Gallery of Art** has several eateries (details 1-202 215 5966; *see p109*). Families appear to prefer the casual styling of the **Cascade Café** (10am-3pm Mon-Sat, 11am-4pm Sun) on the concourse level, where sandwiches and salads are made to order. An espresso or a scoop of gelato is a reason to return in the afternoon. Tucked inside a glass gazebo, itself inside the **Sculpture Garden**, is the **Pavilion Café** (11.30am-3pm Mon-Sat, noon-4pm Sun, or until 6pm June-Sept), a spot for tea or a light lunch. In winter the café does a brisk business in hot chocolate as skaters sip around the frozen fountain.

The **National Air & Space Museum** (*see p118*) radically overhauled its tired restaurant in 2003. The world's most-visited museum now boasts a huge fast-food complex, though there is also an adequate sit-down restaurant, the Wright Place.

If you want something less institutional, you'll have to get off the Mall. Back at the east end, head up Seventh Street. If you want a **Starbucks**, look for the red brick building with a gold dome (1-202 628 5044, open 7am-7pm daily). One block north, at D Street,

is **Andale** (1-202 783 3133), chef Alison Swope's Mexican-inspired venture. Ask for a seat near the window and queso fundito to start. **Footnotes Café** (*see p126*) at Olsson's Books & Records is good for home-made soups, fresh sandwiches and a java recharge.

At the corner of Seventh and E Streets is **Jaleo** (*see p126*), great for tapas, sangría and a burst of energy. Its Tex-Mex neighbour **Austin Grill** (*see p141*) serves beef tacos and crab quesadillas. One block west is an outpost of **Teaism** (*see p129*), the teahouse-cum-eaterie. The bento boxes filled with cucumber salad and poached salmon on rice are excellent, and there's even ostrich burger if you're feeling adventurous. In the afternoon, have a chai shake and a salty oat cookie. For those who prefer something stronger, try the **Gordon Biersch Brewery** at the corner of Ninth and F (1-202 783 5454). Garlic fries go well with each of the beers brewed on the premises (once a bank, now on the register of National Historic Places). Children are welcome.

Further west on Pennsylvania Avenue, you'll find the upscale **Capital Grille** (1-202 737 6200). Look for the sides of beef ageing in the window. Two blocks away sits **Les Halles** (1-202 347 6848), a cheery bistro for steak-frites and better-than-average coffee and dessert. Look for the long awning.

The area around the MCI Center is blooming with family-friendly restaurants like **Fuddruckers** (hamburgers; 734 Seventh Street, NW, 1-202 628 3380) and **Ruby Tuesdays** (upbeat burgers, sandwiches and salads to feed a crowd; 712 Seventh Street, NW, 1-202 347 0276). **Legal Seafood** (704 Seventh Street, NW, 1-202 347 0007), meanwhile, has one the best

---

Minh's offers a respite from the busy streets of Arlington suburban sprawl. The food is consistently delicious, at very fair prices. We're suckers for the rice vermicelli bun, offered with a choice of grilled steak, chicken or shrimp, dressed up with a cooling mix of mint, bean sprouts and cucumbers. Wash it down with a Vietnamese iced coffee, made with condensed milk.

Pho 75

1721 Wilson Boulevard, between Rhodes & Quinn Streets, Rosslyn (1-703 525 7355). Rosslyn Metro. **Open** 9am-8pm daily. **Main courses** $5-$7. **No credit cards.**

'Pho' is Vietnamese for soup – and in this case, it's a highly aromatic beef stock. Soup is the only thing on the menu here. No matter – you can have it many different ways, depending on your choice of beef, from flank or brisket, to more daring tendons and organs. Staff bring over your meat with the soup, rice noodles and a plate of beansprouts, basil, lime and jalapeño peppers. To complete the ritual, there's a host of condiments at your disposal, including oyster and chilli sauce and vinegar. Park yourself at one of the long cafeteria-style tables and get slurping. Don't forget to order an iced coffee, made with viscous condensed milk.

children's menus in town: from a hot dog to one-pound lobster, at a kids'-sized price. The chowder is excellent.

As well as being an architectural gem, not to mention a bustling commuter hub, **Union Station** (1-202 289 1908, www. unionstationdc.com) houses a retail mall, a basement-level food court (sushi, curries, burgers, pizza, cookies) and several restaurants. Sit-down options framing the marble atrium include the Creole-laced and overrated **B Smith's**, Southwestern-tinged **Thunder Grill**, **America** and **Center Café**. **Pizzeria Uno** serves deep-dish Chicago-style pizzas, while **Johnny Rockets** serves shakes and burgers in 1950s-style kitsch. **Au Bon Pain** and its rival **Corner Bakery** have sandwiches, soups, fruit juice, muffins and plate-sized cookies to go. That should keep you going.

Alternatively, head further north to Logan Circle, home to upscale grocer **Whole Foods** (*see p169*). It's a haven of organic produce – from artisanal cheese to Argentinian beef – plus sushi, sandwiches and smoothies to go. Also good for picnic fare are **So's Your Mom** (Adams Morgan; *see p132*) and **Dean & Deluca**, in Georgetown (*see p169*).

Singh Thai

2311 Wilson Boulevard, at North Adams Street (1-703 312 7118). Court House Metro. **Open** 11.30am-3pm, 5-10pm Mon-Thur, Sun; 11.30am-3pm, 5-11pm Fri, Sat. **Main courses** $8-$16. **Credit** Disc, MC, V.

Once upon a time, a Thai guy bought a coffee shop run by an Algerian guy. Before long he started offering a few Thai dishes for lunch alongside the regular lattes and muffins. Then the food became so popular that he closed the coffee shop and opened a full-service restaurant. The food, cooked by his mum, is still delicious and gets the tongue dancing. In fact, the only drawback is the size: the dining room is so small that this place is known locally as 'Teeny Thai.'

Thai Square

3217 Columbia Pike, between Glebe Road & South Highland Street (1-703 685 7040). Ballston Metro then 10B, 23A, 24P bus. **Open** 11.30am-10.30pm Mon-Thur, Sun; noon-11pm Fri, Sat. **Main courses** $7-$15. **Credit** AmEx, MC, V.

You won't find trendy versions of Thai dishes at Thai Square: the food is authentic, traditional and served in a very straightforward manner. The dining room is small – a bit like someone's living room

– and gets packed quickly with families and friends of the staff. Try any of the curries, the eggplant/tofu number that's always on the specials list, or the roasted duck.

Latin/Caribbean

Mexicali Blues
2933 Wilson Boulevard, at Garfield Street (1-703 812 9352/www.mexicali-blues.com). Clarendon Metro. **Open** 11am-10pm Mon-Thur, Sun; 11am-4am Fri, Sat. **Main courses** $4-$11. **Credit** MC, V.
They pack 'em into this friendly corner spot, with its Christmas lights, bright colours and festive Latin tunes. The food is as authentic as you're going to get in this part of the world – all prepared by an intent group of señoras milling about in the semi-open kitchen. A little bit Mexican (flautas, enchiladas, sopes), a little bit Salvadorean (pupusas, tamales), the menu has plenty of starters that work well as bar snacks or as an ad hoc dinner.

Steakhouses

Ray's the Steaks
1725 Wilson Boulevard, at North Quinn Street (1-703 841 7297/www.rays-steaks.com). Court House or Rosslyn Metro. **Open** 5.30-10pm Tue-Sat; 5.30-9pm Sun. **Main courses** $18-$47. **Credit** AmEx, MC, V.
The name may be a pun but meat is no joke to owner Michael Landrum. Steak is what Ray's serves – and we're talking choice cuts at remarkable prices. The meat is aged on the premises, an unpretentious room in a plain-spoken strip mall in Rosslyn. Skip the starters and cut to the chase. Chateaubriand for two is a steal at under $40. This ripe tenderloin arrives ruby-centered surrounded by mushrooms and asparagus in season. If you can't manage dessert after that, key lime pie is available to go. Reservations are essential.

American/Creole

Black's Bar and Grill
7750 Woodmont Avenue, between Old Georgetown Road & Cheltenham Drive (1-301 652 6278). Bethesda Metro. **Open** 11.30am-2.30pm, 5-10pm Mon-Thur; 11.30am-2.30pm, 5-11pm Fri; 5-11pm Sat; 5-9.30pm Sun. **Credit** AmEx, Disc, DC, MC, V.
Bethesda is not suburban. The diverse and glam crowd making whoopee over candy-coloured cocktails and gumbo at Black's would laugh such a suggestion off. The kitchen here offers a sophisticated taste of the American Gulf Coast with fresh oysters (a terrific deal at happy hour), shrimp tacos and duck enchiladas. The calamari, fried and dusted with

parmesan is as wicked as a stolen kiss; the key lime pie, sweeter. Indoors, outdoors or at the bar, seating is always at a premium. Reservations are required.

Ice-cream

Gifford's Ice Cream & Candy Co
7237 Woodmont Avenue, between Elm Street & Hampden Lane (1-301 907 3436). Bethesda Metro. **Open** 11am-11pm Mon-Thur, Sun; 11am-midnight Fri, Sat. **Credit** MC, V.
If Bethesda has a heart, it's probably this old-fashioned ice-cream shop above the arthouse cinema. Gifford's offers a lick of nostalgia – its recipes are unchanged since 1938. In the age of Baskin-Robbins, it offers a reasonable 18 flavours. Some favourites, like eggnog and summer melon, are seasonal. Happily, though, most of them, like the beloved peppermint stick and Swiss chocolate, are year-round winners.

Lebanese

Bacchus
7945 Norfolk Avenue, between Cordell & Del Ray Avenues, Bethesda, MD 20814 (1-301 657 1722). Bethesda Metro. **Open** noon-2pm, 6-10pm Mon-Thur; noon-2pm, 6-10.30pm Fri; 6-10.30pm Sat; 6-10pm Sun. **Credit** AmEx, MC, V.
When the weather allows, the best place to tuck into platefuls of refined Lebanese meze is Bacchus's leafy private courtyard; choosing isn't easy, though, with a 50-dish meze menu. Warak einab (rice, mint and onions swaddled in cabbage leaves), houmous dusted with sumac, and baba ganoush (a mashed aubergine dip) are tailor-made for adventurous vegetarians. Bacchus also serves fried smelt the length of your thumb. And, if meze is not enough, main course kebabs are succulent. An opulent, busy feast, terrific for groups.
Other locations: 1827 Jefferson Place, NW, Dupont Circle (1-202 785 0734).

American

Red Dog Café
8301 Grubb Road (1-301 588 6300). Silver Spring Metro. **Open** 7am-10pm Mon-Thur; 8am-11pm Fri, Sat; 8am-8pm Sun. **Credit** Am Ex, MC, V.
The dog's name is Madison. Give her a pat. The menu is equally friendly: muffins and smoothies at breakfast; pulled pork sandwiches at lunch, and cedar-plank roasted salmon at dinner. True, this homey, if upscale, American eatery is more expensive than some low-key spots, but its wag is worth it. The primary coloured walls: cheery cherry, apple and lemon, are covered with an ever-changing display of paintings.

Bars

Where to neck Guinness and network.

People in DC take their watering holes as seriously as everything else. Most of the classic old establishments have a loyal following, but are friendly enough to newcomers. Every year seems to bring a few new establishments worth checking out.

Bars are usually open until 2am Monday to Thursday and Sunday (after which time alcohol is not allowed to be served). On Fridays and Saturdays, some stay open till 3am or 4am (especially those that double as dance clubs), but alcohol can't be sold after 3am.

The legal drinking age in the US is 21, and, for the most part, it's strictly enforced, especially in Adams Morgan and Georgetown, which get a lot of college-age traffic. In those areas, if you don't have a passport or driver's licence, you probably won't get in the door. So bring along a photo ID with you – even if you're just going to have a glass of wine with your food and look over 30.

In 2002, the Metro extended its hours at weekends, and it now runs until 3am on Friday and Saturday nights, although the last train from your station is often earlier than that. If you're partying late, it's often easier to get a cab home. For gay-oriented bars and clubs, see *pp197-201*.

The best Bars

For behaving outrageously
Madam's Organ Restaurant & Bar, *see p151*.

For cocktails
Lounge 201, Round Robin Bar. For both, *see p148*.

For home-brewed beer
Capitol City Brewing Company, *see p146*. Gordon Biersch Restaurant & Brewery, *see p148*.

For mixing with politicos
Bullfeathers, *see p152*). Hawk & Dove, *see p146*.

For Scotch selection
Flying Scotsman, *see p148*). J Paul's, *see p152*.

For the view
Sky Terrace, *see p146*.

The White House & around

Old Ebbitt Grill

675 15th Street, NW, between F & G Streets
(1-202 347 4800/www.ebbitt.com). Metro Center
Metro. **Open** 7.30am-2am Mon-Thur; 7.30am-3am
Fri; 8.30am-3am Sat; 8.30am-2am Sun. **Credit**
AmEx, DC, Disc, MC, V. **Map** p284 H6.

This restaurant and bar first opened in 1856 as a
boarding house, and over the following years its
more illustrious guests included presidents Grant,
Johnson, Cleveland and Teddy Roosevelt. Its current location, just a block from the White House,
makes it a popular place for the power lunch (in the
main dining room, that is, not in the atrium).
Patrons' ages tend to edge up into the forties and
fifties, probably largely because of Old Ebbitt's
reputation for oysters and wine. The two bars – one
at the back, one at the front – are always packed,
usually with men who ensure that no nubile young
thing pays for her own drinks.

Sky Terrace

Hotel Washington, 515 15th Street, NW, at
Pennsylvania Avenue (1-202 638 5900/www.
hotelwashington.com). Metro Center Metro. **Open**
May-Oct 11.30am-1am Mon-Sat; 11.30am-midnight
Sun. Closed Nov-Apr. **Credit** AmEx, DC, Disc, MC,
V. **Map** p284 H5.

A tourist-heavy outdoor bar, the Sky Terrace is
worth a visit just for its unequalled view of the
monuments. It's a very popular place to watch the
Fourth of July fireworks, but you can't book until
two weeks in advance.

Capitol Hill & around

Hawk & Dove

329 Pennsylvania Avenue, SE, between Third &
Fourth Streets (1-202 543 3300). Capitol South or
Eastern Market Metro. **Open** 10am-2am Mon-Thur,
Sun; 11am-3am Fri, Sat. **Credit** AmEx, DC, Disc,
MC, V. **Map** p285 L7.

The Hawk & Dove is the classic Capitol Hill bar,
attracting partisan staffers who enjoy the political
atmosphere as much as the pool games. It's a hunting lodge-esque relic from the Vietnam War era
(hence the name, which recalls the heated debates
from those days). Political memorabilia has to compete with game trophies (aka dead animals). Today,
it attracts a slightly older and wealthier Hill crowd
than the Tune Inn (*see below*) next door – in other
words, plenty of thirtyish types in suits – though
the free food at happy hour is a big draw for the
young and hungry.

Politiki/Penn Ave Pour House

319 Pennsylvania Avenue, SE, between Third
& Fourth Streets (1-202 546 1001/www.
pennavepourhouse-dc.com). Capitol South
Metro. **Open** 4.30pm-1.30am Mon-Thur, Sun;
4pm-2.30am Fri, Sat. **Credit** AmEx, Disc, MC, V.
Map p285 L7.

Three bars in one, Washington's once full-time tiki
bar has turned its ground floor into the Penn Ave
Pour House, the city's only Pittsburgh-themed bar.
We're talking Iron City on draft, the Steelers (football team) on the TVs, and puppets from *Mr
Roger's Neighborhood* on the walls. But not everything has changed. The basement, Politiki, is still
a tiki lounge that serves exotic drinks in kitschy
glasses; the top floor is still decorated with World
War II posters and a wall-sized tribute to pin-up
Jane Russell. Regardless of theme, this is a popular
spot for sports fans and Hill workers. Quizzo, the
bar's Tuesday night quiz show, attracts many of
the Hill's know-it-alls.

Tune Inn

3332 Pennsylvania Avenue, SE, at Fourth Street
(1-202 543 2725). Capitol South Metro. **Open**
8am-2am Mon-Thur, Sun; 8am-3am Fri, Sat.
Credit AmEx, DC, Disc, MC, V. **Map** p285 L7.

The Tune Inn is one of the few places in DC that
starts serving beer at 8am – and you'll probably
need a pint to deal with the rowdy blue-collar crowd
and the sometimes surly staff. No microbrews here
– this place regularly wins awards for being
Washington's best dive, with prices to match.
Political gurus James Carville and Mary Matalin
came here on their first date before getting married
and working for opposite sides of the aisle.

Union Station & around

Capitol City Brewing Company

2 Massachusetts Avenue, NE, between North Capitol
& First Streets (1-202 842 2337/www.capcitybrew.
com). Union Station Metro. **Open** 11am-2am Mon-
Thur, Sun; 11am-3am Fri, Sat. **Credit** AmEx, DC,
MC, V. **Map** p285 K6.

There are three Cap City branches in the
Washington area. This branch is located inside the
former Postal Square Building, a grand marble
edifice that served as the Federal City Post Office
until 1986. Inside, the branches look a bit alike, with
copper kettles and exposed pipes, but it's the wide
selection of lagers, stouts and top-fermented ales
that are the draw. These include half a dozen
or so brewed on the premises. Cap City brews
primarily ales; it produces pilsners only a few
times each year. Indecisive patrons can try sample
portions of four beers.

Other locations: 1100 New York Avenue, NW,
between H & I Streets, Downtown (1-202 628 2222);
2700 South Quincy Street, Arlington, VA (1-703
578 3888).

The Dubliner

Phoenix Park Hotel, 520 North Capitol Street,
NW, at Massachusetts Avenue (1-202 737 3773/
www.phoenixparkhotel.com/dining.htm). Union
Station Metro. **Open** 7am-1.30am Mon-Thur;
7am-2.30am Fri; 7.30am-2.30am Sat; 7.30am-
1.30am Sun. **Credit** AmEx, DC, MC, V.
Map p285 K6.

Brickskeller. *See p149.*

Eat, Drink, Shop

A clubby two-storey Irish pub in a hotel, this long-standing stalwart tends to be patronised by besuited men in their 40s and 50s, mainly politicians and lobbyists. Later at night, the crowd gets a little younger and a little more mixed, but not enough to keep some young single women from feeling uncomfortable. It's a lively spot to enjoy a pint of Guinness and live Irish music.

Flying Scotsman
233 Second Street. NW, between C Street and Louisiana Avenue (1-202 783 3848/www.flyingscotsman-dc.com). Judiciary Square Metro. **Open** 11am-2am Mon-Thur, Sun; 11am-3am Fri, Sat. **Credit** AmEx, MC, V. **Map** p285 K6.
This Scottish-themed restaurant and bar opened in late 2003 and quickly garnered a loyal clientele of lobbyists, Federal workers and Hill staffers who come for the fun ambience, great food and selection of drinks, including a list of quality Scotches and hard-to-find beers. The popular kitchen dishes out everything from fish and chips to leg of lamb. There's a pool table and dartboard, and a no-smoking rule on the first floor.

Lounge 201
201 Massachusetts Avenue, NE, at Second Street (202-544-5201). Union Station Metro. **Open** 4pm-2am Tue-Thur; 4pm-3am Fri; 6pm-3am Sat. **Credit** AmEx, MC, V. **Map** p285 L6.
It's Martini time! While there is no shortage of expense-account steakhouses and $2 Bud happy hours on Capitol Hill, there was little in between before Matt Weiss opened this thoroughbred in 2003. Complete with deco interior and flat-screen TVs (tuned to headline news – this is the Hill), this is *the* after-work spot for staffers older than 25 and under 50. Order old school cocktails like Greyhounds (vodka and grapefruit juice) and Pink Squirrels (anyone's guess).

The Federal Triangle

Round Robin Bar
Willard Inter-Continental Hotel, 1401 Pennsylvania Avenue, NW, at 14th Street (1-202 637 7348). Metro Center Metro. **Open** 11am-1am Mon-Sat; 11am-midnight Sun. **Credit** AmEx, DC, Disc, MC, V. **Map** p284 H6.
Think old-fashioned gentlemen's club. This expensive, charming, dark green bar is a dressy, cocktails kind of place – mint juleps, gin rickeys, no beer on tap – and it's lobbyist central; in fact, it's said the term 'lobbying' was invented here, because influence-seekers used to hang out in the lobby waiting to speak to President Grant after he'd had lunch in the restaurant. Portraits depict some of the Willard's most prominent guests: Walt Whitman (who immortalised the bar in his appeal to Union troops during the Civil War), Mark Twain, Nathaniel Hawthorne and President Abraham Lincoln, who lived at the hotel for two weeks before his inauguration.

Downtown

Fadó Irish Pub
808 Seventh Street, NW, between H & I Streets (7890066/www.fadoirishpub.com/dc.html). Gallery Place-Chinatown Metro. **Open** 11.30am-2am Mon-Thur, Sun; 11.30-3am Fri, Sat. **Credit** AmEx, DC, Disc, MC, V. **Map** p285 J5.
Fadó – Gaelic for 'long ago' – is a kitschy Irish pub that's rich on atmosphere and host to many younger professionals out for fun before and after concerts or sporting events held at the nearby MCI Center. Its rooms are decorated to reflect various supposedly Irish themes: Victorian, library, cottage and Celtic, with most decorations brought over from the Emerald Isle. The bar hosts Celtic rock shows, trivia nights, and soccer and rugby matches. Food consists of such traditional staples as corned beef and cabbage; there are moderately priced stouts, whiskies and lagers to gulp down.

Gordon Biersch Restaurant & Brewery
900 F Street, NW, at 9th Street (1-202 783 5454/www.gordonbiersch.com). Gallery Place-Chinatown Metro. **Open** 11.30am-midnight Mon-Thur, Sun; 11.30am-2am Fri, Sat. **Credit** AmEx, DC, Disc, MC, V. **Map** p285 J6.
The California microbrew chain's first appearance in the region is an impressive one. Inside a beautifully restored 1890s bank, four traditional German lagers are brewed on site – no stouts or ales, though. All of the stellar beers, which can be matched to the food, like wine, comply with the Reinheitsgebot, a 1516 German law that regulates beer-making.

Kelly's Irish Times
14 F Street, NW, between North Capitol Street & New Jersey Avenue (1-202 543 5433/www.kellys irishtimes.com). Union Station Metro. **Open** 10.30am-1am Mon-Thur, Sun; 10.30am-3am Fri, Sat. **Credit** AmEx, DC, Disc, MC, V. **Map** p285 K6.
The Irish Times has the same Emerald Isle theme as the Dubliner next door, but it might as well be a world away. It may be relatively quiet during the day, but at night, when it's filled with young Hill staffers and American and Catholic University students, it's one of the places in DC known for its hook-up factor: as in, if you want to, you can't fail to. Live Irish music on Thursdays, Fridays and Saturdays.

Dupont Circle

The Big Hunt
1345 Connecticut Avenue, NW, between M & N Streets (1-202 785 2333). Dupont Circle or Farragut North Metro. **Open** 4pm-2am Mon-Thur; 4pm-3am Fri, Sat; 4pm-midnight Sun. **Credit** AmEx, MC, V. **Map** p282 G4/5.
Once upon a time, this was an über-hip hangout for DC's underground. Now, its motto – 'happy hunting ground… for mates, food and drink' – seems to say it all. The bar caters mostly to Dupont's and

The name of the game

Quiz nights, drag bingo, happy hours for pets: Washington, DC's bar owners are creative to say the least when it comes to ways of pulling in the punters, entertaining them and – most important – encouraging them to come back for more.

If you're a quiz fan you've come to the right town. The Quizzo Trivia Night at **Politiki/Penn Ave Pour House** (see p152) is popular on Tuesday evenings, with two full quizzes in less than 90 minutes. The Monday Night Challenge at **Fadó Irish Pub** (see p148) hosts anywhere between 50 to 80 players on a good night. And it's trivia on Tuesday nights at **Stetson's Famous Bar and Restaurant** (1610 U Street, NW, between 17th Street & New Hampshire Avenue, 1-202 667 6295) too.

Open mic nights are another source of entertainment. **Bar Nun/Club 2000** (see p210) has been hosting Monday-night open poetry readings for many years. Something louder and more raucous?

There's always drag bingo at **Club Chaos** (see p198) in Dupont Circle on Tuesday night.

Or, if you prefer your entertainment more mellow and musical, head to **Felix & the Spy Lounge** (2406 18th Street, NW, between Belmont Road & Columbia Road, 1-202 483 3549) on Wednesday for Sinatra night. There's live Irish music galore at the **Dubliner** (see p146) and **Kelly's Irish Times** (see p148), while jazz musicians sometimes grace **Aroma** (see p152). **Velvet Lounge** (see p151), meanwhile, is a live music venue that also functions happily as a neighbourhood bar.

And if going out just isn't the same without your furry friend, you can always take him to the Doggy Happy Hour every Wednesday at the **Adams Mill Bar and Grill** (1813 Adams Mill Road, NW, between Columbia Road & ania Place, 1-202 332 9577), where Washingtonians and their pets socialise on the outdoor patio ($10 donation to the Washington Humane Society requested).

Eat, Drink, Shop

Downtown's yuppie crowds; drinkers beware the singles who take the bar's name to heart. On the other hand, the beer list is long and respectable and the atmosphere is laid back. The bar has pool tables and excellent music, and can fill to the brim at weekends. Its special concoction of Guinness ice-cream is an added lure.

Brickskeller

1523 22nd Street, NW, between O & P Streets (1-202 293 1885/www.thebrickskeller.com). Dupont Circle Metro. **Open** 11.30am-2am Mon-Thur; 11.30am-3am Fri; 6pm-3am Sat; 6pm-2am Sun. **Credit** AmEx, DC, Disc, MC, V. **Map** p282 G4.

This labyrinthine saloon claims to have the world's largest selection of beers: more than 1,000 brands from all over the world, from America to Africa. Not, of course, that all 1,000 of these often-expensive bottles are available at the same time – seasonal varieties, availability and shipping play havoc with the menu. Still, the Brickskeller is a popular place for friends to meet and sample the diverse menu of brews – ordering a Bud light may draw stares. The food is typical bar fare, featuring buffalo burgers and fish and chips.

Buffalo Billiards

1330 19th Street, NW, at Dupont Circle (1-202 331 7665/www.buffalobilliards.com/dc/). Dupont Circle Metro. **Open** 4pm-2am Mon-Thur; 4pm-3am Fri; 1pm-3am Sat; 4pm-1am Sun. **Credit** AmEx, MC, V. **Map** p282 G4.

A subterranean pool hall with what feels like acres of pool tables, as well as snooker tables, dartboards, board games and a cigar counter. It's also a huge happy hour spot. For patrons looking to lounge with the locals, there are many couches strewn. At night the suits morph into gangs of pals in jeans.

Tabard Inn

1739 N Street, NW, between 17th & 18th Streets (1-202 833 2668/www.tabardinn.com). Dupont Circle Metro. **Open** 11.30am-2.30pm, 6-10pm Mon-Thur; 11.30am-2.30pm, 6-10.30pm Fri; 8-10am, 11am-2.30pm, 6-10.30pm Sat; 10.30am-2.30pm, 6-10pm Sun. **Credit** AmEx, DC, MC, V. **Map** p282 G4.

Famous in Washington for its unique, eclectic style, the popular Tabard Inn has a comfy, unique bar, set in a cosy, living room-like front room where patrons can sip wine and brandies relaxing on old sofas in front of an old-fashioned log fireplace. The slender bar in the adjacent room tends to be home to regulars.

Trio's Fox & Hounds

1533 17th Street, NW, between Church & Q Streets (1-202 232 6307). Dupont Circle Metro. **Open** 11am-2am Mon-Thur, Sun; 11am-3am Fri; 10am-3am Sat. **Credit** AmEx, Disc, MC, V. **Map** p282 G4.

A local pub that's dim and cave-like, with hardcore drinkers hunched over the bar. It becomes a real biergarten in warm weather, when crowds pack the patio and swarm the jukebox. This is a place for lingering, a reputation that the sometimes painfully slow staff takes a little too seriously.

The Reef.

Adams Morgan

See also p133 **Tryst.**

Bedrock Billiards

1841 Columbia Road, NW, between 18th Street & Belmont Road (1-202 667 7665). Dupont Circle Metro, then 42 bus or Woodley Park-Zoo Metro. **Open** 4pm-1.30am Mon-Thur; 1pm-2.30am Fri; 1pm-2.30am Sat; 1pm-1.30am Sun. **Credit** AmEx, MC, V. **Map** p282 G3.

Unpretentious pool hall/games room (with 30 pool tables, Scrabble, Connect Four and other childhood faves), which aims for a prehistoric look with caveman drawings on the green walls (these often get replaced with photos, murals and paintings from local artists). The decor isn't a reflection of the clientele, which mainly consists of under-30 folks from the area. This is mostly a beer-drinking crowd that doesn't take itself too seriously.

The Reef

2446 18th Street NW, between Belmont & Columbia Roads (1-202 518 3800). Woodley Park-Zoo/Adams Morgan Metro, then 98 bus or Dupont Circle Metro then 42 bus. **Open** 4pm-2am Mon-Thur; 4pm-3am Fri, Sat. **Credit** AmEx, MC, V. **Map** p282 G3.

Fish tanks as decorations, trippy fluorescent lighting, long lines to get in: all are hallmarks of the Reef, which has risen quickly to fashionable fame since its opening in spring 2002. Owner Brian Harrison, formerly a bartender at nearby Bedrock Billiards, took six enormous fish tanks and filled them with aquatic life from his own collection. The second-storey floor-to-ceiling windows offer a good vantage point for watching the foot traffic on 18th Street. The bar showcases an eclectic selection of beers – nothing in bottles – and is spacious enough to facilitate mingling among regulars, who often already know each other, and newcomers. The entrance is hard to find (no conspicuous sign) and you will have to wait to get in at weekends, but it's worth it.

Madam's Organ Restaurant & Bar

2461 18th Street, NW, at Columbia Road (1-202 667 5370/www.madamsorgan.com). Dupont Circle Metro, then L2 bus or Woodley Park-Zoo/Adams Morgan Metro, then 98 bus. **Open** 5pm-2am Mon-Thur, Sun; 5pm-3am Fri, Sat. **Admission** $2-$5. **Credit** AmEx, Disc, MC, V. **Map** p282 G2.

The 'Sorry We're Open' sign used to mock Madam's Organ's old neighbours, who finally succeeded in pushing this we-love-to-thumb-our-nose-at-everyone establishment several blocks north to get rid of the noise. (Its new neighbours have tried to force the bar to wipe the huge mural of a large-breasted, red-headed woman off the side of the building but so far it has stayed put.) As the bar's motto goes, this is 'where the beautiful people go to get ugly' – and ugly it gets: the crowds dance (or attempt to, in the tiny space) to live music, play pool on the second floor and hook up shamelessly. Redheads – make that red-headed women – get half-price Rolling Rock. In the summers, the top-floor patio opens up.

Tryst

2459 18th Street, NW, between Columbia & Belmont Roads (1-202 232 5500/www.trystdc.com). Dupont Circle Metro, then 42 bus or Woodley Park-Zoo/ Adams Morgan Metro, then 90, 92, 93, bus. **Open** 6.30am-midnight Mon-Thur; 6.30am-3am Fri, Sat; 8am-12.30am Sun. **Credit** MC, V. **Map** p282 G3.

For all the hanging out done in Adams Morgan, the area had been missing a true hangout until Tryst came along. A laid-back café by day, Tryst transforms itself into a packed 18th Street bar at night. *See also p132.*

Shaw: U Street/14th Street Corridor

The Bohemian Caverns

2001 11th Street NW, at U Street (1-202 299 0801/ www.bohemiancaverns.com). U Street/African-American Civil War Memorial/Cardozo Metro. **Open** 6pm-1am Tue; 8pm-2am Wed; 9pm-2am Thur; 9.30pm-3am Fri, Sat. **Credit** AmEx, MC, V. **Map** p282 J3.

After nearly 30 years of vacancy, this throwback of a bar reopened in 2000. The chandelier-hung main floor restaurant is complete 1920s glamour. The lower-level Caverns Jazz Lounge is a nightclub and has its own street entrance; upstairs, you'll find another space with a bar and a dancefloor. *See also p205.*

The Common Share

2003 18th Street, NW, at U Street (1-202 588 7180). Dupont Circle Metro, then L2 bus or U Street/African-American Civil War Memorial/

Cardozo Metro, then 90, 92, 93 bus. **Open** 5.30pm-2am Mon-Thur; 5.30pm-3am Fri, Sat. **Credit** Disc, MC, V. **Map** p282 G3.

There are two ways to find the Common Share: look for the mass of bikes outside (it's bike courier central), or for the long line that snakes several doors down. Bang on the border of Adams Morgan and U Street, the Common Share caters to interns, students and underpaid twentysomethings who affectionately call this dive the Two-Dollar Bar: every drink is $2 and comes in pints, all the time. Don't expect to get a seat (on the garage sale-reject furniture) unless you get here when the doors open.

Polly's Café

1342 U Street, at 14th Street, NW (1-202 265 8385). U Street/African-American Civil War Memorial/Cardozo Metro. **Open** 6pm-1.30am Mon-Thur; 6pm-2.30am Fri; 10am-2.30am Sat; 10am-12.30am Sun. **Credit** MC, V. **Map** p282 H3.

Polly's lives up to its café name, with a cozy atmosphere, a fireplace and terrific home-made cookies. As the patio sculpture of two people sharing a drink suggests, couples abound, though things get a little rowdier at around 11pm, when the late-night happy hour gets rolling.

Stetson's

1610 U Street, NW, between 16th & 17th Streets (1-202 667 6295). U Street/African-American Civil War Memorial/Cardozo Metro. **Open** 4.30pm-1am Mon-Thur; 4.30pm-2.30am Fri; 5pm-2.30am Sat; 5pm-1.30pm Sun. **Credit** AmEx, MC, V. **Map** p282 H3.

U Street's neighbourhood bar long before anyone was calling U Street a neighbourhood, Stetson's is just a shade too bright to be a true corner saloon. A former Democratic bar, Stetson's still attracts many politicos – as well as regulars – for the large-screen projector TV, pool tables and darts.

Velvet Lounge

915 U Street, NW, between Vermont Avenue & Ninth Street (1-202 462 3213/www.velvetloungedc. com). U Street/African-American Civil War Memorial/Cardozo Metro. **Open** 8pm-2am Mon-Thur, Sun; 8pm-3am Fri, Sat. **Credit** MC, V. **Map** p283 J3.

Comfy, funky and groovy, the Velvet Lounge has become a popular spot to stop off for a drink, and makes a good place to drop into after a concert at the nearby 9:30 Club. It's like a neighbourhood bar that just happens to have live music: many come to enjoy Martinis and beers with friends, others are there for the music. *See also p205.*

Georgetown

Billy Martin's Tavern

1264 Wisconsin Avenue, NW, at N Street (333 7370/www.billymartinstavern.com). Foggy Bottom-GWU Metro, then 30, 32, 34, 35, 36, Georgetown Metro Connection bus. **Open** 10am-midnight Mon-Thur; 10am-2am Fri; 8am-2am Sat; 8am-midnight Sun. **Credit** AmEx, DC, Disc, MC, V. **Map** p281 E4.

Opened in 1933 and operated by four generations of the Martins family, this dark wood, Irish-inspired tavern is an institution. It's not a kiss-kiss kind of place, but movie stars routinely opt for the safety and relative sanctity of the green plaid upholstery-laden booths or the tiny backroom called the 'Dugout'. VIPs spotted here have ranged from John F Kennedy to Madeleine Albright (both local residents), although Georgetown students, faculty and locals are more likely.

J Paul's

3218 M Street, NW, at Wisconsin Avenue (333 3450/www.j-pauls.com). Foggy Bottom-GWU Metro, then 30, 32, 34, 35, 36, Georgetown Metro Connection bus. **Open** 11.30am-2am Mon-Thur; 11.30am-3am Fri, Sat; 10.30am-2am Sun. **Credit** AmEx, DC, Disc, MC, V. **Map** p281 E5.

In good weather, young DC professionals fight for the seats of choice along the open windows facing M Street. They're also drawn to the good raw shellfish and the 55 varieties of Scotch. Like almost every other drinking hole in Georgetown, this bar also gets its share of students.

Sequoia

3000 K Street NW, at Wisconsin Avenue (1-202 944 4200). Foggy Bottom-GWU Metro, then 30, 32, 34, 35, 36, Georgetown Metro Connection bus. **Open** 11.30am-11.30pm Mon-Sat; 10.30am-10.30pm Sun. **Credit** AmEx, Disc, MC, V. **Map** p281 E5.

This enormous bar and restaurant is where DC's beautiful people go to see and be seen. The interiors are spacious, with high ceilings and tall windows. The outside bar, which looks out over the Potomac River and has views of Georgetown University and the Kennedy Center, is a popular nightspot cum pickup joint in the summer, crowded with singles, university students and tourists. The drinks are fairly reasonably priced, the fashion is a notch above casual-expensive.

Third Edition

1218 Wisconsin Avenue, NW, between M & Prospect Streets (1-202 333 3700/www.thethirdedition.com). Foggy Bottom-GWU Metro, then 30, 32, 34, 35, 36 bus. **Open** 5pm-2am Mon-Thur; 5pm-3am Fri; 11.30am-3am Sat; 11.30am-2am Sun. **Credit** AmEx, DC, Disc, MC, V. **Map** p281 E5.

The inspiration for the bar in *St Elmo's Fire*, the Third is packed with its own cast of twentysomethings these days. Equally popular with local students and people from outside the area, the dancefloors are hot and sweaty on weekends. In good weather, the outdoor tiki bar is very popular.

Cleveland Park

Aroma

3417 Connecticut Avenue, NW, between Newark & Ordway Streets (1-202 244 7995). Cleveland Park Metro. **Open** 6pm-2am Mon-Thur, Sun; 6pm-3am Fri, Sat. **Credit** AmEx, DC, Disc, MC, V. **Map** p281 F1.

After making its name as a cigar bar, Aroma has become a modernist local hangout. The amoeba-shaped tables and leopard skin-clad couches are packed at weekends, as crowds turn out for a mix of live jazz, DJs spinning loungey tunes, excellent mixed drinks, and some of the best bartenders in the city. Aroma is located along the trendy commercial strip on Connecticut Avenue, competing with many nearby venues. Still, it stands out, drawing many looking for an alternative to the Irish-heavy bars.

Ireland's Four Provinces

3412 Connecticut Avenue, NW, between Newark & Ordway Street (1-202 244 0860/www.irelands fourprovinces.com). Cleveland Park Metro. **Open** 5pm-1am Mon-Thur, Sun; 4pm-3am Fri; 5pm-3am Sat. **Credit** AmEx, DC, Disc, MC, V. **Map** p281 F1.

Probably DC's most popular Irish bar, the 4 Ps is more likely to be filled with college students and yuppies swilling Guinness than old men with brogues. There is a neighbourhood element here, luring many families – including children – with its welcoming atmosphere. But on weekends, suburbanites crowd in to sing 'Brown Eyed Girl' with live musicians and sample the Guinness burgers. Go during the early part of the week to play darts and linger over one of the dozen beers on offer.
Other locations: 105 West Broad Street, Falls Church, VA (1-703 534 8999).

Nanny O'Brien's

3319 Connecticut Avenue, NW, between Macomb & Newark Streets (1-202 686 9189/www.nannyobriens. com). Cleveland Park Metro. **Open** 4pm-1.30am Mon-Thur; 4pm-2.30am Fri; noon-2.30am Sat; noon-1.30am Sun. **Credit** AmEx, DC, Disc, MC, V. **Map** p281 F1.

Much smaller (and more crowded) than the Four Provinces across the street, Nanny's is closer to an 'authentic' Oirish pub than most bars in the city. The traditional music sessions, held every Monday night, are legendary. Three dartboards in the back attract many locals and some of the city's sharpest shooters.

Southeast

Bullfeathers

410 First Street, SE, between D & E Streets (1-202 543 5005). Capitol South Metro. **Open** 11am-2am daily. **Credit** AmEx, DC, Disc, MC, V. **Map** p285 L7.

'Bullfeathers', President Teddy Roosevelt used to snort every time he wanted people to know they were full of it. It's an all-too-appropriate name for this place, which is full of trash-talking Hill aides, interns and politicos drinking up a storm. Thursday nights are popular, and shoptalk is so prevalent that TV crews have to check their cameras at the door.
Other locations: 112 King Street, Alexandria, VA (1-703-836 8088).

▶ For Washington's best lounges, *see pp210-13* **Nightlife**.

Shops & Services

Forget the monuments – where's the merch?

Cady's Alley: design district.

Washington's late-'90s boutique explosion has seasoned, creating a critical mass of serious shopping that has begun feeding on itself, enticing even more new shopkeepers to open their doors. Over the past few years, a small nation of brainy spendthrifts has rediscovered DC and begun bedding down in a raft of new condominiums and lofts going up throughout town. Somebody's got to furnish all those flats, put clothes in those closets and pamper all those people, right? And, of course, what's good for locals is a boon to visitors, too, especially those with money to burn.

SHOPPING DISTRICTS

Georgetown lies at the spiritual, if not geographical, centre of DC's shopping universe. In recent years the old port has become a whole new town, expanding its row of fussy antique stores on upper Wisconsin Avenue, NW, filling in the margins around lower Wisconsin with speciality shops surrounded by global retail

chains (not least in the Shops at Georgetown Park), and recently gutting and renovating the old row of buildings on western M Street, NW, and christening it as Cady's Alley, a home-furnishings hub with the defensible pluck to call itself 'Washington's Design District'.

From Georgetown, if you have enough stamina (and money) left, you can easily walk to **Dupont Circle**, with its collection of favourite old storefronts and a fair number of new ones springing up. Here you can buy used books, records, art, hats, kimonos, make-up, beads and any number of trinkets you never knew you'd need – and eat to your heart's content too.

Once you're done with Dupont, you have a few choices. You can go a few blocks east, to the row of new furniture and decorative arts dealers in the **14th Street Corridor**, and then carry on up to **U Street**, where the better goods are old rather than new. Or you can head north on 18th Street to **Adams Morgan**, where, between the thumping bars and slacker-chic cafés, you'll find cool threads, fast bicycles, tribal arts and more. Or you can stroll from Dupont down **Connecticut Avenue** towards the White House and pick up electronics, perhaps a guitar, a Brooks Brothers shirt, or a really pricey watch.

If you choose the last path, you'll be wending towards **Downtown**, which is worlds improved since the dark days of its 1990s depression. The success of the MCI Center arena and the completion of the new convention centre have helped to import a lot of newish stores and restaurants, particularly in Downtown's east end.

Capitol Hill, hidden up behind the US Capitol at the eastern side of the National Mall, has a few of its own charms, the most conspicuous being the historic Eastern Market, an outsized shed of fresh produce vendors with a fantastic food counter for breakfast or lunch. If you have time for a rummage, the neighbourhood also has its share of antique and junk shops.

If you fancy a splurge, take a cab north to the high-end stores that sporadically line **Wisconsin Avenue** from the Glover Park neighbourhood, south of the cathedral, up through Friendship Heights to Bethesda. When you cross the District line at Western Avenue into Maryland, the sales tax rate drops from 5.75 per cent of the value of your loot to five per cent. The sales tax is also 5.5 per cent if you head

Goodwood.
See p156.

over the Potomac River to shop in Virginia. Here, you'll find your favourite megastores (Target, Best Buy) at Potomac Yards, a clot of chain stores at the **Fashion Centre at Pentagon City**, and numerous clothing, accessory and furnishings shops in **Old Town Alexandria**. With all this shopping, how does any work get done in this town?

One-stop shopping

Malls

Chevy Chase Pavilion

5335 Wisconsin Avenue, NW, at Western Avenue, Friendship Heights, Upper Northwest (1-202 686 5335/www.ccpavilion.com). Friendship Heights Metro. **Open** 10am-8pm Mon-Sat; noon-5pm Sun. **Credit** varies.
Feeding off the better stores across the street at Mazza Gallerie (*see below*), this minor mall offers mainly clothing and home stuff, plus a food court. Highlights include Pottery Barn and, for attractive storage solutions, Hold Everything.

Fashion Centre at Pentagon City

1100 South Hayes Street, between Army Navy Drive & 15th Street, Arlington, VA (1-703 415 2400/ www.simon.com). Pentagon City Metro. **Open** 10am-9.30pm Mon-Sat; 11am-6pm Sun. **Credit** varies.
Not bad for an old-school mall, with copious daylight and royal palms in its deep, plunging atrium. Anchored by department stores Macy's and Nordstrom, this mall offers better (but not the best) apparel, gifts, and speciality goods from 160-odd

national franchises such as the Gap, the Limited and Kenneth Cole, and is surrounded by big-box discount stores (Marshalls, Best Buy, Costco) to its east and a flank of decent shops (Bombay, Sur La Table) in a too-cute outdoor mall to its west.

Mazza Gallerie

5300 Wisconsin Avenue, NW, between Western Avenue & Jenifer Street, Friendship Heights, Upper Northwest (1-202 966 6114/www.mazzagallerie.com). Friendship Heights Metro. **Open** 10am-8pm Mon-Fri; 10am-7pm Sat; noon-5pm Sun. **Credit** varies.
Stores here run from snooty (Neiman Marcus) to congenially high-end (Saks Fifth Avenue's men's store) to over-a-barrel discount (Filene's Basement). Also houses a Williams-Sonoma ($30 cookie decorating kits!), Foot Locker, fine china at Villeroy & Boch, and a multi-screen cinema.

Shops at Georgetown Park

3222 M Street, NW, at Wisconsin Avenue, Georgetown (1-202 298 5577). Foggy Bottom-GWU Metro then 30, 32, 34, 35, 36, 38B and Georgetown Metro Connection bus, or Dupont Circle Metro then D2, D4, D6, Georgetown Metro Connection bus. **Open** 10am-9pm Mon-Sat; noon-6pm Sun. **Credit** varies. **Map** p281 E5.
Tucked, improbably, underground (though two floors are above) between M Street and the C&O Canal, this skylit, air-conditioned mall takes on a life of its own just off Georgetown's hectic streets. It houses a respectable gathering of clothing chains such as H&M and J Crew, fancy toiletries at Crabtree & Evelyn, and frivolous gadgets at the Sharper Image. Skip the meagre food court and visit Dean & Deluca (*see p169*) next door on M Street.

Shops at Union Station

50 Massachusetts Avenue, NE, at North Capitol Street, Union Station & around (1-202 371 9441/ www.unionstationdc.com). Union Station Metro. **Open** 10am-9pm Mon-Sat; noon-6pm Sun. **Credit** varies. **Map** p285 K6.

In the 1980s, before all the airports became malls, the refurbished Union Station assembled a lively range of boutiques and cafés beneath its soaring, coffered vaults. There's not much you won't find elsewhere around town, but it's great for last-minute stops before you board the train, with B Dalton Booksellers, Appalachian Spring for handmade crafts and ceramics, Swatch, Taxco Sterling for jewellery, and several newsstands.

Tysons Corner Center

1961 Chain Bridge Road, McLean, VA (1-888 289 7667/www.shoptysons.com). West Falls Church-VT/ UVA Metro then 3B, 3F, 5B, 28A, 28B bus. By car: Route 66 west to Route 7 west to Tysons Corner. **Open** 10am-9.30pm Mon-Sat; 11am-6pm Sun. **Credit** varies.

Tysons Corner Center and its next-door cousin, Tysons Galleria, helped to spawn the original, 'edge city'. If you can survive the suburban chaos of getting there, you could spend an entire weekend inside TCC's extensive mallways, grounded on one end by Bloomingdale's and on another by Nordstrom, with shops such as Benetton, Lane Bryant and Timberland in between. For the better-fed consumer, the Galleria holds higher-end retailers along the lines of Chanel, Cartier and Saks Fifth Avenue.

Watergate Shops

2650 Virginia Avenue, NW, at 26th Street, Foggy Bottom (1-202 944 3920). Foggy Bottom-GWU Metro. **Open** 10am-6pm daily. **Credit** varies. **Map** p284 F5.

Monica Lewinsky lived in an apartment upstairs at this residential and retail address and, in between her stops at Gap, may have shopped downstairs at, say, Valentino, Saks Jandel or Yves Saint Laurent. Brides-to-be with money to burn should head for the swanky Vera Wang Bridal Boutique.

Department stores

In addition to the following, there's a Nordstrom and Bloomingdale's at Tysons Corner Center (*see above*) and a Macy's at the Fashion Centre at Pentagon City (*see p154*).

Hecht's

1201 G Street, NW, Downtown (1-202 628 6661/ www.hechts.com). Metro Center Metro. **Open** 10am-8pm Mon-Sat; noon-6pm Sun. **Credit** AmEx, Disc, MC, V. **Map** p284 H6.

Hecht's remains the last big retail store standing in Downtown. It's nothing to write home about, but at least it provides the basics – reasonably priced, middle-brow fashions – as well as an outstanding selection of undies, socks, ties, shades and perfume. **Other locations**: 5400 Wisconsin Avenue, at Western Avenue, Chevy Chase, MD (1-301 654 7600).

Lord & Taylor

5225 Western Avenue, NW, at Wisconsin Avenue, Chevy Chase, Upper Northwest (1-202 362 9600/ www.lordandtaylor.com). Friendship Heights Metro. **Open** 10am-9.30pm Mon-Fri; 10am-8pm Sat; 11am-7pm Sun. **Credit** AmEx, Disc, MC, V.

Grown-ups' and children's dress- and sportswear, with broad, basic appeal, by the likes of Calvin Klein and Perry Ellis, plus the requisite cosmetics and jewellery departments. Plus-sizes for women too.

Neiman Marcus

Mazza Gallerie, 5300 Wisconsin Avenue, NW, at Western Avenue, Upper Northwest (1-202 966 9700/www.neimanmarcus.com). Friendship Heights Metro. **Open** 10am-8pm Mon-Fri; 10am-7pm Sat; noon-6pm Sun. **Credit** AmEx, DC, Disc, MC, V.

You can smell the money when you pass through the big glass doors here. With Corneliani men's suits, flirty Anna Sui dresses, Ugg handbags, Prada shoes, Wedgwood dinnerware, and Acqua di Parma at the cosmetics counter, it's all really nice stuff, but, please, why the attitude?

Saks Fifth Avenue

5555 Wisconsin Avenue, at South Park Avenue, Chevy Chase, MD (1-301 657 9000/www.saks fifthavenue.com). Friendship Heights Metro. **Open** 10am-7pm Mon-Wed, Fri; 10am-8pm Thur; 10am-6pm Sat; noon-6pm Sun. **Credit** AmEx, DC, Disc, MC, V.

Luxury a gogo, from casual to couture, with designers such as Marc Jacobs and Michael Kors, and cosmetics by La Prairie, Chanel and Kiehl's. Guys shouldn't miss the Saks men's shop in the nearby Mazza Gallerie (*see p154*). **Other locations**: Tysons Galleria, *see above* (1-703 761 0700).

Discount & factory outlets

Filene's Basement

1133 Connecticut Avenue, NW, between 17th & 18th Streets, Downtown (1-202 872 8430/ www.filenesbasement.com). Farragut North Metro. **Open** 9.30am-8pm Mon-Sat; noon-5pm Sun. **Credit** AmEx, Disc, MC, V. **Map** p284 G5.

Massive markdowns on every category of clothing and accessories by familiar names: sweaters, shirts, wallets and more. Just think of the money you'll save. **Other locations**: National Press Building, 529 14th Street, NW, Downtown (1-202 638 4110); Mazza Gallerie, 5300 Wisconsin Avenue, NW, between Western Avenue & Jenifer Street, Friendship Heights, Upper Northwest (1-202 966 0208).

Potomac Mills

2700 Potomac Mills Circle, Woodbridge, VA (1-703 490 5948/www.potomacmills.com). Hourly bus (weekdays) from Franconia-Springfield Metro/twice daily bus from Dupont Circle or Metro Center Metro (info 1-703 551 1050). By car: Interstate 95 south to exit 163 (at Lorton). **Open** 10am-9.30pm Mon-Sat; 11am-7pm Sun. **Credit** varies.

Eat, Drink, Shop

The retailers at this monster discount mall take on the oversupply of their first-tier locations. The eclectic mix includes Aeropostale, Daffy's, Foot Locker, the Gap, Guess and around 200 others. Bring your skateboards for the Vans Skatepark.

Target

3601 Jefferson Davis Highway, Alexandria, VA (1-703 706 3840/www.target.com). Crystal City Metro then 10P, 11P bus. By car: Interstate 395 south to Route 1 south (aka Jefferson Davis Highway to East Glebe Road intersection). **Open** 8am-11pm Mon-Sat; 8am-9pm Sun. **Credit** AmEx, Disc, MC, V.

It's hard to imagine what basic items you couldn't find at Target, from affordable housewares to auto supplies, budget clothing for all ages, toys, records, and non-perishable foods. Buy some popcorn before you grab a shopping cart – you may be here a while.

TJ Maxx

4350 Jenifer Street, NW, at Wisconsin Avenue, Chevy Chase, Upper Northwest (1-202 237 7616/ www.tjmaxx.com). Friendship Heights Metro. **Open** 10am-9pm Mon-Sat; noon-6pm Sun. **Credit** AmEx, Disc, MC, V.

Mega markdowns on familiar names for guys, gals and kids, with plenty of odds and ends for the house.

Antiques

Most of the fancier antiques stores are in Georgetown, and most of them aren't open on a Sunday. Further smatterings of antiques can be found on Capitol Hill, in Adams Morgan, Dupont Circle and the U Street Corridor. Those listed below tend to have the widest range of good buys at affordable prices.

Arise

117 Carroll Street, NW, between Maple & Willow Avenues, Takoma Park (1-202 291 0770/ www.arisedc.com). Takoma Metro. **Open** 11am-6pm Tue-Sun. **Credit** AmEx, MC, V.

No other store matches the variety and authenticity of the Asian furnishings and apparel sold at Arise. With new shipments of furniture, ceramics, stone ornaments, Buddhas, woven baskets and *ukiyo-e* woodblock prints arriving regularly, repeat visits are a must. Large furniture pieces and kimonos are housed in a warehouse space across the street.

The Brass Knob

2311 18th Street, NW, between Kalorama & Belmont Roads, Adams Morgan (1-202 332 3370/ www.thebrassknob.com). Dupont Cirle then 42 bus or Woodley Park-Zoo/Adams Morgan Metro then 90, 92, 93, L2 bus. **Open** 10.30am-6pm Mon-Sat. **Credit** AmEx, Disc, MC, V. **Map** p282 G3.

Along with its partner, the Back Doors Warehouse on the next block (2329 Champlain Street, NW, 1-202 265 0587), this store sells lighting, functional and ornamental fixtures, and architectural elements that cover pretty much every period of housing in DC.

Goodwood

1428 U Street, NW, between 14th & 15th Streets, Shaw: U Street/14th Street Corridor (1-202 986 3640). U Street/African-American Civil War Memorial/Cardozo Metro. **Open** 5-9pm Thur; 11am-7pm Fri, Sat; 11am-5pm Sun. **Credit** MC, V. **Map** p282 H3.

Scouting the best auctions in the mid Atlantic, Goodwood brings in amazing wood tables, armoires, bookcases and mirrors, plus ornamental follies you won't find elsewhere for the prices. Go on Thursday evening for the picks of the week.

Miss Pixie's

1810 Adams Mill Road, NW, between Calvert Street & Columbia Road, Adams Morgan (1-202 232 8171). Woodley Park-Zoo/Adams Morgan Metro then 90, 92, 93 bus or Dupont Circle Metro then 42 bus. **Open** noon-9pm Thur; noon-7pm Fri-Sun. **Credit** MC, V. **Map** p282 G2.

A neighbourhood institution, this lively storefront hauls in truckloads of country and vintage furnishings each week at extremely reasonable prices. You may take home a gliding porch rocker, a '50s sofa, or cool garden ornaments.

Art supplies

Art Store

3019 M Street, NW, between 30th & 31st Streets, Georgetown (1-202 342 7030/www.artstore.com). Foggy Bottom-GWU Metro then 30, 32, 34, 35, 36, 38, Georgetown Metro Connection bus. **Open** 9am-9pm Mon-Fri; 9am-10pm Sat; 11am-7pm Sun. **Credit** AmEx, Disc, MC, V. **Map** p281 F5.

If you run out of Naples Yellow or Cadmium Red, or need a new stretch of canvas, this is your place.

Utrecht

1250 I Street, NW, at New York Avenue, Downtown (1-202 898 0555/www.utrechtart.com). Metro Center Metro. **Open** 9am-7pm Mon-Fri; 9am-6pm Sat; 11am-6pm Sun. **Credit** AmEx, Disc, MC, V. **Map** p284 J5.

Painters and draftspersons alike will find themselves at home here. Utrecht's own brand of oils, acrylics and watercolours, in particular, come highly recommended.

Books

All the big national chain bookstores have stores in DC. There are two **Borders** downtown (1801 K Street, NW, 1-202 466 4909; and 600 14th Street, NW, 1-202 737 1385), plus a **Barnes & Noble** in Georgetown (3040 M Street, NW, 1-202 965 9880) and downtown (555 12th Street, NW, 1-202 347 0176). Though slightly smaller, the notable local chain, **Olsson's Books & Records**, with stores downtown and near Dupont Circle (418 Seventh Street, NW, 1-202 638 7610; and 1307 19th Street, NW, 1-202 785 1133), packs in nearly as much stock. Listed below are DC's indie and speciality book-sellers.

Cultural commodities

Culture is only one excuse for having a museum. The other, of course, is to have a museum shop. But Washington's museum gift shops aren't simply for tourist souvenirs, but for eccentric little buys that you can't usually find elsewhere. Nearly all of the city's museums have shops, but those listed below are among the most unusual.

Arthur M Sackler Gallery & Freer Gallery of Art

1050 Independence Avenue, SW, between 11th & 12 Streets, The Mall & Tidal Basin (1-202 633 4880/ www.asia.si.edu). Smithsonian Metro. **Open** 10am-5.30pm daily. **Credit** AmEx, Disc, MC, V. **Map** p284 J7.

Books, music and videos relevant to the museum's Asian focus, plus teapots, crystal objects, kimono gift sets, Chinese and Japanese prints and arty umbrellas.

National Building Museum

401 F Street, NW, between fourth & fifth Streets, Judiciary Square area (1-202 272 7706/www.nbm.org). Judiciary Square Metro. **Open** 10am-5pm Mon-Sat; 11am-5pm Sun. **Credit** AmEx, MC, V. **Map** p285 J6.

Often rated the best museum store in DC, the National Building Museum sells a lot of one-off, beautiful items such as toys and gizmos, bowls, pillows, vases, mobiles, posters, neckties, architect-designed watches and many, many design books.

National Gallery of Art

West Building: Constitution Avenue, between Fourth & Seventh Streets, NW; East Building: Constitution Avenue & Fourth Street, NW, The Mall & Tidal Basin (1-202 737 4215/ www.nga.gov). Archives-Navy Memorial, Judiciary Square or Smithsonian Metro. **Open** 10am-5pm Mon-Sat; 11am-6pm Sun. **Credit** AmEx, Disc, MC, V. **Map** p285 J6.

Below ground in both National Gallery Buildings are enormous shops with marvellous books, prints, posters, cards and calendars.

Renwick Gallery of the Smithsonian American Art Museum

17th Street & Pennsylvania Avenue, NW, The White House & around (1-202 633 8998/ 377 2700/http://americanart.si.edu/

renwick/renwick_about.cfm). Farragut North or Farragut West Metro. **Open** 10am-5.30pm daily. **Credit** AmEx, Disc, MC, V. **Map** p284 G5.

A healthy range of books on American crafts, plus prints, are draws here, but the highlights are the ceramic, wood and glass goods, and jewellery that exemplify the museum's mission.

Textile Museum

2320 S Street, NW, between 23rd & 24th Streets, Dupont Circle (1-202 667 0441/ www.textilemuseum.org). Dupont Circle Metro. **Open** 10am-5pm Mon Sat; 1-5pm Sun. **Credit** AmEx, MC, V. **Map** p282 F4.

Books on practically every form of fibre and the woven arts, plus a lovely arrangement of ties, scarves, shawls and other soft things.

Washington National Cathedral

Massachusetts & Wisconsin Avenues, NW, Upper Northwest (1-202 537 6200/ www.cathedral.org/cathedral). 30, 32, 34, 35, 36 bus . **Open** *Sept-May* 10am-5.30pm Mon-Fri; 10am-4.30pm Sat; 8am-6.30pm Sun. *June-Aug* 10am-8pm Mon-Fri; 10am-4.30pm Sat; 8am-6.30pm Sun. **Credit** AmEx, Disc, MC, V. **Map** p281 E2.

For $565 you can pick up an actual oil lamp from the Bronze Age, but for somewhat less you can take home stained-glass reproductions, liturgical material, rosaries, books, cards and the like. Also visit the Greenhouse (for plants) and Herb Cottage (for herbs and other food products) in the grounds. Opening times for the cathedral can vary, so it's best to check first.

Eat, Drink, Shop

ADC Map & Travel Store

1636 I Street, NW, between Connecticut Avenue & 17th Street, Downtown (1-800 544 2659/www.adcmaps.com). Farragut West Metro. **Open** 9am-6.30pm Mon-Thur; 9am-5.30pm Fri; 11am-5pm Sat. **Credit** AmEx, Disc, MC, V. **Map** p284 G5.

A paradise for wanderers, squeezed into a tiny space. The maps cover nearly every region of the world, and there's an extra emphasis on guidebooks to the mid Atlantic region.

Big Planet Comics

3145 Dumbarton Street, NW, between 31st Street & Wisconsin Avenue, Georgetown (1-202 342 1961). Foggy Bottom-GWU Metro then 30, 32, 34, 35, 36, 38B, Georgetown Metro Connection bus. **Open** 11am-7pm Mon, Tue, Thur, Fri; 11am-8pm Wed; 11am-6pm Sat; noon-5pm Sun. **Credit** AmEx, MC, V. **Map** p281 E5.

Underground comics and graphic novels.

Bird-in-Hand Bookstore & Gallery

323 Seventh Street, SE, at Pennsylvania Avenue, Capitol Hill (1-202 543 0744). Eastern Market Metro. **Open** 11am-6pm Wed-Sat. **Credit** AmEx, DC, MC, V. **Map** p285 L7.

Books on art, architecture and design are all available here, as are museum exhibition catalogues.

Candida's World of Books

1541 14th Street, NW, between P & Q Streets, 14th Street Corridor (1-202 667 4811). Dupont Circle Metro. **Open** 10am-10pm Tue-Sat; noon-8pm Sun. **Credit** MC, V. **Map** p282 H3.

A smart shop offering travel guides and atlases, plus language aids, dictionaries and phrasebooks for the linguistically curious.

Capitol Hill Books

657 C Street, SE, at Seventh Street, Capitol Hill (1-202 544 1621/www.capitolhillbooks-dc.com). Eastern Market Metro. **Open** 11.30am-6pm Mon-Fri; 9am-6pm Sat, Sun. **Credit** AmEx, MC, V. **Map** p285 L7.

Capitol Hill Books has two floors of used books – fiction, mysteries, politics, cooking and more – plus rare tomes and first editions.

Chapters

445 11th Street, NW, between Pennsylvania Avenue & E Street, Downtown (1-202 737 5553). Metro Center Metro. **Open** 10am-7pm Mon-Fri; noon-7pm Sat; 2-7pm Sun. **Credit** AmEx, Disc, MC, V. **Map** p284 H5.

Chapters is the independent literary bookstore of DC. New releases are highlighted at the front, and the staff's picks are prominently displayed. The casual atmosphere and friendly proprietors are further draws.

Rich pickings

Bethesda, Maryland, just up the Metro's Red Line from Upper Northwest DC, is a retail hub all on its own. The city basically rolls out a red carpet to shoppers, with stores generally catering to the doctor/lawyer salaries found in households just outside its retail centre. Most of the following stores are in or around the area known as Woodmont Triangle, just outside the Bethesda Metro.

Barry Bricken

4919 Elm Street (1-301 652 9883). Bethesda Metro. **Open** 10am-6pm Mon-Wed, Fri; 10am-8pm Thur; noon-4pm Sun. **Credit** AmEx, MC, V.

Classic designer comforts from the son of a Baltimore trouser-maker. Men and women can choose from an array of tailored cuts in a variety of first-rate fabrics.

Bella Italia

4844 Bethesda Avenue (1-301 654 2667). Bethesda Metro. **Open** 10am-9pm Mon-Thur; 10am-10pm Fri; noon-5pm Sun. **Credit** AmEx, MC, V.

This store, an exponent of the 'slow food' movement, sells truffles in jars and tubes, alongside organic marzipan and fruit jellies. Ceramics by Geribi, D'Arna and Ricceri complete the picture.

Bethesda Florist

4934 St Elmo Avenue (1-301 656 8200). Bethesda Metro. **Open** 8.30am-5pm Mon-Fri; 9am-3pm Sat. **Credit** AmEx, DC, Disc, MC, V.

Nothing freshens a room like a spray of lilies, which you'll find freshly cut here, along with tropicals and gift baskets. Staff can arrange delivery both locally and worldwide.

Lomax Schinzel Antiques

6826 Wisconsin Avenue (1-301 656 1911). Bethesda Metro. **Open** 9.30am-5.30pm Mon-Fri; 9.30am-5pm Sat. **Credit** AmEx, MC, V.

Think Louis XV, Directoire, Regency and Empire and you get the picture. Mahogany, gold leaf, cabriole legs, and claw-and-ball feet are all here.

Maurice Villency

7016 Wisconsin Avenue (1-240 396 0100/www.villency.com). Bethesda Metro.

Kramerbooks

1517 Connecticut Avenue, NW, at Q Street, Dupont Circle (1-202 387 1400). Dupont Circle Metro. **Open** 7.30am-1am Mon-Thur, Sun; 24hrs Fri, Sat. **Credit** AmEx, Disc, MC, V. **Map** p282 G4.
As much the social nucleus of Dupont Circle as a bookstore (with café at the back), the selection is excellent – if you can tolerate the somewhat indifferent staff.

Lambda Rising

1625 Connecticut Avenue, NW, between Q & R Streets, Dupont Circle (1-202 462 6969). Dupont Circle Metro. **Open** 10am-10pm Mon-Thur, Sun. 10am-midnight Fri, Sat. **Credit** AmEx, Disc, MC, V. **Map** p282 G4.
A pioneer in many ways, both in the book business and in DC's gay community. You'll find serious (and frivolous) gay fiction, history (and 'herstory'), self-help and health-care titles, periodicals, plus funny note cards and trinkets.

Politics & Prose

5015 Connecticut Avenue, NW, between Fessenden Street & Nebraska Avenue, Upper Northwest (1-800 722 0790/1-202 364 1919/www.politics-prose.com). Van Ness-UDC Metro then L1, L2, L4 bus. **Open** 9am-10pm Mon-Thur; 9am-11pm Fri, Sat; 10am-8pm Sun. **Credit** AmEx, Disc, MC, V.
Book fans head to Politics & Prose regularly for readings by provocative authors. A fantastic selection

doesn't exclude the tots – they even have their own romp area. And the adults can have coffee too.

Second Story Books

2000 P Street, NW, at 20th Street, Dupont Circle (1-202 659 8884/www.secondstorybooks.com). Dupont Circle Metro. **Open** 10am-10pm daily. **Credit** AmEx, Disc, MC, V. **Map** p282 G4.
A venerable, musty space, chock-full of all kinds of curious used titles, plus second-hand music and prints. Check the sidewalk bins for more bargains.

Yawa Books & Gifts

2206 18th Street, NW, between Wyoming Avenue & Kalorama Road, Adams Morgan (1-202 483 6805). Woodley Park-Zoo/Adams Morgan Metro then 90, 92, 93 bus. **Open** 11am-8pm Mon-Fri; 11am-9pm Sat. **Credit** AmEx, Disc, MC, V. **Map** p282 G3.
Things to read, incense to burn, gifts to give and cards to send – all from Africa.

Cameras & film processing

CVS (*see p172*) also does one-hour developing.

Motophoto

1105 19th Street, NW, at L Street, Downtown (1-202 293 5484/www.motophoto.com). Farragut North Metro. **Open** 9am-7pm Mon-Sat. **Credit** AmEx, MC, V. **Map** p284 G5.

Eat, Drink, Shop

Open 10am-8pm Mon, Wed-Fri; 10am-6pm Tue, Sat; noon-5pm Sun. **Credit** AmEx, Disc, MC, V.
Sleek, modern and utterly gorgeous home furnishings are offered by this New York-based company. Contemporary homewares add to the appeal.

Pirjo

4821 Bethesda Avenue (1-301 986 1870). Bethesda Metro. **Open** 10am-6pm Mon-Sat. **Credit** AmEx, MC, V.
With lines of separates such as Lilith and Rundholtz, plus a sophisticated selection of necklaces, bracelets and the like, this shop draws in customers looking for something understated but unusual.

Sandra's Fine Jewelry

4806 Bethesda Avenue (1-301 652 1997). Bethesda Metro. **Open** 10am-6pm Mon-Wed, Fri; 10am-7pm Sat; 10am-5pm Sun. **Credit** AmEx, MC, V.
In business for more than 30 years, this small store has a large following who return time and again for top-notch craft jewellery.

Underwraps

4928 Hampden Lane (1-301 656 4900). Bethesda Metro. **Open** 10am-6pm Mon-Fri; 10am-5pm Sat. **Credit** AmEx, Disc, MC, V.
Lots of lovely lingerie.

Walpole's

4829 Bethesda Avenue (1-301 913 0002). Bethesda Metro. **Open** 10am-7pm Mon-Sat; noon-5pm Sun. **Credit** AmEx, MC, V.
A haven of exquisite bed and table linens, plus fine cotton items (with an emphasis on Egyptian cotton handcrafted in Italy). Also bath towels, rugs and other personal luxuries.

Wear It Well

4816 Bethesda Avenue (1-301 652 3713). Bethesda Metro. **Open** 10am-6pm Mon-Wed, Fri, Sat; 10am-7pm Thur; noon-5pm Sun. **Credit** AmEx, MC, V.
Wear it Well stocks elegant lines by Womyn and Garfield & Marks, among others, in its collections of suits, tops and trousers, which range from casual to slightly dressy.

Motophoto is great for one-hour photo processing, and passport and visa photos.
Other locations: throughout the city.

Penn Camera

840 E Street, NW, between Eighth & Ninth Streets, Penn Quarter (1-202 347 5777/www.penncamera. com). Gallery Place-Chinatown Metro. **Open** 8.30am-6pm Mon-Fri; 10am-5pm Sat. **Credit** AmEx, Disc, MC, V. **Map** p285 J6.
This old-school camera shop stays more than current with all the equipment a professional photographer could need, but the knowledgeable staff will help get novices started too.
Other locations: throughout the city.

Ritz Camera

1750 L Street, NW, at 18th Street, Downtown (1-202 861 7710/www.ritzcamera.com). Farragut North Metro. **Open** 8.30am-6.30pm Mon-Fri; 10am-5pm Sat. **Credit** AmEx, Disc, MC, V. **Map** p284 G5.
A full-service camera shop and processor. And with 12 District locations, chances are, you're near one.

Electronics

Radio Shack has stores throughout the area; check the phone book for your nearest.

Best Buy

4500 Wisconsin Avenue, NW, at Albemarle Street, Upper Northwest (1-202/www.bestbuy.com). Tenleytown-AU Metro. **Open** 10am-9pm Mon-Sat; 11am-7pm Sun. **Credit** AmEx, Disc, MC, V.
This carnival of mass-media gizmos offers just about anything you want – if it's in stock. Even if it isn't, at least you can compare the prices.

Graffiti Audio-Video

1219 Connecticut Avenue, NW, between M & N Streets, Dupont Circle (1-202 296 8412/www.graffitiaudio.com). Dupont Circle or Farragut North Metro. **Open** 10am-7pm Mon-Sat; noon-6pm Sun. **Credit** AmEx, Disc, MC, V. **Map** p282 G5.
Better TV and audio equipment, with familiar names such as Bose and Sony, among others.
Other locations: 4914 Wisconsin Avenue, NW, Upper Northwest (1-202 244 9643); 7810 Old Georgetown Road, Bethesda, MD (1-301 907 3660).

Fashion

Most of the mainstream clothiers make appearances in the District – Banana Republic, J Crew, Gap and so on. Georgetown has one of nearly all of them, plus choicer chains like Club Monaco, Diesel and Armani Exchange.

Boutiques

All About Jane

2438 18th Street, NW, at Columbia Road, Adams Morgan (1-202 797 9710/www.allaboutjane.com).

Dupont Cirle Metro then 42 bus or Woodley Park-Zoo/Adams Morgan Metro then 90, 92, 93, L2 bus. **Open** noon-9pm Mon, Wed, Thur; noon-9pm Fri, Sat; noon-6pm Sun. **Credit** AmEx, Disc, MC, V. **Map** p282 G3.
It's just a slip of a store, but All About Jane stocks enough cool lines (Juicy, Joie and Tessuto) for fun chicks.
Other locations: 2839 Clarendon Boulevard, Arlington, VA (1-703 243 4424).

Betsy Fisher

1224 Connecticut Avenue, NW, between N Street & Jefferson Place, Dupont Circle (1-202 785 1975/www.betsyfisher.com). Dupont Circle Metro. **Open** 10am-7pm Mon-Wed; 10am-9pm Thur, Fri; 10am-6pm Sat; noon-4pm Sun. **Credit** AmEx, Disc, MC, V. **Map** p282 G4.
Approachable chic, from tailored to saucy. Ensembles, dresses and the rest by the likes of Trina Turk, Rozae Nichols and Yansi Fugel.

Catchcan

5516 Connecticut Avenue, NW, at Morrison Street, Chevy Chase, Upper Northwest (1-202 686 5316). Friendship Heights Metro then E2, E3, E4, E6 bus or Van Ness-UDC Metro then L1, L2, L4 bus. **Open** 10am-5pm Mon-Wed, Fri; 10am-8pm Thur; 10am-6pm Sat; 11am-5pm Sun. **Credit** MC, V.
A catholic array of adornments for the bod (women's clothing, footwear and jewellery), plus Asian and French country furniture, table linens, picture frames and American crafts.

Daisy

1814 Adams Mill Road, NW, between Calvert Street & Columbia Road, Adams Morgan (1-202 797 1777). Dupont Cirle Metro then 42 bus or Woodley Park-Zoo/Adams Morgan Metro then 90, 92, 93, L2 bus. **Open** noon-8pm Mon, Wed-Sat; noon-6pm Sun. **Credit** AmEx, MC, V. **Map** p282 G2.
This frisky girlie shop caters to those with an eye for the breezy. Lots of blouses, dresses, sweaters, pants, belts and hats by Kooba, Frankie B and Shoshanna. The other branch has a shoe boutique.
Other locations: 4940 St Elmo Avenue, Bethesda, MD (1-301 656 2280).

Junction

1510 U Street, NW, between 15th & 16th Streets, Shaw: U Street/14th Street Corridor (1-202 483 0260). U Street/African-American Civil War/Cardozo Metro. **Open** 3-7pm Tue, Wed; noon-7pm Thur-Sat; 11am-5pm Sun. **Credit** MC, V. **Map** p282 H3.
A droll little collectively run boutique selling original designs for men and women, plus vintage pieces, accessories, photography and handmade gifts.

Nana

1534 U Street, NW, between 15th & 16th Streets, Shaw: U Street/14th Street Corridor (1-202 667 6955). U Street/African-American Civil War/Cardozo Metro. **Open** noon-7pm Tue-Sat; noon-5pm Sun. **Credit** MC, V. **Map** p282 H3.

Allan Woods Florist.
See p167.

Nana sells fun, funky dresses, blouses, skirts and more by Classic Girl, Elaine Perlov and Uppsee Daisees, and tosses in Angela Adams handbags and Lilian Hartman jewellery.

Pop

1803A 14th Street, NW, at S Street, Shaw: U Street/14th Street Corridor (1-202 332 3312). U Street/African-American Civil War Memorial/Cardozo Metro. **Open** 11.30am-7.30pm Mon-Fri; 11am-7pm Sat; noon-6pm Sun. **Credit** MC, V. **Map** p282 H4.
Set in a bright little loft, this groovy store is home to such favourites as Ben Sherman, Penguin and Spiewak.

Children

Don't leave the little people out of the style equation. You can find duds and shoes for kids at **H&M** (*see p165*), **Hecht's**, **Lord & Taylor** (for both, *see p155*) and **Target** (*see p156*). There's a **Gap Kids** in Georgetown (1267 Wisconsin Avenue, NW, 1-202 333 2411) and in Chevy Chase. Any **CVS** drugstore (*see p172*) has baby and child sundries galore. And don't forget the museum shops (*see p156* **Cultural commodities**) for one-of-a-kind toys.

Full of Beans

5502 Connecticut Avenue, NW, at Livingston Street, Upper Northwest (1-202 362 8566). Van Ness-UDC Metro then L1, L2, L4 bus. **Open** 10am-5.30pm Mon-Sat; 11am-3pm Sun. **Credit** MC, V.
It's a lucky child whose parents shop at this fun store, which offers mid-range clothing and accessories for infants and older. Cute toys too.

Kids Closet

1226 Connecticut Avenue, NW, at N Street, Dupont Circle (1-202 429 9247). Dupont Circle Metro. **Open** 10am-6pm Mon-Fri; 11am-5pm Sat. **Credit** AmEx, Disc, MC, V. **Map** p282 G4.
Lines by Little Me, Carter's and Absorba, alongside higher-end miniature fashions by Baby Trousseau.

Designer

The greatest concentration of designer clothing lies in DC's better department stores, such as **Neiman Marcus** and **Saks Fifth Avenue** (for both, *see p155*). **Betsey Johnson** keeps her wacky slip dresses at 1319 Wisconsin Avenue, NW (1-202 338 4090). If money's no object, you can visit **Chanel**'s boutique in the Willard Hotel (1455 Pennsylvania Avenue, NW, 1-202 638 5055) and follow up with a trip to **Versace** (5454 Wisconsin Avenue, Chevy Chase, MD, 1-301 907 9400). Women of a certain quiet sophistication shop at **Claire Dratch** (7615 Wisconsin Avenue, Bethesda, MD, 1-301 656 8000) and **Rizik's** (1100 Connecticut Avenue,

NW, Downtown (1-202 223 4050); across the street from the latter is a **Burberry** store (1155 Connecticut Avenue, NW, 1-202 463 3000).

Dry cleaning & laundry

Georgetown Cleaners

1070 31st Street, NW, at M Street, Georgetown (1-202 965 9655). Foggy Bottom-GWU Metro then 30, 32, 34, 35, 36, 38B, Georgetown Metro Connection bus. **Open** 7.30am-7pm Mon-Fri; 8.30am-6pm Sat. **Credit** MC, V. **Map** p281 E5.
Exquisitely careful dry cleaning, laundry, alterations and repairs.

Imperial Valet

1331 Connecticut Avenue, NW, between Dupont Circle & N Street, Dupont Circle (1-202 785 1444). Dupont Circle Metro. **Open** 7.30am-6.30pm Mon-Fri; 9am-3pm Sat. **Credit** AmEx, MC, V. **Map** p282 G4.
In an hour, you can have a hat dry cleaned. In a day, laundry done. Alterations and repairs as well.

U Street Cleaners

1513 U Street, NW, between 15th & 16th Streets, Shaw: U Street/14th Street Corridor (1-202 745 5726). U Street/African-American Civil War Memorial/Cardozo Metro. **Open** 7am-7pm Mon-Fri; 8am-6pm Sat. **Credit** AmEx, MC, V. **Map** p282 H3.
All the usual services, plus surgical cleaning for tough spots and special care for delicates.

Erotic & fetish

Dream Dresser

1042 Wisconsin Avenue, NW, between K & M Streets, Georgetown (1-202 625 0373/www. dreamdresser.com). Foggy Bottom-GWU Metro then 30, 32, 34, 35, 36, 38B, Georgetown Metro Connection bus. **Open** 11am-8pm Mon-Sat. **Credit** AmEx, MC, V. **Map** p281 E5.
Lingerie, bondage gear, whips, nipple clamps... you name it, it's here.

Leather Rack

1723 Connecticut Avenue, NW, between R & S Streets, Dupont Circle (1-202 797 7401). Dupont Circle Metro. **Open** 10am-11pm Mon-Wed, Sun; 10am-midnight Thur-Sat. **Credit** AmEx, MC, V. **Map** p282 G4.
Leather Rack offers pleasure and pain implements geared toward leather daddies. Also has a large selection of videos upstairs.

Hats

Hats in the Belfry

1250 Wisconsin Avenue, NW, between Prospect & N Streets, Georgetown (1-202 342 2006/www.hatsin thebelfry.com). Foggy Bottom-GWU Metro then 30, 32, 34, 35, 36, 38B, Georgetown Metro Connection bus. **Open** 10am-9pm daily. **Credit** MC, V. **Map** p281 E5.

Eat, Drink, Shop

A hat, cap, beret or boater for every head by makes like Bailey, Eric Javits, Kangol and Stetson. Plenty of costume-y choices too.

The Proper Topper

1350 Connecticut Avenue, NW, between Dupont Circle & N Street, Dupont Circle (1-202 842 3055/ www.propertopper.com). Dupont Circle Metro. **Open** 10am-8pm Mon-Fri; 10am-6pm Sat; noon-6pm Sun. **Credit** AmEx, Disc, MC, V. **Map** p282 G4.
The chic hat selection extends itself to both sexes, but women also get combs, jewellery and ephemera. **Other locations**: 3213 P Street, NW, Georgetown (1-202 333 6200).

Jewellery & accessories

Jewelerswerk Galerie

2000 Pennsylvania Avenue, NW, between 20th & 21st Streets, Foggy Bottom (1-202 293 0249). Foggy Bottom Metro. **Open** 10am-7pm Mon-Fri; 10am-6pm Sat. **Credit** AmEx, Disc, MC, V. **Map** p282 G5.
This cool little gallery sells object jewellery made by international artists in a variety of media.

Taxco Sterling

Shops at Georgetown Park, 3222 M Street, NW, at Wisconsin Avenue, Georgetown (1-202 342 9504). Foggy Bottom-GWU Metro then 30, 32, 34, 35, 36, 38B, Georgetown Metro Connection bus. **Open** 10am-9pm Mon-Sat; noon-6pm Sun. **Credit** Disc, MC, V. **Map** p281 E5.

Beautiful doesn't always mean over-the-top expensive in Taxco's well-chosen inventory.
Other locations: 40 Massachusetts Avenue, NE, Capitol Hill (1-202 682 1172).

Tiffany & Co

5500 Wisconsin Avenue, NW, at South Park Avenue, Chevy Chase, MD (1-301 657 8777/ www.tiffany.com). Friendship Heights Metro. **Open** 10am-6pm Mon-Wed, Fri; 10am-8pm Thur; noon-5pm Sun. **Credit** AmEx, DC, Disc, MC, V.
Can't make it home without something shiny packed in a minty blue box? We know the feeling.

Tiny Jewel Box

1147 Connecticut Avenue, NW, between L & M Streets, Downtown (1-202 393 2747/ www.tinyjewelbox.com). Farragut North Metro. **Open** 10am-5.30pm Mon-Sat. **Credit** AmEx, MC, V. **Map** p282 G5.
A vast range of pieces, from classic to contemporary, lines the three floors of Tiny Jewel Box, an old-line downtown favourite. Other adornments include scarves, bags, gloves and gifts.

Menswear

BOSS Hugo Boss

1517 Wisconsin Avenue, NW, between P & Q Streets, Georgetown (1-202 625 2677/www. hugoboss.com). Foggy Bottom-GWU Metro then 30,

Part with the furniture

Thanks, doubtless, to its critical mass of wealth and status, Washington has an uncommon amount of individually owned home stores. If chain domination is cramping your interior style, this is where to come.

Apartment Zero

406 Seventh Street, NW, between D & E Streets, Penn Quarter (1-202 628 4067/ www.apartmentzero.com). Archives-Navy Memorial Metro. **Open** 11am-6pm Wed-Sat; noon-5pm Sun. **Credit** AmEx, Disc, MC, V. **Map** p285 J6.
Cool-hunters shop at Apartment Zero for furniture by the likes of Herman Miller, Artifort and Blu Dot; there's flooring by Interface.

Good Eye

4918 Wisconsin Avenue, NW, between Ellicott & Fessenden Streets, Upper Northwest (1-202 244 8516/ www.goodeyeonline.com). Tenleytown-AU Metro. **Open** noon-6pm Wed-Sun. **Credit** Disc, MC, V.

Appealing to lovers of mid 20th-century throwbacks, Good Eye traffics in mint-condition upholstered and wooden furniture, with a spot-on selection of lighting.

Illuminations

415 Eighth Street, NW, between D & E Streets, Penn Quarter (1-202 783 4888/ www.illuminc.com). Archives-Navy Memorial Metro. **Open** 10am-6pm Mon-Fri; 11am-5pm Sat. **Credit** AmEx, MC, V. **Map** p285 J6.
Two showrooms display lighting made mainly by Artemide.
Other locations: 3323 Cady's Alley, NW, Georgetown (1-202 965 4888).

Millennium Decorative Arts

1528 U Street, NW, between 15th & 16th Streets, Shaw: U Street/14th Street Corridor (1-202 483 1218). U Street/African-American Civil War Memorial/Cardozo Metro. **Open** noon-7pm Thur-Sun. **Credit** AmEx, MC, V. **Map** p282 H3.
Stylish '40s- to '60s-vintage European furniture is stocked at this two-level store,

32, 34, 35, 36, Georgetown Metro Connection bus.
Open 11am-8pm Mon-Sat; noon-6pm Sun.
Credit AmEx, Disc, MC, V. **Map** p281 E4.
Less drapey than they used to be, these suits, shirts and trousers merge excellent materials with reasonable prices.

Brooks Brothers

1201 Connecticut Avenue, NW, between M & N Streets, Dupont Circle (1-202 659 4650). Farragut North or Dupont Circle Metro. **Open** 9.30am-7pm Mon-Fri; 9.30am-6pm Sat; noon-5pm Sun.
Credit AmEx, Disc, MC, V. **Map** p282 G4.
Ever the classicist, Brooks Brothers has a spacious, elegant layout of men's and women's clothes and furnishings. Indulge your inner gentleman (or -woman).
Other locations: 5504 Wisconsin Avenue, Chevy Chase, MD (1-301 654 8202).

Everard's Clothing

1802 Wisconsin Avenue, NW, at S Street, Georgetown (1-202 298 7464/www.everards clothing.com). Foggy Bottom-GWU Metro then 30, 32, 34, 35, 36 bus. **Open** 11am-6pm Mon-Sat.
Credit AmEx, DC, Disc, MC, V. **Map** p281 E3.
The well-dressed man in Washington knows Louis Everard, and Mr Everard knows their measurements, meticulously crafting Italian suits to their specifications. Upstairs there is a women's collection.
Other locations: Omni Shoreham Hotel, 2500 Calvert Street, NW, at Connecticut Avenue, Upper Northwest (1-202 234 5040).

Everett Hall

1230 Connecticut Avenue, NW, between M & N Streets, Dupont Circle (1-202 467 0003/ www.everetthalldesigns.com). Dupont Circle Metro. **Open** 11am-7pm Mon-Sat. **Credit** AmEx, Disc, MC, V. **Map** p282 G4.
Everett Hall creates suits for strapping, sophisticated men. Who could resist his second-skin fabrics, shirts made in Italy and furnishings?
Other locations: Chevy Chase Pavilion, 5335 Wisconsin Avenue, NW, at Western Avenue, Friendship Heights, Upper Northwest (1-202 686 5335).

Rock Creek

2029 P Street, NW, at 21st Street, Dupont Circle (1-202 429 6940). Dupont Circle Metro. **Open** 10am-8pm Mon-Fri; 10am-7pm Sat; 11am-6pm Sun. **Credit** AmEx, Disc, MC, V. **Map** p282 G4.
Metrosexual fashions by Diesel, DKNY, Ted Baker, Paul Smith, Theory et al. Besides sexy club and cocktail wear, the store has excellent furnishings and more than a token selection of swimwear. There's always a friendly face behind the counter too.

Mid-range & budget

H&M

1025 F Street, NW, between 11th & 12th Streets, Downtown (1-202 347 3306/www.hm.com). Metro Center Metro. **Open** 10am-8pm Mon-Sat; noon-6pm Sun. **Credit** AmEx, DC, Disc, MC, V. **Map** p284 J6.

but you'll also find graphic glassware, vases and coaster sets to go with it.

Muléh

1831 14th Street, NW, between S & T Streets, Shaw: U Street/14th Street Corridor (1-202 667 3440/www.muleh.com). U Street/ African-American Civil War Memorial/ Cardozo Metro. **Open** 11am-7pm Tue-Sat; noon-5pm Sun. **Credit** AmEx, MC, V. **Map** p282 H3.
Modern Asian furnishings, with emphasis on renewable materials (rattan, bamboo, grass fibres), clean lines and interesting textures. Prices are bearable.
Other locations: 4731 Elm Street, Bethesda, MD (1-301 941 1174).

Reincarnations

1401 14th Street, NW, at Rhode Island Avenue, 14th Street Corridor (1-202 319 1606). Dupont Circle Metro. **Open** 11am-8pm Tue-Sun. **Credit** AmEx, MC, V. **Map** p282 H3.
A room filled with this store's Harlequin offerings would be a bit much, but in low doses it looks cute.

Tabletop

1608 20th Street, NW, between Q & R Streets, Dupont Circle (1-202 387 7117/ www.tabletopdc.com). Dupont Circle Metro. **Open** noon-8pm Mon-Sat; noon-6pm Sun. **Credit** AmEx, Disc, MC, V. **Map** p282 G4.
Trendy home accessories, including sleek vases, shelving, linens and tableware, plus a few personal items such as jewellery.

Vastu

1829 14th Street, NW, between S & T Streets, Shaw: U Street/14th Street Corridor (1-202 234 8344/ www.vastudc.com). U Street/African-American Civil War Memorial/Cardozo Metro. **Open** 11am-7pm Tue-Sat; noon-5pm Sun. **Credit** AmEx, DC, Disc, MC, V. **Map** p282 H3.
Welcome to warm modernism. Luxurious but not outrageously priced seating, tables and accessories in a showroom that doubles as an art gallery. Super-friendly staff.

Eat, Drink, Shop

The Swedish retailer recently continued its US expansion by opening in DC, selling sportswear and dresswear (including plus sizes) for men, women and kids under its own label.
Other locations: Shops at Georgetown Park, 3222 M Street, NW, at Wisconsin Avenue, Georgetown (1-202 298 6792).

French Connection
1229 Wisconsin Avenue, NW, between M & Prospect Streets, Georgetown (1-202 965 4690). Foggy Bottom-GWU Metro then 30, 32, 34, 35, 36, 38B, Georgetown Metro Connection bus. **Open** *10am-9pm Mon-Wed; 10am-10pm Thur, Fri; 10am-11pm Sat; 11am-9pm Sun.* **Credit** AmEx, Disc, MC, V. **Map** p281 E5.
As its cheeky double-take name (FCUK) suggests, this English high-street chain aspires to a cool, urban image. In reality it's too commercial to be cutting-edge, but it does turn out well-cut, good-quality mens- and womenswear, so who's complaining?
Other locations: Pentagon City, *see p154.*

Zara
1244 Wisconsin Avenue, NW, between M & Prospect Streets, Georgetown (1-202 944 9797). Foggy Bottom-GWU Metro then 30, 32, 34, 35, 36, 38B, Georgetown Metro Connection bus. **Open** *10am-9pm Mon-Sat; noon-6pm Sun.* **Credit** AmEx, Disc, MC, V. **Map** p281 E5.
This Spanish fashion label has taken the European market by storm in just a few years. The men's and women's separates are effortlessly chic, their styles so up-to-date they seem to step straight off the catwalk.

Outdoor

City Bikes
2501 Champlain Street, NW, at Euclid Street, Adams Morgan (1-202 265 1564). Dupont Circle Metro then 42 bus or Woodley Park-Zoo/Adams Morgan Metro then 90, 92, 93, L2 bus. **Open** *10am-7pm Mon-Wed, Fri, Sat; 10am-8pm Thur; noon-5pm Sun.* **Credit** MC, V. **Map** p282 G3.
A cult favourite. Hard-core cyclists in DC, including the legions of bike messengers, come to City Bikes for its excellent bikes, parts and mechanics. More casual cyclists show up to rent bikes and take a spin through the city or nearby Rock Creek Park.

Hudson Trail Outfitter
4530 Wisconsin Avenue, NW, at Brandywine Street, Tenleytown (1-202 363 9810). Tenleytown-AU Metro. **Open** *10am-9pm Mon-Sat; 11am-6pm Sun.* **Credit** AmEx, Disc, MC, V.
Great for every type of sport, stocking an extensive array of hiking clothes, shoes and gear, plus stuff for climbing, kayaking, snow sports and fly fishing. Bicycles and all their hardware are also sold.

Shoes

Georgetown has several good shoe stores, including **Kenneth Cole** (1259 Wisconsin Avenue, NW, 1-202 298 0007), **Steve Madden**

(3109 M Street, NW, 1-202 342 6194) and the **Walking Company** (3101 M Street, NW, 1-202 625 9255).

Church's English Shoes
1820 L Street, NW, between 18th & 19th Streets, Foggy Bottom (1-202 296 3366/www.churchsshoes. com). Farragut North Metro. **Open** *10am-6pm Mon-Sat.* **Credit** AmEx, Disc, MC, V. **Map** p282 G5.
This long-standing English company produces men's handcrafted leather shoes in subdued styles.

Comfort One Shoes
1636 Connecticut Avenue, NW, between Q & R Streets, Dupont Circle (1-202 328 3141/www. comfortoneshoes.com). Dupont Circle Metro. **Open** *10am-9pm Mon-Thur; 10am-11pm Fri, Sat; 11am-8pm Sun.* **Credit** AmEx, Disc, MC, V. **Map** p282 G4.
Ecco, Naot, Birkenstock and Camper and other hippish brands are sold here. Comfort One has several stores in the vicinity, and it prices its shoes as if it were running a monopoly. Convenient but costly.
Other locations: throughout the city.

Shake Your Booty
2439 18th Street, NW, between Belmont & Columbia Roads, Adams Morgan (1-202 518 8205). Dupont Circle Metro then 42 bus or Woodley Park-Zoo/Adams Morgan Metro then 90, 92, 93 bus. **Open** *noon-8pm Mon-Fri; noon-9pm Sat; noon-6pm Sun.* **Credit** AmEx, MC, V. **Map** p282 G3.
Sassy shoes and a fun attitude mark out this homegrown favourite. Expect to find the highest of heels and the flattest of flats, as well as bags, hats and more.

Shoe & luggage repair

Corrective Shoe Repair
1502 21st Street, NW, between Massachusetts Avenue & P Street, Dupont Circle (1-202 232 9749). Dupont Circle Metro. **Open** *8am-7pm Mon-Fri; 8.30am-5pm Sat.* **Credit** AmEx, Disc, MC, V. **Map** p282 G4.
In the heart of the walking city, this shop can fix and waterproof leather shoes and garments, and resole your tired treads.

Lane's
1146 Connecticut Avenue, NW, at M Street, Downtown (1-202 452 1146). Farragut North Metro. **Open** *9.30am-6pm Mon-Fri; 9.30am-5pm Sat.* **Credit** AmEx, MC, V. **Map** p284 G5.
Leather goods in every dimension for the traveller, plus decent desk and office accessories.

Specialist

Backstage
545 Eighth Street, NE, at G Street, Capitol Hill (1-202 544 5744). Eastern Market Metro. **Open** *11am-7pm Mon-Sat.* **Credit** AmEx, MC, V. **Map** p285 M8.
The masses pile in for Halloween, but troupers in DC's enormous theatre make constant trips here for costumes, texts, masks, hair, nails… the works.

Georgetown Formal Wear & Custom Tailor

1083 Wisconsin Avenue, NW, between K & M Streets, Georgetown (1-202 625 2247). Foggy Bottom-GWU Metro then 30, 32, 34, 35, 36 bus. **Open** 10am-7pm Mon-Sat. **Credit** AmEx, Disc, MC, V. **Map** p281 E5.

Black tie required? Head here for a tux or any of the trimmings.

Sporting goods & sportswear

Fleet Feet

1841 Columbia Road, NW, between Biltmore Street & Mintwood Place, Adams Morgan (1-202 387 3888/www.dcnet.com/fleetfeet). Dupont Circle Metro then 42 bus. **Open** 10am-8pm Mon-Fri; 10am-7pm Sat; noon-4pm Sun. **Credit** AmEx, DC, Disc, MC, V. **Map** p282 G3.

Fleet Feet's selection of shoes and togs is first-rate, as shown by the dozens of runners who hang outside the shop on weekends. The prices are good too.

Sports Zone

3140 M Street, NW, at Wisconsin Avenue, Georgetown (1-202 337 9773). Foggy Bottom-GWU Metro then 30, 32, 34, 35, 36 bus. **Open** 10am-10pm Mon-Sat; 11am-6pm Sun. **Credit** AmEx, MC, V. **Map** p281 E5.

This chain sells tracksuits and shoes by Ecko, Adidas and Avirex.

Other locations: throughout the city.

Streetwear

Commander Salamander

1420 Wisconsin Avenue, NW, between O & P Streets, Georgetown (1-202 337 2265). Foggy Bottom-GWU Metro then 30, 32, 34, 35, 36 bus. **Open** 10am-9pm Mon-Thur; 10am-10pm Fri, Sat; 11am-7pm Sun. **Credit** AmEx, Disc, MC, V. **Map** p281 E4.

Goth and punk clothing, hats and accessories by Von Dutch, Gucci and more are available at this underground headquarters.

Urban Outfitters

3111 M Street, NW, between 31st & 32nd Streets, Georgetown (1-202 342 1012). Foggy Bottom-GWU Metro then 30, 32, 34, 35, 36 bus. **Open** 10am-10pm Mon-Sat; 11am-9pm Sun. **Credit** AmEx, Disc, MC, V. **Map** p281 E5.

Fresh-scrub college kids looking for their inner bohos trawl the creaky wood floors of this two-level bazaar for geek fashions and groovy housewares.

Vintage & second-hand

Deja Blue

3005 M Street, NW, between 30th & 31st Streets, Georgetown (1-202 337 7100). Foggy Bottom-GWU Metro then 30, 32, 34, 35, 36, 38B, Georgetown Metro Connection bus.

Open 11am-9pm Mon-Sat; 11am-7pm Sun. **Credit** AmEx, DC, Disc, MC, V. **Map** p281 F5.

Specialising in disused denim, this store also carries a bit of beachwear and island clothing. You may come across some real finds – like old-but-new Levi's, or some cute little shoes. And even Macy's customers have never had such good service.

Meep's & Aunt Neensie's

1520 U Street, NW, between 15th & 16th Streets, Shaw: U Street/14th Street Corridor (1-202 265 6546). U Street/African-American Civil War Memorial/Cardozo Metro. **Open** 4-6pm Thur, Fri; 2-6pm Sat, Sun. **Credit** MC, V. **Map** p282 H3.

Where's that shirt you lost in the sixth grade? Whoops… it's at Meep's, where DC's slackers and band kids flock to get that *Quadrophenia* look. It doesn't sell mopeds, but does have all the other retro-chic essentials.

Polly Sue's Vintage

6915 Laurel Avenue, Takoma Park, MD (1-301 270 5511). Takoma Metro. **Open** 11am-7pm Mon-Fri; 10am-6pm Sat; 10am-5pm Sun. **Credit** MC, V.

Practically any period worth wearing can be found in this wonderful shop, from the age of Dickens through the Cold War. Of special interest are the mid century modern clothes and the sort-of-revived '60s and '70s fashions. Polly Sue's also has gloves, handbags and clutches.

Rage Clothing

1069 Wisconsin Avenue, NW, between K & M Streets, Georgetown (1-202 333 1069). Foggy Bottom-GWU Metro then 30, 32, 34, 35, 36 bus. **Open** 11am-9pm Mon-Thur; 11am-10pm Fri, Sat; 11am-7pm Sun. **Credit** AmEx, DC, Disc, MC, V. **Map** p281 E5.

For $20 you can mount the stairs in this shop and stuff whatever you can fit into a plastic shopping bag (and then pay for it, of course). Yesteryear's fraternity wear (Izod and Ocean Pacific), casual pants and jean jackets are rife.

Florists & garden suppliers

Allan Woods Florist

2645 Connecticut Avenue, NW, at 26th Street, Woodley Park (1-202 332 3334). Woodley Park-Zoo/Adams Morgan Metro. **Open** 9am-7pm Mon-Fri; 9am-6pm Sat. **Credit** AmEx, Disc, MC, V. **Map** p281 F2.

Fresh, seasonal favourites abound at this shop – hydrangeas, peonies, lilies and lilacs in spring and a parade of poinsettias at Christmas time. Also be sure to check out the large cooler that overruns with cut flowers.

Garden District

1801 14th Street, NW, at S Street, Shaw: U Street/14th Street Corridor (1-202 797 9005). U Street/African-American Civil War/Cardozo Metro. **Open** 9am-7pm Mon-p167Sat; 10am-5pm Sun. Closed Jan. **Credit** AmEx, MC, V. **Map** p282 4H.

Eat, Drink, Shop

Grooming Lounge: men-only pampering zone. *See p170.*

Just what the neighbourhood needs – a sweet, compact resource for urban gardeners. Garden District carries plants in all sizes, from bonsai cypresses to flats of bedding plants to river birches weighing several hundred pounds, plus soil, mulch and plant food.

A Little Shop of Flowers

1812 Adams Mill Road, between Calvert Street & Columbia Road, Adams Morgan (1-202 387 7255). Dupont Circle then 42 bus or Woodley Park-Zoo/Adams Morgan Metro then 90, 92, 93 bus. **Open** 9am-7pm Mon-Sat; noon-5pm Sun. Closed Aug. **Credit** AmEx, Disc, MC, V. **Map** p282 G3.
This shop lets its fragrant wares spill out on to the sidewalk. Stop in for a bunch of sunflowers or alstroemeria to freshen your room, or a bouquet of any size for a friend.

Smith & Hawken

1209 31st Street, NW, at M Street, Georgetown (1-202 965 2680/www.smithandhawken.com). Foggy Bottom-GWU Metro then 30, 32, 34, 35, 36, 38B, Georgetown Metro Connection bus. **Open** 10am-6.30pm Mon-Wed, Sat; 10am-9pm Thur, Fri; noon-6.30pm Sun. **Credit** AmEx, MC, V. **Map** p281 E5.
When the staff water the little ivies, creeping figs and gardenias potted up here, the plants are cute. When they don't, they're atrocious. You'll also find garden tools, ornaments, pebbles, moss bales… everything you need for exterior decorating.

The Third Day

2001 P Street, NW, at 20th Street, Dupont Circle (1-202 785 0107). Dupont Circle Metro. **Open** 10am-6.30pm Mon-Fri; 9am-6pm Sat; noon-5pm Sun. **Credit** AmEx, MC, V. **Map** p282 G4.

Of course this store has wonderful houseplants – look at those south-facing picture windows! From jade to ficus, spathiphyllum to cacti, they can help you, too, distinguish yourself as an avid grower.

Food & drink

For more cafés, *see pp122-144.*

Bakeries

Amernick

3313 Connecticut Avenue, NW, between Macomb & Ordway Streets, Cleveland Park (1-202 537 5855). Cleveland Park Metro. **Open** 10am-5pm Mon-Sat. **Credit** AmEx, Disc, MC, V. **Map** p281 F1.
Chef Ann Amernick, formerly of the White House, no less, makes incredible doughnuts, croissants and holiday breads at this neighbourhood bakery.

La Madeleine

3000 M Street, NW, at 30th Street, Georgetown (1-202 337 6975/www.lamadeleine.com). Foggy Bottom-GWU Metro then 30, 32, 34, 35, 36, 38B, Georgetown Metro Connection bus. **Open** 7am-10pm daily. **Credit** AmEx, Disc, MC, V. **Map** p281 F5.
Part of a decent French bakery chain, with all the classics and yummy coffee too.

Marvelous Market

3217 P Street, NW, at Wisconsin Avenue, Georgetown (1-202 333 2591/www.marvelousmarket.com). Foggy Bottom-GWU Metro then 30, 32, 34, 35, 36 bus. **Open** 8am-9pm Mon-Sat; 8am-8pm Sun. **Credit** AmEx, MC, V. **Map** p281 E4.

Delicious breads, rolls, scones and pastries (alas, no biscuits) along with a smattering of packaged goods. The freshly made pizzas, starting at 11am, are worth the (short) wait.
Other locations: throughout the city.

Patisserie Poupon

1645 Wisconsin Avenue, NW, between Q & R Streets, Georgetown (1-202 342 3248). Foggy Bottom-GWU Metro then 30, 32, 34, 35, 36, Georgetown Metro Connection bus or Dupont Circle then D2, D4, D6, G2 bus. **Open** 8am-6.30pm Tue-Sat; 8am-4pm Sun. **Credit** AmEx, DC, Disc, MC, V. **Map** p281 E4.
Patisserie Poupon stocks all your calorific French favourites. Hangover or not, you must arrive early at weekends if you want to grab a table.

Ethnic

DC's suburbs have long since globalised, and these days much of the good ethnic shopping lies in places like Wheaton and Rockville, Maryland, and Arlington and Falls Church, Virginia.

Addisu Gebeya

2202 18th Street, NW, between Wyoming Avenue & Kalorama Road, Adams Morgan (1-202 986 6013). Dupont Circle Metro then 42 bus or Woodley Park-Zoo/Adams Morgan Metro then 90, 92, 93, L2 bus. **Open** 9am-10pm Mon-Sat; 9am-9pm Sun. **Credit** AmEx, MC, V. **Map** p282 G3.
Everything Ethiopian is stocked here, from spices and lentils to spongy *injera* bread and the *teff* flour used to make it.

Casa Peña

1636 17th Street, NW, between Corcoran & R Streets, Dupont Circle (1-202 462 2222). Dupont Circle Metro. **Open** 9.30am-11.30pm daily. **Credit** AmEx, DC, Disc, MC, V. **Map** p282 G4.
Beans, rice, chillies, herbs and just about everything else you need for a hot meal, in addition to meats from the adjacent butcher.

Da Hua

623 H Street, NW, at Seventh Street, Downtown (1-202 371 8888). Gallery Place-Chinatown Metro. **Open** 10am-8pm daily. **Credit** MC, V. **Map** p285 J5.
One of the few authentic Asian shops in Chinatown, offering fresh produce, packaged goods, seasonings and a selection of teas and sweets.

Vace

3315 Connecticut Avenue, NW, at Macomb Street, Cleveland Park (1-202 363 1999). Cleveland Park Metro. **Open** 9am-9pm Mon-Fri; 9am-8pm Sat; 10am-5pm Sun. **Credit** MC, V. **Map** p281 F1.
All these people walking around with crisp, aromatic pizza slices in foil wrappers – where did it come from? Vace, the premier Italian deli in town, which stocks every imaginable kind of freshly made pasta, as well as condiments, meats and wine. Prices are reasonable too.

Fish

Wharf at Maine Avenue, SW

Waterfront-SEU Metro. **Map** p284 J8.
Fish, crab, spices, sauces, you name it… they're at Captain White Seafood (1-202 484 2722), the big fish of this market. Sub-tropical fruits and vegetables sit alongside the piscine goodies at Jessie Taylor Seafood (1-202 554 4173). Slightly cheaper is Pruitt Seafood (1-202 554 2669). Fried seafoods, bisques and chowders are at Maine Avenue Seafood (1-202 479 4188). Custis & Brown Seafood (1-202 484 0168) and Virgo's Fish Market are also worth a look.

Gourmet

Dean & Deluca

3276 M Street, NW, at Potomac Street, Georgetown (1-202 342 2500/www.deandeluca.com). Foggy Bottom-GWU Metro then 30, 32, 34, 35, 36 Georgetown Metro Connection bus. **Open** *Shop* 10am-8pm Mon-Thur, Sun; 10am-9pm Fri, Sat. *Café* 8am-8pm Mon-Thur, Sun; 8am-9pm Fri, Sat. **Credit** AmEx, MC, V. **Map** p281 E5.
Somehow, D&D brought in the quick $15 takeout lunch to this little former market and made DC think it was its own idea. True, the shop's got a lot to be proud of – fresh produce, salads, pastries, meats and more – but prices are higher than you ever thought you'd pay.

Natural foods

Naturally Yours

2029 P Street, NW, between 20th & 21st Streets, Dupont Circle (1-202 429 1718). Dupont Circle Metro. **Open** 10am-8pm Mon-Sat; 11am-6pm Sun. **Credit** AmEx, MC, V. **Map** p282 G4.
A good old-fashioned health food shop, with edibles, nutritional supplements and juices.

Whole Foods

1440 P Street, NW, between 14th & 15th Streets, Shaw: Logan Circle (1-202 332 4300). Dupont Circle Metro. **Open** 8am-10pm daily. **Credit** AmEx, DC, Disc, MC, V. **Map** p282 H4.
This shop certainly knows how to market a markup (although the wine prices are good). You could spend all day in its aisles, leering at the organic bananas, the marinated meats, the non-hormonal dairy products and the deli showcase. If nothing else, grab a smoothie at the juice bar and have a browse.

Wine, beer & spirits

Best Cellars

1643 Connecticut Avenue, NW, between Q & R Streets, Dupont Circle (1-202 387 3146). Dupont Circle Metro. **Open** 10am-9pm Mon-Thur; 10am-10pm Fri, Sat. **Credit** AmEx, MC, V. **Map** p282 G4.

Eat, Drink, Shop

You can find more than 100 different wines for less than $15 a bottle at this user-friendly vendor, which also stocks 'handcrafted' beers and small-batch spirits. Enjoy the free tastings every evening from 5.30pm to 7.30pm, and the food and wine pairings from 2pm to 4pm on Saturdays.

The Wine Specialists

2115 M Street, NW, between 21st & 22nd Streets, Foggy Bottom (1-202 833 0707). Foggy Bottom Metro. **Open** *10am-9pm Mon-Sat.* **Credit** *AmEx, MC, V.* **Map** *p284 G5.*
Wines and more wines, in particular from Italy and California, along with cognacs, armagnacs, calvados and sakés.

Furniture & home accessories

See also p164 **Sitting pretty**.

A MANO

1677 Wisconsin Avenue, NW, at Reservoir Road, Georgetown (1-202 298 7200/www.amanoinc.com). Foggy Bottom-GWU Metro then 30, 32, 34, 35, 36, Georgetown Metro Connection bus or Dupont Circle then D2, D4, D6, G2 bus. **Open** *10am-6pm Mon-Sat; noon-5pm Sun.* **Credit** *AmEx, MC, V.* **Map** *p281 E4.*
Set in upper Georgetown's antiques row, this cosy shop transports you to a world where handmade (hence the name) earthen vessels and decorative items are prized, as well as fine linens. Don't skip the back garden, with its range of outdoor ornaments, wall fountains and follies.

Home Rule

1807 14th Street, NW, at S Street, Shaw: U Street/14th Street Corridor (1-202 797 5544/ www.homerule.com). U Street/African-American Civil War Memorial/Cardozo Metro. **Open** *11am-7pm Mon-Sat; noon-5pm Sun.* **Credit** *AmEx, MC, V.* **Map** *p282 H4.*
You'll spend yourself silly in this arresting little shop, where the walls are lined with the latest kitchen utensils, desk supplies, silk curtains, cleaning gadgets, incredible soaps and lotions, and stocking fillers.

Simply Home

1811B 18th Street, between S & T Streets, Dupont Circle (1-202 986 8607/www.simplyhomedc.com). Dupont Circle Metro. **Open** *noon-9pm Tue-Fri; 11am-9pm Sat; 11am-8pm Sun.* **Credit** *AmEx, Disc, MC, V.* **Map** *p282 G4.*
Brother and sister proprietors Somsak and Nannapat Pollert have distinct roles in this store: she chooses the modish fabrics woven in north-eastern Thailand for garments, linens, bedding and pillows and he conducts the storefront in DC with a showman's precision. Seductive earthenware accessories, candles and teak items fill the balance.

Sur La Table

5211 Wisconsin Avenue, NW, between Ingomar & Harrison Streets, Chevy Chase, Upper Northwest

(1-202 237 0375/www.surlatable.com). Friendship Heights Metro. **Open** *10am-6pm Mon-Wed, Sat; 10am-8pm Thur, Fri; noon-6pm Sun.* **Credit** *AmEx, Disc, MC, V.*
Sur La Table's helpful staff will not only direct you to the kitchen gadget you're looking for, but will brandish some new, interesting one you'll love, like a fat separator or a pasta machine.

Health & beauty

Beauty products, body care & spas

Aveda

1325 Wisconsin Avenue, NW, between N & Dumbarton Streets, Georgetown (1-202 965 1325/www.aveda.com). Foggy Bottom-GWU Metro then 30, 32, 34, 35, 36, 38B, Georgetown Metro Connection bus. **Open** *10am-7pm Mon, Sun; 10am-8pm Tue; 10am-9pm Wed, Thur; 8.30am-8pm Fri, Sat.* **Credit** *AmEx, MC, V.* **Map** *p281 E4.*
Disappear into this well-regarded salon and spa to treat your scalp, wax your brows, have a massage (hot stones optional!) or reward your tired feet. Then take home potions and lotions as a souvenir.
Other locations: throughout the city.

Blue Mercury

1619 Connecticut Avenue, NW, Dupont Circle (1-202 965 1300/www.bluemercury.com). Dupont Circle Metro. **Open** *10am-8pm Mon-Sat; noon-6pm Sun.* **Credit** *AmEx, MC, V.* **Map** *p282 G4.*
You'll feel like Dorothy and co in Oz when you take advantage of the body treatments here, which will put you in just the mood to browse the fine selection of cosmetics, fragrances and moisturisers. The other branch is a store only, not a spa.
Other locations: 1745 Connecticut Avenue, NW, Dupont Circle (1-202 462 1300).

Celadon

1180 F Street, NW, between 11th & 12th Streets, Downtown (1-202 347 3333). Metro Center Metro. **Open** *9am-6pm Mon-Wed, Fri; 9am-7pm Thur; 8.30am-4.30pm Sat.* **Credit** *AmEx, Disc, MC, V.* **Map** *p284 H6.*
Downtown's workaholics defuse their tensions at this zen-like salon and spa, and often leave with a bag of skin and beauty products for carrying on the good work at home.

Grooming Lounge

1745 L Street, NW, between Connecticut Avenue & 18th Street, Foggy Bottom (1-202 466 8900). Farragut North Metro. **Open** *9am-7pm Mon-Fri; 9am-6pm Sat.* **Credit** *AmEx, MC, V.* **Map** *p284 G5.*
Men finally have a spa to call their own in DC. This modern retreat with an old barber shop mood offers haircuts, hot shaves, facials and nail care, plus product lines by Anthony, Dermalogica and Jack Black.

Ilo

*1637 Wisconsin Avenue, NW, between Q Street &
Reservoir Road, Georgetown (1-202 342 0350).
Foggy Bottom-GWU Metro then 30, 32, 34, 35, 36,
Georgetown Metro Connection bus or Dupont Circle
then D2, D4, D6, G2 bus.* **Open** 10am-6pm Tue-Fri;
9am-5pm Sat. **Credit** AmEx, MC, V. **Map** p281 E4.
Accepting an award tonight? This spa provides all
the traditional services, plus medical procedures
such as laser hair removal, microdermabrasion and
Botox to get you ready for your close-up.

Sephora

*3065 M Street, NW, between 30th & 31st Streets,
Georgetown (1-202 338 5644). Foggy Bottom-GWU
Metro then 30, 32, 34, 35, 36 bus.* **Open** 10am-9pm
Mon-Sat; noon-6pm Sun. **Credit** AmEx, Disc, MC, V.
Map p281 E5.
This celebrated French chain is a beauty junkie's
paradise, with skincare, cosmetics and designer
scents for men and women.

The Sports Club/LA –
Splash Spa

*Ritz Carlton Hotel, 1170 22nd Street, NW, at M
Street, Foggy Bottom (1-202 974 6601). Foggy
Bottom-GWU Metro.* **Open** 8am-9pm Mon-Fri;
9am-6pm Sat, Sun. **Credit** AmEx, Disc, MC, V.
Map p284 G5.
Athletes and actors have been spotted at this plush
spa, checking in for facials, massages, body treatments, waxing and the like. No doubt their wallets
feel much lighter when they leave.

Appalachian Spring.
See p173.

Hairdressers & barbers

Axis

*1509 Connecticut Avenue, NW, between Dupont
Circle & Q Street, Dupont Circle (1-202 234 1166).
Dupont Circle Metro.* **Open** 10am-7.30pm Tue-Fri;
9am-7pm Sat. **Credit** AmEx, MC, V. **Map** p282 G4.
The prices seem to keep going up at Axis, but people keep surging through the funky storefront, with
its cheeky window displays, nonetheless.

Christophe

*1125 18th Street, NW, between L & M Streets,
Downtown (1-202 785 2222). Farragut North
Metro.* **Open** 9am-7pm Tue, Wed; 9am-8pm Thur,
Fri; 9am-5pm Sat. **Credit** AmEx, DC, MC, V.
Map p282 G5.
Never in the stories about Christophe, the man him-
self, do you hear about his salon's haircuts. They're
good, and you'll pay dearly.

Evolve

*2905 M Street, NW, between 29th & 30th Streets,
Georgetown (1-202 333 9872). Foggy Bottom-GWU
Metro then 30, 32, 34, 35, 36, 38B, Georgetown
Metro Connection bus.* **Open** 10am-2pm, 3-6pm
Tue-Sat. **Credit** AmEx, Disc, MC, V. **Map** p281 F5.
Two decades of making DC's ladies beautiful attests
to the excellent standards of this salon, which does
hair treatments and facials.

Ipsa

1629 Wisconsin Avenue, NW, between Q & R Streets, Georgetown (1-202 338 4100). Foggy Bottom-GWU Metro then 30, 32, 34, 35, 36 bus. **Open** 9am-5pm Mon; 10am-6pm Tue, Thur, Fri; 10am-7pm Wed; 9am-5pm Sat. **Credit** MC, V. **Map** p281 E4.

A chilled atmosphere at this subdued salon makes for a pleasant visit and a satisfying 'do.

Judy's Beauty Supply

520 Rhode Island Avenue, NE, at Fourth Street, Northeast (1-202 832 1300). Rhode Island Avenue Metro. **Open** 9am-9pm Mon-Sat; 10am-7pm Sun. **Credit** AmEx, Disc, MC, V. **Map** p283 L3.

Weaves in a rainbow of colours, as well as all manner of hair chemicals, perm kits and other needs.

Roche

3050 M Street, NW, at 30th Street, Georgetown (1-202 775 0775/www.rochesalon.com). Foggy Bottom-GWU Metro then 30, 32, 34, 35, 36, 38B, Georgetown Connector bus. **Open** 10am-8pm Tue-Thur; 10am-7pm Fri; 9am-6pm Sat. **Credit** AmEx, MC, V. **Map** p281 E5.

Fashionistas know Roche because they see it written up in the glossies. With its poppy interior and cool attitude, it will send you out a changed person – for the better, that is.

Opticians

A Brighter Image

1720 Connecticut Avenue, NW, between R & S Streets, Dupont Circle (1-202 328 0300). Dupont Circle Metro. **Open** 10am-6pm Mon, Fri; 10am-7pm Tue-Thur; 10am-4pm Sat. **Credit** AmEx, Disc, MC, V. **Map** p282 G4.

This store offers the full complement of eye care, from vision examinations to contact lenses and stylish eyeglasses by Matsuda, Oakley, Alain Mikli, and more. Accepts a broad range of insurance coverage.

Burton Optician

3252 Prospect Street, NW, between Wisconsin Avenue & Potomac Street, Georgetown (965 0346). Foggy Bottom-GWU Metro, then 30, 32, 24, 35, 36, 38B, Georgetown Connector bus. **Open** 10am-6pm Tue-Sat. **Credit** AmEx, MC, V. **Map** p281 E5.

Virginia Burton, proprietor of this small, antique storefront, provides old-world doting and service to buttress her carefully assembled collections of eyewear. When you see the choices, four eyes won't do. You'll want eight, ten, many eyes.

Pharmacies

CVS

6 Dupont Circle, NW, between Massachusetts & New Hampshire Avenues, Dupont Circle (1-202 833 5704). Dupont Circle Metro. **Open** 24hrs daily. **Credit** AmEx, DC, Disc, MC, V. **Map** p282 G4.

Locals have a love-hate affair with this chain drugstore, which has several dozen locations in the area. It carries just about anything you'd need at 2am, but some of the staff can be somewhat clueless. **Other locations**: throughout the city.

Markets

Antiques & flea markets

It seems that people in DC have a mountain of stuff to unload at the city's flea markets, and that there are plenty of willing hands and dollars to take it. The best-known flea market, filled with furniture and oddball artworks, is held from 10am to 5pm every Sunday at Eastern Market (Seventh Street, SE, between Pennsylvania and North Carolina Avenues; Capitol Hill, 1-703 534 7612). On Sundays from 9am to 5pm, the Georgetown Flea Market (parking lot of the Hardy Middle School, Wisconsin Avenue, NW, between S & T Streets, Georgetown, 1-202 396 4989) has a choosier range of furnishings, plus old books, magazines, maps and prints. The 14th & V Flea Market (14th Street, NW, at V Street, Shaw: U Street/14th Street Corridor, 1-202 296 4989) is open both Saturday and Sunday from 9am to 5pm and carries all the usual wares, plus a haul of Africana, jewellery, incense and other small luxuries. These markets accept cash only, but you can usually haggle your way to lower prices.

Farmers' markets

The growing season in the DC region is quite long, hence the ever-flowing bounty of fruits and vegetables, not to mention artisanal cheeses, baked goods and cut flowers available at farmers' markets around town. Eastern Market (*see p94*), held year-round, is the gold standard, open Tuesday to Saturday from 8am to 6pm, and 8am to 4pm Sunday (225 Seventh Street, SE, between C Street & North Carolina Avenue, Capitol Hill, 1-202 544 0083); this market, one of the three remaining structures from the city's 19th-century market system, is at its liveliest on Sundays. At the year-round Freshfarm Market, open 9am to 1pm Sunday (Riggs Bank parking lot, 20th & Q Streets, NW, Dupont Circle, 1-202 362 8889; seasonal locations in Georgetown and Penn Quarter), food vendors all sell food that has been grown, raised or made on their own premises. The same applies to the surfeit of foods at the Takoma Park Farmers' Market (Laurel Avenue, between Eastern & Carroll Avenues, Takoma Park, 1-301 422 0097). All these markets accept cash only.

Music & video

CD Warehouse
3001 M Street, NW, at 30th Street, Georgetown (1-202 625 7101). Foggy Bottom-GWU Metro then 30, 32, 34, 35, 36 bus. **Open** 11am-9pm Mon-Thur; 11am-10pm Fri, Sat; noon-7pm Sun. **Credit** AmEx, Disc, MC, V. **Map** p281 F5.

Stack and stacks of new and not-so-new compact discs and DVDs, including new releases and imports, most of which you can check out before buying. CD Warehouse also buys and trades CDs. Works by local artists are displayed on the walls.

DJ Hut
2010 P Street, NW, at 20th Street, Dupont Circle (1-202 659 2010/www.djhut.com). Dupont Circle Metro. **Open** noon-9pm Mon-Thur; noon-10pm Fri; noon-8pm Sat; 1-6pm Sun. **Credit** AmEx, Disc, MC, V. **Map** p282 G5.

Dance, dance, dance. This DJ destination sells all manner of hip-hop, house, jungle, trance and beats, plus paraphernalia for working turntablists.

Melody Records
1623 Connecticut Avenue, NW, between Q & R Streets, Dupont Circle (1-202 232 4002). Dupont Circle Metro. **Open** 10am-10pm Mon-Thur, Sun; 10am-11pm Fri, Sat. **Credit** AmEx, MC, V. **Map** p282 G4.

Tunes in every imaginable genre are stuffed into Melody Records, a small, owner-operated landmark; the store has the city's biggest collection of world music. Nice, knowledgeable staff make you wish digital music had never dawned, because there's no place like a great record store.

Revolution Records
4215 Connecticut Avenue, NW, at Van Ness Street, Upper Northwest (202 237 2480). Van Ness-UDC Metro. **Open** 10am-8pm Mon; 10am-9pm Tue-Fri; 11am-7pm Sat; 12pm-6pm Sun. **Credit** AmEx, Disc, MC, V.

Run by members of the local indie-rock band Gist, this small but friendly and discerningly stocked shop is particularly strong in hip-hop and alt-rock CDs, both new and used. There's also a small vinyl selection. Live music or DJ sets most weekend afternoons.

Sankofa Video
2714 Georgia Avenue, NW, between Girard & Fairmont Streets, Shaw (1-202 234 4755/ www.sankofa.com). Shaw-Howard U Metro then 70, 71 bus. **Open** 10am-8pm daily. **Credit** AmEx DC, Disc, MC, V. **Map** p283 J2.

The Ethiopian-born filmmaker Haile Gerima owns this store as an adjunct to his film production studio. It stocks a spectrum of titles from around the world, especially Africa.

Video Americain
2104 18th Street, NW, at California Street, Adams Morgan (1-202 588 0117). Dupont Circle Metro. **Open** noon-10pm Mon-Thur; 11am-11pm Fri, Sat; 1-9pm Sun. **Credit** MC, V. **Map** p282 G3.

With more than 15,000 titles suiting nearly every taste in film, this local favourite takes you in with its beguiling arrangement (many directors get their own sections) and pithy commentaries posted around the shelves.

Musical instruments

The Guitar Shop
1216 Connecticut Avenue, NW, between M & N Streets, Dupont Circle (1-202 331 7333). Dupont Circle or Farragut North Metro. **Open** noon-7pm Mon-Fri; 11am-6pm Sat. **Credit** Disc, MC, V. **Map** p282 G5.

Guitar-heads in and around DC consider this long-standing store their own embassy, not least for its rare and exotic items (alongside the standard inventory).

Speciality & gift shops

Appalachian Spring
1415 Wisconsin Avenue, NW, at P Street, Georgetown (1-202 337 5780). Foggy Bottom-GWU Metro then 30, 32, 34, 35, 36, Georgetown Metro Connection bus or Dupont Circle Metro then D2, D4, D6, G2 bus. **Open** 10am-8pm Mon-Fri; 10am-6pm Sat; noon-6pm Sun. **Credit** AmEx, MC, V. **Map** p281 E4.

Why buy household gifts at the national chains when you can find wonderful handmade ceramics, blown glass, carved-wood items, metalwork, blankets and jewellery at this regional crafts boutique?

Georgetown Tobacco
3144 M Street, NW, at Wisconsin Avenue, Georgetown (1-202 338 5100/www.gttobacco. com). Foggy Bottom-GWU Metro then 30, 32, 34, 35, 36, 38B, Georgetown Metro Connection bus. **Open** 10am-9pm Mon-Sat; noon-8pm Sun. **Credit** AmEx, MC, V. **Map** p281 E5.

Tobacco in every form, along with everything you'd ever need for smoking it.

Ginza
1721 Connecticut Avenue, NW, between R & S Streets, Dupont Circle (1-202 331 7991/ www.ginzaonline.com). Dupont Circle Metro. **Open** 11am-7pm Mon-Sat; noon-6pm Sun. **Credit** AmEx, Disc, MC, V. **Map** p282 G4.

Did you leave your heart in Tokyo? This intimate but comprehensive shop sells Japanese household items (dinnerware, etc), plus specialities such as origami paper and garden ornaments, greeting cards, books and clothing at quite reasonable prices.

Sullivan's Toy Store
3412 Wisconsin Avenue, NW, between Norton Avenue & Newark Street, Cleveland Park (1-202 362 1343). Tenleytown-AU Metro then 30, 32, 34, 35, 36 bus. **Open** 10am-6pm Mon, Tue, Sat; 10am-7pm Wed-Fri; noon-5pm Sun. **Credit** AmEx, Disc, MC, V. **Map** p281 D1.

Before the onslaught of Toys 'R' Us, the world was full of toy stores like Sullivan's, which stocks crafts kits, kites and puzzles, plus dolls and action figures.

Eat, Drink, Shop

Arts & Entertainment

Festivals & Events

On the Mall or in the neighbourhoods, there's always something going on.

Smithsonian Annual Kite Festival.

Washington, DC, has all the state ceremonies you would expect of a capital city. But it also has a bursting calendar of less formal occasions, from events associated with the city's big cultural institutions to lively weekends of streetside fun celebrating the diverse districts where the District's real people live – places like Anacostia, Chinatown, Adams Morgan, Dupont Circle, Mount Pleasant, and many more. Keep track of events in town by checking the *Washington Post*'s Friday 'Weekend' section (www.washingtonpost.com/weekend) or the *Washington City Paper* (www.washington citypaper.com). Note that most events are free (unless otherwise stated); phone near the time to check. For information on Washington's various film festivals, *see p185*. For a list of national holidays, *see p264*.

Spring

St Patrick's Day Celebrations

Constitution Avenue, NW, from Seventh to 17th Streets, The Mall & Tidal Basin (information 1-202 637 2474/www.dcstpatsparade.com). Smithsonian, Federal Triangle, L'Enfant Plaza or Archives-Navy Memorial Metro. **Date** 17 Mar. **Map** p285 J6.

DC's St Patrick's Day revelries draw the crowds with a parade of dancers, bands, bagpipes and floats. In true Irish style, the partying continues in pubs around the city. If 17 March doesn't fall on a Sunday, the festivities take place the previous Sunday. Celebrations are also held in Alexandria in Virginia, where they're organised by a charity called Ballyshaners (1-703 237 2199/www.ballyshaners.org).

Annual White House Easter Egg Roll

White House South Lawn, 1600 Pennsylvania Avenue, NW, between 15th & 17th Streets (information 456 2200/456 2322/www.whitehouse. gov). McPherson Square Metro. **Date** 1st Mon after Easter. **Map** p284 H6.

Since 1878, when Congress kicked them off the Capitol lawn, kids aged three to six have been invited to hunt Easter eggs – the count is up to 24,000-plus these days – hidden on the south lawn of the Executive Mansion. A festival on the Ellipse features storytelling and food. The event kicks off at the Southeast Gate at the corner of East Executive Avenue and E Street; it gets very crowded, so arrive early. Make sure the kids are with you around 7-7.30am, when the tickets are handed out (though the actual festivities run from 10am to 2pm).

Easter celebrations

The procession of the Stations of the Cross on Good Friday through Mount Pleasant and Adams Morgan is dramatically Latin. Easter Monday is traditionally a big African American gathering at the National Zoo, remembering the time when African Americans were not welcomed at the Easter Egg Roll.

Smithsonian Annual Kite Festival

Washington Monument Grounds, The Mall & Tidal Basin (information 1-202 357 2700/http:// kitefestival.org). Smithsonian Metro. **Date** Sun late Mar. **Map** p284 H7.

Kite lovers of all ages proudly show off their hand-made contraptions (and the serious ones even take part in competitions). There are also demonstrations with novelty and sport kites by 'kite-making masters'. Usually held on first day of National Cherry Blossom Festival (*see p177*).

Arts & Entertainment

Cherry Blossom

Information 1-202 547 1500/www.nationalcherry blossomfestival.org. **Date** late Mar-mid Apr.
Cherry blossom time is a big deal in Washington. In 1912, 3,000 cherry trees were donated to the city by Mayor Yukio Ozaki of Tokyo as a symbol of friendship between Japan and the United States. These original trees were planted along the Tidal Basin; today, the path that rings the basin becomes clogged with ogling tourists – and even normally blasé Washingtonians. To witness this explosion of colour, try to visit between late March and mid April. Ironically enough, given the World War II fate of the 'friendship' between Japan and the US, the city has become famous for the immigrant blossoms and celebrates with near-pagan worship and a weekend (26 March-11 April 2005) of special events, including a National Cherry Blossom Festival Parade and the Sakuri Matsuri Street Festival, a celebration of Japanese art, food and culture held on 12th Street between Pennsylvania and Constitution Avenues. The atmosphere is congenial and the blossoms are truly wonderful to behold.

Eastern Market Day

Seventh Street, SE, at Pennsylvania Avenue, Southeast (info 1-202 675 9050/www.friendship house.net/marketday.htm). Eastern Market Metro. **Date** 1st Sun in May. **Map** p285 L7.
Neighbourhood festival, held from 11am to 6pm, featuring arts and crafts, games, rides, entertainment and food. All the funds raised go to Friendship House, a local social services agency.

Memorial Day celebrations

Date Memorial Day weekend (last Mon in May).
On the Sunday evening, the National Symphony Orchestra performs a free concert on the West Lawn of the US Capitol (there's another one on Labor Day in September; details on 1-800 444 1324 or www.kennedy-center.org/nso). On Monday, the presidential wreath-laying and memorial services are held at Arlington National Cemetery (1-703 607 8000/www.arlingtoncemetery.org), the Vietnam Veterans Memorial (1-202 426 6841) and the US Navy Memorial (1-202 737 2300 ext 768). Rolling Thunder's Ride for Freedom, a motorcycle parade on Sunday morning, remembers POWs/MIAs and honours those who died in wars involving the United States.

Memorial Day Jazz Festival

Alexandria, VA (information 1-703 838 4844). King Street Metro. **Date** around Memorial Day (last Mon in May).
Quaint Old Town Alexandria is the location for this day-long affair, which features half a dozen or so jazz artists, plus food stalls.

Black Pride

Location varies (1-202 737 5767/www.dcblack pride.org). **Date** Memorial Day weekend (last Mon in May).

Exhibitions, workshops and concerts over four days when around 10,000 African American gays and lesbians hit the city for Black Pride.

Capital Pride

Information 1-202 797 3510/www.capitalpride.org. **Date** early June.
Washington's GLBT community marks Capital Pride Week with parties, pageants, political forums, a Pennsylvania Avenue street festival, the inevitable parade – and even a mini-film festival.

Summer

Also check out the two-week **Shakespeare Free For All** festival held at the Carter Barron Amphitheatre in Rock Creek Park (*see p87*).

Fort Reno Summer Concert Series

Fort Reno Park, NW, between Wisconsin & Nebraska Avenues, Upper Northwest (www.fortreno.com). Tenleytown-AU Metro. **Date** June-Aug.
Both up-and-coming and well-known bands take to the outdoor stage at Fort Reno Park, on a hill overlooking Washington. Concerts are free and bands play for nothing; not surprisingly, long-term funding is a concern. Bring a picnic and soak up the music. No booze or glass bottles allowed.

Marine Band's Summer Concert Series and Evening Parades

West Terrace of the US Capitol, Capitol Hill, The Capitol & around. Capitol South or Smithsonian Metro. **Date** Wed, June-Aug. **Map** p285 K7/p285H7. *US Marine Corps War Memorial, Arlington, VA Rosslyn Metro.* **Date** Thur, June-Aug. **Both** *information 1-202 433 4011/433 6060/ www.marineband.usmc.mil.*
'The President's Own' – once led by John Phillip Sousa – performs free, twice-weekly outdoor concerts, from classical music to brass-band favourites. The action starts at 8pm. On Fridays, the band is a featured element of the showy Evening Parade, which also demonstrates impressive precision formation drills, on the manicured grounds of the Marine Barracks (reservations required; call 1-202 433 6060 or see www.mbw.usmc.mil/parades).

Capital Jazz Fest

Merriweather Post Pavilion, Columbia, MD (info 1-301 218 0404/www.capitaljazz.com). **Date** June.
Billed as the 'world's largest showcase of contemporary jazz music', this outdoor festival serves up food, crafts, and of course some of the best jazz musicians around. David Sanborn, BWB, Earl Klugh, Michael Franks, Dave Koz, and India Arie are among recent headliners. New in 2004: an *American Idol*-style talent challenge with a $5,000 prize.

Mount Pleasant Festival

Mount Pleasant Street, NW, between Irving Street & Park Road, Mount Pleasant (information 1-202 588 5272). Columbia Heights Metro. **Date** 1st Sun in June. **Map** p282 H2.

This lively street fair on pedestrian Mount Pleasant celebrates the hip, diverse neighbourhood north of Adams Morgan. Food vendors, live music, games for kids, crafts and work by local artists. No alcohol.

National Race for the Cure

Starts at Constitution Avenue, NW, at Ninth Street for runners and 12th Street for walkers, The Mall & Tidal Basin (information 1-703-848 8884/www.natl-race-for-the-cure.org). Federal Triangle Metro. **Date** early June. **Map** p284 H6.

It's said to be the biggest five-kilometre run/walk in the world – drawing tens of thousands of participants to raise money for and awareness of breast cancer.

Dupont-Kalorama Museum Walk Day

Information 1-202 387 4062 ext 12/ www.dkmuseums.com. **Date** early June.

Eight museums and houses in Dupont Circle and the neighbouring Kalorama neighbourhood take part in an 'off the Mall' museum day for the public. Free food, music, tours and crafts are added bonuses.

National Capital Barbecue Battle

Pennsylvania Avenue, NW, between Ninth & 14th Streets, Federal Triangle (information 1-301 860 0630/www.barbecuebattle.com). Metro Archives-Navy Memorial. **Date** late June. **Map** p284/p285 J6.

For more than a decade, 'cue wizards have gathered to compete for titles that now carry more than $25,000 of prize money. Tens of thousands throng the nation's Main Street to sample glorious ribs, chicken and every other form of barbecue imaginable. Celebs, music, kids' activities, and much more.

DanceAfrica DC: The Annual Festival

Dance Place, 3225 Eighth Street, NE, at Monroe Street, Northeast (information 1-202 269 1600/ www.danceplace.org). Brookland-CUA Metro. **Date** mid June. **Map** p283 L1.

This two-day festival celebrates African and African American dance with masterclasses, free outdoor performances, crafts and food; the fest culminates with an annual gala performance. Note that an admission price is charged for some events.

Caribbean Festival

Georgia Avenue, NW, between Missouri Avenue & Banneker Park, Mount Pleasant & North (information 1-202 726 2204/www.dccaribbean carnival.com). **Date** last Sun in June.

Since 1993 thousands of islanders and others have lined Georgia Avenue for the DC Caribbean Carnival's big parade, the climax of a week of festivities featuring soca, calypso, steel band music, African drumming, stilt dancers and a few thousand people wearing spectacular Carnival costumes.

Smithsonian Folklife Festival

National Mall, between Tenth & 15th Streets, The Mall & Tidal Basin (information 1-202 357 2700/ recorded info 1-202 633 9884/www.folklife.si.edu). Smithsonian Metro. **Date** last weekend in June and 1st weekend in July. **Map** p285 J7.

This monster festival celebrates the arts, crafts and food of selected US states and other countries (in 2004 Haiti, maritime communities of the US mid Atlantic states, and the music of Latino cultures were the focus). Food and demonstration booths stretch down the National Mall, and there are evening celebrations and music performances. The atmosphere is cheerful, the weather usually hot and sticky, and parking very limited, so use the Metro.

Independence Day

Various venues (information 1-202 789 7000). **Date** 4 July.

Steer clear of this one if you hate crowds (nearly half a million turned up in 2003), or if pervasive security makes you think of Mr Orwell. (The legacy of 9/11 means Fourth of July revellers now encounter a fenced-off National Mall, with 19 checkpoints through which to enter.) Official events begin at 10am at the National Archives, with a dramatic reading of the Declaration of Independence and a demonstration of colonial military manoeuvres. Just before noon, the Independence Day parade starts to wind its way down Constitution Avenue (from the National Archives to 17th Street), and later (5-9.15pm) the grounds of the Washington Monument hosts entertainment – folk music, jazz, marching bands, military singers – and hordes of revellers. The National Symphony Orchestra performs a concert on the West Lawn of the US Capitol building at 8pm and, at roughly 9pm, fireworks are set off over the Washington Monument. Hassles or no, it's a grand sight: the monuments are lovely in the summer dusk, and 2004's barrage involved 2,600 rounds of explosives. Walk to the festivities if you can: Fourth of July crowds eat up parking spots and test the limits of the public transport system. Check local listings for smaller celebrations around the city and suburbs.

Latino Festival

Pennsylvania Avenue, NW, between Ninth & 14th Streets, Federal Triangle (information 1-301 588 8719). Federal Triangle Metro. **Date** last weekend in July. **Map** p284/p285 J6.

DC's enormous Latino population throngs to this two-day festival; visitors can taste the foods and hear the music as hundreds of display booths, food stalls and performers fan out over Pennsylvania Avenue. On the Sunday there's a parade.

Autumn

Kennedy Center Open House Arts Festival/Prelude Festival

2700 F Street, NW, at New Hampshire Avenue & Rock Creek Parkway, Foggy Bottom (1-202 416 8000/www.kennedy-center.org). Foggy Bottom-GWU Metro. **Date** Sun early-mid Sept. **Map** p284 F6.

The Open House – centrepiece of the sprawling Prelude Festival – is a day-long Sunday extravaganza celebrating the Center's birthday and showcasing the diversity of the arts it plays host to. Local and national artists strut their stuff on the plazas, the river terrace overlooking the Potomac, and on the Kennedy Center stages. The 2003 festival celebrated the blues, with artists such as James Cotton and the Daughters of the Blues. Children are kept entertained, too, with a National Symphony Orchestra 'petting zoo' where they get to bow, blow, drum or strum their favourite instruments. The three-week Prelude Fest is the unofficial kickoff of the city's autumn performing arts season, including symphony performances, a jazz series, and the new Page to Stage theatre event, with readings and performances involving no fewer than 30 local troupes.

Adams Morgan Day

18th Street, NW, between Columbia Road & Florida Avenue, Adams Morgan (information 1-202 328 9451/www.adamsmorganday.org). Dupont Circle Metro. **Date** Sat, Sun after Labor Day (1st Mon in Sept). **Map** p282 G3.

For over a quarter of a century, thousands of DC residents have come out to celebrate this community, home to large Latino, white, African and African American populations. Musicians, crafts and ethnic foods are in ample supply.

Black Family Reunion

National Mall/Washington Monument (information 1-202 383 9130/www.ncnw.org/blackfamily.htm). Smithsonian Metro. **Date** early to mid Sept. **Map** p284 H7.

Tens, if not hundreds, of thousands descend on the National Mall each year to celebrate 'the enduring strengths and traditional values of the African American family'. Among the offerings: R&B and gospel concerts; a prayer breakfast; and a festival with a food fair and myriad themed pavilions.

Washington National Cathedral Open House

Massachusetts & Wisconsin Avenues, NW, Upper Northwest (1-202 537 3129/www.cathedral.org/ cathedral). Tenleytown/AU Metro then 30, 32, 35 or 36 bus. **Date** 10am-4pm Sat late Sept/early Oct. **Map** p281 E2.

This event, which celebrates the anniversary of the laying of the cathedral's foundation stone in 1907, is great for kids. As well as demonstrations of stone carving, there are performances by dancers, choirs, strolling musicians, jugglers and puppeteers. Hardier visitors can climb to the top of the central tower for a look at the bells (only one of two times a year you're allowed to do this) and take in the amazing views.

National Book Fair

National Mall, NWk between Seventh and 14th streets (information 1-202 888 714 4696/www.loc. gov/bookfest). Archives-Naval Memorial or Federal Triangle Metro. **Date** early Oct. **Map** p284 H6.

Sponsored by the Library of Congress, the Fair features dozens of authors, illustrators, poets and storytellers, all reading, performing and signing in block after block of pavilions themed around 'Fiction and Imagination', 'History and Biography', 'Mysteries and Thrillers' and so on. Admission is free.

DC in bloom: magnolias and cherry blossom.

Arts & Entertainment

Taste of DC

Pennsylvania Avenue, NW, between Ninth & 14th Streets (information 1-202 789 7002/www.tasteofdc. org). Date Columbus Day weekend (2nd Mon in Oct). Map p284 H6/p285 J6.

Taste of DC, the largest annual outdoor food and music festival on the East Coast, runs for three days over the Columbus Day weekend on Pennsylvania Avenue between Ninth and 14th Streets, which is blocked off to traffic for the purpose. Visitors can sample the fare of more than 40 restaurants from around town. Admission is free; once in, you buy tickets, which are traded for portions of food from the restaurants' booths. The downside: it's pricey ($1-$4.50 per item) and you'll be eating out of a paper cup. But there's also live music, childrens' activities and a good vibe – and the proceeds benefit various charities. One of the city's most popular events.

Annual High Heel Race

17th Street, NW, between S & P Streets, Dupont Circle (information from JR's bar 1-202 328 0090). Dupont Circle Metro. Date on or around 31 Oct. Map p282 G4.

Dupont Circle residents and gawkers from across the city swarm to 17th Street to catch this ultimate drag race, which features outrageously costumed contestants promenading up and down – then sprinting down a two-block stretch in the heart of the capital's gay ghetto. The event itself lasts only minutes, but the street-party atmosphere is festive and the scenery fabulous.

Marine Corps Marathon

Information 1-800 786 8762/www.marinemarathon. com. Date 31 Oct (race starts 8.30am).

The 'Marathon of Monuments' draws runners from around the world, and no wonder: the course winds along the banks of the Potomac, through Georgetown and Rock Creek Park, past the city's most famous sites and monuments, finishing up at the Marine Corps War Memorial. Spectators and supporters turn the route into a 26-mile street party.

Veterans' Day ceremonies

Arlington National Cemetery, Memorial Drive, Arlington Drive, VA (1-703 607 8000/www. arlingtoncemetery.org). Arlington Cemetery Metro. Date 11am Veterans' Day (11 Nov).

A solemn ceremony with military bands, in honour of the country's war dead. Ceremonies are also held at 1pm at the Vietnam Veterans Memorial (details on 1-202 426 6841), Mount Vernon (1-703 780 2000) and the US Navy Memorial (1-202 737 2300).

Winter

National Christmas Tree Lighting

The Ellipse, The Mall & Tidal Basin (information 1-202 426 6841). Federal Triangle Metro. Date early Dec. Map p284 H6.

The president kicks off the holiday season by switching on the lights on the giant National Christmas Tree. For a seat in the enclosure, you'll need a ticket: apply at least six weeks in advance as they run out fast. The ticketless, though, can usually get glimpses from the other side of the fence. The ceremony begins at 5pm; arrive early. From now until New Year's Day, the Ellipse hosts Christmas performances as part of the annual Pageant of Peace.

New Year's Eve celebrations

Events around town range from $20 celebrations at the Kennedy Center (music and dancing in the Grand Foyer) to dinners at some of the area's more upscale dining establishments costing hundreds of dollars. Restaurants and clubs often offer jazz, dinner and a champagne toast for a fixed price (most start taking reservations early).

Martin Luther King Jr's Birthday Celebrations

Information 1-202 727 1186/WPAS concert information 1-202 833 9800/www.wpas.org/. Date 3rd week Jan.

A birthday celebration is held on the steps of the Lincoln Memorial, where Dr King gave his famous 'I have a dream' speech in 1963. The Washington Performing Arts Society (WPAS) hosts an annual children's concert with Sweet Honey in the Rock, who combine gospel, African rhythms and rap into a cappella combinations. A tremendous show.

Chinese New Year

Chinatown, H Street, NW, between Sixth & Ninth Streets, Downtown. Gallery Place-Chinatown Metro. Date late Jan/early Feb, determined by the lunar calendar. Map p285 J5.

Celebrations kick off with a bang – dancers, dragons, firecrackers and parades – and continue, a bit muted, for ten days. Look out for details near the time or contact the Chinese Consolidated Benevolent Association at 1-703 851 5685.

Black History Month

Date Feb.

The Smithsonian Institution (*see p113*) holds special events, exhibitions and cultural programmes throughout the month. For more activities, check newspaper listings and contact the Martin Luther King Library (*see p257*).

Famous birthdays

Information Lincoln 1-202 426 6841/Washington 1-703 780 2000/Douglass 1-202 426 5960. Date Feb.

A trio of famous men's birthdays. A celebration of Abe Lincoln's birthday (12 February) is held at the Lincoln Memorial; Lincoln's Gettysburg address is read and a wreath is laid. For hard-core history buffs only. George Washington's birthday celebration, with a patriotic military programme and a George Washington impersonator, is held (on the third Monday in February) at Mount Vernon, Virginia. The Frederick Douglass birthday tribute is held on or near 14 February at the Frederick Douglass National Historic Site, 1411 W Street, SE, at 14th Street, Anacostia.

Children

The business of the city may seem pretty serious, but there's space for younger visitors to enjoy themselves too.

Go to the Mall, especially on a summer day, and you'll find kids everywhere. It's the museums and monuments that are the attraction (for parents, at least). They're some of the world's finest, and most – including the Smithsonian museums, the Supreme Court and the Capitol – are free. This helps make the city a relatively low-budget destination.

The scale of Washington DC – low-rise buildings, tourist attractions centred in a compact area, and plenty of open space – is inviting, and children are welcome nearly everywhere. To get a taste of the major sights – and avoid transport hassles – consider taking one of the tours offered by a company like Old Town Trolley Tours (*see p61*). The city is also very pedestrian-friendly, so a family walking tour like those offered by Washington Walks (1-202 484 1565, www.washingtonwalks.com) can be delightful, especially in the spring or autumn, before the heat and humidity kick in.

If you have extra time, consider a day trip to Baltimore, an hour's drive north of DC. It's chock full of fun things for kids, including the amazing National Aquarium, as well as Port Discovery, 'the kid-powered museum'. For more on Baltimore, *see pp232-6*.

Babysitting

Childcare in Washington is not cheap, but most large hotels and those with concierge services can provide it, using in-house services or local companies. Last-minute requests can usually be accommodated (with extra fees), but it's best to book ahead. The leading childcare agencies include **White House Nannies** (1-800 270 6266, www.whitehousenannies.com), a well-respected service that uses thoroughly screened, independent carers at a typical rate of $12-$16 per hour plus a $40 referral fee. **Mothers' Aides Inc** (1-800 526 2669, www.mothersaides.com) charges a $50 agency fee a day plus $10-$15 per hour (for a minimum of four hours).

Entertainment

The listings below focus on attractions in or near central DC. For places further afield and in the suburbs, including parks and outdoor recreational facilities, buy a copy of *Going Places With Children in Washington, DC* ($14.95), one of the best specialist guides to Washington for kids. It's available from all decent bookshops.

Eating out

Children are welcome at all but the fanciest restaurants – where you're unlikely to want to take them anyway. For quick budget meals, fast-food restaurants are plentiful and easy to find, but if your kids aren't fussy eaters, you might want to try one of the many moderately priced ethnic restaurants (*see pp122-52*) like the Ethiopian choices found along Adams Morgan's 18th Street or the Chinatown corridor around Sixth and H Streets, NW. A surefire winner for sports-crazy youngsters is the **ESPN Zone** (555 12th Street NW, corner of 11th and E Streets, 1-202 783 3776), with its huge game room worthy of an amusement park.

Arts & Entertainment

Creature discomforts

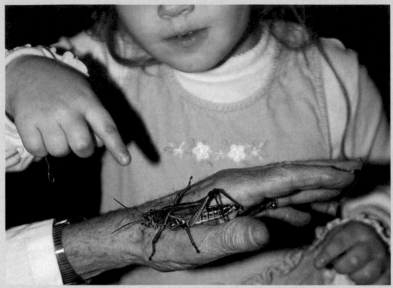

When it comes to creepy, crawly, multi-legged things scuttling around in dark corners, kids usually fall into one of two camps: those who emit bloodcurdling screams while running towards mum and dad and those who stare in wide-eyed, slack-jawed fascination and try to grab the little buggers. Youngsters of the latter variety will find a little slice of nirvana at the **O Orkin Insect Zoo**, dedicated to arthropods, that group of invertebrates that the folks at Orkin (one of America's biggest extermination companies) claim account for up to 90 per cent of all animal species.

Tucked away in a corner on the second floor of the **National Museum of Natural History** (*see p118*), the Insect Zoo is a fascinating treasure that many visitors who come to check out the dinosaur skeletons and the Hope Diamond often completely miss. But if your offspring are the kind who would delight in a close-up look at a pink-toed tarantula, stare for hours at a leaf-cutter ant colony or giggle with delight as a tobacco hornworm crawls up their arm, then this should be your first stop after being greeted by the huge elephant at the museum's rotunda.

One of the main attractions here is the volunteers who bring around a wide variety of critters for patrons to touch and feel. But if a handful of bird-eating spider isn't quite your cup of tea, the maze of arthropod existence is laid out in plenty of other ways. There is a free-ranging bee colony, which produces honey in a window that looks over the Mall, a cave that simulates the environment of zillions of tiny rainforest animals, a tank of underwater creatures and – just to comfort parents – a cut-away house illustrative of the ways our living spaces support entire insect eco-systems.

As with the most of the Smithsonian locations, the Natural History Museum can get quite crowded, especially during the summer, so your best bet for some peaceful bug browsing is to arrive near the 10am opening time or plan to end your day there towards closing time.

National Museum of Natural History

Tenth Street & Constitution Avenue, NW, The Mall & Tidal Basin (1-202 357 2700/ www.mnh.si.edu). Smithsonian Metro. **Open** *June-Aug* 10am-7.30pm daily. *Sept-May* 10am-5.30pm daily. **Admission** free. **Map** p284 J6.

Further afield in suburban Virginia are the two huge Tysons Corner malls, which house the **Rainforest Café** (Tysons Corner Center, 1961 Chain Bridge Road, McLean, 1-703 821 1900), recently voted best kids' restaurant by a local parenting magazine, and **Maggiano's Little Italy** (Tysons Galleria, 2001 International Drive, McLean, 1-703 356 9000), a family-style Italian eaterie whose main dining room is inviting. For lunch, the food court in Union Station is convenient to the Capitol, Supreme Court and the National Postal Museum. The food court in the **Pavilion at the Old Post Office** (1100 Pennsylvania Avenue, NW, between 11th and 12th Streets) is near the museums of Natural History and American History, while the National Gallery of Art (Constitution Avenue and Fourth Street NW, 1-202 737 4215, www.nga.gov) has a nice self-service café with plentiful seating. There is also a branch of **Hard Rock Café** (999 E Street, NW, at Tenth Street, next to Ford's Theatre, 1-202 737 7625). *See also p142* **The lunch bunch**.

Museums

Three Smithsonian museums offer exhibits geared towards children and are consistently rated as kids' favourites: the **National Air & Space Museum** (*see p63*), the **National Museum of American History** (*see p63*) and the **National Museum of Natural History** (*see p63 and p182* **Creature discomforts**). Also popular are the **National Building Museum** (*see p112*) and the **International Spy Museum** (*see p119*). And though it's not a museum *per se*, don't miss the **Bureau of Engraving & Printing** (*see p75*). Children are fascinated by its 35-minute tour, where they can look at currency being printed and even buy a souvenir bag of shredded cash.

Another museum designed mainly for kids is:

National Geographic Museum at Explorers Hall
17th & M Streets, NW, Downtown (1-202 857-7588/ www.nationalgeographic.com/museum). Farragut North Metro. **Open** 9am-5pm Mon-Sat; 10am-5pm Sun. **Admission** free. **Credit** AmEx, Disc, MC, V. **Map** p284 H5.
This free museum is filled with hands-on, science-oriented exhibits for the younger visitor, centring around the Earth Station One interactive theatre and its huge floating model of the earth. Free family programmes are offered each Friday morning.

Animals & the outdoors

Within the District, the best outdoor activity for children, bar none, is a trip to the **National Zoo** (*see p91*). Particularly popular are the zoo's two giant pandas, the prairie dog community and the 11.30am daily sea lion feeding and training. Survival tip: the zoo slopes steeply downhill to Rock Creek from the entrance on Connecticut Avenue, so to avoid a long, hot climb at the end of your visit, plan a circular route that gets you back to the entrance before your kids (and you) run out of energy.

National Aquarium of Washington, DC
US Department of Commerce Building, 14th Street & Constitution Avenue, NW, The Federal Triangle (1-202 482 2825/www.nationalaquarium.com). Federal Triangle Metro. **Open** 9am-5pm daily **Admission** $3.50; $3 concessions; $1 2-10s; free under-2s. **No credit cards. Map** p284 H6.
If you don't have time for a trip to Baltimore to see the superior – but far more crowded and expensive – National Aquarium, this place is worth a visit. Special features are a 'touch tank' containing hermit and horseshoe crabs, and sea snails, sea stars and sea urchins. Also popular, though you might not want to get quite as close, are the shark, alligator and piranha feedings, held at 2pm on alternate days (phone to check). *See also p73*.

Rock Creek Nature Center & Planetarium
5200 Glover Road, NW, at Military Road, Upper Northwest (1-202 895 6070/www.nps.gov/rocr/ naturecenter). Friendship Heights Metro then E2, E3 bus. **Open** 9am-5pm Wed-Sun. **Admission** free.
Rock Creek is a great place for cycling, skating, horse riding and exploring the old mill and the site of the Civil War battle at Fort Stevens. As well as the Nature Center's guided hikes, there's the highly entertaining Creature Feature programme (4pm on Fridays), which takes a close look at the park's wildlife and is highly entertaining. The planetarium (located on the park's western edge) hosts weekend shows, one at 1pm for ages four-plus, the other at 4pm for ages seven-plus.

Shopping

For clothes shops, *see p163*. For a good classic toy shop, try Sullivan's Toy Store, *see p173*.

Sport & fitness

Washington is a fantastic city for bike riding, with miles of family-friendly trails. Try the incredible **C&O Canal Towpath** (www.nps.gov/choh) or the beautiful **Mount Vernon Trail** river ride (www.nps.gov/ gwmp/mvt.html). The latter ends at George Washington's estate, where a tour is offered that younger kids enjoy hugely (*see p244* **Through the keyhold**). Also great are the 11 miles (18 kilometres) of the **Capitol Crescent Trail** and the loop through **East Potomac**

Animal farm: the **National Zoo**. *See p183.*

Park. For maps and details, contact the Washington Area Bicyclist Association (*see p253*). For bike shops, *see p166*. For bike rental, *see p216*.

Theatre & the arts

The 'Saturday's Child' column of the 'Weekend' section of Friday's *Washington Post* cover the current week's performances and other activities for kids in and around DC. Other institutions that occasionally offer children's art and theatre programmes include the **National Gallery of Art** (*see p63*), the **Corcoran Museum of Art** (*see p67*), the **Hirshhorn Museum & Sculpture Garden** (*see p63*) and the **National Building Museum** (*see p112*).

Arthur M Sackler Gallery & Freer Gallery of Art

1050 Independence Avenue, SW, between 11th & 12th Streets, The Mall & Tidal Basin (1-202 633 4880/www.asia.si.edu). Smithsonian Metro. **Open** 10am-5.30pm daily. *ImaginAsia times vary.* **Admission** free. **Map** p284 J7.

The Sackler and Freer galleries, the Smithsonian's two interconnected museums of Asian art, offer ImaginAsia several days a week (call 1-202 357 2700 for the schedule). Children aged six to 14, who must be accompanied by an adult, are given an activity book before entering the exhibition, and take part in an art workshop at the end. For reservations call 1-202 633 0461.

Glen Echo Park

7300 MacArthur Boulevard, at Goldsboro Road, Glen Echo, MD (1-301 492 6229/www.glenechopark. org). Friendship Heights Metro then Ride-On Bus 29.
Until 1968 Glen Echo was a popular amusement park just a trolley ride from Downtown. Today it is preserved by the National Park Service (2pm weekend tours) and run by a non-profit group as a site for theatre, art and dance. It also has a playground, picnic tables, a lovely 1921 carousel (open May-Aug, 10am-2pm Wed, Thur, noon-6pm Sat, Sun; Sept, noon-6pm Sat, Sun) and plenty of places for kids to explore. The following are highlights of Glen-Echo's many child-friendly activities:

The Puppet Company Playhouse (1-301 320 6668, www.thepuppetco.org; 10am, 11.30am Wed-Fri, 11.30am, 1pm Sat, Sun, admission $6). Plays are presented for all ages, most of them adaptations of classic stories for children like Cinderella and The Jungle Book. Reservations recommended.

The Adventure Theatre (1-301 320 5331, www. adventuretheatre.org, 1.30pm, 3.30pm Sat, Sun, admission $7). The DC area's longest-running children's theatre presents one-hour plays for kids aged four and over based on fables, fairy tales, musicals and children's classics, using puppets and actors.

The Discovery Creek Children's Museum (1-202 337 5111, www.discoverycreek.org; 10am-3pm Sat, Sun; admission $5, free under-2s). This small nature centre offers interactive events designed to teach children about nature and geography, as well as wildlife treks through the park.

Kennedy Center

2700 F Street, NW, at New Hampshire Avenue & Rock Creek Parkway, Foggy Bottom (1-800 444 1324/1-202 467 4600/www.kennedy-center.org). Foggy Bottom-GWU Metro. **Admission** varies. **Credit** AmEx, DC, Disc, MC, V. **Map** p284 F6.
Most weekends from October to May (7pm Fri, 11am, 1pm, 3pm Sat, 1pm Sun) the Kennedy Center offers an amazing variety of dance, music and theatre for kids. With subjects as diverse as West African dance and the history of Mexico in song, there is truly something for every taste (although most events are recommended for kids aged five or over). The National Symphony also presents occasional family concerts here.

Saturday Morning at the National

National Theatre, 1321 Pennsylvania Avenue, NW, between 13th & 14th Streets, The Federal Triangle (1-202 783 3372/www.nationaltheatre.org). Metro Center Metro. **Admission** free. **Map** p284 H6.
On Saturdays at 9.30am and 11am, from September to April, the National Theatre offers an eclectic mix of free entertainment for both children and adults. The one-hour events include theatre, music, dance, clowning, juggling, storytelling and magic.

Arts & Entertainment

Film

Washington has caught the multiplex bug, but there's plenty of opportunity to see foreign and independent films too.

Landmark E Street Cinema. *See p187.*

In the rush to fill the American suburbs with megaplex cinemas, Washington was initially ignored. But as the 20th century faded, a building boom commenced – today more than 30 new screens have opened or are under construction in the city, a number only slightly offset by the closure of some older, smaller moviehouses. Most of the new venues feature the same Hollywood fodder that's shown from coast to coast (and beyond), but DC has a growing number of commercial outlets for independent and foreign output. These are complemented by one of the country's most extensive arrays of non-commercial repertory film programmes, which are remarkably popular with the area's well-educated and well-travelled population.

The city has long been a useful location for Hollywood movies, but the crews often spend just a few days in town, filming at conspicuous landmarks before heading back to LA or continuing the shoot in cheaper locales, often in Canada. Still, Hollywood filmmakers keep coming. Steven Spielberg's *Minority Report* tried to make the Federal Triangle futuristic, while Owen Wilson and Vince Vaughn recently brought bad-boy comedy to town for *The Wedding Crasher*. For more on cinema made in DC, *see p186* **On location**.

Local filmmakers often claim that Washington has the country's third-largest film industry, after LA and New York, but few feature films are produced locally. Instead, the emphasis is on documentaries, many made for the cable channels of DC-based Discovery and National Geographic.

There are many local showcases for nonfiction films, including the Silverdocs festival every June at the AFI Silver.

THE CINEMAS
The Loews Cineplex Odeon chain still dominates the city's exhibition market, but new competitors are arriving. Landmark, the leading US arthouse chain, opened the eight-screen **E Street** theatre in early 2004, and United Artists' 14-screen **Gallery Place** megaplex is due to open later in the year. After devoting itself exclusively to closing local movie theatres, in late 2002 Loews inaugurated its first new-generation, stadium-seating DC theatre, the **Georgetown**.

The E Street and Gallery Place cinemas have returned cinema to downtown, which was once full of opulent movie palaces. (The only one that survives is the Warner, now used for music and theatre performances.) Most of the city's cinemas are near Dupont Circle or on upper Wisconsin Avenue; the latter neighbourhood is a little sterile but easily reached by Metro from the city centre. There are also Metro-accessible megaplexes at such suburban stops as Bethesda, Ballston and Silver Spring, but they rarely show films that aren't available within the city limits.

TICKETS AND INFORMATION
Most cinemas have two screenings a night (often starting between 7pm and 7.45pm and 9pm and 9.45pm), often with an extra late show at weekends. AMC Union and Mazza Gallerie, Cineplex Odeon Uptown, Cineplex Odeon Wisconsin Avenue, Loews Georgetown, Loews

Cineplex Odeon Dupont Circle, Loews Cineplex Odeon Outer Circle and Landmark E Street all have weekday matinées; other theatres feature matinées only at weekends (although matinée schedules expand in the summer, when schools are out). Visions Bar Noir and Landmark E Street do weekend cult-film midnight shows.

Most Washington filmgoers don't buy tickets in advance, although it's advisable to do so for opening weekends of heavily promoted new films. Advance tickets for Loews Cineplex, Regal, and UA theatres are available online at www.fandango.com. Buy tickets for AMC and Landmark theaters at www.movietickets.com.

On location

Periodically, someone in Hollywood discovers that not everybody in Washington works in the Capitol or the White House, and makes a film based on that revelation. *The More the Merrier* (1943) is a romantic comedy propelled by the city's wartime housing shortage. *Damn Yankees* (1958) captures the frustrations of Washington Senators baseball fans, and includes some scenes of the now-demolished Griffith Stadium. Although the incident that inspired the tale actually occurred in suburban Maryland, Georgetown provided memorable settings for *The Exorcist* (1973), perhaps the biggest Hollywood hit ever set in DC. In the 1980s, Joel Schumacher came to town to shoot the ramshackle comedy *DC Cab* and was so impressed with Georgetown's Halloween celebration that he soon made another film about vernacular Washington, *St Elmo's Fire*. The 1980s also yielded the disastrous *Good to Go*, an exploitation flick that tried – and failed – to bring DC's go-go funk sound to an international audience.

Still, most Hollywood films set in Washington choose the city as the symbolic residence of American values. Among the most famous of these is *Mr Smith Goes to Washington* (1939), in which naive young senator Jimmy Stewart brings idealism to a city befouled by cynicism – and a country battered by the Depression. Wartime patriotism altered Hollywood's agenda in the 1940s, but soon the studios were again making movies about innocents in corrupt Washington: in 1950's *Born Yesterday*, the dumb-blonde companion of an influence peddler proves she's not so dumb after all when the two take a trip to DC to buy some Congressmen. (Remade in 1993 with a more cynical edge – and a less charming cast – the same story fell flat.)

During the 1950s, Hollywood's most memorable trips to Washington were by UFO. The decade's sci-fi boom was fuelled by an ill-disguised paranoia about the Red Menace, so it could well have been the Soviets rather than extraterrestrials who destroy the city's best-known monuments in 1956's *Earth Vs Flying Saucers* (a precursor to the gleeful destruction of 1996's *Independence Day*). One of the most interesting exceptions to the bug-eyed-monster genre's conventions is *The Day the Earth Stood Still* (1951), which not only has a pacifist message but also scenes set in the everyday Washington far from the Mall.

Hollywood filmmakers didn't find much use for the nation's capital in the 1960s; such dystopian fantasies as *Dr Strangelove* (1962) and *Wild in the Streets* (1968) were more about California than Washington. After the fact, however, one of the most influential films ever made in the city charted the Vietnam era's intrigues: the fact-based *All the President's Men* (1976) which followed the reporters Bob Woodward and Carl Bernstein, who brought down President Richard Nixon, crafted a vision of a shadowy, ominously monumental Washington that has subsequently been borrowed by a dozen thriller directors. The decade ended with *Being There* (1979), in which Peter Sellers plays a slow-witted DC gardener taken as a political savant – a more cynical variation on the innocent-in-the-capital theme.

With the rise of the mature action hero, DC has become a second home to Harrison Ford, who has played a gutsy CIA agent (1992's *Patriot Games*), a gutsy president (1997's *Air Force One*) and a gutsy local cop (1999's *Random Hearts*). The polarising Clinton era brought duelling presidencies: liberals Rob Reiner and Mike Nichols took sympathetic views of an amorous but well-meaning leader in, respectively, *The American President* (1995) and *Primary Colors* (1998), while conservative Clint Eastwood's *Absolute Power* (1996) depicts a depraved president whose adultery leads to murder.

No one's had a go at depicting George Bush in feature films yet, though he has been the target of polemicist and documentary maker Michael Moore in *Fahrenheit 9/11*.

Mainstream films

AMC Union Station

*Union Station, 50 Massachusetts Avenue, NE,
at North Capitol Street, Union Station & around
(1-703 998 4262/office: 1-202 842 3757). Union
Station Metro.* **Admission** $6.50-$9.50. **Credit**
AmEx, Disc, MC, V. **Map** p285 K6.
Located in an intriguing, cavern-like space under
Union Station's waiting room, this cinema contains
nine auditoriums, each named for a vanished
Washington moviehouse. The largest auditorium is
great; the others are good.

Cineplex Odeon Cinema

*5100 Wisconsin Avenue, NW, at Harrison Street,
Upper Northwest (1-202 537 9553). Friendship
Heights Metro.* **Admission** $6.75-$9.50. **Credit**
AmEx, Disc, MC, V.
This cinema is without architectural charm, but it's
almost as large as the Uptown (*below*), with the
biggest flat screen in DC.

Cineplex Odeon Uptown

*3426 Connecticut Avenue, NW, between Porter &
Ordway Streets, Cleveland Park (1-202 966 5400).
Cleveland Park Metro.* **Admission** $6.75-$9.50.
Credit AmEx, Disc, MC, V. **Map** p281 F1.
With the destruction of the last of the downtown
movie palaces in the 1980s, what was once just an
average neighbourhood theatre has become the
city's premier cinema. Blockbusters (and would-be
blockbusters) are the normal fare at this 1936 art
deco theatre, whose 1,500 seats make it the city's
largest. It's known for impeccable projection,
although not everyone applauds the curved screen,
which was originally installed in the 1960s for
Cinerama movies.

Cineplex Odeon Wisconsin Avenue

*4000 Wisconsin Avenue, NW, at Upton Street, Upper
Northwest (1-202 244 0880). Tenleytown-AU Metro.*
Admission $6.75-$9.50. **Credit** AmEx, Disc, MC, V.
This well-designed six-plex is one of the city's newer
cinemas, although it predates the stadium-seating
vogue. The two largest auditoriums are excellent.

General Cinema Mazza Gallerie

*5300 Wisconsin Avenue, NW, between Western
Avenue & Jenifer Street, Upper Northwest (1-202
537 9553). Friendship Heights Metro.* **Admission**
$6.50-$12.50. **Credit** AmEx, Disc, MC, V.
When it opened in 1999, this seven-auditorium cinema was the city's first with stadium seating, boast-
ing large screens and excellent sight lines. Alcoholic
beverages and an expanded snack menu are available in the two 'club cinemas', which have leatherette
seats. The latter auditoriums are restricted to viewers over the age of 21.

Loews Georgetown

*3111 K Street, NW, between 31st Street &
Wisconsin Avenue, Georgetown (1-202 342 6033).
Foggy Bottom-GWU Metro then 30, 32, 34, 35, 36,
38, D2, D4, D6, G2 or Georgetown Connection bus.*
Admission $6.75-$9.50. **Credit** AmEx, Disc, MC, V.
Map p281 E5.
This 14-screen theatre, part of a complex that incor-
porates the old Georgetown Incinerator, has a large,
dramatic lobby. The theatres themselves are stan-
dard stadium-seating houses with large screens.

Foreign & independent films

The Avalon

*5612 Connecticut Avenue, NW, between McKinley &
Northampton Streets, Chevy Chase, Upper Northwest
(1-202 966 6000/www.theavalon.org). Friendship
Heights Metro then E2, E3, E4, E6, L1, L2, L4 bus.*
Admission $5-$9. **Credit** AmEx, Disc, MC, V.
Abandoned by Loews Cineplex, the city's oldest surviving moviehouse was rescued and restored by a
neighbourhood group. Both inside and out, the 1923
structure has more charm than a dozen cookie-cutter
megaplexes. It shows a mix of foreign, independent
and Hollywood fare, as well as classics and kids' films.

Landmark E Street Cinema

*555 11th Street, NW (entrance on E Street, between
Tenth & 11th Streets), Downtown (1-202 452 7672/
www.landmarktheatres.com). Metro Center or Gallery
Place Metro.* **Admission** $6.75-$9.25. **Credit** AmEx,
Disc, MC, V. **Map** p284 E6.
Upon opening, this eight-screen Landmark cinema
immediately became the city's leading arthouse. The
screens are big – even the smallest – and all but one
of the theatres have stadium seating. Landmark also
operates the roomier Bethesda Row in suburban
Maryland, but the downtown cinema's bookings
tend to be more adventurous.

Loews Cineplex Odeon

Dupont Circle *1350 19th Street, NW, near N
Street, Dupont Circle (1-202 333 3456). Dupont
Circle Metro.* **Admission** $6.75-$9.50. **Credit**
AmEx, Disc, MC, V. **Map** p282 G4.
Outer Circle *4849 Wisconsin Avenue, NW, at
Ellicott Street, Upper Northwest (1-202 244 3116).
Tenleytown-AU Metro.* **Admission** $6.75-$9.50.
Credit AmEx, Disc, MC, V.
These two theatres are Loews Cineplex's principal
DC venues for foreign and independent films. The
two-screen Outer Circle has the biggest screen and
the best sight lines; the five-screen Dupont is newer
but a bit cramped.

Visions Bar Noir

*1927 Florida Avenue, NW, near Connecticut
Avenue, Dupont Circle (1-202 667 0090/
www.visionsdc.com). Dupont Circle Metro.*
Admission $6-$9. **Credit** AmEx, Disc, MC, V.
Map p282 G4.
With only two small theatres, this independent cinema has difficulty finding room for its ambitious
mix of programming. Foreign films predominate,
but political documentaries are often shown. This and
Mazza Gallerie are the only two DC moviehouses
that sell alcoholic beverages.

Arts & Entertainment

Repertory

As with most US cities, Washington no longer has any commercial repertory cinemas. It does, however, boast one of the country's most extensive non-commercial rep-film scenes. Keeping abreast of the programmes at these venues is a major undertaking, but not an expensive one: most of them are free. Among the many local institutions that sometimes screen films are the **National Archives** (mainly documentaries from its own collection; 1-866 272 6272); the **DC Jewish Community Center** (Jewish-related films; 1-202 777 3248, www.dcjcc.org/arts/screening room); the **National Museum of Women in the Arts** (usually film series keyed to exhibitions; 1-202 783 5000); and several foreign embassies. See the *Washington City Paper* for listings.

AFI Silver Theatre & Cultural Center

8633 Colesville Road, at Georgia Avenue, Silver Spring, MD (1-301 495 6720/recorded programme information 1-301 495 6700/www.afi.com/silver). Silver Spring Metro. **Admission** $8.50. **Credit** AmEx, MC, V.

The American Film Institute opened this handsome, state-of-the-art complex in 2003. The largest of the three screens is a restored (and reduced) version of the Silver, a 1938 art deco theatre. Although Metro-accessible, the neighbourhood is a little desolate, and thus far the Silver has drawn few patrons. AFI also programmes the National Film Theatre at the Kennedy Center (1-202 785 4600; *see also p222*), which operates intermittently. At both locations, revivals of classic or recently restored movies mix with retrospectives of directors and overviews of national cinemas.

Films on the Hill

Capitol Hill Arts Workshop, 545 7th Street, SE, between E & G Streets, Capitol Hill (1-202 547 6839/www.filmsonthehill.com). Eastern Market Metro. **Screenings** usually 7pm several weeknights. **Admission** $5. **Credit** AmEx, MC, V. **Map** p285 L8.

This programme presents early films, many of them silent, with an emphasis on vintage Hollywood.

Freer Gallery of Art

Meyer Auditorium, Jefferson Drive, SW, at 12th Street, The Mall & Tidal Basin (1-202 357 2700/www.si.edu/asia). Smithsonian Metro. **Screenings** usually 7pm Fri; 2pm Sun. **Admission** free. **Map** p284 J7.

The films shown here come from the countries represented in the gallery's collection, which emphasises Asia and the Middle East. This is one of the best places in town to see movies from India and Iran, but arrive early – the theatre soon fills up with émigrés from those countries. Recently the Freer split a Yasujiro Ozu retrospective with the National Gallery of Art (*see p109*) and AFI. Annual surveys include a Made in Hong Kong season in summer.

Hirshhorn Museum & Sculpture Garden

Seventh Street & Independence Avenue, SW, The Mall & Tidal Basin (1-202 357 2700/http://hirshhorn. si.edu). L'Enfant Plaza Metro. **Screenings** usually 8pm Thur, Fri. **Admission** free. **Map** p285 J7.

The Hirshhorn showcases work by upcoming and experimental directors. Highlights from several alternative festivals are shown annually and filmmakers sometimes show works in progress. Programmer Kelly Gordon was one of the first Americans to champion such directors as Derek Jarman, Peter Greenaway and Tsai Ming-Liang.

Library of Congress

Mary Pickford Theater, Madison Building, First Street & Pennsylvania Avenue, SE, The Capitol & around (1-202 707 5677/www.loc.gov/rr/mopic/pickford). Capitol South Metro. **Screenings** usually 7pm several weeknights. **Admission** free; reservations recommended. **Map** p285 L7.

The Library draws on its own extensive holdings to programme its small cinema. It may have the only copies of some of the early films it shows, although it screens better-known titles in its ongoing series of movies that have been included in the National Film Registry of cinematic treasures.

National Gallery of Art

East Building Auditorium, Fourth Street & Constitution Avenue, NW, The Mall & Tidal Basin (1-202 842 6799/www.nga.gov/programs/film.htm). Judiciary Square or Archives-Navy Memorial Metro. **Screenings** afternoon Sat, Sun; some weekdays. **Admission** free. **Map** p285 J6.

This auditorium has one of the biggest screens and some of the most interesting programming in the city. Film series are sometimes linked to major exhibitions, but the museum also hosts major retrospectives; recent ones include Milestones in Mexican Cinema, and Louise Brooks in Europe. Documentaries about art and related topics are shown on weekdays.

Film festivals

Filmfest DC (www.filmfestdc.org) shows around 75 films, most of them international, during a two-week period beginning in late April. Its organisers also sponsor an overview of Arab films, usually in January. In October and November, the American Film Institute (www.afi.com) presents the **European Film Showcase**, introducing new European films that have recently premiered at festivals.

Other festivals of note include the **Environmental Film Festival** (1-202 342 2564, www.dcenvironmentalfilmfest.org) in March; **Reel Affirmations** (1-202 986 1119, www.reel affirmations.org), a gay and lesbian film festival in October; and **Washington Jewish Film Festival** (www.wjff.org) in December. Check the *Washington City Paper* for listings details.

Galleries

After decades in the doldrums, Washington's small scene is finally packing an artistic punch.

The elegant **Strand on Volta**. See p196.

Historically, Washington's art scene had a problem with provincialism – too many District artists and galleries couldn't see beyond the city limits. Washington's proximity to New York deprived DC of ambitious and energetic young artists, who emigrated northwards in search of international art stardom. But the exodus has slowed, thanks to citywide optimism, a burgeoning new gallery district in the Logan Circle neighbourhood, and an art scene looking towards international influences.

DC also retains its less-polished venues and art events; the city's DIY spirit, so often manifest in local music, bleeds into visual arts, too, as younger artists crowd into alternative spaces and create one-off art shows. Some venues, like **Transformer** and **Signal 66**, follow (fairly) regular monthly exhibition schedules – and their openings have a party atmosphere you won't find at established galleries. Other places, such as the **District of Columbia Arts Center**, host art events about once every two months.

Of late, artists have also been co-opting fallow spaces in downtown office buildings. Recent legislation mandated an arts district in the area around the Penn Quarter; there, new office buildings are required to incorporate an arts component. This stipulation has resulted in one too many lacklustre lobby galleries, but, as in the case of **Gallery at Flashpoint**, has also managed to cultivate a few fine gallery spaces. Elsewhere in town, furniture and design stores have staged mini exhibitions on their walls – so you may run into a show when you least expect it.

Such a blossoming in the local art arena hasn't happened since the 1960s. Back then, Washington Color School artists stained raw canvas with vivid acrylic washes. Although some of that movement's significant players, such as Kenneth Noland, left town to pursue the New York limelight, a handful of Color School pioneers, including Sam Gilliam and Willem de Looper, maintain private studios here. These days, though, the torch has been passed to a younger group whose work leans towards international art trends rather than a rehash of the city's past artistic achievements. Many of these up-and-comers are also responsible for the new alternative spaces.

The best Galleries

For impeccable quality prints by 20th-century masters
Robert Brown Gallery. See p193.

For a cappuccino to go along with the art
Warehouse Gallery. See p190.

For a bustling crowd on opening night
Fusebox. See p194.

For a top-flight vintage photograph
Kathleen Ewing Gallery. See p193.

For world-renowned contemporary work
G Fine Art. See p194.

Arts & Entertainment

Addison/Ripley Fine Art. *See p195.*

Washington collectors, once known for their conservative tastes, are becoming younger and savvier. While the commercial gallery scene is less avant-garde or large-scale than New York's, Washington patrons can still find ambitious work made by local artists as well as national and international ones. In general, the gallery-going community here is casual and supportive (some might argue insular). Artists rub shoulders with Capitol Hill aides and lawyers at the monthly openings in the city's gallery neighbourhoods.

Dupont Circle boasts a dense gallery concentration in townhouses lining R Street between Connecticut and Florida Avenues. The edgier Seventh Street corridor in Penn Quarter bordering downtown, once a studio haven offering cheap rents, has recently witnessed soaring property prices driven by development initiatives that gained galleries wider audiences but made the area prohibitively expensive to resident artists. Georgetown, meanwhile, serves up a hotchpotch of art: galleries varying from avant-garde to conservative cater to both the blue-haired and the blue-bloods. And Logan Circle, the new heart of the scene, shows the most refreshing art the city has to offer.

The city's many embassies and international cultural centres have also begun to step up their programming, and show some of the most cutting-edge work in Washington – the Austrian, Finnish and Swedish embassies are of particular note. *Washington City Paper* is the best publication for gallery listings, including one-off events. Admission for all galleries is free; credit card details are given as virtually all sell works. Note that many galleries are closed on Sunday and Monday. For non-commercial galleries, *see pp105-120*.

Downtown

Gallery at Flashpoint
916 G Street, NW, between Ninth & Tenth Streets (1-202 315 1305/www.flashpointdc.org). Gallery Place-Chinatown Metro. **Open** noon-6pm Tue-Sat; also by appointment. **Credit** MC, V. **Map** p285 J6.
A newcomer on the gallery scene, this space occupies a multi-arts complex sponsored by the city's Cultural Development Corporation. The complex also houses a blackbox theatre and dance studio.

Warehouse Gallery
1021 Seventh Street, NW, between L Street & New York Avenue (1-202 257 5989/www.warehouse theater.com). Gallery Place-Chinatown or Mt Vernon Square/7th Street-Convention Center Metro. **Open** 10am-7.30pm Mon-Sat; also by appointment. **No credit cards. Map** p285 J5.
For upwards of a century, the Rupperts clan has owned this and several other storefronts on the block. In the mid '90s, Molly Ruppert and son Paul started throwing art parties in the former hardware store. Soon they got serious about the art space and renovated it – if that's what you call leaving the walls unfinished and the floors worn. There's a generous skylight now, and some proper walls, along with a full-time café displays works of art on its walls. A next-door space has several floors and is given over to group shows put together by local curators.

Tony Feher shows here, as do local favourites Dan Steinhilber and Robin Rose. Numark's group shows are some of the sharpest in town.

Touchstone Gallery

406 Seventh Street, NW, between D & E Streets (1-202 347 2787/http://gallery.infosrc.com). Archives-Navy Memorial or Gallery Place-Chinatown Metro. **Open** 11am-5pm Wed-Fri; noon-5pm Sat, Sun. **Credit** AmEx, MC, V. **Map** p285 J6.

Touchstone, an artist-owned co-operative gallery, shows works by area artists and lesser-known internationals. Although quality can be a bit hit or miss, the gallery's ample size increases the chances of finding a gem or two on its walls.

Zenith Gallery

413 Seventh Street, NW, between D & E Streets (1-202 783 2963/www.zenithgallery.com). Archives-Navy Memorial or Gallery Place-Chinatown Metro. **Open** 11am-6pm Tue-Fri; noon-7pm Sat; noon-5pm Sun. **Credit** AmEx, MC, V. **Map** p285 J6.

Owner Margery Goldberg's tireless activism against local developers who are trying to advance capitalism before art, combined with her long-standing presence on Seventh Street, have secured her position as a Washington institution. Nevertheless, her gallery, while influential in the neon art scene, consistently shows mediocre painting and craft.

Penn Quarter

Galleries in this burgeoning arts and entertainment district are clustered near the corner of Seventh and E Streets, NW. Monthly Third Thursday joint openings (6-8pm) feature volunteer-led gallery walks and drinks specials at local bars and restaurants.

David Adamson Gallery/Editions

406 Seventh Street, NW, between D & E Streets (1-202 628 0257). Archives-Navy Memorial or Gallery Place-Chinatown Metro. **Open** 11am-5pm Tue-Sat. **Credit** MC, V. **Map** p285 J6.

This gallery revamped its space in 2000 – and it's wooden floor is still looking good. The adjoining printmaking studio collaborates with contemporary art heavyweights such as Jim Dine, Robert Longo and Jack Pierson to create the digital ink-jet prints that are frequently on view here. Painting and print exhibitions by prominent local and national artists make this one of the city's most innovative spaces.

Numark Gallery

625-627 E Street, NW, between Sixth & Seventh Streets (1-202 628 3810/www.numarkgallery.com). Archives-Navy Memorial or Gallery Place-Chinatown Metro. **Open** 11am-6pm Tue-Sat. **Credit** MC, V. **Map** p285 J6.

Cheryl Numark is Washington's power dealer: her gallery openings draw legions of artists and discerning patrons aching to see works by recognised New Yorkers and promising Washingtonians. Her move, in 2003, to a spacious, Chelsea-inspired white cube space only served to enhance her reputation.

Dupont Circle

Most galleries line R Street between Connecticut and Florida Avenues; a handful are tucked in Hillyer Court, an alley south of R Street between Florida Avenue and 21st Street, and a few others stand on Connecticut Avenue. Many of the following are involved in joint gallery openings on the first Friday of the month (6-8pm).

Affrica

2010½ R Street, NW, at Connecticut Avenue (1-202 745 7272/www.affrica.com). Dupont Circle Metro. **Open** 2-6pm Tue; noon-6pm Wed-Sat; also by appointment. **Credit** MC, V. **Map** p282 G4.

Founded in 1979, the gallery has a collection of traditional African fine art that includes statuary, metalwork, textiles and furniture.

Conner Contemporary Art

2nd floor, 1730 Connecticut Avenue, NW, between R Street & Florida Avenue (1-202 588 8750/ www.connercontemporary.com). Dupont Circle Metro. **Open** 11am-6pm Tue-Sat; also by appointment. **Credit** MC, V. **Map** p282 G4.

Since Leigh Conner opened this gallery in 1999, she has been showing prints, photographs, paintings and sculptures by the kind of cutting-edge artists Washingtonians usually travel to New York to see. Recent shows have spotlit Leo Villareal and photographer David Levinthal; a retrospective of DC Color School painters Gene Davis and Tom Downing was well received.

Arts & Entertainment

MOCA DC 1054 31st ST, NW Washington, DC 20007 +1 202-342-6230
Email: MOCADC@hotmail.com
WWW.MOCADC.org

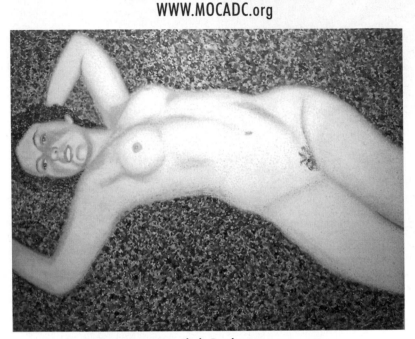

Meredith Reclining

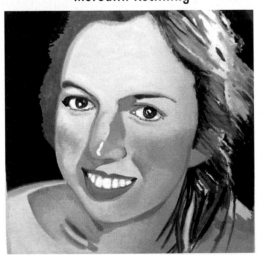

Potrait of Meredith

For further information about MOCA or the paintings, please contact
Michael Clark, Director of MOCA at +1 202-342-6230

Elizabeth Roberts Gallery

*2109 R Street, NW, between Florida & Connecticut
Avenues (1-202 232 1011/www.elizabethroberts.net).
Dupont Circle Metro.* **Open** 11am-5pm Tue-Sat.
Closed Aug. **Credit** MC, V. **Map** p282 G4.
Stepping through the Romanesque arch marking the
entrance to the Elizabeth Roberts gallery, visitors
will be most likely to encounter shows of painting
or sculpture. Locals Roberto Bucci, who makes
pillow paintings, and Jiha Moon, who turns out fan-
tastical drawings, exhibit here.

Fondo Del Sol

*2112 R Street, NW, between 21st Street & Florida
Avenue (1-202 483 2777). Dupont Circle Metro.*
Open 12.30-5.30pm Tue-Sat. **No credit cards.**
Map p282 G4.
Around the corner from the Phillips Collection,
this non-profit gallery dedicates exhibitions and
symposia to arts of the Americas; call for the per-
formance and poetry reading schedule.

Foundry Gallery

*9 Hillyer Court, NW, off 21st Street, between Q & R
Streets (1-202 387 0203). Dupont Circle Metro.*
Open 11am-5pm Wed, Fri, Sun; 11am-6pm Thur,
Sat. **Credit** MC, V. **Map** p282 G4.
DC's oldest co-operative gallery, in the same building as the Gary Edwards Gallery (*see p193*), has
kept the same egalitarian spirit since it opened in the
1970s. As you need only be a member of the gallery
to exhibit, shows vary in quality.

Gallery 10 Ltd

*1519 Connecticut Avenue, NW, at Q Street (1-202
232 3326). Dupont Circle Metro.* **Open** 11am-5pm
Wed-Sat. **Credit** MC, V. **Map** p282 G4.
Many of the District's most respected artists jump-
started nascent careers with shows at Gallery 10.
Now the place shows an older generation of District
artists whose exhibitions vary from undisciplined
to cohesive – you never know what you'll get.

Gary Edwards Gallery

*9 Hillyer Court, NW (1-202 232 5926). Dupont
Circle Metro.* **Open** 11am-5pm Tue-Sat; by
appointment Mon. **No credit cards. Map** p282 G4.
Edwards hawks vintage photographs, including old
NASA space photos and Americana; he also shows
contemporary Russian photographers. Past shows
have included an eye-opening gem of 19th-century
Japanese photography.

Irvine Contemporary Art

*1710 Connecticut Avenue, NW, at R Street (1-202
332 8767/www.irvinecontemporaryart.com). Dupont
Circle Metro.* **Open** 10am-6pm Wed-Sat. **Credit**
AmEx, MC, V. **Map** p282 G4.
Martin Irvine focuses on painting and drawing, with
favourites including Brooklynites Teo Gonzalez and
Andrew Lyght. He also loves South American
artists; a recent show dug up intriguing works by
Chilean-born surrealist Roberto Matta. The gallery
occasionally stages talks and performance works.

Kathleen Ewing Gallery

*1609 Connecticut Avenue, NW, between Q & R
Streets (1-202 328 0955/www.kathleenewinggallery.
com). Dupont Circle Metro.* **Open** noon-5pm Wed-Sat;
also by appointment. **Credit** MC, V. **Map** p282 G4.
Director Kathleen Ewing's unpretentious approach
to art dealing, coupled with her eagle eye, have
earned her a reputation as the city's finest photography dealer. Her laid-back gallery has evolved into
a focal point for local photographers, who regularly
drop in to chat. Since the space opened in 1976,
Ewing's stable of 19th- and 20th-century photographers has grown to include Berenice Abbott, Arnold
Newman, Dana Salvo and DC photographer Frank
DiPerna. She remodelled and expanded in 2002,
nearly doubling the size of the gallery.

Marsha Mateyka Gallery

*2012 R Street, NW, between Connecticut Avenue &
21st Street (1-202 328 0088/www.marshamateyka
gallery.com). Dupont Circle Metro.* **Open** 11am-5pm
Wed-Sat; also by appointment. Closed Aug. **Credit**
MC, V. **Map** p282 G4.
Marsha Mateyka exhibits painting, sculpture and
works on paper by established contemporary
American and European artists. Past highlights have
included museum-quality paintings by Sam Gilliam
and LC Armstrong. The gallery is worth a peek for
its architecture, too: the late 19th-century brownstone's interior features spectacular cherrywood fireplaces, wainscoting and carved wood transoms.

Robert Brown Gallery

*2030 R Street, NW, at 21st Street (1-202 483 4383/
www.robertbrowngallery.com). Dupont Circle Metro.*
Open noon-6pm Tue-Sat. **No credit cards.**
Map p282 G4.
Brown's collection weighs heavy on prints, etchings
and lithographs, and the gallery hosts some big
names: lithographs and drypoint etchings by
German expressionist Max Beckmann and prints
and drawings by well-knowns such as Mel Bochner
and Dan Flavin have all shown in the past.

St Luke's Gallery

*1715 Q Street, NW, between 17th & 18th Streets
(1-202 328 2424). Dupont Circle Metro.* **Open** 10am-
5pm Sat; also by appointment Tue-Fri. **Credit**
AmEx, MC, V. **Map** p282 G4.
Dupont's only Old Master gallery, St Luke's brims
with oils, watercolours and etchings by the likes of
Domenichino, Whistler and Piranesi. The airy townhouse is a favourite with local curators, who cite the
gallery's print collection as the best in the city.

Troyer Gallery

*1710 Connecticut Avenue, NW, at R Street (1-202
328 7189). Dupont Circle Metro.* **Open** 11am-5pm
Tue-Sat. **Credit** MC, V. **Map** p282 G4.
Sally Troyer has condensed her long-established
gallery into a single back room, which is connected
to Irvine Contemporary Art (*see above*) but retains a
separate entrance. Her emphasis of late has been on
pottery, punctuated by small photography shows.

Arts & Entertainment

Logan Circle

Fusebox

1412 14th Street, NW, at Rhode Island Avenue (1-202 299 9220/www.fuseboxdc.com). Dupont Circle Metro. **Open** noon-6pm Tue-Thur; noon-8pm Fri, Sat; also by appointment. **Credit** MC, V. **Map** p282 H4.

Sharp, savvy Fusebox exhibits a stable of solid young talent. Highlights include Brooklyn-based Vincent Szarek's polished sculptures, South African-born Simone Allen's conceptual pieces, and John and Joe Dumbacher's steel and pigment works. Openings are events to see and be seen at.

G Fine Art

1515 14th Street, NW, at Church Street (1-202 333 0300). Dupont Circle Metro. **Map** p282 H4.

Annie Gawlak's gallery began life on M Street, but she's since decamped to hipper pastures. After several months of floating, her new Logan Circle space

Names of the game

While some DC galleries could be accused – justifiably – of playing it safe, the following stand out from the crowd with their interesting programming and sheer charisma.

Sarah Finlay & Patrick Murcia

Pioneers in the now burgeoning 14th Street/Logan Circle neighbourhood, this husband and wife team opened their gallery, **Fusebox** (*see p194*), in September 2001. Despite the sombre mood that autumn, the art community rallied, jamming their inaugural opening. Ever since, the couple's gallery has served as a beacon to the community. With an emphasis on an international cadre of young artists and a sophisticated space to accommodate varied media, Fusebox has raised the bar for visual art in Washington.

Jayme McLellan & Victoria Reis

Both longtime District arts impresarios, the duo teamed up to establish the non-profit **Transformer** (*see p195*) in June 2002. Jayme and Victoria often serve as curators, alternating duties from one exhibition to the next. The tiny space – just about 200 square feet (19 square metres) with an overhead loft-office – hosts a varied programme that includes group shows as well as solos.

Elizabeth Roberts

Though she was just 25 years old when she opened her eponymous gallery (*see p193*) in 2003, Roberts has managed to exceed expectations, presenting a solid exhibitions programme. She favours young up-and-comers, some of which are fellow graduates of American University, where she received her MFA in painting. Older, established Washingtonians get some say as well. Though it's not a gallery of international reach, it is a reliable local venue.

Martin Irvine

Irvine, founding director and associate professor of Georgetown University's Communication, Culture, and Technology Program and longtime private dealer, opened up shop in early 2004. His gallery, **Irvine Contemporary Art** (*see p193*), now takes up part of the space occupied by the venerable Troyer Gallery, and has hosted mostly group shows up until now. When not in the gallery, Irvine can be found trawling the international art fairs of Miami and New York, sniffing out intriguing new faces.

James Strand Alefantis

A native Washingtonian, Alefantis (*pictured*) mastered his networking skills early. After years in restaurant management, he has turned his people skills to gallery ownership – specifically, **Strand on Volta** in Georgetown (*see p196*). If you meet him, you'll know it – he'll have charmed you into his gallery within minutes.

Fuse Box. *See p194.*

is set to open in September 2004. Her programme remains the same: an internationally recognised cadre of contemporary artists, from French legend Daniel Buren to performance artist Vanessa Beecroft.

Signal 66
Blagden Alley, 926 N Street (rear), NW, between Ninth & Tenth Streets (1-202 842 3436/www.signal 66.com). Mount Vernon Square/7th Street-Convention Center Metro. **Open** 1-5pm Wed, Thur; 6.30-8.30pm Fri during exhibitions only; also by appointment. **No credit cards. Map** p282 J4.
You have to trudge down a grubby alley to get to this alternative art space, a former livery stable that can accommodate large-scale art and installations. It's worth it though. You'll find eclectic stuff on view, some of it by the artists who run the place.

Transformer
1404 P Street, NW, between 14th & 15th Streets (1-202 483 1102/www.transformergallery.org). Dupont Circle Metro. **Open** *During exhibitions only* 3-8pm Tue, Fri; 1-6pm Sat; also by appointment. **No credit cards. Map** p282 H4.
This tiny, one-room non-profit space hosts the city's most daring shows. Some are duds, some gems, but each one makes a mark. And don't be alarmed by the gallery's downmarket digs; they're actually an asset: since no wall or window is sacred, artists can transform the place as they like.

Georgetown

Most Georgetown galleries are located on or near M Street, the area's main east–west artery. Six galleries in the Canal Square complex

(1054 31st Street, NW) host joint openings every third Friday of the month; in warmer weather, bands play music.

Addison/Ripley Fine Art
1670 Wisconsin Avenue, NW, at Reservoir Road (1-202 338 5180/www.addisonripleyfineart.com). Foggy Bottom-GWU Metro then 30, 32, 34, 35, 36 bus. **Open** 11am-6pm Tue-Sat; also by appointment. **Credit** MC, V. **Map** p281 E4.
This airy gallery shows and sells high-calibre painting, photography and prints by contemporary American and European artists to an upscale clientele. Gallerists Christopher Addison and Sylvia Ripley make an effort to look for nationally recognised names who might not otherwise show in DC. Their selections, while lovely, are awfully safe. Wolf Kahn shows regularly.

Fraser Gallery
1054 31st Street, NW, at M Street (1-202 298 6450/ www.thefrasergallery.com). Foggy Bottom-GWU Metro then 30, 32, 34, 35, 36 bus. **Open** noon-3pm Tue-Fri; noon-6pm Sat; also by appointment. **Credit** MC, V. **Map** p281 E5.
British expat Catriona Fraser concentrates on photography, but occasionally shows innovative local sculpture and work in other media.

Govinda Gallery
1227 34th Street, NW, at Prospect Street (1-202 333 1180/www.govindagallery.com). Rosslyn Metro. **Open** 11am-6pm Tue-Sat. **Credit** MC, V. **Map** p281 E5.
Although the Govinda Gallery is removed from Georgetown's commercial fray, it's worth a trip to see its signature rock 'n' roll-themed photography and painting shows. The gallery represents the

estate of artist and former Beatle Stuart Sutcliffe as well as rock photographers Bob Gruen and Gered Mankowitz, and often shows classic Stones and Beatles photos. The owner, Chris Murray, adores Cuba and visits frequently, bringing back photos from the island.

Hemphill Fine Arts

1027 33rd Street, NW, at M Street (1-202 342 5610/www.hemphillfinearts.com). Foggy Bottom-GWU Metro then 30, 32, 34, 35, 36 bus. **Open** 10am-5pm Tue-Sat; also by appointment. **Credit** MC, V. **Map** p281 E5.

George Hemphill's contemporary art gallery plays host to many of Washington's strongest artists. Occasional group shows, such as a gripping exhibition of Vietnam War-era photojournalism, add depth to the regular parade of solos. The art here tends towards the decorative, but important works do come through. The gallery plans to decamp to 14th Street/Logan Circle in September 2004.

Maurine Littleton Gallery

1667 Wisconsin Avenue, NW, at Reservoir Road (1-202 333 9307). Foggy Bottom-GWU Metro then 30, 32, 34, 35, 36 bus. **Open** 11am-6pm Tue-Sat. **Credit** AmEx, MC, V. **Map** p281 E4.

This gallery, which was founded by the daughter of studio glass art pioneer Harvey Littleton, shows glasswork that transcends the obvious goblet or bowl (although these are available) by incorporating photo-images and collage.

Museum of Contemporary Art

1054 31st Street, NW, at M Street (1-202 342 6230). Foggy Bottom-GWU Metro then 30, 32, 34, 35, 36 bus. **Open** 1-6pm Wed-Sat; also by appointment. **No credit cards. Map** p281 E5.

Artist Michael Clark's MOCA is DC's answer to the hip, alternative galleries of New York. Don't let the impressive name fool you: this is not a museum. The fluorescent lights and low ceilings may not be much to write home about, but the work shown is risky and innovative. When you visit, you're likely to see vibrant, Pop-art inspired studies of oranges and busts of George Washington by Clark (he prefers to go by his last name). His pictures have attracted a cult following among local collectors.

Parish Gallery

1054 31st St, NW, at M Street (1-202 944 2310/www.parishgallery.com). Foggy Bottom-GWU Metro then 30, 32, 34, 35, 36 bus. **Credit** AmEx, DC, MC, V. **Open** noon-6pm Tue-Sat; also by appointment. **Map** p281 E5.

Specialising in art of the African diaspora, this gallery shows a mixed bag of abstraction and realism; quality varies too.

Strand on Volta

1513 33rd Street, NW, at Volta Place (1-202 333 4663/www.strandonvolta.com). Foggy Bottom-GWU Metro then 30, 32, 34, 35, 36 bus. **Open** 11am-4pm Thur-Sat; also by appointment. **No credit cards. Map** p281 E4.

James Strand Alefantis's airy, one-room gallery exudes Georgetown elegance. His artists aren't stuffy though. One month you'll see playful aeroplane drawings by Los Angeles up-and-comer Jay Stuckey; the next you might view paintings on paper by District abstract expressionist Mindy Weisel.

Elsewhere

Arlington Arts Center

3550 Wilson Boulevard, at Monroe Street, Arlington, VA (1-703 797 4574/www.arlington artscenter.org). Virginia Square-GMU Metro.

After a lengthy renovation and expansion, this non-profit, non-collecting contemporary visual arts centre in Arlington is schedule to reopen in September 2004 in its historic schoolhouse home (phone for details).

Fraser Gallery Bethesda

Suite E, 7700 Wisconsin Avenue, at Middleton Lane, Bethesda, MD (1-301 718 9651/www. thefrasergallery.com). Bethesda Metro. **Open** 11.30am-6pm Tue-Sat; also by appointment. **Credit** AmEx, MC, V.

Georgetown's Fraser (*see p195*) has a suburban sibling. This bright, glass-walled gallery exhibits realist painting and photography.

District of Columbia Arts Center (DCAC)

2438 18th Street, NW, between Belmont & Columbia Roads, Adams Morgan (1-202 462 7833/www. dcartscenter.org). Woodley Park-Zoo/Adams Morgan Metro then 10min walk, or 42 bus. **Open** 2-7pm Wed, Thur, Sun; 2-10pm Fri, Sat. **Credit** MC, V. **Map** p282 G3.

This independent company programmes its small gallery and 50-seat theatre in Adams Morgan with a selection of innovative avant-garde performances and exhibitions that can occasionally border on the incomprehensible.

McLean Project for the Arts

1234 Ingleside Avenue, McLean, VA (1-703 790 1953/www.mcleanart.org). Ballston Metro then 23A, 23C bus. **Open** *Winter* 10am-5pm Tue-Fri; 1-5pm Sat; also by appointment. *Summer* 10am-4pm Tue-Fri; 1-4pm Sat; also by appointment. **Credit** MC, V.

Though located in a posh Virginia suburb, this place shows work worthy of in-town non-profits.

Target Gallery, Torpedo Factory Arts Center

105 N Union Street, at King Street, Alexandria, VA (1-703 838 4565 ext 4). King Street Metro then 28A, 28B bus or Dash bus AT2, AT3, AT5, AT7. **Open** noon-5pm Wed-Sun. **Credit** AmEx, MC, V.

Alexandria's Torpedo Factory Arts Center woos tourists with three floors of studios and galleries. Not so much sophisticated as homespun, the centre's principal appeal is its warm atmosphere.

Gay & Lesbian

Boys and girls come out to play (when they're not busy lobbying, that is).

Walking through, say, Dupont Circle and Logan Circle today, it's hard to think there was a time in the recent past when the future of gay life in the nation's capital was in question. While DC has long had a strong and thriving gay and lesbian community, the inclusive 'place at the table' attitude of the Clinton administration made the city feel like a hometown for its homosexual population, not just a compass point for activism.

The arrival of Bush and the neo-cons was a cause for concern for many, especially those who remember the apathy of Reagan and the elder Bush toward the city's growing AIDS crisis. The younger Bush administration hasn't proved especially gay-friendly: shortly after being appointed, Attorney General John Ashcroft refused permission for the observance of Gay Pride by his employees.

Yet Washington, DC's gay and lesbian community is as vibrant as ever. If anything, the proposed 'marriage amendment' to the United States Constitution, which would only acknowledge marriage as an institution between a man and a woman, has galvanised not only the city's politically minded homosexuals towards activism, but also lit a fire beneath the complacent. Fundraisers to benefit organisations like the Human Rights Campaign, Freedom To Marry, and the Victory Fund – a group supporting the campaigns of pro-gay rights candidates – have become part of the gay social calendar. And if there's one thing the city's gay and lesbian crowd loves, it's a good party. The Washington, DC queer community seems to have had a wake-up call. DC's gays and lesbians don't plan on letting anyone dismantle their place in the District. And judging by the part the community has played in revitalising areas of the city, its doubtful that the straight community would allow such a thing to happen.

The city's gay epicentre, once limited to Connecticut Avenue and Dupont Circle proper, first shifted to 17th Street, NW, particularly between R and P Streets. But the revitalisation of 14th Street and Logan Circle has expanded the District's gay-bourhood again, pushing it further east. Fourteenth Street, touted as the 'Design Corridor', with its new home furnishing stores and art galleries, plus venues like **Caribou Coffee** and **Hamburger Mary's**, has become one of the most stylish places for a stroll.

The action on 17th Street is still colourful, with the reopening of **Cobalt**, the establishment of **Food Bar DC** on its ground floor, and the continued success of their neighbour across the street, **DIK**. Seventeenth Street's anchor, the historic **Annie's Paramount Steakhouse**, still draws a crowd, too.

Moving north to U Street, **Health Bar**, the eaterie housed in the same building as Results The Gym, has turned that gay body-mecca into a one-stop community centre of sorts. The nearby **18th & U Street Diner** is another place where gays and lesbians tend to congregate.

As in any large city the scene is always changing. A party held on Sunday night might move to Thursday with little advance notice. Picking up the current issue of *MW* (that's *Metro Weekly*, by the way) or the *Washington Blade* is the best and easiest way to stay on top of things. So to speak.

Apex

1415 22nd Street, NW, between O & P Streets, Dupont Circle, (1-202 296 0505). Dupont Circle Metro. **Open** 5pm-2am Mon-Wed, Sun; 9pm-2am Thur; 9pm-3am Fri, Sat. **Admission** $1-$6. **Credit** MC, V. **Map** p282 G4.

Another good spot for those nights when the big event isn't what you're up to, Apex has some choice talent in the grooves of DJ Blaine Soileau. The

Bingo at **Club Chaos**.
See p198.

dancefloor isn't gigantic but the beats that draw the boys are often anthem-esque. And that means things can get crowded. A favourite among the young and the restless (and those who like to chase them), Apex also has a video bar in case the sights in the club aren't exciting enough.

Club Chaos
1603 17th Street, NW, at Q Street, Dupont Circle (1-202 232 4141). **Open** 5pm-2am Tue-Thur; Sun; 5pm-3am Fri, Sat. **Admission** free. **Credit** AmEx, DC, MC, V. **Map** p282 G4.
Mustachioed drag kings, Latin drag queens, shirtless dancing hotties and audience-participation party games. No, it's not one of Pedro Almodóvar's earlier films but the drama of Club Chaos. Even on theme nights, the club is very inclusive. Check the *Metro Weekly* or the *Washington Blade* to check out what's going on.

Cobalt/30 Degrees
17th & R Streets, NW (1-202 462 6569/www. cobaltdc.com). Dupont Circle Metro. **Open** 5pm-2am Mon, Sun; 9pm-2am Tue,Wed; 10pm-2am Thur; 10pm-3am Fri, Sat. **Admission** $1-$5. **Credit** AmEx, MC, V. **Map** p282 G4.
Twentysomethings and those who won't admit they're fortysomething gather upstairs around the small dancefloor in Cobalt. Downstairs at 30 Degrees

it's quieter and the attitude is less ageist. Dress among the good-looking crowd throughout leans towards club-fashionable, not club-fabulous. Cobalt/ 30 Degrees is primarily a good place to begin your evening. By 1am most of the boys have moved on.

DC Eagle
639 New York Avenue, NW, between Sixth & Seventh Streets, Downtown (1-202 347 6025/www. dceagle.com). Mount Vernon Square/7th Street-Convention Center Metro. **Open** 4pm-2am Mon-Thur, Sun; 4pm-3am Fri, Sat. **Admission** free. **Credit** MC, V. **Map** p285 J5.
Those familiar with the Eagle standard, set in clubs across the country, will know what to expect. For the uninitiated, DC's version of the popular club offers the usual trappings – pool, pinball and a rock/industrial dance mix. However, what the unfamiliar might find most surprising is the lack of pretence and attitude among the bar's patrons. A great, but dimly lit, club for those who love men in leather (or just the smell of them).

Green Lantern
1335 Green Court NW, behind lot at 1335 L Street, between 13th & 14th Streets, Downtown (1-202 347 4534). McPherson Square Metro. **Open** 4pm-2am Mon-Thur; 4pm-3am Fri, Sat; 1pm-2am Sun. **Admission** free. **Credit** MC, V. **Map** p284 H5.

The big Blowoff

When it comes to music styles, equal opportunity dancefloors are in short supply in most cities nowadays. This DJ only plays electro, that one only spins house, this one is too tweaked out, that one's too high-energy. And when it comes to club patrons, well, it's more of the same. That's why the emergence of Blowoff has been so well received in this town. As Bob Mould, one half of the DJ tag team that is Blowoff, says of the party's diversity: 'It's not just a queer alternative, it's a music alternative.' And he's right on target. Where else can you hear '70s punk, '80s synth pop, '90s techno, French house and new electro all seamlessly referenced in the same night, in the same DJ's set? Mould and DJ partner Rich Morel spin Throbbing Gristle, Liz Phair, Peaches, Loretta Lynn, Deep Dish and Felix da House Cat back to back without missing a beat. Musically, Blowoff brings to mind those nights that turned into mornings, when you spent hours switching back and forth between old vinyl and new CDs as your friends roared their approval and danced around your house.

With the camaraderie of the club-goers and the mingling of Mould and Morel – you'll spot them on the dance floor when they're not spinning their own tunes – the inclusive vibe at this party approaches the fraternal; the love of music is the bond. 'I think that's what makes Blowoff different from other clubs,' says Morel. 'People come specifically for the music.'

Think of the lists Nick Hornby's characters might have made if they were gay and grew up listening to Devo, Sex Pistols, Black Flag and Bowie and you'll get the picture. For Mould this kind of musical appreciation among Blowoff's regulars has a more personal meaning since one of the bands that would definitely be on those lists is Mould's former venture, the legendary Husker Du: 'I have guys come up to me at the club all the time and say, "I saw Husker Du play at the original 9:30 Club back in 1984".' The former skateboard punks who have grown up, hold day jobs on Capitol Hill or in DC's law firms and who now come to dance are also fans of Morel, the same-name moniker of Morel's band.

After a recent makeover, the Green Lantern still draws the same burly types that it always has, especially on Thursday nights when 'shirtless men drink free'. Pool tables, karaoke, a dancefloor and video screens provide plenty of entertainment, but the real action here is the cruising.

JR's

1519 17th Street, NW, at P Street, Dupont Circle (1-202 328 0090). Dupont Circle Metro. **Open** 2pm-2am Mon-Thur, Sun; 2pm-3am Fri, Sat. **Admission** free. **Map** p282 G4.
Bar staff move at lightning speed to serve customers in this tight space. Nightly happy-hour specials and occasional seasonal events (such as the annual Easter bonnet contest) keep the crowd entertained. Videos and pool tables are the main entertainment – aside from cruising, that is – as there's no dancefloor.

Lizard Lounge

1223 Connecticut Avenue NW, between 18th & N Streets, Dupont Circle (1-202 331 4422/www. atlasevents.com/lizard.htm). Dupont Circle Metro. **Open** 8pm-3am Sun. **Admission** free. **No credit cards**. **Map** p282 G4.
This Sunday night party has moved west, in the opposite direction of most of gay DC, and only time will tell if it's a change for the better. Still, Lizard Lounge and its promoter, Mark Lee must be doing something right as the event has been going for six years. In a city where clubs can be yawningly monochromatic, the diversity here brings to mind the colourblind early '80s, when Prince championed the 'Uptown' scene with his lines 'White, black, Puerto Rican/Every body's just-a-freakin'.

Remington's

639 Pennsylvania Avenue, SE, between Sixth & Seventh Streets, Capitol Hill (1-202 543 3113). Eastern Market Metro. **Open** 4pm-2am Mon-Thur, Sun; 4pm-3am Fri, Sat. **Admission** $2-$5. **No credit cards**. **Map** p285 L7.
The waning popularity of the 'new Nashville' and two-stepping craze has made this Capitol Hill bar a little bit easier to walk through. As the District's only gay country music venue, Remington's is still a draw for those who like to Roll the Rug and Do the Tush Push. The club itself is one of the cleanest, friendliest environments in the city, and the recently expanded dancefloor does its best to accommodate all-comers. Dance lessons are available at the beginning of most nights.

Velvet Nation

at Nation, 1015 Half Street, SE, between K & L Streets, Southeast (1-202 554 1500). Navy Yard Metro. **Open** 10pm-6am Sat. **Admission** $8-$12. **Credit** AmEx, MC, V. **Map** p285 K8.

Mould and Morel also have a band-in-progress that shares the name of their DJ effort. Songs by Blowoff, the band, are often worked into the mix at Blowoff, the party. But it's far from a star trip. If anything, these DJs are aware that good music helps to create good memories and the crowd definitely appreciates the thought that goes into the night's set lists.

At full capacity, between the big muscle boys and the big-belly bears, there's not much room to move, let alone dance, but somehow the room manages to thump and grind its way into a sweaty and ecstatic – and often shirtless – mess. 'It's a sexy scene, but it's a fun scene, because when everyone's having fun, everyone is sexy,' says Morel.

And to think it's all achieved without so much as one disco anthem. You'll find no Whitney, Kylie or Mariah on Blowoff's playlists. 'It's a diva-free zone,' Mould says, to which Morel adds, 'Except for me and Bob.'

For the most up-to-date antics of this musical tag team, check local listings or the calendar on their website (www.blowoff.us).

Arts & Entertainment

Cobalt/30 Degrees. *See p198.*

Velvet rules Saturday nights in DC's gay community. Host club Nation offers everything you'd want in a great gay club – superstar DJs, multiple dancefloors (each with their style of music), go-go dancing muscle gods, performances, light shows and throngs of attractive men. The only downside to the club is its location – on the other side of town from where most of the city's gay population lives. Parking is provided and there is security on the premises, but if you're not arriving in a group, go both ways by cab.

Wet

52 L Street, SE, at Half Street, Southeast (1-202 488 1200). Navy Yard Metro. **Open** 8pm-2am Mon-Thur; 8pm-3am Fri, Sat. **Admission** $3-$10. **No credit cards.** **Map** p285 K8.

Wet's showering nude dancers may seem something of a cliché, but that doesn't seem to have made them any less popular. The bar seems to be a favourite for porn stars. Other than that, its pretty typical, as bars where naked men dance under shower sprays go. Housed in the same building as the Edge (*see p211*).

Gyms

Bodysmith

1830 18th Street, NW, at Swann Street, Dupont Circle (1-202 939 0800). Dupont Circle Metro. **Open** varies. **Credit** AmEx, MC, V. **Map** p282 G4.

Bodysmith's personal trainers are well qualified, and judging by the look of the patrons, they do their job well. Best to book ahead, however, as appointments go fast at this small personal training facility. **Other locations:** 1622 14th Street, NW, Logan Circle (1-202 939 0800).

Crew Club

1321 14th Street, NW, between N Street & Rhode Island Avenue, Shaw: Logan Circle (1-202 319 1333). McPherson Square Metro. **Open** 24hrs daily. **Rates** day membership $7. **Credit** AmEx, MC, V. **Map** p282 H4.

A licensed nudist facility, Crew Club caters to those looking for a workout that's uninhibited – or at least undressed. Showers, lockers and towels are all available, as are condoms. There's a TV room too.

Results, The Gym

1612 U Street, NW, between 16th & 17th Streets, Shaw: U Street/14th Street Corridor (1-202 518 0001/www.resultsthegym.com). U Street/African-American Civil War Memorial/Cardozo Metro. **Open** 5am-11pm Mon-Fri; 8am-9pm Sat, Sun. **Rates** day membership $20. **Credit** MC, V. **Map** p282 H3.

Results used to be *the* gym of choice for many in the gay community. The facility is still better than most, but the posing and chatting boys can bring your workout to a standstill during peak hours (6pm onwards). If it's a social scene you want, with patrons as steely and polished as the equipment, you'll be ecstatic. If it's a serious workout you're looking for, hit Results in the off hours. **Other locations:** 315 G Street, SE, Capitol Hill (1-202 234 5678).

Restaurants & cafés

There really aren't any restaurants that are exclusively gay in the District. But there are joints where the community tends to congregate as much for the scene as for the sustenance.

Annie's Paramount Steak House

1609 17th Street, NW, between Q & Corcoran Streets, Dupont Circle (1-202 232 0395). Dupont Circle Metro. **Open** 11.30am-11.30pm Mon-Wed; 11.30am-1.30am Thur; 11.30am Fri-1.30am Sun. **Main courses** $10-$22. **Credit** AmEx, DC, Disc, MC, V. **Map** p282 G4.

This is a DC institution: having served DC's gay community for more than 50 years, it's worth grabbing a burger or a New York strip at Annie's just to be able to say 'I was there'. There's nothing remarkable about the decor or the service – or the food, for that matter. Many of the patrons seem to come to reminisce about the glory of their youth, giving the restaurant even more of a neighbourhood feel. Midnight brunch is served on weekends and holidays, and the kitchen remains open round the clock from Friday night until Sunday night.

Caribou Coffee

1400 14th Street NW, at Rhode Island Avenue, Shaw: Logan Circle (1-202 232 4552/www.caribou coffee.com). Dupont Circle Metro. **Open** 6am-10pm Mon-Thur; 6am-11pm Fri, Sat; 7am-8pm Sun. **Credit** AmEx, Disc, MC, V. **Map** p282 H4.
Yes, it's part of a chain and, no, that chain is not a gay-oriented business. Nevertheless, this Caribou has become a favourite among gay and lesbian locals. It's the kind of spot where heads spin towards the door each time it opens, as everyone looks for a friend or a face they'd like to know better. Weekends are particularly active and it can be hard to get a table. The patio gets equally crowded in summer as it provides a good vantage point for people watching.

Cyber Stop

1513 17th Street, NW, between P & Church Streets (1-202 234 2470/www.cyberstopcafe.com). Dupont Circle Metro. **Open** 7am-midnight Mon-Fri; 8am-midnight Sat, Sun. **Credit** MC, V. **Map** p282 G4.
In the warm weather months you'll find the outdoor tables of this popular Internet cafe dotted with men at work, fingers tapping away on laptops – while they keep an eye on the foot traffic coming down the street. How they get any serious work done, especially when there's a full house, is anyone's guess. If you prefer your coffee with an edge (other than the caffeine) check this place out. Odds are good that you'll be getting checked out before you even log on.

Dupont Italian Kitchen (DIK)

1637 17th Street, NW, at R Street, Dupont Circle (1-202 328 3222). Dupont Circle Metro. **Open** noon-11.30pm Mon-Fri; 11.30am-11.30pm Sat; 11am-10.30pm Sun. **Main courses** $6-$13. **Credit** AmEx, Disc, MC, V. **Map** p282 H4.
It's not the food that keeps this place in business, but rather the prime vantage point it offers for viewing the 17th Street fauna and flora. Meals are modestly priced and the mood is casual (service can be sketchy). It's a great place to spend a lazy afternoon outside, or to socialise on a warm summer night. But note that when patrons get a seat here, they're not likely to give it up in a hurry, and table turnovers can be few and far between. Upstairs is a favourite hang of those of a certain age who don't fancy the loud, late club scene.

18th & U Duplex Diner

2004 18th Street, NW, at Vernon Street, Adams Morgan (1-202 265 7828). Dupont Circle Metro then 42 bus. **Open** 6-11pm Mon, Sun; 6pm-12.30am Tue-Sat. **Main courses** $6-$12. **Credit** AmEx, Disc, MC, V. **Map** p282 H3.
The Duplex Diner, or The 18th & U as it's also known, has the casual feel of the '50s eateries it emulates and a reputation for *au courant* cocktails that

would keep the *Sex And The City* girls happy. Some nights attract more patrons than others; for instance, the Thursday night bar and club crowd often relies on the Duplex as its opening act. The menu lists diner favourites – burgers and fries, natch – but the real draw is the neighbourhood feel.

L'Enfant Café

2000 18th Street, NW at corner of U Street & Florida Avenue, Adams Morgan (1-202 319 1800). Dupont Circle Metro then 42 bus. **Open** 11am-midnight Mon-Thur; 11am-1am Fri; 10am-1am Sat; 10am-midnight Sun. **Main courses** $7.95-$12.95. **Credit** AmEx, Disc, MC, V. **Map** p282 H3.
L'Enfant dishes it best to deliver decent French stalwarts, like boeuf bourguignon, at a reasonable price with reasonable speed. Dimly lit but welcoming and warm, it's an ideal spot to spend a winter afternoon.

Food Bar DC

1639 R Street, NW, between 16th & 17th Streets, Dupont Circle (1-202 462 6200). Dupont Circle Metro. **Open** 5am-10pm Mon-Thur; 5am-11pm Fri; 11am-11pm Sat; 11am-10pm Sun. **Main courses** $3-$23. **Credit** AmEx, MC, V. **Map** p282 H4.
Food Bar DC is an all-in-one address for the city's gay scene. Its location on the street level in the same building as Cobalt means you can eat, drink and dance under one roof. Anyone looking for an ultra-chic hang with a super-modish menu will be disappointed. If you want a reasonable meal in a convenient spot, your needs should be met. Even if you don't eye something on the menu to suit your tastes you'll find plenty of eye candy at the surrounding tables.

Hamburger Mary's

1337 14th Street, NW, between Rhode Island Avenue & N Street, Shaw: Logan Circle (1-202 232 7010). Dupont Circle Metro. **Open** 11am-midnight Mon-Thur; 11am-2am Fri, Sat, 10am-midnight Sun. **Main courses** $7-$10. **Credit** AmEx, MC, V. **Map** p282 H4.
This bar and restaurant is a draw for Logan locals. There are burgers, chicken, salads, sandwiches cocktails and more. Sundays is a popular day.

Health Bar

1612 U Street, NW, between 16th & 17th Streets, Shaw: U Street/14th Street Corridor (1-202 588 9255). U Street/African-American Civil War Memorial/Cardozo Metro. **Open** 7am-2am Mon-Fri; 8am-2am Sat, Sun. **Main courses** $10-$14. **Credit** MC, V. **Map** p282 H3.
Health Bar, in the same building as Results The Gym, has turned this address into a de facto community centre, a one-stop spot for fuelling up, working out, and unwinding. The interior is sleek without being icy; both the long community table and the winding banquette encourage conversation. There are booths, too, for those who prefer a little privacy. The menu does its best to accommodate diets of various kinds. Most of the food – pasta salads, sandwiches and so on – is flavourful enough. Weekend brunches and Monday nights seem to attract the biggest crowds.

Music

The capital sings with a thousand styles.

HR-57: just jazz. *See p206.*

A necessary stop on most touring acts' itineraries, Washington doesn't miss out on many new trends. And the talents fostered in its own backyard have often graduated to the national (or international) stage. Once a backing vocalist and plant propagator at a local nursery, the late Eva Cassidy has posthumously become a superstar. Jazz greats from Duke Ellington to Shirley Horn got their start here, along with R&B stars from Roberta Flack to Ginuwine.

A rockabilly and bluegrass centre in the '50s, '60s and '70s, Washington would, in the mid-'70s, give birth to go-go and, around the turn of the '80s, to the brand of hardcore punk of which locals were so possessive that they styled it 'harDCore'. The '90s saw the revitalisation of the U Street Corridor, known as the 'Black Broadway' in its heyday.

But there has been some backsliding, too, with some jazz nights being ceded to less lofty entertainments. In classical music, smaller organisations have struggled to stay afloat, even as cultural behemoths such as the Washington National Opera and the National Symphony Orchestra have ploughed right along. Rock labels and clubs have closed, but as younger generations take the place of older, new ones will set up shop, and the beat goes on.

VENUES
Washington has a variety of venues for practically every musical taste. The **Kennedy Center** still plays host to those artists who require a more refined setting. The stage at **Lisner Auditorium** on the George Washington University campus is graced by a wealth of talent, and seems to be the locale of choice for international stars like Cape Verde's 'barefoot diva', Cesaria Evora. The **Warner Theatre** is where you'll find acts like Herbie Hancock, and the 10,000-seat Patriot Center at **George Mason University** (far outside the city) gets booked by acts like Hilary Duff and A Perfect Circle.

Mammoth acts – Usher, Prince, Metallica – head straight for the MCI Center (*see p220*), whereas all-day festivals like Lollapalooza, Ozzfest and the HFStival set up shop at Columbia, Maryland's Merriweather Post Pavilion (www.merriweathermusic.com); Bristow, Virginia's Nissan Pavilion (www.nissanpavilion.com) and DC's own RFK Stadium (*see p220*), respectively.

Yet there is no shortage of smaller stages around the District and acts like the Streets, Suzy Bogguss, Engelbert Humperdinck and Franz Ferdinand can all be heard – and seen – in relatively intimate settings, rather than in cavernous arenas.

LISTINGS AND INFORMATION
The free weekly *Washington City Paper* has good music listings. The *Washington Post* has a small 'Lively Arts' section every day, but for planning ahead, consult its more extensive 'Weekend' section (out on Fridays).

Indie city

Ask a white Washingtonian (preferably one under 45 and not carrying a briefcase) what the sound of the city is and eventually talk will turn to Ian MacKaye, his band Fugazi, and his label Dischord Records. A polarising force in local music, MacKaye represents, to his admirers, the rise of politically committed punk that writes its own rules, makes no compromises with the marketplace, conducts its business ethically and, naturally, rocks very hard. To his detractors, MacKaye is the icon of a hidebound, doctrinaire, dour scene that could stand to loosen up a bit and maybe get blotto once in a while.

Although it still has a slate of active bands, foremost among them Q and Not U, Dischord is now nearly 25 years old, and label co-founder Jeff Nelson has moved to Toledo, Ohio. Fugazi is on hiatus as band members raise families and explore side projects, and the recent CD release of 20 of the band's live shows – not to mention the *Twenty Years of Dischord* box set – cements the retrospective mood.

Throughout the 1990s, Dischord shared the scene with Simple Machines and Teenbeat, but the former has closed up shop and though the latter remains active, label head Mark Robinson has decamped to Cambridge, Massachusetts. Rather than conduct business close to home, the most significant local bands these days are on out-of-town labels. The proggy, guitarless, bass-and-organ-heavy Apes put out their latest EP on San Francisco's Birdman Records. The pop-punk of the Washington Social Club has found a home on Badman, also based in San Francisco. Esteemed New York indie Matador released the third studio album of Sabbath-baked power trio Dead Meadow, which formerly recorded for Fugazi bassist Joe Lally's now-defunct Tolotta Records. Puckish-turned-political post-rockers Trans Am have remained with Chicago's Thrill Jockey label for nearly a decade.

When any of these bands play DC, they generally occupy the Black Cat, the 9:30 Club or the Warehouse Next Door.

Tickets for most performances can be obtained direct from the venue. Ticket agencies such as Ticketmaster (1-800 551 7328/432 7328) and ProTix (1-703 218 6500) allow you to order by phone but add high surcharges.

Rock, Roots & R&B

From small rooms to large arenas, DC's stages host every type of rock and pop performance imaginable, including the pretty bog standard. Be warned: there are numerous 'bar band' type spots in the environs of Adams Morgan and Georgetown, where cover bands might punctuate their repertoire of audience-winning hits with one or two original cuts.

Folk, country and bluegrass acts are now generally booked into rock clubs, though the more specialist **Birchmere**, **Iota Club & Cafe** and **Jammin' Java** have more than their share of unplugged acts.

Whatever you're going to see, get tickets well in advance, as many shows sell out quickly. Younger punters should check venues' admissions policies: many require patrons to be 21 or over, though 9:30 Club, Black Cat and Warehouse Next Door admit any age group (no alcoholic drinks served to under-21s). Carry ID.

9:30 Club

815 V Street, NW, at Ninth Street, Shaw: U Street/14th Street Corridor (1-202 265 0930/393 0930/www.930.com). U Street/ African-American Civil War Memorial/Cardozo Metro or 66, 68, 70, 71, 90, 92, 93, 96, 98 bus. **Open** varies. **Admission** varies. **Credit** AmEx, DC, MC, V. **Map** p283 J3.

This mid-sized concert hall has come a long way since its legendary beginnings. Once a cramped dive on F Street, renowned for its heat (and smell), the 9:30 has, since relocating nearly a decade ago, boasted state-of-the-art sound and ventilation, as well as a healthy slate of microbrews. A few long-lived (or reunited) punk and post-punk bands have played both incarnations, among them the Flaming Lips, Wire and Mission of Burma, but these days you're as likely to see Los Lonely Boys, Danger Mouse and MF Doom (not on the same bill, of course) as the Decemberists, Andrew WK and Siouxsie. The open floor and balcony layout is supposed to guarantee unrestricted viewing of the stage from anywhere in the club, and for the most part it succeeds. However, arriving early, scoping out the best vantage point and then standing your ground for the rest of the night is the best way to ensure a good view. The Metro closes at midnight during the week, but buses operate until around 2am; otherwise it might be a good idea to arrange a ride or order a minicab in advance as cabs are scarce on the streets here.

Birchmere

3701 Mount Vernon Avenue, between W Reed Avenue & Russell Road, Alexandria, VA (1-703 549 7500/www.birchmere.com). Braddock Road Metro then 10A, 10B, 10P bus. **Open** from 6pm on gig nights. **Admission** $15-$45. **Credit** AmEx, MC, V.

A bluegrass, folk, and country institution, the Birchmere is one of those venues artists can't bear to outgrow. Patty Loveless might play a couple of nights here in the fall before heading to Wolf Trap in the spring, and Merle Haggard's annual gigs always sell out. This is a listeners' club, not some chicken-wire honky-tonk, and a few house rules apply in the table-service Music Hall: no standing, no smoking, no recording, no talking. It is, however, acceptable to whisper to the waitress a request for bourbon-sauced bread pudding. Rowdier patrons can always head for the bar and the pool tables. From time to time, the Birchmere also serves up the kind of pop, jazz, world music and rock that appeals to a thirtysomething audience.

Black Cat

1811 14th Street, NW, between S & T Streets, Shaw: U Street/14th Street Corridor (1-202 667 7960/www.blackcatdc.com). U Street/African-American Civil War Memorial/Cardozo Metro. **Open** 8pm-2am Mon-Thur, Sun; 7pm-3am Fri, Sat. *Red Room Bar* 8pm-2am Mon-Thur, Sun; 7pm-3am Fri, Sat. **Admission** $8-$20. **Credit** No credit cards (ATM in club). **Map** p282 H3.

As famous for having Foo Fighter Dave Grohl as a backer as it is for the bands it books, the Black Cat has picked up where the old 9:30 left off when it comes to hosting smaller, less mainstream acts, such as Rainer Maria or Beulah or almost any band whose name begins with 'The' and ends in 'ills'. Having moved three doors down the block in 2001, it has maintained its dark, homey vibe while adding a café. A downstairs area – 'Backstage' – hosts spoken-word performances, retro dance parties, independent films, and greener local and out-of-town bands. The indie regulars here can make for a rather focused, undemonstrative crowd; if your idea of fun is toe-tapping, head-nodding and staring at the stage, the upstairs Mainstage is your kind of place.

DC9

1940 Ninth Street, NW, at U Street, Shaw: U Street/14th Street Corridor (1-202 483 5000/www. dcnine.com). U Street/African-American Civil War Memorial/Cardozo Metro. **Open** 8pm-2am Mon-Thur, Sun; 7pm-3am Fri, Sat. **Admission** $5-$15. No advance tickets. **Credit** MC, V. **Map** p283 J3.

This new club's small, vintage-looking first-floor bar leads to a surprisingly large upstairs performance space. It showcases the same sort of local and touring indie bands that play Galaxy Hut and the Velvet Lounge, but in a larger (250 capacity) and more comfortable space.

Dream

1350 Okie Street, NE, at New York Avenue, Northeast (1-202 636 9030/www.welcometodream. com). **Open** 9pm-3am Thur; 6pm-4am Fri; 9pm-4am Sat. **Admission** $10-$40. **Credit** AmEx, MC, V.

Primarily a plush, upscale urban dance club (*see p211*), Dream also occasionally hosts live R&B and

District beat

Ask a black Washingtonian (of just about any age) what the sound of the city is and the response will be 'go-go'. This has nothing to do with bikini-clad women doing the frug in cages circa 1967. The term refers rather to a kind of beat-driven big-band R&B that was pioneered by Chuck Brown and the Soul Searchers and has thrived inside the Beltway for three decades while remaining virtually unheard around the rest of the country. Incorporating elements of funk and hip hop, it features call-and-response shout-outs to the audience and is built on a syncopated rhythm bed that is unmistakeable once you've heard it.

Even if you don't make it out to a club, the District pulses with the go-go beat. All around town, even outside the office buildings of Farragut North, you can see kids banging on upended five-gallon plastic buckets with the huge wooden dowels they use for drumsticks. Go-go is so unshakeable a sound that many

of the old-school acts are still performing several nights a week, every week – not just Brown but also EU and Rare Essence. Newer groups on the circuit include the Backyard Band, the Elevation Band and Ms Spice and the Malenium Band.

The bad news is that the go-go scene has a not-unearned reputation for violence. After shootings outside go-go stronghold Deno's in the summer of 2003, the Alcoholic Beverage Control Board told the club that it could keep either the music or its liquor licence. The go-go got up and went elsewhere.

The best way to keep up with where the bands are playing is to check the listings in *Washington City Paper* or, alternatively, to click through the ad fliers at TMOTTGoGo.com; there's another go-go clearinghouse online at funkmasterj.tripod.com/gogo.htm. As for your own safety, there are no guarantees, but if you don't go looking for trouble, chances are, it won't come looking for you.

hip hop (Joe, Wyclef Jean, Big Tymers). Note that the dress code prohibits athletic wear, no matter how much you paid for it. And many patrons report trouble with condescending staff. It's probably best to drive or take a cab here as there's no Metro nearby and the neighbourhood can be dangerous.

Galaxy Hut

2711 Wilson Boulevard, between Danville & Edgewood Streets, Arlington, VA (1-703 525 8646/ www.galaxyhut.com). Clarendon Metro. **Open** 5pm-2am Mon-Fri; 7pm-2am Sat, Sun. **Admission** free.
Owned by noteworthy local singer-songwriter Alice Despard, this tiny bar offers up-and-coming acts, mostly indie-rock and always for free. With a capacity of only 48, the place fills up easily, but in good weather you can watch the bands from outside, through the club's picture window.

IOTA Club & Cafe

2832 Wilson Avenue, between Edgewood & Fullmore Streets, Arlington, VA (1-703 522 8340/ www.iotaclubandcafe.com). Clarendon Metro. **Open** 11am-2am daily. **Admission** $10-$15. **Credit** AmEx, MC, V.
A good reason to pop across the Potomac to nearby Virginia, IOTA boasts an intimate atmosphere that makes it a great place to hear singer-songwriters such as the child-friendly Dan Zanes or the all-grown-up Ron Sexsmith. Unfortunately, the surroundings can be a little too intimate and it's not uncommon for patrons to be asked to shut up or leave – sometimes by the performers – as even the slightest bit of talking can interfere with the music. The artist-comes-first policy has its benefits: Norah Jones and John Mayer played their first DC shows here. The layout of the club doesn't provide many optimum vantage points, so unless you don't mind standing in between booths and being jostled during the show early arrival is advised.

Jammin' Java

228 Maple Avenue, East Vienna, VA (1-703 255 1566/www.jamminjava.com). **Open** 7am-11pm Mon-Thur; 7am-midnight Fri; 8am-midnight Sat; noon-10pm Sun. **Admission** $10-$22. **Credit** AmEx, MC, V.
A Christian coffeehouse bought out and turned secular, Jammin' Java has earned a place on the folk, blues and roots circuits, with fare ranging from John Renbourn and Jacqui McShee to Roy Book Binder to a regular Monday-night open mic. Owners Luke and Daniel Brindley also occasionally take the stage as pop-rock duo the Brindley Brothers.

Jaxx

6355 Rolling Road, Springfield, VA (1-703 569 5940/www.jaxxroxx.com). **Open** times vary.
Admission $6-$30. **Credit** AmEx, MC, V.
A hard-rock has-been haven par excellence, Jaxx is the room of choice for diehards who would see a Sebastian Bach-less Skid Row and a Glenn Danzig-less Misfits on back-to-back nights. Year after year, bands you didn't think still existed (WASP, Dokken,

Molly Hatchet) crank it up to 11 for the long-haired faithful. Jaxx also regularly hosts up-and-coming local groups, many of which join in a mammoth Battle of the Bands each summer.

Kili's Kafe Lounge

2009 Eighth Street, NW, at Florida Avenue, Shaw (1-202 232 1562/www.kiliskafe.com). U Street/African-American Civil War Memorial/ Cardozo Metro. **Open** 5.30pm-2am Tue; 6pm-2am Wed; 5.30pm-3am Fri; 9pm-3am Sat; 9pm-2am Sun. **Admission** $5-$10. **Credit** Disc, MC, V.
Map p283 J3.
This large, two-storey club is the successor to Kilimanjaro, once DC's leading venue for African and Caribbean music. Mostly recorded sounds so far, but such noted performers as Thomas Mapfumo and Bembeya Jazz have recently appeared.

Velvet Lounge

915 U Street, NW, between Vermont Avenue & Ninth Street, Shaw: U Street/14th Street Corridor (1-202 462 3213/www.velvetloungedc.com). U-Street/ African-American Civil War Memorial/Cardozo Metro. **Open** 8pm-2am Mon-Thur, Sun; 8pm-3am Fri, Sat. **Admission** $3-$12 **Credit** MC, V.
Map p282 J3.
Once almost strictly the province of local bands and their pals in the audience, the Velvet Lounge has branched out towards international cult acts such as the Legendary Pink Dots and Nikki Sudden (of Swell Maps fame), as well as offbeat statesiders including New Orleans jazzers ReBirth Brass Band and Frisco-to-Balto ukulele player Carmaig de Forest. The place still has the feel of a neighbourhood bar that just so happens to have a small stage upstairs. A good place to drop in after attending a show at the nearby 9:30 Club.

Warehouse Next Door

1017 Seventh Street, NW, at K Street, Downtown. (1-202 783 3933/www.warehouse theater.com). Mount Vernon Square/7th Street Convention Center or Gallery Place/Chinatown Metro. **Open** *performance nights* 8pm-2am. **Admission** $5-15. **Map** p283 J5.
Part of a complex that includes a café, a gallery, and two live theatres, this small performance space specialises in experimental varieties of indie-rock and post-punk. It's a good place to catch local luminaries' side projects, and has recently booked such hip out-of-town acts as Deerhoof and Xiu Xiu. When full, the venue can get claustrophobic, but – since it bans smoking – never asphyxiating.

Jazz

Marred by service that can be stroppy, poetry open mics, and evenings when the big event is Belgian beer happy hour, the highly touted return of the legendary **Bohemian Caverns** (2003 11th Street, NW, 1-202 299 0800) hasn't quite brought back the glory days of U Street, but the historic jazz corridor (now Metro accessible) still boasts a few choice locales. And with jazz enshrined as American classical music, the **Kennedy Center** (*see p77*, particularly its Terrace Theater and Terrace Gallery) and the **Smithsonian** (*see p113*) help pick up the slack.

Blues Alley

1073 Wisconsin Avenue, NW, at M Street, Georgetown (1-202 337 4141/www.bluesalley.com). Foggy Bottom-GWU Metro then 30, 32, 34, 35, 36, 38B, Georgetown Metro Connection bus. **Open** 6.30pm-12.30am daily. **Admission** $16-$50. **Credit** AmEx, DC, MC, V. **Map** p281 E5.

Some patrons consider the cover charges here outrageously high for a club that also often imposes a minimum drink order on each table. Others are just so thankful that they have a small space where first-rate acts such as Mose Allison or Pieces of a Dream will perform that money is not an object. Table service can be inconsistent, but if you're coming for the music you'll find the acoustics to be as top-notch as the talent on the stage. A longtime favourite recording spot, the club also offers a series of live discs featuring greats such as Dizzy Gillespie and Stanley Turrentine.

HR-57

1610 14th Street, NW, between Corcoran & R Streets, Shaw: Logan Circle (1-202 667 3700/ www.hr57.org). U Street/African-American Civil War Memorial/Cardozo Metro. **Open** phone for details. **Admission** varies. **No credit cards.** **Map** p282 H4.

From the outside, this store-front club looks like the type of place where a secret handshake is required to gain admittance. But you just need a few dollars to enter, which by the end of the night you'll feel was a bargain. Named after the US House of Representatives' resolution recognising jazz as a national treasure, this unassuming club is about music. You won't find big names here, unless they stop in to jam after Kennedy Center gigs, but you will find huge talent. There's no bar, but a plate of greens and beans can be had for the same price as the cover charge. Hit it on a good night, and you've got the best dinner-and-a-show value in town.

Twins Jazz/Twins Lounge

Twins Jazz *1344 U Street, NW, between 13th & 14th Streets, Shaw: U Street/14th Street Corridor (1-202 234 0072/www.twinsjazz.com). U Street/ African-American Civil War Memorial/Cardozo Metro.* **Open** 6pm-midnight Tue-Thur, Sun; 6pm-1am Fri, Sat. **Credit** AmEx, MC, V. **Admission** $5-$20.

Twins Lounge *5516 Colorado Avenue, NW, at Longfellow Street (1-202 882 2523/www.twinsjazz. com). Fort Totten Metro, then E4 bus.* **Open** 6pm-2am Wed, Fri, Sat. **Admission** $10-$30. **Credit** AmEx, DC, Disc, MC, V.

The twins here are owners Kelly and Maze Tesfaye, though their jazz/supper club also has dual locations. Both are small rooms that regularly feature

local (Lenny Robinson, Callisto) and national (John Hicks, Eddie Henderson) players, though the bigger names usually appear downtown. The headlining cuisine is that of the twins' native Ethiopia, with Caribbean and American dishes rounding out the menu. Some patrons have complained about the cover ($10-$30) and two-drink minimum; to avoid nasty surprises check the website in advance for the night's charge or ask on your way in.

Utopia

1418 U Street, between 14th & 15th Streets, Shaw: U Street/14th Street Corridor (1-202 483 7669). U Street/African-American Civil War Memorial/ Cardozo Metro. **Open** 5pm-2am Mon-Thur; 5pm-3am Fri, Sat. **Tickets** $7-$10. **Credit** AmEx, DC, Disc, MC, V. **Map** p282 H3.

One of the first places to open as part of the Shaw regeneration, this small space has settled into a regular schedule of local jazz and blues every night of the week except Friday. Vocalist Pam Bricker, who occasionally records and tours with chill-out room darlings Thievery Corporation, is solo-billed Wednesdays and shares Sundays with keyboardist Wayne Wilentz and drummer Jim West.

Classical & Opera

Washington, DC's classical music and opera scene tends to reflect the 'by the book' mentality of the city when it comes to the arts. If you prefer more colourful or daring interpretations, you may find performances and productions here less than satisfying.

Companies

Choral Arts Society

1-202 244 3669/www.choralarts.org. **Tickets** $17-$50. **Credit** AmEx, Disc, MC, V.

Under the direction of Norman Scribner, this 190-member chorus has a very popular subscription series for its performances at the Kennedy Center. Occasional international appearances are also part of its itinerary, and it routinely performs locally with the National Symphony Orchestra. Not bad for a bunch of volunteers.

National Symphony Orchestra

1-202 416 8100/www.kennedy-center.org/nso. **Tickets** $40-$75. **Credit** AmEx, DC, MC, V.

The National Symphony, which performs mainly in the Kennedy Center Concert Hall, tries to live up to its name by offering something for everyone, and that's not always easy. Leonard Slatkin is the director of the orchestra and he has focused on making the music more accessible. Sometimes, as with the learning programmes and concerts geared towards children, he hits his mark. Other decisions, like that of naming Marvin Hamlisch as Principal Pops Conductor, are applauded by many but questioned by others. Overall, though, the NSO delivers a variety of engaging performances throughout the year, including composer-themed festivals, most recently one that was devoted to Tchaikovsky.

Washington National Opera

1-202 295 2400/www.dc-opera.org. **Tickets** $45-$290. **Credit** AmEx, MC, V.

Now in its 49th season and under the direction of Placido Domingo, the Washington Opera, resident at the Kennedy Center Opera House, is one of the city's best national performing arts groups. Recent productions include *The Magic Flute* and *Billy Budd*. The season usually sells out to subscribers but there is the chance that a call to the KenCen's box office will result in a lucky score of tickets. All productions have English subtitles.

Main venues

Kennedy Center

2700 F Street, NW, at New Hampshire Avenue & Rock Creek Parkway, Foggy Bottom (tickets & information 1-800 444 1324/1-202 467 4600/ office 1-202 416 8000/www.kennedy-center.org). Foggy Bottom-GWU Metro (free shuttle 9.45am-midnight Mon-Fri; 10am-midnight Sat; noon-midnight Sun). **Box office** 10am-9pm Mon-Sat; noon-9pm Sun. **Peformances** times vary. **Tickets** vary. **Credit** AmEx, DC, MC, V. **Map** p284 F6.

The John F Kennedy Center for the Performing Arts – the national cultural centre of the United States – hosts a great variety of music, particularly on its free Millennium Stage. However, its primary focuses are classical and jazz. A welcome recent addition is the slate of intimate KC Jazz Club shows scheduled for the Terrace Gallery.

The Center has five auditoriums. The Concert Hall is where the National Symphony Orchestra and Washington Chamber Symphony (among others) perform; its acoustics are first class. The Opera House hosts dance and ballet troupes, Broadway-style musical performances, and is the home of the Washington Opera. Productions in the Eisenhower Theater tend to have more of an edge, while the Theater Lab and Terrace Theater are the Center's most intimate spaces.

Folger Shakespeare Library

201 East Capitol Street, SE, Capitol Hill (1-202 544 7077/www.folger.edu). Capitol South or Union Station Metro. **Open** *Library* 10am-4pm Mon-Sat. **Performances** times vary. **Tickets** vary. **Credit** AmEx, MC, V. **Map** p285 L7.

The Globe this isn't, though the convincing back-lit canopy does manage to convey the appearance of an outdoor theatre from Shakespeare's time. The Folger Consort presents period recitals of medieval, Renaissance and baroque chamber music. Interesting for the casual fan and a must for anyone with a passion for lyres and lutes.

Velvet Lounge. *See p205.*

National Academy of Sciences

2100 C Street, NW, at 21st Street, The Northwest Rectangle (1-202 334 2436/www7.national academies.org/arts/). Foggy Bottom-GWU Metro. **Performances** times vary. **Tickets** free. **Map** p284 G6.

A favourite of chamber ensembles, this space hosts groups such as the Jupiter Symphony Chamber Players and the Mendelssohn String Quartet. Free performances are offset by the first-come-first-serve basis of the seating. Navigating the one-way streets around the Academy can be tricky so either take a cab or study your map before you set out.

Other venues

Museums & galleries

Venturing out to the city's numerous museums and galleries can present the unexpected – choral and musical performances to accompany the visual arts on display.

Corcoran Gallery of Art

500 17th Street, NW, at New York Avenue, The White House & around (1-202 639 1700/ www.corcoran.org). Farragut West Metro. **Performances** times vary. **Tickets** vary. **Credit** AmEx, MC, V. **Map** p284 G6.

Music at the Corcoran Gallery is best enjoyed in the setting of the modest Hammer Auditorium, where cabaret singers and jazz groups have taken over from chamber ensembles. The Sunday Morning Gospel Brunch, which is held in the main lobby, is very popular, but if you're expecting an environment where the music is in the background, be warned: it can be extremely loud, irritatingly so depending on your taste, and the musicians are often placed opposite the ticket/information desk, making for

Arts & Entertainment

awkward transactions. This event is best attended solo as conversation is impossible. *See also p106.*

Phillips Collection

1600 21st Street, NW, at Q Street, Dupont Circle (1-202 387 2151/www.phillipscollection.org). Dupont Circle Metro. **Performances** *Sept-May* 5pm. **Tickets** concert included with museum admission. **Credit** AmEx, Disc,MC, V. **Map** p282 G4.

The Phillips, as it's known, carries with it a certain status that seems to lift it above the other, smaller venues in town. Its Sunday afternoon concerts are fittingly first-rate as well. If it's name-recognition you're looking for, you won't always find it here. However, if it's an excellent performance of chamber music in an environment where it's truly appreciated, you won't be disappointed.

Smithsonian Institution

Various buildings of the Smithsonian Institution (1-202 357 2700/www.si.edu). For listings, see p113.

As part of its varied programme, the Smithsonian regularly sponsors music events that can range from jazz performances and chamber music recitals to the two-week Folklife Festival in late June and early July. Call ahead for locations as they can change depending upon the seating required. Also of interest are the performances on the early instruments that are part of the permanent collection in the Museum of American History and the Friday evening IMAX Jazz Café at the Museum of Natural History.

Churches & synagogues

Several of the city's churches, cathedrals and synagogues open their doors for special performances. Others are known for the calibre of the choirs at their weekend services. In addition to those listed below, the **Church of the Epiphany** (1317 G Street, between 13th & 14th Streets, NW, Downtown, 1-202 347 2635) has an outstanding musical programme.

Basilica of the National Shrine of the Immaculate Conception

400 Michigan Avenue, NE, at Fourth Street, Northeast (1-202 526 8300/www.nationalshrine. com). Brookland-CUA Metro. **Performances** times vary. **Tickets** free. **Map** p283 L1.

Occasional choral performances or carillon and organ recitals are healthily attended. Another reason to venture in: though it remains officially undocumented, parishioners attending masses in a side chapel during the early '80s claimed that a statue of the Virgin Mary would appear to be smiling during mass, and then resume its stony look at the end. Hype? Hope? Who knows.

St Augustine Roman Catholic Church

1419 V Street, NW, at 15th Street, Shaw: U Street/14th Street Corridor (1-202 265 1470/ www.saintaugustine-dc.org/music.html). U Street/ African-American Civil War Memorial/Cardozo Metro. **Performances** times vary. **Tickets** free. **Map** p282 H3.

As the Mother Church of the local African American Roman Catholic community, St Augustine's is best known for its stunning Easter vigil service. While the performances by the church's music and dance ministry are stellar, endurance of near-miraculous capacity is required for attendees as this service can last over four hours. Those looking for something a bit less time-consuming but every bit as soul

Kennedy Center. *See p207.*

stirring should look into the church's Sunday 12.30pm mass. Led by the more sedate choir and choral group, the latter complete with ensemble accompaniment of bass, guitar and drums, the service becomes a mix of Gospel, old-time revival and traditional mass.

Washington National Cathedral
Wisconsin & Massachusetts Avenues, NW, Upper Northwest (1-202 537 6200/www.cathedral.org/ cathedral). Tenleytown-AU Metro then 30, 32, 34, 35, 36 bus or Dupont Circle Metro then N2, N4, N6, N7 bus. **Performances** times vary. **Tickets** free. **Map** p281 E2.

Don't let the word 'national' in the name mislead you. There's nothing particularly noteworthy about the services here. Yes, the Cathedral Choral Society does indeed perform, and often with special guest accompanists or vocalists. And yes, there are performances – evensong, solo recitals, and so on – with a certain degree of regularity. However, many of these are presented in the spirit of ecumenicism, and the 'all-inclusive' nature can make for a very long, and not always inspired, event unless you're one of the converted.

Multi-use Venues

George Mason University Center for the Arts
Roanoke Lane & Mason Drive, Fairfax, VA (1-703 993 8888/www.gmu.edu/cfa). **Tickets** $17.50-$84. **Credit** AmEx, Disc, MC, V.

It's a shame that one of the area's best concert facilities is located so far out of the District. Until the issue is addressed, however, folks will have to drive out to the George Mason campus for some of the best in music, experimental drama (presented here by the Theater of the First Amendment company) as well as modern dance. The main hall seats nearly 2,000 and has hosted artists from the Canadian Brass to Dr John to the Dresden Philharmonic. The university's 10,000-seat stadium, the Patriot Center, hosts big-name musical acts as well as sports matches.

Library of Congress
Independence Avenue, between First & Second Streets, SE, The Capitol & around (1-202 707 5502/ www.loc.gov). Capitol South Metro. **Performances** times vary; most begin 8pm. **Tickets** free. **Map** p285 L7.

The problem with a number of Washington venues is that the standard of architecture and acoustics don't always match. The Coolidge Auditorium in the Jefferson Building, however, rises to the occasion on both counts. Programming is intriguing and intimate: genres performed here run the gamut from classical to country to world music, with acts ranging from the Brodsky Quartet to Buddy and Julie Miller to Laura Cantrell and the Phong Nguyen Ensemble. Free admission makes performances even more accessible.

Lincoln Theatre
1215 U Street, NW, between 12th & 13th Streets, Shaw: U Street/14th Street Corridor (1-202 328 6000/www.thelincolntheatre.org). U Street/African-American Civil War Memorial/Cardozo Metro. **Tickets** $10-$50. **Credit** AmEx, MC, V. **Map** p282 H3.

DC's one-time answer to Harlem's Apollo Theater, this magnificent structure has received a new lease of life thanks to the continuing renewal of U Street. The site of jazz performances and neo-'Chitlin Circuit' theatre, the Lincoln also plays host to annual events like Reel Affirmations (Gay and Lesbian Film Festival, *see p188*) and various pageants, concerts and lectures.

Lisner Auditorium
730 21st Street, NW, at H Street, Foggy Bottom (994 6800/concert line 994 1500/www.gwu.edu/ ~lisner). Foggy Bottom-GWU Metro. **Tickets** prices vary. **No credit cards**. **Map** p284 G5.

This concert hall, located on the campus of George Washington University, plays host to a variety of performers and performances. Dance troupes and opera companies have taken the stage here, as has Senegalese singer Youssou N'Dour. Author readings and rock shows are scheduled as well, sometimes on the same night, as when Dave Eggers split the bill with They Might Be Giants.

Warner Theatre
13th & E Streets, NW, The Federal Triangle (1-202 783 4000/www.warnertheatre.com). Metro Center Metro. **Tickets** prices vary. **Credit** AmEx, Disc, MC, V. **Map** p284 H6.

Built in 1924, the Warner Theatre has seen a variety of acts on its stage. The early deco design of the auditorium gives it either a decadent gaudiness or a stately individuality, depending on the performance. Comedian Steven Wright has been scheduled here, as have Hanson, Sweet Honey in the Rock, and – sad but true – Michael Flatley's *Lord of the Dance*.

Wolf Trap
1645 Trap Road, Vienna, VA (1-703 255 1900/ www.wolf-trap.org). West Falls Church Metro then Wolf Trap shuttle bus. **Tickets** $10-$70. **Credit** AmEx, Disc, MC, V.

Calling itself 'America's National Park for the Performing Arts', Wolf Trap consists of two essentially separate performance spaces – the Barns and the Filene Center. Don't let the name, the Barns, fool you. Yes, the space is rustic, but that doesn't mean you'll be sitting on a milking stool. The acoustics here are top notch, as are the seating and facilities. The Filene Center is the sprawling outdoor concert facility with lawn and pavilion seating. The scope of the performances at both spaces is broader than that at many venues in the District that also use the name 'national'. Depending on the night, you might catch the resident opera company tackling Salieri's *Falstaff*, Renée Fleming performing with the National Symphony Orchestra, or Del McCoury laying down some high-lonesome bluegrass.

Arts & Entertainment

Nightlife

Big Apple eat your heart out.

If it's been said once, it's been said a hundred times: when it comes to nightlife, Washington isn't New York. True, but the fact is that it doesn't want to be. The city has incorporated musical and aesthetic trends from all over the world and mixed them together to develop its own distinctive flavour. Here you can find your perfect dance/chill-out club, whether you're a relaxed or hard-core clubber. In the end, though, what DC does best is an upmarket, loungey club scene. Sounds-wise, the mix of international and electronic music from renowned local and American DJs that floods the clubs provides the partygoer with loads of different backgrounds.

Information on club nights and parties can be found in the *Washington City Paper* and the *Washington Post*'s 'Night Watch' column in Friday's 'Weekend' section. Natural-born scruffs should note that much of the DC scene operates a dress code: think slightly posh or stay in line. Jeans, sneakers and hats are frequently taboo. The legal drinking age in the US is 21. It is strictly enforced in DC. Though many clubs will let under-21s in, they can't buy booze.

The best Clubs

For elite Europhiles
18th Street Lounge, *see p211*.

For non-stop dancing
Dream, *see p211*; H2O, *see p212*; or Platinum, *see p212*.

For hip hop lovers
Republic Gardens, *see p213*.

For late-night chilling
Red, *see p213*.

For new-school ravers
Nation, *see p212*; or The Edge, *see p211*.

For relaxed Latin loungers
Chi-Cha Lounge, *see p211*; or Wednesday night at Zanzibar on the Waterfront, *see p213*.

For wannabe New Yorkers
MCCXXIII (1223), *see p212*.

Clubs & lounges

Bar Nun/Club 2000
1326 U Street, NW, between 13th & 14th Streets, Shaw: U Street/14th Street Corridor (1-202 667 6680). U Street/African-American Civil War Memorial/Cardozo Metro. **Open** 8pm-2am Mon; 6pm-2am Tue-Fri; 9pm-3am Sat, Sun. **Admission** $5-$10. **Credit** AmEx, DC, MC, V. **Map** p282 H3.
If you're looking for a reprieve from the super-disco scene, Bar Nun (and its new sister venture, Club 2000) will do nicely. No real special effects are employed here; the emphasis is on the beats – and heavy at that. Those who remember getting lost in a trance from hypnotic house grooves will find the experience transcendental. The crowd is serious about its music, but not so serious about itself – a refreshing attitude for a club of this calibre. Bar Nun occasionally books other events into the space, so call ahead.

The Blue Room
2321 18th Street, NW, between Kalorama & Belmont Roads, Adams Morgan (1-202 332 0800/ www.blueroomdc.com). Woodley Park-Zoo/Adams Morgan Metro then 90, 92, 93 bus. **Open** 7pm-2am Tue-Thur, Sun; 7pm-3am Fri, Sat. **Admission** varies (usually $5-$10 after 10pm Fri, Sat). **Credit** AmEx, MC, V. **Map** p282 G3.
A hangout for Adams Morgan's beautiful people, the Blue Room is equal parts lounge, bar and restaurant, with a tiny dancefloor thrown in for good measure. The restaurant is pleasant enough, but it's the bar and loft upstairs that keep the crowds coming back. Blue walls and lighting are offset by large velour couches, flickering candles, and movies like *Breakfast at Tiffany's* projected on to a screen on the wall. DJs play house and acid jazz at weekends, so the volume is sometimes too loud for conversation.

Bravo! Bravo!
1001 Connecticut Avenue, NW, between K & L Streets, Downtown (1-202 223 5330/www.bravo bravodc.com). Farragut North Metro. **Open** 11am-9pm Mon, Tue, Thur; 11am-3am Wed, Fri, Sat. **Admission** $10. **Credit** AmEx, DC, Disc, MC, V. **Map** p284 G5.
For almost ten years this unassuming nightclub – less than three blocks from the White House – has been attracting upwards of 400 polished dancers on Wednesday and Saturday (Latin) and Friday (world music) nights. The mood is flirty; the music is a combination of Spanish-language club hits and up-tempo remixes that doesn't quit until 4am. This is one of the few 18-and-over dance nights in the city. Lighting is harsh and security tight.

Arts & Entertainment

Bukom Café

2442 18th Street, NW, between Belmont & Columbia Roads, Adams Morgan (1-202 265 4600/www. bukom.com). Dupont Circle then 42 bus. **Open** 4pm-2am Mon-Thur; 4pm-3am Fri, Sat. **Admission** free. **Credit** AmEx, Disc, MC, V. **Map** p282 G3.
The crowd is West African and black American but everyone's welcome to get lost in the sway. The Ghanaian menu is reason alone to come here (try the beef wrapped in cassava leaves) but arrive after 10pm and it's standing room only: be prepared to dance with whoever's next to you. Nightly bands play reggae, soca and funk.

Chi-Cha Lounge

1624 U Street, NW, between 16th & 17th Streets (1-202 234 8400). Dupont Circle Metro. **Open** 5.30pm-1.30am Mon-Thur, Sun; 5.30pm-2.30am Fri, Sat. **Admission** usually free. **Map** p282 H3.
Ecuadorean entrepreneur Mauricio Fraga-Rosenfeld has taught DC to relax to a Latin beat. Since opening Chi-Cha, he's expanded to Dupont Circle (Gazuza), Foggy Bottom (XX) and Arlington (Gua-Rapo). All follow the same formula: deep velvet couches, candlelight, Andean tapas, sangría, Latin jazz and sheesha pipes filled with honey-cured tobacco. Chi-Cha hosts live bands from Sunday to Thursday; on these nights there's a $15 minimum consumption fee. No hats, ties or sportswear. That's right, no ties.

Cocoa

2020 P Street, NW, at Hopkins Street, Dupont Circle (1-202 872 8886/http://cocoadc.com). Dupont Circle Metro. **Open** 10pm-2.30am Fri, Sat. **Credit** MC, V. **Map** p282 G4.
You're welcome to dine at this Dupont newcomer, housed in an elegant brownstone, but you're better off heading upstairs to chill out to the DJ sounds. The scene is upscale indie: mod couches, electronica and pretty girls. All in all, it's an excellent late-night stop for an after-dinner drink. If you can get in, that is – it's as tiny as the bean it's named for.

Dream

1350 Okie Street, NE, at New York Avenue, Northeast (1-202 347 5255/www.welcometodream. com). **Open** 9pm-3am Thur-Sat. **Admission** $10-$40. **Credit** AmEx, MC, V.
Currently one of the most popular dance clubs in town, Dream is a nightmare to reach (best to drive or take a cab, as there's no Metro nearby and the area can be dangerous). A refurbished four-storey warehouse in an industrial neighbourhood off New York Avenue, the club is an evening's commitment. But it's worth it – if you dress to impress the doormen, that is. Inside are myriad bars, rooms pumping hip hop, world music, salsa, house and trance. P Diddy, Beyoncé et al occasionally wave from the balcony.

The Edge

56 L Street, SE, at Half Street, Southeast (1-202 488 1200/www.edgewet.com). Navy Yard Metro. **Open** 8pm-2am Mon-Thur; 8pm-3am Fri, Sat. **Admission** $3-$7. **No credit cards. Map** p285 K8.

This club hosts any number of gay-themed parties during the week but plays to a mixed crowd on Friday and Saturday. The majority dance till it hurts, but for those who want some downtime there are couches near the fireplace, board games in the lounge and an outdoor deck that's great in summer. Don't leave the club to find a cab home; the neighbourhood is pretty unsafe.

18th Street Lounge

1212 18th Street, NW, between M Street & Jefferson Place, Dupont Circle (1-202 466 3922). Farragut North or Dupont Circle Metro. **Open** 5.30pm-2am Tue-Thur; 5.30pm-2.30am Thur, Fri; 9.30pm-2.30am Sat. **Admission** $5-$10. **Credit** AmEx, MC, V. **Map** p282 G5.
It used to be no-go for the terminally unhip at this love-it-or-hate-it lounge, which is run by Rob Garza and Eric Hilton of Thievery Corporation. The plain wooden door with a gold handle – right next to Candey Hardware, and unmarked – was always locked and you couldn't see in, though the bouncers could see out. Nowadays, the occasional jeans-wearer will actually be allowed in to sit on couches and listen to the DJs spin the latest in house and techno, but it's still best to dress up.

Five

1214B 18th Street, NW, between M Street & Jefferson Place, Dupont Circle (1-202 331 7123). Dupont Circle or Farragut North Metro. **Open** 9pm-3am Wed; 10pm-2am Thur; 9pm-5am Fri; 10pm-5am Sat; 6am-noon alternate Sun. **Admission** $5-$10. **Credit** AmEx, MC, V. **Map** p282 G5.
Five tends to attract the poshly dressed folk who can't push their way into 18th Street Lounge. With its three large dancefloors, it's the ideal choice for those whose main interest is dancing to hip hop, top 20 or trance. More a commercial club than a bar, this is one of the only dance places in DC to consistently offer a floor with trance music. Fridays and Saturdays are perfect for those looking to dance until the wee hours of the morning.

Habana Village

1834 Columbia Road, NW, between Biltmore Street & Mintwood Place, Adams Morgan (1-202 462 6310/www.habanavillage.com). Dupont Circle Metro then 42 bus. **Open** 6.30pm-3am Wed-Sat. **Admission** $5. **Credit** AmEx, DC, MC, V. **Map** p282 G3.
This multi-level salsa palace caters to most whims, with a couple of lounges, multiple dancefloors and live sounds. The music, clientele and decor will appeal to Latin lovers but also those who've grown tired of the largely Anglo-focused clubs in Adams Morgan. For details of dance classes, *see p216*.

Heaven & Hell

2327 18th Street, NW, at Kalorama Road, Adams Morgan (1-202 667 4355). Dupont Circle Metro then 42 bus. **Open** 7.30pm-2am Mon-Thur, Sun; 7pm-3am Fri, Sat. **Admission** $5 (includes 1 drink). **Credit** AmEx, DC, Disc, MC, V. **Map** p282 G3.

Arts & Entertainment

This club has a well deserved reputation for throwing the best '80s party in town, on Thursday nights. After getting your glow-in-the-dark halo at the door, head up the stairs to Heaven and immerse yourself in retro land. If you're looking for a young singles meat market and a trite but fun theme night, this is the place to be. Whatever you do, avoid Hell (downstairs, of course) – it's a small bar where nothing interesting ever happens.

H2O

800 Water Street, SW, between Seventh & L Streets, Southwest Waterfront (1-202 484 6300). Waterfront-SEU Metro. **Open** 5-11pm Thur; 5pm-3am Fri; 9pm-3am Sat. **Admission** varies. **Credit** AmEx, Disc, MC, V. **Map** p285 J8.

Owner Abdul Khanu (of Platinum fame) has transformed a tired seafood restaurant into a glistening waterfront club with nightly specials and a parade of superstar DJs. The 42,000sq ft club is a warren of private nooks and expansive dancefloors. More than 1,500 people come through on a regular night. 'International Fridays' feature a complimentary buffet for early arrivals, and salsa bands long into the night. 'Soul Food Saturdays' are designed to feed the body and spirit – pick up a bag of hot rum buns as you leave. In terms of clientele, it's as varied as a Benetton ad, so you won't be surprised to hear that the club hosts a monthly gospel brunch.

Mantis

1847 Columbia Road, NW, at Mintwood Place, Adams Morgan (1-202 667 2400). Dupont Circle Metro then 42 bus. **Open** 5.30pm-1.30 am Mon-Thur, Sun; 5.30pm-2.30am Fri, Sat. **Credit** AmEx, MC, V. **Map** p282 G3.

A large gold Buddha presides like a harvest moon over this apple-green lounge in Adams Morgan. Philippe Starck chairs and modular leather furniture provide a playful space to sip Cosmos and nibble on better-than-average diversions like tuna lollipops and calamari. In the basement a small DJ space gets things moving at around 10pm.

MCCXXIII (1223)

1223 Connecticut Avenue, NW, at 18th Street, Dupont Circle (1-202 822 1800/http://www.club1223. com). Dupont Circle or Farragut North Metro. **Open** 11.30am-2am Mon-Thur, Sun; 5pm-3am Fri, Sat. **Admission** $10. **Credit** AmEx, Disc, MC, V. **Map** p282 G5.

The Roman numerals reveal the address of this exclusive nightspot, which reaches three storeys above busy Connecticut Avenue. Interior columns support high ceilings above myriad couches and a dancefloor the size of a postage stamp. Celebrities such as Michael Jordan, George Clooney and various Saudi princes have been spotted enjoying this exclusive playground, and it's also the domain of professional athletes – and the women who date them. On Thursdays and Fridays African American professionals dressed to impress get here by 7pm and get inside for the $15-premium open bar and free buffet (otherwise, a contemporary menu is available).

Mie N Yu

3125 M Street, NW, between 31st Street & Wisconsin Avenue, Georgetown (1-202 333 6122). Foggy Bottom-GWU Metro then 30, 32, 34, 36, Georgetown Metro Connection bus. **Open** 5pm-1.30am Mon, Tue; 11.30am-1.30am Wed, Thur, Sun; 11.30am-2.30am Fri, Sat. **Admission** free. **Credit** AmEx, DC, Disc, MC, V. **Map** p281 E5.

If you have the patience and the billfold, a trip down the Silk Road can be a kick. Launched as a restaurant, the bar culture all but takes over after 11pm. Skip the fussy food (is anyone ever hungry for quail stuffed with figs?) and camp out in any of the overdressed oriental theme areas (the Turkish tent is fab). The house cocktail menu is a good read, but like the quail, unnecessary. The fun here is the people-watching: richie rich undergraduates and ex-wives. Stick with wine or beer and count the accents.

Modern

3287 M Street, NW, between 33rd & Potomac Streets, Georgetown (1-202 338 7027). Foggy Bottom-GWU Metro then 30, 32, 34, 36, Georgetown Metro Connection bus. **Open** 9pm-2am Thur; 9pm-3am Fri, Sat. **Admission** varies; up to $10. **Credit** AmEx, MC, V. **Map** p281 E5.

Another of John Boyle's successes (Nation, Five, Mie N Yu), this club is popular with young Georgetown. Of the places to chill out, the favourite has to be the ring of leather cubes around the sunken bar. Order into the well and the bartenders hand up your bevs. The hanging bubble chair off the dancefloor is the best seat in the house. This subterranean club can be hard to find – look for the line.

Nation

1015 Half Street, SE, between K & L Streets, Southeast (1-202 554 1500). Navy Yard Metro. **Open** 9pm-2.30am Thur; 10pm-5am Fri; 10pm-6am Sat. **Admission** $10-$25. **Credit** AmEx, MC, V. **Map** p285 K8.

In its former days, this renovated warehouse was a veritable institution among club kids and technophiles. Today the club carries on booking the most renowned international DJs – house, jungle, trance – for its Friday night 'Buzz' party, and the sound and projection system is still top-notch. However, following a series of police raids, Buzz has started to lose its original atmosphere. But on Friday nights – for those who can tolerate swarms of dancing 18-year-olds with glow sticks – those DJs still spin some of the East Coast's best electronic music. Saturday's Velvet Nation (*see p200*) is one of DC's best gay nights. The area's dodgy, so don't wander around outside trying to find a taxi.

Platinum

915 F Street, NW, between Ninth & Tenth Streets, Downtown (1-202 393 3555/www.platinumclubdc. com). Gallery Place-Chinatown or Metro Center Metro. **Open** 10pm-3am Thur-Sat; 10pm-2.30am Sun. **Admission** $10-$15; free for women before 11pm Fri; sign up for free admission on website. **Credit** AmEx, MC, V. **Map** p285 J6.

Madam's Organ

Without question, this is one of the city's most beautiful clubs. Built as a bank at the turn of the last century, the space has endured several incarnations. Whatever the name, the fashionably dressed crowd remains under the 40 mark. Once the lights, smoke and dance music start, the effect is entrancing. Don't sit down unless you want bottle service ($50-$500).

Red

1802 Jefferson Place, NW, at 18th Street, Dupont Circle (1-202 466 3475). Dupont Circle or Farragut North Metro. **Open** 10pm-5am Tue, Thur; 10pm-2am Wed; 10pm-6am Fri, Sat. **Admission** varies; up to $15. **Credit** AmEx, MC, V. **Map** p282 G5.

Undoubtedly the most chilled after-hours club in town. Red's cave-like dance space gives the place a dark, loungey feel, and the music – from progressive to tribal to deep house – packs in the city's clubbers. If you can survive the intensity of the small dancefloor, Red is a weekend must at any time of night. Otherwise, show up after 1.30am to experience some true after-party relaxation.

Republic Gardens

1355 U Street, NW, between 13th & 14th Streets, Shaw: U Street/14th Street Corridor (1-202 232 2710). U Street/African-American Civil War Memorial/Cardozo Metro. **Open** 5.30pm-1.30am Wed, Thur; 6.30pm-2.30am Fri, Sat. **Admission** free Wed, Thur; $10 Fri; $20 Sat. **Credit** AmEx, MC, V. **Map** p282 H3.

Republic Gardens remains Washington's upscale lounge for African Americans. Born in U Street's heyday, the 1920s, the club saw performances by Charlie Parker, Pearl Bailey and native son Duke Ellington. It closed in the 1960s, reopened in the '90s and, after extensive renovations and new management, was reborn in 2003. Dine in the Mahogany Room, rest up or play pool in the Library, or dance on whatever patch of floor you can claim. The Gardens can get packed but the crowd's a gorgeous one.

Zanzibar on the Waterfront

700 Water Street, SW, between Sixth & Seventh Streets, Southwest Waterfront (1-202 554 9100). Waterfront-SEU Metro. **Open** 5pm-2am Wed, Thur; 5pm-3am Fri; 9pm-4am Sat; 9pm-2am Sun (Sky Lounge only). **Admission** varies; up to $15. **Credit** AmEx, MC, V. **Map** p285 J8.

This club has reclaimed the waterfront. Sit near the wide windows at lunchtime and watch the boats chug by; return for Tuesday night's jazz sessions. Wednesday night's salsa party welcomes wonks in suits and hotties in little dresses. Take the free dance lesson at seven o'clock, and you can be using your new moves by eight. On Saturdays, twentysomethings hold court. The restaurant serves Afro-Caribbean food. The Sky Lounge is a popular spot for hanging out – you'll pay a bit extra but the view makes it worthwhile.

Comedy & cabaret

On Sunday nights **Madam's Organ** (*see p151*) hosts magician Alan Nu. He wanders from table to table breaking watches (and repairing them). Indie rock hangout **Black Cat** (*see p204*) occasionally books performance artists – the acts lean towards the avant-garde.

Improv

1140 Connecticut Avenue, NW, between L & M Streets, Downtown (1-202 296 7008/www.dcimprov.com). Farragut North Metro. **Open** *Shows* 8.30pm Tue-Thur; 8pm, 10.30pm Fri, Sat; 8pm Sun. **Admission** $15-$35. **Credit** AmEx, MC, V. **Map** p284 G5.

The best-known and most-loved comedy club in town plays host to some of the hottest names in the business. The most common assessment of Improv is that the the service is disappointing but the material hysterical. In other words, it's worth the wait.

Arts & Entertainment

Sport & Fitness

Hike, bike, swim or join a gym – DC sure knows how to work up a sweat.

Preparing to paddle at **Fletcher's Boat House**. *See p215.*

Active Sports & Fitness

Boating

The Potomac and Anacostia rivers, as well as the Tidal Basin, provide plenty of opportunities to get out on the water. The Tidal Basin tends to be the calmest of the three, and boating there will afford you spectacular views of the city. The Potomac is filled with rapids, and is thus extremely challenging – not a place for beginners. If you're looking for some top-notch tumble-around-the-rapids kayaking, Great Falls, on the Maryland-Virginia border, is the best spot. It's just a few miles from downtown DC, with a popular launch at the Old Angler's Inn, below the falls on the Maryland side; there are also launch sites in Virginia. **Springriver** (5606 Randolph Road, off Rockville Pike, Rockville, Maryland, 1-301 881 5694, www.springriver.com) rents out kayaks.

In Alexandria, Virginia, the **Mariner Sailing School** (Belle Haven Marina, off George Washington Parkway, 1-703 768 0018, www.saildc.com) offers sailing courses and boat hire; for sea kayaking – tours and rentals – try the **Atlantic Kayak Company** (1201 North Royal Street, between Third Street & Bashford Lane, 1-703 838 9072, www.atlantickayak.com).

Out of town, but within an hour's drive, there are lots of other lakes, bays and rivers to explore. In West Virginia you'll find good white-water rafting at Harper's Ferry on the Shenandoah River: **Historical River Tours** (1-410 489 2837, www.historicalrivertours.com) runs day trips for $39-$57; **River Riders** (1-800 326 7238, www.riverriders.com) also organises rafting trips, plus tubing (riding the river sitting in a large rubber ring).

Cunningfalls State Park (1-301 271 7574) in Thurmont, Maryland, is home to one of Maryland's largest waterfalls – a cascade of 27 feet (eight metres). Kayaks and canoes can be rented here too.

Annapolis, Maryland, home of the US Naval Academy, is a very water-oriented town. Chesapeake Bay is extremely popular for sailing, as is fishing and bird watching in the Bay's endless inlets. Sailing boats can be hired

After a few days spent indoors, exploring Washington's many monuments and museums, it's well worth hopping on a bike – or into a kayak – and getting some fresh air. DC offers countless ways to spend an outdoor afternoon, including rollerblading along the Tidal Basin or joining a walking tour of one of the city's historic neighbourhoods. Alternatively, why not skip town altogether and head out to one of the region's natural paradises for some hiking, climbing or white-water rafting? The city will seem a world away.

Whatever you do, don't leave town without catching a Wizards (basketball), Redskins (American football) or Capitals (hockey) game. Washingtonians take their major-league teams very seriously. That said, the official sport of the city should really be soccer. With a growing Latino population, the sport has become a huge spectator sport, with most games packing the houses.

from **South River Boat Rentals** (1-410 956 9729, www.southriverboatrentals.com), while **JWorld** (1-800 966 2038, www.sailjworld.com) runs sailing courses.

Below are some places for tours, classes and rentals within the DC area.

Fletcher's Boat House

4940 Canal Road, NW, at Reservoir Road, Upper Northwest (1-202 244 0461/www.fletchersboathouse.com). Bus D4. **Open** 7.30am-6pm daily. **No credit cards. Map** p280 B3.

Take a canoeing class, or just rent a canoe or rowing boat ($11 per hour) for use on the C&O Canal or the Potomac River.

Jack's Boathouse

3500 K Street, NW, under the Key Bridge, Georgetown (1-202 337 9642). Rosslyn Metro. **Open** 8am-sunset daily. **No credit cards. Map** p281 E5.

This outfit offers a range of rowing boats, canoes and kayaks for use on the Potomac at $15 per hour, or $35 per day.

Thompson Boat Center

2900 Virginia Avenue, NW, at Rock Creek Parkway, Foggy Bottom (1-202 333 9453/www.thompsonboatcenter.com). Foggy Bottom-GWU Metro. **Open** 7am-6pm Mon-Sat; 8am-5pm Sun. **Credit** MC, V. **Map** p284 F5.

Just off Rock Creek Parkway, across from the Kennedy Center. From April to November you can hire canoes, sea kayaks and sculling shells (from $8 an hour) – the last only if you are certified.

Tidal Basin Boathouse

1501 Maine Avenue, SW, at Jefferson Memorial, The Mall & Tidal Basin (1-202 479 2426). Smithsonian Metro. **Open** 10am-6pm daily. **Credit** MC, V. **Map** p284 H7.

Rent a paddleboat ($8 an hour for a two-seater) to go around the Tidal Basin. This is particularly enjoyable in cherry blossom season.

Washington Sailing Marina

1 Marina Drive, off George Washington Memorial Parkway, Alexandria, VA (1-703 548 9027). **Open** *Summer* 9am-6pm daily. *Winter* 10am-5pm daily. **Credit** Disc, MC, V.

Sailboats are available by the hour ($10-$19) for trips on the Potomac River. You must be certified or have enough experience to pass a written exam. You need to drive or take a taxi to get there.

Cycling

Washington has an extensive network of paved bike trails. Marked with green signs with a picture of a bike, trails are mostly flat, making cruising on two wheels a breeze. We list some of the most popular below. However, there aren't too many dirt trails for the hardcore enthusiast.

ADC produces a map showing all bike trails and on-street bike routes within the Beltway; it is available at most bike shops or the ADC Map & Travel Store (*see p158*). The Washington Area Bicyclist Association (Suite 1030, 733 15th Street, NW, 1-202 628 2500) also has maps and trail brochures. They're listed online at www.waba.org. If you're planning on travelling by Metro, note that you can take your bike on the trains between 10am and 2pm and after 7pm during the week and all day on weekends and holidays. Also, all Metro buses are equipped with bicycle racks on their fronts.

C&O Canal Towpath

In Georgetown, just north of the Thompson Boat Center in Foggy Bottom (*see above*), there's a turn-off from the Rock Creek Trail (*see below*) west along the Chesapeake & Ohio Canal Towpath, a packed gravel path that runs 184 miles (296km), all the way to Cumberland, Maryland. There are frequent campsites along the way. Skinny tyres are not recommended.

Capital Crescent Trail

DC's most crowded trail, this 11-mile (17.5km) path runs through Northwest Washington. You start off at the Thompson Boat Center (*see above*) and take the Georgetown Branch Trail (made of crushed rock, not paved) to join up with the Rock Creek Trail between Georgetown and the suburb of Silver Spring out in Maryland.

Mount Vernon Trail

A popular and scenic ride is to George Washington's family home, Mount Vernon, 19 miles (30km) southwest of DC. From the Lincoln Memorial, take the south (downstream) side of the Arlington Memorial Bridge and head south along the Potomac. En route, it runs through charming Old Town Alexandria. If you want to cut the trip in half, you can rent bikes from Big Wheel Bikes in Alexandria (2 Prince Street, at Strand Street, 1-703 739 2300).

Rock Creek Trail

This relatively easy trail runs from Hains Point – where the Washington Channel and the Potomac and Anacostia rivers meet – up the east bank of the Potomac, taking in the National Mall and Rock Creek Park, to Lake Needwood in the Maryland suburbs, 25 miles (40km) from the Mall. It gets hillier towards Maryland, and is often crowded. In the park, Beach Drive north of Blagden Avenue is closed to cars at weekends and on holidays.

W&OD Trail

This trail heads due west from the Mount Vernon Trail (*see above*) for nearly 50 miles (80km) along a former railway track (the Washington & Old Dominion Railroad), through parks and past old train stations. The intersection is just past National Airport, but it's confusing, so it's advisable to bring along a map.

Arts & Entertainment

Bike rental & tours

One-speed cruiser bikes can be rented by the hour or the day at **Fletcher's Boat House** (*see p215*), while **Thompson Boat Center** (*see p215*) has cruisers and 21-speeds. Or try **Bike the Sites**. For the best mountain biking, you'll need to get out of town – look for Scott Adams' *Washington Mountain Bike Book* at any bike shop. Some good rides are accessible by bike path, but many are best reached by car.

Bike the Sites

Tour starts at the Old Post Office Pavillion, 1100 Pennsylvania Avenue, NW, Downtown (1-202 842 2453/www.bikethesites.com). Federal Triangle Metro. **Rates** phone for details. **Credit** AmEx, MC. V. **Map** p284 H7.
This company arranges various city tours by bike, including a five-hour, eight-mile (12.5km) 'capital sights package' for $50-$55 per person (reserve online; price includes bike and helmet hire). A piece of advice: think twice about taking this tour in the humidity of summer. The company also organises tours to Mount Vernon and can arrange customised tours for larger groups.

Dance

Some performance spaces, including the **Kennedy Center** (*see p222*), also hold classes. The Spanish ballroom in **Glen Echo Park** holds popular swing dances on Saturdays (*see p102*).

African Heritage Dance Center

4018 Minnesota Avenue, NE, at Benning Road, Northeast (1-202 399 5252). Minnesota Avenue Metro. **No credit cards**.
Drop-in evening classes (all $10) in traditional African dance, with live music.

Habana Village

1834 Columbia Road, NW, between Biltmore Road & Mintwood Place, Adams Morgan (1-202 462 6310). Dupont Circle Metro then 42 bus. **Open** phone for details. **Rates** phone for details. **Map** p282 G3.
Salsa lessons are held at 7.30pm from Wednesday to Friday. Phone for details of other classes.

Joy of Motion

1643 Connecticut Avenue, NW, at R Street, Dupont Circle (1-202 387 0911/www.joyofmotion.org). Dupont Circle Metro. **Credit** AmEx, MC, V. **Map** p282 G4.

On your trail

You don't have to go far out of town to find great hiking: cool forests, meandering streams and rushing waterfalls are in plentiful supply within a short drive from the city. A word of warning: it's wise to pack bug spray if you plan to be out after dusk – mosquitoes are in abundance. Here are our top five hikes in the Washington area. Driving times listed are from downtown DC.

The four-mile (six-kilometre) **Billy Goat Trail** is in Great Falls National Park (9200 Old Dominion Drive, McLean, Virginia, 1-703 285 2965, fee for park entrance $5 per car). This rocky trail – there's some scurrying over rapids involved – cuts through the lush towering trees that line the Potomac River in Great Falls Park. Don't miss the sandy 'beach' along the trail, or the delightful views of Mather's Gorge, a white-water rafter's playground. Driving time: 30 minutes.

The **Red Trail** in Calvert Cliffs State Park (off Maryland 24 in Lusby, Maryland, 1-301 872 5688) winds its (fairly flat and easy) way through the park to the sandy beach of Chesapeake Bay, a good spot to pick up fossils and sharks' teeth. The tall Miocene cliffs, rising over the Bay at 100 feet (30 metres), are very dramatic. Driving time: 45 minutes.

In the Shenandoah National Park (Skyline Drive is most easily accessible from Warrenton, Virginia, 1-540 999 3500) is **Piney Branch Trail**. Lining this moderate wooded hike are a few waterfalls, but to reach them you have to get off the trail and follow the river. In the summer, bring your swimsuit: a few of the waterfalls have pools at the bottom that are big enough for swimming. Driving time: one hour. Visit www.swimmingholes.org for the locations of other local swimming holes.

The **Chimney Rock and Wolf Rock Circuit** in Catoctin Mountain Park starts at Cunningham Falls (14039 Catoctin Hollow Road, Thurmont, Maryland, 1-301 271 7574). It's a three-and-a-half-mile (five-kilometre) round trip and includes some steep climbs. The rewards are spectacular views and, at the highest point, the sight of Maryland's highest waterfall, which plunges 78 feet (24 metres). Driving time: one hour.

A five-mile (eight-kilometre) hike along the **Northern Peaks Trail** at Sugarloaf Mountain (7901 Comus Road, Dickerson, Maryland, 1-301 874 2024) takes you to a rocky outcropping with sweeping views of Potomac and Shenandoah rivers in Harper's Ferry, West Virginia. Driving time: 45 minutes.

Drop-in classes for $13-$14 in jazz, ballet, modern, flamenco and belly dancing, among others. **Other locations**: Suite 202, 7702 Woodmont Avenue, Bethesda, MD (1-301 986 0016); 5207 Wisconsin Avenue, NW, Friendship Heights (1-202 362 3042).

Liz Lerman Dance Exchange

7117 Maple Avenue, near Carroll Avenue, Takoma Park, MD (1-301 270 6700/www.dance exchange.org). Takoma Metro. **Open** 9am-5pm Mon-Fri. **Rates** $12 per class. **Credit** MC, V.
As well as professional-level modern and ballet classes, this studio offers technique classes and short-term themed classes. Visitors are welcome to drop in for a single class.

Fishing

It's possible to fly-fish in beautiful, rural rivers within a few hours' drive of the city. Those who enjoy sea fishing can join excursions on Chesapeake Bay from Annapolis (trips run from the end of April to the end of November, and it's best to phone at least a day or two in advance).

Right in DC, plenty of people drop a line into the Potomac River. A popular fishing spot is Hains Point, where the Anacostia flows into the Potomac. It's not advised to eat the bottom-feeders such as catfish or carp. You'll need a licence to fish, from DC, Virginia or Maryland. A one-year DC licence costs $7.50. They're sold at Fletcher's Boat House (*see p215*), among other places.

Rod & Reel Charters

Route 261 & Mears Avenue, Chesapeake Beach, MD (1-301 855 8450/www.rodnreelinc.com). **Open** *Late Apr-late Nov* 5am-8pm daily. Closed late Nov-late Apr. **Credit** (for full boat only) MC, V.
Located at Chesapeake Beach, this company runs six- to eight-hour trips for upwards of six people, from $37 per person.

Golf

These three public courses all rent out clubs.

East Potomac Golf Course

972 Ohio Drive, SW, between 15th Street & I-395 (1-202 554 7660). **Open** 7.30am-9.30pm daily. **Rates** *9 holes* $8-$14 Mon-Fri; $11-$17 Sat, Sun. *18 holes* $20 Mon-Fri; $25 Sat, Sun. **Credit** MC, V. **Map** p284 J9.
In East Potomac Park, on the spit of land between the Washington Channel and the Potomac River, is this 18-hole golf course and driving range. Enjoy the views of the monuments from the green. The easiest way to get there is by cab.

Langston Golf Course

2600 Benning Road, NE, at 26th Street, Northeast (1-202 397 8638). Stadium-Armory Metro. **Open** dawn-dusk daily. **Rates** *9 holes* $14

Let's dance: **Kennedy Center**. *See p216.*

Mon-Fri; $17 Sat, Sun. *18 holes* $20 Mon-Fri; $25 Sat, Sun. **Credit** MC, V.
This 18-hole course along the Anacostia River is DC's only public course with water holes.

Rock Creek Golf Course

1600 Rittenhouse Street, NW, at 16th Street, Upper Northwest (1-202 882 7332). Bus D31. **Open** dawn-dusk daily. **Rates** *9 holes* $12.50 Mon-Thur; $15.50 Fri-Sun. *18 holes* $18.25 Mon-Fri; $23 Sat, Sun. **Credit** MC, V.
An 18-hole course in woody, hilly terrain right in the middle of Rock Creek Park.

Gyms

DC Jewish Community Center

1529 16th Street, NW, at Q Street, Dupont Circle (1-202 518 9400/www.dcjcc.org). Dupont Circle Metro. **Rates** $15 per day. **Credit** AmEx, MC, V. **Map** p282 H4.
Day membership gives you access to the swimming pool and fitness machines; water aerobics, yoga and aerobics classes are extra.

Gold's Gym

409 Third Street, SW, between D & E Streets, Southwest (1-202 554 4653/www.goldsgym.com). Federal Center SW Metro. **Open** 6am-11pm Mon-Fri; 8am-10pm Sat; 8am-6pm Sun. **Rates** $15 per day; $50 per wk. **Credit** AmEx, Disc, MC, V. **Map** p285 J7.
Has branches in DC, Arlington and the suburbs.

National Capital YMCA

1711 Rhode Island Avenue, NW, at 17th Street, Dupont Circle (1-202 862 9622/www.ymca.com). Farragut North Metro. **Open** 6am-11pm Mon-Fri; 8am-7pm Sat; 9am-6pm Sun. **Rates** *YMCA members* $7 per day. *Non-members* $15 per day. **Credit** MC, V. **Map** p282 G5.

This trendy YMCA is affiliated with some area hotels, but otherwise only allows members of other YMCAs to use its facilities, such as the 25m pool and seven floors of weights and fitness machines. Classes in aerobics and basketball are also available.

Washington Sports Clubs

1990 M Street, NW, at 20th Street, Foggy Bottom (1-202 785 4900). Dupont Circle Metro. **Open** 6am-10pm Mon-Fri. **Rates** $25 per day. **Credit** AmEx, MC, V. **Map** p284 G5.

This club has weights, machines, a sauna and squash courts.

Other locations: throughout the city.

YWCA

624 Ninth Street, NW, at G Street, Downtown (1-202 626 0710). Gallery Place-Chinatown Metro. **Open** 6.30am-9pm Mon-Fri; 8.30am-4.30pm Sat; 10am-4.30pm Sun. **Rates** *YWCA members* $8 per day. *Non-members* $12 per day. **Credit** AmEx, MC, V. **Map** p285 G6.

The YWCA has a swimming pool, gym and sauna and offers a range of classes from yoga and pilates to martial arts and kickboxing.

Horse riding

Real horse country is just beyond the suburban sprawl of Virginia, but the following caters to horse-lovers in town.

Rock Creek Park Horse Center

5100 Glover Road, NW, at Military Road, Upper Northwest (1-202 362 0118/www.rockcreekhorse center.com). Friendship Heights Metro then E2, E4 bus. **Open** phone for details. **Rates** (approx) $30 for 1hr guided ride (over-12s); $20 for 15min pony ride. **Credit** MC, V.

Guided trail rides and pony rides in the corral. To get there, it's best to take a cab or cycle.

Ice skating

During DC's short cold season, a tiny temporary ice-skating rink is set up at **Pershing Park** (1-202 737 6938) on Pennsylvania Avenue, NW, between 14th and 15th Streets, near the White House. The **National Gallery of Art's Sculpture Garden** ice rink on the Mall (at Seventh Street and Constitution Avenue) is open in winter. Phone the gallery on 1-202 737 4215 for more details. In Maryland, a rink opens at **Bethesda Metro Center Plaza**, at the central intersection of Old Georgetown Road and Wisconsin Avenue.

RFK Stadium, home of DC United. *See p220.*

Fort Dupont Ice Arena

3779 Ely Place, SE, off Minnesota Avenue, Southeast (1-202 584 5007/www.fdia.org). Bus U6. **Open** noon-2pm Fri; 2.30-4.20pm Sat, Sun (other times vary; phone for details). **Rates** admission $4; skate rental $2. **No credit cards**.

Fort Dupont, just over the Anacostia River, used to be run by the Park Service. When it got on the budget death list, parents pulled together and turned it into a non-profit organisation to bring ice skating to kids.

In-line skating

DC's best in-line skating venue is probably **Beach Drive**, north of Blagden Road in Rock Creek Park, which is closed to traffic on weekends. Now that traffic is blocked from Pennsylvania Avenue in front of the White House, skaters, particularly those practising hockey, use the block regularly. Washington's bike paths (*see p215*) are also popular, although they're often too narrow for a real workout, with cyclists and joggers coming from all directions. For more information, visit www.skatedc.org.

Hockey Stop

5544 Nicholson Lane, Rockville, MD (1-301 770 4500). White Flint Metro. **Open** 11am-7pm Mon-Fri; 10am-6pm Sat; noon-5pm Sun. **Credit** Disc, MC, V.

Five minutes from Rock Creek Park, this shop rents skates for $15 a day.

Pick-up games

Washington is teeming with amateur sports clubs and pick-up games (those where anyone's welcome) of everything from baseball to Frisbee to rugby to field hockey. The sand pits along the **Rock Creek Parkway** between the Kennedy Center and the Lincoln Memorial are the place for volleyball matches, while practically the entire **Mall** turns into a mass of softball fields on summer evenings. Other likely spots for games include the **Ellipse**, just south of the White House, and the fields around the **Lincoln Memorial**. For event listings – races, festivals and local club contacts – get a copy of *MetroSports Magazine* (free in street boxes) or check its website at www.metrosportsdc.com.

Rock climbing

The best rock climbing is way out in West Virginia, notably **New River Gorge**, a five-hour drive from the city. Closer in, there are cliffs to be scaled at **Great Falls**, on both the Virginia and Maryland sides. As well as the indoor climbing wall at **Sportrock II**, there is a much smaller one at **Results The Gym** (1612 U Street, NW, 1-202 518 0001). Sportrock also offers day climbing trips to the close-in cliffs at **Carderock** on the Potomac River.

Sportrock II Climbing Center

5308 Eisenhower Avenue, at Van Dorn Street, Alexandria, VA (1-703 212 7625/www. sportrock.com). Van Dorn Street Metro. **Open** noon-11pm Mon-Fri; 11am-8pm Sat, noon-8pm Sun. **Rates** $18 per day. **Credit** MC, V. Sportrock II has a 14,000sq ft climbing wall and provides gear and area information.

Tennis

There are plenty of first-come, first-served courts at parks and schools around the area. If others are waiting, playing time is limited to 30 minutes or an hour.

East Potomac Tennis Center

1090 Ohio Drive, SW, at Buckeye Drive, Southwest (1-202 554 5962). Smithsonian Metro then 20min walk. **Rates** $8-$30.70 per hr. **Credit** MC, V. **Map** p284 H8.
Next to the Potomac at Hains Point, the Tennis Center has three indoor hard courts and nine clay and ten hard courts outdoors. It's easiest to get to the Center by cab.

Rock Creek Tennis Center

16th & Kennedy Streets, NW, Upper Northwest (1-202 722 5949). Bus S1, S2, S3, S4, S5. **Open** 7am-11pm daily. **Rates** $8-$29.75 per hr. **Credit** MC, V.

This public centre just east of Rock Creek Park has ten hard courts and 15 clay courts. A bubble covers half the hard courts during winter. Reservations are recommended. There's a decent pro shop here too.

Yoga

SpiralFlight – A Center for Yoga & the Arts

1726 Wisconsin Avenue, NW, between R & S Streets, Georgetown (1-202 965 1645/www.spiral flightyoga.com). Bus 30, 32, 34, 35, 36. **Open** phone for details. **Rates** $25 per class. **No credit cards**. **Map** p281 E4.
Classes in just about every type of yoga, from Ashtanga to Hatha, as well as pilates and belly dancing. Drop-ins are welcome.

St Mark's Yoga Center

St Mark's Church, Third & A Streets, SE, Capitol Hill (1-202 546 4964). Capitol South Metro. **Classes** 7.45pm Mon; 12.15pm, 7.45pm Wed; 6.30pm Thur; 10am Sat; 4.30pm Sun. **Rates** free 1st class; $12 per class thereafter. **No credit cards**. **Map** p285 L6.
Yoga classes are held in this church basement throughout the week.

Spectator Sports

Tickets for practically all professional sporting events in Washington are distributed by Ticketmaster (1-301 808 4300). There is a service charge for all purchases.

American football

If you want to see the Washington Redskins, three-time Superbowl champions, you'll have to pay for the privilege. There's a 20-year waiting list for season tickets – and all seats are season tickets. That leaves the rest of the world to scour the *Washington Post* classifieds or deal with touts at the gate. You have a slightly better chance of seeing a game if you travel to Baltimore, to watch the Baltimore Ravens (ex-Cleveland Browns), who brought a Superbowl victory to Maryland in 2000. Their tickets go on sale for the whole season in August. Phone 1-410 261 7283 for the latest information. The football season runs from August to January.

FedEx Field

Landover, MD (1-301 276 6050). Landover, Addison Road or Cheverly Metro then shuttle bus on game days.
This vast 80,116-seat bowl, in a nearby Maryland suburb, is the home of the Redskins.

M&T Bank Stadium

Near Camden Yards & Inner Harbor, Baltimore, MD (1-410 230 8000).

Arts & Entertainment

Take a Marc train from Union Station to Camden Yards in Baltimore; the journey takes around 45 minutes. Be warned that Marc shuts down mid-evening, so make sure you're not going to miss the last return train. Alternatively, take an Amtrak train to Baltimore's Pennsylvania Station; the stadium is a ten-minute cab ride away.

Baseball

DC has no home-grown baseball team, but the Baltimore Orioles pack fans from DC into Camden Yards in Baltimore. You can get there by car, by Amtrak rail service (or by Marc on weekdays). The season runs from April to September; tickets are available from Ticketmaster (*see p219*).

Oriole Park at Camden Yards
333 West Camden Street, Baltimore, MD (1-888 848 2473).

Basketball

The Washington Wizards of the NBA and the Washington Mystics of the WNBA (the women's equivalent) play at the MCI Center in Downtown. At the men's games you may catch a glimpse of Jerry Stackhouse, the acrobatic shooting guard from the University of North Carolina. Tickets are usually easy to get and cost $10-$775 for the Wizards, or as low as $4 for the Mystics. The men play from November to May, the women from May to September.

MCI Center
601 F Street, NW, at Seventh Street, Downtown (1-202 628 3200). Gallery Place-Chinatown Metro. **Open** times vary. **Map** p285 J6.
This swanky, $200-million, 20,000-seat stadium is a first-class place to watch games, and also has shops and sports memorabilia.

Hockey

The Washington Capitals play in the MCI Center from October until April. The ever-promising Caps don't usually sell out and tickets cost $20-$140. Phone the MCI Center (*see above*) for match information. Tickets are available from Ticketmaster (*see p219*).

Horse racing

Laurel Park
Racetrack Road, off State Route 198, Laurel, MD (1-301 725 0400/www.marylandracing.com). **Tickets** *grandstand* $3. **No credit cards**.
Halfway between Baltimore and DC, this is where ponies and thoroughbreds race much of the year. You'll need a car to get there.

Pimlico Race Course
Winner & Hayward Avenues, Baltimore, MD (1-410 542 9400/www.pimlico.com). **Tickets** $3. **No credit cards**.
The Preakness Stakes are held at this track on the third Saturday in May. Other thoroughbred races are held – not every day – from April to September. To get there you'll have to drive or take a train to Baltimore's Penn Station and then catch a cab.

Rosecroft Raceway
6336 Rosecroft Drive, off Brinkley Road, Fort Washington, MD (1-301 567 4000/www.rose croft.com). **Tickets** $3. **No credit cards**.
The place to go for year-round harness racing. The only way to get there is by car.

Soccer

Who said Washingtonians don't appreciate soccer? The fans go crazy for DC United, Washington's very good pro team, which plays major-league soccer from March to November at the RFK (Robert F Kennedy) Stadium – they won the MLS Cup in the first two years of the league's existence. There's also an incredibly dynamic Latino League, which fills suburban fields every weekend. The Taca Cup is this league's championship, a multi-day tournament held at the RFK Stadium in late July or early August. Contact the Cup sponsor, Taca Airlines (1-202 589 0811), for details.

RFK Stadium
22nd & East Capitol Street, NE, Northeast (office 1-202 547 9077/DC United office 1-703 478 6600/www.rfkstadium.com). Stadium-Armory Metro. **Open** 8.30am-5.30pm Mon-Fri. **Tickets** vary. **Credit** MC, V.
Tickets are available from the DC United office or through Ticketmaster (*see p219*).

Swimming

Some people recommend avoiding swimming in the Potomac and Anacostia rivers, but lots of locals can be seen cooling off in the Potomac during summer.

There are nearly three dozen (highly chlorinated) indoor public swimming pools in DC; look in the government listings (blue-edged) in the *Yellow Pages* under 'District of Columbia, Parks and Recreation', or phone Aquatic Services on 1-202 576 8884.

Outdoor pools are usually open from Memorial Day (May) to Labor Day (September). The best are the Capitol East Natatorium (635 North Carolina Avenue, SE, 1-202 724 4495) and Francis Pool (25th & N Streets, NW, 1-202 727 3285). Some health and fitness clubs (*see p217*) have pools that are open to the public for a daily fee.

Theatre & Dance

Deranged Southern belles, anti-war polemics, Greek tragedies: Washington's theatre scene is nothing if not dramatic.

Studio Theatre. *See p223.*

It's been a mixed century so far for Washington theatre. Big companies have launched or completed major expansion campaigns, while the future of one landmark house – the Source Theatre Company – seems uncertain to say the least. There's been turmoil among the city's famously scrappy small troupes as well, with one ambitious young company disbanding (the deliciously naughty Cherry Red Productions). The city, which has a thriving black middle class, still boasts just one professional theatre company devoted to exploring the African American experience (**African Continuum Theatre Company**) – and that company struggles to stay afloat.

On the whole, though, DC's theatres have shaken off the effects of 9/11, and the stage scene here remains one of the healthiest in the United States – the second healthiest, if you believe the organisers of the Helen Hayes Awards, who count upwards of 80 producing companies in the metropolitan area.

And while the museums and monuments still draw the biggest swarms of out-of-town visitors, locals are increasingly spotting a new species of seasonal migrant: the cultural tourist. The **Kennedy Center**'s smash-hit Sondheim Festival attracted musical theatre junkies from around the world in the summer of 2002, and a similar endeavour in 2004 brought fans and

critics from afar to get reacquainted with the smothering mothers and deranged belles of Tennessee Williams. In January 2004, the **Signature Theatre** drew Rodgers & Hammerstein devotees from all over to assess the world premiere of a heavily revised *Allegro*, the '50s concept musical that was the duo's first major flop.

The summer-long Potomac Theater Project at the **Olney Theatre Center** draws regional audiences with bracing fare along the lines of Sarah Kane's *Crave* and Howard Barker's *Scenes From an Execution*. And on Capitol Hill, the **Folger Theatre** has recently played host to star performers (including Michael Learned) and celebrity audience members (including Kenneth Branagh) with such high-profile productions as *Elizabeth the Queen* and *Melissa Arctic*, the latter a world-premiere reworking of *The Winter's Tale* from white-hot dramatist Craig Wright. All in all, with its vibrant cross-section of troupes and its huge variety of performances, the capital city is more than ever a capital place to catch theatre.

LISTINGS AND INFORMATION

For comprehensive information on dates, times and venues, check the *Washington City Paper* (searchable listings are at www.washingtoncitypaper.com), the

Arts & Entertainment

GALA Hispanic Theatre. *See p227.*

Washington Post (www.washingtonpost.com), or the Helen Hayes Awards site (www.helenhayes.org). Look for flyers in coffeehouses, theatres, and bookshops like Olsson's (*see p156*). Try **Ticketplace** (1-202 638 2406/www.cultural-alliance.org/tickets/) at the Old Post Office Pavilion on Pennsylvania Avenue for last-minute half-price tickets, and consider **dcplay** (www.dcplay.org) if you'd like to join other fans for a group outing.

Theatre

Major venues

Arena Stage
1101 Sixth Street, SW, at Maine Avenue, Southwest (1-202 488 3300/www.arenastage.com). Waterfront-SEU Metro. **Box office** 10am-8pm Mon-Sat; noon-8pm Sun. **Tickets** $40-$45. **Credit** AmEx, Disc, MC, V.

The city's theatrical grande dame and a pioneer in the American resident theatre movement may be emerging from a half-decade of torpor. Blessed (and cursed) with an affluent, establishmentarian audience, artistic director Molly Smith has disappointed some critics since coming on board in 1998, programming unchallenging audience-pleasers, musicals and the occasional half-baked concept piece, with only a few redeeming bold ventures scattered among them. Recent signs of life, though, have included a blues-infused Zora Neale Hurston discovery (the never-before-seen *Polk County*) and a swaggering staging of Brecht's anti-war polemic *A Man's a Man*, mounted just as the chickens of Iraq were coming home to roost. There is also a hugely ambitious $100-million expansion plan that will upgrade facilities, create a new-play incubator space, and wrap the existing Fichandler and Kreeger theatres in a glittering glass box.

Kennedy Center
2700 F Street, NW, at New Hampshire Avenue & Rock Creek Parkway, Foggy Bottom (1-800 444 1324/1-202 467 4600/www.kennedy-center.org). Foggy Bottom-GWU Metro then free shuttle 9.45am-midnight Mon-Fri; 10am-midnight Sat; noon-midnight Sun. **Box office** 10am-9pm Mon-Sat; noon-9pm Sun. **Tickets** $5-$105. **Credit** AmEx, DC, MC, V. Map p284 F6

As part of its broad-spectrum programming, the national cultural centre puts on a full theatre season each year. It's mostly imports and tours – not since the '70s has the house had a resident company – but now and again the imports are remarkable. The Royal Shakespeare Company has visited regularly in recent years (Gregory Doran's *Taming of the Shrew* was the triumph of the 2003-04 season), and it is returning in 2005 with Vanessa Redgrave in Euripides' *Hecuba*. Home-grown productions are picking up too: at the time of writing, James Earl Jones and Diahann Carroll had been announced for a staged reading of *On Golden Pond*, and Patti LuPone was set for a semi-staged concert of the Marc Blitzstein gem *Regina* in March 2005. And with ex-Covent Garden guru Michael Kaiser at the helm, expect more splashy summer festivals along the lines of the Sondheim and Williams blowouts. *See also p207.*

National Theatre
1321 Pennsylvania Avenue, NW, between 13th & 14th Streets, The Federal Triangle (1-202 628 6161/www.nationaltheatre.org). Federal Triangle or Metro Center Metro. **Box office** *Performance days* until performance begins. *Non-performance days* 10am-6pm Mon-Sat; noon-6pm Sun. **Tickets** $15-$75. **Credit** AmEx, DC, Disc, MC, V. **Map** p284 H6.

One of the city's oldest theatres (it dates back to 1835), the National has a history as a Broadway tryout house, but in recent decades it has been home mostly to fluff – when it doesn't sit empty, that is. When *Cats* comes to town (and yes, it still comes to town occasionally), this is its preferred sandbox. Other recent tenants: tours of *Mamma Mia!, Movin' Out, Rent* and *Chicago*.

The Shakespeare Theatre

450 Seventh Street, NW, between D & E Streets, Penn Quarter (1-202 547 1122/www. shakespearedc.org). Gallery Place-Chinatown Metro. **Box office** *Performance days* 10am-6pm Mon; 10am-6.30pm Tue-Sat; noon-6.30pm Sun. *Non-performance days* 10am-6pm Mon-Sat; noon-6pm Sun. **Tickets** $17-$66. **Credit** AmEx, Disc, MC, V. **Map** p285 J6.

Led for nearly two decades by noted director Michael Kahn and hailed by the *Economist* as 'one of the world's three great Shakespearean theatres', the Shakespeare Theatre is probably the leading classical company in the US – and now it's adding a $77-million, 800-seat house to its portfolio. It currently stages five major works each season, serving up not just intelligent, inventive Bardolatry (a greed-is-good '80s take on *Timon of Athens* and a race-reversed *Othello* starring Patrick Stewart), but plays by the likes of Schiller (a magnificent 2002 *Don Carlos*), Ben Jonson (an uproarious *Silent Woman*), O'Neill (a titanic *Mourning Becomes Electra*), and Euripides (JoAnne Akalaitis' controversial *Trojan Women*). The house also makes a speciality of Tennessee Williams: Kahn's late-'90s *Sweet Bird of Youth*, with Elizabeth Ashley and Michael Hayden, was must-see theatre of the purplest sort. Stars of film, television, and the international stage appear here regularly: Keith Baxter, Kelly McGillis, Dixie Carter, Hal Holbrook and Judith Light are among the big names who've joined this exceptional resident company. The Shakespeare Theatre's new space, nearly twice as large, is just around the corner at 650 F Street, NW.

Studio Theatre

1333 P Street, NW, at 14th Street, Shaw: Logan Circle (332 3300/www.studiotheatre.org). Dupont Circle or U Street/African-American Civil War Memorial/Cardozo Metro. **Box office** *Performance weeks* 10am-6pm Mon, Tue; 10am-9pm Wed-Sat; noon-8pm Sun. *Non-performance weeks* 10am-6pm Mon-Fri. **Tickets** $20-$40. **Credit** AmEx, Disc, MC, V. **Map** p282 H4.

Slick productions, smart directors and substantial plays (occasional cerebral musicals too) make the Studio Theatre a serious player on DC's dramatic scene. An exquisite *Invention of Love* was a recent highlight (Stoppard reportedly stopped in to see it), and if Caryl Churchill didn't catch Studio's 2004 production of her *Far Away*, she should've. Co-founder and artistic director Joy Zinoman draws her share of controversy, but she's built an almost absurdly healthy organisation: four years after a multimillion-dollar expansion, Studio bought two adjacent buildings and began a $12-million expansion that will add a third 200-seat theatre and a black-box space (set to open November 2004) plus more room for the company's respected acting conservatory.

Other theatres & companies

Folger Theatre

201 East Capitol Street, SE, between Second & Third Streets, The Capitol & Around (1-202 544-7077/ www.folger.edu). Capitol South Metro. **Box office** noon-4pm Mon-Sat. **Tickets** $15-$45. **Credit** AmEx, MC, V. **Map** p285 L7.

When the Shakespeare Theatre decamped downtown, the Folger lay fallow for a year or two. But it has since re-emerged, and its stable of regular directors (including British actor Richard Clifford) produces solid, intelligent fare. It was here that Lynn Redgrave developed what became the Broadway hit *Shakespeare For My Father*, and here that mischievous DC Shakespearean Joe Banno dramatised Hamlet's internal debates by splitting the title role into four parts – and casting women in three of them.

Ford's Theatre

511 Tenth Street, NW, between E & F Streets, Downtown (1-202 347 4833/www.fordstheatre.org). Gallery Place-Chinatown or Metro Center Metro. **Box office** 10am-6pm Mon-Fri. **Tickets** $29-$45. **Credit** AmEx, Disc, MC, V. **Map** p284 J6.

President Lincoln's assassination – in 1865, during a performance of *Our American Cousin* – shut this house for a century, but crusading producer Frankie Hewitt helped bring its stage back to life in the late 1960s. Much of what Ford has offered since is easy-to-swallow, family-oriented fare, but now and again producers surprise serious theatre-goers with an edgy imported production (Anna Deavere Smith's *Twilight: Los Angeles, 1992* had its DC run here) or a home-grown gem like 2003's superb *1776* revival. In the wake of Hewitt's death, Ford's has tapped Paul Tetreault, formerly of Houston's Alley Theatre, to run the shop, and he's reportedly bent on beefing up the season. The 2004-5 lineup features respected director Mark Lamos, plus the acclaimed Deaf West co-production of *Big River* that wowed LA and New York in 2003.

Olney Theatre Center

2001 Olney-Sandy Spring Road (Route 108), Olney, MD (box office 1-301 924 3400, information 1-301 924 4485/www.olneytheatre.org). **Box office** 10am-6pm Mon-Sat; noon-5pm Sun. **Tickets** $10-$31. **Credit** MC, V.

It's a hike, but the 45-minute drive to this suburban Maryland house can be worth the trouble. Founded as a summer theatre in the 1930s, it has seen performances by a startlingly starry roster: Helen Hayes, Tallulah Bankhead, Olivia de Havilland, Hume Cronyn, Jessica Tandy, Uta Hagen and Ian McKellen are just a few of the names. These days, Olney's season is largely subscriber-friendly fluff, but once or twice a year artistic director Jim Petosa will programme something startling: a gorgeous *Camille*, David Hare's agonised *Racing Demon*, the hypnotic Calderón adaptation *Sueño*, a take on Zola's *Thérèse Raquin*. And the politically charged Potomac Theatre Festival each summer is a sure bet.

*Just because the playwright's dead
doesn't mean the show should be too.*

THE
**SHAKESPEARE
THEATRE**
In the Nation's Capital

Artistic Director **Michael Kahn**
Managing Director **Nicholas T. Goldsborough**

Photo of the cast from
The Silent Woman by Richard Termine.

Construction has begun on a new 440-seat main stage, completing a campus that will have no fewer than four performance spaces.

Round House Theatre

Bethesda: 7501 Wisconsin Avenue, at Waverly Street, Bethesda, MD (box office 1-240 644 1100/ information 1-240 644 1099/www.round-house.org). Bethesda Metro. **Box office** noon-5pm Mon-Fri. *Silver Spring: 8641 Colesville Road, between Georgia Avenue & Fenton Street, Silver Spring, MD (1-240 644 1099). Silver Spring Metro.* **Box office** noon-5pm Mon-Fri.
Both: **Tickets** $10-$38. **Credit** AmEx, MC, V.

Charles Mee's zany *Wintertime*, August Wilson's *Fences*, and Stephen Adly Guirgis's brutal *Jesus Hopped the 'A' Train* were all part of the 2003-4 season at the ambitious Round House, an established company bold and successful enough to have opened not one but two new houses in recent years. Its main home is in the close-in suburb of Bethesda, but it also offers a regular slate of performances (including a cabaret series) near the other end of the Metro's Red Line, in a black-box space at the AFI Silver complex in Silver Spring. Among shows set for 2005: *Life x 3*, from Yasmina Reza, and *Columbinus*, a world-premiere piece conceived as a response to the Columbine school massacre.

Signature Theatre

3806 South Four Mile Run Drive, at Oakland Drive, Arlington, VA (1-703 218 6500/www.sig-online.org). Pentagon Metro, then 22A, 22B, 22C, 22F bus (weekdays only). **Box office** 10am-6pm Mon-Fri. **Tickets** $28-$30. **Credit** AmEx, Disc, MC, V.

Signature's signature is first-rate Sondheim, but it does plenty besides, staging drama, comedy, and quirky musicals old and new in an intimate theatre. Landmark productions include the first *Assassins* outside New York and a *Passion* that put the house on the map with New York critics, not to mention a pre-Broadway workshop of *Over and Over*, a musicalised *Skin of Our Teeth*. (Kander and Ebb, the Broadway legends behind that show, are honorary board members at Signature, as are Sondheim and Cameron Mackintosh.) Recent outings include a knockout *Hedwig and the Angry Inch* and the revival of Rodgers & Hammerstein's *Allegro*. On tap for 2005: a prodigiously rich season including *Pacific Overtures*, Jon Robin Baitz's *Ten Unknowns*, and world premieres from Tony-nominated composer Michael John LaChiusa, TV director Paris Barclay and Washington-based playwright Norman Allen. The company is on a $7-million fundraising kick, preparatory to moving into a new home in early 2006.

Woolly Mammoth Theatre Company

AFI Theater, Kennedy Center, 2700 F Street, NW, at New Hampshire Avenue & Rock Creek Parkway, Foggy Bottom (1-202 393 3939/www.woollymammoth.net). Foggy Bottom-GWU Metro then free shuttle, 9.45am-midnight Mon-Fri; 10am-midnight Sat; noon-midnight Sun). **Box office** 10am-6pm Mon-Fri. **Tickets** $24-$29. **Credit** AmEx, MC, V. **Map** p284 F6.

This brash and often brilliant company has been pushing boundaries (both theatrical and personal) at the Kennedy Center while its $7 million, 265-seat downtown home is being finished. The new house, at 649 D Street, NW (near the corner of Seventh Street), was due to open in autumn 2004, not quite in time to launch the company's 25th-anniversary season. It wrapped up its 24th season with the world premiere of Angus MacLachlan's *The Radiant Abyss*, a Woolly commission; other notable playwrights who've called Woolly home include *Six Feet Under* scribe Craig Wright and that poet of neurosis, Nicky Silver.

Small companies

Washington is a terrific theatre town: there are far too many fringe-y, flaky, fearless small companies to list here. But look for anything involving the Actors Theatre of Washington (queer-themed stuff, www.atwdc.org), American Century Theater (neglected 20th-century greats, www.americancentury.org), Charter Theatre (www.chartertheatre.org), Catalyst (www.chaw.org/catalyst.htm), Quotidian Theatre (understated plays about the everyday, www.quotidiantheatre.org), Synetic (gorgeous movement-based theatre, www.synetic.org), and the Theater Alliance (www.theateralliance.com), to name only a few. Again, check listings at *Washington City Paper* (www.washingtoncitypaper.com) and Helen Hayes (www.helenhayes.org) for a comprehensive rundown.

For the following companies, fixed addresses are given where possible; for information about performances by roving companies, call the number listed. Note that box office hours have not been given; it's generally a case of leaving a message on the answerphone for the company to call you back.

African Continuum Theatre Company

Information: 3523 12th Street NE, Second Floor (1-202 529 5763/www.africancontinuumtheatre. com). **Tickets** $15-$28. **Credit** AmEx, MC, V.

Rough-edged new plays, solid forays into the tough territory of August Wilson and Athol Fugard, and rousing takes on Zora Neale Hurston's *Spunk* and Endesha Ida Mae Holland's *From the Mississippi Delta* – it's all in a season's (or two) work for ACTCo, which often produces fine work on a tight budget. A lacerating staging of Fugard's *Blood Knot* has perhaps been the company's finest hour so far; if it can stay afloat long enough to move into the $14-million Atlas Performing Arts Center under development on H Street, NE (where it will share space with several other arts organisations), it may well be responsible for many another moment to remember.

Arts & Entertainment

GALA Hispanic Theatre

Warehouse Theater, 1021 Seventh Street, NW, between L Street & New York Avenue, Downtown (1-202 234 7174/www.galatheatre.org). Mount Vernon Square or 7th Street-Convention Center Metro. **Tickets** $28. **Credit** AmEx, MC, V. **Map** p285 J5.

Resident at the Warehouse until its uptown home at the rehabilitated Tivoli Theatre (at Tivoli Square in Columbia Heights) is finished in late 2004, GALA stages Spanish-language classics like Calderón de la Barca's *La Dama Duende* and Garcia Lorca's *Blood Wedding*, plus modern plays by writers such as Venezuela's Gustavo Ott (*Evangélicas, Divorciadas y Vegetarianas*). Visiting Latin American artists regularly join the company; performances are generally in Spanish with a simultaneous translation delivered via headset for English speakers.

Rorschach Theatre

Information: 1421 Columbia Road, NW, #303 (1-202 452 5538/www.rorschachtheatre.com). **Tickets** $12. **No credit cards.**

The rambunctious Rorschach company finds interesting plays and intriguing spaces, and applies its nervy vision to both. For the most part, it's a success; the company serves up everything from Arthur Laurents (*A Clearing in the Woods*) to Serbian wunderkind Biljana Srbljanovic (*Family Stories: A Slapstick Tragedy*). Recent outings have included a hallucinatory adaptation of Bulgakov's *Master and Margarita*: produced in an uncooled church hall at the height of a sweltering DC summer, it was riveting, even as one wanted to faint. Check listings for current production locations.

Source Theatre Company

1835 14th Street, NW, between S & T Streets, U Street/14th Street Corridor (1-202 462 1073/www.sourcetheatre.com). U Street/African-American Civil War Memorial/Cardozo Metro. **Tickets** $25. **Credit** MC, V. **Map** p282 I14.

After 20-plus years of financial struggle (and plenty of artistic success) on the 14th Street theatrical corridor, this venerable company closed 'temporarily' in early 2004, though it insisted it would still produce its annual Washington Theatre Festival – a summer tradition featuring readings and productions of more than 70 new plays, a junior festival for young playwrights and a competition for the best ten-minute play. At the time of writing, however, no information was available about the festival or the theatre's future.

Washington Shakespeare Company

Clark Street Playhouse, 601 South Clark Street, at Sixth Street South, Arlington, VA (1-703 418 4808/www.washingtonshakespeare.org). Crystal City Metro. **Tickets** $10-$35. **Credit** AmEx, MC, V.

Not to be confused with the deep-pocketed Shakespeare Theatre, this highbrow-on-a-shoestring troupe has ten seasons of the Bard – not to mention Beckett, Marlowe, Stoppard, Albee and more – under its scruffy belt. And it's good: hits of the 2003-04 season included a fine *Waiting for Godot* and a luminous adaptation of *Lady Chatterley's Lover*. The company's latest project is a series of staged readings of Shakespeare's plays – all 37 of them.

Washington Stage Guild

Arena Stage at 14th & T, 1901 14th Street, NW, at T Street, Shaw: U Street/14th Street Corridor (1-240 582 0050/www.stageguild.org). U Street/African-American Civil War Memorial/Cardozo Metro. **Tickets** $20-$28. **No credit cards.** **Map** p282 H3.

Forced out of its longtime lodgings several years ago by DC's rocketing rents, this respected company still draws a loyal crowd with smart stagings of Shaw (a politically well-timed *On the Rocks* was a 2004 high point) plus other literary-minded fare. Playwrights featured recently have included Ferenc Molnar, TS Eliot, and Steve Martin – yes, that Steve Martin. The Stage Guild has recently been operating out of an Arena Stage-owned space at 14th and T Streets, NW, and it seems likely to survive until it can find a home of its own.

Dance

The MacArthur Foundation's 2002 'genius grant' to DC dance guru Liz Lerman signalled what cognoscenti already knew: that Washington boasts a robust, healthy and surprisingly diverse dance scene. Larger venues – namely the Kennedy Center (*see p222*), Warner Theater, George Washington University's Lisner Auditorium and George Mason University's Center for the Arts (for all, *see p209*) – bring in world-renowned companies, from domestic powerhouses such as Dance Theatre of Harlem and the American Ballet Theatre to international legends like the Kirov Ballet, the Royal Danish Ballet and the Hamburg Ballet.

Meanwhile, at smaller spaces, vibrant and sometimes surprisingly accomplished local troupes flourish. Modern dance specialists **CityDance Ensemble** (www.citydance.net/ 1-202 238 0172) is one of five companies in residence at Joy of Motion dance studio. **Carla Perlo and Company** and **Deborah Riley** are among a handful in residence at DC's pre-eminent space for modern classes and avant garde performance, **Dance Place**. Each June, this venue stages the DanceAfrica DC festival (*see p178*) a lively mix of local and international dancers, drummers and artisans giving performances and masterclasses. The George Washington University dance department (1-202 994 8072) hosts an international festival of improvised dance every December as well as occasional workshops and master classes by visiting artists. Howard University also offers occasional masterclasses (1-202 806 7050), as does the Kennedy Center.

Heads it is. A performance at **Dance Place**.

Companies & venues

Phone for schedules of dance classes at the venues below.

Dance Place

3225 Eighth Street, NE, between Kearney & Monroe Streets, Northeast (1-202 269 1600/www.dance place.org). Brookland-CUA Metro. **Tickets** $16. **Credit** AmEx, MC, V.

DC's 'hub of dance activity' (according to the *Washington Post*) offers morning and evening classes in modern and African dance, and doubles as a performance space, often featuring emerging artists. A recent season included the KanKouran West African Dance Company, Elevator Repair Service, and the Cleveland Contemporary Dance Theatre, among many others. Dance Place is home for several modern companies and the organisation conducts a host of community outreach projects throughout the District.

DC Dance Collective

4908 Wisconsin Avenue, NW, near Ellicott Street, Upper Northwest (1-202 362 7244/ www.dcdancecollective.com). Friendship Heights or Tenleytown-AU Metro. **Tickets** $10. **Credit** MC, V.

In 1999, Nancy Newell and her company TAPestry broke off from Joy of Motion (*see below*) and set up shop down the block. DC Dance Collective now hosts performances and offers various kinds of classes, ranging from hip hop, jazz and African, to Middle Eastern, ballet, break dancing and, of course, tap. Bakaari Wilder, pop star Mya, and tap great Dianne Walker turned up here for a 2004 tribute to the late Gregory Hines.

Joy of Motion

1643 Connecticut Avenue, NW, at R Street, Dupont Circle (1-202 387 0911/www.joyofmotion.org). Dupont Circle Metro. **Tickets** $10-$15. **Credit** AmEx, MC, V. **Map** p282 G4.

Joy of Motion offers a wide range of classes, including jazz, modern, swing, pilates, yoga, belly dance and flamenco. In addition to its existing three locations, a new studio is planned for the Atlas

Performing Arts Center (*see p225*). Resident companies (including Dana Tai Soon Burgess, CityDance Ensemble, Ziva's Spanish Dance Ensemble and the hip hop Jam Crew) perform at the Jack Guidone Theatre, the Wisconsin Avenue venue.
Other locations: 5207 Wisconsin Avenue, NW, Friendship Heights, Upper Northwest (1-202 362 3042); 7702 Woodmont Avenue, Suite 202, Bethesda, MD (1-301 986 0016).

KanKouran West African Dance Company

1-202 528 1213/www.kankouran.org.

One of the strongest of the area's many African dance outfits. Classes in West African dance and drumming are offered throughout the week at Liz Lerman Dance Exchange (*see below*).

Liz Lerman Dance Exchange

7117 Maple Avenue, near Carroll Avenue, Takoma Park, MD (1-301 270 6700/www.danceexchange.org). Takoma Park Metro. **Tickets** $12. **Credit** MC, V.

Alterna-dance legend Lerman founded this multi-cultural, multigenerational company (the largest and best-known in DC) in 1976, before such adjectives had become clichés. She still creates some of the most innovative work in the area, and several company members, particularly artistic director Peter DiMuro, are impressive choreographers in their own right. The company's studio in the hippy enclave of Takoma Park, Maryland, offers classes focused primarily on modern technique.

Washington Ballet

Information: 3515 Wisconsin, Avenue NW (1-202 362 3606/www.washingtonballet.org). **Tickets** $25-$85. **Credit** Disc, MC, V.

The Washington Ballet presents a solid season of contemporary and classic ballets by the likes of Niles Christie, Krzysztof Pastor and George Balanchine every year from September to May, in addition to an annual production of the *Nutcracker* for two weeks around Christmas time. The company has danced around the world; local performances tend to be held at the Kennedy Center (*see p222*) or at the larger venues downtown. Classes (from beginner to advanced) are offered to the public during the week.

Trips Out of Town

Getting Started

How to get out of town.

Arthur Ashe's statue...

ARTHUR R. ASHE, JR
1943-1993
...de Champion, Author, Humanitarian
...de Virginia Heroes Incorporated
...d Virginia

Within easy reach of Washington DC is a vast and varied hinterland of forested mountains, mile upon mile of beaches, islands, and more, extending deeply into the neighbouring states of Maryland and Virginia. The landscape of this large capital region is widely – and sometimes wildly – varied, from the beaches of Chesapeake Bay in the east to the foothills of the Blue Ridge Mountains in the west. There are also several separate urban areas within the region. In fact, there is something out there beyond the Beltway for almost everyone.

We've divided the chapter into themed sections: urban escapes, war sites, historic homes, the great outdoors. In some cases these overlap geographically: Richmond, for example, is near some Civil War battlefields and the James River plantation houses. See the map on pp274-75 to help plan your excursions – references for each location are given in the text.

Transport

By car

This being the US of A, the car is king – and, fortunately, the regional road network is excellent. Visitors should be forewarned, however, that in the immediate vicinity of Washington – and well beyond it, on some major routes, such as I-66 – traffic can be extremely heavy in weekday commuting hours. The national car rental companies all have Washington outlets, and there are several local firms (see p253).

By rail

Union Station is the hub of an above-average network of suburban and long-distance trains.

Union Station

50 Massachusetts Avenue, NE, at North Capitol Street, Union Station & Around. Union Station Metro/80, 96, 97, D1, D4, D6, D8, X1, X8 bus. **Map** p313 K/L 5/6.

Amtrak

Information & reservations 1-800 872 7245/ www.amtrak.com.
Amtrak provides excellent connections to north-eastern cities, including the hourly Metroliner express trains to Baltimore (45 minutes) and New York City (three hours 15 minutes), and to points south. For journeys to destinations in this chapter, you seldom need to buy or book ahead. Amtrak also has frequent services to Fredericksburg, Richmond and Williamsburg, all in Virginia.

Marc

Information 1-800 325 7245/ www.mtamaryland.com/marc/marc.asp.
Marc, a primarily commuter rail service operated by the Maryland Depart of Transportation, connects Washington to Baltimore and Montgomery County, Frederick County and nearby Western Virginia. However, the one-hour trip takes longer than Amtrak and trains are most frequent during the weekday commuter rush, much less so at other times.

Virginia Railway Express

Information 1-703 684 0400/www.vre.org.
A limited Virginia commuter service on two lines, linking Washington to Fredericksburg and Manassas respectively. It's almost entirely inbound during the morning and outbound in the afternoon.

Trips Out of Town

By bus

Greyhound Bus Lines
1005 First Street, NE, at L Street, Northeast (1-800 231 2222/1-202 289 5154/www.greyhound.com). Bus 80, 96, D3, D4, D8.
Buses exist, but are far less satisfactory a means of getting around the region. Greyhound, the sole-surviving nationwide bus carrier, has services to Baltimore, Richmond, Fredericksburg and Williamsburg, as well as an express service to New York City. The terminal is located in a not particularly appetising area north of Union Station.

By boat

Boats are an option for travelling to some destinations, including Mount Vernon and the Chesapeake Bay islands – for details of the latter, *see p246* Chesapeake Bay & the Maryland Shore.

Spirit of Washington Cruises
Pier 4, Water Street, SW, at Sixth Street, Southwest (1-202 554 8000/www.spiritofwashington.com). Waterfront-SEU Metro. **Map** p313 J8.
Service to and from Mount Vernon from Pier 4 on Washington's Southwest Waterfront. The trip takes about five and a half hours. Fare ($34; $23-$33 concessions; free under-6s) includes admission to the mansion and grounds. The same company organises dining and dancing cruises on the Potomac.

Information

See also the tourist information sections in the **Trips Out of Town** chapter, *see pp232-48.*

Automobile Association of America
701 15th Street, NW, at New York & Pennsylvania Avenues, The White House & around (1-202 331 3000/www.aaa.com). Metro Center Metro. **Open** 8.30am-5.30pm Mon-Fri. **Map** p312 H5.
Excellent maps, guidebooks (with accommodation and restaurant listings) and campground guides – and they're free if you're a member or belong to an affiliated organisation, such as the British AA.

Delaware Tourism Office
99 Kings Highway, Dover, DE (1-800 441 8846/ 1-302 739 4271/www.visitdelaware.net). **Open** 8am-4.30pm Mon-Fri.

Maryland Office of Tourism Development
217 East Redwood Street, Baltimore, MD (office 1-410 767 3400/call centre 1-800 394 5725). **Open** 8am-5pm Mon-Fri.

Virginia Tourism Authority
1629 K Street, NW, between 16th & 17th Streets, Downtown (1-202 872 0523/ www.virginia.org). Farragut West Metro. **Open** 8.30am-5pm Mon-Fri. **Map** p312 H5.
Virginia office: *901 East Byrd Street, Richmond, VA (office 1-804 786 4484/call centre 1-800 932 5827/www.virginia.org).* **Open** 8.30am-5pm Mon-Fri.

... on Monument Avenue, **Richmond**. *See p236.*

Trips Out of Town

Historical sites, forests, coastline – all within striking distance of DC.

Urban Escapes

Baltimore

At some point back in the 20th century, Mayor William Donald Schafer of Baltimore decided to bestow a flattering title on Maryland's metropolis. To the probable mystification of most other Baltimoriens, 'Charm City' was his choice. True, there is much in which this city at the uppermost reach of Chesapeake Bay can take pride. It was one of the earliest true cities in America, a thriving port from the very beginning and later an important manufacturing centre. It was briefly the seat of government of the fledgling nation and the site of numerous historic events, including the battle that gave the United States its national anthem. But charm? As rich as Baltimore's history might be, the city seemed, even to the eyes of locals, a gritty hangover from an earlier and messier industrial era. That image, however, has changed significantly over the last few decades. The city – most especially its historic core – has experienced a renaissance.

Nowadays, Baltimore is not only outgrowing a longstanding inferiority complex in respect to its younger neighbour 40 miles (64 kilometres) to the south, but has become a popular day or weekend destination for Washingtonians.

The major draw is the old port area on the **Inner Harbor**. No longer a depressing urban jungle of rundown factories and warehouses, it has been transformed into the sparkling Harborplace, a lively civic centre of shops and restaurants. Nearby is the world-class **National Aquarium in Baltimore**, with aquatic delights including a daily dolphin show (phone for times). The adjacent wharfside **Baltimore Maritime Museum** is the mooring place for the frigate *USS Constellation*, the last Civil War-era warship still afloat, as well as two veterans of World War II, the Coast Guard cutter *Taney*, the last survivor of Pearl Harbor, and the *USS Torsk*, the submarine that fired the last torpedo of the conflict.

Glass-walled offices in the new high-rise business district form a glittering backdrop for Harborplace. For an overview, take the lift to the 27th-floor observation deck of the **World Trade Center** (aka 'The Top of the World'); at 423 feet (129 metres) it's the world's tallest

Star-Spangled Banner Flag House. *See p234.*

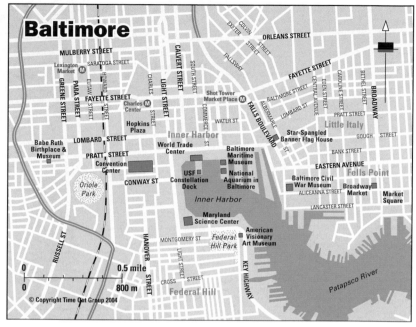

Baltimore

MULBERRY STREET

Lexington Market Ⓜ SARATOGA STREET

ORLEANS STREET

COLVIN STREET

EXETER STREET

FALLSWAY

FAYETTE STREET

GREENE STREET

PARA STREET

EUTAW STREET

HOWARD STREET

CALVERT STREET

CHARLES STREET

SOUTH STREET

LIGHT STREET

COMMERCE STREET

EDEN STREET

CENTRAL AVENUE

CAROLINE STREET

BETHEL STREET

BROADWAY

FAYETTE STREET

Charles Center Ⓜ

Hopkins Plaza

Shot Tower Market Place Ⓜ

BALTIMORE STREET

ALBEMARLE

FALLS BOULEVARD

LOMBARD STREET

PRATT STREET

Little Italy

GOUGH STREET

WATER ST

Star-Spangled Banner Flag House

ST

Babe Ruth Birthplace & Museum

LOMBARD STREET

PRATT STREET

Convention Center

CONWAY ST

World Trade Center

Inner Harbor

Baltimore Maritime Museum

BANK STREET

EASTERN AVENUE

Fells Point

Oriole Park

USF Constellation Dock

National Aquarium in Baltimore

Baltimore Civil War Museum

ALICEANNA STREET

Broadway Market

Market Square

HANOVER STREET

RUSSELL ST

Inner Harbor

LANCASTER STREET

Maryland Science Center

MONTGOMERY ST

Federal Hill Park

American Visionary Art Museum

LIGHT STREET

KEY HIGHWAY

0   0.5 mile

0   800 m

STREET

CROSS STREET

Federal Hill

Patapsco River

© Copyright Time Out Group 2004

---

pentagonal building. Along nearby streets, typical Baltimore row houses with marble front stoops have been restored to something approaching their former charm. Next door are **Little Italy**, which has managed to hang on to some of its ethnic identity in the shadow of downtown's burgeoning skyscrapers, and funky **Fells Point**, a portside neighbourhood dating back to the city's beginnings that might almost make a British visitor think of home, what with cobbled streets carrying names such as Albemarle, Chester, Exeter, Lancaster, Shakespeare and Thames ('Thaymes' with a 'th' to the locals).The city's original waterfront, it takes its name from one William Fell, an English shipbuilder who, recognising its potential, purchased the deepwater site in 1726. It quickly became the area's commercial centre. Fells Point still counts many buildings dating from the late 18th and early 19th centuries. Restored Georgian- and Federal-style houses often have private courtyards. The Broadway Market (Broadway, between Fleet and Lancaster Streets), which dates back to the 18th century, is a pungent maze of stalls selling virtually every comestible imaginable.

Otherwise, the Point is noted for two specialities: antique shops – although the city's largest concentration of shops, known as 'Antique Row', is along North Howard Street

to the north of Harborplace – and drinking establishments. There are dozens of the former, selling everything from conventional old stuff to marine artefacts to threads with a past. The watering holes are almost as numerous and make the Point the heart of the city's nightlife.

Historic sites in the harbour area include the **Star-Spangled Banner Flag House**, the 1793 home of Mary Pickersgill, who stitched the stars and stripes on to the huge flag that flew over Fort McHenry during the 1814 British bombardment. There are guided tours of the house, furnished with Federal-period antiques, and a museum. (The actual banner has been undergoing painstaking restoration at Washington's Smithsonian Institution. It is scheduled to be returned to public display at the National Museum of American History in 2006.) Exhibits at the **Baltimore Civil War Museum** highlight the city's ambivalent role in the bitter 1861-65 struggle between North and South. Baltimore was a station on the 'underground railroad' by which fugitive slaves escaped to the North, but also home to many Confederate sympathisers. There were riots when Union troops passed through the city.

And for something bizarrely different, there is the **Babe Ruth Birthplace**, a cramped rowhouse in a scruffy neighbourhood that was home to the young 'Sultan of Swat', a hero to American boys of all ages during the 1920s and '30s for his prowess on the baseball field, but noted for boozing and lechery off the field. Crammed with memorabilia of the game and the man, the house is of interest primarily to those obsessed with both.

While not the birthplace (Boston was), Baltimore is the burial place of another American of very different renown, Edgar Allan Poe. His final resting place is Westminster Hall & Burying Ground, the cemetery of the First Presbyterian Church (West Fayette Street and Greene Street). There are guided tours of the churchyard and catacombs (phone 1-410 728 5545 for details).

The **Walters Art Gallery** is one of the best fine art museums in the US, with a collection including medieval, Renaissance, 18th- and 19th-century, Islamic and Asian art. The **Baltimore Museum of Art** has a notable collection of modern paintings and sculpture from Van Gogh to Warhol and Rodin to Nevelson. At the **American Visionary Art Museum**, across the harbour in South Baltimore, the focus is on untrained but inspired artists working outside accepted norms. Also in the South Baltimore neighbourhood is the **Maryland Science Center**, with three floors of exhibits and hands-on science demonstrations that are of interest to both adults and children. Not much further on, guarding the harbour entrance, is **Fort McHenry** (*see p239*), the legendary – for Americans – fortress that withstood a British naval assault in 1814, inspiring the national anthem.

American Visionary Art Museum

800 Key Highway (1-410 244 1900/www.avam.org). **Open** 10am-6pm Tue-Sun. **Admission** $9; $6 concessions; free under-5s. **Credit** MC, V.

Babe Ruth Birthplace & Museum

216 Emory Street (1-410 727 1539/www. baberuthmuseum.com). **Open** *Apr-Oct* 10am-5pm daily. *Nov-Mar* 10am-4pm daily. Open until 7pm when Baltimore Orioles playing home game. **Admission** $6; $3-$4 concessions. **Credit** AmEx, Disc, MC, V.

Baltimore Civil War Museum

601 President Street (1-410 385 5188/www. mdhs.org/explore/baltcivilwar.html). **Open** 10am-5pm daily. **Admission** $4; $3 concessions; free under-13s. **Credit** MC, V.

Baltimore Maritime Museum

Pier 3, Pratt Street (1-410 396 3453/www. baltomaritimemuseum.org). **Open** 10am-6pm daily. **Admission** $7; $3-$6 concessions; free under-5s. **Credit** AmEx, MC, V.

Baltimore Museum of Art

10 Art Museum Drive (1-410 396 7100/ www.artbma.org). **Open** 10am-5pm Wed-Fri; 10am-8pm Sat-Sun. **Admission** $7; $5 concessions; free under-19s. **Credit** AmEx, MC, V.

Maryland Science Center

601 Light Street (1-410 685 5225/www.mdsci.org). **Open** *Sept-May* 10am-5pm Tue-Fri; 10am-6pm Sat; noon-5pm Sun. *June-Aug* 10am-6pm Mon-Wed, Sun; Thur-Sat 10am-8pm. **Admission** *Museum only* $4. *IMAX only* $7.50. *Museum & 1 IMAX film* $10. **Credit** AmEx, MC, V.

National Aquarium in Baltimore

501 East Pratt Street (1-410 576 3800/ www.aqua.org). **Open** *Jan, Feb, Nov, Dec* 10am-5pm Mon-Thur, Sat, Sun; 10am-8pm Fri. *Mar-June, Sept, Oct* 9am-5pm Mon-Thur, Sat, Sun; 9am-8pm Fri. *July, Aug* 9am-6pm Mon-Thur, Sun; 9am-8pm Fri-Sat. **Admission** $17.50; $9.50-$14.50 concessions; free under-3s. **Credit** AmEx, Disc, MC, V.

Star-Spangled Banner Flag House

844 East Pratt Street (1-410 837 1793/ www.flaghouse.org). **Open** 10am-4pm Tue-Sat. **Admission** $6; $4-$5 concessions. **Credit** Disc, MC, V.

USS Constellation

Pier 1, 301 East Pratt Street (1-410 539 1797/ www.constellation.org). **Open** *May-mid Oct* 10am-6pm daily. *Mid Oct-Apr* 10am-4pm daily. **Admission** $6.50; $3.50-$5 concessions; free under-6s. **Credit** AmEx, MC, V.

Walters Art Gallery

600 North Charles Street (1-410 547 9000/ www.thewalters.org). **Open** 10am-5pm Wed-Sun. **Admission** $8; $5-$6 concessions; free under-18s. **Credit** MC, V.

World Trade Center

401 East Pratt Street (1-410 837 8439). **Open** 10am-6pm Wed-Sun. *Summer* 10am-6pm Mon-Fri, Sun; 10am-9pm Sat. **Admission** $5; $2-$4 concessions; free under-3s. **Credit** MC, V.

Where to eat & drink

Harborplace has several places to eat and drink, most of them crowded during the summer months. Further afield, but often more fun, are Little Italy and Fells Point But face it: this is still Baltimore on the Bay, where seafood is king and crab cakes are a virtual cult. **Phillips** (301 Light Street, 1-410 685 6600, main courses $7-$65) is a large and popular eaterie with a great harbour view, terrace dining in season and seafood. At **City Lights** (301 Light Street, 1-410 244 8811, main courses $14-$24), crab cakes and crab soup are specialities. **Rusty Scupper** (402 Key Highway, 1-410 727 3678, main courses $6-$10 lunch, $14-$21), across Inner Harbor from Harborplace, also does seafood plus prime rib and such. **Joy America Café** in the American Visionary Art Museum (800 Key Highway, 1-410 244 6500, closed Mon, main courses $9-$16 lunch, $22-$26 dinner) offers a creative organic menu that complements the museum's eclectic art collection.

Though in a rather bleak location on the border of Little Italy, **Della Notte** (801 Eastern Avenue, 1-410 837 5500, main courses under $10 lunch, $18-$38 dinner) is highly rated for its house-baked breads and extensive wine list. In the same area, but lower key and more intimate, is **Da Mimmo** (217 South High Street, 1-410 727 6876, main courses $15-$35 lunch, $30-$45 dinner). **Bohager's** (701 South Eden Street, 1-410 563 7220, closed Mon-Wed, $25 buffet) has an eclectic decor and menu, and is popular with younger diners. **Bertha's** (734 South Broadway, 1-410 327 5795, mains $6-$20) serves English beer and local brews. It's touristy, sure, but good, and the locals love it too. Purely pub possibilities include **Wharf Rat** (801 South Ann Street, 1-410 244 8900, main courses $7-$22) and **Cat's Eye Pub** (1730 Thames Street, 1-410 276 9866), the latter heavily into things Irish.

Where to stay

The Inner Harbor has its share of reliably acceptable but typically plastic chain operations. Places with more personality include **Admiral Fell Inn** (888 South

Broadway, 1-410 522 7377, doubles $199-$329), a renovated 1790s inn on the Fells Point waterfront; it has 80 guest rooms furnished in Federal style. Nearby is the **Inn at Henderson's Wharf** (1000 Fell Street, 1-410 522 7777, doubles $179-$259), a former tobacco warehouse on the Inner Harbor side (with views) of Fells Point with 38 guest rooms, some with period furnishings. Both have water taxi connections.

Resources

Hospital
Johns Hopkins, 600 North Wolfe Street (1-410 955 5000/www.hopkinsmedicine.org).

Internet access
Port City Java, 666 East Fort Avenue (1-410 986 0366). **Open** 6.30am-6pm Mon-Thur; 6.30am-8pm Sat; 8am-6pm Sun.

Post office
900 East Fayette Street (1-410 347 4202).

Tourist information
Baltimore Visitors' Center, 401 Light Street, MD 21202 (1-410 837 4636/1-800 282 6632). **Open** 9am-6pm Mon-Fri; 9am-7pm Sat, Sun.

Getting around

By rail
Baltimore has both a limited subway line and a light-rail surface system. The first, serving primarily local commuters, is not of much use to most visitors. But

Inner Harbor, Baltimore. *See p232.*

The lively Baltimore neighbourhood of **Fells Point**. See p233.

those arriving from Washington by rail can take the light rail from Penn Station to the Pratt Street stop, which is within easy walking distance of Harborplace.

By boat

Boats are an obvious choice for checking out Inner Harbor attractions. Water taxis operated by Water Taxi (1-410 563 3901, www.thewatertaxi.com) make several stops around the harbour. Hours of operation vary seasonally. Tours of the harbour and beyond last several hours aboard the *Bay Lady* and *Lady Baltimore* (301 Light Street, 1-410 727 3113) and the schooner *Clipper City* (Inner Harbor, 1-410 539 6277, www.sailingship.com). Sailings are seasonal.

Getting there

By car

Baltimore is about an hour's drive from Washington. Take I-95 north to I-395, exit 53, which quickly becomes Howard Street (take care not to shoot off to the left on to Martin Luther King Jr Boulevard). Continue north on Howard a short distance (a football stadium and the Camden Yards baseball stadium will be on your left) to Pratt Street. Turn right and continue past Charles and Light Streets to Harborplace, on the right.

By train

Amtrak (1-800 872 7245, www.amtrak.com) and Marc (1-800 325 7245) trains from Washington arrive at Penn Station (1500 North Charles Street). Amtrak's regular service ($15 one-way) takes about 45mins; its Metroliner and Acela Express services are faster – about 35mins – and more expensive ($39-$42 one-way). Both leave about every hour; the last train from DC is at 10pm, the last from Baltimore to DC is at 12.40am during the week, later on Fri and Sat.

Marc trains ($7 one-way) run Mon-Fri only from 6am to about 10pm, leaving about every half-hour during rush hour and every hour otherwise. They also serve Camden Station, within walking distance of Inner Harbor, during weekday rush hours.

Richmond & around

Richmond (map p274 E2) can mean different things to different people. For some, the erstwhile capital of the Confederate States of America is a virtual shrine, replete with many reminders of the 'Lost Cause' and an al fresco hall of heroes. Monument Avenue, the main thoroughfare of the city centre, is lined with larger-than-life statues of Robert E Lee, 'Stonewall' Jackson and other captains of the Confederacy in full uniform with ready swords, plus a latterday local hero, the late tennis great Arthur Ashe. The decision to add this native Richmond son to the line-up was a controversial business, both for traditionalists who thought the space should be reserved for heroes of the Confederacy and for many African Americans, who felt he might not have appreciated the company he was keeping.

For those who don't live in a bygone age, though, Richmond is a midsize provincial city that moves at a less frenetic pace than Washington, a scant two-hour drive to the north. But it is not without its own quiet appeal. This is the South, as is apparent in the soft accents and the architecture. The stately houses with decorative balconies looking out on Monument Avenue's statuary call to mind

Trips Out of Town

distant New Orleans rather than nearby DC. Yet Richmond is also a city of the present, a thriving business centre with a high-rise skyline of gleaming modern office buildings. Monument Avenue is the east-west axis of the city, becoming Franklin Street once you're past the statues and dead-ending at Capitol Square with its pillared **Virginia State Capitol**. Designed by founding father Thomas Jefferson in his architect mode, the building has served as a seat of government for Virginia since 1788, as well as for the Confederacy from 1862 to 1865. Also on Capitol Square is the 'White House of the Confederacy', the wartime residence of the secessionist South's first and only president, Jefferson Davis. Richmond is packed with other historic structures and landmarks, most of them relating to the Civil War; contact the Richmond Region Visitors' Bureau (*see p239*) for information and directions to the sites.

The collections of the **Virginia Museum of Fine Arts** include works from Africa, Asia and the ancient world, as well as works by modern American artists.

America's master of the macabre, Edgar Allan Poe, was a longtime resident of Richmond, first coming to prominence as editor of the local *Southern Literary Messenger*. The **Edgar Allan Poe Museum**, celebrating his life, is in the oldest house in the city (built 1737).

Richmond may not be bright lights, big city, but it is not without its livelier side. Head for **Shockoe Slip**, a three-block strip of Cary Street sloping down from the financial district

Plantation houses

On a 20-mile stretch of scenic State Route 5 between Richmond and Williamsburg is a string of historic plantation houses, set like jewels in a necklace along the James River (map p275 E2/3). All are still privately owned (some occupied by descendants of the original owners) and open to the public – although in some cases only at specific times or by appointment. While it is theoretically possible to take a (very) quick look at one or two on a day visit to Richmond, anything more requires an overnight stay. Admission to each house averages $8.50, less for children and seniors. Note that you can also view the homes and nearby Civil War battlefields from the air with Historic Air Tours (1-800 822 9247) in Williamsburg.

Driving from Richmond towards Williamsburg, the first house you reach is **Shirley Plantation** (501 Shirley Plantation Road, 1-804 829 5121, www.shirley plantation.com, open 9am-5pm daily), the oldest plantation in Virginia, dating from 1613 (although work on the present house did not begin until 1713). It is noted for its unusual 'flying' staircase, which rises three storeys from the centre hall without visible means of support.

Next comes **Berkeley Plantation** (12602 Harrison Landing Road, 1-804 829 6018, www.berkeleyplantation.com, open 9am-5pm daily), said to be where Thanksgiving was first observed in 1619. The present 1726 house is the ancestral home of the Harrison family, which produced two US presidents and a signatory of the Declaration of Independence. The terraced boxwood gardens are of special note.

Nearby is **Westover** (7000 Westover Road, 1-804 829 2882, grounds open 9am-6pm daily), built in the 1730s by William Byrd II, and known for its elegant proportions and sweeping view of the James River. The house is open during Historic Garden Week in April and for group tours by appointment; grounds are open daily.

Originally part of Byrd's own holdings, **Evelynton** (6701 John Tyler Highway, 1-800 473 5075, open 9am-5pm daily) is a Georgian Revival house that has been home to the Ruffin family since the 1840s. One of the family is reputed to have fired the first shot in the American Civil War.

A relatively modest mansion compared with its neighbours, **Belle Air Plantation** (11800 John Tyler Highway, 1-804 829 2431) dates from the 1670s. It is open only for group tours by appointment.

At the end of the line is **Sherwood Forest Plantation** (14501 John Tyler Highway, 1-804 282 1441, www.sherwoodforest.org, open 9am-5pm daily), home of John Tyler, the tenth president. The restored 1730s frame house, furnished with his possessions, is still occupied by a descendant.

To reach the houses, take I-95 from Washington to Richmond, then take State Route 5 east. The plantations are clustered a few miles to the west and east of Charles City, and are marked from the highway.

to the banks of the James River. In the 19th century, the area was a bustling centre of the tobacco and milling industries. Ornate warehouses along the narrow cobblestone streets have been renovated and now house restaurants, clubs, boutiques and galleries. Along with adjacent but much less atmospheric Shockoe Bottom, this is the centre of the city's life and nightlife. The **Farmers' Market** (Main and 17th Streets) in the Bottom dates back to the 17th century. You can tour the historic areas by bus.

One reason for visiting the Richmond area lies an hour's drive to the east – **Williamsburg** (map p275 E3), Virginia's renowned colonial capital. With lavish funding from the Rockefeller family beginning in the 1930s, the town's core has been restored as accurately as possible to its appearance in the late 18th century. The half-square-mile (1.3-square kilometre) historic area contains several hundred restored or reconstructed buildings, from the elegant brick Capitol and Governor's Palace to taverns and private homes. With costumed 'interpreters' strolling about pretending to be gentlemen, housewives, tradesmen and whatever, the effort at bringing an earlier era to life can get a bit thick, but all in all it makes for a diverting show. There's a **Busch Gardens & Water Country USA** amusement park nearby, themed – strangely, given all the local history – around 17th-century Europe. There is a nod to modern times, however, in the form of a 'hypercoaster' featuring nine drops of a total of 825 scary feet.

Also worth a look are nearby **Yorktown** (map p275 E3), where the defeat of besieged British General Cornwallis by a combined American-French force ended the American Revolution, and **Jamestown** (map p275 E3), location of the first (1607) permanent British settlement in North America. And there's still more. Winding along the James River between Richmond and Williamsburg is a string of imposing pre-Civil War plantation homes, some dating back to the early 1700s. A half-dozen of the finest are open to the public (*see p237* **Plantation houses**).

You could also make a stop at **Fredericksburg** (map p274 C2), the halfway point between Washington and Richmond. Also dating from the colonial era, it was George Washington's boyhood home. The historic town centre is surrounded by tacky urban sprawl, but contains some locations of interest. Notable is the **Mary Washington House**, home of Washington's mother. Various Civil War battlefields are located just to the west of town (*see pp239-41*).

Busch Gardens & Water Country USA

1 Busch Gardens Boulevard, Williamsburg, VA (1-800 343 7946/www.buschgardens.com). **Open** varies; phone for details. **Admission** $46.95; $39.95 concessions; free under-3s. **Credit** AmEx, Disc, MC, V.

Edgar Allan Poe Museum

1914 East Main Street, Richmond, VA (1-804 648 5523/www.poemuseum.org). **Open** 10am-5pm Tue-Sat; 11am-5pm Sun. **Admission** $6; $5 concessions. **Credit** MC, V.

Mary Washington House

1200 Charles Street, Fredericksburg, VA (1-540 373 1569). **Open** *Mar-Nov* 9am-5pm Mon-Sat; 11am-5pm Sun. *Dec-Feb* 10am-4pm Mon-Sat; 11am-5pm Sun. **Admission** $5. **No credit cards**.

Virginia Museum of Fine Arts

200 North Boulevard, Richmond, VA (1-804 340 1400/www.vmfa.state.va.us). **Open** 11am-5pm Wed-Sun. **Admission** $5.

Where to stay & eat

The **Jefferson Hotel** (101 West Franklin Street, 1-804 788 8000, doubles $205-$249) is an elegantly renovated Beaux Arts-era palace in the heart of downtown Richmond. The **Berkeley Hotel** (1200 East Carey Street, 1-804 780 1300, rates $125-$205) is also beautifully restored and located in Shockoe Slip, which has much to offer when you step out the door.

The most interesting places to eat are in the Shockoe Slip area. Across from the Berkeley, the **Tobacco Company Restaurant** (1201 East Carey Street, 1-804 782 9555, main courses $7-$12 lunch, $18-$30 dinner) – once what its name proclaims – has been restored with a funkily elegant touch: plenty of gleaming old wood panelling, and leafy plants suspended above a three-storey atrium. The eclectic menu strives for creativity, and sometimes achieves it. **Sam Miller's** (1210 East Carey Street, 1-804 644 5465, main courses $10-$32) is an inviting small restaurant specialising in seafood and beef. **La Grotta** (1218 East Carey Street, 1-804 644 2466, closed Sat & Sun lunch, main courses $8-$15 lunch, $15-$30 dinner), tucked incongruously into the corner of the Richbrau premises (*see p239*), does pasta, seafood and game. For Mediterranean food, head to **Café Europa** (1409 East Carey Street, 1-804 643 0911, main courses $6-$12, $6-$23 dinner), which dishes up mainly Italian specialities, plus Spanish tapas. The **Hard Shell** (1411 East Carey Street, 1-804 643 2333, main courses $5-$8 lunch, $13-$30 dinner), does great seafood, along with live music (jazz, R&B) from Tuesday to Saturday. 'Not your traditional Irish pub' is the claim of **Sine Irish Pub & Restaurant** (1327 East Carey Street, 1-804 649 7767, main courses $8-$16), and the menu substantiates it with honey blackened breast of chicken and baby back ribs. Still, it's very much a pub vibe. Another place for good beer is the **Richbrau Brewing Company** (1214 East Carey Street, 1-804 644 3018, main courses $6-$10 lunch, $10-$23 dinner), a cavernous microbrewery with pub menu.

In Williamsburg, the determinedly colonial atmosphere in the restored eateries can be a bit much, but it's all part of the Williamsburg experience. Cases in point are **Chowning's Tavern** (109 East Duke of Gloucester Street, 1-800 447 8679, lunch only, main courses $7-$13) and **Shield's Tavern** (422 East Duke of Gloucester Street, 1-800 447 8679, main courses $7-$13 lunch, buffet £16.95 or $37.50 dinner). Best bet if you want to avoid all that, at a price, is the **Regency Dining Room** (136 Francis Street, 1-800 447 8679, main courses $11-$17 lunch, $27-$40 dinner) in the very elegant Williamsburg Inn.

Resources

Tourist information
Fredericksburg *Fredericksburg Visitors Center, 706 Caroline Street, Fredericksburg, VA 22401 (1-800 678 4748/1-540 373 1776/www. fredericksburgvirginia.net).* **Open** *Summer* 9am-7pm daily. *Winter* 9am-5pm daily.

Richmond *Richmond Region Visitors Center, 405 North Third Street, Richmond, VA 23219 (1-804 783 7450/www.richmondva.org).* **Open** 9am-5pm daily.

Williamsburg *Williamsburg Convention & Visitors Bureau, 421 North Boundary Street, Williamsburg, VA 23185 (1-757 253 0192/ 1-800 368 6511/www.visitwilliamsburg.com).* **Open** 8.30am-5pm Mon-Fri.

Getting there

By car
From Washington, take I-95 south (be warned that this is one of the most heavily travelled highways along the East Coast). For Fredericksburg, take exit 130; the historic town centre is a little more than a mile to the east on State Route 3. For Richmond, continue south on I-95 to exit 78. For Williamsburg, take I-64 from downtown Richmond to exit 238, following the green and white 'Colonial Williamsburg' signs to the visitors' centre. Or, if time permits, take the more leisurely State Route 5, which winds along the James River and past the historic plantation homes.

By train
Amtrak serves Fredericksburg, Richmond and Williamsburg. From Washington, journey time to Richmond is around 2hrs; there are seven trains daily

each way (six on Sat). Round-trip fare is around $58. Journey time to Fredericksburg is an hour. There are a couple of trains a day between Richmond and Williamsburg (three on Fridays); journey time is 75-90mins and the round-trip fare is $36. Historic Main Street station in downtown Richmond is set to reopen soon and will serve some of these trains. Until then all trains stop at a suburban station that is inconvenient for the town centre.

War Sites

Battlegrounds in three wars that have been fought on American soil lie within relatively short distances of DC. This is especially true of the Civil War (1861-65), the bloodiest conflict in the nation's history. Sites associated with the two 'English' wars, the American Revolution and the War of 1812, are less numerous but still historically significant. The sites below are listed according to the chronological order of the battles that took place at each. Most have visitors' centres and helpful explanatory signs.

Yorktown Colonial National Historical Park
Colonial Parkway & State Route 238, Yorktown, VA (1-757 898 3400). **Open** 9am-5pm daily. **Admission** $5; free under-17s. **Credit** MC, V. **Map** p275 E3.

Yorktown on the York River 12 miles (19km) south-east of Williamsburg was the location of the climactic land and sea battle of the American Revolution. British General Charles Cornwallis, besieged by a combined American and French army under General George Washington and cut off from reinforcement by the victory of French ships over a British flotilla at the entrance to Chesapeake Bay, was compelled to surrender on 19 October 1781. Siege works and the house where the surrender terms were negotiated can be seen on self-guided tours.

Fort McHenry
End of East Fort Avenue, Baltimore, MD (1-410 962 4290/www.nps.gov/fomc). **Open** *Summer* 8am-7.45pm daily. *Winter* 8am-4.45pm daily. **Admission** $5; free under-17s. **Credit** MC, V.

This was not the scene of the decisive battle of the next British-American dust-up, but it has its place in history. In this engagement, the Americans were the defenders against a British naval force attempting to take the city. Bombarded throughout the day and night of 14 September 1814, the fort held out and the British ships withdrew. Baltimore was saved and Americans gained a national anthem. Francis Scott Key, a young lawyer who happened to be aboard one of the British ships to negotiate the release of a captured friend, was inspired by the sight of his country's badly torn flag still flying at dawn on the 14th to write the lyrics of 'The Star Spangled Banner'. The present expanded fort on the site dates from the Civil War.

Fort Washington Park

13551 Fort Washington Road, Fort Washington, MD (1-301 763 4600/www.nps.gov/fowa). **Open** dawn-dusk daily. **Admission** $5 vehicle or $3 individual. **No credit cards.**

Fort Washington, on the Maryland side of the Potomac River between Washington and Mount Vernon, is notable for what didn't happen. Built to protect the city from attack by sea, the fort proved useless in 1814 when British forces captured and burned Washington. The problem lay not with the strength of the fortifications but with the location. The British cleverly sailed up an undefended parallel river, the Patuxent, and marched overland the few miles to Washington. So much for preparedness. The present fort on the site, replacing the original, dates from 1824 and is considered a choice example of early 19th-century coastal fortifications.

Manassas National Battlefield Park

6511 Sudley Road, Manassas, VA (1-703 361 1339/ www.nps.gov/mana). **Open** 8.30am-5pm daily. **Admission** $3; free under-17s. **No credit cards.** **Map** p274 B2.

Manassas/Bull Run is the site of two Civil War engagements known by different names in South and North; in the former it is that of the nearest community, Manassas, and in the latter the nearest significant stream, Bull Run. At the very beginning of the war, in July 1861, a Union force moved on rebel-held Manassas, a railroad junction. So confident of victory was the Washington elite that gentlemen and their ladies, packing picnic lunches, rode out in carriages to watch the spectacle. The Northerners were routed in a ten-hour battle by a spirited Confederate counter-attack, sending the excursionists racing back to the city in panic. It was déjà vu when larger and more experienced armies clashed in August of the following year – without spectators this time. The convincing Southern victory set the stage for an invasion of the North.

Antietam/Sharpsburg

State Route 65, Sharpsburg, MD (1-301 432 5124/www.nps.gov/anti). **Open** *June-Aug* 8.30am-6pm daily. *Sept-May* 8.30am-5pm daily. **Admission** $3; free under-17s. **No credit cards. Map** p274 A2.

The battle that took place here is known in the North by the first name, a creek that was the focus of much of the fighting, while in the South the nearby town of Sharpsburg gets the nod. The battle in mountainous western Maryland was the first Confederate attempt to invade the North and saw the bloodiest single day of the entire war on 17 September 1862, when the dead, wounded and missing of both sides exceeded 23,000. Emboldened by his victory at Second Manassas/Bull Run, General Robert E Lee had moved north but was met by a superior Union force. Neither side could claim a clear victory, but Lee's losses were so severe that he was forced to withdraw to Virginia. There was a crucial diplomatic consequence. The British government, poised to recognise the Confederacy, decided to hold off a

bit. It also gave President Lincoln the opportunity to issue the Emancipation Proclamation, freeing all slaves in states in rebellion against the Union.

Fredericksburg National Military Park

1013 Lafayette Boulevard, Fredericksburg, VA (1-540 373 6122/www.nps.gov/frsp). **Open** *Site* 9am-5pm daily. *Exhibit shelters* 10am-6pm Mon, Fri-Sun. **Admission** $4; free under-17s. **No credit cards.** **Map** p274 C2.

Fredericksburg, located roughly halfway between Washington and Richmond, was the setting of the next confrontation. Seeing an opportunity to launch a general offensive against a weakened Lee, Union forces struck at the strategically situated town on the Rappahannock River in the middle of December 1862 but were repulsed by the Confederate defenders. The three-day battle allowed Lee to recoup and resume the offensive. The site is part of the Fredericksburg & Spotsylvania National Military Park, which also includes the nearby Chancellorsville (*see below*), Wilderness and Spotsylvania Court House battlefields.

Chancellorsville National Military Park

9001 Plank Road, Chancellorsville, VA (1-540 786 2880/www.nps.gov/frsp/cville.htm). **Open** *Summer* 8.30am-6.30pm daily. *Winter* 9am-5pm Mon-Fri; 9am-6pm Sat, Sun. **Admission** $4; free under-17s. **No credit cards. Map** p274 C2.

A ten-day engagement took place at this site to the south of Fredericksburg in late April and early May 1863. It was a stunning Confederate victory over a Union army more than twice as large, thwarting the Northern drive on Richmond and emboldening Lee to launch his second invasion of the North two months later. It was also a grievous loss for the South, with the accidental fatal shooting by his own men of General 'Stonewall' Jackson, Lee's most effective commander.

Gettysburg National Military Park

97 Taneytown Road, Gettysburg, PA (1-717 334 1124 ext 422/www.nps.gov/gett). **Open** 6am-10pm daily. **Admission** free. **Map** p274 A2.

Gettysburg is in southern Pennsylvania, a two-hour drive north of DC. The battle here was the consequence of Chancellorsville and, in retrospect, the turning point of the war. Hoping to deliver a devastating blow to Northern morale by defeating the Union army on its own ground, Lee had moved north with a large force. The Confederates sent a scouting party into the town on the morning of 1 July 1863, encountering an advance patrol of Union General George Meade's Army of the Potomac, and the battle was on. It continued for four days, with the Southerners driving Meade's men back. But Union lines held on and on 4 July, Lee, having suffered heavy losses, was forced to withdraw. It was the bloodiest battle of the war, claiming more than 50,000 casualties. After Gettysburg, Lee was in constant

Fort McHenry. *See p239.*

A railroad hub through which supplies moved to Richmond, 23 miles (37km) to the north, was Ulysses Grant's next target. He began a ten-month siege in June 1864. At one point, Union volunteers from Pennsylvania's coal mines dug a 500-foot shaft beneath the Confederate lines and packed it with powder. The resulting explosion killed hundreds of Southern soldiers. Only the failure of the Union troops to follow through quickly saved the city. The crater left by the blast can be seen today. Lee was finally forced to withdraw on the night of 2 April 1865. The battlefield is accessible from I-95 and I-295.

Richmond National Battlefield Park
3215 East Broad Street, Richmond, VA (1-804 226 1981/www.nps.gov/rich). **Open** 9am-5pm daily. **Admission** free.

Richmond, the primary Union goal, was a continuing battle that lasted for more than three years. It was launched early in May 1862 with the Peninsular Campaign, when the Union used its naval superiority to land troops via Chesapeake Bay on the peninsula between the James and York rivers south of Richmond. The drive was within six miles (9.5km) of the Confederate capital when Lee counterattacked. He relieved pressure on the city, but was unable to dislodge Northern forces from the peninsula. The campaign is particularly notable for the first battle between iron-clad warships, the Union *Monitor* and the Confederate *Virginia* (originally a captured Union wooden ship, the *Merrimac*, which had been fitted with armour plate). It was a draw, but changed the course of naval history. All told, the Union made six attempts to take Richmond before Grant launched his Overland campaign in 1864. With the fall of Petersburg the following year, it became impossible to defend the capital and it was evacuated. Lee surrendered to Grant one week later.

retreat. Britain, along with France, lost all enthusiasm for recognising the Confederacy. In November, President Abraham Lincoln journeyed to the battlefield to dedicate a National Cemetery and deliver his Gettysburg Address, a brief but eloquent oration considered the greatest ever delivered by an American.

Wilderness & Spotsylvania Court House
Wilderness Battlefield National Military Park, State Route 20, Wilderness, VA **Map** p274 C2. *Spotsylvania Court House Battlefield, State Route 613, Spotsylvania, VA (1-540 786 2880/373 6122/www.nps.gov/frsp).* **Map** p275 D2. *Both* **Open** 9am-5pm daily. **Admission** $4; free under-17s. **No credit cards.**

Wilderness, an aptly named tangle of jungle-like overgrowth a few miles west of Chancellorsville, was the beginning of the end for the Confederacy. Abraham Lincoln had at last found his winning general in Ulysses S Grant, who battled Lee's depleted army for two days at the beginning of May 1864. Neither side gained the advantage but Grant launched the battle plan he followed to the end, moving towards Richmond whether he could claim victory or not. The battle at Spotsylvania Court House, beginning just two days after Wilderness, continued for two weeks, claiming some 30,000 casualties. Again, neither side 'won,' but Grant ground forward. Before visiting the sites, drop into the visitors' centre at nearby Chancellorsville battlefield (*see p240*) or the main visitors' centre in the town of Fredericksburg (*see p239*).

Petersburg National Battlefield
1539 Hickory Hill Road, Petersburg, VA (1-804 732 3531/www.nps.gov/pete). **Open** 9am-5pm daily. **Admission** $5 per person or $5 per vehicle. **Credit** AmEx, MC, V. **Map** p275 E2.

The Great Outdoors
You might think that the greater Washington-Baltimore metropolitan area, the fourth-largest population concentration in the entire US, might be a bit short on mountain greenery and other bucolic delights. You would be wrong. Within easy reach of the area's urban centres are some truly wondrous natural settings.

Maryland's shore and the Chesapeake Bay are dealt with separately, *see pp246-8.*

Great Falls & Riverbend Parks

Located ten miles (16 kilometres) north-west of downtown DC, on the other side of the Potomac River, is **Great Falls Park** (map p274 B2, 1-703 285 2966). Set at the point

The Potomac goes wild at **Great Falls Park**. *See p241.*

where the foaming river races through an obstacle course of massive boulders, the park has hiking and bridle trails, picnic facilities and a visitors' centre with historical and geological exhibits. Adjoining **Riverbend Park** (1-703 759 9018) is less developed. Aside from a visitors' centre with minimal exhibits on local wildlife, there's not much there except a boat ramp and some ten miles (16 kilometres) of trails. It's a great place for nature walks and bird-watching. There are guided walks on a random schedule; call for details.

Resources

Tourist information

See p243.

Getting there

By road

Take either the 14th Street Bridge or Theodore Roosevelt Memorial Bridge across the Potomac to the George Washington Memorial Parkway. Take the Parkway north to the intersection with State Route 123. Exit on to 123 west and continue to Georgetown Pike (State Route 193). Continue on the Pike another 12 miles (19km) to the entrances to Great Falls and Riverbend parks, on the right.

Shenandoah National Park & around

The undisputed jewel among the capital area's easily accessible outdoor attractions is **Shenandoah National Park** (map p274 C1, 1-540 999 3500). Straddling Virginia's Blue Ridge Mountains for more than 100 miles (160 kilometres), the park takes its name from the valley and river to the immediate west of the craggy range. Shenandoah, in the language of the native Americans occupying the area when European interlopers arrived, translates roughly as 'daughter of the stars'. The park's visual delights include sweeping views, swift mountain streams, waterfalls and mountain valleys shadowed by forested peaks, some of which rise to more than 4,000 feet (1,219 metres).

Skyline Drive follows the crest of the range for the entire length of the park. There are 75 look-out points along the route where motorists can pull off to take in the views. In the autumn, changing foliage puts on a spectacularly colourful show, usually peaking during the last weeks of October. Traffic at that time can bring to mind rush hour in DC, and there is a lesser visitor peak in the spring when the azaleas and dogwoods bloom. But for most of the year, the park is a refuge from urban stress, laced with more than 500 miles (840 kilometres) of trails. Some permit horses; riding is available from **Skyland Stables** (Skyland Lodge, 1-540 999 2210). Fishing is allowed in some stream (*see also p217*). Current accessible areas and other information can be ascertained at park entrances and several visitors' centres along Skyline Drive, or visit the park's website, www.nps.gov/shen. Park admission is $10 per vehicle.

Nearby **Massanutten Mountain** (1-540 289 9441), in the George Washington National Forest (map p274 B1), has great scenery and several hundred miles of trails for hiking, riding and biking. Also in the area are several natural caverns accessible to the public. The most developed is **Luray Caverns** (map p274 C1, 1-540 743 6551, www.luraycaverns.com), south of the town of Luray. Other options are **Endless Caverns** (map p274 C1, 1-800 544 2283, www.endlesscaverns.com) and **Shenandoah Caverns** (map p274 C1, 1-540 477 3115, www.shenandoahcaverns.com), both off I-81 in the vicinity of nearby New Market.

The Shenandoah, as well as the Tidewater area east of Fredericksburg, are also big on river sport. Take your pick – canoe, kayak, raft or tube – numerous outfitters are ready to set you up for a whitewater adventure or a leisurely float. In Bentonville, try **Shenandoah River Outfitters** (6502 South Page Valley Road, 1-540 743 4159, www.shenandoah-river.com) or **Downriver Canoe Company** (884 Indian Hollow Road, 1-800 338 1963, www.downriver.com). In Front Royal, head to **Front Royal Canoe Company** (information from PO Box 473, 1-540 635 5440, www.frontroyal.com). In Fredericksburg, In Fredericksburg, **Friends of the Rappahannock** (1-540 373 3448) offers canoe river tours.

Where to stay

In Strasburg, a village originally settled by German immigrants in the 1720s, the **Hotel Strasburg** (213 South Holliday Street, 1-800 348 8327, 1-540 465 9191, doubles $83-$180) is a restored Victorian landmark with 29 antique-furnished rooms. To reach the hotel, continue on I-66 beyond the entrance to Shenandoah National Park to I-81 south and exit 298, then two miles (three kilometres) south on US 11. Five miles (eight kilometres) north of Strasburg on US 11, at Middleton, is **Wayside Inn** (7783 Main Street, 1-540 869 1797, www.alongthewayside.com, doubles $99-$159), a rambling structure filled with antiques. Its several dining rooms serve regional cuisine;

the house speciality is peanut soup (yes, really). **Skyland Lodge** (Mile 41.7 Skyline Drive, 1-800 778 2851, doubles $59-$177) is located at the highest point (3,680 feet/1,122 metres) on Skyline Drive. It has lodge suites, rustic cabins, a decent restaurant and spectacular views. **Big Meadows Lodge** (Mile 51.2 Skyline Drive, 1-800 778 2851, doubles $86-$122) has 25 rooms in the beautifully panelled main lodge and another 72 in multi-unit lodges and rustic cabins; it, too, has a restaurant. **Lewis Mountain Cabins** (Mile 57.5 Skyline Drive, 1-800 778 2851, doubles $87-$94) is a more outdoorsy option.

Resources

Tourist information

Luray *Luray-Page County Chamber of Commerce, 46 E Main Street, Luray, VA (1-540 743 3915/ www.luraypage.com).* **Open** 9am-5pm Mon-Sat; noon-4pm Sun.

New Market *Shenandoah Valley Visitors Center & Travel Association, I-81 exit 264, New Market, VA (1-800 847 4878/www.shenandoah.org).* **Open** 9am-5pm daily.

Virginia State Parks, Department of Conservation & Recreation *203 Governor Street, room 213, Richmond, VA (1-800 933 7275/www.dcr.state.va.us).* **Open** 9am-7pm Mon-Fri. Hiking and camping information and reservations.

Getting there

By car

Of the several entrances to Shenandoah National Park, the most convenient from Washington is at its northern tip, 90mins or less via I-66 to exit 6, then south 3 miles (5km) on US 340 to Front Royal.

Catoctin Mountain Park

Maryland has its own back-to-nature retreat, although on a much smaller scale than Shenandoah, in Catoctin Mountain Park (map p274 A2). Located near the small town of Thurmont (about 90 minutes by car from Washington or Baltimore), it is not so much nature preserved as restored. Farmers, loggers and others scratching a living from the land had largely denuded the area before the National Park Service acquired it in 1935. Since then, the park's 5,700 acres have been returned to something like their original state. But it's this park's neighbour that gives it a cachet even Shenandoah might envy. The park wraps around Camp David, the rustic retreat of American presidents, originally constructed for Franklin D Roosevelt, who named it 'Shangri-la'. The less fanciful Dwight Eisenhower renamed it after his grandson. This is where presidents escape Washington for a bit of peace and quiet, and entertain distinguished guests. But trust us, you won't find the exact location on any map of the area. The Secret Service has seen to that. What you will find at Catoctin are trees and more trees, hiking and bridle trails, fishing creeks, picnic areas and, in winter, skiing and snowshoeing.

The haunt of moonshiners during Prohibition (1919-33), the park has preserved the Blue Blazes Still as an artefact. Park rangers give talks at weekends during June and September. Maps, trail guides and information on current park events can be obtained at the visitors' centre (6602 Foxville Road, Thurmont, 1-301 663 9388) off State Route 7.

Through the keyhole

The Washington area has arguably the greatest concentration of historic homes in the US. Many are associated with early presidents, four of the first five (the 'Virginia dynasty') having been Virginians. Maryland, although considerably smaller and as yet without a president to call its own, also has some notable residences. The sites mentioned below are merely the tip of an exceedingly large iceberg. Some, such as Mount Vernon, are less than an hour's drive south from downtown DC and could easily be visited in a day; others, such as Monticello, are more distant and might warrant an overnight stay.

A pleasant 14 miles (23km) south of DC via the George Washington Memorial Parkway (which ends at the visitors' entrance), **Mount Vernon** (map p274 C3, 1-703 780 2000, www.mountvernon.org; open Apr-Aug 8am-5pm daily; Mar, Sept, Oct 9am-5pm daily; Nov-Feb 9am-4pm daily) is the most celebrated and visited historic home in the country. George Washington has gone down in history as a soldier and statesman, but he devoted the greater part of his life to improving the estate he had inherited from an older half-brother, seeking to recreate an English manor house on the banks of the Potomac River. The faithfully restored plantation house contains original furniture and many of the first First Family's belongings. The gardens have been planted in colonial style. A major project in recent years has been the re-creation of a colonial-era farm where crops of Washington's day are raised using the simple implements of the time. Washington and his wife, Martha, lie in a tomb between the house and the colonial farm.

Mount Vernon is jammed with tour groups during the spring and summer; if you are visiting at this time, go in the afternoon when the crowds thin out. Autumn, when the weather is mostly glorious, is much better.

Nearby are other interesting sites with Washington associations. A few miles to the west via the Mount Vernon Memorial Highway is **Woodlawn Plantation** (map p274 C3, 9000 Richmond Highway/US 1, 1-703 780 4000, www.woodlawn1805.org, open 10am-5pm daily, closed Jan, Feb), an elegant brick mansion built by Washington as a wedding present for his adopted daughter, Nelly Parkes Custis, and his favourite nephew. A Federal-style variation on Georgian architecture, the hilltop house is much more stylish and livable than Mount Vernon. In the grounds is another showplace residence, but with no connection to Washington and of a very different time. The **Pope-Leighey House** is a small gem by modern master Frank Lloyd Wright. The house was designed to order in the 1930s for a lowly journalist earning $50 a week to demonstrate that Wright's brand of visionary architecture could be adapted to the lifestyles of ordinary people as well as the very wealthy. The house was moved to its present location when the original site was overrun by highway construction.

Another five miles (eight kilometres) to the south, off US 1, is **Gunston Hall** (map p274 C2/3, 10709 Gunston Road, Mason Neck, 1-703 550 9220, www.gunstonhall.org, open 9.30am-5pm daily), the home of Washington's friend George Mason, a drafter of the US Constitution so principled that he refused to sign the document because it lacked specific guarantees of individual liberties. These were later added as the Bill of Rights, the first ten of (to date) 27 amendments to the original document. Compared with Mount Vernon, this two-storey brick house is distinctly modest – and oddly modern. With a few additions, notably indoor plumbing, it could be very comfortable by today's standards. The restored ground-level rooms are considered outstanding examples of late colonial interior design.

Where to eat & stay

The extensive **Cozy Country Inn** (103 Frederick Road, Thurmont, 1-301 271 4301, doubles $52-$160, main courses $6-$20 lunch, $14-$20 dinner) provides daily lunch and dinner buffets and hearty country breakfasts on weekends. You can also stay overnight, in rooms named after Winston Churchill and other world figures who have dropped in at Camp David over the years.

Resources

Tourist information

See p247.

To the west of DC, near Leesburg, lies **Morven Park** (map p274 B2, 17263 Southern Planter Lane, 1-703 777 2414, www.morvenpark.org, guided tours hourly noon-4pm Mon, Fri-Sun). The home dates from 1781, but the original modest stone house was greatly enlarged during the 19th century. The present, lavishly furnished Greek Revival mansion includes a Museum of Hounds & Hunting and a collection of horse-drawn carriages.

Monticello (map p275 D1, State Route 53, 1-434 984 9822, www.monticello.org, open 8am-5pm daily), a two-and-a-half-hour drive from DC, is almost as celebrated as Mount Vernon. This domed hill-top mansion just outside Charlottesville was the home of the third president, Thomas Jefferson. A largely self-taught but talented architect, he also designed it. The house and its contents reflect Jefferson's interests in books, science and other intellectual pursuits. He is buried in the adjacent family cemetery. Charlottesville itself is a town of more than passing interest, with a history going back to colonial times. It is home to the University of Virginia, which ranks among the top publicly funded universities in the US and was founded by Jefferson, who also designed its original buildings.

Near the town of Orange, about 25 miles (40 kilometres) north of Charlottesville, **Montpelier** (11407 Constitution Highway/ State Route 20, open Nov-Mar 9.30am-4.30pm daily, Apr-Oct 9.30am-5.30pm daily, map p275 D1) was the home of James Madison, the fourth president. Also designed by Jefferson, the house embodied his classical vision. Later owners, including the immensely wealthy Du Pont family, expanded and significantly altered the original structure. Extensive restoration that began in 2003 is stripping away most of the additions to restore the house to its original size and Federal-period appearance.

Parts of the house will remain open to visitors while the work is in progress; it's scheduled for completion in 2007.

Tourist and hotel information for the area is available from the **Charlottesville/ Albemarle Convention & Visitors Bureau** (600 College Drive, Charlottesville, 1-877 368 1102/www.charlottesvilletourism.org, open 9am-5pm daily). **The Association for the Preservation of Virginia Antiquities** (204 West Franklin Street, Richmond, 1-804 648 1889/www.apva.org, open Mon-Fri) has information on 24 historic houses statewide.

Noteworthy Maryland residences include **Bel Air** (12207 Tulip Grove Drive, Bowie, 1-301 809 3089, open noon-4pm Wed-Sun) in Washington's Maryland suburbs. About 20 miles (32 kilometres) from downtown DC, the oldest parts of Bel Air date from 1740. Known as the 'house of governors' because it has been home to two provincial and state governors, the 34-room mansion has been restored and furnished with period antiques. Bel Air has a long association with racing: the first thoroughbreds in America were brought here from England, and the stables later produced several Triple Crown winners. The Stable Museum is located in the grounds.

Darnall's Chance (14800 Governor Oden Bowie Drive, 1-301 952 8010, guided tours, 10am-4pm Fri, noon-4pm Sun) was built in 1704 by a relative of the Calvert family, Maryland's titled English founders. Then surrounded by an estate of more than 100 acres, the house is now in the centre of the town of Upper Marlboro (map p274 B3). It was the birthplace of several members of Maryland's illustrious Carroll family, including a signatory of the Constitution and America's first Roman Catholic bishop. The original red-brick mansion was extensively remodelled during the 19th century in the Greek Revival style.

Getting there

By car
From Washington's Beltway, take I-270 north to Frederick. Continue north on US 15 for 17 miles (27km), exiting on to State Route 77 just south of Thurmont. The park entrance and visitors' centre are 2 miles (3km) to the west.

Little Bennett Regional Park

Closer in to Washington than Catoctin Park, Little Bennett Regional Park has almost the same acreage (3,500) as Catoctin but is much less developed. Other than the 14 miles (22 kilometres) of tree-shaded trails and a scattering of playgrounds, there is not very much in the way of facilities. However, this is a great place to relax in the shade, catch a few rays in the open areas, toss a ball or a frisbee around or even pitch a tent for the night.

Resources

Tourist information
See p247.

Getting there

By car
From the Beltway, take I-270 north 16 miles (26km) to the Boyds exit at Clarksburg. Bear right at the bottom of the ramp and continue to the stoplight, turning left on to State Route 355. Continue 0.25 miles (0.4km) to the park entrance.

Chesapeake Bay & the Maryland Shore

When the talk turns to the great outdoors, Maryland's Chesapeake Bay and shore areas are in a category of their own. Most of Maryland is defined by water, especially that of the Bay. Geographically, it divides the state into east and west, but in all other respects it is the focus of Maryland's identity. The long finger of water reaching northwards from the Atlantic makes Baltimore a world port. It also yields year after year an abundant harvest of seafood, notably the famous blue crab, a popular dish in the capital area (for good places to eat crab in DC, *see p127* **Get your claws out**). More than a score of rivers empty into it and its many inlets create ideal sites for recreation facilities and nature reserves. And it's all within an hour or so of fast-paced Washington.

Annapolis & the West Shore

The capital of Maryland since 1695 and briefly (1783) of the very young United States, **Annapolis** (map p274 B3) is the queen of the Bay area. A modern city has grown up around the colonial core, but the historic city is for the most part preserved. The narrow streets around the old harbour are lined with what is claimed to be the largest concentration of Georgian houses in the country. Annapolis is no longer the busy port it once was, but the sea remains very much a part of its identity. Marinas, sailing schools and charter services make it a recreational centre. It is also the home port of the **US Naval Academy**, which, despite heightened security at military installations since 9/11, remains open to the public. Naval memorabilia, a Freedom 7 space ship and a model ship collection are among the attractions. Visitors may observe the noon formation of midshipmen held Monday to Friday, weather permitting, during the academic year. Guided tours are available.

Several tours, self-guided and otherwise, of the whole Annapolis historic area are also available. Check at the City Dock information booth for details.

South of Annapolis, the Chesapeake's less publicised West Shore stretches more than 100 miles (160 kilometres) to Point Lookout, where the Potomac River flows into the Bay. Along the way are pleasant beaches at locations including Bay Ridge, Mayo, North Beach and Chesapeake Beach. They may lack the cachet and action of Eastern Shore sun 'n' surf meccas, but are more appealing to many visitors for that very reason. Towards the end of the peninsula, and a few miles inland, lies **St Mary's City** (map p275 D3), the fourth-oldest permanent English settlement in the US and first capital of Maryland.

Point Lookout State Park (map p275 D4, 301 872 5688), located on the site of a pre-Civil War resort, is a popular recreation area with beaches, fishing pier, nature trails and picnic facilities.

US Naval Academy

Armel-Leftwich Visitor Center, 52 King George Street (1-410 263 6933). **Open** *Mar-Dec* 9am-5pm daily. *Jan, Feb* 9am-4pm daily. *Guided tours* 10am-3pm Mon-Fri; 9.30am-3pm Sat; 12.30pm-3pm Sun. **Admission** free. *Guided tours* $7; $5-$6 concessions. **Credit** MC, V.

Where to stay

Maryland's capital city has its full share of chain hotels. For the real Annapolis experience, it's better to go for the small hotels in the historic old town. **Gibson's Lodging** (110 Prince George Street, 1-410 268 5555, doubles $99-$189) is a rambling B&B with 18 rooms and two suites in three period houses. Close to the waterfront and convenient for restaurants, **Governor Calvert House** (58 State Circle, 1-800 847 8882, doubles $99-$239) is across the street from the Maryland State House, where the US Congress once met. The main house, built for an 18th-century colonial governor, plus a newer annex contain 54 rooms, with antique and reproduction furniture.

Where to eat

As might be expected, Annapolis has a large selection of seafood-oriented restaurants – some on the rough-and-ready side, others upscale. **McGarvey's** (8 Market Space, 1-410 263 5700, main courses $6-$10 lunch, $16-$25 dinner) and **O'Brien's** (113 Main Street, 1-410 268 6288, main courses $8-$26) are both saloon-type establishments where you're likely to run into off-duty Naval Academy midshipmen.

Outside Annapolis, try the following in the town of Ridge, midway between St Mary's City and Point Lookout. Both are big on local seafood, especially crab in high season (June-August). **Courtney's** (48290 Wynne Road, 1-301 872 4403, main courses $6 lunch, $9-$25 dinner); **Scheible's Crab Pot** (48342 Wynne Road, 1-301 872 0028, main courses $5-$9 lunch, $9-$24 dinner).

Resources

Tourist information

Annapolis *Annapolis & Anne Arundel County Conference & Visitors Bureau, 26 West Street, Annapolis, MD (1-410 280 0445/www.visit-annapolis.org).* **Open** 9am-5pm daily.
Maryland Department of Natural Resources *580 Taylor Avenue, Annapolis, MD (410-260-8009).* **Open** 8.30am-4.30pm Mon-Fri.
Hiking, camping and fishing information.

Getting there

By car

From downtown DC to Annapolis, take US 50/301 (decrepit New York Avenue to the city limits) east 30 miles (48km). It's a 45-minute drive outside of rush hour. To continue down the West Shore from Annapolis, take State Route 2 south, merging with State Route 4 at Sunderland. After crossing the Patuxent River at Town Point, turn south on to State Route 235 and continue to Ridge and Point Lookout. Signs along the way will indicate exits to beaches and St Mary's City.

The Eastern Shore

Across the Chesapeake Bay Bridge (map p274 B3/4) from Annapolis is the Eastern Shore, a very different and much more visited area than its western counterpart. The Eastern Shore occupies the central and largest portion of the Delmarva Peninsula that separates Chesapeake Bay from the Atlantic Ocean. Eastern Shore residents fancy themselves as somewhat apart from the rest of the state. Whatever, it is a choice piece of real estate. Short but broad rivers empty into the Bay from the east and the deeply indented shore is fringed with islands, many barely rising above sea level.

Taking some of the more interesting points from north to south, the first reached after crossing the bridge is **Wye Island** (map p274 B4, information 1-410 827 7577), site of a state natural resources facility open to the public for hiking, fishing and picnicking. **Tilghman Island** (map p274 C3, information 1-410 822 4606), one of the most picturesque points on the Bay, is a few miles to the south. An old fishing community, it is far from a

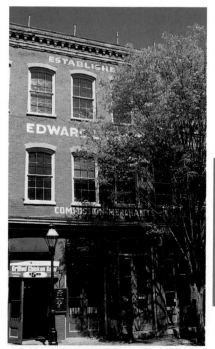

Richmond's **Shockoe Slip**. *See p237.*

museum piece. Fishermen still set out daily to dredge for oysters in the old, tall-masted sailing boats known as skipjacks.

Next stop is **Blackwater National Wildlife Refuge** (map p274 C4, information 1-410 228 2677) on a peninsula south of the town of Cambridge (map p274 C4) and east of the adjoining Hooper Islands. The 20,000-acre refuge is one of the best areas in the mid-Atlantic region for migratory waterfowl, eagles and other birds. There are paved roads and two hiking trails. The roads continue into a marshy area recalling the Florida Everglades and two of the three-island Hooper chain.

Further south is **Deal Island** (map p275 D4, information 1-800 521 9189), which, like Tilghman still a commercial fishing centre. Adjoining the community is Dames Quarter Marsh, another wildlife preserve especially attractive to bird-watchers.

Smith Island (map p275 D4), ten miles (16 kilometres) offshore, can be reached only by boat, from Crisfield on the mainland. The island is part of a cluster of islets lying so low that the thought of high tide can make a visitor uneasy. There are three small communities and a rudimentary road system on the island. But it's more fun to get around by foot or bicycle. Several operators provide passenger ship service from Crisfield to Smith Island; services operate year-round except during storms or, on the rare occasions when there is ice in the Bay. Smith Island Cruises (1-410 425 2771, www.smithisland cruises.com) operates June through October from nearby Somers Cove Marina. There are several restaurants on the island, some open only in warm weather. Accommodation is also available, likewise seasonally. For details, contact the Smith Island Center (1-410 425 3351).

At the end of the line – and in waters claimed by the state of Virginia – is **Tangier Island** (map p275 D4, 1-800 863 2338). It claims to be the crab capital not merely of the Bay, but the world. The few hundred inhabitants speak with an accent that linguists have traced to 17th-century Cornwall. Also requiring a short cruise, either from Eastern Shore points or the Virginia mainland, Tangier is another still-thriving community of fishermen. The town sprawls across three of Tangier's five islets, and as well as the colourful harbour there is a long sandy beach. **Tangier Island Cruises** in Crisfield (1001 West Main Street, 1-800 863 2338, 1-410 968 2338) sails daily at 12.30pm from Crisfield Municipal Dock, tickets are $22. The round trip can be made in a day, but sailing times will give you only a few hours at best on the island. The company also offers overnight stays for $295 per couple, including accommodation at the Holiday Inn and a buffet lunch both days. There's also the 'mail boat', preferred by locals, which is cheaper but more spartan and makes only one journey daily, meaning an overnight stay.

Tangier & Rappahannock Cruises (468 Buzzard Point Road, Reedville, VA, 1-804 453 2628) runs day trips to Tangier from Reedville on the Virginia shoreline. Phone for details of other trips.

Where to stay & eat

If you have time, do your best to stay overnight on Tangier Island. Eating options include **Hilda Crockett's Chesapeake House** (1-757 891 2331), which is also a B&B (doubles $100, including one meal). You can also stay at **Shirley's Bay View Inn** (1-757 891 2396, doubles $90, including breakfast).

Resources

Tourist information
See p247.

Getting there

By car & boat
Follow US 50/301 from Annapolis across the Chesapeake Bay Bridge, remaining on US 50 after US 301 diverges to the north. For **Wye Island**, continue nearly 3 miles (5km), then turn right on to Carmichael Road and continue for just over 5 miles (8km) to the bridge across Wye Narrows to Wye Island.

For **Tilghman Island**, from the US 50 and US 301 split, continue 16.5 miles (26km) on US 50 to the intersection with State Route 322 north of the town of Easton, bearing right and continuing another 2 miles (3km) to State Route 33. Continue for 22 miles (35km), through the village of St Michaels and across the Kapps Narrows drawbridge to the island. The road continues another 3 miles (5km) to Blackwalnut Point.

For **Blackwater**, at the US 50/301 split, continue south 34 miles (55km) to Cambridge, crossing the Choptank River. Take State Route 16 for 7 miles (11km) to the intersection of State Route 335. Turn left; it's 5 miles (8km) to the visitors' centre.

For **Deal Island**, at the US 50/301 split, go south 66 miles (106km) to Salisbury. From Salisbury, take US 13 south 12 miles (19km) to the intersection of State Route 363 (Deal Island Road) at the town of Princess Anne. Take 363 east 17 miles (27km) to Deal Island.

For **Smith Island** and **Tangier Island**, continue on US 13 after Princess Anne for another 5 miles (8km) to the Westover exit. Take State Route 413 south to the Crisfield dock.

Directory

Features

Directory

Getting Around

Arriving & leaving

By air

Three airports serve Washington.
**Washington Dulles International
Airport**, 25 miles (40 kilometres) out
in the suburbs of Virginia, handles
the longer flights into the region,
including most international flights.
**Baltimore-Washington
International Airport** (or BWI)
is a lot closer to the first half of its
name but easily accessible from
Washington by public transport,
and is popular for its cheaper fares
and more bearable traffic. **Ronald
Reagan Washington National
Airport** (most people still use the
non-political, old name 'National') is
the closest to DC, located just across
the Potomac River from downtown,
and gives a great view of the
monuments as you fly in; it's used
mostly for short- and medium-haul
flights within the US and Canada.

The airports have their own official
websites, but for general information,
including ground transportation,
shops and services, hotels and maps,
go to www.quickaid.com.

Super Shuttle

*1-800 258 3826/1-202 296 6662/
www.supershuttle.com.*
Offers door-to-door shared van
service between all three airports
and anywhere in the area. Prices
run from $15 to $30 for the first
passenger and from as little as $5 for
each additional passenger going to
the same place. It's helpful to know
the zip code of your final destination.

MAJOR AIRLINE
CONTACT DETAILS

Note that most airlines now offer
cheaper fares through their websites.
Air Canada
*1-800 361 5373/
www.aircanada.ca.*
American Airlines
1-800 433 7300/www.aa.com.
British Airways
*1-800 247 9297/www.british
airways.com.*
Continental Airlines
*Domestic 1-800 525 0280/
international 1-800 231 0856/
www.continental.com.*
Delta Air Lines
1-800 221 1212/www.delta-air.com.

Northwest Airlines
*Domestic 1-800 225 2525/
international 1-800 447 4747/
www.nwa.com.*
Southwest Airlines
1-800 435 9792/www.southwest.com.
SwissAir
1-877 359 7947/www.swiss.com.
United Airlines
1-800 241 6522/www.united.com.
US Airways
1-800 428 4322/www.usair.com.

To & from
Dulles Airport

*1-703 572 2700/www.metwash
airports.com.*
The quickest and cheapest way
to downtown DC is by getting the
Washington Flyer Bus (1-888
927 4359, www.washfly.com), which
operates between Dulles and the
West Falls Church Metro stop (20-
to 30-minute ride) at the western end
of the Orange Line. It costs $8 one-
way, $14 round trip, and runs at
least every half hour (from 5.45am
to 10pm Mon-Fri, and between
7.45am and 10pm on weekends).
From here you can continue your
journey into the city centre on the
Metro. The **Washington Flyer
Taxi** company has the sole
concession to operate out of Dulles
(unless incoming passengers have
a prearranged pick-up with another
cab company). A ride from Dulles to
downtown DC costs about $40 plus
tip. All Washington Flyer cabs take
credit cards. The above-mentioned
Super Shuttle is a good alternative.

To & from BWI

*1-800 435 9294/1-410 859 7111/
www.bwiairport.com.*
Getting to Washington from BWI can
often be expensive, a hassle, or both.
A cheap combination (best if you
have little to haul) to downtown DC
is the shuttle-train-Metro option.
Take the free shuttle bus (marked
BWI Rail, 1-410 672 6169) from
the BWI terminal to the train station
about a mile away, then catch a Marc
($5 one-way) or Amtrak (from $20)
train south 25 minutes to Union
Station, from where you can get
on the Metro. BWI is also served
by cabs, private car companies and
the **Super Shuttle** (*see above*), but
beware of the long waits for the
latter. You can get complete BWI
ground transport information from

the booth in Pier C or by calling
1-800 435 9294. A cab from BWI
to downtown Washington costs
about $55 plus tip.

To & from
National Airport

*1-703 417 8000/www.metwash
airports.com.*
National Airport is served by the
Metro subway system (Yellow and
Blue lines). It's about a 20-minute
ride to downtown. Going by cab is
another option: signs outside each
baggage claim area will direct you
to the taxi stand. The taxi stand
operator will point you to a particular
cab depending on whether you're
going to DC, Virginia or Maryland.
Virginia-licensed cabs can take you
anywhere; DC- and Maryland-
licensed cabs can't serve Virginia.
The fare is determined by meter
in Maryland and Virginia cabs,
by mileage in DC cabs. All pick-ups
from National Airport add a $1.25
surcharge. A cab to downtown
Washington costs about $12 plus tip.

By rail

A train from New York City (Penn
Station) to Washington takes roughly
three hours and costs about $75 each
way for an unreserved ticket and
$110 each way for a reserved seat.
For more information on trains, call
Amtrak at 1-800-872 7245 or go to
www.amtrak.com. All trains to DC
arrive at Union Station, which has
its own Metro station.

By bus

You can also catch the bus from New
York to DC. The downside is that
the journey takes longer (about five
hours), but the upside is that it's
really cheap – around $42 each way.
Greyhound buses (1-800 229 9424,
www.greyhound.com) leave from a
terminal in a grimmish area north of
Union Station, and arrive at the Port
Authority Bus Station in New York.

By car

Washington is served by several
major highways, including the 270,
the 66 and Interstate 95, which runs
the length of the east coast from

Miami to the Canadian border. At Washington, the 95 splits into the 495-95 and 95, looping the metropolitan area as the Capital Beltway.

A useful resource when planning a car journey is www.mapquest.com. If you type in your address (it only works in mainland USA) and the address in Washington you want to drive to, Mapquest will give you detailed directions, complete with maps and the distance between turns.

Navigation

The District of Columbia used to be a perfect ten- by ten-mile (16- by 16-kilometre) diamond, until Virginia took back its land contribution in 1846. Now DC's jagged western border is the Potomac River. The District is surrounded by Maryland on all other sides. In practice, however, the DC border is more significant for administrative reasons than geographical: the metro area spreads into the neighbouring states.

The city is divided into four quadrants – NW, NE, SE and SW – which meet at the US Capitol, the geographical centre of Washington before the 1846 land retrocession to Virginia. North, South and East Capitol Streets, and the National Mall to the west, radiate out from the Capitol and serve as quadrant dividing lines.

On one level, the District is completely rational in its layout. Numbered streets run north and south on both sides of the Capitol, with intersecting lettered streets and a few named streets tossed in, running east to west, for about 50 square blocks. The higher the number, and the further on in the alphabet the letter, the further away the street is from the Capitol. This grid system fades when the alphabet ends (when words beginning with A through Z replace the lone letters).

But as straightforward as this seems, there is a crucial nuance. Because the naming system radiates from a central point, there are two First Streets (and Second, etc), one on either side of North/South Capitol Street – and ditto for lettered streets, one north and one south of the Mall (aside from A and B Streets, which don't appear in all four quadrants). This means that there can therefore be four different places – one in each quadrant – where, say, a Fourth Street and a G Street intersect, so you need to know which quadrant you're aiming for. This is why we have given the quadrant after every address in our listings, and this is also how you should give directions to a taxi driver (say 'Northwest' not 'NW'). Northwest is by far the biggest quadrant.

Street numbers correspond to cross streets; thus 800 C Street will be on C Street at Eighth Street (or rather, the eighth block from the US Capitol); 890 C Street will be on the 800 block but closer to Ninth Street. For addresses on numbered streets, you can also work out the location. For instance, 400 Eighth Street will be at the fourth block from the US Capitol. In practice this means you can count up the alphabet – ie 400 Eighth Street will be at D Street. There are some exceptions to this rule, however: the letter 'B' (or, strictly speaking, the 200 block) is counted even though there are no B Streets in central Washington (there are named streets in their places – Constitution Avenue in NE and NW and Independence Avenue in SE and SW). Note also that there is no J Street, so it's ignored. For locating yourself, it's useful to remember that E Street is at 500, K is 1000, P is 1500, and U is 2000. Above W Street, the counting depends on the number of blocks, regardless of what the streets are named, although they are generally in alphabetical order. Woven into the grid of lettered and numbered streets are diagonal avenues, all named after American states – Pennsylvania Avenue, Massachusetts Avenue, and so on – that can easily cause drivers and walkers severe disorientation. Some diagonals can be a fast way across town, but most hit confusing traffic circles designed more for horse-and-buggy contraptions than modern travel, or run into parks or important buildings (such as the White House) that cause them to dogleg disconcertingly. Note that I Street is often written 'Eye' Street in order to avoid confusion with 1st/First Street.

Most hotels provide adequate tourist maps, but much better is the *ADC Washington DC Visitor's Map*, which helpfully shows the shapes of the buildings on the Mall and subway entrances. It's very good for central DC, but shows almost nothing of the NE or SE quadrants, and does not include Arlington. Most bookstores stock maps, and gas stations have large-scale driving maps. Or visit the terrific ADC Map & Travel Store (*see p158*).

You don't really need a car in DC. It's a pedestrian-friendly city and most of the main monuments and museums are well served by public transport. Taxis are reasonably priced and easily flagged down in the centre. Parking in downtown DC and near popular nightspots is often a hassle. And while a car can be the best way to get out of town, beware: rush-hour traffic is hell.

For information on driving into neighbouring states, *see p230*.

Public transport

The **Washington Metropolitan Area Transit Authority** runs the entire DC-area public transport network. For information on the Metrorail subway system and buses, call 1-202 637 7000 (hours of operation: 6am-10.30pm Mon-Thur; 6am-11.30pm Fri; 7am-11.30pm Sat; 7am-10.30pm Sun) or go to its website at www.wmata.com.

Metro

The **Metrorail** (or, more commonly, Metro) subway system is a clean, safe and reliable public transport system. Trains run from 5.30am from Monday to Friday and from 7am on Saturday and Sunday. The system closes at midnight Sunday to Thursday and at 3am on Saturday and Sunday mornings, but the last trains from the suburbs may depart before that. Holiday schedules vary. At busy times, trains come as often as two minutes apart. But even if everything is running on time, the scheduled waits at nights and weekends can be up to 20 minutes. Most signs and announcements use the line's final station as the identifier for platforms and trains – though not all trains go as far as the last station, so you need to know which direction you're heading.

You'll find a Metrorail map on p288; also use the handy RideGuide on the Metro website (www.wmata.com), or pick up the **Metro Pocket Guide**, which usefully lists the nearest Metro station to the monuments and other points of interest. A voice-operated telephone **RideGuide** is also available by calling 1-202 637 7000.

Station entrances are marked on the street by square columns with a big white 'M' on top. Throughout this guide, we've listed the Metro stop nearest to each destination. If the Metro station is some distance away, a bus number is also listed, but in practice, and in the daytime at least, it's usually nicer to walk the last part of the journey. Metro lines can run deep and the escalators can be very long. The network is, however, wheelchair-accessible via elevators. If the elevators are broken at a particular station, a bus service will run from a nearby location. Check at the information kiosk before boarding for the latest information on elevator breakdowns.

Fares & passes

The minimum price of a Metro trip is $1.35 but fares depend on when and how far you travel – and can almost double for some rides during rush hours. Fares are printed on a big board on the information kiosk in each station. Under-4s travel free.

Payment is by Farecard: you put up to $20 or your credit card into a machine, which pops out a flimsy card with a magnetic stripe on the front. Use the card to enter and exit the Metro turnstiles. The price of each trip is subtracted and the remaining amount printed on the card until there's not enough value left to go anywhere. You can then transfer the remaining amount to a new card using the same machines you buy cards from. You can't get into the Metro without at least $1.35 on your card. If you don't have enough to get out at a particular station, use the ExitFare machines just before the exit turnstiles, which take only $1 or $5 bills.

A particular bargain is the $6 one-day pass for unlimited trips (valid after 9.30am Mon-Fri, and all day at weekends). They are sold at some hotels, major grocery stores, most Metro stations and online at www.wmata.com. If your visit is going to last longer than a week, look into Metrochecks, which are available in denominations of $1, $5, $10, $20 and $30. These vouchers are accepted by more than 100 different transportation services – trains, buses and van pools – throughout the region. Check www.wmata.com/riding/metrochek/metrochek.cfm for more information.

The lines

Red Line: serves the Maryland suburbs north of DC and runs through the downtown business district. The Zoo, Union Station and UDC (University of the District of Columbia) are on this line.
Green Line: serves Anacostia, the U Street district, Howard University and the eastern Mall area.
Blue Line: serves Arlington, Alexandria, National Airport, the RFK Stadium and most downtown memorials and museums. It parallels much of the Orange Line and some of the Yellow.
Yellow Line: serves Fairfax County (Virginia) via Alexandria to the Mall. Includes National Airport.
Orange Line: serves the suburbs from western Virginia to eastern Maryland. Parallels the Blue Line through most major tourist sights.

Buses

The bus system, also run by the Washington Metropolitan Area Transit Authority, covers the city well and is heavily used by locals, especially for commuting. Metrobuses cost $1.25, or 35¢ with a subway transfer (get one after you

enter the Metro but before you get on the train – look for a machine near the top of the escalators to the platform). You need exact change; dollar bills are accepted. Bus stops are marked by three horizontal stripes in blue, white and red. Metrorail passes are not valid on the bus, with the exception of certain weekly deals. A regional one-day pass costs $3 and is good for an entire day of bus trips (and covers $1.20 of the $2.50 fare on Express bus routes). A good timetable and route tool is available on the Metro website (www.wmata.com/timetables/default.cfm).

The greater Washington area has different local bus systems in the area. Alexandria and Fairfax Counties in Virginia and Montgomery, Prince George's and Prince William Counties in Maryland each run their own public transport or ride-share systems. To reach these services, call Metro (1-202 637 7000) for phone numbers and more information.

Useful bus routes

One popular area served better by bus than Metro is Georgetown: catch a 30, 32, 34, 35 or 36 bus marked 'Friendship Heights' running west on Pennsylvania Avenue. The same buses serve the Upper Northwest area along Wisconsin Avenue, parts of which are far from any Metro stop.

For Adams Morgan, including busy 18th Street, take the 90, 92 or 93 (U Street/Garfield line) bus from Woodley Park-Zoo/Adams Morgan Metro, or the 42 (Mount Pleasant line) bus from Dupont Circle Metro. (Adams Morgan is also within walking distance from Columbia Heights Metro).

Trains

Both **Amtrak** and **Marc** (Maryland Rail Commuter Service) operate out of DC's Union Station. Amtrak connects with cities all over the US, including Baltimore, and also has stops at Alexandria in Virginia and at Rockville and New Carrollton in Maryland. There are several trains daily to New York, Philadelphia and Boston, on which you're allowed to reserve seats, and the fancy new Acela Express (www.acela.com), which is taking on planes in the battle of the east coast intercity executive market.

Marc is a commuter train running from Union Station to parts of West Virginia and Maryland (including Baltimore). The Penn line goes to Baltimore's northern suburbs and runs from 5.54am to 10.35pm on weekdays (every 30 minutes during rush hour, every hour otherwise).

It does not run at weekends. The Camden line stops at Camden Yards (Baltimore's baseball stadium) and runs only during morning and evening rush hours (6.42-8.05am and 4.13-7.35pm). Marc stops at some Metro stations in Maryland. Fares between DC and Baltimore are $7 one-way, $15 round trip. Both Amtrak and Marc serve the BWI Airport station, from where you take a free shuttle bus the short journey to the terminal.

Union Station

50 Massachusetts Avenue, NE, at North Capitol Street, Union Station & around (Amtrak 1-800 872 7245/ 1-202 484 7540/www.amtrak.com/ Marc 1-800 325 7245/www.mta maryland.com/schedules/index.cfm). **Map** p285 K/L 5/6.

Taxis

As elsewhere in the States, driving a taxi is a typical job for recent immigrants, so it's not uncommon to get a driver who needs directions, especially if you're going somewhere slightly off the beaten track.

There are no taxi ranks, but you can usually find cabs outside hotels and it's easy to flag down a DC-licensed cab around most central parts of the city. Cabs for hire have a light on top and the company name on the door. To call a cab in the District, try **Diamond** (1-202 387 6200) or **Yellow Cab** (1-202 544 1212).

Cab fares are based on how many zones you travel through (maps should be displayed in every cab), plus extra charges for additional passengers, rush-hour travel, calling for a cab and travelling during designated snow emergencies. Baggage charges are usually 50¢ for each largeish, grocery-sized handbag after the first one and $2 for each big bag. In reality, some cabbies charge, some don't, depending, it seems, on their mood. The minimum fare possible under the zone system (for one person, flagging the cab, no bags, not at rush hour or in the snow) is $5 plus tip. That will get you all the way from Capitol Hill to Dupont Circle – and it seems to be this trip that brings the smouldering resentment about the zone system into the open. Most cabbies can't wait to see the congressionally mandated zones disappear.

In Maryland and Virginia, cabs run on meters. Cabs licensed for these areas can legally only pick up passengers in DC on a pre-arranged basis – and only take them to the jurisdiction in which they are licensed. That might be why, no matter how hard you're waving on a DC street, that empty cab went right on by.

Diplomatic impunity

Washingtonians both love and loathe the diplomatic corps. The nations of the world throw open their embassies for benefits, or for concerts or exhibitions free to the public. Yet for more than two centuries DC has had a less jolly experience of diplomatic immunity.

The concept of extraterritoriality – that the laws of a host nation don't apply to diplomats from elsewhere – famously healed a tiff between Queen Anne and bellicose Czar Peter the Great in 1708. The US adopted it in 1790, with some colourful experiences to follow. By the late 19th century an untouchable breed of dissolute diplomats, generally young attachés, serially seduced and abandoned impressionable American lasses. Napoleon III's representative, Sartain, 'persisted in firing at cats and rats from the back windows of his house, thus endangering the lives of persons in the adjacent back yards'. The cops could do nothing.

In more recent times, irritants abounded. Ambassadorial wives, unable like everyone else to find a Georgetown parking space, took to double-parking on M Street during rush hour while they popped into their favourite boutique. Immunity expanded exponentially, from ambassadors to their aides to their families to subordinate staff. By the 1970s, even embassy cooks and gardeners brandished Get Out Of Jail Free cards.

Pressed, the State Department reluctantly restricted the Immunati, but it's still a practical rule to beware those in striped trousers, especially in traffic. Locals instinctively steer clear of any vehicle stigmatised by a distinctive red, white and blue licence tag labelled with the letter D, for diplomat (though drunk, danger, or death also spring to mind). Too many have had their cars rear-ended without recourse. Smaller fry get a C for consul, S for staff, or A for United Nations secretariat (the latter mostly menacing motorists and pedestrians in New York).

Driving

The Washington area (especially between DC and Virginia) is not a great place to drive. The traffic circles are confusing and some streets, notably Rock Creek Parkway, change direction in rush hours. Read carefully the times posted in the middle of 'Do Not Enter' and 'No Turns' signs; at other times, entrance is allowed. Unless there's a sign saying otherwise, you can make a right turn when the lights are red.

Parking

There are plenty of off-street pay parking lots around town: **Monument Parking** (1-202 833 9357) has seven locations; **Parking Management Incorporated** (PMI, 1-202 785 9191) has many more. Street parking ranges from difficult to impossible, especially near the Mall, downtown and in popular nightlife areas such as Georgetown and Adams Morgan. The parking police are notoriously pedantic. Add to all this the regular street shutdowns for presidential motorcades and you'll see why nearly a third of District residents don't own a car.

For up-to-the-minute traffic conditions, see www.trafficland.com. Tune to WTOP (1500 AM, 107.7 FM) for traffic reports every ten minutes.

Vehicle hire

For getting right out of town, driving is often the best option. Most major car rental companies have offices in and around DC. Almost every rental agency will require a credit card and matching driving licence, and few will rent to anyone under 25. The price quoted won't include tax, liability insurance or collision damage waiver (CDW). If you already have an insured car in the US, your own liability insurance may cover the rental. Ask about discounts, available to members of the AAA (as well as British AA members), AARP (American Association of Retired Persons) and other organisations.

The following are national car rental companies with locations in DC:
Alamo
1-800 462 5266/www.freeways.com.
Avis
1-800 230 4898/www.avis.com.
Budget
1-800 527 0700/
www.budgetrentacar.com.
Dollar
1-800 800 4000/www.dollarcar.com.
Hertz
1-800 654 3131/www.hertz.com.
National
1-800 227 7368/
www.nationalcar.com.
Thrifty
1-800 847 4389/www.thrifty.com.

Cycling

DC is great for easy cycling. Many parts of the city, including much of the Mall and downtown, are flat (though there's Capitol Hill at the eastern end of the Mall). And if you don't mind a less-than-direct route, you can avoid the hillier parts of the city (in particular, north of Florida Avenue – both NE and NW – and Upper Northwest). A web of bike paths can take you to out-of-centre spots, and riding from museum to monument will save your feet hours of ache (though you'll have to lock your bike to a signpost or railings). For more information on biking in and around DC, get in touch with the **Washington Area Bicyclist Association** (1-202 628 2500, www.waba.org).

Walking

Dawdlers beware! Washington has its fair share of aggressive walkers. Drivers can also be a major hazard, cutting up pedestrians even when the traffic lights are in their favour. Walking is a great way to get around, but remember that summers are hot and muggy, and while the Mall might like look like a nice gentle stroll, it's actually two miles (three kilometres) long, with a hill at the Capitol end.

Directory

Resources A-Z

Addresses

See p251 **Navigation**.

Age restrictions

You have to be 21 to drink alcohol in DC, Maryland and Virginia. Note that the law is very strictly enforced, with severe penalties. Be sure to carry ID with you (*see p256*).

Attitude & etiquette

Washington is unquestionably a major tourist destination, so if you wear jeans, trainers and carry a small rucksack you should feel right at home. It is also, of course, a major business centre, and walking around downtown you'll see lawyers in suits and other members of a well-dressed workforce. If you dress up a little, you'll blend in better.

DC residents are usually very preoccupied with their own little niche. They read the *Washington Post* on the Metro, mind their own business on the sidewalk and get upset when tourists stand on the left side of the escalator instead of the right. But if you do stop someone on the street to ask for directions, they will generally be happy to oblige.

Business

There was a time, not that long ago, when the business scene in Washington could pretty much be covered in one word: government. Not only was the federal presence far and away the dominant industry, but dealing with it was the primary purpose of most private-sector activity. Government is still the 800lb gorilla of the DC jungle, but a number of A-list corporations, such as US Airways, have their headquarters in the Washington area. A high-tech industry has established itself along the so-called Dulles Corridor, turning the expressway linking the city with Dulles International Airport in the Virginia suburbs into something of a Silicon Valley East (AOL Time Warner has a headquarters here, and some Virginians' car tags bear the business bureau catchphrase 'internet capitol'). The business epicentre is downtown's K Street, lined with glassy office buildings. DC now has more office space than any other American city aside from New York.

That said, while Washington may have made the big time, standard operating procedures are lower-key than in comparable cities, especially New York. There are similarities, such as the ubiquitous power lunch, but the overall style is less frenetic. In fact, as viewed from New York, Washingtonians have no style. The idea is to dress down: dark (preferably blue) suits, and ties with a touch of red. In summer, when the heat and humidity threaten to reach meltdown levels, light-hued poplin and seersucker suits are almost a uniform. Year-round, by far the preferred accessory is a neck chain from which dangles a photo-ID card – it's virtually a badge of belonging.

Conventions

Washington Convention Center

801 Mount Vernon Place, NW, between Seventh & Ninth Streets, Downtown (1-800 368 9000/1-202 249 3000/www.dcconvention.com). **Map p285 J5.**
The largest single building in the city, this new centre opened in 2003 to rave reviews and booming business. Its 52,000sq ft (4,836sq m) ballroom and $4-million art collection make it worth a peek for casual visitors, many of whom stop in at the restaurants and retail outlets on-site.

Couriers

All the major international couriers, in addition to several locally based enterprises, are active in DC. For other outfits, check the *Yellow Pages* under 'Air Cargo & Package Express Service', 'Delivery Service', or, for local deliveries, 'Messenger Services'.

Federal Express
1-800 463 3339/www.fedex.com. **Credit** AmEx, DC, Disc, MC, V.

Skynet Worldwide Courier
1-703 759 0090/www.skynetmia. com. **No credit cards**.

United Parcel Service
1-800 742 5877/www.ups.com. **Credit** AmEx, MC, V.

Libraries

See p257.

Publications

The top domestic business papers are readily available in Washington, while foreign publications can be found at larger newsstands. Local journals worth a look include the weekly *Washington Business Journal* (http://washington.bizjournals.com/washington), which also contains a useful 'Resource Directory' section. For more on the local media scene, *see p257.*

Useful organisations

For details of the **Washington DC Convention & Tourism Corporation**, *see p263*. For the **US Customs Service**, *see p255*.

Travel advice

For up-to-date information on travel to a specific country – including the latest news on safety and security, health issues, local laws and customs – contact your home country government's department of foreign affairs. Most have websites packed with useful advice for would-be travellers.

Australia
www.dfat.gov.au/travel

Canada
www.voyage.gc.ca

New Zealand
www.mft.govt.nz/travel

Ireland
www.irlgov.ie/iveagh

UK
www.fco.gov.uk/travel

USA
http://state.gov/travel

Directory

District of Columbia Chamber of Commerce

First floor, 1213 K Street, NW, at 12th Street, Downtown (1-202 347 7201/www.dcchamber.org). McPherson Square Metro. **Open** 8.30am-5.30pm Mon-Fri. **Map** p284 H5.

Greater Washington Board of Trade

Suite 200, 1725 I Street, NW, between 17th & 18th Streets, Downtown (1-202 857 5900/ www.bot.org). Farragut North or Farragut West Metro. **Map** p284 G5. The Board of Trade functions as a regional co-ordinating organisation for DC, northern Virginia and suburban Maryland.

US Department of Commerce

14th Street & Constitution Avenue, NW, The Federal Triangle (1-202 482 2000/www.doc.gov). Federal Triangle Metro. **Open** 8am-5.30pm Mon-Fri. **Map** p284 H6.

Consumer

Whenever possible, pay with a major credit card so you can cancel payment or get reimbursed if there is a problem (be sure to keep receipts or a form of documentation). Consider travel insurance that includes default coverage to protect yourself against financial loss.

Call for Action

1-301 652 4357.
Helps with many kinds of consumer problems, though it's only open 11am-1pm Tue-Fri.

DC Department of Consumer Protection

1-202 442 8475.
Regulates certain businesses in DC, such as tour guides.

Customs

A visa waiver form (I-94W) is generally provided by the airline during check-in or on the plane and must be presented to Immigration at the airport of entry in the US. International visitors should allow about an hour in the airport to clear Immigration. For more on visas, *see p264 and p261* **New passport regulations**.

A customs declaration form (6059B) is also provided on international flights into the US; this must be filled out and handed to a customs official after Immigration (keep it handy). Current US regulations allow foreign visitors to import the following duty-

free: 200 cigarettes or 50 cigars (Cuban cigars are generally not allowed), 1 litre of wine or spirits (over-21s only), and a maximum of $100 in gifts. You can take up to $10,000 in cash, travellers' cheques or endorsed bank drafts in or out of the country. Anything above that you must declare on a customs form, or it risks seizure. It is illegal to transport most perishable foods and plants across international borders. If you are carrying prescription drugs, make sure they are labelled, and keep a copy of your prescription with you.

US Customs Service

1300 Pennsylvania Avenue, NW, at 13th Street, Penn Quarter (1-202 354 1000/www.customs.gov). Federal Triangle Metro. **Open** 8.30am-5pm Mon-Fri. **Map** p284 H6.

US Immigration & Naturalization Service

4420 North Fairfax Drive, Arlington, VA (1-800 375 5283/ www.cis.gov). **Open** 7.30am-2.30pm Mon-Fri.

Disabled

Washington is good at providing facilities for all types of tourists, including the disabled and elderly. Most museums, monuments and memorials are accessible to visitors using wheelchairs and many have other facilities to help disabled travellers. Nearly all streets in the downtown area have wide sidewalks with kerb cuts for greater accessibility. The Metro has excellent facilities for visitors with vision and hearing impairments or mobility problems. All stations are theoretically wheelchair-accessible, although elevators are not always in service. *See also p251.*

An extremely useful website is www.disabilityguide.org, which rates DC's hotels, restaurants, malls and sights according to accessibility. It's run by **Access Information** (1-301 528 8664). The **Washington DC Convention & Tourism Corporation** (*see p263*) also has information and a free brochure on city accessibility. The New York-based **Society for Accessible Travel & Hospitality** (1-212 447 7284, www.sath.org) offers advice for disabled travellers throughout the US.

Tour operators

Outfits organising holidays for disabled travellers include **Access Adventures** in Rochester, NY (1-585 889 9096) and **Sprout**, in New York City (1-212 222 9575, 1-888 222 9575, www.gosprout.org).

Drugs

Hard and soft drugs are illegal in Washington, as in the rest of the US. In practice, however, arresting people for possession of small amounts of soft drugs is not a high priority of DC police. Drug busts are usually limited to dealers and high-profile public gatherings such as concerts.

Electricity

The US electricity supply is 110-120 volt, 60-cycle AC, rather than the 220-240 volt, 50-cycle AC used in Europe. Plugs are standard two-pins. An adaptor and, in some cases, a voltage converter (available at airport shops and hardware stores) are necessary to use foreign electrical appliances. Check www.voltagevalet.com for answers to most electrical questions.

Embassies & consulates

Note that most visa services keep shorter hours than the business hours listed. For other embassies/ consulates, consult the *Yellow Pages*.

Australia

1601 Massachusetts Avenue, NW, at 16th Street, Dupont Circle (1-202 797 3000/www.austemb.org). Dupont Circle Metro. **Open** 8am-5pm Mon-Fri. **Map** p282 H4.

Canada

501 Pennsylvania Avenue, NW, at Sixth Street, Penn Quarter (1-202 682 1740/www.canadianembassy. org). Archives-Navy Memorial or Judiciary Square Metro. **Open** varies. **Map** p285 J6.

Ireland

2234 Massachusetts Avenue, NW, at Sheridan Circle, Dupont Circle (1-202 462 3939/www.ireland emb.org). Dupont Circle Metro. **Open** 9am-1pm, 2-4pm Mon-Fri. **Map** p282 F4.

New Zealand

37 Observatory Circle, NW, at Massachusetts Avenue, Upper Northwest (1-202 328 4800/ www.nzemb.org). Dupont Circle Metro. **Open** 8.30am-12.30pm, 1.30-5pm Mon-Fri. **Map** p281 E3.

United Kingdom

3100 Massachusetts Avenue, NW, at Whitehorse Street, Upper Northwest (1-202 462 1340/ www.britianusa.com). Dupont Circle Metro then N2, N4, N6 bus. **Open** 9am-5.30pm Mon-Fri. **Map** p281 F3.

Directory

Emergencies

The number for ambulance, fire, police and other emergencies is **911** (free from public phones).

Gay & lesbian

Washington is home to a thriving, well-established gay and lesbian community. For information about groups and what's on, consult the *Washington Blade* (also available at www.washingtonblade.com).

The bookshop **Lambda Rising** (*see p159*) serves as an unofficial gay and lesbian resource centre.

Health

Accident & emergency

Emergency treatment in the United States is provided on receipt of hard cash. It is often rumoured that many emergency rooms won't even see you unless you show them a credit card first. This is, in fact, illegal: emergency rooms are only allowed to turn you away if your injury is not considered an emergency, though they will do all they can to make you pay up. Taking out full medical cover is still imperative, ideally with a large and reputable company that will pay upfront rather than reimburse you later.

The hospitals listed below all have 24-hour emergency rooms.

Contraception & abortion

Several branches of the CVS chain (*see p172*; or call 1-800 746 7287 for your nearest branch) are open 24 hours a day. Like other pharmacies, they sell condoms and can fill out prescriptions for other contraceptives. If you need advice about abortion, call **Planned Parenthood** on 1-202 347 8512 or go to its website, www.ppmw.com.

Dentists

DC Dental Society

1-202 547 7613/www.dcdental.org.
The DC Dental Society can refer you to a local dentist for treatment.

Doctors

Doctors Referral

1-800 362 8677/
www.1800doctors.com.
Can recommend a local doctor.

HIV & AIDS

National HIV/ AIDS Hotline

1-800 342 2437.

Elizabeth Taylor Medical Center

1701 14th Street, NW, at R Street, Shaw: Logan Circle (1-202 745 7000/www.wwc.org). McPherson Square Metro. **Open** 8am-10pm Mon-Fri. **Map** p282 H4.
Part of the Whitman Walker Clinic – a pioneering institution offering many services to people with HIV and other sexually transmitted diseases – the Elizabeth Taylor Medical Center provides counselling to AIDS patients and their families. The excellent website is full of useful information.

Hospitals

Children's National Medical Center

111 Michigan Avenue, NW, between North Capitol Street & Georgia Avenue, Shaw (1-202 884 5000/ www.cnmc.org). Brookland-CUA Metro then H2, H4 bus. **Map** p283 K2.

Georgetown University Medical Center

4000 Reservoir Road, NW, at Wisconsin Avenue, Georgetown (1-202 687 5100/http://gumc. georgetown.edu). Dupont Circle Metro then D6 bus. **Map** p281 E4.

George Washington University Hospital

901 23rd Street, NW, at Washington Circle, Foggy Bottom (1-202 715 4000/www.gwhospital.com). Foggy Bottom Metro. **Map** p284 G5.

Opticians

See p172.

Pharmacies

See p172.

Helplines

Alcoholics Anonymous
1-202 966 9115.
Auto Impound
1-202 727 5000.
Dental Emergency
1-800 362 8677.
Mental Health Crisis Hotline
1-703 527 4077.

Non-emergency Metropolitan Police
311/www.mpdc.dc.gov.
Poison Center
1-800 222 1222.
Rape Crisis Center
1-202 333 7273.
Substance Abuse Hotline
1-800 234 0402.
Suicide Prevention Center
1-800 784 2433.
US Capitol Police
1-202 228 2800.
US Park Police
1-202 619 7300/www.nps.gov/uspp.

ID

Unless you're driving or drinking alcohol, there isn't any law that says you must carry identification with you, but it makes sense to do so anyway. Keeping your passport with you is always risky in case you lose it, but a driver's licence is usually a good idea, especially as everyone under the age of 40 seems to get carded – for entry into nightclubs, in particular – in DC.

Insurance

Non-nationals should arrange baggage, trip-cancellation and medical insurance before they leave home (but first check what your existing home and medical insurance covers). Medical centres will ask for details of your insurance company and policy number if you require treatment, so keep this information with you.

Internet

Libraries (*see p257*) are a good bet if you need a local place to get online for the web or to pick up email. There are also many internet cafés – Kramerbooks (*see p159*) has free email access – and some shops have internet access. Online guide www.cybercafes.com is useful for finding cybercafés worldwide. In addition, your existing ISP may have a Point of Presence (POP) that will let you connect to the internet at local call rates. Alternatively, setting up an account with Compuserve (www.compuserve.com) or AOL (www.aol.com) gives you access to local POPs throughout the US. If all you want to do is access your email while in Washington, but don't want the hassle of setting up a new ISP account, you can set up the 'POP [Post Office Protocol] Mail' feature of Microsoft's free Hotmail (www.hotmail.com) service to fetch your mail instead. You can then access your mail from any computer with an internet connection. Many hotels now have net access via a communal terminal or have rooms with dataports (for facilities at individual hotels, see the Where to Stay chapter on pp42-57).

For a list of useful websites, *see p265*.

Left luggage

All three of the area's major airports (for details, *see p250*) have effectively done away with luggage storage at their facilities in light of the US Homeland Security Department's new regulations following 9/11. The airport may be able to advise you on other facilities available.

Legal help

In the legal capital of the country, more than one person out every seven is a lawyer. If you can't afford a pricey Washington lawyer, stop by the Legal Aid Society of the District of Columbia, where legal aid lawyers can provide free legal assistance.

Legal Aid Society

Suite 800, 666 11th Street, NW, at G Street, Downtown (1-202 628 1161/www.legalaiddc.org). Metro Center Metro. **Open** 9am-7pm Mon; 9am-3pm Tue-Thur. **Map** p284 J6.

Libraries

Washington is a good town for library lovers, as it's home to a range of sites from the Library of Congress to specialised libraries in each Smithsonian museum. Many national and international organisations also have their headquarters in DC, complete with archives. The universities all have excellent libraries and the city maintains a vibrant public library system, with 27 branches, many close to Metro stops.

Martin Luther King Jr Memorial Library

901 G Street, NW, at Ninth Street, Downtown (1-202 727 1111/ www.dclibrary.org). Gallery Place-Chinatown Metro. **Open** 9.30am-9pm Mon-Thur; 9.30am-5.30pm Fri, Sat; 1-5pm Sun. **Map** p285 J6.

Library of Congress

First Street & Independence Avenue, SE, The Capitol & around (operator 1-202 707 5000/public information 1-202 707 8000/www.loc.gov). Capitol South Metro. **Open** varies. **Map** p285 L7.
As the central library for the US, the Library of Congress makes it its business to have a copy of almost

everything printed. However, it may take a very long time to find one small book among the nearly 100 million items on 535 miles of shelves, even when the staff do the search for you. The library is open to the public, but you must first wait in line for a library card and an extensive security check. Take at least one photo ID. Note that opening times vary for the different buildings within the complex. *See also p69*.

University libraries

Opening times for the following vary, so phone before setting off.

American University Bender Library

4400 Massachusetts Avenue, NW, at Nebraska Avenue, Upper Northwest (1-202 885 3200/www.library. american.edu). Tenleytown-AU Metro then M4 bus. **Map** p280 C1.
Full-service university library, good for international affairs, social sciences, art, science and technology, among other subjects.

Catholic University of America Law Library

3600 John McCormack Road, NE, at Michigan Avenue, Northeast (1-202 319 5155/www.law.cua. edu/library). Brookland-CUA Metro. **Map** p283 L1.
Outstanding legal research library.

Georgetown University Lauinger Memorial Library

1421 37th Street, NW, at L Street, Georgetown (1-202 687 7452/ http://gulib.lausun.georgetown.edu). Dupont Circle Metro then G2 bus. **Map** p281 D4.
Comprehensive collections include colonial and American Catholic history, and intelligence and covert activities. A medical library and law library are also on the campus. Photo ID is required.

University of Maryland-College Park Libraries

College Park Campus, Baltimore Avenue, College Park, MD (1-301 405 0800/www.lib.umd.edu). College Park Metro then C2, C8 bus. Six libraries and special collections, including historic preservation, National Public Broadcasting archives and East Asia collection.

Lost property

If you leave something on the bus or subway, chances are you won't see it again, but you could try calling the **Washington Metro Transit**

Authority Lost & Found on 1-202 962 1195 or submitting a claim online at www.wmata.com. It's also worth checking at the nearest police station to see if it's been handed in.

Media

The conventional wisdom as the new century dawned was that affluent mainstream Americans had become less inquisitive and more complacent and unconcerned about what happens in Europe, Asia and even their own country, but the twin spectres of terrorism and war have changed that outlook somewhat. But then, complacency was never the order of the day in Washington itself, which consumes news as avidly as it produces it.

This is the one US city where many people actually watch the political chat shows run every Sunday by the main TV networks and offered every day by the growing ranks of cable news channels – notably, the abrasive, right-wing Fox News cable channel, which has been winning viewers at the expense of such polite operations as CNN (now part of Washington's multimedia superpower AOL Time Warner). There's even a local radio station that carries an audio version of the C-SPAN cable channel's Congressional coverage (WCSP, 90.1 FM; *see also p258* SPAN-ing the country).

With all the major American news organisations and many foreign ones in residence in DC, news crews are a common sight around town. Reporters can be spied doing 'stand-ups' in front of many official buildings, most frequently the White House and the Capitol. Newsmakers frequently appear at the **National Press Club** (13th Floor, 529 14th Street, NW; 1 202 662 7500, http:// npc.press.org), although only some of these events are open to the public.

Newspapers & magazines

Dailies

The Godzilla of local print journalism is the **Washington Post**, whose clout is the object of some awe and much resentment. Nonetheless, the *Post* has the highest market penetration of any major US daily, although its executives fret, with reason, that its power is waning with younger Washingtonians. The *Post*'s coverage exemplifies the inside-the-Beltway mentality, with heavy emphasis on politics and policy and a poorly concealed scepticism that anything else really matters. By the standards of US newspapers, international coverage is strong, and over recent years the paper has greatly expanded its coverage of business and technology because of the local high-tech sector's rapid growth. By contrast, genuinely local news and the arts are often treated with indifference. On Fridays, however, the *Post* publishes its 'Weekend' section, with extensive arts and entertainment listings. This, along with the *Washington City Paper* (*see below*), is what most Washingtonians turn to for current entertainment information.

Owned by cronies of the Rev Sun Myung Moon, the **Washington Times** offers an extreme-right view of events, with front-page stories that are often amusingly partisan. Although some commend its sports coverage, the paper is read principally by paleo-conservatives and people who really, really hate the *Post*. Although its locally printed copies offer little that's designed specifically for Washingtonians, the **New York Times** has a significant DC readership. The paper is most popular on Sundays, when its arts and feature writing trounces the *Post*'s. Most large US newspapers

are available in local street boxes, but only the **Los Angeles Times** prints a special daily DC edition. **USA Today**, the country's only national general-interest daily, is produced at Tysons Corner, Virginia, but its terse stories, graphics-heavy presentation and middle-American mindset are not much to local taste.

Weeklies

Geographical or cultural subdivisions of the metropolitan area are served by many weekly tabloids, including some suburban ones owned by the *Post*, but the only such weekly of regional significance is **Washington City Paper**. Founded in 1981 and owned by the Chicago Reader, this 'alternative' free weekly has softened its approach in recent years. Although it covers local politics, the paper is read mostly for its arts coverage, listings and adverts.

The **New Republic**, a longtime liberal journal that in the 1980s became 'neo-liberal', has shifted a bit back towards the left recently. Its most recognisable voice, however, is that of British-born gay conservative Andrew Sullivan.

His feisty website – well worth a look – can be found at www.andrewsullivan.com.

Roll Call and **The Hill** compete for the small but influential readership that makes national policy in the Capitol and its adjacent office buildings. These tabloids occasionally break major stories, but to outsiders most of the coverage will seem arcane.

The District's gay community is served by the weekly **Washington Blade**, which is a good source of local and national news on the gay and lesbian scene. More comprehensive, though, is **MW** (Metro Weekly), which includes listings for bars, clubs, guest DJ spots and parties. It also takes a more gossipy, dishy tone than the *Blade*. Both are free and readily available.

Monthlies

The **Washingtonian** is professional but seldom provocative, except in its coverage of the *Post*. It specialises in service journalism and tepid profiles, pitched to an overwhelmingly suburban readership.

SPAN-ing the country

Politics matter, but not everyone wants to spend all their time in DC checking out the interiors of Congress and seeing senators in the flesh. As is often the case in the US, television has come to the rescue. Your very best guide to Washington's corridors of power may be a deceptively placid but obviously extremely intelligent man named Brian Lamb. It was Lamb who, in the late 1970s, conceived the idea of making the machinery of democracy transparent to the American public via real-time, uninterrupted, commentary-free broadcast of the proceedings of the US House of Representatives. Lamb prevailed on the burgeoning cable television industry to commit to funding the enterprise as a public service and, in March 1979, C-SPAN (Cable-Satellite Public Affairs Network) turned one camera on the proceedings of the House and sent it out over the wires to an audience of 3.5 million households.

The legislative branch stood revealed in all its scriptless mundanity, like an early Warhol film. But the effect was mesmerising: the trivia; the painful humanity; the empty floor to which, for the most part, the majority of elected representatives address their remarks (most legislative work being done

in the offices and meeting rooms of Capitol Hill – rendering floor proceedings nothing more than a formality).

But it was real, and true, and word spread among the hard-core political junkies of America that uncut DC was there to be seen. Now reaching over 60 million households, the original channel has grown to include C-SPAN 2 (which covers the Senate as opposed to the House of Representatives) and C-SPAN 3 (which has a more literary and historical bent to its coverage), C-SPAN Radio and elaborate webcasting. Virtually every television cable service in the country now carries at least one C-SPAN channel.

The organisation's offerings have expanded to include live Senate debates (in 1986), leading to highlights like gavel-to-gavel coverage of the Gulf War resolution of 1991 and the acrimonious Clarence Thomas Supreme Court nomination hearings later that year. Much the same coverage can also be found on networks like CNN and MSNBC, but C-SPAN's determinedly deadpan, point-the-camera-and-let-it-run style continues to set it apart.

For viewing information call 1-765 464 3080, or go to www.c-span.org.

Directory

Two locally published magazines with global agendas are **National Geographic** and **Smithsonian**, which are circulated to members of their respective organisations and are also sold at newsstands. Their articles on science, history and other subjects of enduring importance – and National Geographic's exceptional photography – exemplify the side of DC that is not consumed by the latest poll numbers.

A pioneering 'neo-liberal' policy journal, the **Washington Monthly** was once known as much for grooming young journalists as for anticipating Washington policy shifts, but these days it is little-read.

Among the monthlies devoted to arts and entertainment, *One* covers dance clubs, fashion and upscale dining; the **Washington Diplomat** chronicles the international set, and **On Tap** is intoxicated by beer and places to drink it.

Outlets

Washington has more newspaper and magazine outlets than you might at first think. Many large office buildings have newsstands, often concealed in their lobbies so that only workers and regular visitors are aware of them. Outdoor newsstands (along with sidewalk cafés) were illegal in Washington for much of the 20th century, and since the ban was lifted in the 1960s most attempts to establish them have failed – which explains why the sidewalks at major intersections are overwhelmed by newspaper vending machines.

Among the larger newsstands – and the ones with the best selection of foreign publications – are the **Newsroom** (1803 Connecticut Avenue, NW), **News World** (1001 Connecticut Avenue, NW) and **Metro Center News** (1200 G Street, NW). The city's numerous **Borders** and **Barnes & Noble** outlets (*see p156*) have extensive periodical selections; **Tower Records** (2000 Pennsylvania Avenue, NW, Foggy Bottom; 1-202 331 2400) has the best choice of music and youth-culture titles.

Television

Washington's airwaves carry all the usual suspects: **NBC** (WRC, Channel 4); **Fox** (WTTG, Channel 5); **ABC** (WJLA, Channel 7); **CBS** (WUSA, Channel 9); **UPN** (WDCA, Channel 20) and **WB** (WBDC, Channel 50). These offer the familiar sitcoms, cop and hospital dramas, and growing numbers (because they're cheap to produce) of news magazine shows. The local news programmes on Washington's commercial TV outlets are supposedly less lurid than in most American cities, although that's

hard to imagine. There are also three local public TV stations featuring the customary line-up of *Sesame Street*, British drawing-room dramas and highlights from Riverdance: WMPT (Channel 22), WETA (Channel 26) and WHUT (Channel 32). The latter also runs some Spanish-language shows, while a fourth public station, WNVC (Channel 56), specialises in international programming, from classic Japanese films to the day's news in Mandarin, Polish and French.

On cable, the fare is also commonplace, although it varies sightly among local jurisdictions. National channels based in Washington include **BET** (Black Entertainment Television) and the **Discovery Channel**, as well as the latter's documentary offspring – Animal Planet, the Learning Channel and the History Channel. Washingtonians watch more C-SPAN (*see p258* **SPAN-ing the country**) and C-SPAN 2 (with live coverage of Congress and other public affairs programming) than most Americans; channels seen only locally include the extensive local news coverage of **NewsChannel 8**.

Radio

The current world climate demands that visitors to Washington remain in touch with news and information, and the easiest way to do that is by tuning to the city's excellent all-news station, **WTOP** (available on 820 and 1500 AM, and 107.7FM), which also offers traffic and weather updates every ten minutes. Beyond that, the city is upscale, urban and has a large African American population, so local radio stations play more classical and hip hop and less country music than in most parts of the US. Since the Federal Communication Commission weakened regulations restricting the number of stations that could be owned by large corporations, however, regional diversity in US radio programming is dwindling. Increasingly, stations are tightly formatted to attract a chosen demographic, often with a carefully test-marketed subset of oldies: 'classic rock' (**WARW**, 94.7 FM), 'big oldies' (**WBIG**, 100.3 FM) and 'urban' oldies (**WMMJ**, 102.3 FM). Formerly a pioneering 'underground' and then 'alternative' rock outlet, **WHFS** (99.1 FM) is now as tightly (and unadventurously) programmed as the 'album rock' of **WWDC** (101.1 FM) or the 'hot adult contemporary' of **WRQX** (107.3 FM). 'Urban contemporary' (hip hop and soul) music is heard on **WKYS** (93.9 FM), **WPGC** (95.5 FM) and **WHUR** (96.3 FM). Of the three, WPGC is the

rowdiest, while WHUR goes for a somewhat older audience. The leading Top 40 station is **WWVZ** (103.9 FM); its new rival is **WIHT** (99.5 FM). **WGMS** (103.5 FM) is the city's commercial classical station. The top two public radio stations, **WETA** (90.9 FM) and **WAMU** (88.5 FM), broadcast much of the news and arts programming of Washington-based **National Public Radio** (NPR). The former also plays classical music; the latter offers public-affairs talk shows and weekend folk and bluegrass music. The once-radical **WPFW** (89.3 FM) still mixes jazz and politics, but has become tamer.

College radio, a free-form catalyst in many markets, is insignificant here; the University of Maryland's **WMUC** (88.1 FM) can be received only in the north-eastern suburbs.

Washington is also the home of **XM**, the country's first digital satellite radio service. It broadcasts 100 channels of CD-quality music programming for those who have purchased the special receivers.

Money

As elsewhere in the US, credit cards are virtually a necessity in Washington. If you want to rent a car or book a ticket over the phone, you will need a major credit card. They are accepted almost universally in hotels, restaurants and shops, though occasionally you will find a gas station, small store or cinema that only takes cash. Visa and MasterCard are the most widely accepted cards, with American Express a distant third. Credit cards are also useful for extracting instantaneous cash advances from ATMs and banks. However, where US account holders pay a flat service charge for getting cash this way, UK companies' charges vary – and you pay interest, of course.

The cost of a holiday in DC compares favourably with other US destinations because there are few admission charges to pay at museums and galleries. Out of season, accommodation can be cheap too.

ATMs

Automated Teller Machines are located outside nearly all banks, inside all malls and major shopping areas and now in many bars and restaurants. They are the most convenient and often the most cost-effective way of obtaining cash – but remember that most charge at least a $2 service fee on top of any charges levied by your home bank,

Directory

so don't withdraw small increments throughout the day. All you need is an ATM card (credit or debit) – and your usual PIN number. Check with your bank before leaving home to find out if they are linked to any DC banks and what the fees will be.

Banks

The following branches are central.

Bank of America

1501 Pennsylvania Avenue, NW, at 15th Street, The White House & around (1-202 624 4253). McPherson Square Metro. **Open** 9am-3pm Mon-Thur; 9am-7pm Fri. **Map** p284 H6.

Riggs National Bank

1503 Pennsylvania Avenue, NW, at 15th Street, The White House & around (1-301 887 6000 for all locations). McPherson Square Metro. **Open** 9am-3pm Mon-Thur; 9am-5pm Fri. **Map** p284 H6.
The best branch for foreign exchange.

Currency

The United States' monetary system is decimal-based: the US dollar ($) is divided into 100 cents (¢). Coins and dollars are stamped with the faces of US presidents and statesmen. Coin denominations are the penny (1¢ – Abraham Lincoln on a copper-coloured coin); nickel (5¢ – Thomas Jefferson); dime (10¢ – Franklin D Roosevelt); quarter (25¢ – George Washington); the less common half-dollar (50¢ – John F Kennedy) and the 'golden' dollar (depicting Sacagawea, a Native American woman who acted as a guide to 19th-century explorers Lewis and Clark). You may also come across the smaller 'Susan B Anthony' dollar coin, a failed attempt to introduce dollar coins.

Bills, or notes, are all the same size and come in $1 (George Washington); $5 (Abraham Lincoln); $10 (Alexander Hamilton); $20 (Andrew Jackson); $50 (Ulysses S Grant); and $100 (Benjamin Franklin) denominations.

The US Mint recently changed the look of the bills; both old and new bills are in circulation and are valid. Older bills have smaller portraits, while newer ones have bigger, more cartoonish portraits.

Exchange

Some – but not many – banks will exchange cash or travellers' cheques in major foreign currencies. The most convenient place to exchange money is the airport when you first arrive – but banks will often give better rates.

Travelex, American Express and Thomas Cook (5335 Wisconsin Avenue, NW, 1-202 237-2229) also exchange currency and sell travellers' cheques. Most hotel desks will do the same thing – handy if you're stuck late at night. You can also use travellers' cheques as payment in shops and restaurants, which seldom ask for ID (though banks and exchange offices do).

American Express

1150 Connecticut Avenue, NW, between L & M Streets, Downtown (1-202 457 1300). Farragut North Metro. **Open** 9am-5.30pm Mon-Fri. **Map** p284 G5.
Call 1-800 721 9768 for purchase or refund of travellers' cheques.

Travelex

1800 K Street, NW, at 18th Street, Foggy Bottom (1-202 872 1428/ www.us.thomascook.com). Farragut North Metro. **Open** 9am-5pm Mon-Fri. **Map** p284 G5.
Also has branches at Union Station; at the corner of 14th and I Streets; and Dulles and National airports. The central number is 1-800 287 7362.

International networks

Cirrus/MasterCard (1-800 424 7787) and Plus/Visa (1-800 843 7587) are also linked, respectively, to Maestro and Delta, which let the card function as a debit card to pay for goods and services. Credit and debit cards can be used in ATMs (call the above numbers to find out your nearest), but only debit cards can be used to get cash back when making a purchase.

Lost/stolen

In the event of a lost or stolen card, call the company immediately to deactivate it and also to request a replacement. Travellers' cheques can be replaced via a local office.
American Express cards *1-800 528 4800.*
American Express travellers' cheques *1-800 221 7282.*
Diners Club *1-800 234 6377.*
Discover *1-800 347 2683.*
MasterCard *1-800 307 7309.*
Thomas Cook travellers' cheques *1-800 223 7373.*
Visa *1-800 336 8472.*

Tax

The general consumer DC sales tax is 5.75 per cent; it's five per cent in Maryland and 4.5 per cent in Virginia. The tax on restaurant meals is ten per cent and is added later to the advertised menu price, while the tax on hotel and motel rooms is 14.5 per cent.

In general, business hours in DC are 9am to 5pm Monday to Friday. Most shops are open 10am to 5 or 6pm Monday to Saturday and noon to 6pm on Sunday. Even in the business-heavy downtown area, most shops are open at the weekend. From Monday to Saturday, mall stores usually stay open until 9pm. On the whole, banks open at 9am and close at about 3pm on weekdays only. Restaurants are usually open for lunch from 11am to 2pm and for dinner from 5 to 10pm, but many are open all day. In Adams Morgan, Georgetown and Dupont Circle, some bars and eateries don't close until 2 or 3am.

Police

There are three main phone numbers you should know in case you need to reach the police. The first number, **911**, is used in cases of emergencies: for instance, if a crime is in progress or has just occurred, and also if you see a fire or medical emergency or a major vehicle crash; it is also the number for violent crimes.

The police non-emergency number, **311**, is for minor vehicle crashes, property crimes that are no longer in progress, and animal control problems. If you have a need for any other city service, call 1-202 727 1000.

Postal services

Post offices are found throughout the city; call 1-202 635 5300 or check the phone book to find your nearest. They are usually open 8am-5pm on weekdays; some open for limited hours on Saturdays. Mail can be sent from any of the big blue mailboxes on street corners, but if you are sending a package overseas that is heavier than 16oz, it must be sent directly from a post office and accompanied by a customs form. **Thomas Cook** and **American Express** (for both, *see above*) provide a postal service for their clients.

National Capitol Station Post Office

City Post Office Building, North Capitol Street & Massachusetts Avenue, NE, Union Station & around (1-202 523 2628). Union Station Metro. **Open** 7am-midnight Mon-Fri; 7am-8pm Sat, Sun. **Credit** AmEx, MC, V. **Map** p285 K6.

General Mail Facility

900 Brentwood Road, NE, at New York Avenue, Northeast (1-202 635 5300). Rhode Island Avenue Metro.

New passport regulations

All travellers entering the United States under the Visa Waiver Program must present a machine-readable passport (MRP), which has been the standard issue (burgundy) passport in the UK since 1988. However, at some point in the future, all visitors to the US will be required to present a passport with a biometric identifier (a microchip encoded with information such as fingerprints). The deadline for this requirement was, at the time of writing, under review. At a congressional hearing on 21 April 2004, the State Department lobbied for a two-year postponement of the original deadline, which stated that any passport issued after 26 October 2004 would require a biometric identifier. Call your nearest US Embassy or check http://unitedstates visas.gov or www.travel.state.gov/vwp.html for a final decision.

Meanwhile, all Visa Waiver Program travellers should expect to have their fingerprints scanned and have a digital photo taken when they arrive. This extra measure is supposed to add just 15 seconds to the arrival process, but queue times have increased. Also, children can no longer travel on their parents' passports.

Travellers who need a visa for the US and are travelling after 26 October 2004 will need to submit biometric data for an identifier, which will be added to their visa. Allow plenty of time – up to three months – for visa applications to be processed.

Open 8am-8pm Mon-Fri; 8am-6pm Sat; 10.30am-6pm Sun. **Credit** AmEx, MC, V.
The main postal facility, but quite a way from downtown. A letter sent Poste Restante will end up here; better to have it sent to a specific post office (you'll need the zip code). Mail is held 30 days.

Religion

As you might expect in the nation's capital, there is a diverse mix of people in Washington, from all religions. Many of the following keep irregular hours, so it's best to call first before setting off.

Adas Israel Congregation

2850 Quebec Street, NW, Cleveland Park (1-202 362 4433/ www.adasisrael.org). Cleveland Park Metro. **Map** p281 F1.
Conservative Jewish.

Basilica of the National Shrine of the Immaculate Conception

400 Michigan Avenue, NE, at Fourth Street, Northeast (1-202 526 8300/ www.nationalshrine.com). Brookland-CUA Metro. **Map** p283 L1.
The biggest Catholic church in the western hemisphere. *See also p208.*

Foundry Methodist Church

1500 16th Street, NW, at P Street, Dupont Circle (1-202 332 4010/ www.foundryumc.org). Dupont Circle Metro. **Map** p282 H4.

Islamic Center

2551 Massachusetts Avenue, NW, at Belmont Road, Kalorama, Adams Morgan (1-202 332 8343). Dupont Circle Metro then N2, N4, N6 bus. **Map** p282 F3.

New York Avenue Presbyterian Church

1313 New York Avenue, NW, between 13th & 14th Streets, Downtown (1-202 393 3700/ www.nyapc.org). McPherson Square Metro. **Map** p284 H5.

St John's Episcopal Church

1525 H Street, NW, opposite Lafayette Square, The White House & around (1-202 347 8766/ www.stjohns-dc.org). McPherson Square Metro. **Map** p284 H5.

St Matthew's Cathedral

1725 Rhode Island Avenue, NW, between Connecticut Avenue & 17th Street, Dupont Circle (1-202 347 3215). Farragut North Metro. **Map** p284 G5.
Roman Catholic.

Washington Hebrew Congregation

3935 Macomb Street, NW, at Massachusetts Avenue, Cleveland Park (1-202 362 7100/www.whc temple.org). Cleveland Park Metro. **Map** p281 D1.
Reformed Jewish.

Washington National Cathedral

Massachusetts & Wisconsin Avenues, NW, Upper Northwest (1-202 537 6200/www.cathedral.org/ cathedral). Bus 30, 32, 34, 35, 36. **Map** p281 E2.
Episcopal. *See also p88.*

Safety & security

Apart from the large-scale security concerns and restrictions that come from being the capital of the United States, the areas of DC that are notorious for crime are parts of the Southeast and Northeast quadrants plus pockets of the Northwest, mostly east of 16th Street and north of Columbia Road, far from the main (and even most of the secondary) tourist sights. The threat of crime near the major visitor destinations is minuscule. The area around the Capitol is very heavily policed, and Metro trains and stations are also well-patrolled and virtually crime-free. Adams Morgan and the U Street/14th Street Corridor are much too heavy with traffic to be considered dangerous (the panhandlers are mostly harmless; feel free to ignore them), but the sidestreets surrounding them can be dodgy after dark, as can some streets near Union Station and around Capitol Hill. Stick to the heavily populated, well-lit thoroughfares when walking in these areas at night. Generally, as in any big city, you should take the usual security precautions. Be wary of pickpockets, especially in crowds. Look like you know what you're

Directory

doing and where you're going – even if you don't. Use common sense and follow your intuition about people and situations. If someone does approach you for money in a threatening manner, don't resist. Hand over your wallet, then dial 911 or hail a cab and ask the driver to take you to the nearest police station where you can report the theft and get a reference number to claim insurance and travellers' cheque refunds.

Smoking

Fewer and fewer people in the US smoke, and DC is no exception. It is illegal to smoke on public transport, in public buildings, theatres, cinemas, restaurants (except in designated smoking areas) and most shops. If you want to smoke, best to go outside.

In 2002 Montgomery County Council in Maryland followed the example set by California and voted to ban all smoking in bars and restaurants.

Study

While not a full-blown university town like Boston, DC does have its share of colleges and universities. The major ones are listed below, but there are many smaller institutions, branch universities and schools in suburban Virginia and Maryland. Most of these schools conduct summer courses in politics, international relations and other programmes directly relating to the city's weighty political scene. For libraries, see p257.

American University

4400 Massachusetts Avenue, NW, at Nebraska Avenue, Upper Northwest (1-202 885 1000/www.american. edu). Tenleytown-AU Metro then M4 bus. **Map** p280 C1.
Over 11,000 students attend this university in residential Washington. It has strong arts and sciences programmes, and a law library.

Catholic University of America

620 Michigan Avenue, NE, at Harewood Road, Northeast (1-202 319 5000/www.cua.edu). Brookland-CUA Metro. **Map** p283 K2.
Catholic University received a papal charter in 1887. Its diverse programmes include architecture, engineering and law.

Georgetown University

37th & O Streets, NW, Georgetown (1-202 687 0100/www.georgetown. edu). Dupont Circle Metro then G2 bus. **Map** p281 D4.
Georgetown attracts students from all over the world to its prestigious international relations, business, medical and law schools.

George Washington University

1 & 22nd Streets, NW, Foggy Bottom (1-202 994 1000/www.gwu.edu). Foggy Bottom-GWU Metro.
Map p284 G5.
GWU houses law and medical schools and has strong programmes in politics and international affairs.

Howard University

2400 Sixth Street, NW, at Georgia Avenue, Shaw (1-202 806 6100/
www.howard.edu). Shaw-Howard University Metro. **Map** p283 J2.
About 10,000 students attend this predominantly African American university, studying medicine, engineering, dentistry, social work and communications.

University of the District of Columbia

4200 Connecticut Avenue, NW, at Van Ness Street, Upper Northwest (1-202 274 5000/www.udc.edu). Van Ness-UDC Metro.
UDC was formed in 1974 as a land-grant institution with an open admissions policy. Not as prestigious as most of its neighbours, it nonetheless has a variety of programmes, including arts, sciences and law.

Telephones

Dialling & codes

The area code for DC is 202. To make a call within the District, you need only dial the seven-digit local number, not the 202 area code.

Maryland and Virginia are more complicated. The area codes for the city of Alexandria and the counties of Arlington and Fairfax in Virginia are 1-703 and 1-571. In Maryland, Prince George's County and Montgomery County both use 1-301 and 1-240 area codes. Calls from any one of these area codes to another, as well as within one area code, are classed as local, but you must dial the area code, even if you're dialling from DC. Some calls are treated as local, others long distance. Non-Washingtonians will probably not know which is

On the alert

Following the September 11, 2001 terrorist attacks on New York and the Pentagon, the Department of Homeland Security devised a five-tier system known as the Homeland Security Advisory System for assessing potential terror threats and communicating the level of caution the public needs to observe. The suggested procedures apply mainly to law-enforcement officials, although the public is asked to take notice of the advice and respond with common sense. As with any city at any time, if you spot someone or something that looks odd, speak up.

The levels are as follows: **Green**, meaning there's a low risk of an attack; people are urged know where they can take shelter in

an emergency. **Blue** (Guarded Risk) advises that you should be watchful of dodgy activity (as ever) and keep your emergency supplies (drinking water, non-perishable food) up to date. **Yellow** (Elevated Risk) is the commonest default level, and means you should have a Plan B for coming or going anywhere in case routes are blocked. **Orange** (High Risk) warns of delays entering public buildings and transport systems while people and their baggage are inspected. **Red** (Severe Risk) means an attack is imminent or under way. Roads and entire areas may be declared off-limits. You should tune to the news and stay put in a secure place and execute your emergency plans.

which, but you will always get through by dialling the '1' first, and if it is a local call you will only be charged for a local rate. For this reason we have included the 1 prefix before all numbers.

Numbers to other parts of the US always require the 1 prefix before the area code. This is also the case for numbers beginning 1-800, 1-888 and 1-877, which are all toll free within the US, though note that your hotel may still bill you a flat fee. Most are also accessible from outside DC and – at the usual international rates – from outside the US.

Public phones

Yes, even in an age when it's not possible to go a block without seeing someone with a mobile phone pressed to their ear, there are still public pay phones in DC. To use a public phone, pick up the receiver, listen for a dial tone and feed it change (35¢ for a local call). The operator is free, as is directory assistance on a Verizon phone (other companies may charge 35¢). If you use a payphone for long distance or international calls, use a phonecard (available at supermarkets, drugstores and convenience stores everywhere) or calling card. Otherwise, you will need a lot of change – a quarter is the highest denomination a payphone will accept. After you dial the number a recorded voice will tell you how much you need to put in. Some payphones, especially at airports and big hotels, accept credit cards.

Most hotels charge a flat fee of 50¢-$1 for telephone calls – including local and even toll-free calls – which can quickly add up. You can get round this at some hotels by using a house phone and asking the operator to connect you to your number. Alternatively, look for payphones, usually located in the lobby or near the restrooms. If you need to make a long-distance or international call, you will often have to leave a cash deposit or credit card at the hotel desk. The rates will be high, however, so you are better off using a phonecard.

MCI WorldCom (1-800 265 5328) lets you use MasterCard. American Express or Discover. Brits will find it is cheaper to do this to call home than to use their own domestic phone chargecard (eg BT Chargecard).

Operators & assistance

For local directory assistance within the DC metro area, dial 411. For national long-distance enquiries, dial 1 + [area code] + 555 1212 (if you don't know the area code, dial

0 for the operator). For international calls, dial 011 then the country code (UK 44; New Zealand 64; Australia 61 – see the phone book for others). For collect (reverse charge) calls, dial 0 for the operator.

If you use voicemail, note that the pound key is the one marked # and the star key is *. On automated answering systems, 0 often gets you to a real-life operator.

Mobile phone rental

US readers with mobile phones should contact their mobile phone operators about using their phone in Washington. All five UK mobile phone operators have roaming agreements with major US operators, so, in theory, you should be able to use your mobile in Washington. In practice, though, it's not quite that simple (unless you have a tri-band phone, in which case you need only ask your operator to enable their phone's roaming ability). The US uses a different frequency for its digital mobiles than most of the rest of the world, so single- or even dual-band European phones won't work there.

There are two basic solutions to this problem. The first is to rent a US-compatible phone (either in the UK or the US) and put the SIM card from your UK mobile into it. The second solution is to rent a phone in Washington, with an airtime contract. You don't get to use your UK number, but the call charges should be a lot less. For information on local cellular rental, try InTouch USA (www.intouchusa.com), which features next-day Washington-area delivery or check the *Yellow Pages* under 'Cellular Telephone Equipment & Supplies'. The following UK mobile operators have roaming information on their websites:

O2 (in UK: 08705 678 678/ www.o2.co.uk).
Orange (in UK: 07973 100 150/ www.orange.co.uk).
3 (in UK: 0870 733 0333/ www.three.co.uk).
T-Mobile (in UK: 0845 412 5000/ www.tmobile.co.uk).
Vodafone (in UK: pay monthly 0870 070 0191/pay as you talk 0870 077 6655/www.vodafone.co.uk).

Time

Washington, DC, operates on Eastern Standard Time (the same time zone as New York and Miami), which is five hours behind Greenwich Mean Time (London) and three hours ahead of Pacific Standard Time (Los Angeles). Clocks go forward one hour on the first Sunday in April to daylight saving time and back one

hour on the last Sunday in October. To find out the exact time, call 1-202 844 2525.

Tipping

Cab drivers and waiters are generally tipped 20 per cent – more for exceptionally good service. Bartenders expect 50¢-$1 per drink. Hairdressers get ten per cent, bellhops $1 per bag and hotel maids $1-$2 per day.

Toilets

Malls, museums, bookstores and some grocery stores have toilets; clothes shops almost always do not. In restaurants you may have to buy a drink in order to use them.

Tourist information

Brits can call the Washington DC Convention & Tourism Corporation's London outpost on 020 8877 4521 for an information pack, or the Capital Region Brochure Line on 01234 767928.

Like other US cities, Washington employs street cleaners who are also versed in essential information for visitors – look out for them at the main sights, highly visible in their red or gold jackets.

Washington DC Convention & Tourism Corporation

4th Floor, 901 Seventh Street, NW, at I Street, Downtown (1-202 789 7000/www.washington.org). Metro Center Metro. **Open** 9am-5pm Mon-Fri. **Map** p285 J5.
A good starting point for information.

DC Chamber of Commerce Visitor Information Center

Ronald Reagan Building & International Trade Center, 1300 Pennsylvania Avenue, NW, between 13th & 14th Streets, The Federal Triangle (1-202 328 4748/ www.dcvisit.com). Federal Triangle Metro. **Open** 8.30am-5.30pm Mon-Sat. **Map** p284 H6.
Tonnes of information and advice.

International Visitors Information Service

Meridian International Center, 1630 Crescent Place, NW, at 16th Street, Adams Morgan (1-202 667 6800). U Street/African-American Civil War Memorial/Cardozo Metro. **Open** 9am-5pm Mon-Fri. **Map** p282 H3.

Directory

Brochures, maps and resources for international visitors, including a 'language bank' (for translations) with 42 languages (1-202 939 5538).

Local weather
1-202 936 1212.

National Park Service
1-202 426 6841/www.nps.gov.

Smithsonian information
1-202 357 2700.
Information on all the Smithsonian's museums.

Traveler's Aid
1-703 773 6361/ www.travelersaid.org.
Network of travel support, with locations at Union Station, and National and Dulles airports.

Visas & immigration

If you are a citizen of the UK, Ireland, Australia, New Zealand, Japan or most western European countries (check with your local US embassy or consulate), have proof of intent to leave (such as a return plane ticket) and are visiting the US for less than 90 days, you need only a valid passport and visa waiver form (*see p255*) to enter the country. Canadians and Mexicans do not need visas but must have legal proof of their residency and valid identification. Citizens of other countries or people who are staying for longer than 90 days or who need a work or study visa should contact their nearest US consulate or embassy well before the date of travel (note that visitors

requiring visas will also have to submit biometric data; for details *see p261* **New passport regulations**).

The US embassy in London has a recorded message service (020 7499 9000) for all general visa enquiries. The website (www.usembassy.org.uk) also has information. Also see www.visafaqs.com.

When to go

The best time to visit Washington is autumn, avoiding the humidity and heat of summer and the colder winter weather. April is, in theory, a lovely time to come – early in the month, the cherry blossoms are in flower at the Tidal Basin. However, it's also DC's busiest month for tourism. In autumn, the trees turn brilliant shades of orange, red and yellow, and the weather is pleasant. Perhaps most importantly, the massive crowds of tourists are scarcer in autumn than in mid summer. If you do visit in summer, be sure to drink plenty of water so you don't get dehydrated, and start sightseeing early in the day to avoid long lines in the heat. Daytime summer temperatures average 86°F (30.2°C) but feel hotter because of the high humidity; aim to be inside an air-conditioned building at midday. Winters are fairly mild, but even a light snowfall can bring the city to a standstill. Don't be surprised if there are long periods of bitter weather and occasionally heavy snow. Otherwise, winter days can be bright and clear, even warm in the direct sun.

If you want to see government in action, remember that in addition to Christmas and Easter breaks, Congress is in recess during August and the Supreme Court from May to September.

National holidays

New Year's Day (1 January); **Martin Luther King Jr Day** (third Monday in January); **Presidents Day** (third Monday in February); **Memorial Day** (last Monday in May); **Independence Day** (4 July); **Labor Day** (first Monday in September); **Columbus Day** (second Monday in October); **Election Day** (first Tuesday in November); **Veterans Day** (11 November); **Thanksgiving Day** (fourth Thursday in November); **Christmas Day** (25 December).

Women

Women travelling alone inevitably face more safety concerns than men or women in groups. Washington is no different from any other big city so take the usual precautions. Many men interpret a woman sitting alone in a bar as a woman wanting to be picked up. If you'd rather be alone, answer any advances with a firm but polite 'no'.

Local contacts

National Organization for Women
2nd Floor, 733 15th Street, NW, at H Street, Downtown (1-202 628 8669/www.now.org). McPherson Square Metro. **Open** 9am-5pm Mon-Fri. **Map** p284 H5.
Plenty of information on a variety of issues. Can refer women travellers to rape crisis centres and counselling services and provide lists of feminist events. Its members are very active liberals in the political scene.

Average monthly climate

Month	Max (°F/°C)	Min (°F/°C)	Rainfall Inches/cm	Humidity %
Jan	42/5.6	26/–3.4	2.7/6.9	62
Feb	45/7.3	27/–2.8	2.7/6.9	60
Mar	56/13.4	37/2.8	3.2/8.1	59
Apr	66/19	46/7.8	2.7/6.9	58
May	76/24.6	56/13.4	3.7/9.4	64
Jun	84/29.1	66/19	3.8/9.6	66
July	88/31.3	71/25.2	3.8/9.6	67
Aug	86/30.2	70/21.2	3.9/9.9	69
Sep	80/26.9	62/16.8	3.3/8.4	70
Oct	69/20.7	50/10.1	3.0/7.6	67
Nov	58/14.5	41/5	3.1/7.9	65
Dec	47/8.4	31/–0.56	3.1/7.9	64

Directory

Further Reference

Books

Non-fiction

Dance of Days
Mark Andersen & Mark Jenkins
Two decades of punk in DC.

All the President's Men
Carl Bernstein & Bob Woodward
The story behind the Watergate scandal.

Washington Goes to War
David Brinkley
The history of Washington during World War II.

Lies and the Lying Liars That Tell Them
Al Franken
The left-wing's new poster boy examines the 'rhetoric of the Right'.

Personal History
Katherine Graham
The autobiography of the erstwhile publisher of the *Washington Post*.

Dream City: Race, Power and the Decline of Washington, DC
Harry Jaffe & Tom Sherwood
An in-depth look at how race and power-lust corrupted local politics.

The Beat
Kip Lornell & Charles Stephenson, Jr
Go-go's fusion of funk and hip hop, DC's music.

Parliament of Whores
PJ O'Rourke
America's most scabrous commentator gets to grips with the US political system, as practised in Washington.

George W Bushisms: The Slate Book of the Accidental Wit and Wisdom of Our 43nd President
Jacob Weisberg
Self-explanatory.

Plan of Attack
Bob Woodward
The inside story of the George W Bush administration's planning for the 2003 invasion of Iraq, by the famous reporter.

Shadow: Five Presidents & the Legacy of Watergate
Bob Woodward
Though-provoking bestseller on how the Watergate affair affected subsequent presidential scandals.

Fiction

Thank You for Smoking
Christopher Buckley
Send-up of TV pundits and political special-interest groups.

Echo House
Ward Just
The story of three generations of a powerful Washington family, written by a former *Washington Post* reporter.

The Tenth Justice
Brad Meltzer
Bestselling thriller based on the travails of an ambitious young clerk to a Supreme Court justice.

Murder in the Map Room (and other titles)
Elliott Roosevelt
Series of White House murder mysteries written by FDR's son, with First Lady Eleanor Roosevelt as the problem-solving sleuth.

Empire
Gore Vidal
A historical novel based on Theodore Roosevelt's Washington, Vidal's epic brings America during the Gilded Age into vivid focus.

Drum-Taps
Walt Whitman
Whitman's war poems were directly influenced by his work in Civil War hospitals in Washington.

Reference

The Guide to Black Washington
Sandra Fitzpatrick & Maria R Goodwin
Places and events of significance to DC's African American heritage.

Buildings of the District of Columbia
Pamela Scott & Antoinette J Lee
Detailed architectural history of DC, from the Revolutionary War to post-World War II, with photos, drawings and maps.

AIA Guide to the Architecture of Washington, DC
Christopher Weeks
Concise descriptions and photos of DC's most notable structures, including 100 built since the mid '70s.

Film & television

Though there are other shows set in DC, it's the Emmy Award-winning *The West Wing* that has taken centre stage. The show follows the daily life of fictitious Democratic President Jeb Bartlet (played by Martin Sheen) and, in particular, his staff. Log on to www.nbc.com/westwing for details.

For films shot around the District, *see p186* **On location**.

Websites

Listed below are stand-alone websites. Many tourist information services, museums and attractions have their own sites, which are given in the listings of their respective entries elsewhere in this guide.

Washington Post
www.washingtonpost.com.
The Post makes every word it prints available online, although stories are moved after two weeks to the archives, access to which requires a fee.

Washington City Paper
www.washingtoncitypaper.com.
Much of this paper's content is not online, but its listings and classifieds are available in a searchable form.

WTOP News
www.wtopnews.com.
The city's leading all-news radio station's excellent website includes breaking news and helpful links to weather and traffic reports, as well as a listen-live option.

DC Watch
www.dcwatch.com.
For outsiders seeking a sense of the passion and perplexity of civic affairs in America's 'last colony', this site gives an exhaustive introduction.

Congress
http://thomas.loc.gov.
Links to lots of useful Congressional information, including days-in-session for the House and Senate, full text of bills being considered and a listing of how congressmen and -women voted on specific issues.

Directory

Index

Note: Page numbers in **bold** indicate section(s) giving key information on a topic; *italics* indicate photographs.

a

1001 Pennsylvania Avenue 39
abortion 256
accommodation 42-57
  best hotels 42
  boutique hotels 48-49
  rates & services 42
  by price
  budget 55-57
  expensive 45-53
  moderate 53-55
  very expensive 43-45
  see also p271
  accommodation index
Adams, John 10
Adams Morgan 85
  accommodation 51, 56
  bars 150-151
  festival 179
  restaurants 131-134
African-American DC
  history 11, 13-15, 86
  Martin Luther King 16, 19, 63
  museums 98, 99
  population 18
age restrictions 254
airports & airlines 250
Alexandria 97-101
Alexandria Black History Museum 98
American football 219
American Visionary Art Museum 234
Anacostia 95
Anacostia Museum for African American History & Culture 112
Anderson House 37
Anderson, Marian 16, 64
Annapolis 246
Annual High Heel Race 180
Annual White House Easter Egg Roll 176
Antietam 240
antiques 156, 172
aquarium 183

architecture 34-39
  20th-century 38-39
Archives II 104
Arena Stage 222
Arlington, VA 96-97
  accommodation 51, 57
  National Cemetery 96, **102-103**
  restaurants 141-144
Arlington House 35
Army-Navy Club 39
art & artists 189, 194
art supplies 156
Arthur M Sackler Gallery 63, 105, **106**, 157, 184
Arts & Industries Building 63
Arts Club of Washington 77
ATMs 259

b

Babe Ruth birthplace 233, 234
babysitting 181
bakeries 168
Baltimore 232-236
  Civil War Museum 233, 234
  Maritime Museum 232, 234
  Museum of Art 234
Baltimore-Washington International Airport 250
banks 260
barbers 171-172
Barry, Marion 19, 20
bars 145-152
  best 145
  with entertainment 149
  opening hours 145
  see also p271 bars index
Barton, Clara 103, 104
baseball 220
basketball 220
battlegrounds 239-241
Bead Museum 118
Bel Air 245
Bethesda, MD 103
  accommodation 51-53, 57
  restaurants 144
  shopping 158-159

bicycle tours 61
  see also cycling
birthdays, famous 180
Black Family Reunion 179
Black Fashion Museum 112
Black History Month 180
Black Pride 177
Blackwater National Wildlife Refuge 248
Bladensburg 104
Blair House 67
boat tours 61
boats 214-215, 231
Bonus Army 15, *15*
book shops 156-159
books, reference 265
Boy Scout Memorial 63
Brookland 92
Bureau of Engraving & Printing 75
Burnham, Daniel 37, 38
Busch Gardens & Water Country USA 238
buses 231
Bush, President George W 20, 28, *28*
business information 254-255

c

C & O Canal towpath 88, 215
cafés *see* restaurants
cameras 159
Camp David 243
Candian Embassy 82
Capital Beltway 101
Capital Jazz Fest 177
Capital Pride 177
Capitol, US 32, 34, 35, *63*, **69**, *69*, **72**
Capitol area 69-72
  accommodation 53, 55
  bars 146
  restaurants 138
Capitol Hill 93-94
car hire 253
Caribbean Festival 178
Carlyle House 34, **98**
Carter Barron Amphitheatre 87

Catholic University of America 91
Catoctin Mountain Park 243-245
Cedar Hill 95
Chancellorsville National Military Park 240
Cherry Blossom festival 177
Chesapeake Bay 246-248
Chevy Chase 104
children 181-184
  babysitting 181
  entertainment 181
  restaurants 181-183
  museums 181-183
  shopping for 163
  sport 183
  theatre & the arts 184
Chinatown 78
Chinese New Year 180
Christ Church 34, 93
Christ Church, Alexandria 98, *99*
churches 261
CIA 13
cinema *see* film
City Museum of Washington, DC 78, **118**
Civil War 12
  battlegrounds 239-241
Clara Barton National Historic Site 103, 104
classical music 206-209
Cleveland Park 91
  bars 152
climate 264
Clinton, President Bill 28-29, *29*
clubs *see* nightlife
College Park 104
Congress 26-28
Congressional Cemetery 94
Constitution 26
consulates 255
consumer information 255
contraception 256
conventions 254
Corcoran Museum of Art 67, **106**, 116, 207
couriers 254
Court of Appeals 82

Index

Advertisers' Index

Please refer to the relevant sections for contact details

Section sponsored by

 Smithsonian Institution

Maps

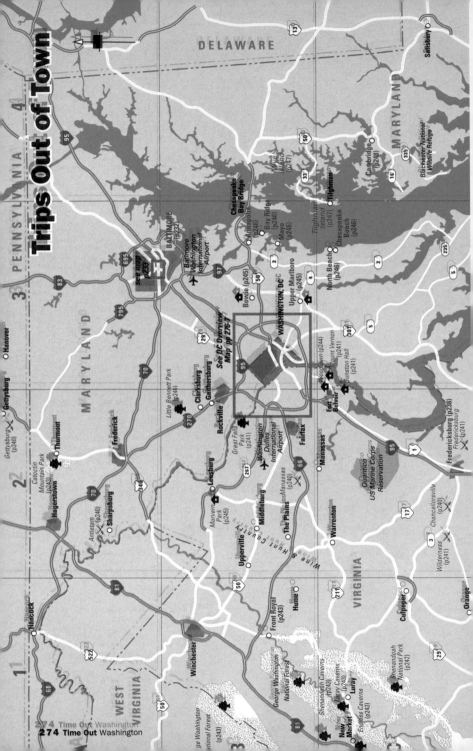

Trips Out of Town

DELAWARE

Salisbury

PENNSYLVANIA

MARYLAND

Hanover

Gettysburg (p240)

Thurmont

Catoctin Mountain Park (p243)

Hagerstown

Sharpsburg (p240)

Antietam (p240)

Hancock

WEST VIRGINIA

Winchester

George Washington National Forest (p243)

Frederick

Little Bennett Park (p246)

Clarksburg

Gaithersburg

Rockville

Leesburg

Great Falls Park (p241)

Morven Park (p245)

Middleburg

Uppervile

The Plains

Wine & Hunt Country

Warrenton

Front Royal (p243)

Hume

Luray (p243)

Luray Caverns (p243)

Shenandoah Caverns (p243)

Endless Caverns (p243)

New Market (p243)

Shenandoah National Park (p242)

VIRGINIA

Culpeper

Orange

Chancellorsville (p240)

Wilderness (p241)

Fredericksburg (p238) Fredericksburg (p241)

Quantico US Marine Corps Reservation

Manassas

Manassas (p240)

Fairfax

Washington Dulles International Airport

WASHINGTON, DC

See DC Overview Map pp 276-7

Bowie (p245)

Upper Marlboro (p245)

Mount Vernon (p241)

Gunston Hall (p241)

Fort Belvoir

Woodlawn (p244)

Baltimore (p232)

See map p233

Baltimore Washington International Airport

Chesapeake Bay Bridge

Annapolis

Bay Ridge (p246)

Mayo (p246)

North Beach (p246)

Chesapeake Beach (p246)

Tilghman Island (p247)

Tilghman

Kent Island (p247)

Cambridge (p248)

Blackwater National Wildlife Refuge

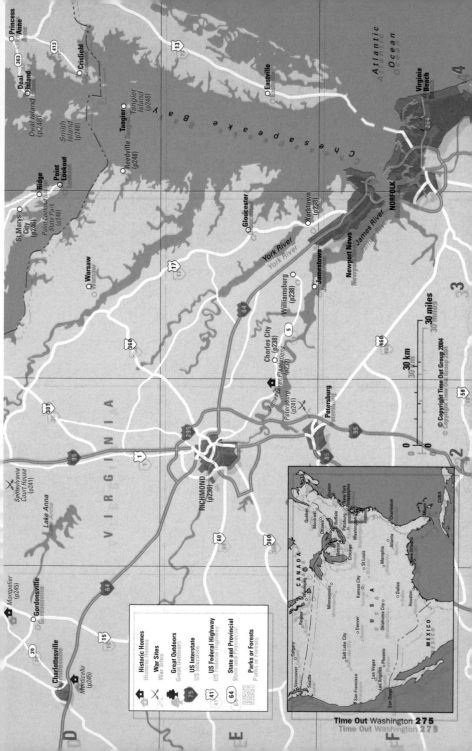

Princess Anne

363

413

Deal
Island

Deal Island (p248)

Cristfield

13

Smith
Island
(p248)

Tangier
Island
(p248)

Eastville

Tangier
(p248)

Reedville
(p248)

C h e s a p e a k e   B a y

Point
Lookout

A t l a n t i c
O c e a n

Virginia
Beach

NORFOLK

Ridge

St Marys
City (p246)

Point Lookout
State Park (p246)

Gloucester

Yorktown
(p228)

4

Warsaw

17

York River
York River

Jamestown
(p238)

Newport News

James River
James River

Williamsburg (p238)

360

64

Charles City
(p238)

5

3

301

1

James River Plantations
(p239)

Petersburg
(p241)

466

58

30 km
30 km

30 miles
30 miles

© Copyright Time Out Group 2004
© Copyright Time Out Group 2004

95

295

RICHMOND
(p236)

Spotsylvania
Court House (p241)

Lake Anna

35

83

0
0

2

Montpelier
(p245)

64

60

366

V I R G I N I A

Gordonsville
(p)

15

Charlottesville
(p245)

20

Monticello
(p245)

D

E

F

Historic Homes
Historic Homes

War Sites
War Sites

Great Outdoors
Great Outdoors

US Interstate
US Interstate

US Federal Highway
US Federal Highway

State and Provincial
State and Provincial

Parks or Forests
Parks or Forests

75

441

64

CANADA

U S A

MEXICO

CUBA

Vancouver
Seattle
Calgary
Winnipeg
Ottawa
Montreal
Quebec
Buffalo
New York
Washington
Pittsburgh
Boston
Chicago
Detroit
San Francisco
Salt Lake City
Denver
Kansas City
St Louis
Memphis
Charleston
Atlanta
Las Vegas
Los Angeles
Phoenix
Oklahoma City
Dallas
Houston
San Diego
New Orleans

DC Overview

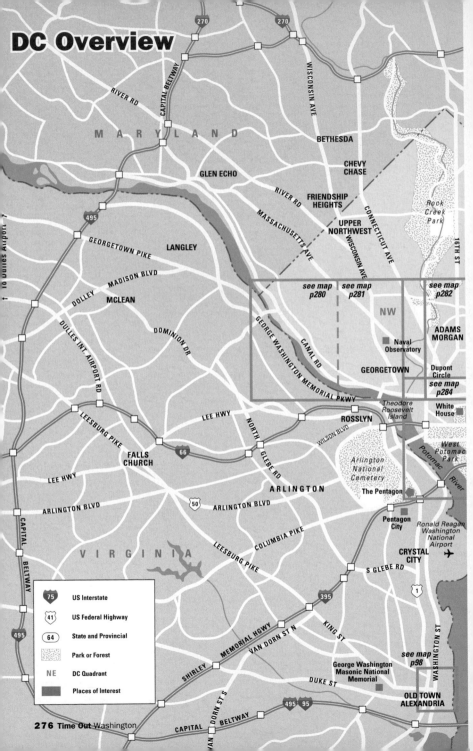

270

270

WISCONSIN AVE

RIVER RD

CAPITAL BELTWAY

M A R Y L A N D

BETHESDA

GLEN ECHO

CHEVY CHASE

FRIENDSHIP HEIGHTS

RIVER RD

UPPER NORTHWEST

CONNECTICUT AVE

WISCONSIN AVE

Rock Creek Park

16TH ST

495

GEORGETOWN PIKE

MASSACHUSETTS AVE

LANGLEY

MADISON BLVD

DOLLEY

MCLEAN

DOMINION DR

DULLES INT'L AIRPORT RD

To Dulles Airport

see map p280

see map p281

see map p282

NW

ADAMS MORGAN

Naval Observatory

GEORGE WASHINGTON MEMORIAL PKWY

CANAL RD

GEORGETOWN

Dupont Circle

see map p284

LEESBURG PIKE

LEE HWY

NORTH GLEBE RD

Theodore Roosevelt Island

White House

West Potomac Park

Potomac

ROSSLYN

WILSON BLVD

66

FALLS CHURCH

LEE HWY

ARLINGTON BLVD

50

ARLINGTON BLVD

ARLINGTON

Arlington National Cemetery

The Pentagon

Pentagon City

River

Ronald Reagan Washington National Airport

1

COLUMBIA PIKE

LEESBURG PIKE

CRYSTAL CITY

V I R G I N I A

S GLEBE RD

CAPITAL BELTWAY

495

395

MEMORIAL HGWY

SHIRLEY

VAN DORN ST N

KING ST

see map p98

WASHINGTON ST

George Washington Masonic National Memorial

DUKE ST

VAN DORN ST S

CAPITAL BELTWAY

495 95

OLD TOWN ALEXANDRIA

Legend

75	US Interstate
41	US Federal Highway
64	State and Provincial
	Park or Forest
NE	DC Quadrant
	Places of Interest

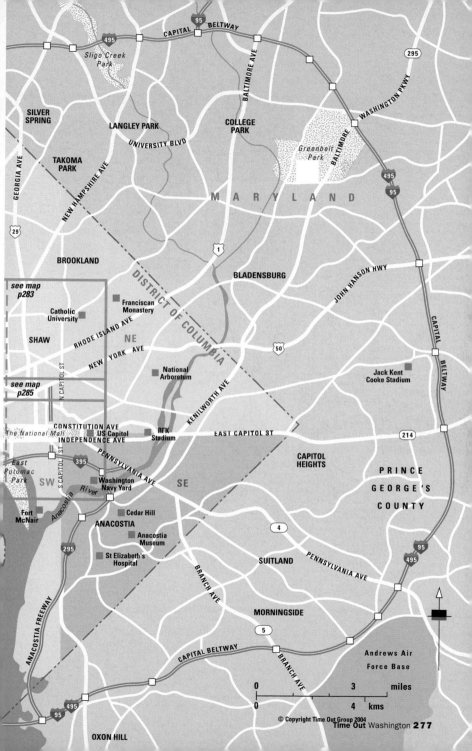

CAPITAL BELTWAY

495

95

295

Sligo Creek
Park

SILVER
SPRING

LANGLEY PARK

BALTIMORE AVE

COLLEGE
PARK

WASHINGTON PKWY

BALTIMORE

Greenbelt
Park

495

95

GEORGIA AVE

TAKOMA
PARK

UNIVERSITY BLVD

NEW HAMPSHIRE AVE

M A R Y L A N D

29

BROOKLAND

1

BLADENSBURG

JOHN HANSON HWY

CAPITAL BELTWAY

see map
p283

Catholic
University

Franciscan
Monastery

DISTRICT OF COLUMBIA

SHAW

RHODE ISLAND AVE

NE

50

Jack Kent
Cooke Stadium

NEW YORK AVE

N CAPITOL ST

see map
p285

National
Arboretum

KENILWORTH AVE

CONSTITUTION AVE

US Capitol

RFK
Stadium

EAST CAPITOL ST

214

The National Mall

INDEPENDENCE AVE

S CAPITOL ST

PENNSYLVANIA AVE

CAPITOL
HEIGHTS

P R I N C E

395

G E O R G E ' S

East
Potomac
Park

Washington
Navy Yard

C O U N T Y

SW

Anacostia   River

SE

Fort
McNair

Cedar Hill

4

ANACOSTIA

295

Anacostia
Museum

SUITLAND

PENNSYLVANIA AVE

95

495

St Elizabeth's
Hospital

BRANCH AVE

ANACOSTIA FREEWAY

MORNINGSIDE

5

A n d r e w s   A i r
F o r c e   B a s e

95

495

CAPITAL BELTWAY

BRANCH AVE

0   3   miles

0   4   kms

© Copyright Time Out Group 2004

OXON HILL

Time Out Washington **277**

A UNIQUE AMERICAN

The National Museum of the American Indian

opened on the National Mall on September 21, 2004 – the newest and perhaps most unique of the Smithsonian Institution's 18 world renowned museums in Washington, D.C. The Mall building encompasses 254,000 square feet. Throughout the museum you'll see over 8,000 amazing works from scores of Native cultures, drawn from our hemispheric collection of more than 800,000 objects.

EXPERIENCE

But this vibrant place is much more than just a collection of objects. It's a place where you can watch Native artists at work, purchase authentic arts and crafts, sample Native-inspired cuisine from all over North America and watch live performances of both traditional and contemporary theater and dance. In short, the National Museum of the American Indian is a place where you can truly experience the Native cultures of the Americas. Join us on the National Mall.

Smithsonian
National Museum of the American Indian
www.AmericanIndian.si.edu

DC Neighbourhoods:
NW and Upper Northwest

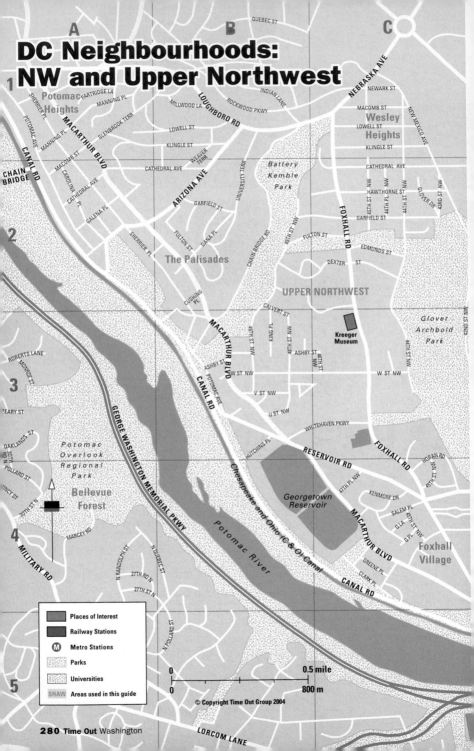

A   **B**   **C**

QUEBEC ST
INDIAN LANE
NEBRASKA AVE
NEWARK ST

1

Potomac
Heights
PARTRIDGE LA
MANNING PL
MILLWOOD LA
ROCKWOOD PKWY
LOUGHBORO RD
MACOMB ST
LOWELL ST
Wesley
Heights
NEW MEXICO AVE

SHERRIER PL
MANNING PL
GLENBROOK TERR
LOWELL ST
KLINGLE ST
KLINGLE ST

POTOMAC AVE
MACARTHUR BLVD
MACOMB ST
CATHEDRAL AVE
WEAVER TERR
ARIZONA AVE
UNIVERSITY TERR
Battery
Kemble
Park
CATHEDRAL AVE

CHAIN BRIDGE RD
CAROLINA
CATHEDRAL PL
GALENA PL
45TH NW
44TH NW
44TH NW
HAWTHORNE ST
43RD ST N
GLOVER DR

2

GARFIELD ST
45TH NW
GARFIELD ST

SHERRIER PL
FULTON ST
DANA PL
CHAIN BRIDGE RD
45TH NW
FULTON ST
FOXHALL RD
EDMUNDS ST

CUSHING PL
The Palisades
DEXTER ST

UPPER NORTHWEST

42ND ST NW

CALVERT ST
Glover
Archbold
Park

MACARTHUR BLVD
45TH ST NW
KING PL
45TH ST NW
Kreeger
Museum
46TH ST NW
45TH ST NW

3

ROBERTS LANE
MONROE ST
CANAL RD
POTOMAC AVE
W ST NW
ASHBY ST NW
W ST NW

PEARY ST
V ST NW

OAKLANDS ST
U ST NW
WHITEHAVEN PKWY
FOXHALL RD

POLLARD ST
HUTCHINS PL
RESERVOIR RD
HOBAN RD

QUINCY ST
30TH ST N
Potomac
Overlook
Regional
Park
GEORGE WASHINGTON MEMORIAL PKWY
Chesapeake and Ohio (C & O) Canal
47TH PL NW
45TH ST NW
KENMORE DR

Bellevue
Forest
Georgetown
Reservoir
MACARTHUR BLVD
SALEM PL
O LA
45TH ST NW
O PL

4

MARCEY RD
Potomac River
GREENE PL
Foxhall
Village

MILITARY RD
N RANDOLPH ST
27TH RD N
CANAL RD
CLARK PL

N QUEBEC ST
27TH ST N
CLARK PL

	Places of Interest
	Railway Stations
M	Metro Stations
	Parks
	Universities
SHAW	Areas used in this guide

N POLLARD ST

0   0.5 mile

0   800 m

© Copyright Time Out Group 2004

5

LORCOM LANE

DC Neighbourhoods: NW and NE

F   G   H

1

Woodley Park

National Zoological Park

PORTER ST
PINEY BRANCH PKWY
ADAMS MILL RD

NEWTON ST
MONROE ST
LAMONT ST
KILBOURNE PL
KENYON ST
IRVING ST
HOBART ST
HARVARD ST

Mount Pleasant

SPRING RD
PERRY PL
OGDEN ST

NEWTON ST
MONROE ST
PARK RD

MOUNT PLEASANT & NORTH

Columbia Heights

IRVING ST

QUINCY ST
KANSAS AVE

KENYON   ST

COLUMBIA RD

2

Woodley Park-Zoo/Adams Morgan

WOODLEY RD
CONNECTICUT AVE
CATHEDRAL AVE
CALVERT ST

CALVERT   ST
Adams Morgan
BILTMORE ST

ADAMS MORGAN

ONTARIO PL
LANIER PL
ONTARIO RD
FULLER ST
EUCLID ST

HARVARD ST

GIRARD ST
FAIRMONT ST
EUCLID ST

SHAW

GIRARD ST

CLIFTON ST

Rock Creek Park

See page 281

MINTWOOD PL
BELMONT ST
KALORAMA RD
WYOMING AVE
CALIFORNIA ST

COLUMBIA RD
ASHMEADE PL
20TH ST NW

CHAMPLAIN ST
CRESCENT PL
KALORAMA RD

Meridian Hill Park (Malcolm X Park)

CHAPIN ST
BELMONT ST
W   ST   NW

FLORIDA   AVE
CLIFTON ST

3

Rock Creek

KALORAMA CIRCLE
WYOMING AVE
TRACY PL
CALIFORNIA ST
BANCROFT PL

Kalorama

KALORAMA RD
WYOMING AVE

CONNECTICUT AVE

CALIFORNIA ST
VERNON PL
SEATON PL

16TH ST NW
14TH ST NW
13TH ST NW
12TH ST

SHAW: U STREET/ 14TH STREET CORRIDOR
U ST NW
U St-African-Amer Civil War Memorial/ Cardozo

11TH ST
10TH ST

MASSACHUSETTS AVE
ROCK CREEK AND POTOMAC PKWY

SHERIDAN CIRCLE

FLORIDA AVE
18TH ST

WILLARD ST
CORCORAN   ST
CHURCH ST

CAROLINE ST
WALLACH PL

JOHNSON AVE

RIGGS PL

VERMONT   AVE

4

Phillips Collection

DUPONT CIRCLE

Dupont Circle
DUPONT CIRCLE

RIGGS PL

CHURCH ST

SHAW: LOGAN CIRCLE

LOGAN CIRCLE

Q ST NW
P ST NW
N ST NW
OLIVE ST

27TH ST NW
25TH ST NW
23RD ST
22ND ST
NEW HAMPSHIRE AVE
CONNECTICUT AVE

MASSACHUSETTS AVE
RHODE   ISLAND   AVE

SCOTT CIRCLE

KINGMAN PL

P   ST

MASSACHUSETTS AVE

B'nai B'rith Klutznick National Jewish Museum

National Geographic Society

THOMAS CIRCLE

DOWNTOWN

5

Watergate Complex

K   ST   NW

WASHINGTON CIRCLE

FOGGY BOTTOM

Foggy Bottom-GWU

PENNSYLVANIA   AVE

George Washington

JEFFERSON PLACE
DE SALES ST

Farragut North
Farragut West

21ST ST
19TH ST

Renwick Gallery

McPherson Square

FRANKLIN SQUARE

NEW   YORK   AVE

JACKSON
MADISON

LAFAYETTE SQUARE

VERMONT   AVE
14TH ST NW
13TH ST

See Page 284

MOUNT PLEASANT & NORTH

Georgia Ave-Petworth

QUINCY ST

CREEK CHURCH RD

QUEBEC PL

PRINCETON PL

MORTON ST

PARK PL

KENYON ST

WARDER PL

IRVING ST

COLUMBIA RD

HORBART PL

GRESHAM PL

GIRARD ST

GEORGIA AVE

FAIRMONT ST

EUCLID ST

Howard University

HOWARD PL

COLLEGE ST

BRYANT ST

Howard University Hospital

OAKDALE PL

ELM ST

THOMAS ST

FLORIDA AVE

Shaw-Howard University

RHODE ISLAND AVE

US Soldiers & Airmans Home

IRVING ST

Children's National Medical Center

MICHIGAN AVE

McMillan Reservoir

McMILLAN DR

CHANNING ST

BRYANT ST

ADAMS ST

NORTH CAPITOL ST

GIRARD ST

Glenwood Cemetery

Prospect Hill Cemetery

CHANNING ST

BRYANT ST

ADAMS ST

LINCOLN RD

THOMAS ST

TODD PL

SEATON PL NW

RANDOLPH PL NW

QUINCY PL

FRANKLIN ST

BATES ST

NEAL PL

RIDGE ST

SHAW

Mt Vernon Sq/7th St-Convention Center

Washington Convention Center

MT VERNON SQUARE

JUDICIARY SQUARE AREA

NEW YORK AVE

PATTERSON ST

PIERCE ST NW

See Page 285

MASSACHUSETTS AVE

Catholic University of America

Shrine of the Immaculate Conception

MICHIGAN AVE

Theological College

Brookland

Brookland CUA

Trinity College

NORTHEAST

GIRARD ST

FRANKLIN ST

EWARTS ST

DOUGLAS ST

CHANNING ST

BRYANT ST

ADAMS ST

RHODE ISLAND AVE

Rhode Island Avenue

SEATON PL NE

S ST NE

RANDOLPH PL NE

NORTHEAST

NEW YORK AVE

PENN ST

FLORIDA AVE

PATTERSON ST

PIERCE ST NE

DELAWARE AVE

NORTH CAPITOL ST

Union Station

G ST NE

UNION STATION & AROUND

Legend

■	Places of Interest
■	Railway Stations
Ⓜ	Metro Stations
	Parks
	Universities
SHAW	Areas used in this guide

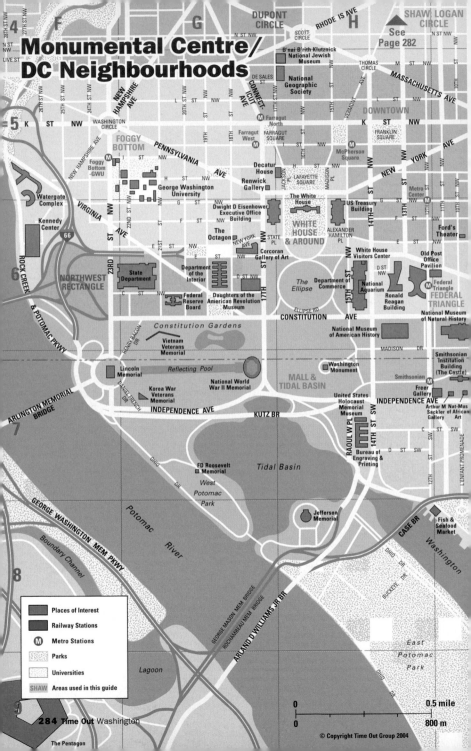

Monumental Centre/ DC Neighbourhoods

See Page 282

DUPONT CIRCLE

SHAW LOGAN CIRCLE

RHODE IS AVE

SCOTT CIRCLE

THOMAS CIRCLE

MASSACHUSETTS AVE

DOWNTOWN

B'nai B'rith Klutznick National Jewish Museum

National Geographic Society

DE SALES

FRANKLIN SQUARE

Farragut North

Farragut Square

K ST NW

Farragut West

McPherson Square

NEW YORK AVE

WASHINGTON CIRCLE

FOGGY BOTTOM

PENNSYLVANIA AVE

Foggy Bottom -GWU

George Washington University

Decatur House

Renwick Gallery

LAFAYETTE SQUARE

The White House

Metro Center

Watergate Complex

Dwight D Eisenhower Executive Office Building

WHITE HOUSE & AROUND

US Treasury Building

ALEXANDER HAMILTON PL

Ford's Theater

Kennedy Center

The Octagon

NEW YORK AVE

White House Visitors Center

Old Post Office Pavilion

VIRGINIA AVE

Corcoran Gallery of Art

E ST NW

Federal Triangle

ROCK CREEK & POTOMAC PKWY

NORTHWEST RECTANGLE

State Department

Department of the Interior

The Ellipse

Department of Commerce

National Aquarium

Ronald Reagan Building

FEDERAL TRIANGLE

National Museum of Natural History

Federal Reserve Board

Daughters of the American Revolution Museum

ELLIPSE RD

CONSTITUTION AVE

Constitution Gardens

National Museum of American History

MADISON DR

HENRY BACON DR

Vietnam Veterans Memorial

Washington Monument

MALL & TIDAL BASIN

Smithsonian Institution Building (The Castle)

Lincoln Memorial

Reflecting Pool

Smithsonian

Freer Gallery

DANIEL FRENCH DR

Korea War Veterans Memorial

National World War II Memorial

United States Holocaust Memorial Museum

INDEPENDENCE AVE

Arthur M Sackler Gallery of African Art

ARLINGTON MEMORIAL BRIDGE

INDEPENDENCE AVE

KUTZ BR

RAOUL W PL

L'ENFANT PROMENADE

OHIO DR

FD Roosevelt Memorial

Tidal Basin

Bureau of Engraving & Printing

West Potomac Park

GEORGE WASHINGTON MEM PKWY

Boundary Channel

Potomac River

Jefferson Memorial

CASE BR

Fish & Seafood Market

Washington

OHIO DR

BUCKEYE DR

East Potomac Park

GEORGE MASON MEM BRIDGE

ROCHAMBEAU MEM BRIDGE

ARLAND D WILLIAMS JR BR

Lagoon

Legend	
	Places of Interest
	Railway Stations
Ⓜ	Metro Stations
	Parks
	Universities
SHAW	Areas used in this guide

284 Time Out Washington

The Pentagon

0   0.5 mile

0   800 m

© Copyright Time Out Group 2004

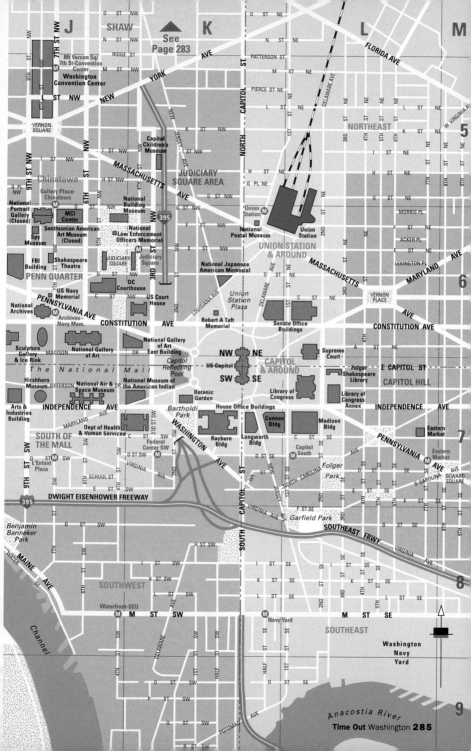

Street Index

Street Index

System Map

Legend

- Red Line • Glenmont to Shady Grove
- Orange Line • New Carrollton to Vienna/Fairfax-GMU
- Blue Line • Franconia-Springfield to Largo Town Center
- Green Line • Branch Avenue to Greenbelt
- Yellow Line • Huntington to Mt Vernon Sq/7th St-Convention Center

Station in Service Transfer Station Planned Station

Virginia Railway Express Commuter Rail Parking

N

 No Smoking
 No Eating or Drinking
 No Animals (except service animals)
 No Audio or Video Devices (without earphones)
 No Litter or Spitting
 No Dangerous or Flammable Items